DISABILITY IN HIGHER EDUCATION

A Social Justice Approach

Nancy J. Evans
Ellen M. Broido
Kirsten R. Brown
Autumn K. Wilke

JB JOSSEY-BASS™
A Wiley Brand

Published by Jossey-Bass
A Wiley Brand
One Montgomery Street, Suite 1000, San Francisco, CA 94104-4594—www.josseybass.com

Jossey-Bass books and products are available through most bookstores. To contact Jossey-Bass directly call our Customer Care Department within the U.S. at 800-956-7739, outside the U.S. at 317-572-3986, or fax 317-572-4002.

Wiley publishes in a variety of print and electronic formats and by print-on-demand. Some material included with standard print versions of this book may not be included in e-books or in print-on-demand. If this book refers to media such as a CD or DVD that is not included in the version you purchased, you may download this material at http://booksupport.wiley.com. For more information about Wiley products, visit www.wiley.com.

Library of Congress Cataloging-in-Publication Data

Names: Evans, Nancy J., 1947– author. | Broido, Ellen M., 1965– author. |
    Brown, Kirsten R., author. | Wilke, Autumn K., author.
Title: Disability in higher education : a social justice approach / Nancy J. Evans,
    Ellen M. Broido, Kirsten R. Brown, Autumn K. Wilke.
Description: San Francisco, CA : Jossey-Bass, 2017. | Includes
    bibliographical references and index.
Identifiers: LCCN 2016044997 | ISBN 9781118018224 (cloth) | ISBN 9781118415689 (epub) |
    ISBN 9781118418543 (epdf)
Subjects: LCSH: People with disabilities—Education (Higher)—United States. |
    College students with disabilities—United States.
Classification: LCC LC4813 .E83 2017 | DDC 378.0087—dc23
LC record available at https://lccn.loc.gov/2016044997

Cover design: Wiley
Cover image: ©binik/Getty Images

Printed in the United States of America

FIRST EDITION

HB Printing

CONTENTS

LIST OF TABLES AND FIGURES

Tables

Figures

ACKNOWLEDGMENTS

Collectively, we thank the students and colleagues who gave life to this book and who supported us as we researched and wrote it. Throughout our journey as educators and student affairs practitioners, we have been inspired by and learned from you. We are also grateful to our partners and spouses who cooked dinners, shoveled snow, scanned documents, edited drafts, moved houses, drove to coffee shops in different states, and tolerated all the time we spent on "that damn book." This book would not exist without our talented editor, and we thank Alison Knowles, at Jossey-Bass, for her unwavering patience with this project. The writing and editing process can be isolating, frustrating, time-consuming, and hard—yet through all of this, our silly, playful cats invaded the weekly author meetings, jumped on keyboards, and kept us company, sitting on our laps during the solitary hours. We acknowledge their warmth and sense of humor, and we are grateful for the connection they brought to our team.

We thank Susan Rankin, who graciously provided her data and analyses to support our chapters on campus climate for faculty and staff (Chapter 7) and students (Chapter 9) and championed our completion of the book. We also express our thanks to the campus disability professionals we met with while researching this book. In particular, we thank Michael Hudson and his staff members at Michigan State University, Jennifer McMahon at the San Diego Community College District, Paula Doss and Fred Bellinger at the University of California at San Diego, Jeff Vernooy (now deceased) at Wright State University, Joyce Stern and Angie Story and the staff members at Grinnell College, and the participants who requested that we not identify them or their institutions. They were exceedingly helpful in informing us about how campuses might best serve students, staff, and faculty with disabilities. We also thank the numerous participants of the multiple individual research studies that underlie much of the writing in this book. Note that all individuals' names used in this text, other than those of the authors, writers and professionals to whom we give attribution, are pseudonyms. Finally, we acknowledge the reviewers who contributed to making this book a stronger final product, in particular Maria Peña, who provided multiple rounds of feedback and expanded our thinking. Nancy Evans thanks her partner, Jim Trenberth, for his constant support during the preparation of this book. Ellen Broido thanks her partner, Jo Campbell, for her patience and support over the years spent working on this book; her former research assistants, Kirsten Brown and Katherine Stygles, for their assistance in locating material for the book; and Kirsten especially for stepping into a coauthorship role. Kirsten Brown is grateful for the love and support of her family: Jack, Hellen, Karen, Jeff, Lynn, Pete, baby Jack, and partner Kevin Wyne; she is also thankful for the opportunity to learn from this wonderful team of coauthors. Autumn Wilke thanks her partner, Alesha Magee, for the long hours spent at coffee shops and support throughout the writing process, her former faculty adviser and mentor Nancy Evans for inviting her to participate in this project, and the other disability staff at Grinnell College for their collective wisdom.

PREFACE

A social justice approach to disability in higher education means beginning with the assumption that people's abilities and rights to contribute to and benefit from higher education are not dependent on their bodies or psyches conforming to dominant norms. It means that we believe the barriers to success in higher education lie in the structural, organizational, physical, and attitudinal aspects of our institutions. In this book, we deliberately approach disability from a social justice perspective, recognizing the multifaceted nature of disabled people's lives, while attending to the contributions and potentials of students, staff, and faculty with disabilities. We also pay attention to the attitudinal, organizational, and physical barriers impeding success; to history, law, and policy; to functional limitations and the challenges posed by people's minds and bodies; and to advocacy, struggle, and social change. In particular, we recognize that the experience of disability is mediated by other social identities people hold and the many roles they take on, both within and outside higher education. In addition, in this book we examine the role of people who are not disabled in creating and maintaining social systems, policies, and norms that circumscribe the lives of individuals with disabilities, as well as the ways that those with and without disabilities can reduce or eliminate those barriers.

Our approach differs from most other writing on disability in the context of higher education, in which disability commonly is understood as deficit, limitation, or inability. Even those who work to create an inclusive, socially just society frequently use metaphors that reinforce perceptions of the incapacity of people with disabilities (e.g., using "color-blind racism" to describe people who say they are unaware of racial differences; Nocella, 2009). As Mingus (2011) noted,

> People usually think of disability as an individual flaw or problem, rather than as something partly created by the world we live in. It is rare that people think about disability as a political experience or as encompassing a community full of rich histories, cultures, and legacies (para. 1).

In this book, we strive to do just that. In addition, this book differs from other texts on disability by recognizing and exploring diversity within disabled communities. Moreover, we take an intentionally interdisciplinary approach, drawing on both the research and experiential literature from a variety of disciplines, while noting the paucity and dated nature of disability research that foregrounds the experiences of people with disabilities in higher education (E. V. Peña, 2014). Finally, we approach disability as a campuswide issue rather than the sole province of disability resource providers.

We need a better approach to understanding disability in higher education for multiple reasons. First, the numbers and percentages of people with disabilities entering college are rising, with 2011 data indicating 11.1% of college students having a disability (National Center for Educational Statistics, 2016b), almost double the numbers from the mid-1990s (although there is considerable variability in disability statistics, as discussed in Chapter 4). Second, despite the increasing enrollment of disabled students into higher education, people with disabilities continue to be underrepresented in the workforce, including at colleges and universities, as we expand on in Chapter 7. These two dynamics are compounded because few staff or faculty members know how to work effectively with people with disabilities as students, colleagues, or supervisees. Finally, few colleges or universities have systematically identified and eliminated institutional and cultural barriers to the success of their constituencies with disabilities. In this book, we provide the information necessary to begin to create campus environments supportive of the success of all their members.

Audience

The primary audiences for this book are disability resource providers and student affairs practitioners who work with students with disabilities (i.e., all student affairs practitioners), faculty and academic affairs administrators, and master's and doctoral students who are studying social justice and disability issues. We believe the book will be particularly useful to scholars and faculty who teach courses on social justice and/or disability, both inside disability studies programs and in education, health and human services, social work, and human development programs. Scholars studying disability also will find this book to be an important resource because we bring together material from multiple disciplinary perspectives; present new data and interpretations; and integrate history, theory, and practice from a social justice perspective. This book will be of help as well to scholars who are pursuing new and important areas for future disability research, practitioners seeking a reference manual written from an intersectional perspective, faculty interested in course textbooks and supplementary material, students who are entering the field wanting disability-specific knowledge, and individuals without disabilities looking to deconstruct ableism on their campuses. Finally, we believe this book will be useful to those working to help students with disabilities make the transition from high school to higher education.

Positionality

As we begin a book that takes a social justice approach to understanding disability in higher education, we recognize the importance of locating ourselves as authors. We believe that readers need some understanding of the experiences, influences, and values we bring to our own approaches to disability and the ways those approaches shaped the content of this book.

We hold several social locations in common. Each of us is a White, cisgender woman with a great deal of education. All of us were raised and have lived most of our lives in the United States. We each identify as having one or more disabilities. We all have cats. We each have worked in student affairs (although in different functional areas). We all have extensive histories in social justice work, view ourselves as advocates, and view student affairs work in general and disability work specifically from that perspective. While we all have served as college instructors, for two of the four of us (Nancy and Ellen), this was or is our primary professional role. Autumn and Kirsten have taught in addition to their main employment. In addition, we have unique histories that have shaped how we came to write this book and how we conceptualize disability, both personally and as a theoretical construct. Below, each of us explains her history.

Nancy J. Evans

I had polio as a four-year-old during the last big polio epidemic before development of the polio vaccine. I grew up in a poor family: my father was a tenant farmer who left school after the sixth grade, and my mother was the daughter of Norwegian immigrant farmers. My first memories are of my parents leaning over my bed at the medical center an hour from my home, where I was treated by a prominent orthopedist, nationally known for his work with polio patients. Still, my mother experienced lifelong guilt feelings because (a) she was sure I had caught the polio virus on a trip to her family home in Minnesota just before I became sick, and (b) our family's financial status made it impossible for her to take me to the Mayo Clinic in Minnesota for treatment. My back and legs were paralyzed, and I spent nine months in a rehabilitation hospital learning to walk with crutches and the back and leg braces I have worn since I was four years old. I also had many surgeries between the ages of 4 and 13 to straighten my legs and feet, which required hospitalization, rehabilitation, and periodic home schooling.

I had my last major surgery at age 13 and was home-schooled during my eighth-grade year by a young teacher who also taught at the local school. She spent a great deal of time with me and was a major influence on my life, encouraging me to excel in my schoolwork and go on to college. My father was killed in an accident when I was just starting ninth grade. My mother, who was not used to making decisions, was overwhelmed and unsure of her role as a single parent with two teenagers. Since she worked first evening and then night hours, we were left on our own a lot. Because of my teacher's influence and my mother's lack of self-confidence, I became an independent and resilient teenager, making my own decisions, ignoring my impairment for the most part, and focusing on the aspect of my life in which I could excel: academics.

Because of my disability, the New York State Department of Vocational Rehabilitation would pay my college tuition and costs as long as I attended an in-state college. However, the private college I had my heart set on attending "discouraged" me from enrolling because they did not think I could handle its rather hilly campus. Devastated, I instead attended SUNY-Potsdam (now Potsdam State University), where I felt welcomed. Potsdam provided an excellent environment in which to expand my horizons, become involved in the civil rights and antiwar protests of the 1960s, and become a student leader, including student government president.

Immersed as I was in student government and protest, I had no clue what I would do with my life after I graduated from college in 1970. Based on the advice of my student government advisor, I finally decided on a career in student affairs, completed a master's degree, worked in the field for several years, completed a PhD, and became a faculty member. Throughout these young adult years, I rarely thought about my identity as a disabled person, other than the affect I assumed my disability had on my social relationships, particularly with men. Another belief my mother passed on to me was that men would not be interested in me romantically. That belief was dispelled when I met my life partner while we were both teaching at Western Illinois University. Together we worked through many of the issues and false messages I had regarding my appearance and ability to contribute to a relationship; we were married in 1997.

I learned about the concept of social injustice as an undergraduate during the civil rights and antiwar movements and developed close friendships with several gay men in graduate school and my first professional position. When I began teaching, it was apparent to me that the student affairs literature base was focused almost exclusively on students whose backgrounds were privileged. Believing that student affairs professionals needed to know about minoritized students as well, I began adding information about these students through panels, assignments, and discussions. Later, I focused my scholarship on the experiences of lesbian, gay, bisexual, and transgender (LGBT) college students and social justice in general. Reflecting now, I believe that I was doing this work related to other marginalized individuals because I was not yet ready to explore the issues I personally faced as a disabled person.

It was not until I began teaching at Iowa State University (ISU) that I needed to address my identity as a disabled person. I had gradually lost strength in both my legs and my arms and I began experiencing significant pain. I was at a point of needing to make the transition from walking with crutches to using a wheelchair at work. This decision felt like "giving in" to my disability, and I agonized over it. At that time, ISU's disability resource coordinator, who was also taking classes in the student affairs program, became an important ally in the process of turning my feelings around to the point where I was not only comfortable with myself as a disabled person who used a wheelchair, but could also openly share my experiences in classes, presentations, and writing. I am so grateful that he constantly confronted the oppression people with disabilities experience and modeled speaking up for one's rights in professional settings.

Currently I am experiencing the challenges of post-polio syndrome, which most polio survivors experience as they reach their 60s. I went on permanent disability leave in 2013 since I no longer had the energy to manage my faculty role effectively. I continue to learn and grow by immersing myself in the disability and social justice literature, and I bring social justice and critical realist positions to my personal and professional work.

Ellen M. Broido

My diagnosis of diabetes as a four-year-old profoundly shaped multiple aspects of my experience and identity, although it has taken me many years to recognize those influences and I am sure there is more to learn. I grew up in a family in which I was encouraged to treat diabetes as "no big deal" and to ensure no one was inconvenienced by it. I also had the socioeconomic privilege to access quality health care and cutting-edge treatment. I had contact with other kids with diabetes while attending a camp for diabetics for two weeks each summer; that experience was a counterbalance to the rest of the year, where diabetes was a solitary, isolating experience I was taught to treat as a mild annoyance and a manageable medical condition. I absorbed the message to minimize others' awareness of the impact of diabetes on my life, accept the myth of being able to do it all, and never considered myself to have a disability. However, due to diabetes, I lost my vision in one eye while a master's student and was told to expect to lose my remaining sight in the near future. Shortly after, I was exposed to material about disability in the context of a course on social justice, and for the first time I recognized the commonality between my own experiences and those whom I had previously considered to be "other" people with disabilities.

This dawning understanding of a social justice perspective on disability, work with others who shared social justice approaches, and research on other aspects of social justice grounded my professional work in higher education in social justice. Later, as I began to do research on disability in higher education, my thinking was influenced by multiple theorists and researchers who were using critical approaches to disability.

My other social identities, as a person who has racial, economic, educational, and cisgender privilege, and someone minoritized because of my sexual orientation, gender, and religious affiliation, also influence how I experience disability. My understanding of disability and approach to the material in this book is shaped by the combination of my own identity and experiences as a disabled person, my other social identities, my contact with others doing social justice work on disability and other issues, and theoretical and empirical literature.

Kirsten R. Brown

From a very young age, being dyslexic was an inescapable part of my self-identity. In grammar school, some of my most embarrassing memories involved spelling exams. As an adult working in academia, I constantly struggle to produce written work that others might interpret as grammatically correct. Yet my identity and positionality are more than just a monolithic picture highlighted by learning differences; culturally, I inhabit a space where my white skin, able body, cisgender appearance, advanced education, heterosexual relationship, and middle-class position provide some cover for my dyslexic grammatical blunders. The privilege that these positions afford, coupled with an immersion in disability research and an empathetic family, allows me to occupy a space where writing is a practice, not a perfection. As a social justice advocate, I view my spelling errors as an opportunity to deconstruct stigma associated with disability by making the hidden visible to students in my classes and colleagues.

Autumn K. Wilke

Disability was not an aspect of my life that I began to fully embrace until I was an adult in my first full-time job. As a graduate student, I was diagnosed with generalized anxiety disorder, panic disorder, and an adjustment disorder. I attended weekly therapy sessions with an individual therapist and weekly group therapy sessions to attempt to manage my symptoms, and I told no one about my struggles. Anxiety had been a constant part of my life, but it had not affected me in such a pronounced way until graduate school. As a teenager, I had internalized many of the messages regarding mental health that are prevalent in society, and I continued to view my mental health through this lens. I saw my daily struggles with anxiety as an internal flaw that I had to manage. I did not seek accommodations or support from my faculty or supervisors even though I was familiar with the accommodations process, having received academic accommodations for severe migraines as an undergraduate student.

In my first full-time position, I had the pleasure of working with a number of incredibly talented students who also experienced a myriad of struggles with mental health, and as I challenged their own internalized perceptions of their mental health, I began to challenge my own. I sought a new therapist and added a new diagnosis, obsessive-compulsive personality disorder—which helped to explain many of my experiences that were not fully encompassed by my anxiety disorders. I also began to recognize the ways in which my other privileged identities as a white, cisgender, middle-class woman affected my access to not only health care resources, but also to accommodations in the workplace and professional legitimacy even with the stigma many people attach to mental health disabilities.

Organization of the Book

We deliberately organized this book to move from foundational philosophical, historical, theoretical, and legal concepts; through exploration of the albeit limited literature on the interaction of disability with other aspects of identity and experience; to a focus on environmental issues; before focusing on very practice-oriented chapters. We believe that effective, socially just disability work requires understanding why particular strategies do or do not work in particular settings and with particular individuals and groups, and that "why" comes from philosophy, history, theory, and laws. While we recognize that some readers may want to jump directly to strategies for particular functional areas of campus, we encourage all readers to engage with the preceding chapters so they can best tailor their work in light of the foundational material.

This book begins with an Introduction in which we discuss our social justice framework, language that we have chosen to use in this book, and the additional theoretical perspectives that underlie the text. The book has four parts: "Foundational Concepts" (chapters 1 through 4, addressing history, theory, law, and ways of classifying disability); "Population-Specific Experiences" (chapters 5 through 7, focusing on social identities, diverse populations and campuses, and faculty and staff with disabilities); "Environmental Issues" (chapters 8 through 12, focused on the campus environment, campus climate, universal design, assistive technology, and instructional issues); and "Serving Students" (chapters 13 through 15, on disability resource offices, student affairs units, and transition-related topics). Each chapter starts with a vignette or quote from one of us or from students, faculty, or staff who offered invaluable contributions to our research for this book. Each chapter closes with discussion questions that serve as tools for reflection and practical application of the issues and concepts described in the chapter. The Conclusion to the book presents a new framework for a socially just approach to disability in higher education and strategies to implement the framework.

Introduction

In the Introduction, we describe what we mean by a social justice approach to disability, frame the language we use in the book, discuss language to avoid, and provide a rationale for the material we have chosen to include. We close by suggesting that a social justice approach accepts that bodies and minds come in a wide variety of forms and advocate that all people are deserving of respect and equality regardless of how they function (Nocella, 2009).

Part 1: Foundational Concepts

In the first chapter, we provide an overview of the history of disability in the United States. We review both the social context in which the education of people with disabilities took place and the major events in the development of higher education that affected disabled individuals. In Chapter 2, we present the various models of disability that have guided society's understanding and treatment of people with disabilities over time and currently. We also examine how disability models can inform student affairs professionals and faculty who work with students with disabilities.

In Chapter 3, we discuss how disability law and legal initiatives play a significant role in shaping the educational experiences of people with disabilities. We provide a brief historical overview of four foundational pieces of legislation pertaining to disability and education and then focus on current and upcoming legal issues, including accessible technology, auxiliary aids, standardized testing, barrier removal, housing, emotional support animals, and accommodations for temporary disabilities. We conclude by discussing socially just approaches to interpreting disability law.

Chapter 4 is focused on different individual and social factors that influence how people think about and experience disability. We review the broad variability within and among forms of impairment. We conclude by providing definitions of and reviewing statistics on the prevalence of forms of impairment found most often in college student populations.

Part 2: Population-Specific Experiences

In Chapter 5, we address the influences of the multiple identities of individuals with disabilities. We examine as well the concept of disability identity and provide an overview of several theories of disability identity development that can inform student affairs professionals and faculty who work with students with disabilities. In addition, we examine numerous ways that race, gender, sexual orientation, and social class influence the individual experiences of people with disabilities in the college and university environment.

In Chapter 6, we continue the theme of multiple aspects of disabled students' identity and focus on lived experiences that affect different student populations' access to and experience within higher education. We discuss topics salient to disabled students who are also adult learners, community college students, English language learners, first-generation college students, international students, single-parent students, student athletes, transfer students, undocumented students, and students who are veterans.

Chapter 7 has a focus on the specific experiences and context of university staff and faculty members with disabilities. It contains an overview of case law, legislation, and regulations regarding employment and reporting, as well as climate issues specific to faculty and staff, and concludes with recommendations for policy and practice. This chapter will be of particular interest to human resources staff, as well as staff and faculty who have disabilities or who have colleagues with disabilities.

Part 3: Environmental Issues

The third part of the book addresses multiple aspects of the campus environment. In Chapter 8, we discuss aspects of the campus environment and the effects they have on students with disabilities. Specifically, we examine the ways in which the human aggregate (faculty and students), the organizational structure (university policies and practices), and the physical environment (architecture, landscape, and location) affect the performance, satisfaction, and well-being of students with disabilities and recommend ways in which these aspects of the environment can be modified to better address the needs of disabled students.

The focus of Chapter 9 is on how disabled students experience the campus climate and the effects that the climate has on those students. We include in this discussion a summary of a recent multicampus study of campus climate experienced by students with disabilities and a model for transforming campus climates to be more welcoming for this student population.

In Chapter 10, we examine the concept of universal design and its application to various aspects of the campus environment, as well as to instruction. We explore the relationship of universal design and social justice and describe specific programs that provide resources and materials to assist college and university staff in developing universally designed initiatives.

In Chapter 11, we explore how technology can improve the autonomy and independence of many individuals, including those with disabilities. Technology is increasingly present in the day-to-day functioning of colleges and universities, and when it is employed in an accessible manner, it can be a strong tool for the retention and positive experiences of students, faculty, and staff with disabilities. In this chapter we outline categories of technology, tips for usage, and guidelines for reviewing accessibility.

In Chapter 12, we examine current classroom practices for working with students with disabilities, critique existing methods, and explore the implications of universally designed instruction for the education of students with disabilities. We include examples of good practice for instructing disabled students and other nontraditional students who also benefit from universal design.

Part 4: Serving Students

In Chapter 13, we focus on disability resource offices and their staff. We describe the administrative, service provision, and outreach roles that are critical to student success and community education and the role of disability resource practitioners in advocating for social justice.

In Chapter 14, we examine current practices and socially just approaches to engaging and supporting students with disabilities in higher education. We start by discussing current research on retention of students with disabilities and describe the importance of universal design in student affairs. Then we provide an overview of functional areas within student affairs, using specific examples and existing research to demonstrate effective uses of universal design.

In Chapter 15, we address the transitions into, during, and out of postsecondary education for students with disabilities. We also continue the discussion of student affairs functional areas in relation to admissions, orientation, transfer students, study abroad, career services, and graduate school preparation. In particular, we highlight the roles that vocational rehabilitation and K-12 education play in the transition process and call attention to the lack of research focused on the transitions that occur while in college.

Conclusion

We conclude by presenting seven core principles of a socially just approach to disability in the specific context of higher education. We explain how those principles might manifest to create a higher education environment free from ableism.

ABOUT THE AUTHORS

Nancy J. Evans is professor (on permanent disability) in the School of Education at Iowa State University, where she previously taught in and coordinated the college student affairs program. She holds an MFA from Western Illinois University in theatre, a PhD from the University of Missouri-Columbia in counseling psychology, an MSEd from Southern Illinois University-Carbondale in higher education-college student personnel, and a BS from the State University of New York at Potsdam in social science. Professional positions she has held include associate professor of counselor education, counseling psychology, and rehabilitation at the Pennsylvania State University; associate professor of counselor education and college student personnel at Western Illinois University; assistant professor of higher education and student affairs at Indiana University; counseling psychologist and assistant professor at Bowling Green State University; residence counselor at Stephens College; and assistant dean of students at Tarkio College. Evans has received the following awards from ACPA—College Student Educators International: Lifetime Achievement Award, Voice of Inclusion Award, Diamond Honoree, Senior Scholar, Contribution to Knowledge Award, and Annuit Coeptis Senior Professional. She also received the Legacy of the Profession Award from NASPA-Student Affairs Administrators in Higher Education and the Research Award from the Association for Assessment in Counseling and Evaluation. Iowa State University has presented her with the following awards: Thielen Award for Service to the Division of Student Services; Award for Superior Service to Alumni; Superior Research Medallion, College of Education; and Superior Teaching Award, College of Education.

Evans has been actively involved in ACPA throughout her career, serving as its president from 2001 to 2002, cochair of the 2009 Next Generation conference, chair of Books and Media Board, editorial board member of the *Journal of College Student Development*, and chair of the Commission on Professional Preparation. Her other books include *Student Development in College* (2nd edition), with Deanna S. Forney, Florence Guido, Lori Patton, and Kristen Renn; *Developing Social Justice Allies*, with Robert D. Reason, Ellen M. Broido, and Tracey L. Davis; *Foundations of Student Affairs Practice*, with Florence A. Hamrick and John Schuh; *Toward Acceptance*, with Vernon Wall; *Student Development in College*, with Deanna S. Forney and Florence Guido-DiBrito; and *Beyond Tolerance*, with Vernon Wall. Evans's scholarly interests center around the experiences of minoritized groups, particularly disabled students and LGBT students, on college campuses.

Ellen M. Broido is associate professor in Bowling Green State University's Higher Education and Student Affairs program, with an affiliate appointment in Women, Gender, and Sexuality Studies. She holds an EdD from the Pennsylvania State University in counselor education, an MSEd from Indiana University in both college student personnel administration and counseling and counselor education, and an AB from Columbia College of Columbia University in biology. She has held professional positions including coordinator of University Studies/student affairs partnerships and assistant professor of University Studies at Portland State University, residence director and judicial coordinator at the University of Massachusetts–Amherst, and chemistry teacher at the Bishop's School. Broido has received several awards from ACPA, including the Disability Leadership Award from the Standing Committee for Disability, the Annuit Coeptis Emerging Professional award, and recognition as an Emerging Scholar. Bowling Green State University has presented her with the President's Award for Collaborative Research and Creative Work.

Broido has contributed to ACPA throughout her career, serving as a member of the governing board, editor and chair of the Books and Media Board, directorate body member of the Commission on Professional Preparation, and member of the editorial board of the *Journal of College Student Development* and several presidential task forces. She wrote *Developing Social Justice Allies* with Robert D. Reason, Nancy J. Evans, and Tracey L. Davis. Broido's research and writing interests span a range of social justice issues in the context of higher education, including disability activism; experiences of students with disabilities; experiences of classified, administrative, and faculty women; gendered dynamics in faculty service; ally development; and LBG student issues.

Kirsten R. Brown is a student affairs professional at the University of Wisconsin-Madison and a part-time faculty member in sociology at Madison College. She completed her PhD in higher education administration and student affairs at Bowling Green State University. She also holds a master's in sociology from the University of Wisconsin-Milwaukee and a bachelor of science from Carroll College. Brown was awarded the Disability Leadership Award by ACPA's Standing Committee on Disability in recognition of her research contributions. She is active in several professional organizations and has presented nationally at ASHE, NAFSA, and ACPA. Her research agenda addresses issues of access, diversity, and outcomes in higher education. Specifically, she is interested in practices that support the retention and success of students with disabilities in postsecondary education. Brown's recently published work focuses on neuro and learning diversity, autism spectrum disorder (ASD), and disability research methods.

Autumn K. Wilke is an academic affairs professional at Grinnell College working as the assistant dean for disability resources. She completed her MEd in educational leadership and policy studies at Iowa State University. She also completed a certificate in postsecondary disability services from the University of Connecticut. Wilke was awarded the Annuit Coeptis Emerging Professional Award by ACPA. She has been active in the directorate body of the ACPA Commission for Social Justice Educators and AHEAD's Standing Committee on Member Development.

INTRODUCTION: A SOCIAL JUSTICE FOUNDATION

In this introduction, we lay the foundation for the rest of the book. We define what we mean by a social justice approach to disability and how it relates to additional approaches that frame this text. Furthermore, we explain our choice of vocabulary and provide definitions of key terms. This information is necessary to understand and contextualize the material that follows in the rest of this book.

A Social Justice Lens

A social justice approach explicitly recognizes and challenges the ableism present in individuals, institutions, and society. Griffin, Peters, and Smith (2007) defined *ableism* as "a pervasive system of discrimination and exclusion of people with disabilities ... privileg[ing] temporarily able-bodied people and disadvantag[ing] people with disabilities" (p. 335). Ableism, like other forms of oppression, operates on multiple levels, including the interactions between individuals; in institutions (e.g., institutions of higher education and specific employment settings); social systems (e.g., educational and legal systems); and social-cultural norms, expectations, and assumptions (Hardiman, Jackson, & Griffin, 2007). Ableism includes the assumption that "certain abilities are essential" (Hutcheon & Wolbring, 2012, p. 40) to "normal" existence. Examples include the assumption that all people have the ability to dress themselves, focus on one topic at a time, spell correctly, or be alert in all settings. Ableism points out that certain forms of assistance are stigmatized (e.g., assistance with accessing printed material, using a tablet to communicate, or using a personal assistant to bathe), while other forms of assistance are seen as unremarkable (e.g., assistance with choosing one's major or applying for financial aid). By stigmatizing only particular forms of assistance, ableism makes invisible the fact that all people are interdependent, relying on each other for multiple forms of help.

Evans and Herriott (2009) argued that the goals of a social justice approach to disability include the elimination of ableism and the critique, redefinition, or expansion of what is considered normal so that all types of physical, mental, and sensory differences are accepted and appreciated. A social justice approach accepts that bodies and minds come in a wide variety of forms and advocates that all people are deserving of respect and equality regardless of how they function (Nocella, 2009). L. Brown (2014) explained that this means creating

> a world in which all supports are natural supports provided unquestioningly, without the feeling of legal or contractual obligation, but because of a sense of human dignity and decency, and where those supports are not viewed as accommodations for a standard system but natural and normal facets of a universally designed system. (pp. 44–45)

In addition, a social justice approach to disability explicitly examines the diversity of experiences, roles, and identities of disabled people, recognizing that people's experiences are shaped by multiple aspects of their social identities. For example, a student with a learning disorder (LD) who was raised in an economically privileged family and community may experience that disability very differently from a student who grew up in a family and community with inadequate financial resources. These differences might arise from greater financial access to private testing and supports and fewer assumptions that the disability was a consequence of poor parenting (given the common assumption that wealthier families parent more effectively than parents with lower income; "Choose Your Parents Wisely," 2014), although there is strong evidence to the contrary (see Dermott & Pomati, 2015). Hence, a social justice perspective takes an intersectional approach and considers the whole person, including factors beyond disability.

Within social justice paradigms, oppression is presumed to manifest on personal, institutional, and social/cultural levels. Thus, in this book, we explore personal attitudes about disability—those held by people without disabilities and by disabled people themselves. We examine institutional structures, programs, and policies as these are the institutional manifestations of ableism. Additionally, we argue for approaches to disability on campus that recognize the ways in which all members of the higher education community, those with and without disability, have been socialized to view disability and the ways that socialization is reflected in the organizational systems, norms, and assumptions that shape higher education.

In using a social justice approach, we recognize the influential role of the environment in creating ableism, as argued by social constructionist perspectives on disability. We also acknowledge that people's bodies and minds can at times create challenges that even the most inclusive environments cannot solve. S. J. Williams (1999) and Shakespeare (2014), among many others, have noted that even in completely inclusive, universally designed environments, people may experience functional limitations because of their bodies and minds. In short, we believe it is necessary to consider the biological realities of people's bodies and minds, as well as the environment, in understanding and addressing disability and ableism.

While social justice is the foundational approach of this book, our thinking is expanded by several other complementary theoretical perspectives; we present a brief overview here, and they are detailed in Chapter 2. For example, our understanding of the importance of both the body and the environment comes from the critical realist approach to disability (Danermark, 2002). In addition, critical disability theory has informed our approach, particularly its recognition that disabilities are not static, and explicit attention to ways that disability interacts with other aspects of social identity (Corker, 1998; Shildrick, 2012).

Our social justice approach also aligns closely with the newly articulated disability justice movement. Arising in the late 2000s, the disability justice movement explicitly addresses the absence of people from multiple marginalized groups (particularly people of color and lesbian, bisexual, gay, and transgender people) from the discourse on disability and from leadership roles in the disability rights movement. Additionally, it challenges the dominant disability rights perspective that the goal of disability activism should be independence, recognizing that interdependence is inherent in all aspects of human existence (Mingus, 2011).

Critical realism, critical disability theory, and disability justice are distinct approaches, yet they are mutually compatible and provide important refinements and extensions of each other. Throughout this book, we use foundational concepts from all four theoretical approaches. Furthermore, we as authors also hold an understanding of broader theoretical perspectives and social systems that surround higher education; thus, readers will notice connections to feminism, theories of privilege, critical race theory, and sociological perspectives. Despite this broad view, we recognize that our frameworks, experiences, and most of the research we draw on in this book are grounded in Western perspectives; as we reiterate in the Conclusion, there is much to be learned from non-Western frameworks and experiences.

Language

The language we use to describe disability, impairments, people, and environments carries historical legacies and reflects social, political, and moral values. In this section, we describe and define some of the terms we use in this book, some of the words we have deliberately chosen not to use, and the rationale for our choices. Words and phrases that are considered respectful and inclusive in one social, geographical, theoretical, or historical context can be triggering and offensive in another. We recognize the importance of language in creating shared understanding, acknowledge that not everyone welcomes the words we use, and see the explanation of our choices as an opportunity for dialogue rather than an assertion of absolute or permanent definitions.

As is the experience of multiple other minoritized groups, disabled people differ from each other in multiple, meaningful ways, including different preferences for language choices. While our intent has been to be simultaneously as inclusive, as precise, and as descriptive as possible, we know our usage reflects our own experiences, values, and sociohistorical context and that some readers may find our usage alienating, disrespectful, dated, or otherwise problematic. Even we as the authors of this book are not always in agreement about our use of language, and our understandings and choices have evolved over the course of writing this book.

People with disabilities have been labeled many different ways over time, including as *handicapped*. The use of the word *handicapped* to refer to people with disabilities often is misunderstood as deriving from disabled people holding their caps out to beg for alms (i.e., holding their caps in their hands, hence, hand-i-cap), but this is erroneous (Handicaprice, 2011). According to Stiker (1999), the word *handicap* originated in horse racing to designate ways to equalize chances of winning. At the beginning of the 20th century, the word began more generally to signify disfavor, disadvantage, or hindrance and to be applied to people with disabilities (Disability, 2015). The word, as a description of people, is considered disrespectful in most contexts, but is appropriately used to describe aspects of an environment that create challenges or difficulty. Thus, a small font size on a PowerPoint presentation is a handicap for those with some forms of visual impairment.

We use *impairment* to refer to the ways in which people's bodies or minds differ from what society deems "normal" or "typical." *Impairment* therefore refers to specific physical, psychological, sensory, cognitive, or health conditions, whether present at birth or acquired later. That said, some people, particularly those in the Deaf community and those with various forms of learning disabilities, do not view their differences as impairments but as equally effective ways of communicating, thinking, and processing information. The use of the capital D in *Deaf* indicates reference to members of a linguistic and cultural group rather than a form of impairment.

The terms *neurodiverse, neurodivergent,* and *neuroatypical* refer to forms of neurological functioning that differ from dominant assumptions caused by autism, dyslexia, brain trauma, medication, and numerous other sources (Antonetta, 2007; Walker, 2014).

We use *disabled* to refer to the ways in which people's activities are restricted by their environments (and thus, as a synonym for *handicap*), and *disability* as the noun form of *disabled.* Shakespeare (2014) pointed out that the distinction between *impairment* and *disability* is incomplete and unstable, and readers will note we vary our usage throughout the text.

We agree with the critical realist perspective that disability is a consequence of individual and environmental causes, as well as their interaction (Shakespeare, 2014). Disability may be a result of environmental barriers, including policy (e.g., people are required to stand to work in certain jobs), physical design (e.g., laboratories can be reached only by taking the stairs), or attitudes (e.g., not hiring a hearing-impaired student to be a resident assistant because the employer assumes the student could not perform the job). Furthermore, disability may result from people's impairments or an interaction of the person and the environment (Lewin, 1936).

In our usage of *disability*, we differ from the social constructionists, who would argue that disability is solely a consequence of environmental barriers (Sherry, 2007), and adherents of the medical and rehabilitation models, who would argue that *disability* and *impairment* are different words for the same thing (Drum, 2009), a problem located in an individual's mind or body. We also recognize that disability may function as an identity label (Shakespeare, 2014; Sherry, 2007), although many, perhaps most, people who are legally or medically considered to have a disability do not identify as disabled (Shakespeare, 2014). Our usage is consistent with that used in the United Nations Convention on the Rights of Persons with Disabilities: "Persons with disabilities include those who have long-term physical, mental, intellectual, or sensory impairments which in interaction with various barriers may hinder their full and effective participation in society on an equal basis with others" (United Nations General Assembly, 2007, Article 1).

In this book, we use both *person-first* and *disability-first* language. This choice reflects the multiple audiences of this book. Person-first language (e.g., *people with* disabilities) was promulgated within the rehabilitation professional community at least as early as 1975 (Manus, 1975), although some credit a letter to the editor of *BusinessWeek* in 1988 (Eblin, 1988) with introducing this phrasing to a broader audience. However, this usage was quickly rejected in other circles, particularly the Deaf, autistic, and blind communities (see, e.g., the 1993 resolution from the National Federation of the Blind rejecting the use of person-first language for blind people, reprinted in Jernigan, 2009).

We agree with Gable (2001), who wrote about disability-related language usage in the United States, stating:

> For many years, person-first language has prevailed, and for good reasons. Person-first language requires one to privilege the individual as a person with full humanity. In person-first language, educators use phrases such as student with a disability and students with learning disabilities. The person-first movement grew out of disability activists' press for social recognition of biased language that dehumanizes people about whom references to disability were made (Blaska, 1993; Bogdan & Biklen, 1977; Zola, 1993). Disability-first language has recently reemerged among many disability studies scholars, but it is used in two ways. Some scholars and disability activists are using disability-first language (e.g., disabled person or disabled woman) to show disability pride (Gabel, 1997; Linton, 1998). This trend is similar to the gay pride trend of recent years. Other disability scholars are using disability-first language to represent the power of the social consequences of particular ways of being. In this usage, privileging disability symbolizes the oppressive or discriminatory social conditions facing disabled people (Abberley, 1987; Linton, 1998; Peters, 1996; Shakespeare, 1997). (p. 32)

Gable's (2001) arguments have been repeated by other scholars (e.g., Albrecht, Seelman, & Bury, 2001b; Shakespeare, 2014) and increasingly by disability activists (e.g., Ladau, 2014). Additional rationales for using disability-first language include arguments made by Collier (2012), who argued that "sticking a word in the shadow of a noun can create the impression that there is something inherently wrong with it, that it should be hidden" (p. E939), and by Titchkosky (2011), who wrote, "The desire to shore up a firm separation between people and disability, by privileging the former and diminishing the latter, points to an image of disability as a kind of danger" (p. 53). (We note that in the United Kingdom, disability-first language has been the norm within the disability-rights community since its beginning.)

Other scholars (e.g., Hutcheon & Wolbring, 2012) take additional linguistic approaches, using language such as "ability diverse," and "those with presumed impairments" (p. 39), reflecting their grounding in a social constructionist perspective. In this book, we chose not to reproduce linguistic hierarchies of meaning; rather, we employ both person-first and disability-first language because we honor both positions. In working with students, faculty, and staff, we strongly advocate for using the individual's preferred language.

We use the term *functional limitation* to describe the ways in which people's activities are limited or restricted, whether by impairment or environment. Thus, a person with dyslexia may be functionally limited in her or his ability to read quickly or spell accurately. Environments influence functional limitations; a person with a mobility impairment may move easily on level ground but find it difficult to be as quick or cover the same distance if the footing is uneven. Note that a variety of impairments may result in the same functional limitation.

Language We Avoid

We choose not to use language that implies people with disabilities are, because of their disability, tragic, pitiful, or otherwise less than human. Phrases such as "afflicted with," "suffers from," and "overcomes" are problematic because they imply that people with disabilities are inherently miserable and that disability is fundamentally a deficit. Phrases that inaccurately limit the agency of disabled people also should be avoided. For example, people "use" wheelchairs, rather than being "confined" to wheelchairs, or "wheelchair bound." We also avoid using language that heroizes, idealizes, or ascribes positive traits to people merely because of their impairments. For example, people with disabilities are not inherently stronger or more determined, brave, or courageous than anyone else. Use of these adjectives in the absence of knowledge about a specific person's personality or character is as dehumanizing as the terms listed at the start of the paragraph. Disabled people are people, with the same distribution of strengths and flaws as all other humans. Numerous listings of additional examples of respectful and inclusive, as well as problematic, language are available on the Internet, and we encourage readers new to disability issues to review those sources.

Conclusion

Our goal in writing this book is to expand the conversation about disability in higher education beyond the traditional narrative of the deficits of people with disabilities, legal compliance, and academic accessibility; to challenge those in higher education to consider what truly inclusive practice across the range of the collegiate experience might look like; and to center the experiences of students, staff, and faculty with disabilities. The frameworks and language presented in this introduction form the foundations of that dialogue.

PART ONE

FOUNDATIONAL CONCEPTS

CHAPTER ONE

A HISTORY OF DISABILITY
IN HIGHER EDUCATION

I grew up before the passage of the ADA [Americans With Disabilities Act]. Although I learned to be self-sufficient and mentally strong, I certainly experienced the effects of discrimination that the ADA later addressed. For instance, the college I had my heart set on attending advised me not to enroll since, because of my disability, they did not believe I could be successful there. Instead of giving up on college, however, I found a school that was willing to admit me, ended up graduating with a 3.23 GPA, and became student government president. Unconsciously, I think I needed to prove that I could succeed regardless of what the first school told me.

—Nancy, faculty member

I n this chapter we present a history of disability in the United States, with particular attention given to disability in higher education. We started this book by writing a chronological history of disability in higher education, and about 120 pages into that chapter we stopped. (A chronology is in the chapter appendix.) We cannot tell you all of that rich, deep, and diverse history in this book, because the history of disability in higher education is a book unto itself—and to shorten or condense that rich struggle down to a single chapter is unethical. We would not be authors of this book, or even people with a college degree, if it were not for the disabled people who came before us; they made higher education a possibility for women like us with physical, learning, and mental health impairments. So rather than trying to squeeze 200 years of history into one chapter, we have selected three historical themes that show why social justice is imperative. In doing so, we know that the scope of the three themes or stories represented in this chapter—Deaf education, the influence of war veterans, and disability activism—is limited and represents only a fraction of the disability history of the United States. However, our goal is not comprehensive coverage; rather, we use these stories to illustrate why social justice is necessary. Furthermore, although attitudes about disability have evolved to some extent, astute readers will notice that bias, prejudice, and the prize of normalcy continue to exist and have systemic legal and societal impacts on the inclusion of people with disabilities.

Disability cannot be understood without examining the many historical connotations leading to different ways of viewing, interacting with, and treating individuals who have been labeled "disabled" (Nielsen, 2012). Burch and Sutherland (2006) pointed out that "social values and cultural perceptions have strongly framed what qualifies as a disability and have influenced the responses" (p. 129). While individuals with disabilities have always experienced their situations in various ways, what has been shared among disabled individuals throughout history and across categories of impairment are "experiences of cultural devaluation and socially imposed restriction [and] of personal and collective [struggle] for self-definition and self-determination" (Longmore & Umansky, 2001, p. 4).

In addition to excluding people with disabilities from most of the privileges of citizenship, the concept of disability itself was used to exclude other groups from citizenship, namely women, people of color, and immigrants (Baynton, 2001). Each of these groups was assumed to have physical, emotional, intellectual, and/or psychological flaws that precluded their ability to carry out the responsibilities of full membership in society (Baynton, 2001). And in arguing for full rights to participate in society, these groups used the argument that they were *not* disabled, thereby suggesting that it was legitimate to discriminate against those who did have physical, mental, or psychological impairments (Baynton, 2001).

Historically, position in society has largely dictated who was educated and how that education occurred. As Bryan (1996) stated, "In American society, education is a prerequisite to almost any endeavor one may undertake" (p. 15). While opportunities for higher education became broader over time, the further people were from positions of power, the less likely they were to be afforded the benefits of a college education (Thelin, 2011), which continues to be the case. And as we discuss in this chapter, people with disabilities have, for the most part, been very far from positions of power and have had to fight to legitimate their very existence in society, as well as their right to an education. Indeed, in the leading book on the history of higher education in the United States, *A History of American Higher Education* (2011), its author, John Thelin, made no mention of the education of students with disabilities or of laws that have mandated the inclusion of disabled students, such as the Americans With Disabilities Act (ADA).

Here, we offer a counternarrative: we proudly show how disabled students, faculty, and staff have been an important part of higher education by examining the themes of Deaf education, veterans, and disability rights activism. We chose these themes because they have influenced the education of students with disabilities in important ways. First, Deaf children were the first group of children outside the boundary of those considered physically "normal" to receive an education. They were also the only group to have an institution of higher education specifically established to provide them with a college education. Second, throughout history, war veterans who became disabled as a result of their service to their country changed the nature of the student body entering higher education. To prepare disabled veterans for careers they could enter, state and federal governments established policies to fund their pursuit of higher education, leading to increased numbers of disabled students on college campuses and the development of programs and services to support them. Finally, disability activism illustrates the roles that disabled individuals have taken to enhance their education and establish their civil rights and equitable treatment in society.

Deaf Education

During the colonial era, higher education was primarily for wealthy White males, particularly those intended for careers in political leadership or the clergy. Colleges, in effect, established which individuals would make up the elite members of colonial society (Thelin, 2004). Certainly the chances that disabled individuals would receive any type of education were almost nonexistent. One exception was the deaf offspring of a few of the wealthiest Americans who were sent to deaf schools that had been established in Europe in the 1700s (Leigh, 2009). Deaf education in the United States itself began in 1817 and has shaped and influenced the inclusion of disabled people in education.

Early Deaf Education

During the Second Great Awakening, a period of spiritual resurgence and zeal that occurred in the United States between the 1790s and 1830s, a belief in people's ability to become better human beings through education and moral enrichment, emerged ("Educating the Senses," 2014). This positive belief system led to a social reform movement in which upper- and middle-class urban inhabitants worked to improve the conditions of the poor, the sensory impaired, the mentally and psychologically disabled, and others whom they perceived to be spiritually impoverished (ushistory.org, 2016). The development of common schools was a result of this philosophy (Warder, 2014). Horace Mann, labeled the Father of the Common School Movement, who served as secretary of the Massachusetts Board of Education starting in 1837, believed that the best way to achieve "the moral and socioeconomic uplift" of all citizens was to establish universal, free, nonsectarian, and public educational institutions—common schools (Warder, 2014).

At this time in Europe, several Catholic clergy became interested in finding ways to communicate with deaf and blind individuals and developed sign language and braille to do so (Griffin, Peters, & Smith, 2007; Patterson, 2009; Stiker, 1999). In the United States, as a result of the Second Great Awakening, evangelical Protestants took on the mission of educating deaf and blind children about Christianity using the same tools (Burch, 2001; "Educating the Senses," 2014; Nielsen, 2012). By the late 1840s, advocates for disabled children, especially Samuel Gridley Howe and Hervey Wilber, argued that in the appropriate setting, these children, as well as children who were psychologically or cognitively impaired, could be educated and prepared for work (Nielsen, 2012). Disabled children were considered "trainable" if they were in controlled settings where they could receive moral and humane treatment (Byrom, 2001; "Educating the Senses," 2014; Stiker, 1999; Trent, 2009). As a result, special schools for disabled children emerged during the 19th century.

At the urging of several parents of deaf children, the first school for disabled children in the United States, the Connecticut Asylum for the Education and Instruction of Deaf and Dumb Persons (which became known as the American Asylum for the Deaf), was founded in 1817 in Hartford, Connecticut (Cerney, 2013). The parents, led by Mason Fitch Cogswell, convinced Thomas Hopkins Gallaudet, a hearing minister, to travel to Europe to learn how to educate deaf individuals and then to open the school in Connecticut (Crowley, 2014). In Europe, he met Frenchman Laurent Clerc, who was himself deaf and had graduated from the National Institute in Paris, where he learned sign language, and he convinced Clerc to return to Connecticut with him and teach at his school (Cerney, 2013; Crowley, 2014). Additional residential schools for deaf children developed across the northern and midwestern states (Cerney, 2013). While children who attended residential deaf schools received an education, it was mostly vocational and few were prepared to enter college (Griffin et al., 2007).

Fewer deaf schools were opened in the southern states during the 1800s, and those that were available were racially segregated and of lower quality (Nielsen, 2012). The problem of the lack of schools for deaf children in the South was compounded by the reluctance of wealthy White southerners to send their children to racially integrated deaf (and blind) schools in the North that were often run by abolitionists (Burch & Sutherland, 2006; Nielsen, 2012).

Although deaf schools in the West and North were integrated by the mid-1800s, southern deaf schools were not (Nielsen, 2012). Indeed, it was 1869 before the first deaf school for Black children was opened in North Carolina (Chronology, 2009; Landecker, 2014). Like mainstream public schools, deaf schools remained segregated from Reconstruction through the 1950s, with Louisiana being the last to integrate in 1978 (Burch & Sutherland, 2006; Landecker, 2014).

Deaf schools established for southern African Americans received only minimal financial support from state and local sources and were substandard in both facilities and teaching as a result. Black teachers generally had little training in deaf education, and many created their own unique sign language dialects, different from American Sign Language (ASL) and often from the dialects used in other Black deaf schools (Nielsen, 2012). These differences were significant enough that once deaf schools were integrated, Black children could not understand their White teachers and classmates (Landecker, 2014). These differences contributed to the segregation of the African American deaf community, although deaf African American graduates of deaf schools did build relationships with each other and a sense of Deaf community among themselves (Nielsen, 2012).

This difference continues to be a concern for African American d/Deaf students, who often cannot understand White interpreters and generally have family members who are not certified interpreters sign for them (Fleischer & Zames, 2011). Other ethnic deaf groups face similar issues if the sign language they have learned is not ASL, such as members of Latinx and Asian Deaf communities. Some funding became available in 1996 to train Black interpreters at LaGuardia Community College, but little effort has been extended to address the limited understanding of minority group members (Fleischer & Zames, 2011).

Oralism Versus Manualism

Around the middle of the 19th century, oralism was introduced into deaf schools in the United States (Cerney, 2013). This method of communication, which involved the use of lipreading and speech rather than sign language, originated in Europe and was advocated by the educators Horace Mann and Samuel Gridley Howe, who observed this method of educating deaf students during a trip to Germany in 1843 (Edwards, 2001). Howe opened an oral school for the deaf in Massachusetts in 1867, and throughout the rest of the 19th century and into the 20th century, deaf educators battled over the preferred method of communication for deaf students, with oralism becoming prominent by the end of the 19th century (Edwards, 2001).

Oralists viewed sign language as "disorderly, irrational gesticulation"; they argued that "real thought and learning could only take place through oral and written language" (Longmore, 2003, p. 42). Most hearing educators supported oralism for another reason: they believed it would lead to the assimilation of Deaf students into mainstream society (Burch, 2001). They reasoned that if sign language were eliminated, then deaf individuals would have to communicate using spoken language, which would weaken the development of a separate Deaf culture and community. The oralists preferred that deaf people assimilate into the spoken community, where they would be less of a threat to mainstream culture (Cerney, 2013; Longmore, 2003). Led by Alexander Graham Bell, hearing educators and politicians argued that such communities would contribute to Deaf people marrying and producing more deaf children, which would lead to the continuance of a "defective race of human beings" (Cerney, 2013, p. 475).

However, Deaf people themselves overwhelmingly preferred sign language since they viewed it to be of Deaf origin and therefore their natural language (Edwards, 2001). As such, it was best taught by Deaf educators and provided employment for Deaf adults (Burch & Sutherland, 2006). The reality was that teaching speech to deaf children took an enormous amount of time, required almost one-to-one tutoring, took significant time away from the teaching of academic subjects, and was successful only if the child had become deaf after learning the English language (Longmore, 2003). Profoundly deaf students who could not learn speech were labeled "oral failures" and placed in vocational classes with no opportunity to take academic classwork that might lead to a more challenging career (Van Cleve, 2009). Deaf students continued to learn sign language from the remaining Deaf teachers who taught vocational classes and from older children teaching it to the younger ones (Burch, 2001). They used sign language to communicate outside the classroom and after they left school, thereby thwarting attempts to undermine the development of Deaf community and culture (Baynton, 2009).

A final blow for those in favor of using sign language to teach deaf children came in 1880 at the International Congress on the Education of the Deaf in Milan, Italy, when the 164 educators in attendance, only 1 of whom was deaf, voted to abolish the use of sign language in deaf schools and use oralism exclusively (Griffin et al., 2007; Leigh, 2009). Griffin et al. (2007) noted that in 1867, all deaf schools in the United States taught sign language; by 1907, no schools did. Oralism was used almost exclusively in deaf schools in the United States between the 1890s and the 1920s (Burch & Sutherland, 2006).

Resistance to Oralism. During the Progressive era (1890s–1920s), a strong sense of community developed among blind and Deaf individuals who had been educated in residential schools over the previous 50 years (Burch, 2001; Kudlick, 2001). After graduating from these schools, blind and Deaf adults formed alumni associations, advocacy groups, and other organizations and developed publications to continue to keep in touch with each other and address topics that particularly interested them (Edwards, 2001; Kudlick, 2001). Eugenicists, however, fought against the establishment of Deaf and blind communities, arguing that they would contribute to the growth of these "defective" populations (Burch, 2001). Oralists, most of whom were part of the eugenics movement, also encouraged more deaf students to go to public or day schools, where they could interact with hearing students and would have less opportunity to become a part of a Deaf community (Cerney, 2013). Deaf communities, in turn, worked to disprove the beliefs of the eugenicists and to gain their rights to the same treatment as other U.S. citizens (Burch, 2001).

While it appeared at the close of the 19th century that oralists had defeated manualists (users of sign language) with regard to the language that would be taught in deaf schools, several factors contributed to a resurrection of sign language in the teaching of deaf children. In 1891, Gallaudet College started a school to train teachers for the deaf. Although the school accepted mainly male students who could hear, it also ensured that teachers learned sign language as well as oral methods of teaching the deaf (Burch, 2001). Students in deaf schools continued to practice Deaf culture, learn sign language from each other and from Deaf vocational teachers who remained at the schools, and advocate for their own culture and language once they graduated by expressing their views in independent newspapers (Burch, 2001). As Nielsen (2012) stated, "American Sign Language … remained alive and vibrant due to the sometimes covert, sometimes overt, insistence and resistance of deaf people" (p. 98).

The Reemergence of Sign Language in Deaf Schools. The Great Depression marked the beginning of a resurgence in the use of sign language in deaf residential schools (Burch, 2001). Beginning in 1929, the Deaf community succeeded in having superintendents appointed to head these schools who were more supportive of Deaf interests, arguing that oral programs had not produced positive academic results for deaf students. In addition to providing deaf children with a better education by reinstating sign language, the hiring of Deaf-supportive superintendents helped to promote a more positive identity for Deaf individuals that helped to combat the negative view of Deaf people as defective and deviant that had emerged under oralist superintendents.

By 1939, sign language was again being taught in Deaf schools in many states, and Deaf teachers were hired to teach in these schools (Burch, 2001). Between the end of World War I and the beginning of World War II, as many as 75% of Gallaudet College's graduates became teachers at deaf schools. These teachers, who became important role models for their deaf students, were largely responsible for strengthening the Deaf culture and community and undermining oralism. Poor economic conditions in the United States during the Depression also contributed to the development of a strong Deaf community, since students remained longer at residential Deaf schools because their parents could not afford to bring them home for visits and employment was hard to secure (Nielsen, 2012; Patterson, 2009).

Another factor in the reinstatement of sign language was the popularity of John Dewey's child-centered educational philosophy in the 1930s, which weakened the oralist approach and introduced scientific assessment to determine the effectiveness of school programs (Burch, 2001). Testing of deaf children's hearing at 29 schools in 1924–1925 led to the conclusion that speech ability was related to the age at which the child became deaf, how much residual hearing the child had, and how long the child had had speech training, factors that Deaf people had claimed were important since oralism was introduced.

In 1965, *A Dictionary of American Sign Language on Linguistic Principles* was published by Stokue, Croneberg, and Casterline (as cited in Cerney, 2010). This publication legitimized ASL and contributed to the move away from oralism in the schools (Cerney, 2010; Fleischer & Zames, 2001).

The Effects of Mainstreaming on d/Deaf Students

In 1975, the Education for All Handicapped Children Act was passed, requiring that "all children should receive a 'free, appropriate public education' in the 'least restrictive environment'" (Cerney, 2010, p. 472). While this law pleased parents whose deaf children could now live at home and attend a public school, it was devastating for the residential schools where for generations

Deaf students had learned their language and culture and developed a community (Cerney, 2010). This law has resulted in a loss of funding for residential schools, along with a loss of enrollments.

As important, Cerney (2010) argued, the "system of assimilation" found in public schools fights against the desire of the Deaf community to be viewed as "a unique and culturally viable minority group" and isolates deaf children from others who understand that culture and use sign language (p. 472). During his interviews with disability activists, Charlton (1998) learned from Deaf individuals that they had not had one teacher in their 12 years of public education who was proficient in sign language. In another instance, which resulted in the 1982 *Hendrick Hudson Central School District v. Rowley* Supreme Court case, a Deaf student sued the school district for not providing a full-time interpreter (Fleischer & Zames, 2001). Rather, the school had provided the student with a part-time interpreter and tutors. Because the student was performing adequately academically, the Court ruled in favor of the school system, declaring that there was "no congressional intent to achieve equality of opportunity or services," although this rationale countered the Individuals with Disabilities Education Act (IDEA), discussed in Chapter 3, which required that disabled children be provided with an educational plan that would allow them to achieve their "maximum potential" (Fleischer & Zames, 2001, p. 189).

In the 1980s, the courts were inconsistent regarding cases focusing on what constituted a "least restricted environment," with some ruling that segregated schools for disabled children were legal, while others pushed for integration and mainstreaming (Fleischer & Zames, 2001). A third opinion the courts provided, which applied to physically disabled and deaf children, was that physical accommodations, created however the school wished, took precedence over issues related to least restrictive environments. The latter ruling meant that d/Deaf children could be placed in special education or any other segregated location within the school.

Research completed in the 1980s documented that since deaf children of deaf parents had been exposed to complete language usage through sign from birth, they were better at language concepts than deaf children of hearing parents (Fleischer & Zames, 2001). Therefore, deaf students who have learned sign language as a first language are well prepared to learn English as a second written language. One expert, Marcia Bernstein, stressed that anyone who teaches d/Deaf individuals should be proficient in ASL (Fleischer & Zames, 2001). As a result, a number of state-supported schools and charter schools for d/Deaf students now require that all teachers instruct mostly in ASL (Fleischer & Zames, 2001).

Higher Education for Deaf Students

With the significant number of deaf schools in the United States by the mid-19th century, a strong network of advocates pressed for opportunities for deaf high school graduates to have the opportunity to attend college (de Lorenzo, 2009). In 1864, at the urging of Edward Gallaudet, the son of Thomas Gallaudet, Congress authorized Columbia Institution for the Instruction of the Deaf, Dumb, and Blind to confer college degrees under the name the National Deaf-Mute College (renamed Gallaudet College in 1894 in honor of Edward Gallaudet's father, Thomas Hopkins Gallaudet, and Gallaudet University in 1986; de Lorenzo, 2009). Gallaudet was fully accredited in 1957 and began a graduate program in 1962 (J. W. Madaus, 2000). Its purpose was to provide opportunities for d/Deaf students to gain the knowledge and skills to undertake professional employment (de Lorenzo, 2009; J. W. Madaus, 2000, 2011). Initially, blind students were also admitted to the institution, but just a year later, they were transferred to the Maryland Institution at Baltimore (Griffin et al., 2007).

After the Civil War, more colleges and universities began admitting women (Nielsen, 2012). Gallaudet admitted women when it was established, but in 1871 the college became male only (de Lorenzo, 2009). With pressures increasing, in 1886 women were again admitted to Gallaudet on an experimental basis for two years (de Lorenzo, 2009; Nielsen, 2012). There was no dormitory for the women, who lived instead in the president's home. They could not leave campus without a chaperone or join extracurricular literary societies since it was viewed as improper for them to associate with men (Nielsen, 2012). Although the valedictorian of the class of 1893 was a woman, Agatha Tiegel, the first woman at Gallaudet to graduate with a four-year degree, doubt about the intellectual capabilities of women continued. In a speech to the college, Tiegel gave a passionate address, "The Intellect of Women," in which she proclaimed the equality of women with regard to ability and intellect, as well as their right to an education (Nielsen, 2012). Women continued to enroll at Gallaudet despite pressure from men against coeducation (Nielsen, 2012).

Although a few African American students enrolled in the precollege program at Gallaudet immediately after its founding, they did not graduate from the college (de Lorenzo, 2009). Segregation increased around the turn of the century and in 1903 African American students in the precollege program were transferred to the Maryland School for Colored Deaf Mutes in Baltimore (de Lorenzo, 2009). After a lawsuit by parents, African American deaf students were finally admitted to the Gallaudet precollege program again in 1952 (de Lorenzo, 2009). With support from Deaf mentors, a Black student,

Andrew Foster, was admitted to the college in 1951 (de Lorenzo, 2009); in 1954, he became the first Black student to graduate from Gallaudet.

National Technical Institute for the Deaf. In 1965, the National Technical Institute for the Deaf (NTID) was established by Congress. Rochester Institute of Technology was selected in 1966 to house this institute, which was designed to prepare d/Deaf students for successful employment in technical fields (Griffin et al., 2007; J. W. Madaus, 2000). It opened in 1968 with 70 d/Deaf students enrolled ("History of NTID," n.d.). In addition to programs in technology, in 1969 NTID began the first program in the country to train interpreters ("History of NTID," n.d.).

Deaf President Now!. In 1988, students at Gallaudet College engaged in one of the most important protests in disability history (J. B. Christiansen, 2009). The cause of the protest was the selection of a hearing president for the college by Gallaudet's board of trustees (Griffin et al., 2007). The students found it particularly troublesome that in the 124 years of its existence, Gallaudet had never had a d/Deaf or hard-of-hearing president (Fleischer & Zames, 2001). During the search for a new president, Deaf leaders both on and off campus, including alumni, engaged in a campaign to have a d/Deaf president selected (J. B. Christiansen, 2009). At the end of the search, 9 of the 67 candidates who applied were d/Deaf. Of the 3 finalists interviewed, 2 were d/Deaf. The board selected Elizabeth Zinser, the candidate who was not d/Deaf. When the decision was announced on flyers rather than by a member of the board, the crowd that had gathered to hear the news was outraged, and a protest was held at the hotel where the trustees were staying. After a week of demonstrations, meetings, and marches, during which no classes were held and media covered the events extensively, Zinser stepped down. The board met again and selected one of the d/Deaf finalists, I. King Jordan, as the next president (J. B. Christiansen, 2009; Nielsen, 2012). In addition, when the chairperson of the board of trustees resigned, the first d/Deaf board chairperson was named (J. B. Christiansen, 2009).

The Deaf President Now! (DPN) movement was significant for many reasons. It was a significant event in the history of self-advocacy by the Deaf community (J. B. Christiansen, 2009; Longmore, 2009). Second, it was an important event not just among Deaf activists but also for disability rights activists as a whole; it gave other disabled people encouragement to continue their initiatives (J. B. Christiansen, 2009; Fleischer & Zames, 2001; Pelka, 2012). It was particularly instrumental in changing the political climate that allowed the ADA to be approved just two years later (J. B. Christiansen, 2009;

Fleischer & Zames, 2001; Shapiro, 1993). A final observation by Fleischer and Zames (2011) referred to the effect that the movement had on d/Deaf people themselves. Prior to DPN, d/Deaf people who could speak were perceived to hold the most political power in the Deaf activist community. After DPN, being a Deaf child of Deaf parents gave a person credibility in the new radicalized Deaf community, as did using ASL (Fleischer & Zames (2011).

The Second Gallaudet Protest. When Jordan retired from the presidency of Gallaudet in 2006, controversy again arose over his successor, Jane K. Fernandes, a Gallaudet University administrator (de Lorenzo, 2009). Although Fernandes was deaf, various constituencies, including students, faculty, staff, and alumni, questioned her leadership style, previous policy decisions, and how well she represented Deaf cultural identity. Protesters occupied buildings, camped on the campus green, and closed down the campus, causing suspension of classes. The board of trustees rescinded Fernandes's appointment and instead appointed Robert Davila, a Gallaudet alumnus who had previously served as vice president at Gallaudet. This protest, de Lorenzo (2009) suggested, demonstrated the turmoil that Gallaudet was experiencing internally to define its role in the 21st century, particularly given the technological advances, such as closed captioning and the Internet, that currently allow d/Deaf students to attend almost any college they choose.

Cochlear Implants

One of those innovations was cochlear implants. The first experimental surgeries in the United States to embed cochlear implants occurred in 1961, although deaf children did not start receiving them until after 1977 (Christiansen & Leigh, 2009). Cochlear implants, which include both external and surgically implanted internal parts, are designed to assist individuals to hear when hearing aids are not successful. They are now small enough to fit behind the ear but remain quite expensive. Members of the Deaf community have challenged the use of cochlear implants since they do not see deafness as an impairment and believe that they live meaningful lives using ASL, which is part of their Deaf culture. They particularly protest the implantation of cochlear devices in very young children who cannot make their own decision to have an implant. Waiting until a child is old enough to make a decision is problematic, however, since the younger a person is when the surgery is performed, the better the cochlear implant will work. In 2000, however, the National Association of the Deaf softened its opposition to pediatric cochlear implants because so many individuals were getting them and found them helpful (Leigh, 2009). Deaf parents of deaf children with implants also reported that their children were able to navigate quite well in both the hearing and the Deaf worlds (Leigh, 2009).

Deaf Culture: An Aspect of Social Justice

The theme of d/Deaf education demonstrates several important aspects of social justice, including the right to choose a preferred language; the importance of intersectionality, including race, gender, and social class in determining access; the multiple avenues of discrimination; and the opportunity for a rich, vibrant culture. Deaf culture is perhaps the oldest and strongest disability culture; it first developed in the United States in deaf residential schools in the mid-19th century and grew as ASL was formalized as the language of Deaf people, particularly through their long and tumultuous fight to maintain it in the face of oppression (Kuppers & Wakefield, 2009). According to Leigh (2009), Deaf people have rejected allowing hearing people to define them and instead "view the world ... from a Deaf center, one that reflects a different normality" (p. 14). In its valuing of differences, this idea of a different normality is certainly one that social justice advocates support.

Influence of War Veterans

The United States is a country born out of war, and since its inception over 200 years ago, military conflicts have been a constant factor in its history. From the Revolutionary War to the current conflicts in Iraq and Afghanistan, either active military engagement or the aftermath of war seems to have always been present. A major impact of war is always the veterans who return with some type of impairment, physical or psychological. How to respond to disabled war veterans has been a major issue facing the country for centuries. Certainly, veterans deserve some sort of compensation for their service. Deciding what that compensation will be has been one dilemma the government has faced. How to return veterans to a productive life has been another, addressed by both the government and the medical field. Where disabled veterans fit into society has been a third, and perhaps more nebulous, question that has had to be resolved by society itself.

Early Influences

The philosophy of the Enlightenment, which lasted until the beginning of the 19th century, led to a more rational view of disability than the previous

perspective grounded in religious beliefs (Trent, 2009). The Revolutionary
War Pension Act of 1818 "established disability as a legal and social welfare category" (Nielsen, 2012, p. 54). The War Pension Act also helped legitimize the
medical paradigm; individuals who administered veterans' pensions "began to
require that doctors (rather than local shop owners, neighbors, or ministers)
determine impairments" (Nielsen, 2012, p. 66).

The Civil War led to significant changes in both the northern and southern
United States, including an alteration in how society viewed disability (Logue,
2009; Nielsen, 2012). The war led to the deaths of 620,000 people and left
hundreds of thousands with physical and psychological disabilities, including
around 45,000 amputees (Logue, 2009; Nielsen, 2012). Major decisions had
to be made regarding the futures of these veterans. In addition, the post–Civil
War years were a time of upheaval as the country shifted from predominantly
rural to mostly urban, and the economy, which had been mainly agrarian,
became largely industrial. Reconstruction led to increasing numbers of
former African American slaves moving to the North to seek employment
(Nielsen, 2012).

Disabled Veterans. Since a great number of disabled veterans were amputees,
their immediate need was for devices to assist them with mobility. During
and after the war, a great number of medical devices, such as improved prostheses and wheelchairs, were patented (Logue, 2009; Nielsen, 2012). These
devices were a great help to all individuals with mobility impairments, not
just veterans.

Securing employment was difficult for disabled veterans (Nielsen, 2012).
Although 20,000 disabled military men had successfully served in the Invalid
Corps, which was established in 1863 to take on job responsibilities behind the
lines so that able-bodied soldiers could be sent to fight, employers were less willing to hire them after the war (Nielsen, 2012). A federal law, Section 1754, was
passed to give disabled veterans preference in civil service work, which assisted
some individuals who were qualified for intellectual work (Nielsen, 2012). Most
veterans, however, were not equipped to take on intellectual employment and
struggled after the war to find jobs they could do. Many ended up in poor-
houses or asylums (Nielsen, 2012).

Former Slaves. Former slaves who were disabled often had no alternative but
to remain on the plantations of their former masters and work for their room
and board (Nielsen, 2012). Emancipated African Americans also faced the
misperceptions of Whites that freedom led to their becoming ill and insane,
resulting in many being placed in segregated insane asylums in the South,

where they received inferior treatment and experienced horrible living conditions (Nielsen, 2012).

World War I

R. K. Hickel (2001) noted the importance of World War I in establishing disability as "an expansive but contested category" (p. 236) for providing financial support to U.S. citizens. Because of the huge numbers of individuals debilitated by the war, new ways of thinking about and managing the consequences of disability were needed. Progressive principles used to address disability caused by industrial accidents were incorporated into strategies developed to assist war casualties (R. K. Hickel, 2001). For instance, the basic concepts associated with workers' compensation were incorporated in War Risk Insurance, which ensured that disabled veterans had the same benefits as disabled workers injured on the job.

Disability became defined as "functional impairment," that is, reduced bodily function that prevented individuals from being able to engage in productive labor and manage their lives (R. K. Hickel, 2001; Longmore, 2003; Pelka, 2012). In 1921, federal legislation created the Veterans Bureau with authority over pensions and made physicians responsible for determining if benefits were deserved (R. K. Hickel, 2001; Pelka, 2012). Physicians began approaching disability "in terms of diagnosis, prognosis, and treatment" (R. K. Hickel, 2001, p. 237). This view of disability, which evolved into the rehabilitation—or functional limitations—model of disability (see Chapter 2), led to the development of policies that "created a large stigmatized and segregated category of persons and held it in a permanent state of clientage" (Longmore, 2003, p. 206).

Veterans, who were unhappy with this view of disability, argued that their pensions should be based on their "obligations toward [their] dependents, [their] local communities, and the state"—expectations built on "a life of labor, moral integrity, and patriotic loyalty in a just and democratic society" (R. K. Hickel, 2001, p. 253) rather than on a medical diagnosis. In addition, racial bias was evident in the distribution of benefits to Black disabled veterans (R. K. Hickel, 2001). Only half of the Black veterans who sought assistance received it, with justification for turning these veterans down being that Blacks were more susceptible to illness and were congenitally weak so their impairments were innate rather than war related (R. K. Hickel, 2001).

Rehabilitation. At the beginning of the 20th century, a new way of addressing the needs of people with physical disabilities began to unfold. Labeled "rehabilitation," this approach focused on providing vocational training for "crippled" individuals (Byrom, 2001). Associated with rehabilitation was the image of disability as a "deficiency to eradicate" (Stiker, 1999, p. 124). The leaders of the rehabilitation movement in the United States viewed "cripples"—individuals with mobility impairments, such as amputees and paraplegics—as both a social and an economic problem because they were economically dependent on others (Byrom, 2001). Despite this impression, people who became disabled as a result of war or industrial injuries were often willing and even eager to find work to support themselves and their families (Pelka, 2012). While the goal of all rehabilitationists was to enable physically impaired persons to become self-sufficient, *social* rehabilitationists, who generally did not have medical backgrounds, tended to focus on changing societal attitudes regarding disability, while *medical* rehabilitationists used medical procedures such as moral education, orthopedic surgery, and other medical methods "to correct flaws in disabled people" (Byrom, 2001, pp. 333–334). Each group, however, saw both approaches as necessary (Byrom, 2001) in order to help those who were physically impaired assimilate into mainstream society (Stiker, 1999).

After the end of World War I, disabled veterans became the main clientele of rehabilitationists. To determine the needs of disabled soldiers, researchers from a Cleveland social service agency conducted a survey of disabled people in the city (Nielsen, 2012). Expecting all of these individuals to be incapable of financially supporting themselves, they were surprised to find that 65% of the physically disabled individuals they surveyed were self-supporting and living reasonably "normal" lives (Nielsen, 2012). As a result, rehabilitation professionals worked with disabled veterans to become "successful cripples" rather than "begging type of cripples" (Nielsen, 2012, p. 128). Their primary goal became enabling veterans to become employed (Nielsen, 2012).

To address the concern that disabled veterans would become a "social burden" (Ward, 2009, p. 52), federal legislators passed three laws that provided veterans with benefits that would put them in a better position to seek employment (J. W. Madaus, 2000). The first, in 1917, was the Vocational Education Act, which established the Federal Board for Vocational Education and led several states to also establish vocational rehabilitation agencies to address the needs of the disabled World War I veterans (J. W. Madaus, 2000). In 1918, the federal government passed the Smith-Sears Veterans Vocational Rehabilitation Act, which established and paid for state vocational training programs (S. Brown, 2008; R. K. Hickel, 2001). The Smith-Fess Civilian Vocational Rehabilitation Act of 1920 extended vocational rehabilitation to disabled civilians over the age of 16 who demonstrated the potential to successfully become employed; however, in most states, the services provided were not particularly well developed (S. Brown, 2008; R. K. Hickel, 2001; Scotch, 2001a; Ward, 2009). Society, remember, often considered these disabled individuals to be "bad cripples" who begged on the streets and would never become "good citizens" who could support themselves (Nielsen, 2012, p. 128). These views were especially apparent in the case of White women and people of color (Nielsen, 2012).

Vocational rehabilitation centers, such as the Red Cross Institute for Crippled and Disabled Men in New York City, which was established in 1917 for disabled adult men, had as another important goal to educate the general public about physically disabled people "so that they [would] be regarded from the standpoint of their capabilities rather than their disabilities" (Byrom, 2001, p. 144). Unfortunately, employers often rejected this argument and refused to hire disabled individuals (Nielsen, 2012). Instead, those trained to join the "mainstream workforce" often had to settle for work in sheltered workshops that were established by private, nonprofit organizations or were government supported (Dunlavey, Magliulo, & Marotta, 2009). In these workshops, disabled men worked under close supervision doing assembly, repair, and production of products for far less money than other workers in the hope that this employment would lead to better positions in the community (Byrom, 2001; Dunlavey et al., 2009). Unfortunately, that rarely happened, and they remained in these segregated work environments (Dunlavey et al., 2009). Sheltered workshops, then, "served as a symbol of the cripple's inferior status in the job market" (Byrom, 2001, p. 145).

Higher Education Opportunities for Disabled Veterans. The Veterans Vocational Rehabilitation Act of 1918, while primarily designed to prepare disabled veterans for work, sometimes provided postsecondary education and training as a means to achieve this goal (J. W. Madaus, 2000). Veterans engaged in study in areas such as industry, trade, and agriculture (J. W. Madaus, 2011). Professional training was also available to veterans who had some college education (J. W. Madaus, 2011). For instance, the Ohio Mechanics Institute in Cincinnati, which at that time offered two- and four-year college programs (Ohio Mechanics Institute, n.d.), enrolled over 400 World War I disabled veterans (J. W. Madaus, 2011). These students began a national organization to self-advocate for further support for disabled veterans, Disabled American Veterans (DAV), which is still active (DAV, n.d.; J. W. Madaus, 2011).

World War II and Its Aftermath

As men and women left private employment for military and government service, worker shortages at home led to the employment of around 300,000 people with disabilities in wartime industry (Nielsen, 2012; Pelka, 2012). In addition to providing disabled people with steady incomes, employment also led to improved self-images. In society as a whole, opinions about people with impairments improved after World War II. Nevertheless, although disabled people were no longer viewed as worthless and unfit as they had been previously, now disabled people—largely soldiers at this time—were seen as unfortunate, objects of charity, and pitiable (Beilke & Yssel, 1999; Griffin et al., 2007; Imrie, 1997; Ward, 2009).

Advances in medicine, especially the development of antibiotics to treat infection, resulted in significantly longer life expectancies, even for severely injured soldiers (Pelka, 2012). As veterans returned from the war maimed and traumatized, they were institutionalized for medical treatment and rehabilita-tion. But the goal of institutionalization now was to find ways to "fix" these vet-erans, especially those with the "least difficulties" (Ostiguy, Peters, & Shlasko, 2016; Ward, 2009, p. 52), so they could reenter society and support themselves and their families while contributing to the rapidly expanding U.S. economy in the 1950s (Bryan, 2013; Ward, 2009).

An important after-effect of World War II and the Korean conflict was the rapid expansion of rehabilitation institutions, technology, and medical inno-vations, supported by increased governmental funding for vocational rehabili-tation, that allowed young people with impairments resulting from war service, polio, and accidents to live longer and be more mobile as better wheelchairs and prostheses became available (Scotch, 2001a; Ward, 2009). Veterans, polio survivors, and other individuals with impairments started to defy the image others held of them as weak, helpless, and passive and sought to establish a new view of themselves as self-sufficient (Ward, 2009). Many formed advocacy groups, including the Blinded Veterans Association in 1945 and the Paralyzed Veterans of America in 1947 (Pelka, 2012).

Expansion of Higher Education Opportunities. After World War II, the first significant numbers of individuals with disabilities were admitted into colleges and universities (J. W. Madaus, 2000). They were largely war veterans receiving educational benefits through the Vocational Rehabilitation Amendments of 1943, which increased educational and vocational assistance to disabled people, and the Serviceman's Readjustment Act of 1944 (the GI Bill), which expanded opportunities for all veterans to attend college, as well as providing them with low-interest home loans and a stipend while looking for work (S. Brown, 2008; L. J. Davis, 2015b; J. W. Madaus, 2000, 2011). By 1946, veterans, many of whom had disabilities, were 52% of the total college pop-ulation (J. W. Madaus, 2011). Disability resource offices were established in response to the needs of these students (Beilke & Yssel, 1999; S. Brown, 2008; J. W. Madaus, 2000).

Lack of Accessibility on College Campuses. Few, if any, college and university campuses provided physical access to individuals with disabilities prior to the end of World War II (J. W. Madaus, 2000). Students with disabilities who enrolled in higher education found alternative ways to negotiate campuses, usually by enlisting friends or family to help, but occasionally demonstrating to administrators that they were worthy of assistance (see Fleischer & Zames, 2001, p. 36, for one such story). At UCLA, one of the first universities to admit disabled veterans after World War II when 18 paraplegic veterans enrolled for the 1946–47 academic year (J. W. Madaus, 2000), a group of nondisabled veterans volunteered to carry these students into inaccessible buildings (S. Brown, 2008). At the University of Illinois, an influential administrator transformed the campus into a community that was accessible to students with disabilities (S. Brown, 2008).

Tim Nugent and the University of Illinois Program. In 1947, William Kleashers, deputy commander of the American Legion, requested help from the University of Illinois to enable disabled veterans to attend college at the Mayo Army General Hospital in Galesburg, Illinois (S. Brown, 2008). This fully accessible hospital was leased to the university and became the Galesburg Undergraduate Division. Its dean hired a graduate student in educational psychology and administration, Tim Nugent, himself a disabled veteran, to develop a program for the disabled veterans (S. Brown, 2008). It began in 1948 as the first program for disabled students on a college campus (Griffin et al., 2007).

Significant resistance from administrators and even the state governor, Adlai Stevenson, who were afraid that the University of Illinois would become known more for its disabled students than its academic programs, threatened the program's existence in 1949 by closing the Galesburg campus (S. Brown, 2008). A legal technicality saved the program: since 14 wheelchair-using students had been promised two years of college and had received only one year at that time, the program was moved to the Urbana campus of the University of Illinois. The campus was not accessible to them, and accommodations were quickly made to add ramps to six classroom buildings, provide the students with keys to elevators in the student services building and the library, and house them in an old World War II barracks that had ramps at both ends and a community bathroom in the middle (S. Brown, 2008).

The program, which Nugent directed from 1948 to 1960, became known for serving students with severe impairments, including those with spinal cord injuries, post-polio paralysis, muscular dystrophy, and cerebral palsy (S. Brown, 2008). In addition, Nugent convinced the university to require that all new buildings be accessible to wheelchairs long before any other university took this step. When new residence halls were built, they required several rooms in each building and all bathrooms and common areas to be accessible. Nugent also established a service fraternity inclusive of men and women students with disabilities. This group worked, independent of the university, to socially integrate disabled students and address problems they encountered. Another innovation that Nugent introduced was wheelchair sports teams, which became varsity sports in 1954 funded by the Veterans Administration, the state Division of Vocational Rehabilitation, and private donations, since the university refused to fund them (S. Brown, 2008).

Obtaining both adequate funding and space were constant battles with the university during the early years of the Disability Resources and Educational Services program. However, after a group of disabled students invited Governor William Stratton to speak at their annual awards banquet in 1954 and he praised the rehabilitation work the university was doing, the university never again questioned the need for the program (S. Brown, 2008).

Wheelchair ramps and curb cuts were among the many changes first introduced at the University of Illinois to improve access for students who used wheelchairs (Pelka, 2012). Other innovations begun over the years for disabled students at the university included counseling services, preregistration, a student rehabilitation center, accessible buses, a transitional living program for students who had severe mobility impairments, an on-campus living center for students who needed assistive services, and the first study-abroad program for students with disabilities (S. Brown, 2008).

Other universities across the country followed the lead of the University of Illinois in establishing programs for disabled students in the 1950s. Among the earliest initiators were Southern Illinois University, the University of Missouri, the University of Minnesota, City University of New York, Florida State University, the University of Michigan, Wayne State University, Hunter College, and Kansas State Teachers College (now Emporia State), all of which had established programs by 1959 (S. Brown, 2008; J. W. Madaus, 2000). These schools were the exception, however, as most administrators and faculty believed that providing severely disabled students with a college education was not a worthwhile endeavor since they were unlikely to succeed academically or obtain employment after college (J. W. Madaus, 2011). In a 1957 national survey by Condon reviewed by J. W. Madaus (2000), 31 colleges and universities out of 181 respondents reported having an organized program for students with disabilities. Since these early programs were designed to serve disabled veterans, their focus was on eliminating physical barriers for mobility-impaired students rather than considering other types of impairments (J. W. Madaus, 2000).

Aftermath of the Korean Conflict

The Korean conflict resulted in over 100,000 disabled U.S. veterans (J. W. Madaus, Miller, & Vance, 2009). Unfortunately, educational benefits that had been available to World War II veterans had been reduced and no longer covered all the costs of higher education. As a result, fewer disabled veterans took advantage of these benefits to attend college (Rumann & Hamrick, 2009). However, after the Korean War, additional college and universities implemented services to assist disabled veterans, although many institutions of higher education continued to refuse to admit students who used wheelchairs because their campuses were inaccessible (J. W. Madaus et al., 2009).

Impact of the Vietnam Conflict

Veterans of the Vietnam conflict, returning home in the 1960s and 1970s, received—at best—a low-key welcome since many U.S. citizens opposed this war (Ackerman & DiRamio, 2009; Rumann & Hamrick, 2009). More than 153,000 veterans returned from Vietnam with injuries, including many whose conditions were caused by chemical weapons, which created new types of impairment (J. W. Madaus et al., 2009). Unemployment of disabled veterans after the Vietnam War was twice as high as that of nondisabled veterans, according to a U.S. Department of Labor report in 1974 (cited in J. W. Madaus et al., 2009), because of their lack of training and failure to complete college.

As after earlier wars, one solution to this problem was provided by the government in the form of legislation. In 1974, Congress passed the Vietnam Era Veterans' Readjustment Assistance Act, which increased educational benefits (J. W. Madaus et al., 2009). However, many veterans felt unwelcome on college campuses, which often served as hubs of antiwar protests (Rumann & Hamrick, 2009). In addition, the Vietnam War also led to congressional passage of the Rehabilitation Act of 1973 (Nielsen, 2012). This legislation addressed the civil rights of disabled individuals with the inclusion of Section 504, which led to significant advancement for disabled students as a whole (see the next section).

The Conflicts in the Middle East

Because of improvements in military equipment, medical innovations, and evacuation systems, about 85% of the soldiers deployed to the Middle East during the Persian Gulf War in the 1990s and the conflicts in Iraq and Afghanistan during the 21st century have survived (J. W. Madaus et al., 2009). In addition to amputations and other injuries that affect the body, more than 40% of these disabled veterans returned home with traumatic brain injury (TBI) and posttraumatic stress disorder (PTSD), sometimes along with other impairments (DiRamio & Spires, 2009). While as a whole, these veterans are being honored for their service, higher education institutions, along with the rest of society, have not been well prepared to respond to veterans with these impairments and assist them in reintegrating into civilian life (Ackerman & DiRamio, 2009; Rumann & Hamrick, 2009). One initiative to address PTSD, Severely Injured Military Veterans: Fulfilling Their Dream, was developed and funded by the American Council on Education to assist severely wounded veterans in their transition from wartime service to higher education by providing them with mentors known as *champions* (DiRamio & Spires, 2009).

The government has responded to disabled veterans of the Middle Eastern conflicts by again changing benefits. In 2008, the Post-9/11 Veterans Educational Assistance Act (also known as the New GI Bill) became law (J. W. Madaus et al., 2009). This comprehensive law, which went into effect on August 1, 2009, replaced the variety of other educational benefits previously available to veterans and brought the level of benefits back up to the post-World War II level for veterans who have served since September 11, 2001 (J. W. Madaus et al., 2009; Rumann & Hamrick, 2009).

Veterans and Social Justice

The treatment of veterans throughout the history of the United States is a fitting example of why social justice is such an important concept for educators to understand and practice. While citizens express support and concern for "our veterans," services have never (and still do not) lived up to the level of patriotism espoused in this country. War also reminds us of how quickly individuals can lose their privilege and become members of an oppressed class, in this case, disabled people. Throughout history, once able-bodied privilege has been taken away, individuals have also lost their rights to equitable health care, employment, education, and inclusive treatment in society, despite the laws and provisions for services that the government has provided after the fact. Perhaps most important, social justice is necessary in order to enable veterans to gain control of their own lives again rather than being controlled by government regulations, institutional policy, and societal attitudes.

Disability Activism

The eugenics movement, which lasted from about 1880 until the end of World War II, viewed disabled people as evolutionary "defectives" and considered them part of "the degenerate class," which included all types of "undesirable" people (L. J. Davis, 2006, pp. 7–9). As Nielsen (2012) reflected, "The ideal American citizen was defined in increasingly narrow and increasingly specific physical terms" (p. 101). Preventing the "defective classes" from interacting with "normal" members of society and from producing defective and degenerate offspring were goals of the eugenics movement. These steps were accomplished by restrictive marriage laws, institutionalization, blocking immigration, involuntary sterilization, and the most extreme measure, euthanasia (Nielsen, 2012; Pernick, 2009; Ward, 2009). From 1930 through the 1940s, eugenics extremists in Germany and elsewhere were arguing that the human "race" was polluted by these "defective" people who should be sterilized or killed rather than merely institutionalized to keep them out of sight (Griffin et al., 2007).

Early Disability Rights Initiatives

Beginning in the 19th century, individuals with disabilities pushed back against eugenics, establishing their own communities and fighting to create a more positive view of themselves in society (Burch, 2001; Kudlick, 2001). Members of the Deaf community were the first to establish state political organizations as well as a national organization, the National Association of the Deaf in 1880, to fight the move toward oralism already discussed in this chapter (Longmore, 2009; Pelka, 2012). Their efforts expanded in the early 20th century to address other forms of discrimination such as federal civil service hiring practices (Longmore, 2009).

Blind people also formed their own politically focused organizations in the 19th century, including the American Blind People's Higher Education and General Improvement Association, which was established in the mid-1890s by graduates of a number of midwestern state schools (Kudlick, 2001; Longmore, 2009). From 1900 through 1903, this organization published *The Problem*, a magazine designed to publicize conditions that blind individuals faced and their actual ability to function in society (Kudlick, 2001; Longmore, 2009).

In the early decades of the 20th century, polio epidemics arose, leading to the impairment of many thousands of people in the United States. Although later scholars have determined that it is likely that Franklin Delano Roosevelt, who would become president in 1933, actually had Guillain-Barré syndrome (Goldman, Schmalstieg, Freeman, Goldman, & Schmalstieg, 2003), he was diagnosed at the age of 39 as having polio and became an advocate and role model for others who were diagnosed with this disease; however, he publicly hid his disability because he feared that he would not be elected if citizens were aware of it (Longmore, 2003). The New Deal that Roosevelt introduced saw the establishment of a number of federal programs, some of which provided assistance to disabled people and some of which excluded them (Scotch, 2001a).

Activism During the Great Depression

By the end of the eugenics movement in the 1930s and 1940s, more disabled individuals were tired of the discrimination they had faced for their entire lifetimes and began to see themselves as worthy of better treatment in society (Nielsen, 2012). Using the labor movement as a model, several organizations made up of disabled people began to play the role of advocates and activists for better treatment and respect from the larger U.S. society, particularly with regard to employment (Pelka, 2012).

For instance, the National Association of the Deaf (NAD), as well as the National Fraternal Society of the Deaf, actively addressed "insurance discrimination, job discrimination, driving restrictions, lack of vocational training, and other issues the Deaf community identified as vital" (Nielsen, 2012, p. 134). At the same time, the National Federation of the Blind (NFB), founded in 1940, was focused on the right of blind people to organize and run their own organization rather than being controlled by sighted individuals who had previously controlled organizations for the blind (Pelka, 2012). The NFB and other organizations of the blind were active in lobbying the government for employment for blind individuals and less restrictive social welfare regulations, as well as guide dog and "white cane" laws to provide blind people with freedom of movement in public settings, the first initiatives in the country to advocate for access and accommodation laws (Dunlavey et al., 2009; Longmore, 2009).

The League of the Physically Handicapped, formed in 1935 in New York City, actively protested against policies that made physically disabled people ineligible for jobs with the Works Progress Administration; its efforts resulted in jobs for 1,500 physically disabled workers (Longmore, 2003, 2009; Pelka, 2012). It was the first national political organization made up of members from more than one disability group in the United States (Longmore, 2009).

Established in 1940, the American Federation of the Physically Handicapped lobbied for an end to discrimination in the private employment sector

(Pelka, 2012). It was successful in getting a law passed in 1945 establishing the National Employ the Physically Handicapped Week, which was expanded in 1952 to become the President's Committee on Employment of the Physically Handicapped (later the President's Committee on Employment of People with Disabilities). This committee became a permanent organization in 1955 (Pelka, 2012). Throughout the disability rights movement, this committee played an important role in bringing disability activists together to share perspectives (Longmore, 2009; Pelka, 2012). As Nielsen (2012) commented, "Throughout the Depression and extending into the Cold War period, people with disabilities and their allies laid important groundwork that later disability rights activists would build on" (p. 133).

Ed Roberts and the Berkeley Movement

After World War II, physically disabled activists focused on obtaining the right to attend college (Longmore, 2009). In 1962, Ed Roberts, a quadriplegic polio survivor who used a wheelchair and an iron lung, became the first student with significant impairments to enter the University of California–Berkeley after successfully suing the institution for access and integration (Fleischer & Zames, 2001; Lampros, 2011; Nielsen, 2012). Berkeley officials required Roberts to live in the infirmary rather than in a residence hall, however (Fleischer & Zames, 2001; Nielsen, 2012). After hearing of Roberts's admittance, 12 other students with severe disabilities also enrolled at Berkeley and lived in the infirmary with him. The third floor of the Berkeley infirmary became the home for an activist group of disabled students, who successfully advocated for making the Berkeley campus and the city more accessible (Lampros, 2011). They also argued for personal attendants so they could live independently while enrolled in college (Nielsen, 2012).

Roberts assisted his former college advisor, Jean Wirth, in writing a grant proposal to the Department of Health, Education, and Welfare for a minority student dropout program to improve services for disabled students, which they obtained (Fleischer & Zames, 2011; Madeus, 2000). In 1970, this $81,000 grant, plus $2,000 from the university, formalized a student group called the Rolling Quads (later named the Disabled Students Union) and established the Physically Disabled Students Program at Berkeley, which provided support including personal attendants and wheelchair repair (Fleischer & Zames, 2011; J. W. Madaus, 2000; Nielsen, 2012; Pelka, 2012). Graduates of Berkeley and other institutions that were among the first to provide services for disabled students, including Illinois and Boston University, became important leaders of the disability rights movement in the 1970s (Longmore, 2009).

The Emergence of the Disability Rights Movement

The Berkeley movement was one of only a few initiatives in the period between the 1940s and 1960s as most of the disability groups formed in the 1940s lost momentum because of internal strife and burnout (Pelka, 2012). It was not until the 1970s that people with disabilities again began taking the lead in determining their own fate (Griffin et al., 2007). Enlightened by the civil rights movements of the 1960s (Fleischer & Zames, 2001), the disability rights movement of the 1970s and beyond transformed how disabled people thought about themselves and how others viewed them (Bryan, 2013). Its first goal was to demonstrate to society that people with disabilities were marginalized and therefore oppressed by the social structure of U.S. society (J. A. Winter, 2003). Once awareness was achieved, the movement worked to eliminate marginalization of disabled people and "to empower them to influence social policies and practices so as to further the integration and full inclusion of individuals with disabilities into the mainstream of American society" (J. A. Winter, 2003, p. 37), as well as to achieve autonomy over their own lives. An important aspect of the disability rights movement was exemplified by its slogan, "Nothing about us without us," which stressed the value that disabled people placed on participating in the decisions that would affect them (Ostiguy et al., 2016).

Several events converged in the early 1970s that set the disability rights movement in motion: the influence of the civil rights movements, the independent living movement, the parents' movement for integrated education, and the Rehabilitation Act demonstrations.

The Civil Rights Movements. The civil rights movements of African Americans, women, and lesbian and gay individuals in the 1960s and 1970s led to increased awareness of the rights of all people to equity and fairness among people with disabilities (Nielsen, 2012; Scotch, 1988). The movements were similar in that all were "struggles for fairness of opportunity among people who became fed up with their control and denigration ... by the larger society" (McCarthy, 2003, p. 210). Disabled people were encouraged by these movements to pursue their own political rights, full citizenship, and self-determination during the 1970s. Disabled activists learned from the strategies used by other groups to secure their rights (Fleischer & Zames, 2011; Pelka, 2012; Scotch, 1988). These movements also motivated people with different impairments to work together as one large movement for disability rights (Nielsen, 2012).

The Independent Living Movement. Meanwhile at Berkeley, Ed Roberts and the Rolling Quads moved out of the infirmary in 1972 and into the Berkeley community, where they established an agency self-governed by disabled residents, the Center for Independent Living (Bryan, 2010; Fleischer & Zames,

2011). This concept rapidly spread around the country in the 1970s and 1980s (Meade & Serlin, 2006) based on "the principle of self-determination, consumer control, and deinstitutionalization" (Nielsen, 2012, p. 163). Independent living centers (ILCs) offered peer counseling and coordinated personal assistants, while lobbying for accessibility, civil rights, and funding to support independent living (Longmore, 2009).

Another positive effect of the development of ILCs was the inclusion of individuals with severe impairments, challenging vocational rehabilitation practices that had focused largely on assisting less disabled clients in preparing for and finding employment while ignoring severely disabled individuals who were relegated to living in institutions (Ostiguy et al., 2016; Scotch, 2001a). Oliver (1990) noted that ILCs changed the definition of *independence* from doing things by oneself to making decisions for oneself and being in control of one's life.

Lucy Gwin, the editor of the bimonthly magazine *Mouth: The Voice of Disability Rights,* pointed out that Ed Roberts and the others who established ILCs were all White males from "comfortable" families who had "been transformed over night into second-class citizens" by the polio virus (Fleischer & Zames, 2001, p. 41). She reflected in an interview,

> What caused them to question their second-class status? They'd hatched out of privilege and protection into a world that was changing radically... The independent living revolution arose among privileged white boys. And bless them, those boys stormed the barricades to free us [people with disabilities] from *the medical model.* (Gwin, 1967, pp. 26–27, in Fleischer & Zames, 2001, p. 41)

During the 1990s, ILCs extended their services to people with sensory, cognitive, and psychological impairments, as well as people of all ages and ethnic backgrounds, as the deinstitutionalization movement left many individuals searching for homes in the community (Longmore, 2009). Current issues facing ILCs include the ability to identify and hire personal attendants, securing funding for in-home care rather than requiring people with disabilities to be cared for at residential treatment facilities, and securing enough accessible housing (Ostiguy et al., 2016). Resources to support ILCs seldom are adequate to keep up with the numbers of people with disabilities who wish to live in them, especially if these people are financially insecure (Ostiguy et al., 2016).

The Parents' Movement for Integrated Education. As late as the 1960s, states were failing to provide adequate education to disabled children (Fleischer & Zames, 2001). As many as one in eight children with disabilities did not receive any education at all, and over half of all disabled children failed to receive special educational services to be successful in school (Fleischer & Zames, 2001).

While school districts did start taking more responsibility for educating children with disabilities starting in the early 1950s, parents often viewed this "education" to be babysitting or an act of "charity" (Ward, 2009, p. 53). Parents urged schools to provide better education that would enable their disabled children to attend college or successfully seek employment (Ward, 2009).

The parents' advocacy movement, which began in the 1950s and 1960s, focused on lawsuits and legislation to achieve its goals of inclusive education for their children with disabilities (Longmore, 2009), often using *Brown v. Board of Education* as an arguing point for integrating education to include children with disabilities (Griffin et al., 2007). But as the 1960s began, little progress had been made toward integrating public K–12 education (Pelka, 2012).

In 1971, however, *Pennsylvania Association for Retarded Children v. Commonwealth of Pennsylvania* led the courts to accept a consent decree that stated for the first time that disabled children had the right to free public education (Pelka, 2012). This decree encouraged activists across the country to file lawsuits in support of right-to-education legislation, which convinced Congress to pass the Education for All Handicapped Children Act in 1975 (Griffin et al., 2007; Pelka, 2012). This law guaranteed all disabled children pre-K through high school a free and appropriate education in the least restrictive environment (Kalivoda, 2009; J. W. Madaus, 2000).

After the passage of this law, activists lobbied for appropriate funding from the federal government; they also filed lawsuits to force compliance by school districts (Longmore, 2009). Parents of disabled children advocated in particular for mainstreaming children with disabilities into classrooms with nondisabled children (Longmore, 2009). In response to the Education for All Handicapped Children Act of 1975, the Supreme Court ruled in the case of *Burlington School District v. Department of Education* that schools were responsible for paying for enrolling disabled children in private programs if the courts determined that such a program was the least restrictive environment in which to provide a disabled child with an appropriate education (Griffin et al., 2007).

The Education of the Handicapped Act Amendments, renamed the Individuals with Disabilities Education Act (IDEA), passed in 1990. It strengthened the original bill mandating that each student's needs be individually addressed through an individual education plan (IEP; Kalivoda, 2009). Not all parents have viewed the IDEA favorably, however. Some advocates argued that experts played too large a role in developing IEPs, devaluing the role of parents in determining what their disabled child needed in the educational setting, particularly if the parents were members of minoritized groups (Fleischer & Zames, 2001). Deaf parents, in particular, have expressed concern about integrating their children into hearing classrooms where they are not allowed to use sign language. They have argued that education in a Deaf setting is the least restrictive environment for their children (Ostiguy et al., 2016).

Perhaps the largest problem facing parents of disabled children is the lack of compliance of school systems with provisions of the IDEA. In a national Council on Disability report conducted in 2000, every state was found to be out of compliance with the IDEA (J. A. Winter, 2003). Systematic monitoring is necessary to overcome this issue. Despite the failure of some schools to fully implement the IDEA, this act has significantly improved the education of disabled children and has been a major factor in the large increase in numbers of disabled individuals attending college since its passage (J. W. Madaus, 2011).

Rehabilitation Act Demonstrations. In 1972, President Richard Nixon pocket-vetoed the Rehabilitation Act, which would have given priority to severely disabled individuals in the rehabilitation system by setting up independent living centers for living and working in their communities. This led members of the cross-disability organization, Disabled in Action, to protest in New York City while the younger, more activist members of the President's Committee on Employment of the Handicapped (PCEH) held a night-long vigil at the Lincoln Memorial in Washington, DC (Longmore, 2003; Pelka, 2012). When Nixon vetoed the bill the second time in 1973, members of PCEH held a march in protest (Longmore, 2003). The vetoes also spurred younger members of various disability organizations to join together to form alliances across disability categories, recognizing that they were all fighting for the same goals (Bryan, 2010; Longmore, 2003).

In 1973, Nixon finally signed the third version of the Rehabilitation Act passed by Congress after members of Congress had decreased the funding level for programs for individuals with serious disabilities and dropped the provision for independent living centers (Longmore, 2003). Included in the bill, however, was Section 504, which outlawed discrimination against "otherwise qualified" disabled individuals in federally funded programs (Longmore, 2009). This provision of the bill was added near its conclusion by Senate staffers with minimal experience with disability issues "who nonetheless recognized that prejudice was a problem for disabled Americans" (Longmore, 2003, p. 104). Only one person commented on it during all the debates and hearings held prior to the vote, and few people, including Nixon and his advisors, became aware of its antidiscrimination language (Longmore, 2003; Nielsen, 2012). Only the National Federation of the Blind, which had taken a strong civil rights approach to disability issues for several decades, stressed the importance of Section 504 to disabled people (Longmore, 2003). However, when it came time to fund the bill, disabled people began to see its value (Nielsen, 2012).

Because of concern over the costs of providing accessibility, especially at colleges and universities, the government avoided issuing implementation regulations for the Rehabilitation Act for four years under three presidents (Longmore, 2009; J. W. Madaus, 2000). Efforts to get these regulations into effect mobilized advocacy among leaders of the disabled community who made up the PCEH (Scotch, 1988). At this committee's 1974 meeting, they established the American Coalition of Citizens with Disabilities, the first successful cross-disability advocacy organization (Longmore, 2009; Scotch, 1988). This group's activism culminated in April 1977 with one-day sit-ins in Washington, DC, and 10 other U.S. cities, as well as occupation of the Department of Health, Education, and Welfare (HEW) in San Francisco, which lasted 25 days (Longmore, 2003; Pelka, 2012). Finally HEW secretary Joseph Califano signed the regulations to implement Section 504 (Fleischer & Zames, 2011; Longmore, 2003, 2009; Nielsen, 2012).

This sit-in succeeded for a number of reasons, including the previous experience of many of its leaders in other activist movements (e.g., free speech, antiwar, feminist, and racial civil rights) and what they had learned from the tactics these other groups used (Fleischer & Zames, 2001; Nielsen, 2012). They also had support from traditional disability organizations, such as Easter Seals and United Cerebral Palsy, as well as religious leaders and less expected groups, including labor unions, gay men, Chicano activists, and the Black Panthers (Longmore, 2003; Nielsen, 2012). As a result, this protest led to sophisticated coalition building during the 1980s that eventually led to passage of the ADA (Longmore, 2009). Section 504 was the first civil rights law that protected the rights of disabled students, faculty, and staff in higher education (Kalivoda, 2009). (See Chapter 3 for further discussion of its implications for higher education.)

Disability Rights Issues After Section 504

In the 1980s, disability rights were a less visible public issue than they had been in the previous decade (Scotch, 1988). However, important legal and political issues did arise that shaped the future of disability activism and contributed to the passage of the ADA.

Court Decisions Regarding Section 504 Implementation. Although Section 504 had a major impact on the access of students with disabilities to higher education, many questions had to be answered related to its implementation (Pelka, 2012). Many schools were reluctant to implement aspects of the legislation because they perceived that it would be costly and time-consuming (J. W. Madaus, 2000). Even after funding to implement Section 504 was released, compliance on college and university campuses was minimal (Kalivoda, 2009). J. W. Madaus (2011) reported that a backlash occurred with significant legal action.

The courts dealt with cases focusing on "documentation of disabilities, reasonable accommodations, definitions of 'major life activities,' and the impact of mitigating measures on the impact of a disability" (J. W. Madaus, 2011, p. 11). In 1984, one of these court cases, *Grove City v. Bell*, led the Supreme Court to rule that Section 504 applied only to specific funded programs rather than the entire institution (J. W. Madaus, 2000; Safransky, n.d.). In 1987, Section 504 was amended under the Civil Rights Restoration Act to reverse this decision (J. W. Madaus, 2000; Safransky, n.d.). This amendment stated that Section 504 applied to the entire institution if any of its programs received federal funding, reversing the decision the Court handed down in *Grove City v. Bell*. The Civil Rights Restoration Act's prohibition of discrimination against disabled students in higher education provided a foundation for legal action to protect the rights of students with disabilities if institutions were unwilling to provide accommodations voluntarily (J. W. Madaus, 2000). However, many court cases, to the dismay of many disability activists, narrowed the scope of Section 504 at a time when the political landscape was becoming increasingly conservative (L. J. Davis, 2015a; Scotch, 1988).

Addressing Political Conservatism in the Reagan Era. Ronald Reagan, elected president in 1981, was "skeptical, if not downright hostile" (Pelka, 2012, p. 28) to the involvement of the federal government in efforts to advance civil rights. Among his efforts to defund aspects of President Lyndon Johnson's Great Society, the administration began making threats to amend or revoke regulations implementing both Section 504 of the Rehabilitation Act of 1973 and the Education for All Handicapped Children Act of 1975 (L. J. Davis, 2015a).

Several leaders in the disability movement were children of wealthy members of the Republican Party, including Patrisha Wright, Mary Lou Breslin, and Justin Dart. Using this fact of birth to their advantage, disability rights activists from the Disability Rights Education and Defense Fund (DREDF), led by Wright, and the Disability Rights Center, led by Evan Kemp Jr., worked with insiders in the Reagan administration to gain information regarding the administration's specific plans (L. J. Davis, 2015a). This information was leaked to members of DREDF, who began intense lobbying and grassroots campaigning to stop their efforts (L. J. Davis, 2015a; Griffin et al., 2007). After the administration received over 40,000 cards and letters, they abandoned their attempt to repeal this disability rights legislation (L. J. Davis, 2015a).

Passage of the ADA

By the late 1970s, disability activists were clear that more legislation was needed to bring buildings into compliance and raise consciousness to accomplish their goals of access and equity (Meade & Serlin, 2006). While Section 504 effectively addressed the "easy" issues, such as architectural and transportation accessibility, it did not lead to increased employment, a major issue facing disabled people (Fleischer & Zames, 2001). Disability activists consistently lobbied for a stronger law that would allow them to confront discriminatory employers (Fleischer & Zames, 2001).

The ADA was introduced in 1988 by two congressmen, Senator Lowell Weicker, a Republican from Connecticut, and Representative Tony Coelho, a Democrat from California (L. J. Davis, 2015a; Mezey, 2009). The bill passed in the Senate but was defeated in the House (Mezey, 2009). The introduction of the bill did raise awareness among members of Congress, as well as citizens in general, of the challenges that disabled people in society continued to face (Mezey, 2009). The ADA was reintroduced in May 1989 after President George H. W. Bush became president by Representative Steny Hoyer, a Democrat from Maryland, and Senators Tom Harkin, a Democrat from Iowa, and Ted Kennedy, a Democrat from Massachusetts (L. J. Davis, 2015a; Mezey, 2009). The goal of the ADA was to advance "the civil rights of people with disabilities" by establishing "a 'national mandate' to end discrimination against people with disabilities and to guarantee that the federal government would play a key role in enforcing the law" (Mezey, 2009, p. 48).

DREDF was among the leaders of the movement to pass the ADA (L. J. Davis, 2015a). Because of their efforts, particularly those of Patrisha Wright, disability rights was on the agenda of a significant number of other civil rights organizations, including the influential Leadership Conference on Civil Rights, for the first time (Pelka, 2012). While Kemp was working inside the administration, Wright had been meeting and collaborating with other activist civil rights groups to raise their awareness of the ADA and the issues facing disabled Americans (L. J. Davis, 2015a). Their involvement was important in lobbying Congress while the ADA was being considered (Davis, 2015a).

Important as well were disability activists across the country. Justin Dart, a leading disability activist, and his wife, Yoshiko Dart, traveled throughout the United States collecting stories from people with disabilities for the

"Disability Discrimination Diaries" that he used to generate support from the public for passage of the ADA (Fleischer & Zames, 2011). In addition, as the ADA was being considered in Congress, over 8,500 disability activists signed and paid for a full-page ad in the *Washington Post* urging their legislators to pass the ADA and to reject amendments that would legalize unacceptable discrimination that some members of Congress were attempting to add to the bill. The ad was personally delivered to every congressional office and the president (Fleischer & Zames, 2001). With this backing, the ADA was successfully guided through Congress by Senator Harkin and Representative Hoyer, passing the Senate 76–8 and the House 377–28 (Fleischer & Zames, 2001).

Justin Dart, often referred to as the Father of the ADA, described the passage of the ADA this way:

> A ragtag hodgepodge of advocates with disabilities, families, and service providers, who had never completely agreed on anything before, joined together with a few farsighted members of the older civil rights movement, business, the Congress, and the Administration to defeat the richest, most powerful lobbies in the nation. (Fleischer & Zames, 2001, p. 92)

Fleischer and Zames (2001) went on to name some of these lobbyists. They included the "National Federation of Independent Business, U.S. Chamber of Commerce, the *New York Times, Wall Street Journal,* the Restaurant Association, Greyhound Buses, and the entire transportation community, as well as conservative elements of the Republican party" (Fleischer & Zames, 2001, p. 92). Pelka (2012) stated, "Quite simply, the Americans with Disabilities Act of 1990 marks the political arrival ... of the national disability rights movement" (p. 29).

The ADA had a major influence on increasing the numbers of students with disabilities attending higher education (J. W. Madaus, 2000). It extended rights to every aspect of the operation of college and university campuses, providing access to all facilities, services, and programs they offered. As a result, colleges and universities have been forced to adapt and provide the programs that disabled students need. Unfortunately, these changes were much too slow and often required not only activism on the part of students and faculty with disabilities but, too often, lawsuits to win their rights. (For an in-depth and engaging history of the ADA, see L. J. Davis, 2015a.)

Working for the Passage of the ADA Amendments Act

As with Section 504, the ADA did not totally live up to its expectations, largely because the rulings of an increasingly conservative Supreme Court limited the meaning of some of the vague phrases used in the law, such as "disability," "reasonable accommodations," and "undue burden" (Mezey, 2009). Cases such as *Sutton v. United Airlines* (1999), *Murphy v. United Parcel Service* (1999), and *Toyota Motor Manufacturing v. Williams* (2002) restricted who qualified as disabled and therefore limited how and to whom it applied, particularly in employment (J. W. Madaus, 2011; Mezey, 2009).

To address these issues, bipartisan legislation, the Americans With Disabilities Act Amendments Act (ADAAA), was introduced to clarify the original intent of Congress in passing the ADA (Fleischer & Zames, 2011). This legislation was supported by a broad coalition of disability and civil rights organizations, war veterans, the U.S. Conference of Catholic Bishops, the National Association of Manufacturers, and the U.S. Chamber of Commerce, which previously had opposed the ADA (Fleischer & Zames, 2011).

Once again disability activists played a large role in publicizing the legislation and encouraging citizens to support its passage. On November 15, 2006, a bus tour, The Road to Freedom, left Washington, DC, on a 25,000-mile road trip to advocate for the passage of the ADA Restoration Act, an earlier version of the ADAAA (Fleischer & Zames, 2011). It was led by Jim Ward, the founder and president of ADA Watch and the National Coalition for Disability Rights. The trip lasted 18 months and made 20 stops, accompanied by a second bus that held a traveling exhibit about disability rights. Ward believed that a grassroots initiative such as this would remind people that their voices were powerful in the electoral process. He provided the people he met with call-in numbers, website addresses, and petitions so they could let Congress members know they supported the ADAAA. Senator Harkin, one of the sponsors of the ADA, spoke on the floor of Congress about the Road to Freedom campaign, noting that it was instrumental in the passage of the ADAAA (Fleischer & Zames, 2011). The law passed in 2008, with implementation taking place on January 1, 2009 (Mezey, 2009).

In the ADAAA, Congress clarified language used to define disability, provided expanded examples of what conditions should be considered disabling, and explained the role of mitigating measures in determining eligibility (J. W. Madaus, 2011). Institutions of higher education are just beginning to see the impact of the ADAAA as cases make their way through the courts and are interpreted by the Office for Civil Rights (Goren, 2016).

Disability Activism and Social Justice

By the end of the 20th century, the disability rights movement had changed how disability was viewed in the United States from a "medical, charity model" to a "minority rights issue" (Ward, 2009, p. 52). The self-advocacy involved in this movement also led to changes in self-perception among people with disabilities as they developed minority group consciousness and a strong positive sense of themselves (Castañeda & Peters, 2000; Longmore & Umansky, 2001).

Disability activism as it happened over the history of the United States exemplifies social justice. Disabled individuals and groups that fought for equity and justice demonstrated that they were people to be respected and included in U.S. society. They worked to overcome the oppression they experienced, educate those around them, and ensure that those who came after them would be treated as full, participating, and valued citizens of this nation.

Conclusion

Critical to the three movements highlighted in this chapter—deaf education, the influence of war veterans, and disability activism—are themes of liberation, justice, interdependence, and respect, ideas that are core aspects of the social justice approach. Deaf people, veterans, and disabled activists (including Deaf and veteran activists) all worked to liberate themselves and others who were part of the populations they represented from the oppression that they experienced in society. All three groups advocated for equity and justice to live their lives freely and to be treated fairly. They also worked together with other members of their groups and their allies to achieve their goals. Finally, the core principle underlying their activism was to be viewed with respect by those in society. Their stories and the themes that appear in them have special meaning within the framework of social justice, as we detail in Chapter 2.

The history of disability is rich, extensive, and powerful. It demonstrates the varied ways in which disability has been viewed in society and the manner in which disabled members of society have been treated. It is not always pretty or easy to read. Yet it demonstrates the resilience of people faced with challenging circumstances and their ability to turn those circumstances around. Disabled people have found ways to succeed in a society where they have not always been wanted or welcomed. To truly understand the experiences of people with disabilities today, understanding the past through the eyes of their predecessors is valuable in that it provides a clearer sense of the work that is yet to be done and the strategies that may be or may not be effective to move nearer to completing it.

Discussion Questions

1. How has U.S. history influenced educational access for people with disabilities?
2. What barriers have people with disabilities experienced in access to education and legal protections?
3. Why is a historical understanding important for framing a socially just approach to disability in higher education?
4. How have the historical narratives described in this chapter influenced the culture of your institution in regard to access and policies for people with disabilities?
5. What is the specific history of disabled people studying and working on your campus?

Appendix: Significant Moments in the History of Disability in the United States

Year	Disability Moment	Historical Context
1700–1800		Age of Enlightenment
1775–1783	Continental Congress promised pensions to disabled veterans.	Revolutionary War
1790s–1830s	Evangelical Christians took on the mission of educating deaf and blind children.	Second Great Awakening
1817	American Asylum for the Deaf opened.	
1818	Revolutionary War Pension Act passed.	
1840–1870		Second Industrial Revolution
1850s	Oralism introduced in deaf schools.	
1861–1865		Civil War
1865–1877		Reconstruction era

Year	Disability Moment	Historical Context
1864	Congress authorized Columbia Institution for the Instruction of the Deaf, Dumb, and Blind (later Gallaudet University).	
1867	Exclusively oralist Clarke School for the Deaf opened in Massachusetts.	
1869	Institution for Colored Deaf and Dumb and Blind opened in North Carolina.	
1880	International Congress on the Education of the Deaf met in Milan, Italy. National Association of the Deaf established.	
1880–1945	Eugenics movement in the United States.	
1890s–1920s		Progressive era
1893	First woman, Agatha Tiegel, graduated from Gallaudet.	
1894	First documented case of polio in the United States (in Vermont).	
1895	American Blind People's Higher Education and General Improvement Association formed.	
1896	First eugenics law prohibiting marriage of certain disabled.	
1902	Helen Keller became first deaf-blind person to graduate from college; published her autobiography in 1903.	

(*continued*)

Year	Disability Moment	Historical Context
1907	Indiana passed first forced sterilization law. Sign language removed from all U.S. schools.	
1917	The Vocational Education Act established the Federal Board for Vocational Education.	United States enters World War I
1918	Smith-Sears Veterans Vocational Rehabilitation Act passed.	
1920	Smith-Fess Civilian Vocational Rehabilitation Act passed. Disabled American Veterans formed.	
1921	Federal legislation created Veterans Bureau.	
1930s	Resurgence of sign language in deaf schools.	Great Depression
1933	Election of the first U.S. president with a physical disability.	F. D. Roosevelt elected president
1935	League of the Physically Handicapped formed. Vocational rehabilitation programs received permanent authorization under the Social Security Act.	
1937–1955	Polio epidemics spread across the United States.	
1938	President F. D. Roosevelt established March of Dimes.	
1940	The American Federation of the Physically Handicapped founded. National Federation of the Blind formed.	

Year	Disability Moment	Historical Context
1941–1945	300,000 people with disabilities employed in wartime industry.	United States in World War II
1943	Congress passed the Vocational Rehabilitation Amendments (i.e., the Barden-LaFollette Act). Public Law 16 passed.	
1944		Serviceman's Readjustment Act (GI Bill)
1945	Blinded Veterans Association formed.	
1947	Paralyzed Veterans of America formed.	
1948	Disability Resources and Educational Services program at the University of Illinois at Galesburg gained official recognition from the university. Later moved to the main campus at Urbana-Champaign.	
1950–1953		Korean War
1952	President's Committee on Employment of the Physically Handicapped (later President's Committee on the Employment of People with Disabilities) formed.	
1954	Andrew Foster became the first Black student to graduate from Gallaudet. Congress passed Vocational Rehabilitation Amendments of 1954.	*Brown v. Board of Education of Topeka*

(*continued*)

Year	Disability Moment	Historical Context
1960s–1970s		Civil rights movements
1961	American Council of the Blind formed.	
	First experimental cochlear implant surgeries performed.	
1962	Edward Roberts, a veteran of World War II, was the first quadriplegic person to enroll at the University of California, Berkeley.	
1963	Vocational Education Act passed.	
1965–1975		Vietnam War
1965	The National Technical Institute for the Deaf, established by Congress; it opened in 1968.	
	A Dictionary of American Sign Language published.	
1970	Judith Neumann and other disability activists in New York City formed Disabled in Action.	
	Ed Roberts and Rolling Quads receive a U.S. Department of Education grant to establish the Physically Disabled Students Program, which became the nucleus of the first Center for Independent Living in 1972.	
1971	*Pennsylvania Association for Retarded Children v. Commonwealth of Pennsylvania.*	

Year	Disability Moment	Historical Context
1972	*Mills v. Board of Education.* Disability activists hold demonstrations in Washington, DC, San Francisco, and other cities to protest veto of Rehabilitation Act.	
1973	Section 504 of the Rehabilitation Act passed.	
1974	Vietnam Era Veterans' Readjustment Assistance Act passed.	
1975	Education for All Handicapped Children Act (Pub. L. 94–142) signed by President Gerald Ford. Kurzweil Reader invented.	
1977	The American Coalition of Citizens with Disabilities sit-ins in Washington, DC, and 10 other U.S. cities; 25-day occupation of the Department of Health, Education, and Welfare office in San Francisco. Association on Handicapped Student Service Programs in Postsecondary Education (AHSSPPE) founded; renamed Association on Higher Education and Disability (AHEAD) in 1992.	

(*continued*)

Year	Disability Moment	Historical Context
1979	*Southeastern University Community College v. Davis* Disability Rights Education and Defense Fund founded.	
1981–1983	Reagan administration threatened elimination of Section 504 and Education for All Handicapped Children Act.	Ronald Reagan elected U.S. president
1985	U.S. Department of Education sponsored the National Longitudinal Transition Study.	
1987	Congress passed Civil Rights Restoration Act over President Reagan's veto.	
1988	Deaf President Now! movement at Gallaudet University. Americans With Disabilities Act introduced in Congress.	
1989	Revised versions of ADA introduced in Congress. Center for Universal Design created.	
1990	Americans With Disabilities Act passed. Soldiers report symptoms of Persian Gulf syndrome. Congress amended Education for All Handicapped Children Act, renaming it the Individuals with Disabilities Education Act; reauthorized in 1997.	Persian Gulf War
2003		U.S. invasion of Iraq began

Year	Disability Moment	Historical Context
2004	U.S. Access Board published updated ADA Accessibility Guidelines.	
	President George W. Bush signed the Assistive Technology Act.	
2006	Second controversy at Gallaudet over hiring of president.	
2008	Americans With Disabilities Act Amendments Act signed; effective January 1, 2009.	
	Higher Education Opportunity Act passed.	
	Post-9/11 Veterans Educational Assistance Act (the New GI Bill) passed.	

Source: Content drawn from Chronology. (2009). In S. Burch (Ed.), *Encyclopedia of American disability history, vol. I* (pp. xxiv–lvi). New York, NY: Facts on File. Additional material drawn from references cited in this chapter.

CHAPTER TWO

DISABILITY MODELS

As a wheelchair user who had polio when I was young, I have experienced well-meaning individuals tell me that if I just pray and live my life as God wishes me to, I will be cured, the implication being that I must not be living a "Godly" life since I still need a wheelchair for mobility. These beliefs are a good example that the moral model continues to guide people's thinking.

—Nancy, faculty member

M ost disability models are closer to paradigms than they are to theories in that they present a certain way of viewing disability based on people's perceptions, beliefs, and experiences rather than research data. Definitions and conceptualizations of disability presented in models reflect the worldview of specific time periods and cultures (Drum, 2009). As such, disability is a social construction, the meaning of which shifts over time and place and is influenced by political ideology, economic conditions, and cultural values (Meade & Serlin, 2006; Olkin, 1999). Olkin (1999) explained that "each [model] has a perspective on what 'the problem' of disability is, who holds the problem, and avenues that best address the problem" (p. 24). How U.S. society has perceived disability over the course of the country's existence has provided the foundation for how individuals with disabilities have been viewed and treated, as well as the expectations and assumptions held by individuals with disabilities themselves.

Interactions between individuals with disabilities and various societal institutions, including the family, community, workplace, and educational system, are dictated largely by the meaning that society attaches to disability during a specific period in history. Different assumptions about disability—that is, disability models—have influenced whether individuals with various disabilities were able to attend college at specific times during the history of the United States and their experiences after they enrolled. Scholars have also based research on specific models to verify the ideas they include.

In this chapter, we first review the moral, medical, functional limitations, social, and minority models as major disability perspectives that have guided thinking and action over time. We discuss them in the order in which they became important in society, noting factors that were influential in their development. We then outline critical disability theory and critical realism as two models that have influenced our thinking and have potential to contribute to the understanding and practice of disability scholarship and disability support. We next highlight the social justice model, which we believe has particular utility in higher education settings. Then we briefly discuss two emerging models, the disability justice model and the interactionist model, that introduce useful ideas not found in other models. The appendix at the end of this chapter summarizes key points of the models we describe. Older models do not disappear when new models arise. Many of these models coexist in society currently, and there are still vestiges of the earlier models, as Nancy's experience discussed at the start of the chapter demonstrates.

While disability models vary greatly in how they conceptualize disability, Scambler and Scambler (2010) posited that a theme connecting diverse perspectives is the idea of chronic illnesses and disabilities as "assaults on the lifeworld" (p. 1). This broad understanding of disability allows for a variety of disability models, each of which interprets the contributions of biological, psychological, and social factors in its own way. Disagreement over disability policy, legislation, and practice can be attributed to differences in how disability is defined and conceptualized by individuals using different disability models (Scotch, 2009). Understanding the principles associated with each of the major models is therefore necessary prior to exploring how disability is understood and addressed in higher education.

Established Models

We begin by providing overviews of established models of disability that have guided understanding of disability since the start of the Common Era (moral model), the 19th century (medical model), the beginning of the 20th century (functional limitations model), and the 1960s and 1970s (social model and minority group model).

Moral Model

Proponents of the moral model view "disability [as] a defect caused by moral lapse or sins" (Olkin, 1999, p. 25). As early as the beginning of the Common Era, the Jewish culture linked physical defects to the "sins" committed by individuals and believed that it was up to individuals to cure themselves since their actions had caused the defects (Stiker, 1999). During medieval times when religious beliefs and practices dominated the thinking and actions of Western civilization, people believed that disability was God's punishment for "sin, failure of faith, moral lapse, or evil" (Olkin, 1999, p. 25) committed by individuals themselves or members of their families. Physical impairments could also be "the work of the devil" (Drum, 2009, p. 27). Because they were viewed as the result of the individual's moral misbehavior, defects brought shame on the individual and the family (Olkin, 1999). As a result, during the Middle Ages, people who were viewed as defective were "shunned, condemned, or used for entertainment purposes, e.g, as court jesters" (Drum, 2009, p. 27).

During the late 1800s, disability and its related effects, such as poverty, unemployment, and dependence on others, continued to be viewed as a result of fate, God's punishment, or individual moral weaknesses (K. W. Hickel, 2001). Because disabled people were viewed as weak, flawed, and having brought their conditions on themselves, government agencies as well as private charities refused to provide aid to adults disabled in later life, although they did assist children with disabilities and veterans of military service (K. W. Hickel, 2001).

While the moral model is not the most prevalent view of disability today, vestiges of it remain in today's language, culture, and beliefs (Olkin, 1999). For instance, one often hears the phrase, "It is God's will," when a child is born with an incurable illness or a person becomes paralyzed as a result of an automobile accident. Western culture is permeated with the belief that disability is "bad" and, as a result, individuals with physical and mental impairments must have done something "wrong" that contributed to their condition. This attitude is especially evident when individuals are viewed as having played a direct role in their impairment, such as those with AIDS, Type 2 diabetes, obesity, or addictions. In such cases, it is viewed as acceptable to blame these individuals for their disabilities and even to exclude them from protection under the Americans With Disabilities Act Amendments Act (ADAAA; e.g., those with drug addiction who have not stopped using drugs). In addition, pop culture (e.g., television programs, movies, and popular books) often portrays disabled characters as villains or evil persons (Longmore, 2003). Arguments against providing government assistance to people with disabilities are frequently based on similar thinking (Shapiro, 1993).

Olkin (1999) provided another viewpoint originating from the moral model: "the myth of disability as mysticism" (p. 25). This belief suggests that when individuals lose one of their senses, other senses are heightened, such as the blind seer in the ancient Greek play *Oedipus* who provided the king with a prophecy regarding the future. Similarly, some people believe that as a result of surviving the adversity of living with a physical impairment, individuals will develop special spiritual, emotional, or reflective powers (Olkin, 1999).

Medical Model

Many factors converged during the mid-1800s that led to the development of the medical model. Most important was the beginning of the scientific and medical fields during the late 1700s and their refinement throughout the 1800s (Castañeda, Hopkins, & Peters, 2013). A second factor was the emergence of the concept of the "average man" whose characteristics and qualities were assumed to be "correct" or "normal" (L. J. Davis, 2006, p. 6). Any deviation from the average was viewed as deviant, abnormal, and in need of correction in order for a person to be acceptable in society. In addition, scientific advances during the 1800s led to a better understanding of diseases and their causes (Drum, 2009). Thus, by the late 1800s, disability was considered a public health issue, and people came to believe that it could be treated by physicians in institutions designed for that purpose (Drum, 2009). By the early 20th century, social service agencies, educational institutions, health care personnel, and policymakers formalized the medical model of disability and placed disability under the authority of medical and quasi-medical professionals (Nielsen, 2012). From these beginnings, the medical model evolved and remains a major paradigm for understanding, treating, and working with people with disabilities. A number of variations of the medical model exist (see Altman, 2001; Masala & Petretto, 2008); our overview focuses on principles associated with the majority of these approaches.

Adherents of the medical model view disability as "a medical problem that resides in the individual ... a defect in or failure of a bodily system and as such is inherently abnormal and pathological" (Olkin, 1999, p. 26). If the person is to fully function as a human being, this defect must be "cured or eliminated" (Siebers, 2008, p. 3). Fine and Asch (1988/2000) listed the following assumptions of the medical model: (a) disability is located only in the body, (b) a person's problems are caused by the person's impairment, (c) disabled persons are "victims" who must learn to handle the circumstances they face, (d) how disabled persons view themselves and compare themselves to others centers around their disabilities, and (e) people who have disabilities need help and support.

The medical model is linear (Minaire, 1992). Disabilities are caused by diseases, illnesses, traumas, or internal biological conditions (Drum, 2009) that create pathologies defined as physiological or cognitive impairments that make persons different from those who are considered "normal" (Meade & Serlin, 2006). The resulting symptomologies are the limitations people experience in their ability to perform everyday activities people of a similar age can complete, such as personal self-care, attending school, managing a household, or maintaining employment (Longmore & Umansky, 2001). Thus, users of the model focus "on the disease process itself, with the goal of curing the disease and returning the patient to normal functioning" (Lutz & Bowers, 2003/2007, p. 13). Therefore, a university's disability resource office staff using a medical perspective would focus on students' access to appropriate health care.

Rather than viewing individuals with disabilities as people, adherents of the medical model see them as "social embodiments of their physical disability: they are dysfunctional or quasi-functional or nonfunctional bodies to be repaired or, if not, then managed with bureaucratic and economic efficiency" (Meade & Serlin, 2006, p. 3). It is up to the medical professional to decide how to cure the disabled person's problem and the disabled person must do exactly what is prescribed in order to "get well" (Pfeiffer, 2000/2007, p. 7), taking on what Parsons (1951) labeled the "sick role" (p. 23). By taking on the sick role, individuals do not have the same social obligations as others in society, such as employment or household management, because they are "sick," but they also give up their rights to those who are caring for them (Pfeiffer, 2000/2007). If they do not obey the regimen prescribed by their physician or are not "cured" of their illness, they must accept the blame for their failure "to respond to treatment" (Drum, 2009, p. 28). Scambler and Scambler (2010) observed that under the medical model, the lives of individuals with disabilities can be affected as much by fears of stigmatization as by the direct effects of the exclusion from society they experience as a result of being excused from their social responsibilities.

A number of critiques of the medical model can be found in the literature. Imrie (1997) noted that focusing exclusively on the biological aspects of disability ignores factors such as culture, environment, and politics that play an important role in disability and its effects on individuals directly and by way of the attitudes and prejudice that result from these aspects of society. Lutz and Bowers (2003/2007) also suggested that while the medical model can be useful in the diagnosis and initial treatment of diseases, it does not take into consideration other factors that affect individuals with disabilities over the course of their life span. Psychologists have also expressed concern that the medical model does not take into consideration that psychological distress from prejudice and discrimination can contribute to how individuals experience and respond to disability (Marks, 1997). Disability activists reject the idea of equating disability with illness or abnormality. Many find the views and resulting treatment disabled people receive from members of the medical community as oppressive and marginalizing (Bricher, 2000).

Strict adherents of the medical model, who are concerned only with curing the illnesses or physiological abnormalities exhibited by individuals with impairments, are most likely to view disabled individuals as unfit to attend college or work in any capacity. One of the reviewers of a draft of this book (M. Peña, personal communication, August 5, 2016) shared an experience that she had with this type of thinking when she began working at a college in 1989: "I had to go before the college board, introduce myself, and talk about my college degrees, [and] then proceeded to tell them about my learning disability. One of the board members said, 'Having a learning disability and going to college are mutually exclusive.'" Since they are viewed as being sick, disabled people are considered unfit to take part in the normal activities expected of a college student or employee.

Within the medical model, there is no expectation that society will make adjustments to change people's attitudes or improve the environment so that people with disabilities can participate fully. People with disabilities are expected to rely on medical intervention, such as medication, therapy, or other forms of treatment, to address the symptoms and problems associated with their impairment. Another experience that our reviewer, M. Peña (personal communication, August 5, 2016), recalled was an employer who, upon learning that she had a learning disability, asked her if she took a pill for that. Those who adhere to the medical model also believe that if there is no current intervention to treat the impairments of disabled individuals, they must adjust to being outsiders and wait for a cure for their ailment.

Functional Limitations (Rehabilitation) Model

The concept of rehabilitation first appeared around 1880 with the development of hospital-schools to prepare crippled children to function in society (Byrom, 2001). Adherents of this approach viewed disability as a deficiency that could be overcome with assistance from professionals whose role was to treat the social and medical problems these children faced (Burch & Sutherland, 2006). The rehabilitation approach was expanded to address the increasing number of disabled veterans after World War I (Strauss, 1965).

Stiker (1999) pointed out that "the notion of 'rehabilitation' [implied] returning to a point, to a *prior* situation" (p. 122), suggesting that disability was a deviation from the norm of nondisabled existence and that the goal of rehabilitation was returning the disabled individual to this state. During the early 20th century, the focus shifted from its original emphasis on social rehabilitation, providing education and training so that disabled individuals could find a place to fit in society, to medical rehabilitation, which consisted of surgical and technological intervention to correct the impairments of disabled persons (Byrom, 2001).

In the functional limitations (or rehabilitation) model, the main argument is that disabilities cause limitations in a person's ability to perform specific functions of daily life (Bryan, 2002). Like the medical model, the functional limitations model of disability is exclusively focused on the person; the individual, rather than society, is rehabilitated (Imrie, 1997). But as Nagi (1965) explained, unlike the medical model, which focuses on pathology and cure, the rehabilitation model focuses on functional limitations and disabilities. Functional limitations may include difficulties moving, breathing, working, or caring for oneself independently (Bickenbach, Chatterji, Badley, & Üstün, 1999). The functional limitations model is essentialist in nature; it does not acknowledge that the culture, situation, or environment can influence the extent to which functional limitations affect people's ability to do things (Imrie, 1997). Adherents of the model also see disability as dichotomous; that is, there are only two kinds of people in the world—those who have functional limitations and those who do not (Drum, 2009). Only those who do not have functional limitations—the able-bodied—can be successful (Imrie, 1997).

The goal of this model is to improve disabled people's functional capabilities so that they are "restored to their previous condition," that is, the usual human condition of "ordinariness" (Michalko, 2002, p. 152). Unlike the medical model, the functional limitations model does not address the underlying condition that caused the impairment; rather, the emphasis is on improving the individual's functional capacity (Drum, 2009). To do so, rehabilitation personnel assess functional limitations and develop rehabilitation plans that focus as much as possible on restoring individuals to their former level of functioning and assisting them in adapting to their environments (Bryan, 2002). As Michalko (2002) pointed out, in today's society, people tend to be judged by how well they are able to carry out activities, "make a living," and contribute to society. There appears to be a hierarchy of disability, with physical and occupational functioning being the most important to address in rehabilitation (Imrie, 1997). As such, "the problem of disability ... becomes the problem of inability" (Michalko, 2002, p. 156). Disability resource office staff working from a functional limitations model would focus on providing accommodations, adaptive equipment, and individual coaching to enable students with disabilities to "overcome" their functional limitations and accomplish their academic goals, succeed in college, and enter the workplace.

There are a number of criticisms of the functional limitations model. From a social justice perspective, the functional limitations model, as with the medical model, places power and control in the hands of medical personnel who determine what tests and treatments should be administered to address the individual's functional limitations and when the individual's functional capacity has improved enough to consider the rehabilitation a success (Lutz & Bowers, 2003/2007). The reliance on testing by disability resource staff to verify learning disabilities and allow students to secure accommodations is based on the functional limitations model. In addition, the individual must be a "good patient" and comply with the instructions the rehabilitation professional provides. Disabled persons who cannot successfully regain full function remain dependent on others for care and are left "in a chronic role of dependency" (Lutz & Bowers, 2003/2007, p. 12). They are socialized into accepting the idea that they are "inferior" to those who are not disabled and behave in ways that conform to the stereotypes and behaviors that others expect (Imrie, 1997). In addition, the rehabilitation model does not value individual difference. Individuals with disabilities that make them unique must be rehabilitated so they are similar to everyone else and can assimilate in society (Stiker, 1999).

Others point out that the functional limitations model ignores the effects of aspects of the environment by focusing only on internal bodily limitations (Bickenbach et al., 1999; H. Hahn, 1991). It also fails to consider ways to change the environment to suit disabled persons by expecting the disabled person to adjust to the environment (Bryan, 2002). For instance, vocational rehabilitation services, which many disabled individuals rely on for assistance in attending college or securing employment, assisted Nancy when she determined that she could not negotiate the amount of walking required in her position at Penn State. They provided her with a motorized scooter to use on campus. Rather than recommending that the university adjust her work environment by moving her classes to the building in which her office was located, they considered only ways to adjust her personal mobility.

Medical personnel working from a rehabilitation perspective have also been criticized for focusing so much on the causes of conditions affecting disabled individuals that they tend to segregate them into disease categories and separate them from other people with different disabilities rather than bringing them together to address common issues, such as discrimination and environmental barriers (Bryan, 2002). In addition, reducing a person to a condition ignores other aspects of the whole person (Bryan, 2002).

Social Model

The social model of disability originated in the United Kingdom and was based on *Fundamental Principles of Disability* (1976), a document written and published by a disability activist group, the Union of the Physically Impaired against Segregation. Academics in the United Kingdom, especially Michael Oliver, Colin Barnes, and Vic Finkelstein, formalized the ideas set out in the document to create the social model of disability, the most often cited version of which was written by Oliver (1990). The social model was developed as an alternative to the medical and functional limitations approaches to which many disability activists objected (Drum, 2009). Many variations of the social model have evolved since the 1980s, including materialist (Finkelstein, 1980), cultural (Barnes, 1991; Shakespeare, 1994), and feminist (C. Thomas, 1999) versions (Tregaskis, 2002). The social model was introduced primarily for use by disability professionals and activists. As a result, Oliver (2004) stressed that it was not a disability theory. Often referred to as the "big idea" of the disability movement in the United Kingdom, the social model had a major influence on building the collective disability consciousness of its members by getting disabled people to think about their commonalities and the barriers they all faced (Oliver, 2004).

Barnes (1991) defined *disability* as "the loss or limitation of opportunities to take part in the normal life of the community on an equal level with others due to physical and social barriers" (p. 2). Thus, disability is a socially constructed concept, its meaning based on the perceptions of those making up society (Llewellyn & Hogan, 2000; Olkin, 2011b). Proponents of the social model argue that disability is located in the social environment, which they view as exclusionary and oppressive, rather than in the body (Marks, 1999). Social modelists define the environment broadly as including physical, economic, and political factors, as well as social dimensions (Tregaskis, 2002). They understand disability as the barriers that individuals with impairments have to address in all aspects of their lives, including work settings, housing options, education opportunities, civil rights, transportation, and access to the architectural environment (C. Thomas, 2004).

Initially impairment was not important to social modelists in that they saw disability as "wholly and exclusively social … [and] disablement [as having] nothing to do with the body" (Oliver, 1996, pp. 41–42). Later writers modified this position, defining impairment as "limitation in a person's physical, mental or sensory functioning [that] ... only become[s] salient and disabling in specific settings" (Marks, 1999, p. 80). Social modelists, however, continue to believe that "*disability* is the overriding priority for ... the disabled people's movement" (C. Thomas, 2004, p. 24). Disability resource office staff working within the social model would be interested only in environmental barriers such as inaccessible buildings, lack of captioning on videos, or inaccessible technology rather than any factors related to students themselves.

The main goal of adherents of the social model is to make sense of and change "disabling socio-political and cultural practices" (Goodley, 2004, p. 123). Social modelists also argue against segregated, special, or adapted facilities for disabled people since such facilities send a message that disabled individuals are different from other members of the community and cannot fit in the "normal" world (Marks, 1999). Instead, they advocate using universal design (see Chapters 10 and 12) to modify the mainstream environment so that it is accessible to all individuals, with or without disabilities (Marks, 1999).

The strengths of the social model are that it introduced a new way for professional disability workers and researchers to think about disability and raised new research questions amenable to different methodological approaches to better understand the concept of disability (Llewellen & Hogan, 2000). The social model depathologized disability by focusing on the social environment rather than internal ailments or injuries while addressing what they believed to be the true cause of disability: prejudice and discrimination (Fougeyrollas & Beauregard, 2001). The model also secured some basic changes in society to allow access and inclusion for people with disabilities (Oliver, 2013; Olkin, 2011b).

There are a number of concerns about the social model as well. Critics have focused on the role of impairment and personal stories within the social model, with some arguing that their inclusion would lessen the model's effectiveness and others suggesting they are critical to a fuller understanding of disability (Shakespeare & Watson, 1997). Abberley (1987) critiqued the minimization of impairment, arguing that like disability, it too was socially produced. Others, particularly feminists, posited that the body should be considered since it has an effect on a person's experiences (C. Thomas, 2004). Shakespeare (2006a) explained that individuals with degenerative conditions or conditions that cause pain and discomfort would certainly be well aware of the negative aspects of impairments. For instance, Ellen has noted that even when she is working at a camp for children with diabetes, designed to remove all social barriers, she still experiences fluctuations in blood sugar that limit her functioning.

C. Thomas (2004) viewed the type of social barriers addressed in the social model as too limited, in that only material barriers found in the external social world were considered. Marks (1999), as well as C. Thomas (2004), argued that there are also psychoemotional aspects of disability, specifically the effects of social interactions between the "powerless impaired" and the "powerful nonimpaired," such as families, communities, health services, and educational services, when they make impaired people feel helpless, worthless, unattractive, and so forth. Abberley (1987), as well as Marks (1999) and Vernon (1998), pointed out that the social model ignores individual differences in race, gender, and other social identities, as well as historical time, when considering the effects of the environment on those with disabilities. Finally, Shakespeare (2006a) suggested that the idea that removing all social barriers would erase disability was unrealistic. Anastasiou and Kauffman (2011) explained that removing all barriers for persons with one type of impairment, not a particularly realistic idea itself, could create barriers for persons with another type of impairment. For instance, creating curb cuts for wheelchair users makes following sidewalks with a cane difficult for people who are blind, and allowing emotional support animals into residence halls for students with psychological disabilities presents challenges for students with pet allergies.

Minority Group (Sociopolitical) Model

Also referred to as the sociopolitical model, the minority group model is an expansion of the social model, which proponents in the United States believed used too narrow a view of the environment (Drum, 2009). The minority group model grew out of the disability rights movement in the United States in the 1970s (H. Hahn, 1988; Smart & Smart, 2006). Those associated with this movement distrusted the medical model and medical professionals who controlled all decisions regarding the treatment of disabled persons, leaving disabled individuals with no voice in decisions that affected their lives (Lutz & Bowers, 2003/2007). Disability rights activists also argued that nondisabled academics who had no knowledge of the issues facing people with impairments were often biased and that disabled researchers should take the lead in conducting research about disability since they understood the issues (Longmore, 2003). As a result, disabled academics in the United States, especially Harlan Hahn and Paul Longmore, promoted the new "minority group" approach, which led to its predominance in the 1970s and 1980s as a basis for research and the development of the field of disability studies in the United States (H. Hahn, 1985, 1988; Longmore, 2003).

The goal of this movement was to transfer the "burden of disability" (Lutz & Bowers, 2003/2007, p. 14) from people with impairments to society by creating a sense of community among people with disabilities and strengthening laws to combat discrimination and change public policy (H. Hahn, 1985). Similar to members of other minority groups based on race, gender, or sexual orientation, proponents of the minority group model argued that people with disabilities experience commonalities such as oppression, alienation, and discrimination (H. Hahn, 1991; Longmore, 2003; Scotch, 2000/2009). H. Hahn (1988) argued that nondisabled people oppress disabled people for violating two critical values of Western society in the 20th century: physical attractiveness (in the case of physical disabilities) and individual autonomy. H. Hahn added that "the social stigma of a disability fundamentally derives from the fact that the resulting functional impairments may interfere with important life activities" (p. 43). Disability resource staff working within the context of the minority group model are likely to stress the importance of building awareness among students with disabilities of the oppression and discrimination they face on campus and within society. They would be likely to create consciousness-raising groups and encourage an activist orientation among students for obtaining rights and policies to create a more just environment.

Impairment and disability are considered to be different concepts within the minority group model (Nielsen, 2012). While not explicitly defined in the model, *impairment* is used to refer to a mental or physical disease, injury, or ailment affecting the person's body or mind; *disability* is defined as "the product of the interaction between individuals and the environment" (H. Hahn, 1991, p. 17). People's surroundings, rather than their bodies, are the sources of the limitations they face (H. Hahn, 1988), and social context greatly influences how disability is viewed and treated (Nielsen, 2012). H. Hahn (1991) went on to explain that "disability is not a personal defect or deficiency [but rather it is] primarily the product of a disabling environment" (p. 17). As such, it is the environment that must be adjusted to meet the person's requirements rather than the person adapting to the environment (Bryan, 2002). H. Hahn (1988, 1991) saw societal attitudes as the most powerful environmental factor affecting people with disabilities. He offered three postulates to this proposition: (a) negative attitudes are the major cause of the barriers that people with disabilities face, (b) public policy drives all aspects of the environment, and (c) social attitudes are influential in the creation of public policy.

The minority group model is particularly important in the history of disability since it was instrumental in the passage and enactment of disability rights laws and the development of disability activism in the United States

(Drum, 2009; Longmore, 2003). It also does a better job than the medical and functional limitations models of explaining the daily experiences of disabled people, since in most cases, prejudice and discrimination have more of an impact on lives than do functional limitations (Scotch, 2000/2009; Smart & Smart, 2006). H. Hahn (1985) also pointed out that the minority group model is more complex than either the medical or social models since it considers the interaction of the person and the environment rather than only one of these factors.

The minority group model nevertheless also has some weaknesses. Batavia and Schriner (2001) viewed it as "over simplified," suggesting that it leaves out consideration of important factors including individual, family, and cultural variables that influence a person's ability "to live independently and productively" (p. 692). Lack of attention to the role of the individual's body is also a point of contention (Drum, 2009; Imrie, 1997), as is the narrow focus on public policy approaches to reduce discrimination toward disability (Imrie, 1997). Many critics have argued that the variability of impairments and the difficulties of coming together as a group act against the development of a minority group consciousness (S. R. Jones, 1996). Perhaps the most salient criticism of the minority group model in the view of social justice educators is its construction as a deficit model that supports the stereotype of individuals with disabilities as being victims in need of support (S. R. Jones, 1996).

Critical Approaches to Disability

Two more recent models have strong potential for shaping the work of disability professionals and scholars: critical disability theory and critical realism. Both fit under the umbrella of critical theory.

Critical Disability Theory

Critical disability theory (CDT) is a framework that emerged from postmodern and postconventional critiques of existing disability theories (Corker, 1998; Corker & Shakespeare, 2002; L. Davis, 2002; Meekosha, 2006; Meekosha & Shuttleworth, 2009; Shildrick, 2009, 2012). Foucault (1977, 1980) championed critical perspectives, yet disability studies theorists did not adopt his ideas until the 1990s (Corker, 1998, 1999; Corker & Shakespeare, 2002) and only very recently has CDT entered the higher education and student affairs literature (Meekosha & Shuttleworth, 2009; Peña, Stapleton, & Schaffer, 2016; Vaccaro, Kimball, Wells, & Ostiguy, 2015).

Although critical of the medical and functional limitation models, CDT arose primarily as a challenge to the perceived hegemony of the social model (L. Davis, 2002). Specifically, Corker (1999) argued that thinking about disability only as a form of social oppression was incomplete, explaining, "In its efforts to produce a collective notion of disability, disability studies has inadvertently reproduced the kind of representations and theoretical structures that it has historically claimed to challenge" (p. 629). CDT scholars questioned metanarratives (L. Davis, 2002), particularly those within the social model that prescribe dichotomies such as individual/society or impairment/disability (Corker & Shakespeare, 2002; Meekosha & Shuttleworth, 2009; Shildrick, 2012). Scholars working within a CDT framework also critiqued ideas associated with the minority model, noting that a "conundrum in disability research is the assumption that all participants in a particular study will form part of a collective 'disabled identity'" (Smith-Chandler & Swart, 2014, p. 424).

As a model, CDT is complex and multifaceted; here we focus on four core components. First, in CDT, *disability* is defined as "slippery, fluid, [and] heterogeneous" (Shildrick, 2009, p. 4). This definition allows disability to change over time and be intersectional; that is, it is shaped by other aspects of social identity, meaning, for example, that a particular form of disability experienced by an Asian American may differ from how that disability is experienced by an African American (Shildrick, 2009). As Smith-Chandler and Swart (2014) stated, "We contend that there is no single, universal, fixed, stable disabled identity and that experiences differ in terms of both individual and contextual factors" (p. 424). A definition of disability that is fluid and temporal can be useful in higher education settings, in that it allows that disability might be recently acquired, or recently diagnosed, or might change in impact over the collegiate experience. Furthermore, it encourages practitioners to take an intersectional approach and understand why some students may not identify as disabled even though they may have an impairment. For instance, rather than assuming a student who refused to accept accommodations for a learning disability was being stubborn and unrealistic about his ability to succeed with the disability, a disability resource professional using a critical disability theory approach might probe to understand why the student felt this way and how learning disabilities were viewed in his family and culture.

Second, CDT includes local knowledge as a method of understanding the lived experiences of people with disabilities (Meekosha & Shuttleworth, 2009). Given the importance of campus climate, locally situated knowledge is imperative for anyone working with disabled people in higher education settings. For example, knowing that snow removal along accessible paths is prioritized by facilities staff is valuable, and not to be assumed when coming from a campus where these paths either were not prioritized or there was no snowfall.

Third, CDT educators value emancipation and spotlight issues of human rights and social justice (Meekosha & Shuttleworth, 2009). Practitioners may assume that important social justice topics for disabled people primarily relate to employment, education, and physical access. CDT goes beyond the political focus of other theoretical frameworks by bringing social justice into areas that are meaningful for disabled people, such as culture and sex (Meekosha & Shuttleworth, 2009). For instance, individuals with many types of disabilities are frequently and falsely assumed to be asexual; thus, health and education providers should have critical discussions with all clients about healthy sex practices. Those working within a CDT framework encourage campus sex education programmers to include diversity in relation to how people with impaired bodies have sex and foster a disability culture by inviting speakers and promoting disability pride events.

Finally, scholars using a CDT framework posit that both impairment and environment are important and that a relational discourse occurs between embodiment and disability (Meekosha & Shuttleworth, 2009). Unlike other theoretical frameworks that isolate impairment, CDT allows for a "causal relationship between impairment and disability" (Corker, 1999, p. 632). For example, the social model would posit that Kirsten's spelling impairment is caused by the environment, and practitioners using that model would focus on changing the environment by creating access to spell-checking or other adaptive software. CDT allows a more complex and fluid understanding of a relationship between the inability to spell and the environment. Practitioners employing CDT would recognize that in some environments, the impairment will dominate and environmental alterations, such as spell-checkers or writing on a dry erase board during a meeting, are not useful. Furthermore, by having an embodied component, CDT honors the frustration Kirsten feels when she spells a word so poorly that a spell-checking program cannot even guess what she wants. Hence, using CDT, a professional working in higher education might gain a better understanding of why there are times when impairment matters more, why there are times when environment matters more, and why there are times when the interactions between impairment and society make functional limitations more or less difficult to manage.

CDT offers professionals in higher education settings a unique set of tools to understand disability experiences in a more complex and intersectional manner. Notably, CDT provides a framework that allows faculty, staff, and others in higher education settings to consider identity, intersectionality, campus environments, impairment, and visible and nonvisible representations;

it offers powerful tools to break down hierarchies and include underrepresented voices. Within CDT, students, scholars, and researchers prefer and frequently use disability-first terminology (e.g., "disabled student"), although some also purposefully employ person-first language (e.g., "student with a disability") in specific situations (Meekosha & Shuttleworth, 2009; Shildrick, 2009). For example, person-first language can be used to show pride or reclaim disability, "move away from the preoccupation with binary understandings" (Meekosha & Shuttleworth, 2009, p. 50), or deconstruct hierarchies of knowledge via discourse analysis (Shildrick, 2009). The use of disability-first language may be uncomfortable, especially in student affairs, which remains a field where the dominant norm emphasizes using person-first language.

Another challenge in using CDT is that fluid or temporal definitions of disability may be challenging to employ within identity-based centers or in developing identity politics. In addition, the tendency of postmodern scholars to use complex and inaccessible language might make CDT inaccessible to individuals without an advanced understanding of philosophical thought (K. Brown, Broido, Stapleton, Evans, & Peña, 2016).

CDT offers unique social justice opportunities but also may pose difficulties for engaging undergraduate students, staff, and community members. Higher education professionals and scholars wishing to integrate CDT in their practice and research should engage with the theoretical lens beyond the limited overview provided in this book. In particular, we direct interested readers to consider Gillies and Dupuis (2013) as an example of how to use CDT to frame a participatory action research study, Meekosha and Shuttleworth (2009) as a resource to better understand social justice implications, and E. V. Peña et al. (2016) as a framework for exploring intersectionality.

Critical Realism

Unlike the other models reviewed in this chapter, critical realism is not a model of disability but a philosophy of science. We include it here because, as applied to the study of disability, it requires that we reintegrate consideration of the physical realities of the body and mind with the constructivist focus on structural and social systems (Shakespeare, 2014). Critical realism arose as an explicit philosophy of science during the 1970s (Bhaskar, 1998) but is grounded in the work of multiple Western philosophers writing across the 20th century (Danermark, Ekström, Jakobsen, & Karlsson, 2002). It was developed to address the limitations of both essentialist perspectives and those of constructivist perspectives in ways that would "serve progressive politics" (Moya, 2000, p. 3).

Applied to disability studies to address shortcomings of the social model (Shakespeare, 2014), critical realism is a paradigm that holds that reality exists in ways that allow us to make causal truth claims. Both physical and social phenomena are thought to exist independent of observers' and participants' perceptions of them. However, understandings of truth and reality are shaped by individuals' identities and experiences such that "the conditions and social relations of the production of knowledge influence its content" (Easton, 2010, p. 120). Thus, "critical realists propose ... there exists a reality 'out there' independent of observers ... [and that] the world is socially constructed but not entirely so" (p. 120).

A second key concept in critical realism is the multilayered nature of reality. Phenomena such as disability have multiple, mutually influencing layers: the molecular, the physiological, the psychological, the social, and the structural/cultural (S. J. Williams, 1999). These layers influence each other, but in nondeterministic ways. Danermark (2002), who has to date made the greatest use of critical realism in writing about disability, gave the example of two people who have a hearing impairment with the same physiological origin. Depending on their linguistic memory, the quality of their sight and light levels in their environment, and their coping skills, they will have varying degrees of functional impairment. Their families and friends will react in multiple ways to their impairment, some in ways facilitative of communication and others in ways less so. The two people may live in different countries, one of which provides extensive support to those with limited hearing and another without such resources. These mechanisms are independent of one another but do influence each other. Understanding hearing impairment requires recognition of the multiple, mutually shaping but independent layers of reality. Disability within a critical realistic perspective, then, is "a relationship between intrinsic factors (impairment, personality, motivation, etc.) and extrinsic factors (environments, support systems, oppression, etc.)" (Shakespeare, 2014, p. 76).

Writers using a critical realism framework (e.g., Shakespeare, 2014) to discuss disability have argued it is important to consider both the body/mind and the social/cultural experience when trying to understand disability and respond to it, as well as to consider the influence of context, knowing that no context-free claims about reality can be sustained (Danermark & Gellerstadt, 2004; Pilgrim, 2014). Shakespeare (2014) made clear that disability cannot be solely understood as a social construction, writing that "even with the removal of barriers and the provision of support, impairment will remain problematic for many disabled people" (p. 85). For instance, a critical realist in student affairs encouraging a student with a chronic disability to become involved on campus would want to ensure that the student took under consideration not only her specific interests and the accessibility of the organizations she was considering but also factors associated with her physical condition, such as fatigue.

The critical realist approach has two primary limitations. The first is the inaccessibility of the model. Most books and articles about critical realism are written using language inaccessible to those without training in metaphysics and the philosophy of science. The second is that critical realism appears to have made little inroad into the practice of social science. While it is easy to find writing about critical realism, it is more challenging to find research that employs a critical realist approach, especially disability research. Very little writing provides guidance on how to conduct a study from the perspective of critical realism. Articles published in the *Journal for the Theory of Social Behavior*, the primary outlet for critical realist writing, are overwhelmingly theoretical, with very few empirical pieces.

Social Justice (Ableist or Disability Oppression) Model

The social justice (or ableist, or disability oppression) model of disability is based on concepts associated with the overall social justice movement in the United States, which borrowed ideas from the separate civil rights, women's, and New Left movements of the 1960s and 1970s (L. A. Bell, 2013). In this model, concepts such as social justice, liberation, and oppression are used to analyze, evaluate, and transform systems of social behavior, discriminatory institutional structures, and cultural practices (M. Adams, Bell, & Griffin, 2007). The University of Massachusetts Social Justice Education Program has been particularly influential in developing and promoting this model. With the exception of conceptual work introduced by writers associated with the University of Massachusetts program and some research conducted in the United Kingdom, little writing and almost no research in the field of social justice has focused on ableism (Nocella, 2009).

Rather than focusing on *disablism*, which F. K. Campbell (2009) defined as "a set of assumptions (conscious and unconscious) and practices that promote the differential or unequal treatment of people because of actual or presumed disabilities" (p. 4), social justice model adherents "prefer the term *ableism* to define the oppression of people with disabilities" (Griffin, Peters, & Smith, 2007, p. 335). Rauscher and McClintock (1997) explained that throughout history, ableism has functioned to "create an environment that is often hostile to those whose physical, emotional, cognitive, or sensory abilities fall outside the scope of what is currently defined as socially acceptable" (p. 198).

F. K. Campbell (2009) added that ableism equates able-bodiedness with normalcy; by contrast, disability is viewed as abnormal, dependent, and deficient. As such, disabled individuals often cannot fulfill the social and economic roles that society expects, and their talents are not acknowledged (Castañeda et al., 2013; S. R. Smith, 2009). Implicit in the ableist perspective is the belief that disability is a negative status and should be eliminated or rehabilitated if possible (F. K. Campbell, 2009).

Another label for this approach, *disability oppression theory*, is used to describe the dynamics associated with the discrimination and injustice that are directed toward people with disabilities in an ableist society (Castañeda & Peters, 2000). Rather than attempting to "fix" people with disabilities so that they will "fit" into an ableist society, advocates of disability oppression theory promote addressing the oppressive culture so that all individuals are accepted as they are (Castañeda & Peters, 2000; Nocella, 2009). Hutcheon and Wolbring (2012) posited that the concept of ableism is helpful in two ways: it helps to explain the experiences of "ability-diverse" (p. 47) individuals and allows for more effective examination of policy and its effects.

Similar to other forms of oppression, ableism works on cultural, institutional, and individual levels (Castañeda et al., 2013; Griffin et al., 2007; Rauscher & McClintock, 1997). Cultural beliefs, including those regarding beauty, independence, and normality, affect how individuals with disabilities are viewed and treated in society. The policies, practices, and norms established in institutions such as the family, religion, law, housing, health care, and government create barriers for people with disabilities. Individual attitudes such as paternalism, pity, sympathy, disgust, and others expressed toward disabled individuals contribute to feelings of discomfort and distrust that people with disabilities experience in an ableist society (Griffin et al., 2007). The social justice model outlines how people with disabilities overcome these forms of oppression as they move toward empowerment as a result of the establishment of equitable access and accommodation within society and the creation of social structures where all people are able to take on equally important tasks and meaningful roles while connecting with other people interdependently (Castañeda & Peters, 2000).

Three major components unique to the social justice model of disability are its focus on privilege and oppression as major influences in shaping how disability is viewed and experienced in U.S. society; its emphasis on diversity and intersectionality of the disabled individual's experiences, roles, and identities; and its intentionally educational mission. Social justice advocates point out that throughout time, nondisabled individuals have held the privilege and power to decide how disabled people, as the oppressed group, will be viewed and treated (Evans, 2008). L. A. Bell (2013) explained that oppression of individuals with disabilities has four qualities. It is *pervasive* in that inequality is "woven throughout social institutions as well as embedded within individual consciousness" (p. 22). It is *restrictive* in that lives of individuals with disabilities are constricted by structural and material barriers. It is *hierarchical* as members of the dominant nondisabled group are advantaged by disempowering the oppressed disabled group. Finally, it is *internalized* by disabled individuals as well as nondisabled dominant group members.

Oppression has three dimensions: context, application, and consciousness (Hardiman, Jackson, & Griffin, 2013). As already noted, oppression in the form of ableism can occur at the individual level, through the attitudes and behaviors of individuals; it can take place in institutional settings, including family, government, education, religion, and the legal system; and it is also located at the social/cultural level when expressed as values, beliefs, and norms. Oppression is applied in these same locations—individually through attitudes and behaviors; institutionally through laws, policies, and practices; and societally through values, beliefs, and customs. Finally, the dimension of consciousness indicates that oppression can be intentional or unintentional. Similarly, social justice educators and advocates can address oppression in each of these contexts and locations. For instance, diversity courses should include units on disability to dispel students' negative attitudes, misinformation, and stereotypes about people with disabilities; social justice advocates can review policies and practices in areas such as admissions, residence life, and student activities to ensure that they are equitable for all students (see Chapters 14 and 15); and advocates can point out underlying values and beliefs that may appear in campus media, such as newspapers, handbooks, and websites.

The second aspect of the social justice model addressed much more extensively than in other models is diversity and the intersectionality of experiences, roles, and identities. As S. R. Smith (2009) pointed out, in addition to structural injustice, discrimination against disabled individuals is also caused by "identity exclusion" (p. 25), when nondisabled individuals assume what the experience of disabled people is rather than considering the variation in experiences that disabled individuals actually have. Proponents of the social justice model stress the diversity of people with disabilities, including their broad range of physical, emotional, and mental capabilities; their other social identities; and their various personality characteristics, as well as the different social contexts in which they live (Castañeda et al., 2013; Evans, Assadi, & Herriott, 2005).

All of these variables influence people's worldviews, self-perceptions, and how others perceive and treat them. Taking into consideration individuals'

various social identities, including gender, race, religion, age, sexual orientation, and social class, in relation to their impairments is especially important
for understanding the meaning that the individual, other people, and society
will attach to their disabilities (Castañeda & Peters, 2004; Griffin et al., 2007).
For instance, because the norms of behavior for young African American children are different from those for White children, African American children
are much more often diagnosed as having attention deficit disorder than are
White children (see Chapter 5 for further discussion of identity). As Hardiman et al. (2013) stated, "Our various social identities interrelate to negate
the possibility of a unitary or universal experience of any one manifestation of
oppression" (p. 30).

The social justice model is intentionally educational, unlike other models
we have addressed. MacKinnon, Broido, and Wilson (2004) listed three important dimensions of social justice advocacy in education. Applied to disability,
they are (a) providing support to students with disabilities; (b) educating both
students with disabilities and those who are not disabled about the existence
of disability oppression, working with them to create an environment that
values differences, and teaching them to advocate for their own and others'
liberation; and (c) working to change institutional structures and policies that
support oppression of those with disabilities.

Four goals are associated with the social justice model: elimination of
ableism, redefinition of normal, respect and equity, and development of a
positive disability identity. Eliminating ableism involves changing the physical
and social environment so that disabled individuals can function effectively
(Griffin et al., 2007). Implementing universal design principles both in
and out of the classroom is one strategy for accomplishing this goal at
the institutional level (see Chapters 10 and 12). Legislation to eliminate
discrimination and environmental barriers is another means that the government has used to address ableism (Rauscher & McClintock, 1997; see
Chapter 3 for a discussion of legal aspects of disability.) In recent years, social
justice education has been used to raise individual awareness of ableism and
promote equity, access, and transformation of societal systems to create just
institutions and cultural values of respect and equal treatment for all people
(Hackman, 2008).

Redefining normalcy "so that physical, mental, and sensory differences are
no longer viewed as abnormal" (Griffin et al., 2007) is another goal of the social
justice model. Within the ableist system, certain characteristics of the human
mind and body, constructed as "normal," are privileged; others, associated
with disability, are viewed as deficient and inadequate (F. K. Campbell, 2009).
Individuals with minds and bodies that are not "normal" are excluded by the

dominant nondisabled group from many aspects of economic and social life (Nocella, 2009). To reintegrate individuals with disabilities into society, the narrow definition of what is considered normal needs to be expanded so that their differences are accepted and valued (Rauscher & McClintock, 1997). Social justice educators stress that concepts such as normalcy, average, standardization, and equality are socially constructed and there is no such thing as an objective "norm" or "average" (Nocella, 2009). Rather, all people are different mentally and physically, leading social justice educators to promote "respect of differences not of equality" (Nocella, 2009, p. 155). An example of a narrow definition of what is normal is the assumption that all people should be able to navigate by walking. A social justice approach would suggest that any form of navigation, including using motorized scooters or wheelchairs, is appropriate. Given this assumption, all entrances to buildings would be wide and have automatic door openers; entrances would be approached using sidewalks that were flat or slightly inclined rather than stairs.

The goal of promoting respect and equity, then, is intertwined with respecting difference. Respect entails self-respect as well as respect from others and for others. As L. A. Bell (2013) stated, "Social justice involves social actors who have a sense of their own agency as well as a sense of social responsibility toward and with others, their society, and the broader world in which we live" (p. 21). This vision of society can best be achieved when "the distribution of resources is equitable and all members are physically and psychologically secure" (L. A. Bell, 2013, p. 21). S. R. Smith (2009) argued for a "productive tension" (p. 27) in the creation of "socially just human relations" (p. 27) that would enable nondisabled individuals to identify with and appreciate disabled individuals by engaging with them and sharing positive experiences but also recognize that people with disabilities have a right to expect structural changes in the social and political environment to enable them to successfully negotiate their surroundings. In the postsecondary setting, advocates of the social justice model of disability stress the right of every person to have a fulfilling and successful academic and cocurricular experience in which each person's complete identity and specific experiences are taken into account (Evans & Herriott, 2009). Social justice educators also "seek to create awareness on the campus regarding disability as another expression of human diversity similar to race, social class, gender, and sexual orientation" (Evans & Herriott, 2009, p. 36). Diversity classes and programs that include information regarding disability are effective ways of accomplishing this goal.

Similar to the minority group model, the social justice model is invested in achieving a positive identity among disabled people. Understanding that disability is caused by social, economic, and environmental barriers rather than "conditions" that are psychological or physical in nature allows persons with disabilities to redefine themselves as strong and capable individuals (Rauscher & McClintock, 1997). Within this model, disabled individuals are proud of their differences and work to make others aware of their accomplishments and talents (Rauscher & McClintock, 1997). For example, disabled individuals may develop particular insights as a result of their experiences as "outsiders" that can be of benefit to other people (S. R. Smith, 2009). In the college or university setting, ensuring that students with disabilities are provided with opportunities to engage in cocurricular activities and take on leadership positions enables them to use their skills and talents in positive ways that convey to others that they are capable and encourages development of a positive disability identity.

The social justice model is more complex than earlier models in its understanding of how systems of privilege and oppression affect how individuals with disabilities view themselves and how others view them. It also is much more attentive than other models to the intersectionality of social identities and the unique aspects of each person's life as a disabled person. However, like other models, it does not account for the role played by impairments in the everyday life of many people with disabilities, particularly those who experience chronic illness and pain on an ongoing basis. To begin to address this concern, we next turn to two promising approaches that consider bodily experiences as well as broader disability communities.

Emerging Models

Disability justice and the interactionist model of disability are two emerging models that offer political and multifaceted approaches to understanding disability. In particular, the interactionist model is useful in that it is based on two studies of disabled college students.

Disability Justice

Disability justice is a new framework for disability advocacy, originally conceptualized in 2005 by a group of queer women of color who are also disabled activists (Berne, 2015). Mingus (as cited in Taormina-Weiss, 2013) argued, "Disability justice is a multi-issue political understanding of disability and ableism, moving away from a rights based equality model and beyond just access, to a framework that centers justice and wholeness for all disabled people and communities" (para. 5).

Disability justice activists looked to create a movement that addressed the shortcomings of the disability rights movement, which they saw as focused on White, economically privileged, heteronormative people and approaches (Berne, 2015). The disability justice movement exists primarily online, created by activists rather than scholars; this origin is congruent with the movement's focus on creating change rather than theorizing.

Mingus (2014) captured a core principle of disability justice, writing:

> We recognize that ableism is connected, tied up with and mutually dependent on other systems of oppression and that we cannot end ableism without also ending white supremacy, economic exploitation, colonization, and gender oppression. Disability justice requires that we no longer build single-issue analysis, but instead build frameworks that can hold the complexities of our lives. (p. 110)

Another key idea in disability justice is that of interdependence, a direct challenge to the disability rights argument that people with disabilities want to be independent. Copley (2011) wrote, "Ableism depends on maintaining the myth that we can be self-sufficient if we are strong enough—the myth of independence" (para. 6). In a disability justice perspective, there is recognition of and value in "interdependence, in which other people are necessary for physical, emotional and community health and well-being. Interdependency values our connection to others and communities" (Copley, 2011, para. 6). This emerging model offers new voices and perspectives to understanding disability, particularly as experienced by those with multiple marginalized identities. Disability resource office staff proponents of this model would focus on disabled students as people with many different yet intertwined social identities and stress the importance of working together for change.

Interactionist Model of Disability

Two studies of college students with disabilities served as the basis for an interactionist model of disability developed by Evans and Broido (2011). The first study was a phenomenological exploration of how students with disabilities perceived their involvement in social activities, organizations, and leadership positions, as well as the effects of their experiences on identity development. The second study was a phenomenological exploration of the collegiate experiences of students who had Type 1 diabetes.

Building on Lewin's (1936) interactionist model, Evans and Broido (2011) argued that students' ability to function in an environment is an interaction of the environment, the person, and the person's impairment. Each of these areas is dynamic: environments can range from enabling to disabling, people can make more and less effective choices, and impairments can vary from minimal to significant. The three elements influence each other as well. Environments can support individuals' ability to make effective choices, and individuals can influence their environments; the extent of impairment can influence people's ability to make effective choices, and the choices they make may (depending on the type of impairment) influence the impact of the impairment. The environment can influence the impact of the impairment and to a small degree; the extent of impairment might influence the environment (see Figure 2.1). A student affairs professional using an interactionist perspective would examine the degree to which specific aspects of the campus environment were disabling, the effectiveness of the individual student's choices, and the type and severity of the student's impairment, as well as how these factors all intersect and contribute to the specific situation the student was experiencing. The student affairs educator could help the student to understand that her experiences are fluid and can be changed by altering one or more of these variables.

Conclusion

Returning to Nancy's story that started this chapter, multiple models of disability shape the experiences of students, faculty, and staff with disabilities. Vestiges of the moral model shape the thinking of many individuals, as Nancy learned. Other older models, such as the medical model and the functional limitations model, continue to guide the work of disability resource offices on many college campuses, as well as vocational rehabilitation services that many students use. Therefore, an understanding of all of the models discussed in this chapter is imperative.

L. A. Bell (2013) posited, "Practice is always shaped by theory, whether formal or informal, tacit or expressed" (p. 22). How individuals approach disability, how they identify problems that need to be addressed, how they choose to address them, and the solutions they determine to be appropriate are all influenced by theory (L. A. Bell, 2013), specifically by the models they choose to frame their understanding. We recommend using concepts drawn from more than one model as each can provide helpful insight that another one may not (Bryan, 2002). We do believe, however, that a social justice approach provides the strongest foundation from which to understand the impact of disability and how to address ableism in society since its principles are well developed and the model is based on inclusiveness and respect for all people. Once this foundation has been established, concepts from the critical

FIGURE 2.1. INTERACTIONIST MODEL OF DISABILITY

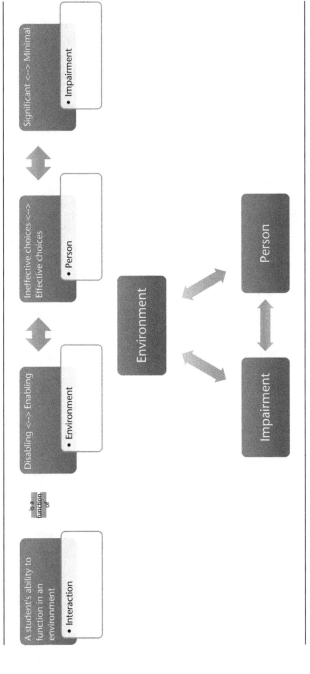

Source: Evans and Broido (2011).

and interactionist models, as well as disability justice, can add to the manner in which disability is understood and ableism is addressed, since they are more fluid and include more complex and dynamic understandings of intersectionality. Throughout this book, we ground our thinking in the social justice perspective, while also using ideas and concepts from various models and theories to explore the wide range of issues that must be addressed when working with disabled students in higher education settings.

Discussion Questions

1. Which models of disability most closely align with or inform current practices on your campus?
2. How might using one of the emerging models of disability inform policies and practices on campus differently than the established models?
3. How do you see the various models of disability being informed by and informing societal expectations of disability?

Appendix: Summary of Disability Models

	Definition of Disability	Main Ideas	Practitioners	Further Reading
Moral	Disability is a defect. It is also defined as "bad"; as a result, individuals with physical and mental impairments must have done something "wrong" that contributed to their condition.	Disability is caused by a moral lapse, sin, or the will of a higher power (e.g., God). People with disabilities bring their impairments and associated suffering on themselves because of their negative actions. If a higher power has caused this, "it is God's will."	Practitioners should know that specific religious beliefs viewed disability as God's punishment or "the work of the devil" (Drum, 2009, p. 27) and know that people with disabilities historically were shunned, used as entertainment, or viewed as weak. They should understand how vestiges of these ideas are present today in the literature, pop culture, and stereotypes.	Drum (2009); Olkin (1999)

(continued)

	Definition of Disability	Main Ideas	Practitioners	Further Reading
Medical	Disability is a product of biology in which a congenital or chronic illness, injury, or some other departure from "normal biomedical structure or functioning has consequences for an individual's activities of daily living and, ultimately, for the individual's ability to participate in society" (Scotch, 2000/2009, p. 602).	Rooted in the scientific method, the problem resides in the individual, who must learn to cope with the impairment. Individuals are placed in stigmatizing categories (e.g., the blind, the learning disabled). Categorization of disability is dependent on medical diagnosis and classification systems. Disabled people are compared to an idealized notion of normality. The focus is on pathology and cure. Decisions are made by medical professionals. Family or professionals are responsible for those who cannot be cured.	Practitioners should be aware that the medical model is traditionally the dominant one. The focus on objectivity and scientific method associated with the model suggests and reinforces ideas of authority. The medical model is not particularly helpful for practitioners as it locates the problem within the individual rather than considering other factors such as the environment, prejudice, and discrimination. It also implies that "something is wrong" with the person rather than honoring natural human variation.	Altman (2001); Masala & Petretto (2008); Scotch (2000/2009)

| Functional limitations | Disability is a deficiency that can be overcome with assistance from professionals whose role is to treat the functional limitations. | Disabilities cause limitations in a person's ability to perform specific functions of daily life. Disability is located in the individual, and the focus is on function limitations (e.g., difficulty hearing). The goal of this model is to improve or restore capabilities so the person is as "normal" as possible. Unlike the medical model, this limitations model does not address the underlying condition that caused the impairment. | Practitioners should know that the functional limitations model places power in the hands of medical authority rather than the individual. This model also contains language that disability resource providers commonly use when assessing appropriate accommodations. The model ignores critical factors such as the environment and the causes of conditions, and it does not value individual differences. | Bryan (2002); Imrie (1997); Michalko (2002) |

(continued)

	Definition of Disability	Main Ideas	Practitioners	Further Reading
Social	Disability is "the loss or limitation of opportunities to take part in the normal life of the community on an equal level with others due to physical and social barriers" (Barnes, 1991, p. 2).	Disability is a social construct. Environmental barriers isolate and exclude people with disabilities from full participation in society. Limitation of activity is caused by social organization rather than impairment. The experience of disabled people is dependent on social context and differs in different cultures and at different times. Goals are barrier removal, including both environmental and attitudinal barriers; making imbalance of power visible; and shifting the burden of disability from disabled people to society.	Practitioners should be aware that the social model depathologizes disability. This model frequently has support from disability activists and can be used to place focus on the campus environment, not the individual. This model is effective when discussing and trying to change physical, attitudinal, and social barriers to access. However, the model does not account for individuals' lived or bodily experiences (e.g., pain).	Barnes (1991); Finkelstein (1980); Oliver (1990); Oliver & Barnes (2012); Shakespeare (2006); Tregaskis (2002)

| Minority group | Disability is "the product of the interaction between individuals and the environment" (H. Hahn, 1991, p. 17). People with disabilities are seen as a minority group oppressed by a nondisabled majority group for violating the norms and values of nondisabled society: physical attractiveness and individual autonomy. | Prejudice and discrimination are causes of problems for people with disabilities. Postulates: (1) "Aversive attitudes are the basic source of the barriers encountered by persons with disabilities"; (2) "All aspects of the environment are shaped or molded by public policy"; (3) "Public policy is a reflection of widespread social attitudes" (H. Hahn, 1991, p. 17). The model focuses on commonalities of people with disabilities. Goals are building a sense of community among people with disabilities and strengthening laws to combat discrimination and change public policy. | Practitioners can use this model to specifically target issues of prejudice and discrimination and expand beyond environmental barriers. This model was successful in obtaining disability rights laws and encouraging activism. The variability of disabling conditions can act against minority group consciousness. Shakespeare (2014) argued that it is not appropriate to assume ideas should transfer from one type of oppression (e.g., race) to another (e.g., disability). The minority model does not challenge deficit-based stereotypes. | L. J. Davis (1995); H. Hahn (1985, 1988, 1991); Longmore (2003) |

(continued)

	Definition of Disability	Main Ideas	Practitioners	Further Reading
Critical disability theory (CDT)	Disability is fluid and can be changed over time. Critical disability theorists choose not to define disability, as many are operating in a postconventional paradigm that inherently questions boundaries and definitions.	Posits that thinking about disability only as a form of social oppression is incomplete and questions metanarratives, particularly those associated with the social and medical models. In particular, CDT allows for the critique of prescribed dichotomies such as impairment/disability or individual/society. Themes include local knowledge, emancipation and human rights, and the relationship between embodiment and disability.	This model encourages practitioners to consider how disability interacts with other aspects of social identity and recognize that the experience of disability shifts over time. Most writing about CDT is intended for academic audiences with existing knowledge of postmodern theory; other readers likely will find the writing style challenging.	Corker (1998, 1999); Corker & Shakespeare (2002); Meekosha & Shuttleworth (2009); E. V. Peña, Stapleton, & Schaffer (2016); Shildrick (2012)

| Critical realism (CR) | Disability is "the outcomes of the interaction between individual and contextual factors, which includes impairment, individual personality, environment, attitudes, policy, and culture" (Shakespeare, 2014, p. 77). | Draws on the ideas of Kant, Marx, and other Western philosophers. Postulates: (a) An independent reality exists, and the world is partly socially constructed. (b) Reality is multilayered in nature. (c) Disability is a relationship between extrinsic and intrinsic factors. | Encourages practitioners to consider multiple aspects of disability, including the physical body, individuals' reactions to their own disability, and social considerations, including others' reactions, policies, and cultural norms. Writing about CR is highly academic and grounded in philosophy, which may be unfamiliar to many practitioners. | Bhaskar (1998); Danermark (2002); Danermark, Ekström, Jakobsen, & Karlsson (2002);Shakespeare (2014) |

(continued)

	Definition of Disability	Main Ideas	Practitioners	Further Reading
Social justice	The concept of ableism is central to social justice. Implicit in the ableist perspective is the belief that disability is a negative status. However, rather than attempting to "fix" people with disabilities so that they will "fit" into an ableist society, advocates address the oppressive culture.	Employs concepts such as social justice, liberation, and oppression to analyze, evaluate, and transform systems of social behavior, discriminatory institutional structures, and cultural practices (M. Adams, Bell, & Griffin, 2007). The focus is on ableism—the oppression of people with disabilities. Postulates: (a) Focus on privilege and oppression. (b) Emphasis on diversity and intersectionality of experiences, roles, and identities. (c) Goal of educating both individuals with disabilities and those who are not disabled about the existence of disability oppression.	Practitioners can use the concept of ableism to analyze and assess their campus environment and departmental policies. Rather than locating the problem within the individual with a disability, practitioners can use the social justice model to change oppressive components of the broader culture, including ideas (e.g., beauty, independence, normality), policies (e.g., laws), and attitudes (e.g., paternalism, pity, sympathy).	M. Adams, Bell, & Griffin (2007); Castañeda & Peters (2000); Evans (2008); Griffin, Peters, & Smith (2007); Ostiguy, Peters, & Shlasko (2016)

Disability justice	Disability is a political experience of oppression, understandable only in interaction with experiences of other social identities (e.g., socioeconomic status, race, gender, sexual orientation).	Disability justice advocates argue that disability is a political experience of oppression that can be understood only in the context of multi-issue commitment to social justice. They argue that access is a baseline, but the goal is transforming society to function for all people and value interdependence.	Disability must be addressed alongside other forms of oppression on campus, including racism, sexism, and other efforts to create more inclusive campuses. All members of the campus should recognize, value, and support interdependent, rather than independent, relationships. Accessibility should be considered a minimal standard, and what is being made accessible must function for all community members.	Berne (2015); Mingus (2014)

(continued)

	Definition of Disability	Main Ideas	Practitioners	Further Reading
Inter-actionist	The experience of disability is a consequence of the interaction of three components: the environment, the person, and the person's impairment. Each component itself varies between more or less enabling, and the components influence each other.	Environments vary in how enabling they are; people's choices range from more to less effective, and people's impairments vary from minimal to significant. Components interact with each other; for example, one environment (fluorescent lighting) can heighten migraines, while the same environment with few audible distractions can be more functional for some people with attention deficit hyperactivity disorder.	Practitioners should be aware that how people experience their disability varies, even within a given day. Interventions should help address environmental barriers, personal decisions, and management of impairment, where possible.	Evans & Broido (2011); Broido (2006)

CHAPTER THREE

DISABILITY, LAW, AND EDUCATION IN THE UNITED STATES

The legal aspects, and ramifications, of my role did not fully sink in until I had to explain recent case law in order to justify a major change to a campus policy.

—Autumn, a coordinator of disability resources

Legal initiatives have played a significant role in shaping the educational experiences of people with disabilities. In this chapter, we examine historical precedent, current and upcoming legal issues, and socially just approaches to addressing disability law in higher education. We start by highlighting key legislation that influenced how disability was defined and perceived in the United States, particularly in relation to education. Then we discuss Section 504 of the Rehabilitation Act, the Americans With Disabilities Act (ADA), the Higher Education Opportunity Act, and the Americans With Disabilities Act Amendments Act (ADAAA) as four foundational pieces of legislation that substantially have and continue to shape access to postsecondary education for people with disabilities. We examine the implications of these laws for administrators, students, and institutions. Looking to the future, we review pending legal topics that will affect access in the next five to 10 years: accessible technology and auxiliary aids, campus facilities, animals in campus housing, international law, temporary accommodations, obesity, and standardized testing. We conclude with a discussion on socially just approaches to interpreting disability law in higher education.

In writing this book, we also acknowledge critiques of law and are aware of a paradox in using law as a method for discussing social justice and accessibility (Connor & Gabel, 2013). Specifically, the law functions as a regulatory social mechanism and thereby creates and enforces normality from a predominantly medical perspective. Furthermore, legal rights do not always rectify inequality (Spade, 2011). From a social justice perspective, it is important to understand the law is an incomplete method of social change, and equity cannot be achieved through legal measures alone.

Historical Overview

It is impossible to divorce disability, education, or law from the broader historical context in which these social structures are nested. As such, they are gendered and raced, and they intersect with a variety of other components of identity, including nationality, sexual orientation, and social class. While we provide a broad overview of the historical context for understanding disability in the United States in Chapter 1, our intent in this chapter is to provide a brief review of legal disability history with the purpose of laying a foundation for understanding the social context in which laws related to postsecondary educational access for people with disabilities were written and enacted. In doing so, we draw on previous authors who have mapped a broad history of disability (e.g., Nielsen, 2012), created a comprehensive list of relevant disability legislation (e.g., Griffin, Peters, & Smith, 2007; Field & Jette, 2007b), produced an in-depth analysis of foundational legislative movements (e.g., Scotch, 2001b), traced discriminatory legislation (e.g., Lombardo, 2008b; Schweik, 2009), and outlined historical disability activism (e.g., Barnartt & Scotch, 2001). These histories situate our inquiry, but we do not seek to reproduce them; rather, the central focus of this chapter is how the law shapes access to and success in postsecondary education for people with disabilities.

Early Laws: Colonialization to 1900

Early legislative initiatives considered persons with disabilities as part of a larger population of the "deserving" poor (Scotch, 2001a, p. 387), as individuals incapable of voting (Schriner & Ochs, 2001), or as those who should not reproduce (Lombardo, 2008a). Much of the legislation during this period treated individuals with disabilities as incapable of the self-sufficiency prized in American society and reflected social definitions of disability that engendered pity, embodied stigma (Goffman, 1963), and required assistance or segregation from the larger society. The vast majority of laws operated under a medical definition of disability and focused on employment concerns.

Economic Opportunity and Integration: 1900–1945

The beginning of the 20th century brought higher education to the masses, with institutions experiencing rapid growth and development as wealthy philanthropists and the Morrill Act of 1890 financed the "age of university-building" (Thelin, 2004, p. 155). During this time, the purpose of higher education also shifted from a method of identifying and confirming White, male, high-class colonials destined for political leadership or the clergy to an industrial, capitalistic perspective that viewed college as a method of achieving socioeconomic mobility and conveying prestige (Thelin, 2004).

In the 1920s and 1930s, disability legislation primarily focused on the topics of economic opportunity and integration for people with disabilities rather than higher education. For example, the Smith-Fess Act was integrated into the New Deal in 1933, expanding programs to include living expense support, and in 1935 vocational rehabilitation programs received permanent authorization under the Social Security Act, extending services to all 48 states (Scotch, 2001b). These programs were imperative in opening doors to higher education, in that they provided income, a means of independent living, and the essential groundwork necessary for future higher education legislation.

Initial Access: 1945–1960

In the second half of the 20th century, laws related to those with disabilities shifted from simple assistance to a more comprehensive model of civil rights protections; however, access to higher education remained elusive. Furthermore, most of the pre-1960s legislation was initiated by "able-bodied civic leaders or by service providers, and such organizations frequently operated on the basis of stereotypes of dependency for the disabled people they sought to represent" (Scotch, 2001b, p. 33).

The end of World War II brought a greater awareness of disabled war veterans at the congressional level (Scotch, 2001b), and the Servicemen's Readjustment Act of 1944 (GI Bill) espoused access to higher education by providing up to four years of college funding for any World War II veteran who met admissions requirements (S. F. Rose, 2012). Although the GI Bill offered the potential for broad access to higher education, many disabled veterans were funneled under Public Law 16, which paid a higher stipend but prioritized wage-based work and rehabilitation over education by requiring that veterans receive permission from a vocational counselor to enroll in college (S. F. Rose, 2012). According to S. F. Rose (2012), "The vocational orientation of Public Law 16 reflected the understanding of disability that had emerged in the early 20th century as synonymous with dependency and the inability to be self-sufficient" (p. 29). Furthermore, the overt focus on male veterans with acquired disabilities and a gender-stratified workforce resulted in disability legislation that ignored women (S. F. Rose, 2012).

An increase in the rate of impairment associated with war and polio epidemics, combined with medical advances that allowed people to live longer, resulted in a greater prevalence of persons with disabilities after World War II (Barnartt & Scotch, 2001). In 1947, a paraplegic veteran, Harold Scharper, negotiated admission to the University of Illinois-Galesburg and a residential living space in married student housing. Scharper paved the way for other students with disabilities to attend the University of Illinois, although Public Law 16 greatly limited enrollment (S. F. Rose, 2012). In 1949, as the state of Illinois closed the Galesburg campus, disabled students successfully demanded access to the Urbana-Champaign location (S. F. Rose, 2012). The Urbana-Champaign program grew under the leadership of disabled veteran Tim Nugent (S. E. Brown, 2008) and became "a prototype for disabled student programs and then independent living centers across the country" (Griffin et al., 2007, p. 427), setting the social precedent for physically disabled students to gain access to a college education. (See Chapter 1 for more information about the establishment of the University of Illinois program.)

Activism: 1960–1975

The 1960s were marked by a wave of activism on college campuses (Thelin, 2004) and within the disability rights movement as illustrated by an increase in disability-specific organizations and the engagement of people with disabilities in the legislative process (Barnartt & Scotch, 2001). Vocal critiques of the medical paradigm emerged as activists argued that disability should be understood as a social condition associated with discrimination and inaccessible environments. These societal changes, coupled with a successful program at the University of Illinois, set the stage, and students with physical disabilities who desired a college education but were denied admission based on discrimination began using the legal system to gain access. Nielsen (2012) reported that "in 1962, the same academic year in which African American James Meredith matriculated at the University of Mississippi after suing for access and racial integration, a polio survivor named Edward Roberts sued UC Berkeley for access and integration" (p. 162). Roberts paved the way for other physically disabled students, and the Rolling Quads became the disability activist group at the University of California–Berkeley (Nielsen, 2012).

Legal initiatives began to have indirect effects on higher education as the courts took up the issue of access to education for students with disabilities in the K-12 system. Although *Brown v. Board of Education* (1954) was brought on the basis of racial segregation, the finding that separate educational facilities are inherently unequal laid a legal foundation that allowed parents to challenge the refusal of public schools to enroll children with disabilities. In 1972, the ruling on *Mills v. Board of Education* held that the District of Columbia could not exclude children with disabilities from public schools and rejected the cost of accommodations as a rationale for denying access to education. Similarly, the U.S. District Court for the Eastern District of Pennsylvania, in *Pennsylvania Association for Retarded Children (PARC) v. Commonwealth of Pennsylvania*, struck down state laws that were used to deny children with disabilities access to public schools (Griffin et al., 2007). Both court cases served as a legal foundation for the 1975 Education of All Handicapped Children Act (Pub. L. 94-142), which mandated free and appropriate K-12 education for all children. This act provided children the opportunity to receive disability testing and required the least restrictive educational environment possible. Although not formally directed at colleges, these legal changes had a time-delayed effect by creating a larger group of disabled students seeking access to higher education (Ryan & McCarthy, 1994a).

Environmental barriers also rose to the forefront of legal activism. The Architectural Barriers Act of 1968 (42 U.S.C. 4151) was the barrier-free movement's first major legislative achievement (Longmore, 2009). This act required that most buildings designed, built, altered, or leased with federal funds must be accessible (Griffin et al., 2007; Longmore, 2009). Since its passage, accessibility issues have been at the forefront of the movement to ensure equal participation in our society (Silver, Bourke, & Strehorn, 1998). The act's enforcement provisions were weak, but further lobbying prompted creation of the Architectural and Transportation Barriers Compliance Board in 1973 to ensure compliance.

Foundational Education Legislation

Section 504 of the Rehabilitation Act of 1973 (Section 504), the ADA, the Higher Education Opportunity Act of 2008 (HEOA), and the ADAAA are foundational legislative initiatives that provided access to higher education for students with disabilities. In this section, we provide a social context for understanding this seminal legislation and discuss important implications for students with disabilities in higher education. Employment legislation is not within the scope of this book; we direct interested readers to Colker and Grossman (2014a) and to the material covered in Chapter 7 on faculty and staff with disabilities.

Section 504 of the Rehabilitation Act of 1973. Motivated by demands to pro-vide services for military veterans, the Rehabilitation Act of 1973 was the first legislation that afforded equal access for people with disabilities to public and private postsecondary institutions (Hall & Belch, 2000). Modeled after Title VI of the Civil Rights Act of 1964 (Scotch, 2001b), Section 504 (Pub. L. 93-112) of the Rehabilitation Act stipulated that programs or activities that receive federal funding cannot deny otherwise qualified people participation in, and benefits of, their services due to their disability, nor could they discriminate against disabled individuals in any way. Dean (2009) explained, "As a result of the legislation, colleges and universities receiving federal funds were required to provide nondiscriminatory, equal access to programs and facilities for individu-als with disabilities" (p. 196). However, equal access was not the original intent, and at the time of its enactment, Section 504 was an "inconspicuous segment of routine legislation" nestled at the end of a law intended to expand vocational rehabilitation (Scotch, 2001b, p. 3). Section 504 generated no public debate, was briefly referenced in House and Senate reports (H.R. Rep. No. 93-500, 1973; S. Rep. 93-318, 1973), and "no public expenditures were projected for Section 504" (Scotch, 2001b, p. 53). Yet the inclusion of Section 504 quickly became significant because the language implied that the federal government, in pursuit of a nondiscrimination policy, should not permit anyone participat-ing in discrimination to benefit from federal assistance.

Enacting Section 504 meant numerous and potentially expensive changes to federally funded projects including building construction, urban mass transit systems, and federal employment practices (Scotch, 2001b). These changes quickly became controversial because they were costly, and "a major battle ... ensued over the promulgation of regulations enforcing it" (Weber, 1995, p. 1093). Four years later, in June 1977, after a lawsuit and 25-day sit-in protest (Nielsen, 2012; see Chapter 1 for more details), the secretary of the U.S. Department of Health, Education, and Welfare signed the regulations associated with Section 504 into effect (Scotch, 2001b).

The application of Section 504 to higher education substantively shaped policy regarding disabled students and employees. Specifically, Section 504 provided legal definitions, banned workplace discrimination, addressed build-ing codes, and prompted the regulatory concept of "reasonable accommoda-tion" (Weber, 1995, p. 1095).

Section 504 (1973) provided a foundational language, defining a person with a disability in the following manner:

> The term handicapped individual means any individual who (a) has a physical or mental impairment which substantially limits one or more of such person's major life activities, (b) has a record of such an impairment, or (c) is regarded as having such an impairment. (29 U.S.C. sec. 794)

This language greatly expanded the definition of disability and placed the focus for determination of disability on the impact of the impairment rather than the existence of it. In addition, for the first time, the legal definition extended coverage to individuals who were perceived as having a disability, thereby including the presumptions of others in the assessment process. While this foundational language used terminology that is no longer considered appropriate (i.e., *handicapped*), the intent of Section 504 and its definition of impairment set legal precedent that was used in subsequent laws (e.g., the ADA).

The regulations associated with Section 504 prohibited state and local governments from discriminating against disabled people with regard to access and use of programs or activities operated by a federally funded entity. This meant that public postsecondary institutions and private institutions that accepted federal funding (i.e., most private higher education institutions) could not discriminate against qualified students who applied to academic programs. Armed with a legislative weapon to battle discrimination in the admissions process, the number of students on college campuses increased. Correspondingly, the field of disability resources evolved as a vehicle for colleges and universities to provide accommodations (Dean, 2009). Section 504 also placed an emphasis on physical accessibility; institutions had to ensure that new buildings were designed and constructed in a manner that was "readily accessible to and usable by individuals with disabilities" (ADA, 2010b, Sec. 12146). In addition, regulations with regard to employment banned discrimination in recruitment, hiring, promotion, pay and benefits, job assignments, training, employer-sponsored social programs, and other work conditions. The law also prohibited discriminatory employment criteria and preemployment inquiries (U.S. Department of Education, 2015). This legislation directly affected faculty and staff whom institutions currently employed and future hiring practices.

Americans With Disabilities Act. Although Section 504 was foundational legislation, it only addressed disability discrimination by recipients of federal funds. Initially passed in 1990 and reauthorized in 2009, the ADA was vital legislation that extended the protections offered in Section 504 to private employers, places of public accommodation, telecommunication, transportation, and services or programs offered by state or local governments (Wilhelm, 2003). The ADA defined a person with a disability in the same manner that Section 504 does. The ADA is composed of several subchapters; specifically, Title II applies to public entities, including states and local governments, and therefore covers public higher education institutions. Private institutions fall under Title III because they are places of public accommodation.

The ADA defined *accommodation* as "any change in the work or school environment or in the way things are customarily done that enables an individual with a disability to enjoy equal opportunities" (U.S. Equal Employment Opportunity Commission, 2011a, para. 11). The courts have been responsible for interpreting the ADA's definition of *reasonable accommodation*; often the courts have been hesitant to force academic institutions to modify programs for fear of impinging on academic freedom or decreasing educational quality. Therefore, the courts have negotiated a balance between accommodations that provide access to students and those that result in substantial modifications that may devalue or decrease academic rigor. The precedent regarding accommodation and academic standards was set by the Supreme Court, prior to the passage of the ADA, in *Southeastern University Community College v. Davis* (1979). The Court stated, "Section 504 imposes no requirement upon an educational institution to lower or to effect substantial modifications of standards to accommodate a handicapped person" (p. 413). Since much of the ADA was modeled after Section 504, later courts have often cited this standard when addressing issues of program modification. For example, the decision in *White v. University of South Carolina-Columbia* (1996) stated that "accommodations must constitute reasonable deviations from the usual requirements which meet the student's needs without sacrificing the integrity of the program" (p. 1295). The question of how much change is a reasonable modification has arisen in several court cases (e.g., *Wynn v. Tufts University School of Medicine*, 1992). Courts have generally deferred to faculty judgment in academic matters as long as the college or university can demonstrate that it has a set of written policies, followed due process, engaged in an interactive process, and "exercised reasonable deliberation" (Kaplin & Lee, 2013, p. 1103). Hence, although students with disabilities may request accommodations, for the accommodation to be deemed reasonable, it cannot decrease academic quality.

It is also important to note that the ADA differentiated between reasonable accommodations and personal services. An institution is not responsible for providing personal attendants, hearing aids, or glasses (Simon, 2000). However, the institution is responsible for providing auxiliary aids such as qualified sign language interpreters, note takers, qualified readers, braille and large-print materials, and adaptive equipment (Simon, 2000). This distinction is important as many of the services that students with disabilities would benefit from or have received in K-12 education, such as a personal organization coach or individual social skills role playing, are considered personal services under the ADA.

The ADA offers a variety of recourses for students with disabilities who are dealing with discrimination. The ADA (2010a) defined discrimination to encompass three key areas: (a) the use of criteria that unnecessarily screen out or tend to screen out individuals with disabilities from the use and enjoyment of goods and services; (b) the failure of a person or institution to make reasonable and nonfundamental modifications to policies, practices, or procedures that will accommodate an individual with a disability; and (c) the failure to take necessary steps to ensure that no individual with a disability is excluded, denied services, segregated, or otherwise treated differently from other individuals (Kaplin & Lee, 2013). Under the ADA, a claim must be made within 180 days of the alleged disability discrimination (*White v. University of South Carolina-Columbia*, 1996). Students can file a complaint under Title II with the Office for Civil Rights (OCR), U.S. Department of Justice (DOJ), or in the courts.

Higher Education Opportunity Act. The Higher Education Opportunity Act of 2008 (HEOA; Pub. L. 110-315) addressed a wide range of legislative issues, including modifying student loan programs, increasing institutional reporting requirements, and revising the federal student aid application process (Cortiella, 2009). The HEOA also contained several provisions that focused on improving access to and success in higher education for students with disabilities. Specifically, it created a national center and allocated grant funding for programs that improve college recruitment, transition, retention, and completion for students with disabilities (Council for Exceptional Children, 2008).

The HEOA also focused on issues of access specifically for students with intellectual disabilities by providing competitive grants to create or develop inclusive-model programs that focus on comprehensive transition and postsecondary programs. The grant competition requires that the program offer a "meaningful credential" on completion and incentivizes inclusive living-learning engagement by awarding preference to proposals that integrate students with intellectual disabilities in campus residential housing (Council for Exceptional Children, 2008, p. 41).

The HEOA placed notable focus on accessible instructional materials (AIM) and used a two-pronged approach to assess and improve equal access. First, the HEOA created grants to encourage "the development of systems to enhance the quality of postsecondary instructional materials in specialized formats and the timely delivery to postsecondary students" (Council for Exceptional Children, 2008, p. 7). Second, the HEOA created the Advisory Commission on Accessible Instructional Materials in Postsecondary Education for Students with Disabilities to address and seek remedies for the challenges encountered by students with print disabilities. The commission's report (2011) recommended that Congress take action on a number of key issues:

> a) establishing a process for creating uniform accessibility guidelines for industry and consumers, b) revisiting the components of existing copyright exception, c) assessing AIM's relationship to current research and instructional materials access taking into account the rights of content owners and d) re-emphasizing the importance of compliance with civil rights laws for institutions of higher education so that the needs of students with disabilities are more adequately addressed by postsecondary educational institutions. (p. 13)

The advisory commission's report highlighted "challenges posed by copyright law" (Kaplin & Lee, 2013, p. 1097) and the complexity of civil rights, a capitalistic marketplace, and rapidly emerging technology involved in securing equal access to instructional materials.

Americans With Disabilities Act Amendments Act. The ADAAA (Pub. L. 110-3-25), effective January 1, 2009, clarified who is considered to have a disability under the law and reduced the amount of documentation individuals must offer when establishing that they have a disability (Heyward, 2011). Simon (2011) explained the ADAAA's dynamic purpose:

> Congress significantly modified the law to reject four landscape changing U.S. Supreme Court decisions (*Sutton* v. *United Airlines,* 1999; *Murphy* v. *United Parcel Service,* 1999; *Albertson's* v. *Kirkingburg,* 1999; *Toyota Motor Manufacturing* v. *Williams,* 2002) because these cases improperly "narrowed the broad scope of protection intended to be afforded by the ADA, thus eliminating protection for many individuals whom Congress intended to protect" (42 U.S.C. § 12101(a)(4)). (pp. 96-97)

Through these modifications, Congress reasserted that students with disabilities can also be talented and academic success does not remove access to accommodations (Simon, 2011).

Because the ADAAA is relatively new, how the courts will interpret legislative guidelines remains unclear. Initial indications are that changes in the ADAAA have at least four implications for higher education. First, the ADAAA prohibited "considering mitigating measures in determining whether an individual's disorder meets the ADA's definition of a disability" (Kaplin & Lee, 2013, p. 1097). Mitigating measures are steps the student would take (e.g., medication, accommodations, or assistive technology) that would decrease the effects of an impairment. This is a direct response to the court cases listed above that narrowed the definition of disability. One likely implication is that students who are twice exceptional (both gifted and disabled) may receive greater coverage and benefits under the ADAAA than they received under the ADA (Colorado Department of Education, 2012). In addition, because the amendments act broadened the definition of disability, case law "decided prior to the effective date of the amendments on the ground that the student was not disabled provide[s] limited guidance as to how courts may rule now that the amendments are in effect" (Kaplin & Lee, 2013, p. 1096). A final implication of the ADAAA is that "courts will be less willing to award summary judgment to colleges, particularly if the claim is that the student's disorder does not meet the act's definition of a disability" (Kaplin & Lee, 2013, p. 1096). In light of these changes, it is important to note that the ADAAA did not change the requirement that applicants and students meet the same academic standards as do nondisabled students.

Legislative Implications

The legislation described holds implications and creates responsibilities for students, educational institutions, and third-party providers (e.g., Amazon). In this section, we describe steps students take to access accommodations and the responsibilities of postsecondary institutions regarding admissions, recruitment, and provision of accommodations. Furthermore, we discuss important legal implications that occur when students make the transition from K-12 to postsecondary education. We address third-party providers in the section on pending and future legal issues and in Chapter 11.

Responsibilities of the Student

Students with disabilities have several legally mandated responsibilities. First, in order to be considered for reasonable accommodations under the ADA, students have to establish that they are qualified to receive the benefits of the public service, program, or activity. People with disabilities are qualified if they satisfy "the academic and technical standards requisite to admission or participation in the recipient's education program or activity" (U.S. Department of Education, 2015, Sec. 104). The courts have established that individuals with a disability must prove they are "otherwise qualified" by showing they can perform the essential duties of the position with or without accommodations (Kaplin & Lee, 2013), which in the case of students, means they can meet the academic requirements of a degree program. *Southeastern University Community College v. Davis* (1979) is the landmark case in which the Supreme Court interpreted the definition of *otherwise qualified* to mean a person "who is able to meet all of a program's requirements in spite of his handicap" (p. 406). Subsequent court rulings (e.g., *Zukle v. Regents of the University of California*, 1999) have upheld this principle. Hence, students with disabilities have to demonstrate that they can perform essential duties and meet the academic and technical standards of the program.

Once admitted, students must inform the college or university of their disability by properly following institution policies, usually by registration with the disability resource office (DRO). The "courts have generally ruled that, unless an institution has knowledge of a student's disability, there is no duty to accommodate" (Kaplin & Lee, 2013, p. 1098). It is important to note that faculty and staff outside the DRO to whom students report their disability have a responsibility to inform students about the institution's policies on requesting accommodations.

After informing the institution, students must demonstrate that they meet three legal prerequisites for accessing reasonable accommodations. First, students need to prove that they have a disability. Under both Section 504 and the ADA, students must prove that they have "a physical or mental impairment which substantially limits one or more ... major life activities" (Section 504, 1973; ADA, 2010a, Sec. 12102). This initial step requires students to provide the academic institution with written documentation confirming they have a physical or mental impairment. Standards for documentation vary; under a social justice model, institutions follow practices outlined by the Association on Higher Education and Disability (AHEAD) and encourage the use of a dynamic narrative intake process as described in Chapter 13. We do acknowledge, however, that the courts have established a precedent of relying on opinions of medical professionals and deferring to social science research, specifically the *Diagnostic and Statistical Manual of Mental Disorders* (DSM; e.g., *Guckenberger v. Boston University*, 1997), and therefore give preference to a medical paradigm when forming opinions.

"Merely having an impairment does not make one disabled for purposes of the ADA," according to the ruling in *Wong v. Regents of University of California* (2005, p. 1067). Students must meet a second legal prerequisite by demonstrating that their disability affects a "major life activity." In response to court limitations on the definition of a person with a disability, the ADAAA expanded the definition of "major life activity" and provided two nonexhaustive lists that meet this definition. Dyer (2011) noted that "the first list includes many activities that the Equal Employment Opportunity Commission (EEOC) has recognized (e.g., walking) as well as activities that the EEOC has not specifically recognized (e.g., reading, bending, and communicating)" (p. 4). The second list outlined bodily functions—for example, normal cell growth and brain, bladder, bowel, digestive, circulatory, endocrine, immune, neurological, and respiratory functions. The ADAAA considers learning a major life activity.

Third, the student must show that the disability creates "a substantial limitation" to that major life activity. The ADAAA expanded previous interpretations because Congress "found that the federal regulations that had defined the term *substantially limits* as 'significantly restricted' communicated a much higher standard of impairment than Congress had intended" (Simon, 2011, p. 97). It remains to be seen how the expanded definition will play out in court.

After a student has self-identified as an individual with a disability and addressed the issues of "otherwise qualified," "major life activity," and "substantially limits," then the process of "reasonable accommodations" begins. Students have the right to request specific accommodations, although the academic institution may deem the request "unreasonable," and, as discussed later in this chapter, the courts have generally deferred to institutions on academic matters.

It is important to clarify that in specific circumstances, Section 504, the ADA, and the ADAAA do not offer disability protection. First, neither alcoholism nor drug addiction is covered if the individual does not qualify for the "safe harbor" provisions by maintaining sobriety and participating in or successfully completing a supervised rehabilitation program (Grossman, Colker, & Simon, 2015). However, in accordance with the Equal Employment Opportunity Commission's (EEOC) interpretation of the ADAAA, alcoholism and drug addiction may be covered as disabilities if the individual is in recovery, is not currently using alcohol or drugs, and the impairment substantially limits a major life activity. Although the EEOC covers employment, the courts have applied similar guidance to institutions of higher education (e.g., *Quinones v. University of Puerto Rico, et al.*, 2015). Questions regarding necessary length of sobriety are made on a "case by case" basis (Grossman et al., 2015, p. 20). From a social justice perspective, Rothstein (2004) stated that when considering alcoholism, "institutions of higher education must balance legitimate concerns about the health and safety of others with the individual's right to be protected against unwarranted discrimination" (p. 126). Hence, a student who is in recovery from alcohol or other drug addiction may be protected under the ADAAA and eligible for reasonable accommodations, such as approval to live in a substance-free residence hall.

Second, it is important to note that legislation does not offer protection to students with disabilities who are dismissed for misconduct (Kaplin & Lee, 2013). The courts are clear: neither Section 504 nor the ADAAA offers protection to students who have threatened to physically harm others (*Mershon v. St. Louis University*, 2006) or who cannot meet behavioral requirements (*Halpern v. Wake Forest University Health Sciences*, 2012). Generally courts "tend to rule that a student who cannot meet the behavior requirements of an internship or residency is not a qualified individual with a disability" (Kaplin & Lee, 2013, p. 1107). Along the same line, "students with disabilities are not free to violate student codes of conduct simply because they have a disability; they must conduct themselves within the social and behavioral constraints of the academic community" (Simon, 2000, p. 77). For example, institutions do not have to provide alternative accommodations when a student is caught cheating on exams (*Strahl v. Purdue University*, 2009). Hence, students with disabilities are held to the same behavioral code of conduct as all other members of the academic community.

Responsibilities of the Educational Institution

Postsecondary institutions also have legally mandated responsibilities. The first group of obligations addresses the admissions and recruiting process. Under Section 504 of the Rehabilitation Act of 1973, the admissions or recruiting processes at educational institutions that receive federal funding cannot discriminate against individuals with disabilities (Kaplin & Lee, 2013). This means that postsecondary institutions cannot inquire about disability before admission, impose a quota or limit on the number or proportion of students with disabilities, or use an admissions test or a criterion that disproportionately affects the admission of students with disabilities unless the standard is a valid predictor of success and alternative, nondiscriminatory options are not available (Kaplin & Lee, 2013).

The second group of obligations addresses the accommodations process. Once students are admitted and have established that they are disabled and qualified, educational institutions have the legal burden to explore accommodations (S. B. Thomas, 2000). The courts outlined several guidelines for postsecondary educational institutions to follow, and the Association on Higher Education and Disability (AHEAD, 2012b) provided recommendations for practice. Here we outline salient points; we also summarize the corresponding case law in Table 3.1. Specifically, institutions must engage with students in an interactive process to clarify individual needs and identify the appropriate accommodations; arbitrary accommodations are not suitable (AHEAD, 2012b). Institutions must participate in "reasonable deliberation" and explore all viable options for accommodation (*Guckenberger v. Boston University*, 1997); "mere speculation that a suggested accommodation is not feasible falls short of the reasonable accommodation requirement" (*Wong v. Regents of University of California*, 1999, p. 818). Decisions about reasonable accommodations are to be made by qualified professionals with training in the field (*Guckenberger v. Boston University*, 1997).

TABLE 3.1. EXAMPLES OF LAWSUITS THAT AFFECT THE IDENTIFICATION AND IMPLEMENTATION OF REASONABLE ACCOMMODATIONS

Impact on Accommodation Process	Case	Date
Decisions regarding accommodations must be made by qualified individuals.	*Guckenberger v. Boston University*	1997
New accommodations policies cannot be implemented without notification to eligible students who may experience a delay or denial of reasonable accommodation as an effect.	*Guckenberger v. Boston University*	1997
There must be a specific grievance process for students if their request for accommodations is denied.	*Guckenberger v. Boston University*	1997
An interactive process must be used to understand the needs of the individual and identify appropriate accommodations.	*Guckenberger v. Boston University* *Vinson v. Thomas*	1997 2002
All viable options for accommodations must be explored.	*Wong v. Regents of University of California*	1999 2005
Accommodations must consider the specific needs of the individual.	*Duval v. County of Kitsap*	2001
Accommodations must be made in a timely manner.	*Button v. Board of Regents of University and Community College System of Nevada*	2008
Interpreters, note takers, scribes, and others must be qualified individuals who deliver service in a consistent manner.	*Button v. Board of Regents of University and Community College System of Nevada*	2008

Once the institution and student have determined reasonable accommodations, the institution is obligated to provide these accommodations in a timely fashion. The individuals providing accommodations, such as interpreters or exam proctors, must be qualified and deliver service in a professional and consistent manner. When institutions are considering changes to accommodation policies, a university cannot create a process or use documentation requirements that would exclude individuals who are disabled. In addition, new accommodations policies cannot be implemented in a way that delays or effectively denies accommodations to eligible students; changes to accommodation policies should be announced to affected students in a timely manner (*Guckenberger v. Boston University*, 1997). Institutions must retain and follow a clearly articulated grievance policy specific to the accommodations procedure (AHEAD, 2012b).

Legal Transitions Between K-12 and Postsecondary Education

Legislation governing the K-12 system and postsecondary education differs greatly in what the law mandates from institutions, how the law engages with the family, and the requirements that the law places on students. As a result of these differences, many students and their families find navigating the transition to college difficult. Understanding legal differences can help students feel better prepared for the change and help professionals in both the K-12 and postsecondary settings support students through the transition (Dean, 2009).

In the K-12 educational system, students with disabilities are covered by the Individuals with Disabilities Education Act (IDEA; Pub. L. 105-17), which legally entitles students to special education on the basis of diagnosis. This legal coverage guarantees evaluation, remediation, and accommodation in the educational environment (Wolf, Brown, & Bork, 2009). In postsecondary education, students with disabilities are covered by the ADAAA and subpart E of Section 504; this legislation guarantees protection from discrimination and equal access for qualified individuals. We summarize key areas of difference affected by legislative regulations in Table 3.2 and then describe three fundamental alterations from high school to college that students and families will notice.

The first notable change involves the role that students take in securing their own accommodations. One of the primary differences is that students must self-identify to the institution through the DRO and advocate for accommodations through a formal request. In contrast, in K-12 education, students play only a small part in securing services for themselves; instead, parents and educators make most of the decisions, and once a disability is identified, the school has the responsibility to identify and implement accommodations.

Differences in locus of responsibility parallel the second major difference between K-12 disability law and postsecondary law: at the postsecondary level, parents and family members have significantly less involvement in the process. The Federal Education Rights and Privacy Act (FERPA; Pub. L. 93-380) requires that students sign a release form before campus administrators can discuss a student's personal information or educational record with family members. Although FERPA protects students' privacy, the communication gap that often results from this law can be a stark contrast from the free flow of information experienced under the IDEA in K-12 settings.

Finally, because students are shifting from a legal framework with the goal of ensuring students' success (IDEA) to a framework that provides access (ADAAA), the transition can also mean that some students who received services in K-12 may face a reduction in eligibility (Wolf et al., 2009). Pragmatically, students may assume that the accommodations they received before

TABLE 3.2. TRANSITION FROM HIGH SCHOOL TO COLLEGE: EXAMPLES OF DIFFERENCES BETWEEN LEGAL COMPLIANCE AND SOCIALLY JUST APPROACHES

Area of Difference	High School	Postsecondary: Legal Compliance	Postsecondary: Socially Just Approach
Legal protections	Individuals with Disabilities Education Act (IDEA) Section 504 of the Rehabilitation Act of 1973 Title II of the ADA (free appropriate public education)	ADAAA Title II or III Section 504 of the Rehabilitation Act of 1973 Department of Housing and Urban Development Regulations Family Educational Rights and Privacy Act (FERPA)	ADAAA Section 504 of the Rehabilitation Act of 1973 Department of Housing and Urban Development Regulations FERPA
Legislative and institutional goals	Enable (ensure) student success—defined as completion of K-12 education	To provide equal access to physical and academic environments	To provide equal access to physical, academic, and social environments and support the success of all students with disabilities in their transition to college.
Accessing disability services	If a staff member or teacher thinks a student has a disability, the school must work with the student and the student's family to create an individual education plan (IEP) and a transition plan.	Students must self-report and actively seek resources from the disability resource office (DRO).	Students must self-report and actively seek resources from the DRO. DRO staff should reach out to students who have disclosed to other staff in order to facilitate accommodation requests. In addition, the DRO should provide information to all students regarding available services. The student must respond to outreach and complete the accommodations process in order to receive services.

(continued)

TABLE 3.2. (CONTINUED)

Area of Difference	High School	Postsecondary: Legal Compliance	Postsecondary: Socially Just Approach
Testing for disabilities	The school provides testing for the student.	The student is responsible for pursuing and paying for testing.	The student is responsible for pursuing and paying for testing. If cost is a barrier, the student should speak with DRO professionals who may be able to help identify alternate funding. DRO offices should also compile a list of testing providers (including low-cost options) in the area.
Documentation	Individual Education Plan Section 504 plan School conducts evaluation to create IEP or Section 504 plan	Current evaluations from applicable professionals, including disability diagnosis and testing results. Often requires document to be within a specified number of years.	Association on Higher Education and Disability (AHEAD) documentation guidelines. DRO office should also use a narrative intake process that places the student's self-report as the primary source of documentation.
Parental role	School is required to include parents in process. Parents advocate and have access to student records.	Under FERPA, college officials are not permitted to discuss educational records with parents once the student is enrolled. Most colleges do not encourage students to sign FERPA waivers.	The student determines if college officials can discuss accommodations with parents with a FERPA waiver. DRO explains the coverage provided by a FERPA waiver and discusses with individual student if parental involvement will provide a substantial benefit to the transition process.

Student role	Identification and the accommodations process is the responsibility of the school and parents. Students must be invited but are not obligated to attend meetings.	Students self-identify to DRO and self-advocate in the accommodations process.	Students self-identify to DRO and self-advocate in the accommodations process. DRO uses a process that helps students learn how to self-advocate through frequent feedback and question prompts.
Institutional role	Include parents; identify and accommodate student.	Provide equal access and reasonable accommodations to individuals who disclose and request accommodation.	Provide equal access and reasonable accommodations to individuals who disclose and request accommodations. Foster student success using principles of universal design. Teach self-advocacy skills, create a disability-friendly campus climate, and advertise DRO to incoming students.
Curriculum	Modifications to curriculum and/or changes to the pace can be made. Frequent testing and assignments are used. Attendance is reported. Grades may be modified based on curriculum.	Modifying essential components of courses and/or curriculum is not an option. Grades are based on the objectives listed in the course syllabus.	Modifying essential components of courses and/or curriculum is not an option. Grades are based on the objectives listed in the course syllabus. Teaching follows principles of universal design.

(e.g., unlimited test time) will continue to move with them through their entire educational experience. It may be difficult for students and families to understand why accommodations and services provided in high school might not be appropriate or offered in college. Because of the substantial changes in not only legal protection but also resulting services, programs that are designed to educate students and their families about the transition are essential for providing students with the tools to succeed in postsecondary education.

Pending and Future Legal Issues

The law is dynamic. As discussed earlier in this chapter, the ADAAA and Section 504 are important because they provide the basis for many institutional policies, processes, and decisions related to accessibility and accommodation. However, institutions that rely solely on information from the ADAAA and Section 504 will quickly find themselves lagging behind best practices in the field. Therefore, it is imperative that DRO professionals pay close attention to their specific state and local laws, emerging case law, and federal guidance. In the next section, we describe the dynamic nature of the law and then delineate several emerging legal issues—accessible technology and auxiliary aids, campus facilities, animals in campus housing, international influences, temporary accommodations, obesity, and standardized testing—as important topics that will shape future accessibility on college campuses. Additionally, in Chapter 14, we discuss the recent legal changes related to harm to self or other and future issues posed by state legalization regarding marijuana in the section on student conduct; in Chapter 6, we describe National Collegiate Athletic Association eligibility for students with learning disabilities as a pending legal topic under athletics.

Understanding the Dynamic Nature of Law

Lawsuits filed through the OCR and through local or state agencies provide DRO staff with additional guidance regarding emerging disability issues in higher education. The OCR is the primary federal agency responsible for enforcing Section 504 at educational institutions and claims made under Title II of the ADAAA (Kaplin & Lee, 2013; OCR, n.d.). The OCR publishes only select resolutions on its web page; however, AHEAD maintains a searchable Wiley OCR database accessible to members only (https://www.ahead.org/membersarea/wiley-terms). Table 3.3 summarizes selected letters from the DOJ and the Department of Education to specific institutions

TABLE 3.3. EXAMPLES OF DEPARTMENT OF JUSTICE AND DEPARTMENT OF EDUCATION, OFFICE FOR CIVIL RIGHTS RESOLUTIONS AND LETTERS

Effect on Educational Institution	Resolution or Letter	Date
Institutions have the right to deny participation if the student exhibits significant unsafe behavior over an extended period of time even with the provision of reasonable modifications, auxiliary aids, or services.	Letter to Glendale Community College	2003
This letter further clarified understanding of the otherwise qualified language in the ADA. It reaffirmed that institutions have the ability to deny admissions to students if they do not meet the minimum GPA requirement for applications.	Letter to Michigan State University	2005
A university may give consideration to a student's request and take steps to provide a reasonable accommodation, but an institution is not obligated to provide unreasonable accommodations or accommodations that cannot be enforced.	Letter to University of Wisconsin–Milwaukee	2006
Students have a right to a clear and prompt process for addressing allegations of disability discrimination. Institutions have a responsibility to conduct a reliable and impartial investigation of the student's grievance, provide the student with adequate notice about the outcome of the complaint, and give the student an opportunity to appeal.	Letter to Loyola University of Chicago Letter to Platt College	2006 2007
Institutions must have a process that is individualized to assess whether a student poses a direct threat to the health or safety of others before limiting or prohibiting access to or participation in an educational program.	Letter to Doane College	2009

following an OCR investigation. These letters provide guidance and resolutions to institutional issues related to interpretation and implementation of the ADA and Section 504.

In addition, the DOJ publishes "Dear Colleague" letters that are intended for a broader audience and address an entire educational category (e.g., secondary education; U.S. DOJ, 2014a). "Dear Colleague" letters are used to provide additional guidance to educators and administrators. Often these letters are a platform to clarify the intent of a specific law or cluster of laws, as was the case with the recent "Effective Communication" letter that we discuss later in this chapter (U.S. DOJ, 2014c).

Case law provides the third method of clarifying the interpretation of existing laws and often offers additional guidance on how to implement vague edicts of existing legislation. An example of case law that greatly informs the work of admissions offices and DROs today is *Pushkin v. Regents of the University of Colorado* (1981), which clarified the definition of *otherwise qualified* found in the decision of *Southeastern University Community College v. Davis* (1979), discussed previously in this chapter. *Pushkin v. Regents* expanded the interpretation of the ADA and concluded that decisions regarding admission and accommodation are individualized and that the decision regarding whether someone is otherwise qualified cannot be based on a stereotype of a particular functional limitation. For example, an institution cannot assume that all students who are blind are not otherwise qualified to participate in an art history program.

Case law that has recently been decided in the courts or is currently on the legal docket gives disability resource staff insight into issues on the horizon and provides guidance for how to implement changes to existing programs, policies, and procedures. At the time of the writing of this book, there were multiple cases spanning several areas of disability in higher education. In addition, practitioners may find that older case law also provides important clarification. Table 3.1 provides an overview of several important cases from the past two decades, and we next discuss current court cases that indicate emerging issues.

Emerging Legal Issues

Accessible technology and auxiliary aids, campus facilities, animals in campus housing, international law, temporary accommodations, obesity, and standardized testing will be critical legal topics.

Technology and Auxiliary Aids. Technology, websites, and the use of auxiliary aids have been a focus of disability court cases for more than half a decade. We discuss Section 508 of the Rehabilitation Act of 1973 and the Telecommunications Act of 1996 in Chapter 11; here we focus our attention on case law and DOJ guidance.

Recent court cases indicate that postsecondary institutions should closely examine the accessibility of their websites and instructional technology. Advocacy groups and legal offices have aggressively pursued many court cases related to accessible technology on behalf of students. This trend informed the DOJ's publication of the "Dear Colleague" letter on effective communication (2014b) and the accompanying FAQ (2014c) document that provides guidance on how institutions, specifically in the K-12 system, interpret the IDEA, the ADA, and Section 504 regarding auxiliary aids.

The first major area addressed in the "Dear Colleague" letter is the use of auxiliary aids, such as an interpreter or scribe, and assistive technology (see Chapter 11 for examples of commonly used assistive technology). This letter, and further guidance from the DOJ, stated that institutions of public education are to provide students with appropriate assistive technology so that communication for students with disabilities is "as effective as communication with all other students" (U.S. DOJ, 2014a, p. 1). The DOJ went on to clarify that the most appropriate auxiliary aid must be determined by giving "primary consideration" to the specific auxiliary aid requested by the individual with a disability (U.S. DOJ, 2014c, pp. 8-9). The courts interpreted this instruction to mean that unless there is a substantial reason that the educational institution cannot provide the requested auxiliary aid, deference should be given to the student's request. The DOJ also clarified financial rules because uninformed administrators occasionally considered cost as a substantial reason to deny the requested auxiliary aid. The DOJ explained that when considering if an auxiliary aid or accommodation presents an undue financial burden, the determination regarding financial burden is made considering "the nature and cost of the aid or service relative to [the] size, overall financial resources, and overall expenses" of the institution, not the DRO (U.S. DOJ, 2014b, para. 37).

Due to the recent nature of the updated guidance from the "Dear Colleague" letter and the letter's current focus on the K-12 system, it is likely that many colleges and universities have not adopted policies and procedures that are in line with this interpretation of the ADAAA. DRO staff will want to pay close attention to the development of future court cases related to effective communication, and giving "primary consideration" to the student is one area where socially just practitioners can work to create change on their campus.

Several recent court cases have focused specifically on access to web-based course materials and course communication. A few recent examples that affect institutions include a settlement between Louisiana Tech and the Justice Department (U.S. DOJ, 2013b), a settlement between the South Carolina Technical College System and the Office for Civil Rights (OCR, 2013c), and a consent decree between the DOJ and Miami University (U.S. DOJ, 2016). These three cases echo earlier agreements reached with the University of California-Berkeley, Pennsylvania State University, University of Montana, Google, and Kindle regarding the accessibility of technology used in the postsecondary environment, including technology operated by third-party vendors (Kaplin & Lee, 2013).

The settlement reached with Louisiana Tech addressed issues related to the timeliness of the availability of online course materials and inaccessible web pages and learning technology (U.S. DOJ, 2013b). The settlement required the university to ensure that all "learning technology, web pages, and course content is accessible in accordance with the Web Content Accessibility Guidelines (WCAG) 2.0 Level AA standard" (U.S. DOJ, 2013b, para. 2) and mandated that the university take measures to train all administrators and instructors on the ADA. This settlement implies that all postsecondary institutions must follow WCAG 2.0 Level AA standards (we discuss these standards further in Chapter 11).

The South Carolina Technical College System failed to meet the requirements of Section 504 and the ADA because its websites were inaccessible to people who are blind, have low vision, or have a print-related disability. Under the terms of the settlement with the OCR, the college system was required to "develop a resource guide that provides information about web accessibility requirements," make the website accessible to all students with disabilities, and "annually review the system's and college's websites and monitor steps taken to correct any accessibility problems identified" (OCR, 2013c, para. 4). This settlement implies that all postsecondary institutions must have accessible websites.

Similarly, Miami University failed to have accessible websites, learning management systems, and curricular material (U.S. DOJ, 2016). In addition to requiring that web content meet WCAG 2.0 AA standards, this consent decree directly addressed the timeliness of communication with students who have vision or hearing disabilities. Specifically, DRO staff must communicate with each student once a month to determine whether the student is receiving accommodations; if the student reports difficulties, DRO staff must schedule an in-person meeting within three business days. Furthermore, the institution must have an accessible technology policy, provide staff with accessible technology training, form a university accessibility committee, and hire an accessible technology coordinator.

At the time of the writing of this book, two cases that bear close attention from institutions of higher learning are the *National Association of the Deaf (NAD) v. Harvard* and *NAD v. MIT*, both filed in January 2015 (National Association of the Deaf, 2015b). The plaintiffs in these cases allege that course content in massive open online courses and information or material free and open to the public, such as archived speeches, should be available in alternative formats that allow access for the d/Deaf and individuals who are hard of hearing (National Association of the Deaf, 2015b). These cases hold implications for institutions that operate open enrollment online courses and provide additional guidance for institutions with materials that are available to the public through the web.

These five cases provide clarification on best practices and legal requirements, confirming the importance of accessible institutional websites and any third-party learning platforms and administrators and faculty being trained regarding their obligations under the ADA. In addition, as indicated in the Louisiana Tech case, institutions should make sure that appropriate training includes information about the importance of timeliness of converting applicable course materials to alternative formats. Institutions that have not reviewed their web content and course learning platforms must make the necessary changes to ensure that their technology meets the requirements outlined under the WCAG 2.0. Institutions should hire professional accessible technology staff to oversee technology compliance and form a university accessibility committee.

Campus Facilities. Accessibility of campus facilities is another area for future consideration. The ADA and Section 504 "place institutions under a continuing obligation to improve campus accessibility and relocate programs... independent of a request for accommodation" (Catlin, McCabe-Miele, Bowen, & Babbit, 2010, p. 2). The requirement for continued improvements to physical accessibility is frequently overlooked by campus administrators and facility managers. This oversight stems from the incorrect assumption that facilities built before 1990 are grandfathered and do not require substantial alteration until they are renovated or replaced. In reality, institutions must address accessibility issues when they are "easily accomplishable and able to be carried out without much difficulty or expense" (ADA, 2010c, Sec. 36.304).

The importance of campus accessibility is prevalent in the 2013 settlement between Mills College and the United States. This settlement required that Mills College follow the guidance listed above and "remove architectural barriers in existing facilities where such removal is readily achievable" (U.S. DOJ, 2013c). As part of this decision, the DOJ gave Mills College a list of items to remedy, requiring that the institution address many of these issues within three years; oversight of the settlement and repairs is effective until 2024.

Additional accessibility legislation involves campus sports arenas and residence halls managed by third parties. For example, the 2008 consent decree between the University of Michigan and the DOJ addressed issues of physical accessibility to football games; as part of the resolution, the University of Michigan added 200 wheelchair and companion seats, increased accessible parking, modified ticketing policies, and upgraded inaccessible restrooms (*Michigan Paralyzed Veterans of America and the United States v. The University of Michigan and The Regents of the University of Michigan,* 2008). Furthermore, campus housing facilities, including bathrooms, showers, and counters, have to be accessible to students using wheelchairs even if a developer or developer's subsidiaries manage the campus residential units (*Kuchmas, et al. v. Towson University, et al.,* 2006).

Institutions that have not done a substantial self-study of campus accessibility are encouraged do so for both legal compliance (Catlin et al., 2010) and social justice reasons. A self-study identifies areas of campus where barriers can be removed to enhance access and allows institutions to "integrate barrier removal, modifications, and relocation plans into the institution's strategic planning, budgeting processes, and academic calendars" (Catlin et al., 2010, p. 6). A self-study is essential to a comprehensive, long-term facilities plan that prioritizes improving campus accessibility.

Animals in Campus Housing. Emotional support animals (ESAs), which are also referred to as assistance, therapy, comfort, or companion animals, present a second housing-related issue. There are important legal differences between service animals and ESAs. In 2010, the DOJ clarified that a service animal is a dog that is "individually trained to do work or perform tasks for the benefit of an individual with a disability including a physical, sensory, psychiatric, intellectual or other mental disability" and the "work or task that the dog performs must be directly related to the individual's disability" (Gluck & Dermott, 2011, pp. 1–2). The regulations also provide that a miniature horse can be used as a service animal if the institution has a facility that can accommodate its size and weight; the horse needs to be housebroken (Colker & Grossman, 2014a). A guide dog that serves an individual with a visual impairment is an example of a service animal. The OCR has ruled that institutions cannot require documentation for service animals but can ask "if the animal is required because of a disability" and "what work or task the animal has been trained to perform" (Colker & Grossman, 2014a, p. 290). Legal precedent clearly establishes that service animals are covered in campus housing and campus facilities under the ADA.

Conversely, the DOJ clarified that ESAs are animals, of any species, that are not trained to respond to an individual by performing a specific task and that provide emotional support and comfort to an individual with a disability. ESAs are not covered under the ADA (Gluck & Dermott, 2011). However, the Department of Housing and Urban Development, which is charged with administering the Fair Housing Amendments Act (FHAct, 1988), outlined a different stance, specifically noting that "disabled individuals may request a reasonable accommodation for assistance animals in addition to dogs, including emotional support animals, under the FHAct or Section 504. In situations where both laws apply, housing providers must meet the broader FHAct/Section 504 standard in deciding whether to grant reasonable accommodation requests" (U.S. Department of Housing and Urban Development, 2011, para. 1). Although both agencies distinguish between the type of work done by service animals and ESAs, the different interpretation between the FHAct and the ADA has created confusion regarding application to higher education (Colker & Grossman, 2014a). As emerging case law has interpreted the FHAct to apply to campus residential housing (*United States v. University of Nebraska*, 2013; *Leland and Fair Housing Council of Oregon v. Portland State University*, 2014), ESA coverage in residential facilities is an important legal topic.

The National Association of College and University Attorneys (Gluck & Dermott, 2011) recommended that institutions address emerging case law, state-specific antidiscrimination laws, and interpretation differences between the FHAct and ADA by carefully reviewing their policies. The recent consent decree between the DOJ and the University of Nebraska-Kearney (*U.S. Department of Justice v. The University of Nebraska at Kearney and the Board of Regents of University of Nebraska*, 2015) demonstrates that institutions must have a housing policy that accommodates requests for ESAs. It is recommended that policies allow the institution to address ESA requests on a case-by-case basis considering the potential positive impact for the student with the disability. Policies should also include language that indicates the requested accommodation is reasonable and adequately supported and that the FHAct applies only to residential housing. Unlike service animals, ESAs usually are not permitted in classrooms (Gluck & Dermott, 2011). The University of Nebraska-Kearney consent decree is particularly instructive since the appendix includes copies of the DOJ-approved policies for reasonable accommodations in university housing and an assistance animal policy that practitioners may use as a template or model when developing or reviewing their institution's policies. (For further reading, see Masinter, 2015.)

International Influences. The ADA typically does not apply abroad; however, some institutions have campuses in other countries (e.g., New York University Shanghai), and therefore an understanding of other countries' legislation is vital. In addition, American institutions are part of a broader global community, making awareness of and participation in international legal policies and practices important. For instance, the Marrakesh Treaty allows organizations supporting the blind, visually impaired, and print disabled in participating countries to import and export accessible texts produced in other countries and create accessible text versions without first having to ask for permission from the copyright holder. This treaty is designed to address the lack of accessible texts for individuals who are visually impaired. At the time this book went to press, Canada had become the 20th country to sign the treaty. President Barack Obama sent the Marrakesh Treaty to the Senate in February 2016; the United States has yet to ratify it (B. Winter, 2016).

The United States has also failed to ratify the U.N. Convention on the Rights of Persons with Disabilities and Optional Protocol, which was adopted in 2006 (United Nations, 2008). This convention was designed "to elaborate in detail the rights of persons with disabilities and set out a code of implementation" (MacKay, cited in "Convention in Brief," 2006, para. 1). Countries that sign the convention agree to "develop and carry out policies, laws and administrative measures for securing the rights recognized in the Convention and abolish laws, regulations, customs and practices that constitute discrimination" ("Convention in Brief," 2006, para. 2). It also guarantees "that persons with disabilities enjoy their inherent right to life on an equal basis with others" (para. 4). President Obama signed the convention on July 30, 2009; the Senate failed to ratify it by a vote of 61–38, 5 votes short of the two-thirds majority needed to pass (Zeitlin, 2013). Although the United States has not ratified this convention, higher education is located in a global world, and practitioners must be aware of legal advancements in the rights of people with disabilities who are beyond our national borders.

Temporary Accommodations. Another emerging area that the courts continue to debate relates to the obligation of disability resource providers, in both education and employment, to provide accommodations for individuals with a temporary illness or injury that is disabling for the duration of the condition. *Summers v. Altarum Institute Corp.* (2014) brought attention to the assumption that individuals with temporarily disabling conditions (lasting fewer than six months) were not covered under the ADAAA or Section 504 might not be correct. This court case and several similar cases handled by the EEOC found that temporary conditions, if they are severe enough to disrupt a major life condition in a substantial way, qualify as disabling. Institutions should take note because these rulings may imply that some students with major injuries (e.g., severely broken arm, severe concussion) could be eligible for temporary accommodations. Further clarification and translation to higher education is necessary; however, institutions should consult with legal counsel and develop a policy rather than dismiss the disability claims of students with temporary illness or injury (Colker & Grossman, 2014b).

Obesity. The existence of discrimination against obese people is well documented (Harker, 2015). However, the legal inclusion of obesity as a disability dates only to 1993, when the court in *Cook v. State of Rhode Island* found that obesity was covered as a disability under Section 504 of the Rehabilitation Act. In *Cook*, obesity was considered a disability because an employer perceived it to be disabling; however, in its decision, the court argued that the plaintiff had successfully made the case that morbid obesity was a true impairment, whether or not it was perceived to be (Browne, Morrison, Keeley, & Gromko, 2010). More recently, the EEOC prevailed in a 2011 employment suit, *EEOC v. Resources for Human Development* (U.S. Equal Employment Opportunity Commission, 2011b) when a consent decree was ordered by a U.S. district court judge, determining that obesity is in and of itself (i.e., even in the absence of any other disability, and regardless of cause) protected under the ADA for employment purposes.

However, the status of obesity as a disability has been contested by both those who argue obesity is a moral lapse (Browne et al., 2010) and those advocating acceptance of people of all body sizes (National Association to Advance Fat Acceptance [hereafter NAAFA], n.d.). Also problematic to the consideration of obesity as a disability is that obesity does not inherently indicate functional limitations; there is extensive evidence that obesity does not necessarily indicate poor health (Solovay, 2000), as the Association for Size Diversity and Health has argued in its Health at Every Size tenets. Nonetheless, for some people, extreme obesity does create impairment, particularly with regard to appropriate seating and access to narrow or small spaces (Solovay, 2000), both issues on college campuses.

To date, almost all court cases that have found obesity to be a disability have been employment discrimination or harassment cases. As such, there is not yet guidance as to whether failure to accommodate obesity will be considered by the courts. A social justice focus means that institutions should provide accommodations related to body size.

Standardized Testing. The provision of standardized exam accommodations by national organizations is a current topic that holds future social justice implications. Notably, a recent consent decree, *Department of Fair Employment and Housing (DFEH) and the United States v. LSAC* (2014) addressed allegations that the Law School Admission Council (LSAC) engaged in widespread and systemic discrimination against individuals with disabilities. Although this settlement does not directly affect postsecondary institutions, it has long-term implications for students taking standardized tests, most notably the LSAT. Under the consent decree, LSAC will no longer mark or flag LSAT scores identifying individuals with disabilities who receive extended time as an accommodation (U.S. DOJ, 2014d). Furthermore, LSAC will address the claim that it routinely denied accommodation requests from individuals with supporting documentation of permanent physical disability and make substantive changes by "streamlining" the accommodations evaluation process, automatically granting most testing accommodations if an individual has previously received accommodations on a standardized exam, and implementing best practices developed by a panel of experts (U.S. DOJ, 2014d). The consent decree sets a precedent regarding stigma associated with using accommodations and provides students with disabilities equitable opportunities to access graduate and professional education.

Conclusion

The law is clearly dynamic; hence, administrators and faculty must create time within their practice to stay abreast of the most recent changes. From a social justice perspective, there is a difference between the letter of the law and the intent of the law. The letter of the law provides a foundation, a baseline of legal protections for individuals with disabilities; the intent of social justice offers a ceiling. For example, although the ADAAA has not historically been interpreted to provide coverage to U.S. citizens in other countries (Kaplin & Lee, 2013), study abroad is a valuable learning experience that all students should have the opportunity to take part in. Practitioners operating in a social justice paradigm should critically examine legal guidance and best practices to understand and make decisions based on the intent of the law.

Furthermore, legal compliance is the responsibility of all campus community members, not just the DRO. Under a social justice paradigm, we strongly advocate that the burden for providing accommodations, including those related to academic instructional materials and technology, does not simply become a task of the DRO; rather, universal design and accommodations are a collaborative process that engages all stakeholders.

Discussion Questions

1. After reviewing some of the current legal issues in higher education and issues on the horizon, what changes do you anticipate will have the largest impact on students with disabilities? Faculty? Disability resource professionals?

2. Why do you think that the ADA has not been updated to provide additional protections for the evolving populations (e.g., students with larger electrical wheelchairs than were used in the 1970s) accessing higher education today?

3. What responsibilities do you think institutions have to help new students transition from coverage under IDEA and Section 504 to coverage under the ADA and Section 504? What might this assistance with transitioning look like?

4. How can the models of disability discussed in Chapter 2 inform legal interpretations?

CHAPTER FOUR

DIMENSIONS OF IMPAIRMENT AND DISABILITY

In responding to a question about if she considered her new diagnosis of ADHD to mean she had a disability, Willie said, "I don't know. I've been thinking about that. I'm not sure. I think it can be in some context but it's not—like, I haven't necessarily—I don't know if I have faced discrimination based on ADHD. Maybe I was treated differently because I was spacey when I was in elementary school, but I haven't had the same kind of experiences that maybe someone with a different disability would. I don't know.

—Willie, an undergraduate student

Disability and impairment can be thought of in many different ways, none of which on its own allows a full understanding of people's experiences of living with disability and impairment. Our attempts to understand people's experiences of disability are further complicated because "institutional definitions of 'disability status' often conflict with the unique ways that disability is embodied in the everyday lives of individuals" (Lightman, Vick, Herd, & Mitchell, 2009, Introduction, para. 1). In this chapter, we provide a number of perspectives to illuminate multiple aspects of and perspectives on impairment and disability. Not all people with disabilities will find each of these frameworks relevant, but collectively they help us understand the multiple ways in which impairments influence people's lives.

Olkin (1999) highlighted multiple frameworks for categorizing disability, including those of diagnosis, system affected, onset, and functional impairment, arguing that "all these factors must be considered in understanding a specific person's disability" (p. 14). We have expanded that list to include the extent of impairment and impact on daily functioning; the course of the impairment; the extent to which people consider themselves a person with a disability; the extent to which the impairment is apparent to others; the duration of the impairment (temporary versus permanent; recent versus established); onset of the impairment (congenital versus acquired, sudden versus gradual); which systems of the body are affected by the impairment; extent of stigma around the type of or cause of disability and extent to which the person is perceived as deserving of the impairment; and extent to which the impairment is perceived as real or legitimate.

In the first section of this chapter, we present a brief overview of each of these dimensions of disability. In the second section, we describe specific categories of impairment that are commonly used to group students with disabilities, provide definitions and descriptions of those disabilities, and offer a brief statistical overview relating to that disability.

It is difficult to write about disability from many of these lenses without using a framework of limitations and disorders. While we advocate for a framework based on self-identification and self-definition, these are not the definitions used in the legal world of accommodation or the medical world of diagnosis and treatment. There is an inherent tension between the need for documentation and medical confirmation of diagnoses for accommodation purposes and a social justice focus on self-definition. In this chapter, more so than the others in this book, we have used medical and legal terms and definitions for disabilities in order to draw on existing literature and research and to enable readers to understand the language used by those who construct key institutional aspects of disabled people's lived experiences.

Creating Categories and Labels

Who has the ability to create and assign labels of impairment and disability is a social justice issue, just as the ability to create and assign gender, sex, and race are social justice issues. Who gets to decide who or what ways of being are "normal" or are "impaired" is a reflection of the models of disability discussed in Chapter 2. If one works within the medical model, medical professionals define and diagnose disability and impairment, deciding which bodily and mental ways of being are categorized as deviant. Within the medical perspective, individuals are not able to decide for themselves whether they have an impairment; they have to be diagnosed by a medical authority. This approach is problematic for multiple reasons, but it has legitimacy in a world in which unverified claims of having an impairment could lead to abuse (Shakespeare, 2014).

Relying on medical practitioners to define disability and impairment and, conversely, health, is problematic first because what medicine considers impaired and healthy is often arbitrary and socially constructed. It changes over time; for example, gay, lesbian, and bisexual identities and behaviors were until quite recently (and in some places still are) considered manifestations of mental illness. Addiction was (and often still is) considered a moral lapse rather than a medical condition. Indeed, the very existence of mental illness has long been argued to be a medicalization of normal human variance (Szasz, 1960/2002).

An additional reason that relying on medical definitions of disability is problematic is the unequal access to medical care and thus diagnosis. At least in the United States, access to appropriate medical screening is largely dependent on adequate income and medical insurance, and is unavailable to large fractions of the population (a further discussion of this issue is presented in Chapter 5). This problem is particularly evident in university settings when students and staff realize they may have learning disabilities. Universities almost always require documentation from a medical or psychological professional, which requires expensive testing.

The ways in which people with disabilities can document their impairments have expanded. Under revised standards in the Americans With Disabilities Act Amendments Act (ADAAA), there are some circumstances in which prior documentation of accommodations (particularly in K-12 settings) is being accepted as sufficient (S. F. Shaw, 2012) rather than requiring current testing and diagnosis. However, external documentation is still required. Among others, Heyward (2011) has argued that

> abdicating responsibility to individuals with disabilities and their advocates is not the solution to meeting the compliance obligations of the ADAAA. The obligation of any campus is to provide meaningful access—not to give individuals whatever they think they need or ask for. (p. 57)

Beyond the question of who assigns the label of impairment and disability lies the distinction between conditions that are diagnosable, those that are diagnosed or claimed, and those that create functional impairment. For example, many of the studies of the mental health of college students ask respondents to indicate if they have particular experiences that are presumed to be (and often are defined as) indicators of psychological impairments. While students may report these experiences (i.e., they are diagnosable based on their reported experiences), that does not mean they have been diagnosed as having or believe themselves to have mental illness. And while some studies do assess whether these experiences have a negative influence on students' abilities to function as students (e.g., American College Health Association, 2014), the majority do not. Thus, in many instances, we do not know whether or to what extent people are impaired by their symptoms. H. Belch (2011) noted, "A mental illness becomes a disability when one's ability to cope successfully is compromised" (p. 75), including interfering with "learning-related activities such as concentrating, reading, and thinking" (p. 75). As we interact with campus community members, we must remember that impairment, diagnosis, and specific experiences or symptoms are not always coincident, and one cannot be presumed to indicate the other.

Categorizing Impairment

Like many others, the World Health Organization (2002) has argued that "disability is always an interaction between features of the person and features of the overall context in which the person lives" (p. 9). Putnam (2005) wrote,

> Individual variance within each of the six conceptual domains of disability identity ... may be related to (a) demographic characteristics, such as race and ethnicity, chronological age, level of formal education attained, economic status, and marital status; (b) social characteristics, such as employment status, social participation, social support, and religiosity; (c) disability characteristics, such as diagnostic condition, age of onset, duration of disability, severity of impairment, and amount and level of functional limitation; and (d) disability characteristics, such as incidence and prevalence of discriminatory experience, interaction with other persons with disabilities, and involvement in disability rights activities. In addition, individual disposition or personality may create variability in response. (p. 194)

Impairments vary tremendously among each other, and for a variety of reasons, individuals experience the same impairments in many different ways. We next provide an overview of some of the many frameworks for considering how impairments are perceived and experienced by people with disabilities and by those around them.

Impairments Vary in Extent and Impact on Daily Functioning

The kind and extent of impairment can alter how much energy people have, how much effort it takes to engage in typical activities, and in what ways people conduct those activities (Albrecht, Seelman, & Bury, 2001a; Kerschbaum et al., 2013; World Health Organization, 2002). There are differences in the extent to which a person's attention deficit hyperactivity disorder, visual impairment, or social anxiety disorder (among many possible examples) influences people's daily lives and the nature of accommodation that will enable them the greatest flexibility. Some forms of impairment have minimal impact on some aspects of functioning but significant impact on others. For example, some learning disabilities can make absorbing information in a lecture setting challenging, but they have minimal influence on the ability to learn in applied settings like labs or internships. People with hearing loss may hear well in quiet settings but need assistance when there is a great deal of background noise. Some may be able to lip-read well in some settings but not others. Other kinds of impairment, for example, depression, have more systemic influences. When creating campus programs and policies to be accessible to the greatest range of users, it is critical to avoid an all-or-nothing perspective on impairment and plan for a range of accommodation options.

The environment can influence the extent of disability (H. Belch, 2011; World Health Organization, 2002). For example, with universal design and proper accommodation, many activities can be conducted with less effort than without accommodation or preclude the need for any accommodation. Similarly, some environments can make tasks more challenging. For example, environments with high levels of background noise may be particularly distracting for people with some forms of learning disabilities. Environments with low-friction floors (tile, wood, or low-pile carpet) are easier for those using manual wheelchairs to navigate than floors with high-pile rugs. Multiple accessible entrances reduce the effort used to get to doors with level entrances and automatic openers.

Another aspect of environmental influence is the way in which others respond to a person's impairment or diagnosis, which can also significantly influence a person's ability to function (Lightman et al., 2009). Others' responses can create both attitudinal and structural barriers for a person with a disability. Managing the stigma associated with HIV infection or learning disabilities or assumptions of the cognitive competence of people who use mobility devices takes both time and energy and reduces people's ability to spend that time and energy on other matters.

The Course of an Impairment May Be Stable, Progressive, Chronic, or Episodic

Rolland (1994) noted that the course of an impairment has a significant influence on how people respond to impairment and can shape what is needed to create environments in which people can thrive. Many college students with disabilities have chronic but stable impairments. As a consequence, any accommodations to create inclusive environments should be appropriate for the duration of their enrollment. Common forms of stable impairments seen in college populations include many forms of learning disabilities, cerebral palsy, acute blindness or deafness (or both), and some forms of spinal cord injuries.

Those whose impairments are progressive or episodic may need different accommodations at different times. In addition, there are psychological consequences to changes in impairment, and, for episodic impairments, the uncertainty of their timing. Thus, those with progressive or episodic impairments may need different psychological support (Rolland, 1994). Forms of progressive impairments are wide ranging and might include multiple sclerosis, muscular dystrophy, rheumatoid arthritis, many forms of cancer, heart disease, post-polio syndrome, Parkinson's disease, Type 2 diabetes, and lupus. Episodic impairments might include irritable bowel syndrome, some mental health and psychiatric conditions, kidney stones, asthma, HIV, and epilepsy.

Not Everyone Identifies as a Person With a Disability

Like many other forms of oppression, people with disabilities may or may not claim disability as a core aspect of their identity (Putnam, 2005). Indeed, there is much evidence (Nario-Redmond, Noel, & Fern, 2013) that most people who might legally be considered disabled do not themselves identify that way. However, also like many other kinds of oppression, dominant group members have retained the right to decide who is and is not disabled and in some cases force identities on people they might not claim. In addition, as Nario-Redmond, Noel, and Fern (2013) argued,

> The medical model's equation of disability with impairment, together with an emphasis on curing the sick (Marks, 1999)[,] have created unique social pressures for persons with disabilities to cope by means of individualistic strategies that distance the self from disability as a social category (Schur, 1998). (p. 469)

Not All Impairments Are Equally Apparent to Others

Some forms of impairment are quickly apparent to observers–for example, those who use mobility-assistance devices and those with speech impairments. Those without immediately apparent forms of disability may have to prove they have disabilities and fight to get assistance or recognition of their disability. For example, people who need accessible parking because of impairments affecting their aerobic capacity or because of nonapparent injuries often report getting dirty looks; others are denied the option to stand during classes or meetings. Those with apparent disabilities often receive assistance they do not want or do not find useful. Those who request accommodation may find that the accommodation provided was not what they asked for and does not meet their needs (Kerschbaum et al., 2013).

Impairments Vary in Duration and Timing

Disabilities vary temporally. Some are temporary; a 2014 U.S. Court of Appeals ruling clarified that temporary disabilities are covered under the ADAAA if they substantially limit a major life activity (*Summers v. Altarum Institute Corp.*, 2014). Others, the primary focus of this book, are permanent aspects of people's lives once they are recognized, although their presentation may vary across a life span. Another key consideration for those working in the college environment is the period of diagnosis or recognition. Some forms of disability may be recently acquired, and people still may be coming to terms with the ways in which that disability will influence their lives. Some forms of disability change rapidly in their early stages and others at later stages. Some people may have lived with disability for all or most of their lives, although adjustment issues can arise at any point (Olkin, 1999). A number of studies have demonstrated that those who have had impairments for longer durations (H. D. Hahn & Belt, 2004; Jemtå, Fugl-Meyer, Öberg, & Dahl, 2009), have congenital onset (Li & Moore, 1998), and especially those "who have been living with disability from an early age compared to those with late-onset conditions" (Nario-Redmond et al., 2013, p. 471) are more likely to have greater acceptance of their disability status and a positive disability identity.

The Onsets of Impairment Vary

Like variance in duration and timing, when and how impairment or disability comes into people's lives influences their experiences. Congenital impairments are those present prior to or at birth, although they may be recognized only later in life (Porth, 2009). Often students and staff members with congenital impairments will have adjusted to these forms of impairment prior to their becoming part of a university community, yet new environments and expectations may require new strategies. Acquired impairments are those arising any time after birth. Many forms of disability arise over a life span, and many students and staff members may be dealing with initial adjustment to acquired disability. In addition, impairments vary in their speed of onset. Some are sudden, as in the case of accidents; others are gradual and may take a long time to be identified or recognized, such as many forms of age-related dementia.

Impairments Can Affect One or More Bodily Systems

Medical model discussions of disability often group impairments by which systems of the body are influenced by the impairment, recognizing that many people experience multiple forms of impairment. For example, the U.S. Social Security Administration's (n.d.) system uses 14 categories:

- Musculoskeletal system
- Special senses and speech
- Respiratory systems
- Cardiovascular system
- Digestive system
- Genitourinary impairments
- Hematological disorders
- Skin disorders
- Endocrine disorders
- Congenital disorders affecting multiple body systems
- Neurological disorders
- Mental disorders
- Malignant neoplastic diseases
- Immune system disorders

The Extent of Stigma Around the Type of or Cause of Disability and Extent to Which the Person Is Perceived as Causing the Impairment Varies

The public has long differentiated between the "deserving" and the "undeserving" in many regards, including in the areas of disability and impairment (Corrigan, Markowitz, Watson, Rowan, & Kubiak, 2003). Those with lung cancer who have histories of smoking cigarettes are perceived to have "caused" or, at a minimum, contributed to their disability, while those who never smoked are not. Children with disabilities are often cast as "innocent victims," while adults with the same conditions are overlooked, and those whose HIV-positive status resulted from sexual contact or drug use are condemned, while those whose status resulted from blood transfusions or prenatal transmission are held blameless. Thin people who have heart disease are thought to have tragically bad luck, while their heavier counterparts are believed to have brought it on themselves. Carpenter and Paetzold (2013) found that people are more likely to affirm accommodation requests when they believe people were not "to blame" (p. 24) for their impairments, a dynamic also evident in case law considering obesity as a disability (Harker, 2015).

In addition, while disability of any type carries stigma (Goffman, 1963; Susman, 1994), certain kinds of impairment carry extreme forms of social stigma. The stigma around drug dependency is exceptionally strong. However, people "who have been successfully rehabilitated and who are no longer engaged in the illegal use of drugs, [or] who are currently participating in a rehabilitation program and are no longer engaged in the illegal use of drugs" (U.S. Commission on Civil Rights, 2000, Ch. 4, para 4) have protection from discrimination within the Americans with Disabilities Act (ADA; *Fowler v. Westminster College of Salt Lake*, 2012). Also, while people having addictions to prescription drugs or alcohol are protected by the ADA even when using these substances, those addicted to illegal drugs are not (U.S. Equal Opportunity Employment Commission, 2009), even though all share the disability of addiction. HIV/AIDS remains a highly stigmatized disability in many settings (Herek, Capitanio, & Widaman, 2003), as are most forms of psychological impairments (Corrigan, 2005).

Impairments Vary in the Extent to Which They Are Perceived as Real or Legitimate

Finally, certain forms of impairment are less commonly accepted as genuine disabilities. In particular, newly recognized or labeled and nonapparent forms of disability (e.g., learning disabilities, chronic fatigue syndrome, psychiatric disabilities) frequently are seen as lacking legitimacy or are perceived as excuses (Lerner, 2004; Shlaes, Jason, & Ferrari, 1999). As discussed in Chapter 3, the status of obesity as a disability is still contested, at least beyond the courtroom. In addition, as we have noted, addiction often is not perceived to be a legitimate disability. Episodic disabilities similarly can be seen as lacking authenticity. When others do not perceive an impairment to be credible, it becomes more challenging to obtain needed, legally mandated accommodations, and differences in performance may be attributed to laziness or lack of effort rather than seen as the consequences of the disability. In higher education, this dynamic is well documented, particularly in the area of learning disabilities, where faculty and peers see claims of learning disability as mechanisms for privileged students to gain advantage over their less resourced and more honest peers (e.g., Lerner, 2004; Lovett, 2010).

Implications

Given the extensive variations we have described, it is important to recognize that creating equitable environments requires both a focus on universal design and an understanding of the unique experiences of the individuals in those environments. People having the same impairment label can have very different experiences of disability.

Impairments Commonly and Increasingly Seen in College Populations

Ascertaining how many people have impairments and disabilities, how many have specific forms of impairment, and how many of those are college students is far more difficult than it would at first seem. Fujiura and Rutkowski-Kmitta (2001) pointed out that quantifying disability is complicated by the "enormous range of concepts, method of definition, systems of surveillance, and indeed, humanity ... [and] that discrepancies among approaches underscore the fluidity of the disability concept and the vagaries of classifying human variability into simple dichotomies" (p. 69). These challenges extend to attempts to quantify the numbers of students with disabilities in higher education, and D. Leake (2015) has argued that in the most commonly reported data set on students with disabilities in higher education, the National Post-Secondary Aid Study, disability statistics "are misleading and their dissemination should be discontinued" (p. 73).

As Harbour reported in the 2008 Biennial AHEAD Survey of Disability Services and Resource Professionals in Higher Education,

> There are no US organizations that currently collect statistics about all disabled students in higher education. Unlike elementary and secondary school systems, which have mandated reporting and standardized disability categories under IDEA, higher education service providers usually only collect statistics for their immediate supervisors. Because there are no agreed-upon standards, many statistics vary by office. For example, some administrators may count deaf, deaf-blind, and hard-of-hearing students as having three different types of disabilities. Other campuses may count these students with blind and visually impaired students, reporting them all under a category of students with sensory disabilities. (p. 11)

The issues we have raised compound problems arising from differences in who is asked about disability numbers. Some studies report data collected by disability resource offices, others use National Center for Educational Statistics (NCES) data, and still others use student self-report on anonymous surveys. Thus, conclusive reports of total numbers of students with disabilities in higher education and specific breakdowns by type of disability are at best approximations (see D. Leake, 2015, for an extended discussion of the challenges in determining these values and critiques of some commonly cited data sources).

It is important also to recognize there is notable variation in disability statistics by institutional type, control, and size and that the numbers of students with disabilities include only students who identified themselves to their institutions as having a disability. This challenge is compounded by the fact that 63% of postsecondary students who were identified in secondary school as having a disability no longer report they consider themselves to have a disability. Another 8.5% who do still consider themselves to have a disability choose not to identify themselves as such to their postsecondary institutions (Newman et al., 2011).

With those caveats, we provide in Tables 4.1 and 4.2 reported values for the most prevalent forms of impairments on U.S. higher education campuses, as well as for acquired brain injuries and autism spectrum disorder (where data exist), two relatively less common but growing forms of disability in higher education. These values should be taken as imprecise estimates, but they are the best data currently available. We then provide brief descriptions of those impairments.

The following list of definitions is not comprehensive of the types of impairments held by members of university communities. We have focused on those most prevalent in current student populations and on two forms, acquired brain injury and autism spectrum disorders, that have increasing presence.

TABLE 4.1. PERCENTAGES OF ALL COLLEGE STUDENTS REPORTING PARTICULAR DISABILITIES

	Higher Education Research Institute 2010 Survey of College Freshmen (Four-Year Institutions Only)	American College Health Association National College Health Assessment, 2014
Percent of all college students who report a disability	14.6%	
(Specific) learning disability	2.9%	4.5%
AD(H)D	5.0%	7.8%
Mental illness/depression/ psychological disorder	3.8%	6.7%
Health impairments/problems	1.8%	5.2%
Orthopedic/physical	2.7% (hearing, mobility, sight, speech, etc.)	1.0%
Deaf/hard of hearing		2.1%
Blind/visually impaired		2.6%
Speech/language disability		0.9%
Other	3.3%	2.1%

TABLE 4.2. STUDENTS BY DISABILITY TYPE AS A PERCENTAGE OF ALL STUDENTS WITH DISABILITIES

	Raue and Lewis, 2011 (Two- and Four-Year Institutions; Students ID Selves to Institution; Data From 2008–2009)	Kasnitz, 2011 (Disability Service Professionals)	Higher Education Research Institute, 2011 (2010 Survey of College Freshmen, Four-Year Institutions only)
(Specific) learning disability	31%	28.16%	19.9%
AD(H)D	18%	20.21%	32.3%
Mental illness/ depression/ psychological disorder	15%	15.59%	26.0%
Health impairments/ problems	11%	9.25%	12.3%
Orthopedic/physical	7% (mobility)	6.20% (mobility)	18.5% (hearing, mobility, sight, speech)
Deaf/hard of hearing	4%	3.25%	
Blind/visually impaired	3%		
Traumatic brain injury	2%		
Autism/autism spectrum disorder	2%		
Other			3.3%

Acquired Brain Injury

Acquired brain injury (ABI) includes both traumatic brain injury (TBI) and cerebral vascular accidents (e.g., strokes), as well as other injuries to the brain resulting from lack of oxygen, concussions, and other causes. These injuries may cause "altered cognition, affect, and/or sensiomotor abilities (often including vision)" (Ciuffreda & Kapoor, 2012, p. 95). *Traumatic brain injury* refers specifically "to an acquired, sudden-onset, nonprogressive and nondegenerative condition, exclusive of birth trauma, affecting neurologic functions" (p. 95). A recent (Krause & Richards, 2014) study of college students found 16% reported experiencing TBI, a common injury in veteran students who have served in combat roles, a growing population on many campuses (Church, 2009). Sports injuries and automobile accidents are also common causes of TBIs (Krause & Richards, 2014).

The effects of TBI are highly variable, and many directly influence students' ability to learn and engage with campus communities, but effective interventions are poorly researched (Hux et al., 2010). Dizziness, headaches, and memory and balance/coordination problems were found more frequently in undergraduates reporting TBIs than in students without a history of TBI (Krause & Richards, 2014).

Attention Deficit Hyperactivity Disorder

Attention deficit hyperactivity disorder (ADHD) "is defined by the DSM as a combination of inattention, hyperactivity, and impulsivity that are developmentally inappropriate for age" (Wolf, Simkowitz, & Carlson, 2009, p. 415). *ADD* (attention deficit disorder) is a previously used term for one of three forms of ADHD, and while still used in lay language, it is now formally known as ADHD–predominantly inattentive type (Lange, Reichl, Lange, Tucha, & Tucha, 2010). Across a variety of studies, between 4% and 8% of college students have ADHD, with roughly twice as many men as women reporting characteristics. Students with ADHD often have other forms of impairment as well, with just over 60% of students in a national study of the entering class of 2010 who reported two or more disabilities having ADHD as one of their diagnoses (Higher Education Research Institution, 2011).

Autism Spectrum Disorders

Autism spectrum disorders (ASD), also often called "autism," are "a class of complex neurodevelopmental disorders affecting social and communication skills, behavior, and sometimes cognitive development" (Pinder-Amaker, 2014, p. 125). Formerly considered three different diagnoses—autistic disorder, Asperger's disorder, and pervasive developmental disorder not otherwise specified—the 2013 revision to the *Diagnostic and Statistical Manual of Psychiatric Disorders* now combines them into a single disorder with a spectrum of symptoms (Pinder-Amaker, 2014).

Autism, along with other neurological conditions, including dyslexia and other cognitive processing differences, is considered by some to be a form of neurodiversity. This language reflects a shift away from deficit-driven understandings of these ways of understanding the world (Robertson & Ne'eman, 2008). Walker (2013) noted, "Terms like *neurodiversity, neurotypical,* and *neurominority* allow us to talk and think about neurodiversity in ways that don't implicitly pathologize neurominority individuals" (para. 37).

Many authors (e.g., Adreon & Durocher, 2007; Dente & Coles, 2012; Hewitt, 2011) have noted that the transition to college presents multiple psychosocial challenges for students with ASD, including difficulties relating to social interactions and following verbal directions. Students with ASD enroll at college at lower rates than students with many other forms of impairment, as Wei, Wagner, Hudson, Jennifer, and Javitz (2015) noted:

> Nationally, the combined 2-year and 4-year college enrollment rates for youth with ASDs was 32%, the third lowest among youth in 12 special education disability categories and much lower than that of youth in the general population (70%; Shattuck et al., 2012; Wei, Yu, Shattuck, McCracken, & Blackorby, 2013). (p. 1)

Estimates of the prevalence of ASD in the college student population vary substantially, but most fall between 0.7% and 1.9% of all college students (White, Ollendick, & Bray, 2011).

Chronic Health Conditions

The term *chronic health conditions* refers to a wide variety of disabilities, all "long-lasting conditions that can be controlled but not cured" (Center for Managing Chronic Disease, n.d.). Commonly recognized chronic health conditions are allergies, asthma, diabetes, Crohn's disease, epilepsy, and heart disease. The prevalence of chronic illness is increasing due to several interacting factors, including more people surviving childhood health conditions because of greater access to care and advances in treatment options (Halfon & Newacheck, 2010). In addition, "concepts of health and disease and definitions of what constitutes a childhood chronic illness have also changed" (Halfon & Newacheck, 2010, p. 665), and they include a wide range of impairments. Chronic health conditions can be stable, episodic, or progressive; may have onsets in childhood or during the traditional college years; and often are hidden forms of disability.

d/Deaf and Hard of Hearing

These labels refer to distinguishable groups. People who identify as Deaf claim a culturally distinct identity around their use of (typically American) sign language; common knowledge, beliefs, and practices based in Deaf culture; and politicized identities. Their identity is defined by what they can do rather than by an absence or loss of hearing (Padden & Humphries, 1990). Like other cultural groups, *Deaf* is capitalized. When spelled with a lowercase "d," *deaf* refers "to the audiological condition of not hearing" (p. 2). When referring to both groups simultaneously, current usage is to place the lowercase "d" first (e.g., d/Deaf). According to the University of Washington's Disabilities, Opportunities, Internetworking, and Technology Program (DO-IT) program (2014), "'Hard of hearing' refers to a hearing loss where there may be enough residual hearing that an auditory device, such as a hearing aid or FM system, provides adequate assistance to process speech" (para. 3). Hearing loss is a consequence of a wide variety of conditions, and while often undiagnosed, is thought to be one of the most common forms of disability among faculty and staff (Roufs, 2012; Tidwell, 2004). People who are deaf or hard of hearing rarely use ASL; those who are Deaf almost always do.

Learning Disabilities

While the IDEA does not pertain to higher education, many higher education institutions retain its definition of *specific learning disability*. As defined in the Individuals with Disabilities Education Act, *specific learning disability* refers to "a disorder in one or more of the basic psychological processes involved in understanding or in using language, spoken or written, which ... may manifest itself in the imperfect ability to listen, think, speak, read, write, spell, or to do mathematical calculations" (Individuals with Disabilities Education Improvement Act, 2004, p. 118). Some examples of commonly recognized specific learning disabilities are dyslexia, dysgraphia, and dyscalculia, but the category includes many other forms of learning disabilities that relate to how sound and language are processed by the brain and how visual information is understood, among others. The prevalence of learning disabilities has been rising over the past decades (HERI, 2011).

Psychological Disabilities and Mental Health Conditions

The language referring to this disability is far from consistent, and various literatures refer to psychiatric disabilities, mental health impairments, mental illness, and other terms. Like chronic health conditions, psychological impairments can be stable, episodic, or progressive; may have onsets in childhood or during the traditional college years; and often are hidden forms of disability.

Mental health concerns are a large and growing disability on college campuses, and as the figures we present indicate, perhaps almost half of all college students may experience one or multiple forms of psychological disability, although many fewer have been diagnosed as having a disability, self-identify as having a disability, or identify themselves to campuses. A major national study of both college-attending and non-college-attending 19- to 25-year-olds (Blanco et al., 2008) found that almost half of all young adults, both those in and not in college, "met DSM-IV criteria for at least one psychiatric disorder in the previous year" (p. 6). While noting that prevalence rates of psychological impairments mirror those of same-age peers in the general population,

Hunt and Eisenberg (2010) wrote that counseling staff report "increased severity among the case mix" (p. 5) of students using campus counseling centers. Data from the 2014 National College Health Assessment (American College Health Association, 2014), collected from almost 80,000 students attending a diverse set of higher education institutions, indicate that 29% of male and 43% of female respondents reported ever receiving psychological or mental health services from a counselor/therapist/psychologist.

The increasing prevalence of mental health concerns in college populations may be a consequence of greater use of and more effective interventions during childhood and adolescence, enabling more young adults with psychological impairments to continue on to college than had been true in the past. In addition, the observed rise in the use of campus-based counseling services may well be a consequence of increased willingness to seek help for mental health concerns (Hunt & Eisenberg, 2010).

Students with psychological impairments face particular challenges as students. Compared to students generally and students with other forms of impairment, students with psychological disabilities are particularly at risk for dropping out of higher education (Hartley, 2010), despite having similar grade point averages (Brockelman, 2009), perhaps because they have been found to have lower scores on measures of life satisfaction and social support from friends and family and less control over their ability to reach their goals (Dong & Lucas, 2014). Multiple studies indicate that very few students who are accessing treatment for psychological disabilities identify themselves to campus disability service offices (Collins & Mowbray, 2008), and thus they may not be getting appropriate support.

There is a wide range of psychological impairments in the college population. The most common forms of psychological disabilities in this population are substance use disorders (29.15% of college students), personality disorders (17.68% of college students; these include avoidant, dependent, obsessive-compulsive, paranoid, schizoid, histrionic, and antisocial personality types), anxiety disorders (between 10% [Hunt & Eisenberg, 2010] and 11.94% [Blanco et al., 2008] of college populations), and mood disorders (between 17% [Hunt & Eisenberg, 2010] and 10.62% [Blanco et al., 2008] of college students, including major depressive disorder, dysthemia, and bipolar disorder).

Substance use disorders are a form of psychological disability (National Institute on Drug Abuse, 2010) that includes both abuse of (use that creates problems) and dependence (addiction) on alcohol, nicotine, and other drugs (Young, Nakashian, Yeh, & Amatetti, 2006). In a nationwide study of mental health of young adults, Blanco and his colleagues (2008) found that substance use disorders are the most common forms of psychological impairments in college student populations, and college students show greater levels of alcohol abuse and dependence than their same-aged non-college-attending peers, although less nicotine or drug abuse and dependence. Despite the prevalence of alcohol or drug disorders (abuse or addiction, or both) in college students, very few (5.36%) sought treatment in the prior year.

Nonprescription use and abuse of prescription drugs is a recently recognized phenomenon. According to ACHA's 2014 National College Health Assessment, roughly 3% of students report nonprescribed use of antidepressants, 6.2% nonprescribed use of painkillers, 3.5% use of sedatives, and 8.3% use of stimulants (particularly drugs prescribed for ADD). Zullig and Divin (2012), drawing from 2008 ACHA data, found 13% of college students reporting some form of nonmedical prescription drug use and that these students had "significantly greater odds of reporting depressive symptoms and/or suicidality" (p. 893) than their peers not taking nonprescribed prescription drugs.

According to the ACCESS Project at Colorado State University (2010), "Anxiety disorders are chronic conditions that produce feelings which may interfere with a person's ability to carry out normal or desired activities" (p. 1). There are multiple forms of anxiety disorders, including "General Anxiety Disorder (GAD), Post-traumatic Stress Disorder (PTSD), Acute Stress Disorder (ASD), Obsessive Compulsive Disorder (OCD), Panic Disorder, Social Anxiety Disorder (SAD), and a variety of phobias" (p. 1).

In contrast to many other forms of disability, depression in college students is extensively studied, perhaps in part because it is so prevalent and because of its strong connection to suicidal behavior. In a large, but single-institution study, researchers found depressive symptoms in all but 16.5% of the students, with 29.6% reporting mild, 30.6% moderate, 16.6% moderately severe, and 6.6% severe depression (Garlow et al., 2008). In a more recent multi-institutional study, Hunt and Eisenberg (2010) found "17% of students had positive screens for depression according to the Patient Health Questionnaire–9, including 9% for major depression, and 10% of students had a positive Patient Health Questionnaire screen for an anxiety disorder (panic or generalized anxiety disorder)" (p. 4).

Mobility Impairment

According to the ACCESS Center at Colorado State University (2010), "Mobility impairment refers to the inability of a person to use one or more of his/her extremities, or a lack of strength to walk, grasp, or lift objects" (p. 1). People with mobility impairments may intermittently or consistently use equipment, including canes, walkers, and wheelchairs, to enable or ease mobility.

Mobility impairments may be congenital or arise at any point in life. They are caused by a wide variety of conditions, including "multiple sclerosis, cerebral palsy, spina bifida, diabetes, muscular dystrophy, and paraplegia ... [as well as] cardiac conditions, chronic back pain, active sickle cell anemia, diabetes, and respiratory disorders such as cystic fibrosis" (University of Michigan, Services for Students with Disabilities, n.d.). According to 2013 data from the American Community Survey (W. Erickson, Lee, & von Schrader, 2015), in the U.S. adult (16 to 64 years old) population, among those having at least a high school diploma or the equivalent, 6.8% of the population reported an ambulatory impairment, giving a rough estimate of those eligible to attend college.

Surprisingly little is written specifically about mobility impairment in the literature on higher education, with Wessel, Jones, Blanch, and Markle's (2015) article as a notable exception. They studied multiple aspects of the college experience for wheelchair users and their parents and found a physically accessible campus, a supportive disability services office, and relevant majors were critical in deciding which college to attend. They also reported that students experienced "typical" transitions to college (e.g., concerns regarding course selection and time management, greater independence) and concerns unique to those who use personal care attendants (including locating and supervising them). Finally, the authors found that these students experienced greater social integration than many had had in primary and secondary schools.

Conclusion

People with disabilities and impairments are vital members of university communities. Although they have many common experiences, they also have extensive variation in their experiences of impairment. The multiple frameworks, statistics, and descriptions reviewed in this chapter provide numerous lenses through which differences in the experience of disability and impairment may be highlighted. An ongoing awareness of these multiple lenses will aid community members in developing campuses that are inclusive and supportive of disabled students, staff, and faculty.

Discussion Questions

1. Think of a student with a particular form of impairment you interact with regularly. How do the differences described in the first part of the chapter (e.g., extent of impact, recency of diagnosis, whether the impairment is

progressive, level of stigmatization) influence how the student might experience the impairment? How might this differ for a staff or faculty member with a disability?

2. How might we address the barriers to support experienced by those with more stigmatized forms of disability?

3. Common assumptions about what forms of impairments are most prevalent in college students (mobility and sensory impairments) differ greatly from reality (most college students with impairments have learning and psychological disabilities). What are the consequences of this misperception? How is this a social justice concern? What social justice perspectives help us understand this dynamic and create more equitable campuses?

4. Data on students with disabilities in higher education are difficult to collect and compare, even at the level of basic demographics. How might we develop more reliable, trustworthy data on our campuses and nationally?

PART TWO

POPULATION-SPECIFIC EXPERIENCES

CHAPTER FIVE

DISABILITY IDENTITY DEVELOPMENT AND MULTIPLE ASPECTS OF IDENTITY

[We must escape] from the demand that disability simply get added to the oft-cited trilogy of gender, race, and class. Disability is certainly gendered, raced, and classed through everyday talk, and disability also intersects with sexuality, ethnicity, age, family status, and all other forms of difference. But citing and adding difference to difference will not necessarily reveal how daily existence needs and makes these differences; how it needs and makes some differences notable some of the time, in some places, and other differences neither noticed nor viable. (Titchkosky, 2007, pp. 7–8)

In this chapter and the next, we explore how identities, some visible, some not, intersect and interact with disability. We begin by describing what we mean by *intersectionality* and *multiple aspects of identity*. Then we outline and critique the limited disability identity models, including the paucity of research on the disability identity of college students. Next, we describe changes that occur between K-12 and postsecondary education, when students move from being identified as disabled by parents or teachers to self-identification. Then we address the intersection of disability and the social identities of socioeconomic status, gender, race, sexual orientation, and religion. (In Chapter 6, we develop the conversation by focusing on student populations, such as international students, with unique educational experiences). We conclude by discussing social justice and intersectional approaches to higher education.

Multiple and Intersecting Social Identities

We engage these topics with the understanding that multiple aspects of identity are not merely additive and that the salience of people's identities changes over time and by context. In addition, people's own identities shift as they acquire disabilities, change class status, or come out. Identity is not stable (Titchkosky, 2007). For example, people with disabilities may identify most strongly as members of the disability community at certain times in their lives; at other times, they may distance themselves from the disability community and experience more salience with another identity (e.g., race, religion). These fluctuations in the salience and awareness of identities inform individuals' day-to-day experiences with the world around them. Furthermore, multiple aspects of identity do not always intersect. However, an awareness of the multiple identities of people with disabilities is imperative for exploring socially just accommodation, support, and development options that take into account people's previous experiences and interactions with the world (Patton, Renn, Guido, & Quaye, 2016).

Taking an intersectional approach is imperative when an individual's experiences are not defined by a single identity but rather by the simultaneous experiences of the multiple identities they hold. Purdie-Vaughns and Eibach (2008) called the simultaneous experience of multiple targeted identities "intersectional invisibility" (p. 378). As a result of not fitting an expected prototype, the experiences of these individuals are overlooked in research and in current literature on their separate subordinated groups. This intersectional invisibility may be experienced by people with disabilities who also hold additional social identities with less relative power and privilege in society (e.g., students who identify as queer or students of color).

Identity and an individual's interaction with the world are "influenced and shaped not simply by a person's race, class, ethnicity, gender, physical ability, sexuality, religion, or nationality—but by a combination of all of those characteristics" (Dill & Zambrana, 2009, p. 6). People's social identities and their understandings of their disability are further influenced by the temporal, "national, geographic, and cultural environments" (Evans, 2008, p. 19). The centrality and meaning of different aspects of identity change as the environment changes (S. R. Jones & Abes, 2013). These contextual influences and shifting salience of various identities, including disability identity, affect an individual's interactions with a particular social group and allow that individual to assign an understanding of the emotional connection to and relative significance of group membership (Tajfel, 1972).

Disability Identity Development in College Students

Disability identity development models explain how people with apparent and nonapparent impairments come to understand themselves in relation to the concept of disability. Various models conceptualize this process in different ways, giving factors such as environment, significant others, and psychological makeup varying weight in the development process. In this section, we discuss and critique four of these models. We start with the understanding that identity, similar to disability, is socially constructed (S. R. Jones & Abes, 2013). S. R. Jones and Abes (2013) explained,

> Viewing identities as socially constructed locates identity development within larger historical, social, political, and cultural contexts and suggests that identity does not exist outside contingent social realities—and therefore that it is constantly changing amid shifting contexts rather than fixed and stable. (p. xx)

Siebers (2008) believed that the presence of disability is a complicating factor in traditional understandings of identity (e.g., gender, race, sexuality) because disability creates a less static image of identity and challenges theorists and practitioners to reconceptualize more static understandings of identity. As a result, theorists have observed that disability can serve as an anchor for understanding the status and impact of other identities (Siebers, 2008). Sherry (2007) expanded on this notion by proposing that disability identity is more complex than the essential binary difference of disabled/nondisabled that many theorists assume.

Disability identity exists as an individual and societal phenomenon. Johnstone (2004) found that disability identity "is most empowering when it is self-described and defined as an individualized experience" (para. 40). As we outlined in Chapter 2, theorists have used multiple models to understand disability. Not all of these models allow for individual self-identification, but rather label an individual as disabled on the basis of societally defined criteria. In some of the models discussed in this chapter, identity development is viewed as a fixed time line—something that is achieved rather than as something that will shift throughout the lifetime of the individual. We view disability identity as a complex and evolving process. The salience of disability in an individual's identity is also likely to shift based on the context in which an individual and sociocultural environment defines disability, and this context will have a profound impact on individuals' recognition and acceptance of their disabilities (Dunn & Burcaw, 2013).

When evaluating or applying disability models, practitioners and researchers must understand the specific populations and environment in which researchers developed their identity models. For example, Forber-Pratt and Aragon's (2013) model is specific to college students with physical disabilities and was developed at an institution with a historical reputation for accessibility and disability advocacy, whereas Davidson and Henderson (2010) used discourse analysis to examine narratives of college students with autism spectrum disorder (ASD) across a variety of institutions. While both of these models share "giving back to the community" or "education of the community" as concepts that occur later within the identity model, there are also clear differences regarding the process of disability disclosure, which might be related to differing levels of support found on the different campuses at which the studies occurred or differences among the reactions of students with apparent and nonapparent disabilities, or both. In addition to reviewing these two models, we describe the ecological identity model proposed by Johnstone (2004) based on his review of the disability identity literature, the narrative identity review and analysis of Dunn and Burcaw (2013), the political identity exploration of Shakespeare (1996) and Putnam (2005), and the multidimensional model of college student disability identity development of Kraus (2008).

Ecological Identity Models

Ecological models of human development (e.g., Bronfenbrenner, 1979, 1993, 1995) allow for the examination of the processes through which individuals interact with the environment to shape their identity (Renn & Arnold, 2003), including students with disabilities (Patton et al., 2016). Tudge, Gray, and Hogan (1997) defined the ecological perspective as "a standpoint for conceptualizing the changing maturing person in relation to a changing environment—social, physical, and psychological" (p. 72). Patton et al. (2016) described ecological models as "a useful heuristic for understanding student development ... [serving] as a terrain on which to map the locations of development across a number of domains" (p. 45). Several theorists have used this approach to explain disability identity development.

Disclosure and Identity. Davidson and Henderson (2010) described four repertoires for understanding the "coming-out" process for autistic students. They viewed this process for autistic students as being similar to the coming-out process for lesbian, gay, bisexual, and transgender people with comparable emotional, physical, and social risks associated with disclosure.

Many other people with disabilities, in addition to autistic people, experience similar "coming-out" processes. The four repertoires that Davidson and Henderson identified are keeping safe, qualified deception, like/as resistance, and education.

We note that individuals who hide their disability status do so for a wide range of reasons, often influenced by the perceived and actual risks associated with disclosure in a particular environment. Lack of disclosure should not be equated with developmental failure as disclosure is a complicated and lifelong process.

The keeping-safe repertoire Davidson and Henderson (2010) identified centers on the assessment by individuals with disabilities of whether an environment is a safe place in which to disclose their diagnosis. Specifically, Davidson and Henderson (2010) explored the result of stigma and misconceptions related to ASD, where individuals may find disclosure risky in employment or other high-stakes environments. As with autistic people, many people with other disabilities make conscious decisions based on the environment as to whether it is physically and socially safe to disclose their disability status.

Davidson and Henderson (2010) described qualified deception as "deception to manage selves, identities, and situations in ways that can diffuse potentially threatening socio-spatial encounters" (p. 161). Some individuals may manage disclosure by sharing an aspect of their disability that appears similar to other disabilities that are less stigmatized than autism. The qualified deception repertoire may be used by individuals in a wider range of contexts than the keeping-safe repertoire and can open up additional experiential opportunities than nondisclosure alone. For example, in the qualified deception repertoire, an individual may be able to explain difficulty with following verbal instructions and ask for written instructions for tasks, a functional impact that can span many different disabilities, whereas in the keeping-safe repertoire, an individual may avoid any situation that would involve verbal instructions.

Davidson and Henderson (2010) described like/as resistance as being similar to the coming-out process of lesbian, gay, and bisexual individuals, serving as a form of resistance to the narrative that there is something inherently wrong with their diagnosis. Specifically, this process involves "resisting what [autistic individuals] see as profoundly offensive claims that their autism might be eradicated, and so they themselves [can be] 'fixed'" (p. 162).

The final repertoire Davidson and Henderson (2010) described is education, which addresses the responsibility felt by some autistic authors, whose work was reviewed as part of the study that Davidson and Henderson conducted, to educate others and eradicate stereotypes and stigma. Davidson and

Henderson described this process of coming out as "taking responsibility for the co-production of positive (political) space" (p. 164).

Personal Constructions of Identity. Johnstone (2004) suggested that "disability as an identity is often a personal construction, a purposive attempt to make meaning of self in the world" (para. 10). Based on a review of literature specific to disability and identity, he described six major categories of disability identity: socially ascribed, disempowering identities; overcompensating identities; identities that shift focus away from disabilities; empowering identities; complex identities; and common identities.

Socially ascribed, disempowering identities were based on the work of Riddell, Baron, and Wilson (2001) who posited that people with disabilities may have few options regarding identity "because of societal labels and ascriptions" (Johnstone, 2004, para. 11). Ascribed labels of disability or specific impairments, when not claimed by the individual, can cause some individuals to experience shame. This identity category is often linked to the medical model, where power and control over those with disabilities are held by nondisabled medical personnel. Because of the stigma associated with disability, people attempt to hide their impairments and experience embarrassment when the impairment is discovered.

Overcompensating identity, Johnstone's (2004) second category of identity, occurs when "people feel the necessity to overcompensate in order to cope with the notion of being disabled" (para. 15). Overcompensation often takes the form of working to succeed at higher levels than people without disabilities, which can result in a stressful and pressured lifestyle.

Identities that shift the focus away from disability is Johnstone's (2004) third category. Johnstone explained that this shift may occur for a variety of reasons, many of which are deeply personal to the individual. Deaf individuals, for instance, often view themselves as part of a linguistic minority rather than as individuals with disabilities. Others may shift focus away from disability through denial, asserting that their impairment or disability does not affect them in a particular context or environment or that it is less significant than others suggest it is.

Empowering identities are those that place disability at the forefront of an individual's holistic identity and recognize disability "as a valued concept in identity formation" (Johnstone, 2004, para. 21). This shift in placement has been bolstered in recent years as the discourse on disability in the United States has moved from emphasis on the medical model to social understandings of disability. For many individuals, empowering disability identities are developed through connections with a disability community and engagement in identity politics.

Complex identities capture the idea that people with disabilities identify themselves in multiple ways, including by race, class, gender, and sexual orientation, as well as disability. Disability and impairment can result in different feelings and outcomes, such as empowerment, pain, or pride. Other labels a disabled person might claim include "tolerant," "survivor," or "sensitive" (Johnstone, 2004, para. 31). Furthermore, people claiming a complex identity would be likely to view their identities as fluid and "subject to fluctuations of self and identity" (para. 32).

Johnstone (2004) reported that the majority of people with disabilities see disability as a *common identity* or culture, built through sharing similar experiences and "negotiating disability in a world oriented largely for (and by) able-bodied people" (para. 34). Deaf people, especially, have developed a Deaf culture that has its own language, similar experiences, and its own organizations. A common disability identity and disability culture help individuals develop positive personal identities and provide support mechanisms through which they process their disabilities. Johnstone also discussed the influence of disability culture on society, including its promotion of the inherent value of people with disabilities.

Stage Identity Models

Stage models provide descriptions of the typical progression of experiences or internal thought processes an individual in a particular identity group will experience. Specific to disabled students, Patton et al. (2016) stated that stage models describe "the developmental trajectories of disabled students [and] focus on how individuals come to understand themselves inclusive of their disability and in relation to others with disabilities" (p. 236).

Model of Social and Psychosocial Identity. Forber-Pratt and Aragon (2013) developed the four-stage model of social and psychosocial identity for understanding identity development among college students with physical disabilities. These stages—acceptance, relationship, adoption, and giving back—describe the developmental trajectory the participants in the study underwent as they entered disability culture. Forber-Pratt and Aragon's model should be read with the understanding that it was developed based on research conducted on one campus, with a small number of students who all had severe physical disabilities and all lived in the same residence hall. Further research should be conducted before extrapolating this model to the spectrum of individuals with disabilities attending higher education in the United States.

The *acceptance* phase that Forber-Pratt and Aragon (2013) identified was designed to capture the development of both individuals who are born with a

disability and those who acquire a disability later in life. Reaching the acceptance phase requires individuals to have an awareness of their disability and
perhaps to have processed through Kübler-Ross and Kessler's (2005) stages
of grief: denial, anger, bargaining, depression, and acceptance. During the
acceptance phase, individuals come to acknowledge their disability and make
conscious decisions, emotionally and in action, to not let their disability limit
their interactions with the world. This process also prompts individuals to
explore and engage with disability culture.

As individuals move into the *relationship* phase, they seek out and form relationships with other individuals with disabilities and further develop a sense of
disability community. Dunn and Burcaw (2013) also noted the importance
of community and relationship building in the formation of disability identity.

The *adoption* phase, as described by Forber-Pratt and Aragon (2013),
"entails individuals adopting the core values of disability culture: independence and social justice" (p. 9). In their study, Forber-Pratt and Aragon
stressed the physical aspects of independence, such as managing personal
hygiene and navigation; they did not expand the model to address executive
functioning aspects of independence that may be critical to the identity
development of individuals with learning disabilities and autistic people.
The development of an understanding of social justice, in either the individual or systemic sphere, was a critical part of this model. Forber-Pratt and
Aragon clarified that in order to progress though this stage, individuals are
not required to engage in political activism; rather, they must recognize the
inequalities that face them and/or members of their community.

The final stage of Forber-Pratt and Aragon's (2013) model of social and
psychosocial identity is *giving back to the community*. In this phase, individuals
move from individual recognition and concerns identified during social justice development in the adoption phase and become active in modeling their
identity for other members of the community "who are still learning the ways
of the group" (p. 12). During this stage, individuals may also engage in more
tangible forms of activism designed to give back to the disability community
through social and legal change.

Multidimensional Model of Identity. Kraus (2008) proposed a model of disability identity in which she attempted to address some of the limitations of
traditional stage models by merging fluidity and stage concepts. Her model
was developed as the result of a phenomenological study of college students
with physical disabilities at a single institution.

To develop the multidimensional model of disability, Kraus (2008) drew
on more traditional stage models and acknowledged that students who have

not recognized their disability status will experience a linear progression of development when in the stages of *ignorance* and *questioning*. Ignorance reflects the period of time when individuals are unaware of disability—not just their own disability but also the overall concept of disability. They begin to explore disability when they themselves become disabled or when "they realize not everyone has a disability" (Kraus, 2008, p. 182). This exploration involves questioning what disability means in the life of the individual and the potential influence of disability in society.

Kraus (2008) posited that students enter into a fluid understanding of disability after they understand that they have a disability. For Kraus, the deviation from more traditional stage models occurs in the third aspect, or stage, of disability. Specifically, Kraus's model allows students who have moved from the first two stages of ignorance and questioning into negotiated identity to have a complex interaction with their disability identity. Negotiated identity involves an understanding of identity that is dynamic and interacts with environmental factors. Kraus (2008) explained that "individuals negotiating disability identity are not simply reacting to their environments, they are also agents of their own development, active players within ever changing environments" (p. 184). Students' negotiated identities exist as the center of intersecting spheres of community, education, involvement, activism, anger, and pride (Figure 5.1).

FIGURE 5.1. NEGOTIATED DISABILITY IDENTITY

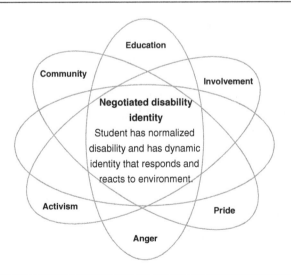

Source: From Kraus (2008). Used with permission.

Each of these spheres informs a student's current negotiated identity. According to Kraus, negotiated identity elicits a sense of motion, allowing the individual an identity that is constantly in flux. Kraus (2008) emphasized that it may be impossible "to discern one sphere from another or to strictly determine how they interact with or influence each other" (p. 184) as a result of the active engagement and influence of individuals on their own environments and identities.

Narrative Identity Models

Dunn and Burcaw (2013) explored disability through a narrative identity lens in order to engage the social-psychological aspects of disability identity development. Dunn and Burcaw (2013) used narratives in existing literature to understand "critical aspects of life with a disability" (p. 148). Themes of communal attachment and affirmation of disability, identity politics and activism, and personal meaning and disability emerged in the literature review that Dunn and Burcaw conducted. These themes, along with other subnarratives of individuals, led Dunn and Burcaw to make recommendations for practitioners, primarily of rehabilitation psychology, to facilitate and recognize identity development in their clients.

Communal attachment and affirmation of disability were identified as primary personal identity development factors for respondents in the studies that Dunn and Burcaw (2013) reviewed. Communal attachment constituted the "favorable feelings toward and a desire to affiliate with a broad community of people with disabilities" (Dunn & Burcaw, 2013, p. 149). Dunn and Burcaw identified the act of coming home or integrating into the community as a reoccurring narrative in the lives of people with disabilities and an important task for internal individual affirmation of the positive aspects of disability.

Identity politics and activism, discussed in the next section in greater detail, was identified as a second narrative in the lives of people with disabilities. Dunn and Burcaw (2013) found this narrative to be spurred by the development of self-worth (affirmation), which "enables people with disabilities to see themselves as possessing the same worth as individuals who have not experienced disability" (p. 150) and thus worthy of political influence and change.

Personal meaning and disability, which Dunn and Burcaw (2013) described as "searching for significance, engaging in sense-making, and finding benefits associated with disability" (p. 150), provides a context for understanding personal acceptance of disability. The development of a personal meaning of disability is closely tied to affirmation, but Dunn and Burcaw identified it as distinct from affirmation because affirmation does not move from acknowledgment of disability to acceptance. Dunn and Burcaw viewed the development of a personal meaning and acceptance of disability as the most important theme in disability identity development.

Political Identity Models

Political identity could be considered in our discussion of ecological identity models; however, because of the number of studies that have focused on the political aspects of disabled people's identities, we have chosen to examine this aspect of identity development separately from the ecological approaches previously reviewed. Shakespeare (1996) described the role of the disability movement in developing a political identity among people with disabilities by providing a collective framework from which to view political action. Putnam (2005) used H. Hahn's (1994) minority group model and Schur's (1998) research on disability rights activism as the foundation for exploring a political disability identity.

Putnam (2005) hypothesized that individuals with a political interest in the disability community and disability rights issues likely recognized themselves as minority group members. Putnam identified six themes related to political disability identity development: self-worth, pride, discrimination, common cause, policy alternatives, and engagement with political action. These themes provided the framework for gauging disability identity through a political lens.

Putnam (2005) viewed *self-worth* and *pride* as important factors for individuals with disabilities in establishing self-esteem and not only adjusting to but embracing their disability. This process included recognizing the positives of individuals' capabilities and ability to influence their own lives. The theme of *discrimination* built on individuals' understanding of their self-worth expanded to a broader understanding of micro and macro discrimination of individuals with disabilities. The recognition of systems of discrimination and identification of common experiences shared with other people with disabilities allowed individuals to see a *common cause* held by themselves and other disabled people. Putnam (2005) described this process of developing a common cause as "the transition from common disability experience [toward] disability-related political agenda" (p. 192). Individuals may experience this transition at different rates, with some individuals moving into a political consciousness early after embracing their disability, whereas others may take years to progress to a collective understanding.

The final two themes, *policy alternatives* and *political action*, describe the desire of people with disabilities who have a political disability identity to make changes to the structures (e.g., policies, environments) that limit the daily lives of many individuals with disabilities. Putnam's (2005) description of *policy alternatives* hinges on the understanding of disability as contextual, where "barriers to disability reduction are identifiable, and if they are appropriately addressed, disability can be mediated and the experience of living with disability can be improved" (p. 193). When individuals recognize the opportunity for mediation through policy change, they show a desire to enact change through verbalization of the possibility of more inclusive policy. Individuals may move beyond acknowledgment of alternatives to current policy to engagement in *political action*. This engagement can be motivated by individual experiences of discrimination, in response to the common experiences of people with disabilities, or in order to gain greater social inclusion.

Critiques of Disability Identity Development Theories

Research on the identity development of individuals with disabilities is lacking in both the amount and the rigor of the research. There is a paucity of true developmental theories applicable to this population. The models describing the identity development of individuals with disabilities in this chapter are among the few existing resources, and many of them are either relatively recent and have not been confirmed or very old, outdated, and unvalidated. In addition, many of the theories described in this chapter were developed through research based on only reviews of existing literature, very small samples, or a specific subset of the disability community. These limitations mean that many of the developmental understandings described in this chapter may not be generalizable to the growing population of students with disabilities on college campuses.

Studies have not looked at the effect of identity development on self-advocacy, requests for supports or accommodation, and other skill sets that are identified later in this book as crucial to the academic and social success of many students with disabilities. Just as models for understanding disability identity are lacking, few studies consider the multiple identities of disabled students. However, some recent work has explored specific identity intersections.

Patton et al. (2016) indicated that the theorization and study of "disability identity and its development has lagged behind those for other minoritized groups in higher education" (p. 233). In the absence of a strong student development literature base, they noted similarities between factors influencing disability identity development and identity development of other minoritized identities, including limited access to resources, the segregation of space, and expectations to conform to the dominant group norms. However, there are multiple important differences between disability identity and other forms of identity that make the application of minoritized identity development and nondisability-specific theories problematic. Specifically, disability status can be acquired at any point in life and forms of impairment can shift over time, disabilities can vary in functional limitations, and disability status varies in how apparent it is to others. Given that disability identity can fluctuate throughout the lifetime of an individual as a result of these factors, we reject trends within the broader student affairs literature to treat people with disabilities as a monolithic group. Students with disabilities have varied experiences, and as a result of the comparatively underdeveloped literature base, we advocate for understanding disabled students—and all other students—as individuals with multiple intersecting identities.

Shakespeare (1996) noted the important difference between being identified as disabled by others and identifying oneself as disabled. He contended that this distinction is critical for understanding and evaluating disability identity. Shakespeare believed that approaches where people with disabilities were identified by others and developed an identity based on that identification grew out of the medical model of understanding disability, which hinges on labeling disabled bodies. Many of the approaches that are informed by self-identification or political activism are more closely aligned with social models of disability, which view the interaction between the self and environment as key to identity development. While there are only a few true disability identity theories, several researchers have discussed factors that may influence students' development and facilitate students' placing their disability identity in the foreground of their experiences.

Self-Identification as Disabled

S. R. Jones and Abes (2013) found that "self-definition is an ever-changing process because of the influence of contexts, which are nested in structures of privilege and oppression" (p. 93). Individuals may have multiple privileged and oppressed identities, and the relative social position of these identities can have an impact on the salience of the identity to the individual (Abes, Jones, & McEwen, 2007; S. R. Jones & Abes, 2013). As a result, "social identities exist within power relationships" (Evans, 2008, p. 19). These power relationships may lead students to alter the ways in which they present themselves and which identities they choose to highlight or downplay (Abes et al., 2007; S. R. Jones & Abes, 2013). A number of factors can affect these choices, including the individual's cultural and family background, concerns about personal safety, and career-related issues (S. R. Jones & Abes, 2013). Vernon and Swain (2002) found that the extent of overt discrimination an individual experienced was directly related to that person's level of awareness and fear associated with a specific social identity. Furthermore, identity does not begin when a student starts college.

Approximately 55% of high school students with documented disabilities enrolled in some form of postsecondary education within eight years of leaving high school (Sanford et al., 2011). However, the number of students who identify themselves as disabled to disability resource offices (DROs) decreases significantly between high school and postsecondary enrollment. "Almost two-thirds (63 percent) of postsecondary students who were identified by their secondary school as having a disability did not consider themselves to have a disability by the time they had transitioned to postsecondary school" (Newman et al., 2011, p. 31) and thus did not identify themselves to the DRO. Furthermore, an additional 9% of students who received services in high school and continued to identify as a person with a disability also decided not to disclose this information to their college or university (Newman et al., 2011). Thus, only 24% of undergraduate students who were identified as having a disability in high school seek services for their disability as they begin college.

One reason for this decline may be the stigma associated with disability, resulting in a reluctance to identify with disability or out oneself as disabled. Baldridge and Swift (2013) noted the careful assessment of social consequences that people with disabilities engage in prior to asking for accommodations. Annamma, Conner, and Ferri (2013) and Samuels (2003) found that perceived social consequences can prohibit individuals from requesting accommodations, especially accommodations that are visible. Students develop an understanding of their identity through their experiences with society, including the primary and secondary educational systems. These experiences influence not only their identification as disabled but also their decisions regarding which institution to attend and what resources to use. Ultimately they may have an impact on a student's collegiate success. Because many students do not disclose their disability or request accommodations at the onset of college, it is important for institutions to create educational environments that are inclusive and to consider the value of programs that educate all students and their parents about the transition to college and available resources.

The decline in disclosure and self-identification from secondary to postsecondary education is most prevalent among students with invisible disabilities (Sanford et al., 2011). As we have already noted in this chapter, disclosure is often a complicated aspect of identity negotiation that can be influenced by the environment, the individual's acceptance of that aspect of identity, and the visibility of the identity. The choice to disclose is one that individuals with more visible disabilities do not have the privilege of making; however, for individuals with invisible identities, there can be a "self-destroying tension between appearance and identity" (Samuels, 2003, p. 233).

Institutions of higher education should carefully consider the ways in which the cultural environment of the institution promotes or hinders students, staff, and faculty from feeling able to identify as disabled in the postsecondary environment. (Greater attention to the unique dynamics of staff and faculty members' disclosure decisions is given in Chapter 7.) DROs that provide a space for students to connect with peers with disabilities and promote social engagement of students in addition to providing accommodations and promoting access will have greater success in engaging students with the office early in their academic career. Faculty who include accessibility statements on their syllabi may find that students feel more comfortable approaching the faculty member to disclose and discuss accommodations. Universally designed environments, discussed in Chapters 10 and 12, provide support for all students regardless of disability status or disclosure.

Social Identities

Social class, race and ethnicity, gender, religion, and sexual orientation are aspects of identity in addition to disability that affect college students. In this section, we present the literature on these social identities and note opportunities for future research.

Often institutions work with students with disabilities and presume that their disability is the only, or the most, salient part of their identity. Underhile and Cowles (1998) found that universities have historically categorized individuals based on individual identities rather than recognizing that individuals hold multiple identities. As a result, institutions have expected that students seek support from offices based on these dissected identities. The problem with this division for people with disabilities is that an individual's disability "is expected to explain all of the life experiences of the individual" (Erevelles & Minear, 2010, p. 129) and presumes a similarity of experience among all students with disabilities.

As discussed in Chapter 1, people with disabilities have been excluded in many overt and covert ways in education in the United States. Laws, testing, and educational systems and structures historically have been built to serve a "normative" group of White, upper-class, able-bodied men. When legal protections were created for people with disabilities, there continued to be an expansion of services for the same normative group within the disabled community (O'Toole, 2004), meaning that advances in disability protection were primarily designed to address the needs of White, upper-class students with disabilities and the needs of groups outside of this norm were overlooked or ignored. As a result, scholarly research, legal advancements, and current practices do not address the multiple social identities of students with disabilities prior to and during college.

Social Class

Socioeconomic status traverses across other aspects of identity (e.g., race). Although it is no longer socially acceptable and in many cases is illegal to discriminate based on race, gender, or disability, the same is not true of economic status, and issues of racial and gender inequality often masquerade as socioeconomic discrimination. For instance, funding for and access to high-quality K-12 education is dependent on property taxes, and this system frequently places racial and ethnic minorities in disadvantaged settings (Kozol, 1992). Because socioeconomic status is a powerful influence on educational outcomes and because discrimination is often justified by income inequality and embedded within our social and institutional structures, we intentionally examine this topic first.

Financial access to college is a concern for many students, with and without disabilities. Burke (1995) found that students with disabilities enroll in postsecondary education at lower rates than their nondisabled peers, and a major factor influencing enrollment is ability or perceived ability to pay for education. "These concerns are magnified for students with disabilities who may need to take additional classes … [or] take more time to study due to their identified disability" (Garrison-Wade & Lehmann, 2009, p. 437). These additional time constraints are compounded for students with disabilities from low-socioeconomic backgrounds that require them to work a significant number of hours in order to fund their education.

Sanford et al. (2011) found that family income is a strong predictor of college enrollment for students with disabilities, particularly at two-year institutions. Students with family incomes below $25,000 per year were significantly less likely to attend college than their nondisabled peers from similar economic means (Sanford et al., 2011). Once they are enrolled in college, family income plays a role in access to accommodations. McGregor et al. (2016)

found that the rate of accommodations for students with learning disabilities is higher for students from wealthy families.

Cheatham and Elliott (2013) surveyed the work of a group of researchers who found that "high school context (private or public) may structurally impact students' academic orientations and educational choices, and that these effects may differ by socioeconomic groups" (p. 96). They also found that students from low socioeconomic backgrounds often rely heavily on secondary education guidance counselors to discuss issues of financial aid and college exploration; however, many of these students go to schools that employ fewer guidance counselors than more affluent schools attended by higher socioeconomic status students. In addition, schools with minimal resources may have significantly fewer resources to support transition planning for students with disabilities. These factors have a negative effect on students' college enrollment (Cheatham & Elliott, 2013) and preparation (J. W. Madaus, Grigal, & Hughes, 2014).

In addition to affecting matriculation, social class also has an impact on secondary educational opportunities that help to prepare students for postsecondary education. These influences are significant for all students but are felt most keenly by students with disabilities (Kozol, 1992). Elementary and secondary institutions in the United States are not funded equally, and schools in high-poverty neighborhoods experience a number of limitations that detract from students' learning (Blanchett, 2006; Kozol, 1992). These limitations include "high turnover of teaching and instructional staff, a high number of uncertified or provisionally licensed teachers, limited or no access to technology, one or no foreign language programs, few educational specialists (e.g., in math, science, or reading),[and] few advanced classes" (Blanchett, 2006, p. 26). Many of the institutions that are deemed high poverty also are institutions that primarily educate students of color, creating a significant overlap of socioeconomic status, race, and educational opportunities (Blanchett, 2006; Kozol, 1992). The funding constraints of schools in low-income districts also reduce the educational resources for identifying, testing, and supporting students with disabilities.

Race and Ethnicity

Students with disabilities in secondary education do not experience a difference in college attendance based on race or ethnicity; 62% of Hispanic, 60% of African American, and 61% of White young adults with disabilities had enrolled in a postsecondary program within six years of completing secondary education, according to a study by Sanford et al. (2011). However, there are racialized discrepancies in diagnosis and receipt of support services in secondary education for students with disabilities that adversely affect their postsecondary experience. In addition, just as discrimination based on racial identity often hides under the guise of discrimination based on income, ableism may be used to justify "differential treatment and rationalize schools' failure to help students [of color] achieve" (Ostiguy, Peters, & Shlasko, 2016, p. 318).

While the college matriculation rates, when combining all types of post-secondary education, of students with disabilities are similar across race and ethnicity (Sanford et al., 2011), these aspects of identity are linked with significant differences in diagnostic experiences and institution level matriculation (Blanchett, 2006; J. Blanks & Hughes, 2013; Erevelles & Minear, 2010). Rates of diagnosis vary significantly by race, with certain forms of impairment more or less often diagnosed in different populations. Reid and Knight (2006) wrote that in the 12 years previous to their research, "the number of students labeled LD [learning disabled] who attend college has increased from 16% to 40% of the college students with disabilities" (p. 20). However, they emphasized, DROs were not seeing an equitable increase for all racial populations (Reid & Knight, 2006) and fewer students of color were entering college with a specific learning disability.

Racially and ethnically diverse students experience a greater amount of misdiagnosis and underdiagnosis than their White peers, particularly in secondary education. However, Erevelles and Minear (2010) and Blanchett (2006) also found that racially minoritized students were overrepresented in special education, remedial, or tracked classrooms and that "Black children constitute 17 percent of the total school enrollment, but 33 percent of those labeled 'mentally retarded'" (Erevelles & Minear, 2010, p. 131). Blanchett (2006) also noted that African American students with disabilities were transferred out of special education classrooms and met academic milestones at lower rates than White students with disabilities. Furthermore, overrepresentation of Latino/a, Native American, and Native Alaskan students in special education was particularly likely to occur in states where many students from these ethnic populations live (Annamma et al., 2013). For example, a student may be tracked into a remedial program on the assumption of a disability but never be properly tested or may be misdiagnosed due to racial bias in current assessment measures.

Blanchett (2006) ascribed these discrepancies to White privilege and racism, which work together to keep the numbers of students from minority ethnic and racial groups disproportionate in special education. For example, Travers, Tincani, and Krezmein (2013) found that Black, Hispanic, and

American Indian students are less likely to be identified as having ASD. They hypothesized that racially diverse students are being misdiagnosed or diagnosed at a later date than their White peers, and they are "less likely to receive a timely clinical diagnosis of autism outside of the school setting and instead may rely on special education screening and assessment process for autism identification" (p. 46), a process that may be heavily influenced by the relative wealth of the school district.

Many secondary schools use methods of determining who has learning disabilities (the discrepancy model) that, combined with institutionalized systems of racism, may explain the overrepresentation of minoritized students in remedial classrooms who receive a label of mental retardation rather than learning disabled (Warner, Dede, Garvan, & Conway, 2002). Warner et al. (2002) emphasized that IQ norms have been based on primarily European American populations. They hypothesized that an exclusionary effect occurs for minoritized populations because of the lack of representation in the normative sample; however, limited research has focused on racial and ethnic populations other than European Americans and African Americans.

The experiences of students of color in secondary education can have a marked effect on help-seeking behavior and resource use at the postsecondary level. Ball-Brown and Frank (1993) found that many minoritized students avoid using disability resources and distance themselves from their disability. This distancing may be the result of negative experiences with the individual education plan process, with special education teachers, and from segregation into remedial classes following identification in secondary education. Vernon and Swain (2002) found that "Black disabled people consistently speak to experiences of segregation and marginalization within services" (p. 79) that reduces their future trust in and use of resources.

Language can also serve as a significant barrier in access to and effective provision of services in postsecondary education (Banton & Hirsch, 2000; Reid & Knight, 2006; Vernon & Swain, 2002). Reid and Knight (2006) found that "linguistic minority students are overrepresented in secondary special education programs" (p. 20). Banton and Hirsch (2000) found that in working with individuals with disabilities from ethnically and linguistically diverse backgrounds, communication issues were influenced by differences in primary language and because non-English-speaking families of students with disabilities are unlikely to come into contact with information about disability services. Vernon and Swain (2002) also noted the importance of recognizing that communication goes beyond "language skills and literacy" (p. 80), and as a result even students born in an English-speaking context might experience communication barriers.

Asian American youth had significantly lower rates of help seeking for psychiatric disabilities, including major depression and anxiety, than did their peers (Wyatt, Ung, Park, Kwon, & Trinh-Shevrin, 2015). Asian American students were at the highest risk for major mental health symptoms and suicidal ideation between ages 16 and 24 during the time when many of these students are entering postsecondary education (Wyatt et al., 2015). Wyatt et al. also found that Asian American and Native Hawaiian/Pacific Islander youth and young adults experience higher rates of suicidal ideation than the national average. This risk, they wrote, may be compounded by cultural norms that limit disclosure of stress, trauma, or challenge to individuals outside the family and by the model minority myth, which perpetuates the idea that Asian Americans should excel academically without effort.

As a result of the wide range of experiences students may have as the result of their racialized identities, colleges and universities should implement policies and practices that are inclusive of students with minoritized racial/ethnic identities and are culturally appropriate. This intentional action includes finding ways to connect the work of intercultural and multicultural staff and DRO staff, recognizing that students require support appropriate to their multiple identities. This work may also be supported by federal TRIO programs on individual campuses, which are mandated to provide support for minoritized students who are first generation or disabled, or both (U.S. Department of Education, 2016). Many of the students supported by TRIO programs are also racially minoritized students. Supporting students with a wide range of identities also must include training faculty and staff on culturally appropriate curriculum, testing, and advising.

Institutions will also want to develop a strong relationship between disability resources and career development resources staff. Students with disabilities often have more difficulty securing employment following graduation than their nondisabled peers; however, evidence also shows that racially minoritized students with disabilities experience additional barriers that their White peers with disabilities do not experience (Bertrand & Mullainathan, 2004). Erevelles and Minear (2010) found that "75 percent of African Americans [with disabilities], compared to 39 percent of Whites [with disabilities], are still not employed three to five years out of [postsecondary] school" (p. 132). This discrepancy indicates that institutions must provide more effective supports for students with disabilities that address both ableism and racism in employment.

It is critical to note that some populations, such as American Indian, Native Hawaiian, Native Alaskan, and Asian American students, have received significantly less study than their White, African American, and Hispanic peers. Students with disabilities from these populations may require additional supports that are not accounted for in this chapter. Practitioners should push for increased research on these populations and develop cultural competencies that support all racially diverse students, including those with disabilities.

Gender

Unlike their nondisabled peers, the gender gap in college matriculation does not exist for students with disabilities; around 60% of both men and women who were identified as having a disability in high school enrolled in postsecondary education (Sanford et al., 2011). This research has assumed binary sex categories and allowed only for students to identify as male or female, making invisible genderqueer and transgender students. Very little research has focused on the matriculation rates for genderqueer and transgender students (Baril, 2015) whose gender identities do not align with the sex or gender they were assigned at birth and even less has focused on identifying challenges or barriers to accessing postsecondary education for students who are genderqueer/transgender and disabled (Baril, 2015).

Faculty, staff, and administrators should expect that there may be social and academic impacts for transgender students, as research in the K-12 system has identified barriers that prevent high school completion for some students who are both transgender and disabled. Greytek, Kosciw, and Diaz (2009) found that 28% of transgender high school students reported being harassed at school for an "actual or perceived disability" in addition to their transgender identity (p. 18) and this rate of harassment is higher than that for their cisgender peers.

In addition to the harassment that many transgender and disabled students experience, the Massachusetts Department of Public Health (2009) found that many transgender people had higher rates of depression, anxiety, and suicidal ideation than their cisgender peers, as well as higher incidences of disability status and experiences of victimization or violence. These health and safety issues are compounded for many transgender and disabled people because of difficulty finding counselors with the expertise and sensitivity to competently treat transgender individuals with ongoing medical or mental health concerns (Sanchez, Sanchez, & Danoff, 2009). These challenges are compounded given that many people presume that being transgender is inherently a mental health disorder.

For many transgender and genderqueer students with disabilities, discriminatory medical experiences serve as a barrier to accessing medical care for their disability, and in general, prior to arrival at college. These same barriers also exist during college for documentation purposes and ongoing care. As a result, institutions, particularly those in rural areas or located in states with limited resources, should develop relationships with medical and mental health care providers with experience meeting the medical needs of transgender students.

Faculty, staff, and administrators also should be educated about the experiences of disabled transgender students to ensure that they are served in the classroom and on campus across their multiple identities. Harley, Nowak, Gassaway, and Savage (2002) stressed the importance of addressing "administrative issues such as name and gender changes and health plans" (p. 533) in order to support students who are both transgender and disabled. Confidentiality and respect for the students' names and pronouns and awareness of trans-specific health and administrative needs in communication regarding disability are important.

As Sanford et al. (2011) noted, men and women with disabilities are accessing higher education at similar rates; however, the lived experiences of cisgender students with disabilities have been shown to vary by gender (Baldridge & Swift, 2013; Gerschick & Miller, 1994; Madigan, 2005; Rousso, 2003). These variances are most notable in regard to help-seeking behavior, past educational experiences, identification as disabled, and coexisting conditions. Specifically, Baldridge and Swift (2013) stated that men with disabilities indicated they were less willing to seek assistance than did women with disabilities, and men may be less likely to access resources early in their college career. Gerschick and Miller (1994) hypothesized that the aversion to help-seeking behavior that some men exhibit is the result of hegemonic masculinity, which "privileges men who are strong, courageous, aggressive, independent, self-reliant, and career-oriented" (p. 34). For some men with disabilities, seeking assistance poses a double threat to this narrative of masculinity by acknowledging the need for help and admitting to a disability, which "society perceives ... [as] weak, pitiful, passive, and dependent" (Gerschick & Miller, 1994, p. 34).

There are gender differences in diagnosis, identification, and receipt of disability services. Madigan (2005) found that "a disproportionately higher number of boys than girls are served in programs for youths with emotional disorders (ED) and learning disorders (LD)" (p. 47). However, Rousso (2003) stated that this phenomenon might be the result of different standards for identification. Rousso found that "in order for girls to receive services [in the K-12 educational system], they had to have more significant levels of disability than boys ... and girls receiving services were often placed in more restrictive educational settings than boys" (p. 19). These factors lead to fewer women having been diagnosed or having previously received services for these particular forms of disabilities when entering college than their male peers. In addition, more women with disabilities have been removed from mainstream courses, which can have a negative impact on their academic and social readiness for postsecondary education.

Of significant concern for postsecondary institutions is the vulnerability of disabled students to violence. In 2003, Rousso found that "disabled girls experience violence within the family, institutions, and community at higher rates than their nondisabled peers" (p. 10). More recently, Cantor et al. (2015) found that students registered with disability resources at large research-extensive institutions were almost twice as likely to experience sexual violence as their nondisabled peers, regardless of gender. Of the survey respondents reporting a disability, 21.4% reported "experiencing nonconsensual sexual contact involving force or incapacitation" (p. 102) compared with 11.3% of their nondisabled peers. When broken down by gender, the numbers are especially alarming: 31.6% of disabled women reported nonconsensual sexual contact compared with 18.4% of their women peers, 8.7% of disabled men compared with 4.2% of nondisabled men, and 34.4% of disabled transgender or gender nonconforming individuals compared with 20.0% of nondisabled transgender and gender nonconforming students.

The prevalence of students with disabilities experiencing sexual violence on campus requires institutions to direct resources to not only supporting students who have experienced trauma but also to explore options for reducing the vulnerability of this population. DRO staff should develop close working relationships with the Title IX and violence prevention staff on campus. Collaboratively, professionals associated with these offices should also train faculty and staff about the protections and supports that would benefit students who are both disabled and have experienced trauma or become disabled as the result of that trauma. Clark and Pryal (2015) stated, "30 to 40 percent of female rape victims will still be suffering from PTSD six months" (para. 4) after experiencing the traumatic event. As a result of the ongoing effects of sexual trauma, Clark and Pryal argued, "Title IX offices need to *presume* that rape will affect a student's performance in class. If that presumption is wrong, and the survivor needs no accommodations from disability support services, so be it" (para. 19). NotAlone.gov (2015) provides guidance to institutions, stating that disability services should be among the resources made available to sexual assault victim-survivors: "Students who have a disability, including those who develop a disability as a result of experiencing sexual misconduct, may be entitled to additional services [beyond interim measures] and supports as accommodations" (p. 1). We also believe that in order to provide socially just access to the college experience for disabled students who have experienced trauma, institutional leaders have an obligation to consider a student's existing accommodations when determining what Title IX interim measures are appropriate for a particular student. For example, if a typical Title IX interim measure would be to allow a student access to a peer's notes to alleviate difficulty with concentration, the Title IX office staff should consider additional supports if the student already receives peers' notes as an accommodation.

Religion

Elhoweris, Whittaker, and Salend (2007) stated, "It is critical for educators to understand the influence of religion or spirituality" (p. 1) on people with disabilities. They found that although many people with disabilities exist on the outskirts of organized religion, religion or spirituality are still important protective factors for some students with disabilities that help them cope with the effects of their disabilities. These protective factors may be especially important for students who develop their disabilities during college. A. B. Blanks and Smith (2009) found that it is important for educators to support access to "religious activities, traditions, and cultural milestones" (p. 301) for individual disabled students who have strong religious identities.

Chen, Brown, and Kotbungkair (2015) found that people with disabilities have been excluded throughout the histories of many sociocultural and religious organizations. This exclusion has primarily been documented among Judaism, Christianity, Islam, and Buddhism. Jewish and Christian religious texts contain depictions of people with disabilities as impure, having been disfavored by Yahweh and God (respectively) or as being a burden to be cared for by society (A. B. Blanks & Smith, 2009). Buddhists may think that "disabilities were a direct result of past life deeds ... subsequently, a disability is usually equated with perpetual pain and suffering" (Chen et al., p. 53). These beliefs may affect a person's disability identity development or the treatment of a person with a disability by other members of the Buddhist community. A. B. Blanks and Smith (2009) found that of the Abrahamic traditions of Islam, Judaism, and Christianity, Islam has the longest history of including people with disabilities in religious practices and communities. Muslims believe all people "are born in the body Allah intends us to have ... Therefore, to dishonor or exclude people with disabilities from civil society or religious life is to disrespect and disregard the will of Allah" (p. 299).

The experiences with religion that students with disabilities have influence the development of their combined identity as people with disabilities and people within their own faith tradition. Students with disabilities may also experience stigma and judgment from individuals in other faith traditions. A. B. Blanks and Smith (2009) found that some students and families of students with disabilities experience "internalized blame and shame" (p. 301), which can be informed by faith-based traditions. This shame can contribute to a lack of participation in accommodation decision processes and a distancing from a disabled identity. As a result, some students may resist disclosing their disability, seeking resources, or even identifying as disabled. In order to combat the stigma that can be associated with disabilities and create strong partnerships with a variety of faith traditions, DRO staff and other student affairs professionals should work closely with staff of the religious life office or organizations on and off campus to support students from religious or spiritual backgrounds who are processing conflicting aspects of their identity in college.

Sexual Orientation

Several authors note the dearth of research on queer, lesbian, gay, and bisexual (LGB) students with disabilities in higher education (e.g., Duke, 2011; Fraley, Mona, & Theodore, 2007; Harley et al., 2002; R. A. Miller, 2015). Slightly more research has been conducted with students in secondary education who are both LGB and have disabilities and on the general disabled LGB population, although most of this research has tended to focus solely on the sexual experiences of LGB people with disabilities (Harley et al., 2002). Duke (2011) found that "only a handful of studies explore the intersection of disability, [homo]sexuality, and gender identity/expression" (p. 3). The limited literature on this topic indicates that disabled queer students face barriers on campus and within the classroom.

LGB students with disabilities may be at greater risk of experiencing academic difficulties than their heterosexual peers with disabilities (Morgan, Mancl, Kaffar, & Ferreira, 2011). Duke (2011) explained that LBG "youth with disabilities commonly experience prejudice and discrimination—based on sexuality, gender identity/expression, and disability" (p. 37). This discrimination occurs in educational settings, medical and mental health clinics, religious settings, and with their peers and families. As a result of the combined influences of ableism and heterosexism, LGB students with disabilities experience an "increased risk of major depression, generalized anxiety disorder, conduct disorder, substance abuse/dependence, multiple disorders, suicidal ideation, and suicide attempts" (Duke, 2011, p. 38).

Many lesbian, gay, and bisexual individuals experience discrimination from medical and mental health providers (Duke, 2011), and as a result, LGB students with disabilities face barriers to diagnosis and treatment of their disability that their heterosexual peers do not. This difference means that fewer LGB students enter college with complete documentation of their disabilities and thus will experience greater barriers in accessing treatment and support for management of their disabilities while in college. Students attending institutions in rural or low-population-density areas or states with a limited number of medical and mental health providers are especially at risk for receiving inadequate care (Duke, 2011).

Henry, Fuerth, and Figliozzi (2010) found that LGB students with disabilities reported facing heterosexist barriers in the campus environment. Students felt they could not be open with the DRO staff about their sexual orientation and that staff providing access services were not open to discussing this aspect of students' lives. Thus, staff of DROs with a social justice focus will collaborate with staff of the campus LGB support office (if such an office exists) and provide training for disability support staff in identity development of LGB individuals. Institutional staff should develop supports for students with disabilities who are in the process of coming out, as Harley et al. (2002) found that this population is especially prone to withdrawing from college.

Inside the classroom, R. A. Miller (2015) found that queer students with disabilities disclosed their queer and disabled identities strategically and contextually. Furthermore, participants in R. A. Miller's study expressed the need to manage others' perceptions of their identities. Students described maintaining a "balancing act" (p. 387) and frequently made decisions about disclosure of their disability identity based on whether the individual or environment was safe and comfortable for other identities. "At times," R. A. Miller (2015) noted, "students deployed their identities strategically to advocate for social change or provide visibility for minority identity groups" (p. 386). Students also reported experiencing microaggressions and discrimination related to their disabilities within the classroom from other students, faculty, and teaching assistants. R. A. Miller's findings highlight the importance of having faculty who are queer and/or disabled. Faculty members' disclosure of their queer and/or disabled status is critical in creating a safe classroom environment. In addition, R. A. Miller's research reaffirmed the importance of diversity training for faculty and teaching assistants.

Areas for Future Research

Henry et al. (2010) found that "individuals with multiple minority status have been underrepresented within the literature because this line of research has typically been limited to a single viewpoint which oversimplifies and produces generalized conclusions that do not account for complex exchanges between multiple identities" (p. 379). While in this chapter we have worked to complicate this oversimplified narrative, we only were able to discuss aspects of a person's identity one at a time. We also did not explore the complexities of intragroup diversity and were limited by the paucity of research focusing on people with disabilities and their multiple identities.

Thorne, McCormick, and Carty (2009) found that the dominant narratives of White, cisgender, upper-class, and able-bodied individuals continue to be perpetuated through the "scholarly research [that] is prioritized and conducted and policies [that] are supported" (p. 8). All of the aspects of identity and experience discussed in this chapter require additional research, but some identities have been especially neglected by researchers, particularly topics relevant to individuals with disabilities who are also Native peoples, transgender people, LGB people, and religious minority students. Although there is a body of literature on socioeconomic status and disability in K-12 education, research in the postsecondary setting is limited. We urge researchers to pay particular attention to these populations as they study college students with disabilities. In summary, students with disabilities are demographically diverse, hold intersecting identities, and have a wide range of functional limitations, making it imperative that all members of campus communities employ a holistic perspective in their work with students with disabilities.

Implications for Higher Education

Hackman (2008) found that in order to create inclusive resources that can mitigate the effects of "socially constructed barriers" (p. 40), educators and administrators should "consider students' racial, ethnic, gender, class, sexual orientation, religious, and disability identities" (p. 40) in relationship to those societal barriers. Without these considerations it is difficult to address the holistic needs of an individual in order to provide an equitable chance for a successful academic experience. This holistic approach to supporting students with disabilities is in line with the social justice perspective of disability that

> considers the interaction of impairment with other social identities, such as gender, sexual orientation, or ethnicity, as well as the environmental contexts in which individuals find themselves and the specific nature of their impairments; in this way, individuals are viewed as multidimensional and unique. (Evans, 2008, p. 15)

Institutions of postsecondary education should consider implementing practices, structures, and policies that support the diverse students with disabilities who are considering and attending the institution. We outline socially just practices for supporting students with multiple minoritized identities in Table 5.1.

TABLE 5.1. SOCIALLY JUST PRACTICES FOR SUPPORTING STUDENTS WITH MULTIPLE IDENTITIES

Practice	Examples	Rationale
Place the DRO in the same location as offices for students with additional or other minoritized identities.	At Penn State, Student Disability Services is part of the larger Educational Equity unit, which includes veteran, multicultural, and TRIO programs. It is located in the same building as the LGBTQA center and Center for Women Students.	The title, physical placement, and institutional alignment of the office all send messages regarding the philosophy of the campus in supporting students, faculty, and staff with disabilities. Placing the DRO in the student health center can increase stigma and perpetuate the consideration of disability as solely a medical problem.
Enhance affordable disability-related services (e.g., disability testing, academic coaching, assistive technology) for students with disabilities with minimal financial support.	Develop a relationship with the local vocational rehabilitation office and state Medicaid to help connect students with off-campus resources that may provide health care and auxiliary aids. Develop a relationship with a learning disability testing center that accepts the campus student insurance. Explore options for financial aid to cover the cost of necessary assistive technology or supplemental campus academic coaching.	Students with disabilities from low-socioeconomic-status backgrounds are at risk for receiving less diagnostic, academic, and adaptive help. Access to these resources can greatly improve the outcomes for these students.
Develop close working relationships with affinity- or identity-based offices.	Partner with offices supporting students with other underrepresented identities at the institution (e.g., multicultural student affairs, international student affairs, religious life, women's center). Encourage inclusion and representation of disability-related student groups on multicultural or diversity leadership councils.	Students with multiple identities need culturally competent support from the DRO. Close working relationships with other offices and ongoing training among the offices will improve the experience and supports for students with multiple targeted identities.
Analyze existing policies, practices, and procedures to remove cultural bias.	Use a regression-based model for reviewing learning disability documentation rather than a discrepancy model. Remove the use of pronouns from letters to faculty or incorporate a student's preferred pronoun and name into letters. Or use *they/them/their* universally in letters.	Some current practices of DROs and colleges/universities likely have higher negative effects on students from multiple targeted identities. Implementing processes to remove cultural bias will improve the rates of students who access services.

	Review imagery and materials provided by the DRO, and ensure that a wide variety of visible identities and experiences are represented.	Best practices for supporting students with disabilities are based on research that primarily has looked at the needs of White, upper-class, cisgender men. In order to improve best practices, research must represent the diverse learners entering postsecondary education.
Encourage socially just research with under-represented populations to better understand the needs of diverse learners.	Gather internal data on the matriculation, persistence, and experiences of students with disabilities. Ensure these internal data include intragroup differences based on other identity factors (e.g., socioeconomic status, race, gender). Include individuals with disabilities in the research process. Hire faculty with disability-related research interests, provide incentives for research on multiple aspects of identity in underrepresented populations, and provide funding for such research.	
Implement universal design for learning (UDL), and incentivize its use by faculty.	Provide training during new faculty orientation. Include the use of UDL in faculty reviews and reward its use in the promotion and tenure process.	Implementing universal design for learning will provide support to all learners and will have especially large gains for students from multiple underrepresented identities, including those with disabilities (Pliner & Johnson, 2004; Edyburn, 2010).
Ensure culturally relevant programming and spaces are accessible to all participants.	Provisions for universal design and accommodations should be built into programming and spaces that support cultural programming, including access to religious holiday celebrations, worship spaces, cultural centers, LGBTQ centers, multicultural programming, and women's centers. Training on accessibility should be provided for staff of these events, and spaces and accessibility should be considered an essential requirement when allocating space for identity-based groups or organizations.	Access to culturally relevant programming will increase support for and decrease isolation among students, increasing the retention of minoritized students.

The process of recognizing individuals with disabilities as multidimensional should begin with the messages the university sends regarding its inclusion of people with disabilities. These messages are conveyed through the inclusion of people with disabilities throughout the college's recruitment and promotional materials and in the location and structure of the DRO. Inclusion of the DRO as a component of campuses' intercultural or multicultural offices that support other forms of campus diversity sends a different message than a DRO housed in the health and counseling center or one housed in an academic success center, potentially a message with a greater social justice implication. The careful placement of the disability resource center can help to reduce stigma and provide more holistic support for students with multiple targeted identities. Stapleton (2015) suggested the inclusion of materials on disability in the women's center and multicultural center library. Similarly, a library maintained by the DRO should contain materials that represent the multiple identities held by students with disabilities.

Reid and Knight (2006) also found that the materials and messages disseminated by DRO staff can subtly exclude students with disabilities. They noted that many documents produced reflect "White Eurocentric notions of merit" (p. 21) and "do not affirm students' cultural contexts" (p. 21). Institutional staff should carefully construct culturally aware and inclusive messages regarding disability resources and students, faculty, and staff with disabilities and find ways to meet the needs of students whose families are not able to leverage support for postsecondary education.

At institutions where faculty, administrators, and staff understand and value identity as multifaceted, the DRO staff will employ a dynamic process that allows all students to share aspects of their broader identity and their unique experiences as students with disabilities. For example, if an individual with a disability is trans, that individual may require more support in finding a competent and supportive medical or mental health provider in the community when transitioning to college than a cisgender disabled student. If an individual with a disability is from a religious, cultural, or ethnic background that views disability as shameful or an inherent flaw, that student may require additional support in structuring conversations with faculty members and may struggle to approach a DRO that requires students to use language of disability to talk about themselves and their accommodation requests.

Conclusion

Consider two students who have disabilities or impairments and seem to be identical with respect to their disability. The students share a diagnosis, have identical descriptions of ways they will be affected in the college environment, and will be taking the same classes. Conventional wisdom in disability resources would suggest that a disability resource staff member, administrator, or faculty member will have very similar interactions with these two students and that they should require identical accommodations and support systems in the classroom. However, as we discussed in this chapter, these students may also be different in meaningful ways; they may have different gender and racial identities and come from different socioeconomic backgrounds. In this chapter, we complicated the conventional wisdom, recognizing the ways that students' multiple and intersecting identities may influence their understanding of disability, their support systems, their coping mechanisms, and the relative impact of their disability in a higher educational setting.

Discussion Questions

1. How might intersecting social identities compound or mitigate the relative impacts of a disability on an individual?
2. How might social identities affect identification of an individual's disability?
3. What training on or awareness of intersecting identities should disability resource providers receive? Faculty? Students? Student affairs professionals?
4. What should disability resource providers do to be cognizant of intersecting identities when working with students with disabilities? How about faculty? Students? Student affairs professionals? How about human resource departments when recruiting faculty and staff with disabilities?

CHAPTER SIX

STUDENT POPULATIONS

And I was trying insulin for the first time and I was trying to do trig homework and that was a real drag. And then when I got out of the hospital it was Passover and my taxes were due. [Laughs] And these are things that only affect adult students.
—Abigail, a student newly diagnosed with diabetes

A conception of disability that does not include the ways in which multiple aspects of identity and experience influence how disability is lived

> erases the widely diverse and rich lives of so many people with disabilities—for whom disability likely matters, but who also define themselves according to and whose lives are shaped by race, sexuality, gender, class, political ideology, athleticism, their favorite hobby, whether or not they like yappy dogs, and the like. (Nielsen, 2012, p. xiv)

Hence, it is imperative to understand how belonging to additional groups or populations (e.g., being a student athlete or adult learner) may influence the unique educational experiences of students with disabilities. Although we describe themes prevalent within the literature, we are aware that not everyone within a population has life experiences reflected within the published academic research and remind readers to expect variation in individual experience.

We recognize, as we did in Chapter 5, that we are constrained by the limited literature that explores the experiences of impairment and disability in conjunction with other aspects of the collegiate experience. Scholarship on disability in higher education is marginalized (E. V. Peña, 2014), and in some areas, our only recourse is to advocate for future research. We also know that our coverage of this topic is incomplete, in that student populations beyond those described in this chapter (e.g., refugees) are affected by interactions between disability and other aspects of their experiences. We recognize that omission makes invisible the experiences of oppressed groups and strongly encourage future research that examines the interaction between disability and student populations that we were unable to include.

We engage these conversations with the distinct understanding that each student embodies multiple identities and roles and "it is not just that we 'all have our differences'; it is, instead, that we attend to differences differently, making them *intersect* in particular ways" (Titchkosky, 2007, p. 3). Furthermore, we are aware that students do not enter the postsecondary environment as a blank slate; rather, they arrive with over 16 years of constructed knowledge and identity-related experiences. Students with disabilities bring with them divergent experiences of inclusion and exclusion, marginalization, stigma, accommodation, and support from their experiences of disability within the K-12 system and, in many cases, their adult lives. In fact, as we discussed in Chapter 5, students who are identified as having a disability prior to attending college may not self-identify as disabled, have an affirming disability identity, or hold any attachment to the larger disability community (Dunn & Burcaw, 2013).

Furthermore, the existing literature frequently treats disability as a single large, lumped category (Stapleton et al., 2014) and thus the commonality of experience for impairment groups is exaggerated (Mercer, 2002). Not all disabilities or experiences of impairment are the same. Researchers who disaggregated categories of disability (e.g., K. Brown, Peña, & Rankin, 2015) found that experiences of campus climate and perceptions of academic success differ according to disability type. However, common threads also exist; people with disabilities face stigma and exclusion from fully participating in a variety of social spaces, including education and employment. Following Vernon and Swain (2002), we hold an awareness of "contradictions of oppression" (p. 92) and are mindful of both commonality and diversity in our understanding of disability as it connects with other unique experiences that students have.

With these considerations in mind, in this chapter we focus on the experiences of disabled students who are also traditional and adult learners, community college students, transfer students, English language learners, students who are first generation, international students, parenting students, student athletes, students of size, undocumented students, and veterans.

Adult Learners

Age is an important part of lived experience and within the broader social structure coincides with privileges and life course milestones. For example, in the United States, age 18 is generally considered legal adulthood. Age also plays an important part in helping traditional-age students access benefits; under the Affordable Care Act, many students are legally entitled to access their parent's health care up until age 26. Furthermore, as people age, their potential to acquire impairments (e.g., hearing loss) increases. In this book, we define traditional-age college students as those who enter postsecondary education between the ages of 18 and 24; we consider adult learners those who enter or return to postsecondary education after the age of 24.

Although we present traditional and adult learners as separate groups, we agree with Kerka (2002) and caution researchers and educators from seeing adult learners as dichotomous from traditional-age learners in postsecondary education. Specifically, Kerka noted numerous overlaps in experience and barriers based largely on the ecological factors in the life of the individual (e.g., identity factors discussed in Chapter 5). For example, theoretical frameworks often assume adult learners will be self-directed; however, "power differences based on race, gender, class, sexual orientation, and disability can limit adults' autonomy" (Kerka, 2002, p. 3), which can, in turn, affect self-direction and self-efficacy.

It is difficult to ascertain the prevalence of adult learners with disabilities, as few national data sets or longitudinal studies track adult learners with the same precision as they do high school students with disabilities (e.g., National Longitudinal Transition Study-2). Rather, data available on adult learners are primarily a snapshot in time. For example, according to the National Center for Education Statistics (NCES, 2016a), in fall 2013 approximately 13% of students at four-year institutions, 27% of students at public two-year institutions, and 53% of students at private two-year institutions were over the age of 25. However, these data describe only the prevalence of adult learners and the type of postsecondary institutions they are likely to attend; NCES does not provide information on the prevalence of adult learners with disabilities. Digging deeper into NCES reports, in the 2011–12 academic year, based on student self-reporting, 18.8% of learners with disabilities were age 24 to 29 and 35.8% of learners with disabilities were age 30 or older (NCES, 2015). Therefore, it is important for practitioners working with adult learners to consider disability, particularly impairments that typically have later-life onset.

The literature on adult education, inclusive of research focused on adult college students, rarely considers disability (Rocco & Delgado, 2011). As discussed in Chapter 4, there may be significant variance in the experiences of individuals with disabilities based on age and recency of diagnosis. However, as individuals age, their understanding of interdependence and use of social supports also changes. Baldrige and Swift (2013) explained, "Growing evidence indicates that older persons have more positive attitudes about seeking help and are more willing to seek it than younger persons ... younger people are more likely to embrace social roles that emphasize strength and self-reliance" (p. 750). Hence, adult or nontraditional learners may be more likely to seek out support from the disability resource office (DRO) and other campus support systems (e.g., tutoring services) while younger students may be less likely.

Although adult learners may be more likely to seek assistance from DROs, adult learners also face unique challenges in postsecondary education. First, adult learners may have completed secondary education without the support of an individualized learning plan, either because they attended prior to widespread implementation of the Individuals with Disabilities Education Act or because they have developed their disability later in life. The lack of prior experience with educational accommodations, combined with a break from the academic environment, may cause difficulty in that adult learners are not able to anticipate or describe the academic impacts of their disabilities. Second, adult learners with learning disabilities may have difficulty articulating their experience (Goss, 2001). Third, "adults with learning disabilities often come back to school with memories of classroom trauma and a history of academic failure which result in great anxiety at the prospect of reentering" (Goss, 2001, p. 8). Finally, as a product of having greater life experience, adult learners are balancing multiple life roles such as parent, spouse/partner, caregiver, employee, or veteran that traditional-age students may not have experienced (Ross-Gordon, 2011). Those working with adult learners with disabilities must be aware of multiple roles and that negative experiences within secondary education, which occurred many years ago, may affect self-esteem and goals and generate stress.

Community College Students

The overwhelming majority of students with disabilities who enroll in postsecondary education attend two-year colleges (Newman, Wagner, Cameto, & Knokey, 2009; Sanford et al., 2011). Data from the U.S. Department of

Education indicated that 20% of students identified with a disability in high school went on to take classes at a community college. In comparison, 9% of students identified with a disability in high school went on to attend a four-year college or university (Wagner, Newman, Cameto, Garza, & Levine, 2005). Enrollment differences by degree focus hold across disability category and type. National data indicated that six years after high school graduation, 41% of students with a learning disability attended a two-year or community college, whereas 15.5% attended a four-year college. This difference in institutional enrollment is also evident for students with intellectual disabilities (21.5% two-year, 6.3% four-year), autism (32.6% two-year, 15.5% four-year), emotional disturbance (29.7% two-year, 7.6% four-year), and orthopedic impairment (45.5% two-year, 22.5% four-year; Sanford et al., 2011). Hence, practitioners and faculty working at two-year institutions support a larger number of students with disabilities, and due to access-based institutional missions and open enrollment admissions policies, students who attend community colleges often have a wider range of functional limitations.

Several factors may contribute to the significantly higher enrollment of students with disabilities at community colleges, including lower tuition, closer proximity to home, less rigorous admissions standards, smaller class size, intent to transfer to a four-year institution, career training, and an educational environment focused on teaching rather than research. Students with disabilities who attend community colleges may share other identities and unique experiences discussed in Chapter 5 and this chapter (e.g., they may be first-generation, parents, and/or adult learners). In addition, a portion of students with disabilities at two-year institutions transfer to four-year institutions; a successful transfer experience is a critical aspect of persistence for students with disabilities who are seeking a bachelor's degree. The strongest predictors of successful transfer from two-year to four-year institutions were the proportion of transfer courses that students took and the percentage of credits that students successfully completed compared to the number of credits they enrolled in (Ponticelli & Russ-Eft, 2009). We discuss the transfer experience later in this chapter; we also highlight transition-related topics in Chapter 15.

The vast majority of community college research on students with disabilities focuses on the transition to college or work (e.g., Ankeny & Lehmann, 2010; see Chapter 15). Less is known about the experiences of students with disabilities while attending community colleges, although there are articles that focus on impairment-specific experiences, particularly those of students with learning disabilities (Norton, 1997), students with autism (e.g., K. R. Brown & Coomes, 2015), and those who are d/Deaf or hard of hearing (e.g., S. G. Johnson & Fann, 2015). In their review of existing publications related to students with disabilities in community colleges, Quick, Lehmann, and Deniston (2003) concluded that there is a need for research that uses participant-oriented methodologies and examines topics such as staff development, accommodations, disability-specific needs, and self-advocacy.

The literature on the success of students with disabilities in community colleges indicates that full-time enrollment, degree aspirations, meeting with academic advisors, and strong grade point averages (GPAs) were positively related to persistence for students with disabilities (Mamiseishvili & Koch, 2012). Furthermore, similar to students with disabilities at four-year institutions, faculty members' knowledge of the accommodations process and attitudes toward students with disabilities (Dona & Edmister, 2001), as well as access to accommodations and campus administrative support (S. G. Johnson & Fann, 2015), were important to academic success. In particular, students attending community colleges placed value on the availability of supports for independence such as transportation and accessible seating and indicated that a sense of belonging was important (Kurth & Mellard, 2006).

Institutional factors associated with a two-year degree focus may significantly shape the campus experience for students with disabilities. For example, as very few two-year campuses offer residential living, most students with disabilities are commuter or nonresidential students. Garland (2015) outlined supports for commuter students with disabilities and noted that siloed institutional structures frequently place disability resource offices and commuter services offices in different locations. Garland noted that practitioners in both functional areas have "several common roles such as helping students navigate campus and community resources, helping students access and engage campus environments, advocating for students when they experience administrative barriers, and helping faculty and staff understand the needs of the students they serve" (p. 57). Garland also suggested cross-training practitioners as one method of improving the experience of students with disabilities.

Moving from student affairs to academic affairs, we agree with Rodas (2016): disability studies courses are a valuable part of the curriculum within the two-year setting because they are a method of building disability culture and also a means of educating students about important social justice topics such as stigma and oppression. Specifically, Rodas, a faculty member and disability scholar, suggested,

> With rare exceptions, community college students who openly identify as disabled are just as likely as their nondisabled peers to reenact oppressive social messages about disability: some perform "supercrip" narratives of independence and ability while others approach

me apologetically about accommodations. In the first instance, the student approaches the learning environment with an expectation of being dismissed or patronized; in the latter, the accommodation is implicitly understood as a "favor," an imposition on the professor rather than an ordinary fact of the classroom. In both instances, there is a denial of the inherent validity of disability as culture and identity and an unconscious rejection of disability as a regular and valuable aspect of human diversity, a feature of urban community college culture that is far less prevalent in the more privileged environments of traditional four-year colleges. (p. 191)

The inclusion of disability studies courses into community college curricula, as part of liberal arts course work and diversity workforce development initiatives, serves critical social justice functions of expanding awareness of disability and building disability community.

Transfer Students

Students with disabilities who transferred were concerned about their self-advocacy skills, access to technology, ability to make new friends, availability of educational accommodations and services for students with disabilities, and the transfer process (L. C. Burgstahler, Crawford & Acosta, 2001). Similarly, disability resource professionals also indicated that poor study skills, inadequate academic preparation, poor self-advocacy skills, lack of financial support, and differences in social life were areas of concern for transfer students (L. C. Burgstahler et al., 2001). Professional disability resource providers also indicated that a lack of role models and mentors with disabilities, moving away from home, and adjusting to a larger, less personal environment were concerns that students did not identify but created challenges for students who transferred from two-year institutions (L. C. Burgstahler et al., 2001).

Disability resource professionals working at four-year institutions can support transfer students by educating admissions staff and making sure that the disability resource office is included on campus tours, attending two-year transfer fairs and creating relationships with disability resource colleagues working at two-year institutions, and creating resources designed to assist transfer students with navigating the new environment. Disability resource professionals working at two-year institutions can support the transfer process by educating themselves about policies of four-year institutions within their geographic region and following best practices regarding documentation standards so that students will not experience a decrease in accommodations when moving into the four-year environment (L. C. Burgstahler et al., 2001).

English Language Learners and English as an Additional Language

It is difficult to ascertain the prevalence of postsecondary students who are English language learners (ELL) and learners for whom English is a second, third, or additional language. In the K-12 system, there are 5 million ELL students (Orosco & O'Connor, 2013), and when combined with English as second language learners (ESL), approximately 11.2 million K-12 students attend U.S. public schools (Trainor, Murray, & Kim, 2016). Although Spanish speakers represent the largest individual population of ELL students, ELL students speak more than 400 languages (Artiles & Ortiz, 2002).

ELL students and students with disabilities represent two of the populations with the lowest high school completion rates and poorest postschool outcomes. Those who are dually identified (both ELL students and students with disabilities) may experience even lower postsecondary gains (Trainor, Murray, & Kim, 2016). ELL students are overrepresented in K-12 special education classrooms (Figueroa, 2002). Yet there is a paucity of literature and comprehensive research studies addressing the overrepresentation of ELL students in special education (Orosco & O'Connor, 2013; Trainor et al., 2016). Furthermore, it is unclear "whether this overrepresentation is the result of actual learner disabilities or whether it is the result of testing procedures that cannot distinguish between disability and bilingualism as causes of learning difficulties" (Figueroa, 2002, p. 51).

Learning disabilities may be more evident in a second or additional language than in an individual's native language (A. R. Erickson, 2008; Schwarz & Terrill, 2000; Shulman, 2002). This may occur because

> a learning disability may be so subtle in a first language that it is masked by an individual's compensatory strategies, e.g., getting general information through the overall context when specific words or concepts are not understood, and substituting known words for words that cause difficulty. (Schwarz & Terrill, 2000, para. 3)

Artiles and Ortiz (2002) and Shulman (2002) found that it is particularly difficult for ELL students with disabilities to be tested accurately for learning disabilities. Artiles and Ortiz went on to state that assessment personnel need to carefully select testing measurements that will accurately diagnose disabilities and not "rely solely on standardized tests normed on monolingual, middle-class White students or even standardized tests normed on bilingual populations" (p. 19).

Figueroa (2002) encouraged testing providers to rely more heavily on observations than on standardized testing measures. Specifically, he recommended,

"Observe the English language learner's behavior and functioning in multiple contexts, observe longitudinally, and rely principally on informed professional judgment in reaching diagnostic conclusions" (p. 51). Figueroa also found that translated tests, regardless of quality, show empirically significant deviations in scores and should not be used for the purposes of diagnosing learning disabilities. Schwarz and Terrill (2000) recommended that providers interview learners and collect information about their work in cases where students are referred for testing for a problem that has persisted over time and has "resisted normal instruction" (para. 11).

Schwarz and Terrill (2000) recommended the following strategies for instructors to support ESL students with learning disabilities:

- Provide highly structured instruction and be predictable in learning patterns.
- Use sequential steps for accomplishing tasks and covering material.
- Use universal design principles, including multiple modes of representing material.
- "Simplify language but not content" (para. 17).
- Reinforce major concepts through visual cues and rephrasing.

Orosco and O'Connor (2013) found that interactive teaching methods, such as "reciprocal teaching and small cooperative learning groups" (p. 516), were especially effective for allowing ELL students with disabilities to engage in the classroom. Johnson Santamaria, Fletcher, and Bos (2002) recommended the use of scaffolding to break down tasks and large assignments.

First-Generation Students

One in six college students attending four-year institutions holds first-generation status (Wurster, Rinaldi, Woods, & Ming Liu, 2013). Low-income first-generation college students are more likely than their peers to have an impairment. According to Engle and Tinto (2008), 14% of students who were both low income and first generation reported a disability on their Free Application for Federal Student Aid. Low-income, first-generation students are also more likely to be members of other unique populations discussed in this chapter than their non-first-generation peers, including ELL students, adult learners, parenting students (Engle & Tinto, 2008; Wurster et al., 2013), and veterans (Wurster et al., 2013).

In comparison with continuing-generation students with disabilities, first-generation students with disabilities had lower GPAs, less family support, and higher levels of financial stress (A. R. Lombardi, Murray, & Gerdes, 2012).

Furthermore, after controlling for background variables (e.g., gender) and college factors (e.g., roommate efficacy), first-generation status remained a significant predictor of GPAs for students with disabilities (A. R. Lombardi et al., 2012). First-generation students with disabilities also were more likely to display risk factors for attrition, including working full time while enrolled, attending part time, and entering education as an older independent student (Engle & Tinto, 2008; Orbe, 2004). In addition, first-generation college students showed higher levels of posttraumatic stress disorder and depression symptoms than their non-first-generation peers (Jenkins, Belanger, Londoño Connally, Boals, & Durón, 2013).

Engle and Tinto (2008) identified best practices for retaining first-generation students, including a first-year experience or impact program that focuses heavily on academic support, highly active advising model, and engagement plans and programming to involve these students in social events on campus. Jenkins et al. (2013) encouraged institutions serving first-generation college students to provide higher levels of on-campus mental health services and to be aware that students presenting with "apparent learning disabilities or attention deficits [should be] screened for PTSD and depression symptoms" (pp. 137–138). As discussed in Chapters 14 and 15, these same practices can have a substantial impact on retention of students with disabilities (H. A. Belch, 2004; M. W. Hadley, 2007; I. H. Lee, Rojewski, Gregg, & Jeong, 2015) and will be especially helpful for students from multiply underrepresented populations.

International Students

International students with disabilities face several unique circumstances in U.S. higher education. It is important to note that many international students will face not only the circumstances discussed in this section but also the challenges related to ELL students. International students also may experience disability differently than their U.S. peers do as a result of differences in culture—particularly in regard to meanings associated with disability, social norms for seeking assistance with academic or social challenges, testing and the accommodations process, and financial issues. Data collected by i-graduate's International Student Barometer in 2010 (Mobility International, 2016a) and in 2015 (i-graduate International Insight, 2015) indicated that 5% of international students studying in the United States report having used disability resources.

As Awoniyi (2014) noted, "International students have at least three different cultures with which to contend when they arrive on a college campus—they have to learn how to balance their native culture, American culture, and the culture of the college or university" (p. 172). Ritchie (2013) emphasized that international students with disabilities have to navigate these new cultures often in a new language while also balancing the need to succeed in their courses. For many students, disclosure of their disability to the DRO may be difficult because of their cultural views of disability, and they may require social and emotional assistance in navigating the accommodations process.

International students with disabilities who may be eligible for a reduced course load under the institutional accommodation policy may face challenges due to the strict nature of visa requirements (Ritchie, 2013). Visa regulations "make only limited provision for temporary reduced course loads due to medical conditions, and are not well suited to students who would require a sustained reduction in course load" (p. 9). In the event that an international student with a disability requires or may require a reduced course load, the DRO and the staff member responsible for the Student and Exchange Visitor Information System (SEVIS) should work closely together in order to advise the student appropriately about options under immigration law (Ritchie, 2013). Similar visa issues may affect students with disabilities who plan to bring personal care attendants with them from their home country (Ritchie, 2013). If students plan to bring attendants, they should communicate this information to both the international student affairs office and the disability office so that the SEVIS officer on campus can assist with obtaining a visa for the attendant. Mobility International (2016b) maintains a comprehensive set of resources for international students and their advisors related to accessibility.

International students who are undiagnosed or underdocumented when they arrive in the United States may face barriers to providing documentation required by some institutions in order to receive accommodations. As with the experiences of ELL students, testing that many international students receive in the United States will be inaccurate because it is not administered in their native language. Furthermore, medical professionals, including those who do educational testing, may have limited cultural competence and may ask culturally insensitive questions. The experience of international students with disabilities is an important area for future research as higher education becomes increasingly globalized.

Parenting Students

Muccigrosso, Scavarda, Simpson-Brown, and Thalacker (1991) and K. H. Jones, Domenico, and Valente (2006) noted limited research on individuals with disabilities in education who are also pregnant or are parents. In their 1991 work, Muccigrosso et al. indicated that students in K-12 special education experience higher rates of teenage pregnancy and at a younger median age than teenagers in the nondisabled population. As a result, more students with disabilities may be accessing higher education as parenting students than their peers (V. Brown & Nichols, 2012). This factor may also result in more students with disabilities entering postsecondary education at a later age, as V. Brown and Nichols (2012) noted that parenting students often return to school as adult learners. The National Center for Education Statistics (2015) reported that 32.5% of students with self-reported disabilities were independent students with dependents during the 2011–12 academic year.

Bedrossian (2016) noted that the Americans With Disabilities Act Amendments Act "clearly obligates disability services offices to accommodate limitations associated with pregnancy and breast feeding as temporary disabilities, although pregnancy itself is not a disability" (p. 6). Brake (1994) described requirements under Title IX and the ADA to provide accommodations for pregnancy in the same manner and to the same degree as other temporary disabilities. For example, if a school provides excused absences and supplemental notes for students who experience concussions, then they must do the same for pregnancy-related health problems.

Bedrossian (2016) stressed the importance of collaborative work between DRO, Title IX, Equal Employment Opportunity, and human resource office personnel in order to accommodate parenting students. (We note these collaborations also would benefit faculty and staff who are pregnant or nursing.) Accommodations suggested by Bedrossian include "priority registration, note-taking/recording, ergonomic seating, classroom relocation and classroom breaks" (p. 6). V. Brown and Nichols (2012) identified policies at institutions supporting pregnant and parenting students, including parking for pregnant students, academic leave, lactation rooms, on-campus day care, parenting guides, and funding for subsidized child care.

There is a paucity of research on pregnant or parenting students with disabilities in education, with existing studies focusing on students in the K-12 system. To our knowledge, no studies (secondary or postsecondary) examine the intersection of parenting, education, and disability for male students. The limited existing literature does indicate, however, the following:

- Students with disabilities may be more likely than their peers to become parents, and to do so at a younger age.
- Parenting students experience greater financial and time constraints than their peers, which can present additional challenges for parenting students who are also disabled.
- Parenting students with disabilities may be at greater risk of dropping out or not being retained.

As a result, institutions of higher education should create inclusive policies and practices (e.g., offering transportation supports, child care options) in order to support the needs of not only parenting students with disabilities but all pregnant and parenting students.

Student Athletes

Student athletes who compete in sports funded by the institution may also be individuals with disabilities, or the student may acquire a disabling condition resulting from athletic participation (e.g., concussions in high-impact sports such as soccer). Student athletes are also a unique population who may have a nontraditional campus experience, including substantive time demands in addition to regular class work, extensive travel, physically demanding workouts, public scrutiny, loneliness, and limited opportunities for anonymity (Carodine, Almond, & Gratto, 2001). Student athletes also must achieve and maintain National Collegiate Athletic Association (NCAA) academic eligibility standards. Achieving the NCAA's academic eligibility standards, in particular NCAA's high school core course requirements, has posed difficulty for students with learning disabilities (e.g., *Matthews v. NCAA*, 2001). These eligibility standards were the subject of a consent decree between the Department of Justice (1998) and the NCAA as the standards adversely screen out students with learning disabilities. Although the NCAA has claimed on several occasions that it is a private entity, several court cases indicate that the organization "operates a place of public accommodation," and therefore is subject to the requirements of the ADA under Title III (Kaplin & Lee, 2013, p. 1866). Furthermore, as we discuss in Chapter 14, students with disabilities must be "provided an equal opportunity to participate in athletics, including intercollegiate, club, and intramural athletics" (Office for Civil Rights, 2013a, p. 2). A social justice perspective encourages practitioners to consider the many competing demands that student athletes with disabilities face and work to support the whole student while advocating for nondiscrimination and access.

Concussions have increasingly become an important topic within high-contact sports, and disability resource professionals are addressing an increasing number of requests for temporary accommodations. Case law indicates that if there is a discrepancy between the student and the institution about participation in competitive athletics, the courts deferred to the postsecondary institution's right to determine medical clearance (*Wright v. Columbia University*, 1981; *Pahulu v. University of Kansas*, 1995; *Class v. Towson*

University, 2015). In all three cases, the court upheld the university's medically conservative position that the students were not qualified to play football either because their participation would have resulted in unreasonable modifications (*Class v. Towson University*, 2015) or playing sports is not a "major life activity" or an "integral part of learning" (Kaplin & Lee, 2013, p. 1357). Practitioners seeking further guidance can consult the NCAA's (2015) guidelines for returning to academics and returning to play after a concussion.

Students of Size

Students of size, also referred to as fat (reclaiming a word with pejorative connotations) or obese (in legal and medical terminology), are frequently an overlooked student population that faces stigma, prejudice, and discrimination. Although the literature on students with disabilities is marginalized in higher education (E. V. Peña, 2014), research on the experience of fat students in higher education is essentially nonexistent. A review of the higher education literature found one master's thesis on the topic (C. E. Stevens, 2011) and a general education course focused on antifat attitudes (Humphrey, Clifford, & Morris, 2015). Within higher education literature, examinations of health and fitness (e.g., Waldron & Dieser, 2010) or body image and self-esteem (e.g., Lowery et al., 2005) are more prevalent, but these articles do not include obese students as the primary participants or directly challenge dominant norms of physical appearance and attractiveness. Much of the nonmedical literature about size is found within the areas of body image (e.g., Spencer, Barrett, Storti, & Cole, 2013; Webb, Fiery, & Jafari, 2016), sociology of the body (e.g., Saguy, 2013), fat studies (e.g., Rothblum & Solovay, 2009), and legal studies (L. E. Jones, 2012; Stover, 2010).

C. E. Stevens (2011) found that fat college students experienced discrimination in three forms: interpersonal interactions, physical structures that created access issues, and places that did not feel safe or comfortable. Discriminatory interpersonal interactions ranged from subtle to overt and included sizist comments, size-related jokes, harassment on the street, name-calling, and unsolicited weight loss advice from members of the campus community (e.g., roommate or supervisor). Inaccessible physical structures on the campus included desk size, aisle width, bus seating, and access to university apparel at the bookstore. An overwhelming majority of participants reported the institution's desks were too small and described the process of trying to fit into the desks as "humiliating" (p. 49). Desk size directly impeded learning as participants described being less inclined to attend classes in rooms with small desks, unwilling to answer questions or draw attention to themselves, and not wanting to participate in activities that required movement like going to the chalkboard. C. E. Stevens noted, "By creating spaces that fat students cannot comfortably fit into, the school is communicating to students that their bodies must be a certain size in order to be the ideal student" (p. 48). Places of safety on college campuses were lacking; participants in C. E. Stevens's study reported feeling particularly vulnerable in dining halls, student health centers, fitness facilities, and specific social settings (e.g., bars, sorority and fraternity events). Notably, feeling "like they were the only fat person there" (p. 54) made respondents highly uncomfortable in social settings because they did not feel they belonged. Students' experiences were gendered; women participants were held to ideal standards of beauty, and sizism affected "fat men's ability to be perceived as masculine" (p. 103).

In the absence of robust scholarly research, higher education media coverage predominantly focuses on negative experiences of undergraduate students. For example, a 2015 article in *Inside Higher Education* described an outreach program at Bryn Mawr College that sent target e-mail invitations to students with higher body mass index, inviting the student to join fitness and nutrition groups. Students' reactions included rebuffing the college for "fat shaming" and voicing discomfort as to why student records were used for targeted marketing ("Did Bryn Mawr Engage in Fat Shaming?" 2015). A 2014 *Chronicle of Higher Education* article (R. Fox, 2014) described how size discrimination limits opportunities for fat women, particularly within science fields and undergraduate research.

The relationship between fat and disability is too complex to include a full discussion of all perspectives within this chapter. Briefly, there are varying opinions within the literature as to whether obesity is a type of disability. Here, we note that disability often has different definitions depending on the theoretical model employed and sociocultural location. For example, using a legal lens, the Equal Employment Opportunity Commission has successfully argued that obesity meets at least one of the three-pronged definitions of disability as outlined in the ADA (see Chapter 3). Conversely, some scholars (e.g., L. E. Jones, 2012; Stover, 2010) present fat people and disabled people as two separate populations that can have "complex intersection" (L. E. Jones, 2012, p. 2005) and share similar experiences of oppression. In particular, Stover (2010) outlined conceptual problems with labeling fatness a disability, including the fact that disability is stigmatized and the fat acceptance movement is seeking to reduce stigma. Furthermore, components of the fat acceptance movement (e.g., Health at Every Size) promote the idea that people can be both fit and fat (National Association to Advance Fat Acceptance, n.d.).

The concept of fitness or health implies distance from conceptualizations and stigma of disability (L. E. Jones, 2012).

In working with students, it is imperative to highlight that both students with disabilities and fat students must address oppression, stigma, prejudice, and discrimination because their bodies or minds violate ideas of normalcy. In particular, for both disabled people (see Chapter 7) and fat people (R. Fox, 2014), discrimination leads to fewer job opportunities and the assumption that the individual is incapable of doing good work. Students with disabilities face bullying (K. Brown et al., 2015), as do people who are fat (Puhl & King, 2013). There are also parallels between theoretical models used to understand disability and fatness. For example, the moral model (fat people are sinful or gluttonous), medical model (obesity is an epidemic), and functional limitations model (interventions include diet and exercise) are frequently and harmfully used to conceptualize the experiences of students in both populations. Furthermore, the themes of resistance, reclamation, and challenging dominant power structures exist within the disability (see Chapters 1 and 2) and fat studies literature (C. E. Stevens, 2011).

Practitioners can support students of size by addressing attitudinal and physical barriers (M. Peña et al., 2016). Specifically, practitioners should be aware of and confront subtle forms of unwelcoming behavior, stigma, fat shaming, and sizism on their campus (M. Peña et al., 2016). C. E. Stevens (2011) stated, "One of the most important things that colleges and universities can do to assure that fat bodies can feel safe and comfortable in the educational environment is by restructuring the classrooms" (p. 104). Physical barriers can include desks, laboratory gloves, or lab coats that are too small; some solutions are integrated seating for all sizes, wide aisles, and clothing that comes in a range of sizes (M. Peña et al., 2016). It is important to note that ADA Standards for Accessible Design (2010), commonly perceived as measures to provide access to students with mobility impairments, also protect access for students of size. Practitioners interested in learning more about students of size and alternative models for assessing well-being can consult the National Association to Advance Fat Acceptance. Given the paucity of empirical literature, this topic is an important area for future research.

Undocumented Students

The literature on undocumented students with disabilities is scarce, and this is clearly an area for future research. In light of these limitations and because undocumented students are also frequently an invisible population on college campuses, we provide a brief general overview of the legal issues, including the

Personal Responsibility and Work Opportunity Reconciliation Act (PRWORA) of 1996 and the Deferred Action for Childhood Arrivals (DACA).

The PRWORA prohibits undocumented individuals from receiving any federal public benefit, including disability and financial aid (Frum, 2007). While DACA protections have provided new pathways to higher education, they have not removed the federal and state exclusions from financial aid (American Immigration Council, 2014). Individual states, postsecondary institutions, and researchers have chosen to interpret this act as applying only to benefits that provide monetary value and have provided support by considering undocumented students as residents and thus eligible for in-state tuition (Colorado Asset, 2015–2016; Frum, 2007). While researchers have not addressed undocumented students' eligibility for protections under the ADA, because accommodations do not have a monetary value, institutions should take a socially just approach to supporting undocumented students with disabilities and provide accommodation support. It is important to note that undocumented students are likely not eligible for supports from vocational rehabilitation and thus are not able to use community resources to have necessary assistive technology purchased for them to use during postsecondary education.

Although PRWORA limits the rights and supports for undocumented students, in the absence of other legal protections, Gildersleeve, Rumann, and Mondragón (2010) emphasized that undocumented students, including those with disabilities, are still entitled to rights under the Fourteenth Amendment. Specifically the Fourteenth Amendment protects individuals' "rights to emergency health care, emergency shelter, and disaster aid; due process related to unlawful search and seizure, arrest, and work-related discrimination and unfair employment practices; and unfair housing discrimination" (p. 8). From a social justice perspective, it is important to note that disability resource providers or others working in higher education do not have a legal obligation to report undocumented students to immigration. Students who are not already DACA registered should be referred to the individual on campus who supports DACA students so that if they are eligible and wish to register, they have an adviser who can help them navigate this process.

Given that "more than 43 percent of DACA-eligible non-applicants indicated that they could not afford the $465 application fee" (American Immigration Council, 2014, para. 26), many undocumented students with disabilities likely have financial barriers prohibiting extensive testing for disabilities. Many undocumented students may also face the barriers discussed in the previous sections on ELL students and first-generation college students.

Veterans

Veterans are unique in their presence on college campuses. Veteran status and disability status are highly correlated; Wurster et al. (2013) found that student veterans with combat exposure were "twice as likely to have a documented disability than their non-veteran student peers" (p. 130). Specifically, 1 out of every 5 veterans who saw combat reported a disability, whereas 1 in 10 nonmilitary students reported a disability (Wurster et al., 2013). Physical disabilities create challenges and changes for a veteran similar to other college students with physical differences; however, mental health disabilities for veterans pose unique challenges for practitioners. Almost 250,000 recent war veterans who have returned from service have been diagnosed with mental health issues from their combat duty (Ackerman, DiRamio, & Garza Mitchell, 2009; Hoge, Auchterlonie, & Miliken, 2006; J. W. Madaus, Miller, & Vance, 2009; Murphy, 2011). Many traditional ways of treating veterans with disabilities have not been successful, specifically with invisible disabilities (Wood, 2012).

Many veterans are undiagnosed or do not meet the criteria for disability status established by the military (Mikelson, 2014), yet their symptoms include experiencing memory loss, trembling, seizures, sensitivity to light and noise, headaches, insomnia, nightmares, depression, trigger events, anxiety, and, often, a tendency to seek alcohol or drugs. These reported symptoms can impede the progress of a college student, many of whom may have families to care for, are older in age, and have never experienced any type of disability-related concern. The Veterans Administration (VA) has high standards for determining disability status (Mikelson, 2014; U.S. Department of Education, 2008), and these standards are drastically different from those established in education. Mikelson (2014) stated that a "determination by the military or the VA that a veteran did not have a disability ... does not necessarily limit a veteran's ability to independently document disabilities and receive academic adjustments in a postsecondary setting" (p. 86).

The most pressing issues that veterans face relate to their experiences and the exposure to trauma that they have had in their military work. These experiences can create a sense of loneliness and "otherness" for veterans as students on college campuses. In fact, even campuses with well-developed veteran services find that veterans may not seek any type of accommodation or support for their symptoms (Mikelson, 2014). The military mentality of self-reliance (Mikelson, 2014) can be an impediment for those trying to return to a college classroom and succeed in their intended postwar career choices.

The most typical diagnostic label given to veterans is posttraumatic stress disorder (PTSD). This label can be a difficult one for soldiers to deal with, and often traditional approaches, such as psychotherapy, may not reach veterans. In addition to the barriers to seeking assistance that veterans may face on college campuses, Mikelson (2014) found that many veterans with less apparent disabilities such as "psychological issues stemming from PTSD may receive no financial assistance from the federal government" (p. 86).

What can disability resource providers do to reach this important cohort of students who have such critical needs for support, not only in their ability to attend college (secure admission, obtain financial assistance) but in their ability to be retained, referred for support, and connected to the appropriate professionals? A study by Vance and Miller (2009) revealed that most veterans on campus were referred to academic resources, disability resources, therapy (or counseling), and veterans affairs offices; however, not all of them used these resources.

Veterans with disabilities may experience additional barriers in accessing resources not faced by their nonveteran peers. These barriers may include the high standards established by the VA for disability status, social norms related to military culture, and stigma. Mikelson (2014) found that veterans often do not understand their rights under the ADA and mistakenly assume that if the VA does not find them eligible for disability benefits, they also are not eligible for educational accommodations. Military culture also "places a high value on self-reliance" (p. 91), and acknowledgment of a disability "may be viewed as a form of weakness" (p. 86). Disability providers cannot use the traditional "wait for the student to disclose" strategies; rather, they need to take an active approach and work closely with other offices supporting veterans (Vance & Miller, 2009). Vance and Miller (2009) suggested that veteran-serving institutions consider hiring a veteran to work in the DRO or to having a joint position in the veteran support office and disability resources.

Veterans may also experience stigma on campus, including from faculty, that can damage the relationship that students with disabilities often need to develop with their faculty. Elliott, Gonzalez, and Larsen (2011) found that one of the most referenced experiences that led to student veterans feeling alienated on campus was upsetting or offensive interaction with professors. Veterans seeking postsecondary education to gain new skills may wish to continue in their work with the military; hence, they may fear being identified with an office that works with students with disabilities. Overcoming the stigma and gaining the trust of veterans may require stronger partnerships between disability resource staff and student veteran organizations on campus, veteran offices (both institutional and in the community), admissions, and orientation programs for returning veterans.

Burnett and Segoria (2009) suggested three levels of collaboration for reaching veteran students with disabilities: (1) collaborations between disability resources offices and Veterans Service Centers, (2) collaboration within organizational structures of the overall academic institution, and (3) collaboration with the community. They suggested that "financial aid, matriculation, student conduct, student health, disability services, veteran services, or any of the myriad of support services may exist in 'silos' disconnected from one another, with diminished ability to achieve truly collaborative support of students, especially students with unique needs" (p. 53). Burnett and Segoria contended that most student affairs or institutional support staff have no idea what military life is like and thus miss opportunities to assist or identify specific support needs.

Support for veteran students with disabilities should be multifaceted. Campuses should develop campuswide committees involving key personnel who may interface with veterans, including a member of the DRO. The charge to such committees should be provided by a high-level institutional leader in order to establish the directive that veterans are an institutional priority. A disability-focused mentoring program is another way to improve success for student veterans (DiRamio & Spires, 2009). Peer-to-peer support can be extremely powerful; disabled student veteran mentors can give back to their colleagues and offer them insight into unique challenges and supports that can affect their success in college. In addition, the development and support of disabled veteran student groups can "support academic and social aspects of campus life and provide peer support" (Mikelson, 2014, p. 93). A final suggestion in creating a learning environment that is conducive to optimal academic success for veterans, particularly those with disabilities, is to establish universally designed instructional materials, as suggested in Chapter 10, which would remove barriers to academic access.

Favorite Hobbies, Yappy Dogs, and Now What?

Returning to Nielsen's (2012) quote at the start of this chapter, it is imperative for practitioners to engage with the "widely diverse and rich lives" (p. xiv) of people with disabilities. Although much of published scholarship categorizes and parses out components of lived experience for unitized study (and we recognize the structure of this chapter follows that dominant academic narrative), we encourage readers not to be restricted by category-based understandings. Not all students in a particular population identify with that group or share the same experiences, yet there is value in understanding trends and patterns within groups.

We also encourage readers to understand and engage with students in a manner that takes into account their varied interests beyond the categories traditionally considered in the academic literature. We think of our own lives, where disability matters—but so do our cats, the board games on Autumn's kitchen table, the Thai dinner we shared with partners, the tennis matches and yoga practice, the audio book recommendations—and we encourage readers to understand that favorite hobbies and yappy dogs matter. Although these topics bring a lighthearted feel to the end of Nielsen's quote, the fabric engaging with activities, animals, and people we enjoy is meaningful.

Methods to Promote an Inclusive Environment

Our purpose in including this chapter and Chapter 5 is to help readers understand students with disabilities in a complex and multifaceted manner. All too often, the first and predominant thing people notice is a wheelchair, a service dog, a stigma, or an accommodation letter. Taking a holistic perspective is an important first step toward promoting an inclusive environment.

Tailored transition programs are a second avenue that practitioners can use to promote inclusion. For example, many of the student populations we have described in this chapter will have additional changes to navigate when entering, transferring, and graduating from college. Programs that anticipate and address some of these specific adjustments are methods of making the environment more welcoming. For example, a bridge program can partner one international student with one upper-level domestic student over the course of a semester or year. This program allows the international student to have a local campus guide, and the domestic student gains international understanding and cross-cultural skills. Similarly, new veterans coming to campus can be paired with returning veterans. Although these programs are not disability specific, the model could be adopted by the DRO for incoming students with disabilities, or students with disabilities can participate in programs that are offered by other departments.

Creating and fostering a disability culture on campus is a third method of creating inclusive communities that value the multiple dimensions of students' identities and experiences. Disability culture is a consequence of "the community that is intentionally created when diverse disabled people come together to affirm the community's varied experiences that nevertheless often result in shared values" (Disability Culture, n.d.), a shared word view, and often a sense of group identity. Although like many other minoritized communities, disability culture springs from a shared history of stigma and oppression, this culture also has a powerful strain of protest and resilience (see Chapter 1). Disability culture is created and shared through a variety of platforms, including literature, stories, art, theatre, film, music, and food. Practitioners can foster disability culture by including disability topics within campus movie festivals, speakers, and activities. Practitioners can also connect with the broader local disability community by making university events (e.g., theatre) accessible for all community members (e.g., provide interpreters).

Future Research

As we described in this chapter, there are several areas where further research is necessary—specifically, populations that we did not mention in this chapter, including students who are refugees, ex-offenders, and students who are attending minority-serving institutions (e.g., tribal colleges, historically Black colleges and universities, and Hispanic-serving institutions). Data on the lived experiences of refugees and ex-offenders and the campus climate of minority-serving institutions could provide meaningful insight into how to better support students. In addition, there is limited information on transfer students with disabilities, in particular the experiences of students who successfully transfer from two-year to four-year institutions. This is a particularly important topic because the vast majority of students with disabilities enter postsecondary education through the two-year system. Tracking time to degree of students with disabilities who transfer would provide useful information on the effect of first institution on time to degree. Furthermore, much of the research on students with disabilities who are parents is notably dated. Given the increasing number of adult learners and centrality of parenting to identity, this is an important area for future exploration.

Conclusion

Students with disabilities are demographically diverse, hold intersecting identities, and have a wide range of functional limitations, making it imperative that disability resource practitioners employ a holistic perspective in their work. Notably, many students do not view themselves as disabled or do not choose to seek services, encouraging the DRO to promote concepts of universal design that will benefit all students, including those with disabilities who do not identify themselves to the DRO. In this chapter, we described specific populations, but we also encouraged readers to go beyond academic categorizations in their work and pay attention to meaningful human interactions that create community. We concluded by noting the importance of fostering connections and future research, as many important populations were omitted from this chapter due to lack of relevant literature.

Discussion Questions

1. How is your campus or office working to support the needs of disabled student populations with unique experiences?
2. Which student populations on your campus may be underserved under current processes and procedures?
3. Which offices does the DRO on your campus currently partner with? Who should those partnerships be expanded to?
4. How might experiences for faculty and staff with disabilities who also belong to these populations mirror the experiences of students? How might their experiences differ?

CHAPTER SEVEN

FACULTY AND STAFF WITH DISABILITIES

When I started working at Iowa State, Lagomarcino Hall was not a disability-friendly building. My office was on the second floor, and there was only one elevator to get there. When it was not working—which was too often the case—my secretary called me and told me I had to work at home. Those in charge of physical plant decided to replace the elevator one summer, but it was six weeks into the fall semester before it was done. They gave me a temporary office on the first floor, but I had no access to the second floor main department offices, our mailboxes, or any of my books and files. I felt extremely isolated. The building also lacked push buttons on the doors, and it was impossible to open the heavy doors since my wheelchair pushed backward every time I tried. I had to wait for someone to come along to open the door for me. Many classrooms were arranged in ways that did not allow me to get to the front of the room without having students help me by moving the furniture. During the winter, the sidewalks were generally shoveled, but the parking lot wasn't plowed very well. It was very difficult to get through the snow to get to the sidewalk and into my building. There were a number of times I was stuck in the snow until someone came by to help push me out of the snowbank. The worst part was there was no one to contact about these problems. Human Resources was supposed to assist faculty with disabilities, but in reality, they knew very little about the issues and how to fix them. Luckily I became friends with the student DRO coordinator, and he informally took care of issues such as these for me. Without his assistance, I am not sure I would have stayed at Iowa State.

—Nancy, faculty member

We acknowledge with gratitude the assistance of Susan R. Rankin in providing portions of her data set and analyses for use in this chapter.

Conversations about disabled faculty and staff on university campuses are rare; when they happen in formal university contexts, they are likely to be about preventing workplace injury and managing the return to work of those who acquired injuries or, less frequently, accommodating existing staff and faculty members who acquire disabilities after employment. In addition to these populations and concerns, we now have younger employees entering the higher education workforce whose schooling, life experiences, and expectations were expanded by the ADA. With equitable hiring and accommodation policies, the population of disabled higher education employees is likely to increase. However, conversations about faculty and staff with disabilities have yet to fully recognize this shift. As Goodwin and Morgan (2012) wrote, despite (relatively) clear procedures for students with disabilities, "few models exist for parallel accommodation to promote the success of faculty members with disabling illnesses" (para. 5); even fewer conversations occur regarding staff members with disabilities. Furthermore, few of these conversations come from a social justice perspective.

In this chapter, we take a social justice perspective, assembling data from a broad range of sources within and outside higher education to provide insight into the experiences of disabled higher education staff and faculty and provide recommendations for ways to create more inclusive environments that support the success of these members of campus communities. Social justice calls on us to be concerned with all members of our communities; this chapter begins to bring disabled staff and faculty into the conversation about inclusive campuses.

Information as basic as the numbers of staff and faculty with disabilities working in higher education is unknown (Anderson, 2007; Olkin, 2011a), and estimates are, most often, just extrapolations from larger population data about employment rates of people with disabilities, which indicate vast under-employment of this population (Brault, 2012). A small exception to this lack of data exists in the sciences, because the National Science Foundation (NSF) tracks the disability status of science and engineering doctorate holders working as academics, including research and teaching faculty, department chairs, deans, provosts, and presidents. Using a stringent definition of disability, the NSF reported that in 2013, approximately 7.3% of science and engineering doctorate holders working in higher education were considered disabled (National Science Foundation, 2015; percentages are calculated from data presented in Table 9–20). NSF data also show that unemployment is higher among scientists and engineers with disabilities than those without: 31.0% of scientists and engineers with disabilities were not in the labor force, 5.2% were unemployed, and only 63.8% were employed, versus 13.5% not in the labor force, 2.9% unemployed, and 83.5% employed for those without disabilities.

According to the NSF, in 2012 (the most current available data), across all disciplines, 5.0% of doctorates were awarded to students with disabilities (percentage calculated from data presented in Table 7–6).

Disabled staff and faculty face multiple challenges on campus; they also have the ability to provide counternarratives about the place of people with disabilities in the world. Although Anderson (2006) wrote specifically about disabled faculty and the classroom, his point extends to the influence of all university employees who "engage the political by living with inaccessible buildings, attitudes, and policies ... Teachers with disabilities live out a highly personal and embodied politics of resistance while serving as a guide to students in the classroom" (p. 375). Anderson argued that when students encounter faculty with disabilities, they inherently engage in experiential education as disability becomes not "an abstract issue but ... a living document" (p. 376).

In this chapter, we explore the experiences of staff and faculty members through multiple lenses, including those of human resource and legal perspectives. We then review empirical literature and first-person accounts of disabled faculty and staff who work in higher education. We specifically focus on policies, training, and campus climate and provide suggestions for ways to make college campuses places where staff and faculty can have successful careers.

Perspectives on Disabled Faculty and Staff

Staff and faculty members who have or acquire disabilities are rarely studied in research on disability in higher education. While later in this chapter we cover material that specifically addresses their experiences, we start by reviewing human resource and legal perspectives pertaining to employees in general. Neither of these perspectives has a social justice focus, but both drive many of the policies and practices that shape the experiences of disabled staff and faculty working in higher education. As we end the chapter, we bring back in a focus on social justice as we make recommendations for practice.

Human Resource Perspectives

The human resource perspective on people with disabilities in the workforce takes two disparate tracks. The first examines disability discrimination and makes the argument that despite the low success rate of disability discrimination claims related to job loss against employers (about 20%), the absolute number of these claims filed with the Equal Employment Opportunity Commission (EEOC), approximately 140,000 between 1992 and 2008 (Roessler,

Hurley, & McMahon, 2010), indicates that many people with disabilities perceived a hostile climate in their current or former workplaces. In particular, people with more stigmatized forms of impairment (e.g., sensory impairments, psychological disabilities, learning disabilities) file claims of compensatory discharge (a legal term referring to a person resigning due to "workplace restriction, constraints, or intolerable working conditions" [Roessler et al., 2010, p. 409]) at rates significantly exceeding those of people with less stigmatized impairments (Roessler et al., 2010). Authors writing in the human resource management literature argue that "decreasing the rate of unlawful termination is one step toward increasing labor force participation for people with disabilities as well as the viability of the organization itself" (Roessler et al., 2010, p. 408).

The second perspective on disability used in the human resource perspective is that of *work disability*, a term that refers to a temporary or permanent withdrawal from the workforce by a person with an impairment. Work disability specifically describes

> when a worker is unable to stay at work or return to work because of an injury or disease. Work disability is the result of a decision by a worker who for potential physical, psychological, social, administrative, or cultural reasons does not return to work. While the worker may want to return to work, he or she feels incapable of returning to normal working life. Therefore, after the triggering accident or disease has activated a work absence, various determinants can influence some workers to remain temporarily out of the workplace, while others return, and others may finally not return to work at all. (Loisel, Anema Feuerstein, Pansky, MacEachen, & Costa-Black, 2013, p. ix)

While the concept of work disability is incongruent with a social justice perspective on disability, it is foundational to human resource approaches to disability and thus highly influential in understanding the experiences of disabled faculty and staff in the workplace.

Loisel and Côté (2013) argued that the ability and willingness to return to work is the result of an interaction of multiple factors: (a) employees' psychosocial traits (e.g., self-efficacy, coping strategies, social support); (b) attitudinal, organizational, and physical aspects of the workplace; (c) health care–related factors (e.g., the impairment itself, medical practitioners' attitudes about the impairment and return to work); and (d) laws, policies, and regulations regarding insurance (both medical and disability) and disability documentation.

Loisel and Côté (2013) made the point that "the negative health and well-being impact of work disability cannot be solved by measures directed towards the workers. System and social disability determinants have been described as having a 'toxic' influence on workers' psychological state" (p. 64), and thus their ability to return to work. Conversely, the actual physical diagnosis by itself has minimal predictive value in determining the ability of an employee to return to work.

The work disability model, while problematic because it explicitly links disability with the inability to work and primarily considers injuries and illnesses that arise within the context of work, is useful in that it recognizes multiple factors beyond impairment as influential in people's ability and willingness to work. The most current versions of work disability models make clear that no forms of impairment inherently prevent people from being effective in the workplace and identify multiple factors that can influence disabled staff and faculty members' success on campus (Costa-Black, Feuerstein, & Loisel, 2013). (Readers interested in gaining a greater understanding of contemporary models of work disability are directed to Costa-Black et al., 2013.)

Legal Perspectives

The legal landscape for people with disabilities is shaped primarily by federal legislation and numerous court cases refining interpretations of legislation. Most relevant here are provisions pertaining to employment law, specifically those prohibiting discrimination in hiring and termination and in the provision of accommodations.

ADA/ADAAA. Like students, higher education staff and faculty members are protected by Section 504 of the Rehabilitation Act of 1973, the Americans With Disabilities Act (ADA), passed in 1990, and the Americans With Disabilities Act Amendments Act (ADAAA), passed in 2008, with final regulations issued in 2016. Title 1 of the ADA protects people with disabilities against

> discrimination in recruitment, hiring, promotions, training, pay, social activities, and other privileges of employment. [The ADA] restricts questions that can be asked about an applicant's disability before a job offer is made, and it requires that employers make reasonable accommodation to the known physical or mental limitations of otherwise qualified individuals with disabilities, unless it results in undue hardship. (42 U.S.C. sec. 121001)

Thus, to be protected, employees "must indicate their need for such accommodation and ... the accommodation itself must not pose an undue hardship on the employer" (Roessler et al., 2010, p. 420). Despite these legal protections, ample evidence indicates that many employees continue to face discrimination based on disability (Carpenter & Paetzold, 2013).

Case Law. Disability discrimination suits in higher education have been largely unsuccessful; more than 90% of cases are resolved in favor of the institution (Abram, 2003; Anderson, 2007), a rate even higher than for disability discrimination cases generally (Roessler et al., 2010). Writing specifically about faculty,

Abram (2003) noted that cases in which universities are required to provide accommodation and in which they are found to have "wrongful[ly] fail[ed] to hire disabled faculty" (p. 6) are rare, and that most cases in which faculty sue their institutions for discrimination are lost at the summary judgment stage, meaning the judge finds an "absence of any genuine issue of material fact, or the inability of a reasonable jury to find for the plaintiff" (p. 6). The procedural requirements for a suit under the ADA are complicated and time limited, and in some cases public colleges and universities have sovereign immunity, meaning they are protected from some lawsuits. Moreover, as Anderson (2007) noted, disability claims are held to a reasonable, rather than strict, scrutiny standard, meaning that an employer has only to demonstrate that a claim is unreasonable (e.g., too costly or too difficult) to be released from any obligation to provide an accommodation.

Although historically employment-related disability court cases were difficult to win, the passage of the ADAAA, which broadened the overly narrow definition of *disability*, should make such suits more successful. It is important to understand that "many proposed lawsuits settle out of court, particularly where the defendant university believes it is likely to lose the suit" (Abram, 2003, p. 16). Additionally, it is difficult to quantify the preventive effects of legislation, that is, "the success or failure of legislation should not be measured by the number of lawsuits filed under the legislation, but by compliance with the legislation" (Abram, 2003, p. 16). The legal guidelines on these points are complicated, vary by state, and continually change with the dynamic nature of the law; readers with a particular interest in this topic are encouraged to seek information on local and current laws from qualified sources.

Reporting Requirements. In 2013, revisions were made by the Office of Federal Contract Compliance Programs (OFCCP) to the regulations implementing the nondiscrimination portion of Section 503 of the Rehabilitation Act of 1973. New requirements included a mandate that contractors determine the number of their employees and job applicants who voluntarily disclose having a disability and implement affirmative action programs for hiring and promotion of qualified individuals with disabilities, with a target of 7% across all job categories (Affirmative Action and Nondiscrimination Obligations of Contractors and Subcontractors Regarding Individuals with Disabilities, 41 C.F.R § 60–741.45, hereafter cited as Affirmative Action). The regulations apply to "every Government contractor that has 50 or more employees and a contract of $50,000 or more" (Affirmative Action, 41 C.F.R § 60–741.40(b)(1)), which includes virtually all institutions of higher education in the United States.

Specifically, employers are required to "invite applicants to inform the contractor whether the applicant believes that he or she is an individual with a disability" (Affirmative Action, 41 C.F.R § 60–741.42 (a)(1)), and again issue the same invitation to disclose after job offers are made (41 C.F.R § 60–741.42 (b)(1)). The language is clear that disclosure is voluntary and that "the contractor may not compel or coerce individuals to self-identify" (41 C.F.R § 60–741.42(d)). Employers are required to make available to the OFCCP the total number of jobs available, the percentage of job applicants who have identified as persons with disabilities, the actual number of people with disabilities hired and who accept jobs, and the percentage of people in the current workforce who have identified themselves as having disabilities.

The regulations not only reiterate existing mandates for nondiscrimination and prohibit harassment of employees with disabilities, but go further in requiring the development of affirmative action plans covering both initial employment and advancement, "including [to] the executive level" (Affirmative Action, 41 C.F.R § 60–741.43). Affirmative action programs include development and dissemination of policy statements and review of existing job definitions to be sure any requirements for physical and mental job qualifications are "job-related for the position in question and are consistent with business necessity" (41 C.F.R § 60–741.43(c)(1)). If employees with known disabilities are having difficulty performing job functions that are reasonably thought to be disability related, the employer can ask if the issues are disability related and, if so, "confidentially inquire whether the employee is in need of a reasonable accommodation" (41 C.F.R § 60–741.43(d)(1)). The policy requires affirmative outreach and recruitment for job vacancies to organizations and groups that are disability related.

The Rehabilitation Act of 1973 now contains a "utilization goal" that 7% of employees be qualified people with disabilities, clearly specifying this is neither "a ceiling or a floor for the employment of particular groups. Quotas are expressly forbidden" (Affirmative Action, 41 C.F.R § 60–741.45). For employers of more than 100 people, this goal applies within each job group.

In response to these regulations, colleges and universities (along with other workplaces) should be asking current and future employees for information about their disability status, which will yield better data about self-reported disability. Intentional outreach to diversify applicant pools and affirmative action efforts may increase the numbers of disabled faculty and staff; close attention to these figures, efforts to retain disabled workers, and employees' responses to these requests for self-identification are warranted.

Barriers That Disabled Faculty and Staff Face in Higher Education

Disabled faculty and staff face attitudinal, policy, and procedural barriers as employees in higher education institutions. We discuss these within the context of social justice.

Attitudinal Barriers

People's ability to be hired despite their disabilities and to access legally mandated accommodations depends on the attitudes of employers, because "employers are to make decisions regarding disability and accommodation matters on an individualized case-by-case basis. As a result, decisions regarding whether an employee's impairment constitutes a disability or whether an accommodation is reasonable may be subject to the influence of personal attitudes and beliefs" (Carpenter & Paetzold, 2013, p. 19).

Carpenter and Paetzold's (2013) research indicated that participants in their study were more likely to grant accommodations to people whose impairment was commonly perceived as a disability than someone whose impairment was less commonly thought of in that way. This research was bolstered by Santuzzi, Waltz, Finkelstein, and Rupp (2014), who argued that those with less known disabilities or whose disabilities were less common in their age group (e.g., stroke in a young adult) often were required to "prove" they really had a disability and had functional limitations that required accommodation.

For a variety of reasons, people with disabilities themselves often fail to request useful, necessary, or legally mandated accommodations (Baldridge & Swift, 2013; Santuzzi et al., 2014). Some accommodations are difficult to hide from coworkers (e.g., an atypical break schedule), and people may choose not to request them to keep their disability status hidden. Many people fear the stigma of disability; people with impairments related to mental health, HIV/AIDS, addiction, and even diabetes are often believed to have brought their condition on themselves through socially condemned behavior and are especially stigmatized (Santuzzi et al., 2014).

While the attitudes of coworkers and supervisors often create barriers for people with disabilities, their own attitudes sometimes compound the situation. People with disabilities are not immune from societal attitudes about disability and may internalize the same stereotypes and stigma as their nondisabled colleagues. In their review of the literature regarding challenges people with nonapparent disabilities face in the workplace, Santuzzi et al. (2014) noted that despite significant benefits of disclosing their disability (including legal protection, increased productivity, and social support), employees with disabilities frequently do not do so, in part because they themselves may not accept that they have a disability or may feel shame about the disability.

Assumptions about what a "normal" educational setting and "normal" workers are like also create barriers for faculty and staff with disabilities. Iantaffi (1996) argued that in academia, value is placed on the quality of people's minds and thinking. On its face, this value would create greater room for people with physical disabilities, although it presents particular challenges for those with psychological impairments (Price, 2011; Pryal, 2014a) and learning disabilities, as well as neurodiverse populations. However, Iantaffi argued that the presence of people with apparent disabilities brings uncomfortable reminders of the importance of bodies and "the presence of disability … becomes threatening" (p. 179). Anderson (2006) added that disability "disrupts" (p. 369) the typical functioning of higher education by introducing accommodations such as "guide dogs, sign language interpreters, and motorized wheelchairs" (p. 369). Iantaffi went on to note that even when a disabled faculty member is able to gain employment in higher education, "her body still contradicts her position and her authority, challenging the assumptions of students and other members of staff, creating a conflict between the mental image people behold when thinking of an academic and her actual 'abnormal' body" (p. 179). These authors make clear that disability disrupts normative assumptions about who is qualified to be a faculty member and how that role is to be enacted.

Potts and Price (1995), using a feminist lens, wrote of the influence of their disabled bodies on their work as academics. They noted,

> The way in which my body enters into and affects the teaching situation as disabled and female highlights how the disruptive materiality of any of our particular bodies becomes most marked at the points when we resist or destabilize the discursive norms of academia. (p. 109)

They argued that whenever academics' bodies depart from norms of whiteness, able-bodiedness, heterosexuality, or maleness, those departures are perceived as a challenge, and people become uncomfortable. This discomfort, specific to academic contexts, creates many of the attitudinal barriers that disabled staff and faculty members face, magnifying concerns present in the larger society about the ability of people with disabilities to be competent workers.

According to Howarth (2007–2008), "excellent deans are perceived as strong, hardworking leaders" (p. 758), while dean candidates who have disabilities "may face spoken and unspoken concerns about stamina, travel, and stress" (p. 759). Such stereotypes restrict people with disabilities from positions that others believe they cannot fulfill, creating a climate in which there are barriers to entry and few role models for staff and faculty with disabilities. These concerns tap into the larger cultural conception of disability. Iantaffi (1996) made the point that

> disability is feared because it is seen as a hopeless situation of passivity, lack of control and of happiness. Distress, ugliness and other negative values are also associated with it. The way society views dependency and independence affects also the academic, and, since academics are seen as independent people, this negative image of disability as a state of dependency does not "fit in" with society's image of higher education. We try, therefore, through action, or non-action, to keep this experience away from the intellectual life led within this establishment, in order to preserve this from any kind of contamination that disabled women's bodies, with all their associated negative values, might bring. (p. 181)

Although Intaffi's argument is specific to faculty, the same dynamic applies to many university employees, particularly those whose work is intellectual, while Howarth's point makes clear that concerns about disability apply to both physical and intellectual aspects of university work.

Olkin (2011a) noted that in the absence of multiple people with disabilities in an environment, disability issues often are overlooked in the development of policy and procedure. Raising disability concerns and pointing out ways in which existing or proposed physical structures, policies, and operating norms are ableist can cause a person to be "seen as a one-note administrator, the one who keeps bringing up the same issues all the time" (p. 208), and consequently being perceived "through a narrow lens as the disability person and nothing else" (p. 208), impeding one's chances for advancement.

Anderson (2007) argued that the foundational attitudinal issue is the misconception that disability is an individual rather than an environmental issue: "When institutions treat disability as something inside a person's body, they fail to see it in the campus environment" (p. 188). Anderson pointed out that while accommodations should be individually tailored, a primary focus on individual accommodations overshadows the ways in which campuses create and limit access for all.

Policy and Procedure Barriers

Structural norms as well as formal organizational policies and practices can be barriers to the full inclusion and success of staff and faculty with disabilities. Some of these are institution-level concerns; others play out across institutions and are discipline or job category concerns.

As Nancy described at the start of this chapter, one barrier employees on many campuses face, should they decide it is safe to disclose their need for accommodation, is knowing how to access that accommodation (Price, 2013). Unlike most student disability resource offices (DRO), there is rarely an obvious place for staff and faculty members to turn to for accommodation; according to Fuecker and Harbour (2011), service may be provided by human resource offices, the campus ADA coordinator, the employee benefits office, the Equal Employment Opportunity Commission office, individual departments, the same office that supports students with disabilities, or even some combination of these offices. Having to make accommodation requests, and thus having to disclose often stigmatized impairments, to multiple people and offices in the process of trying to locate the right one can by itself be enough of a barrier to prevent employees from getting the accommodations they use to fully perform their jobs, as the research on climate shared later in this chapter makes clear.

The source of funding for accommodations that employees need to perform the essential functions of their job is another organizational challenge (Badger, 2009; Olkin, 2011a; Roufs, 2012). When accommodations are paid for at the unit (e.g., department, office) level, they can easily be perceived as benefiting an individual at the expense of the group (e.g., if a department paid for an air filtering system, employees might not be able to spend as much on conference travel), leading to resentment of the disabled employee. Although most accommodations are free or very low cost (Loy, 2015), given limited department and office budgets, they can be perceived as an unfair advantage (Carpenter & Paetzold, 2013).

In part because of the dispersed and campus-specific way in which disabled employees are supported, there is no standardized or centralized reporting of the numbers of faculty and staff with disabilities, their functional limitations, or the kinds of accommodations provided. This absence of data prevents any meaningful understanding of the climate for disabled employees or assessment of the extent to which institutions are creating inclusive climates that support the success of disabled staff and faculty (Olkin, 2011a).

Furthermore, the way time is organized and valued and productivity is evaluated—both organizational issues—can create barriers to disabled employees. Higher education institutions, like the dominant culture in which they are situated, rarely recognize "crip time," defined as "a flexible approach to normative time frames" (Price, 2011, p. 62). Crip time demands

> reimagining our notions of what can and should happen in time, or recognizing how expectations of "how long things take" are based on very particular minds and bodies.... Rather than bend disabled bodies and minds to meet the clock, crip time bends the clock to meet disabled bodies and minds. (Kafer, 2013, p. 27)

Price credited Gill (1995) and Zola (1993) for creating awareness of the ways in which functional limitations may arise in unpredictable ways and for unpredictable durations, playing havoc with norms about time lines and timeliness and challenging the dominant culture's values of speed and quantity of production.

Potts and Price (1995) implicitly argued for recognition of crip time as an accommodation for faculty, writing that impairments of the body may make scholarly activity more difficult because impairments can sap energy and may necessitate alternate ways of teaching and writing that are more laborious and time-consuming. Olkin (2011a) pointed out that any meeting or event she attends in a new place requires scouting out accessible entrances and bathrooms and locating outlets that can power her wheelchair, noting that simply because a space is deemed accessible does not ensure it meets her unique needs. She highlighted the many ways in which she must spend her time that are not required of nondisabled colleagues. Price (2011), writing about the experience of psychological disability, noted that crip time can make collegiality more difficult as unpredictable tolerance for interpersonal interaction experienced by people with some forms of psychological impairments can impede engagement in both planned and spontaneous social activities.

The arguments we have raised challenge ableist assumptions that valuable work is defined primarily by quantity in a given period, completing tasks in normative ways or typical forms of interaction, and that all people can devote equal amounts of time to their work. A social justice perspective requires that we reexamine both the obvious and subtle ways in which organizational norms reinscribe dominant, singular definitions of effective, productive work.

In addition to institutional-level policy and practices, professional policy also influences the experiences of disabled employees. In January 2012 the American Association of University Professors (AAUP), a professional association promoting academic freedom and shared governance in higher education and, on some campuses, a union for faculty and academic professionals, released a report, "Accommodating Faculty Members Who Have Disabilities" (n.d., available outside the AAUP membership wall in Franke, Bérubé, O'Neil, & Kurland, 2012). It suggested policies and guidelines relating to the ADA and hiring, as well as a summary of litigation related to the dismissal of faculty with disabilities. Prior AAUP policy on disability spoke only to termination of disabled faculty. While the 2012 policy is a significant improvement, it still has notable deficits, including, as Kerschbaum et al. (2013) articulated, "fail[ure] to recognize ... that both essential job functions and accommodations are dynamic" (para. 3). Additional limitations include a focus on physical aspects of the environment to the exclusion of other aspects, particularly the technological environment; attention solely to legal compliance with the ADA's "reasonable standard" (e.g., requesting that accommodations be reasonable to the employer) without pushing universities to consider an equal access standard or to address ableism; and failure to recognize the need of some disabled faculty for flexibility and "an acknowledgement of unpredictability with regard to time" (Price, 2013, p. 5). More socially just policy would address many of these limitations, recognizing and accommodating the extensive variability in how faculty (in the particular case of AAUP policy) and staff experience impairment. Such policy would build on concepts of universal design (see Chapter 10), allowing work to be successfully performed in multiple manners, valuing quality of output over consistency in the ways the work is produced.

Experiences of Disabled Staff and Faculty

There is minimal published empirical literature on the experiences of faculty and staff members with disabilities working in higher education settings; a multicampus, interview-based study of disabled faculty and professional staff within a single state system (S. Friedman, 1993); a very small, national, quantitative study of mostly science, technology, engineering, and math faculty (Milchus & Grubbs, 2007); a large, single-institution quantitative study of staff and faculty (Shigaki, Anderson, Howald, Henson, & Gregg, 2012); and an unpublished multicampus qualitative dissertation (J. B. Williams, 2010) on administrators in higher education appear to be the few empirical examinations of this topic. What exists more robustly is a small but growing body of first-person accounts, largely published in newspapers, books, and online. Those writings come overwhelmingly from faculty members; the narratives of student affairs professionals included in the book *Making Good on the Promise: Student Affairs Professionals with Disabilities* (Higbee & Mitchell, 2009) are a rare exception to that pattern.

Personal Narratives

The writings by and about faculty come predominantly from d/Deaf professors and academics with hearing loss and those with various forms of psychological disabilities. The two groups of authors report some shared experiences (personal acceptance of the disability and reluctance to disclose due to stigma associated with the impairment) but also meaningful differences. For example, Pryal (2014a), writing about her own experience of mental illness and drawing on others' published accounts, wrote: "It's hard for me to suggest that graduate students, contingent faculty, or pre-tenure faculty disclose their mental illnesses to their academic colleagues" (para. 19) because of the stigma and prejudice they likely will encounter. Saks (2009) gave similar advice: "Hiding is the prudent course but one should recognize there is no shame in having a mental illness" (para. 21). While authors writing about mental illness do note the benefit of disclosure, including potential peer support and access to accommodations, their experience is that broad disclosure before obtaining tenure is likely to create more problems than it solves. In contrast, writers discussing hearing loss (e.g., Roufs, 2012; Tidwell, 2004) overwhelmingly advocate broad disclosure.

Concerns related to disclosure are not limited to those with stigmatized forms of disability because all forms of impairment carry stigma in some ways. In Vance's (2007) anthology of writing by higher education faculty with disabilities, almost all authors spoke of concealing their disability when that was possible. In some cases, it is because "in my mind it is unseemly to share my situation with others. I don't want any favors, and I don't want to look like I am making excuses" (Greenwood & Wright-Riley, 2007, p. 239). From a different perspective, Slone (2007) wrote in the same book: "I wanted to be seen as an integral and essential part of the department so that when the beast [multiple sclerosis] reared its ugly head my contributions, rather than my disability, would come to the forefront" (p. 269).

A consistent theme in the writing of faculty with disabilities is the challenges related to conferences and work-related travel (e.g., Olkin, 2011a; Price, 2011; Woodcock, Rohan, & Campbell, 2007). For a variety of individual and disability-specific reasons (e.g., lack of interpreters familiar with discipline-specific terminology; absence of barrier-free access to conference facilities; unpredictable physical contact with others; the need for those with impairments that heighten fatigue or restrict mobility to pay baggage fees, use taxis instead of public transportation, tip people who assist with luggage), work-related travel is particularly challenging and often uniquely expensive for many university employees with disabilities. This problem creates barriers to advancement when being known in one's field is a criterion for tenure or advancement. It also limits opportunities for professional development, collaboration with geographically distant colleagues, and the professional engagement that requires presence at committee meetings in these settings. Similarly, it also makes it harder to participate, as either a candidate or a selection committee member, in conference placement activities.

Common themes among the personal narratives of student affairs professionals with disabilities included in Higbee and Mitchell's (2009) book include significant differences in the experiences of practitioners with apparent disabilities and those with hidden disabilities, especially in the job interview process. Being able (personally and organizationally) to set limits, engage in self-care, and advocate for oneself are struggles faced by those whose impairments limit their energy or are exacerbated by stress or lack of rest; often this problem was made more difficult by writers' desire to prove they had no limitations and could accomplish as much work as, and in the same manner as, their nondisabled colleagues. Many writers, paralleling the experience described in Nancy's vignette, spoke of social isolation in the workplace and being seen as "other." Finally, those with adult-onset impairments took several years to accept that they had a disability and learn what their rights were and what accommodations would enable them to be most effective in their work.

Climate

Climate refers to the "subjective view and experience" (C. C. Strange & Banning, 2001, p. 86) of members of an environment and, as used specifically in higher education contexts, "the current attitudes, behaviors, and standards [of faculty, staff, administrators, and students concerning] the access for, inclusion of, and level of respect for individual and group needs, abilities, and potential" (Rankin & Reason, 2008, p. 264). (See Chapter 9 for a more extensive discussion of the concept of climate.) These quantitative approaches support the autobiographical accounts already discussed.

Shigaki et al. (2012) studied perceptions of the climate for staff and faculty with disabilities on a midwestern university campus. They found that respondents with disabilities believed their supervisors and colleagues were significantly less knowledgeable about disability than did their nondisabled peers, and compared to their nondisabled peers, they experienced the campus as less accessible to and less accepting of people with disabilities. Furthermore, a substantial minority of employees with disabilities reported harassment (20%) or discrimination (26%) at the university based on their disability status.

J. B. Williams's (2010) dissertation is perhaps the only empirical work on administrators in higher education who have disabilities. Based on her interviews with 10 mid- and senior-level higher education administrators from institutions across the United States, she found that most described their campus environments as supportive, yet all had experienced incidents in which "they were perceived negatively [by their colleagues] in the context of their disability" (p. 124). J. B. Williams also found that unless the administrators had professional contact with disability services offices on their campus, they "had little working knowledge of the ADA, and its protections for people with disabilities" (p. 125), and thus did not access services they were entitled to and that would have helped them to be successful in their work.

In 2011, Rankin and her colleagues conducted a system-wide study of the campus climate at a 13-campus university in the United States (personal communication, February 14, 2014). Included in the survey were all faculty, staff, and students in the system (see Chapter 9 for results from students). University community members completed 104,208 surveys for an overall response rate of 27%. Faculty had a response rate of 27% ($n = 8,891$), exempt staff 47% ($n = 20,513$), and nonexempt staff 27% ($n = 14,985$; note that the findings reported here combine exempt and nonexempt staff).

The survey questions were constructed based on the work of Rankin (2003). The survey contained 93 questions, designed so that respondents could provide information about their personal campus experiences, their perceptions of the campus climate, and their perceptions of the university's institutional actions, including administrative policies and academic initiatives regarding diversity issues and concerns. The survey was available in both online and pencil-and-paper formats and was offered in English at all campuses, as well as in Spanish and Mandarin at several campuses that requested the additional languages. Some limitations to the generalizability of the data existed, including that respondents self-selected to participate. Moreover, since the university did not collect data regarding disability status, it cannot be determined if the responses from people with disabilities are generalizable to all people with disabilities in the university system.

Of the 8,698 faculty members who responded to the survey, 15.1% ($n = 1,315$) indicated they had one or more disabilities or medical conditions. Of the 51,452 total staff respondents, 11.7% ($n = 6,002$) gave a similar answer. Table 7.1 provides a breakdown of the kinds of disabilities and medical conditions respondents indicated, with medical and mental health/psychological conditions being the most common, followed closely by being hard of hearing. There were meaningful differences between the incidence of particular kinds of disabilities in faculty versus staff, with staff reporting much higher rates of learning disabilities and faculty much greater rates of hearing loss.

Rankin found, consistent with the nonempirical literature, that both staff and faculty with disabilities found the campus climate less comfortable than did those without disabilities, with 8.6% of nondisabled staff indicating they were uncomfortable or very uncomfortable versus 15.8% of staff with disabilities. Faculty with disabilities had a similarly lower level of comfort than did their nondisabled peers (15.6% versus 9.7% reporting either uncomfortable or very uncomfortable). Both staff and faculty with disabilities found their academic department or work unit more uncomfortable than they did the campus as a whole (24.5% staff, 19.4% faculty), rates meaningfully higher than their nondisabled peers (14.2% staff uncomfortable or very uncomfortable, 13.0% faculty).

TABLE 7.1. TYPES OF DISABILITY REPORTED BY FACULTY AND STAFF

Which, If Any, of the Disabilities/ Conditions Listed Below Impact Your Learning, Working, or Living Activities? (Mark all that apply) Disability/Condition	Faculty with Disabilities			Staff with Disabilities		
	Number	Percent Faculty with Disabilities	Percent All Faculty	Number	Percent Staff with Disabilities	Percent All Staff
Medical condition	408	31.0	4.7	1,969	32.8	3.8
Mental health/ psychological condition	254	19.3	2.9	1,176	19.6	2.3
Low vision	94	7.1	1.1	466	7.8	0.9
Attention deficit/ hyperactivity disorder	118	9.0	1.4	674	11.2	1.3
Learning disability	46	3.5	0.5	380	6.3	0.7
Hard of hearing	257	19.5	3.0	794	13.2	1.5
Speech/communication condition	36	2.7	0.4	163	2.7	0.3
Physical/mobility condition that does not affect walking	144	11.0	1.7	735	12.2	1.4
Physical/mobility condition that affects walking	157	11.9	1.8	734	12.2	1.4
Asperger's/autism spectrum	21	1.6	0.2	71	1.2	0.1
Acquired/traumatic brain injury	30	2.3	0.3	118	2.0	0.2
Deaf	6	0.5	0.1	51	0.8	0.1
Blind	4	0.3	0.0	27	0.4	0.1

Disabled faculty members were more than twice as likely as their nondisabled colleagues to report their classroom climates were uncomfortable or very uncomfortable (4.4% versus 1.9%). However, in both cases, the vast majority of faculty found their classrooms to have comfortable climates and there were only trivial differences in the percentage of faculty with and without disabilities reporting positive climates.

Staff and faculty members with disabilities experienced much greater rates of exclusionary (e.g., were shunned, ignored), intimidating, offensive, and hostile conduct (bullying, harassing behavior) than did their nondisabled peers. Specifically, 43.6% of staff reported such experiences (versus 28.4% of their nondisabled staff colleagues), as did 33.1% of faculty (versus 20.5% of their nondisabled faculty peers). Of those, almost half (20.4% of disabled

TABLE 7.2. RATINGS OF CAMPUS CLIMATE FOR PEOPLE WITH DISABILITIES

	Very Respectful or Respectful		Disrespectful or Very Disrespectful		Don't Know	
	Number	Percent	Number	Percent	Number	Percent
Psychological health issues	4,153	59.7	992	14.3	1,812	26.0
Physical health issues	5,249	75.4	713	10.2	1,000	14.4
Learning disability	4,143	60.2	660	9.6	2,080	30.2
Physical disability	4,994	72.7	627	9.1	1,251	18.2

staff members and 14.5% of disabled faculty) indicated that the exclusionary behavior interfered with their ability to work or learn. Clearly such conduct interferes with the ability of the university to conduct its business.

Despite these very real concerns, disabled staff and faculty survey respondents as a whole were positive about the overall campus climate for people with disabilities, with 58.7% indicating they found the campus "disability friendly." Only 12.1% found the campus "not disability friendly." That said, when asked to rate the campus climate for those with particular forms of disability, notable differences were evident. As visible in Table 7.2, respondents felt the campus was far less likely to be respectful of people with psychological health issues than of people with other forms of disabilities, although sizable proportions indicated they did not know (particularly, 26.0% for psychological health issues and 30.2% for learning disabilities).

Taken as a whole, the limited empirical data on the experiences of staff and faculty members with disabilities indicate the pervasiveness of ableist assumptions and norms, lack of knowledge about disability and legally mandated protections, and, while limited, experiences of discrimination and harassment far greater than their nondisabled peers. These data validate and give depth to the autobiographical accounts presented earlier in the chapter.

Creating an Inclusive Climate

Campuses can support the success of staff and faculty who have disabilities in multiple ways. Some strategies give direct support to disabled faculty and staff, others provide training for the larger campus community, and still others require changes to policies and programs. While many of these recommendations apply to both faculty and staff members, much more is written about what supports are helpful to faculty members than about creating inclusive climates for the staff who make up the majority of the higher education workforce.

It is well established in the human resource literature that people with disabilities request workplace accommodations far less often than they feel they need to or have a right to (Baldridge & Swift, 2013; Kulkarni, 2013) and that requests for accommodations are granted more often to high-performing employees and those thought to be blameless for their impairment (Florey & Harrison, 2000). Ensuring that employees know what accommodations are appropriate for their work and how to request them (Fuecker & Harbour, 2011), destigmatizing the process of making these requests, and ensuring that appropriate requests are filled using legal mandates as a minimum, rather than maximum, standard would go a long way to equalizing the workplace for people with disabilities.

The University of Minnesota models an effective way to address these mandates. It has developed a comprehensive program that integrates services from multiple campus units, focusing on creating work spaces that support employees in staying in or returning to work when they have disabilities, injuries, or chronic medical conditions (Fuecker & Harbour, 2011). UReturn

> is the office designated to serve all employees (including faculty and staff) with any disability or medical condition requiring accommodations or workstation adjustments. UReturn obtains and confidentially maintains medical documents, certifies eligibility for services, recommends workstation adjustments or reasonable accommodations, and develops plans for the provision of these accommodations and adjustments for employees with illness or injury. As a neutral party, specialists assist employees and their supervisors in implementing appropriate accommodations/adjustments. (University of Minnesota Disability Resource Center, n.d.)

The UReturn program is notable for multiple reasons. Its philosophy is to maximize the human capital resources of the university by enabling employees to work to their fullest capacity. They found that "the shift from asking 'Who is covered under the law?' to 'What is reasonable for this individual?' is good business" (Fuecker & Harbour, 2011, p. 47). The office is colocated with the student DRO (although with a separate waiting room), ensuring seamless integration as employees and students move between statuses on campus and avoiding duplication of specialized staff. The university's disability insurance provider locates staff within the office, enabling coordination of benefits and services so that many staff members who would otherwise take disability leave are able to remain in the workforce with appropriate accommodation (Fuecker & Harbour, 2011). In addition, the office has a budget for workplace accommodations, ensuring that accommodations do not compete with other unit-level needs. Finally, the focus on early intervention and extensive outreach has resulted in far fewer frustrated employees unable to obtain needed services and creation of a more supportive environment for current and prospective disabled staff and faculty.

The development of a single-stop office for employees with disabilities is one strategy to create a more inclusive campus. There are also strategies that may be easier to implement, which we detail next.

Policy and Procedure Changes

Olkin (2011a) argued that campuses need to fund disability accommodations from a central campus source as an annual line item. As discussed earlier in the chapter, if accommodations are handled at a departmental or division level, they will be perceived as competing with other budget priorities, and disabled staff will be perceived as taking resources away from other employees. Maintaining centralized funding not only forestalls these zero-sum perceptions but properly situates accommodations as a responsibility of the entire campus community.

Including disability as part of the diversity recruitment process is a second strategy. Olkin (2011a) advocated for the development of explicit plans to "recruit, retain, and promote women with disabilities ... [into] all aspects of leadership roles, from mentors to institution president," while being aware of how the language of the job description might "invite or deter" (p. 213) applications from disabled women. Implicit in this recommendation is a call to reconsider essential aspects of the job and consider how crip time can be built into a wider range of leadership positions. She wrote that the absence of faculty and administrative leaders with known disabilities "can discourage students with disabilities from thinking of themselves in leadership roles" (p. 210). While Olkin's arguments are specific to women, the issues she highlighted pertain to people of all genders.

Many authors (e.g., Olkin, 2011a; Shigaki et al., 2012) have pointed out that few employees know how to request accommodations for themselves or for other faculty and staff. Olkin argued that "policies for accommodations should be well delineated and published appropriately and ubiquitously in print and online materials" (p. 212), while Shigaki et al. suggested that universities centralize web-based information about "disability policy and resources ... in a prominent and centralized area of the website" (p. 570). These processes also could be included in new employee orientation and reiterated through periodic electronic communication to members of the university community, perhaps as part of the annual distribution of materials about enrollment for benefits.

Systematically collecting data about disability is a fourth strategy for improving the campus climate for faculty and staff. As is evident throughout this book, data about disability are limited, fragmented, and not comparable; that situation is compounded when looking at data about faculty and staff with disabilities and the campus climate regarding disability. Without knowledge of the "demographics" of disability on campus (e.g., What are the roles of disabled staff and faculty? What is the nature of their disability? What kinds of accommodations are requested?) and the experiences of disabled employees, as well as the attitudes of the larger population about people with disabilities, it is impossible to adequately monitor changes in the campus climate or the accessibility of the campus. However, as campuses do so, "data may have to be aggregated to protect individuals' confidentiality; collecting data across campus and institutions is one way to get greater estimates without jeopardizing identities" (Olkin, 2011a, p. 213).

Disability ought to be considered in larger studies of campus climate, as in the University of California's Campus Climate study (2014). Alternately, campuses can look specifically at attitudes toward faculty and staff with disabilities and how disabled faculty and staff experience the climate, as did both Shigaki et al. (2012) and North Dakota State University's Women with Disabilities Task Force (2012).

Organizational Structure

Centralizing the funding for and provision of disability-related accommodations has been recommended (Olkin, 2011a; Shigaki et al., 2012) for two reasons. First, as we already addressed in this chapter, funding accommodations from departmental budgets can create resentment of the disabled employee. Second, "having a decentralized service structure makes it difficult, if not impossible to maintain systematic collection of aggregate data on disability-related issues or accommodations requested or provided" (Shigaki et al., p. 561). Centralized systems, or providing a line item for accommodations (preferably in combination with the office that provides disability services to students, but potentially just for faculty and staff), make more likely "a broader view for strategic planning, such as identifying what access barriers might be best addressed at a systems level (in concert with a 'social model' approach) versus on an individual basis (reflecting a medical model)" (Shigaki et al., p. 561).

Having a council or committee on disability that reports to a senior university officer (preferably the president) that specifically includes creating a positive climate for staff and faculty with disabilities in its charge also is important. A commitment to, and accountability for, creating environments inclusive of employees with disabilities needs to begin at the top (Olkin, 2011a). Having senior personnel involved is important because they control budgets, set institutional priorities, and can create accountability. While it should go without saying that such a council or committee should have multiple people with disabilities on it, the long history of decisions being made on behalf of people with disabilities in their absence (Fleischer & Zames, 2011) makes it necessary to say so.

Policies for advancement that recognize only singular ways of performing a job and that have inflexible standards of productivity that focus on quantity (Price, 2011) can be barriers to the full inclusion of employees with disabilities. Writing specifically about faculty, Price made a universal design argument, pointing out the benefits to "not only faculty with mental disabilities, but all faculty (except perhaps those few in the positions of greatest power and prestige) [of] ... a radical reconfiguration of the research-teaching-service triad, with a proliferation of differently structured positions according to need, ability, and desire" (p. 137). This argument can be extended to all employees by using multiple criteria for success and allowing as much flexibility as possible in the ways in which people perform, and can be seen to excel in, their essential job functions.

Campus Community Training

Roessler et al. (2010) made several suggestions for ways that workplaces might use training to create climates that enable workers with disabilities to be more successful. Shigaki et al. (2012) suggested that such training "provide[s] basic information on disability issues, supports, and barriers" in multiple settings, including "new faculty orientation, department in-service training, and internet short-courses" (p. 570). These trainings could be provided in much the same way as campuses (ought to) train about Title IX, sexual orientation, sexual harassment, and other mandatory diversity topics. Roessler et al. (2010) recommended "training programs and work site interventions that enable all employees to understand the origins of disability discrimination, identify its presence in the workplace, and respond more positively toward coworkers with disabilities" (p. 421).

Carpenter and Paetzold (2013) pointed out that those with supervisory responsibility need training on how to react to requests for disability accommodations, as many hold "perceptions and personal biases" (p. 18) that lead them to deny legally appropriate accommodations. They argue as well that because accommodations may be perceived as unfair, particularly in competitive contexts, it is important to make clear why accommodations create fairness rather than advantage.

One particularly important place for this kind of training is with search committees. Olkin (2011a) argued that committee members must be trained to include disability in "encouraged to apply" statements, display basic disability etiquette, and know the difference between legal and illegal questions pertaining to a candidate's disability. Furthermore, search committees should be responsive to specific requests for disability accommodations during the interview process, including forms of transportation, breaks during the day, and dietary accommodations. Price (2011) encouraged employers doing initial screening at large conferences to consider conducting interviews in private hotel rooms that are scent free and use nonfluorescent lighting. Eliminating scents, fluorescent lighting, unwelcomed physical contact with strangers, and the distractions of noise and movement creates environments more conducive to people with a wide variety of forms of impairment.

Facilities and Physical Access

Colleges and universities should presume ADA, ADAAA, and state-specific building codes are floors, not ceilings, and seek to extend physical accessibility as broadly as possible, given that most design decisions that increase accessibility for people with disabilities are beneficial to the entire campus population. Campuses also should use principles of universal design in all programs, services, and materials (Shigaki et al., 2012). Physical access needs to extend beyond wheelchair accessibility to include forms of lighting, the chemicals used in building materials and furnishings, and the ability for people to have privacy and quiet.

Support for Disabled Staff and Faculty

There are multiple ways to provide support to faculty and staff with disabilities. Roessler et al. (2010) noted that even three hours working with a rehabilitation counselor can enable employees to better understand their accommodation needs and "their employment rights and of proper procedures for requesting accommodations" (p. 420) and suggested a range of support mechanisms be provided to workers with depression. They argued that in addition to being supportive of a diverse workplace, these measures were cost-effective for corporations given the expenses of lowered productivity and greater sick day use from unsupported workers with disabilities.

Colleges and universities should provide existing faculty and staff who acquire new impairments with information about accessibility options and resources in addition to making this information available during new employee orientation. Because staff and faculty often have long careers at single institutions, many will acquire impairments after employment (Shigaki et al., 2012). In addition, many do not consider themselves to have disabilities. Iezzoni, McCarthy, Davis, and Siebens (2000) reported that 20% of people who use manual wheelchairs and 15% of those who use electric wheelchairs do not identify as having a disability. Both newly disabled and those who do not identify as disabled might not seek accommodations that would increase their success and productivity in the workplace. Such outreach must allow people to control who has knowledge of their disability status and "not link private health information to any given employee" (Shigaki et al., 2012, p. 569). Finally, Pryal (2014b) advocated that in the case of disclosure of presumably stigmatized identities, listeners should not assume that employees find such disclosure difficult and that the person shares the listener's assumption of stigma.

An excellent resource that employees and employers in all settings should be aware of is the Job Accommodation Network (JAN), run by the U.S. Department of Labor's Office of Disability Employment Policy. JAN maintains a website (https://askjan.org/index.html) that houses extensive information about how to create access within a wide range of workplaces, including information specifically for educators (Whetzel & Goddard, 2010). Information is available by type of disability, functional impairment, and general topic (e.g., aging, technology, veterans). JAN provides numerous resources on the ADA, general compliance issues, and assistance for employers and employees in determining and implementing appropriate accommodations. In addition, some disciplines and professions have groups for member with disabilities that can provide support (e.g., American Chemical Society has a Chemists with Disabilities group and ACPA, a student affairs professional organization, has a Coalition for Disability).

Conclusion

As Schur et al. (2014) pointed out, employers provide accommodations to many employees for a wide variety of reasons (e.g., requests to better accommodate family concerns, requests for specific office furniture, provision of child care). From both a social justice perspective and an economic perspective, recruiting and retaining skilled employees, whether they have or develop impairments, is in the interest of all colleges and universities.

In order to determine if we are creating campuses that support the success of all their members, we need better data on their experiences. As yet, there exists minimal empirical literature on disabled faculty, and especially staff, in higher education. Thus, a critical aspect of a socially just approach to disability includes greater support for this research.

Discussion Questions

1. Colleges and universities (as government contractors) are now required to collect data on how many people with disabilities are part of their labor force. How might you encourage faculty and staff with disabilities to identify themselves to the institution? What might be their concerns about disclosing this information, and how would you address those concerns?

2. Many staff and faculty will develop disabilities over the course of their employment at a college or university. How might your institution identify these members and inform them of the supports that are available to them?

3. As discussed in the chapter, we know very little about the campus climate that staff and faculty with disabilities experience. What would be the best (most effective, most inclusive, most complete, most accurate) way to obtain this information in your institutional context? Be sure to consider who would be involved in the development and design of the assessment, what kinds of data would be collected, how you would encourage people to participate, how the findings would be distributed, and the political and resource implications of the process.

PART THREE

ENVIRONMENTAL ISSUES

CHAPTER EIGHT

THE CAMPUS ENVIRONMENT

I think ... a strength of MSU [is that] we work in a lot of teams. ... We ... have someone in housing who does specific assignments for students, so when we have a student we go through their needs assessment and we determine what their needs are in housing and we submit that to that one individual and her supervisor. So she does the actual placement—but she might also involve others. ... We can have a barrier free room but that does not mean that it meets all the needs of that particular student. There are some modifications that may need to be made in addition. So then I will work with the individualized planners, designers, and then the facilities guys who actually get in there and actually make those adjustments. That is literally happening all the time.

—Matt, a disability resource provider

The context in which students attend higher education has an effect on the outcomes of college (C. C. Strange & Banning, 2001). The social psychologist Kurt Lewin (1935) was among the first to conceive of behavior as made up of the person in interaction with the surrounding environment. As Moos (1976) explained, Lewin believed that

> people have needs and the environment has "valences," which may or may not satisfy these needs. One cannot understand an individual's behavior without information about both his [*sic*] needs and the ways in which the environment can satisfy or frustrate these needs. (p. 20)

Moos (1976) considered the environment to be a "social ecology" (p. viii) made up of physical, human aggregate, organizational, and socially constructed components, each of which affects—individually and in relation to each other—how people adapt, adjust, and cope with the situations in which they find themselves. How environments affect people varies on a positive to negative continuum, from "actively *stressful*" to serving as "an active and positive force" (Moos, 1976, pp. 29–30). For students with impairments who attend college, the campus environment is often particularly challenging (C. Strange, 2000).

In the following sections, we examine the physical, organizational, and human aggregate components of the environment, as well as how these components have been perceived (i.e., how they have been socially constructed). We then consider how these components of the environment affect students with impairments, as well as ways to adjust these aspects of the environment to more effectively support disabled students. In Chapter 9, we examine students' perceptions of the overall campus environment, which we call the *campus climate*.

Physical Environment

In his discussion of the physical environment, Moos (1976) considered both natural and human-made elements. Natural aspects of the physical environment include such factors as weather, population density, crowding, and the way natural space is used. The human-made physical environment consists of the architectural environment, including building design, location, and layout; constructed pathways and parking lots; furniture and equipment design within buildings; noise; and air pollution.

The physical environment can be particularly troublesome for individuals with mobility, sensory, and health impairments. Individuals with mobility impairments may have difficulty traversing the campus, negotiating entrances to buildings, and moving through spaces that contain stairs or nonmovable seating. Individuals with hearing impairments may be unable to hear conversations in loud environments, engage in conversations in classrooms, or understand when emergency alarms go off. Those with visual impairments may be unable to identify pathways between buildings, read material posted on whiteboards in classrooms, or determine when snow is blocking entrances to buildings. Long distances between buildings or air pollution can affect the energy level of students with health impairments.

Given the number of lawsuits that have been filed on behalf of impaired students, it is clear that the physical environment creates barriers for students with impairments (Associated Press, 2011; Crisp, 2014; Jimenez & Rosynsky, 2013; National Federation of the Blind, 2010; Parry, 2010d, 2010e, 2011; U.S. Attorney's Office, 2013). (See Chapter 3 for further information.) These lawsuits have cited numerous violations of the Americans With Disabilities Act (ADA) that affect wheelchair users, such as sloped parking lots that were too steep to navigate, lack of handrails on ramps, and improperly placed paper dispensers in bathrooms cited in a lawsuit against Radford University in Virginia (Associated Press, 2011). Issues facing wheelchair users that led to a lawsuit against Southern University included rough surfaces and paths that may cause blind and visually impaired students, as well as students who use wheelchairs, to lose their balance; elevators that were locked at night, preventing access to night classes; classrooms, bathrooms, auditoriums, and stadiums that were inaccessible to wheelchair users; counters that were too high for students who use wheelchairs to see over; and water fountains that wheelchair users could not reach (Crisp, 2014).

The lawsuit against Mills College in California discussed in Chapter 3 required the following adjustments to better meet the needs of wheelchair users: appropriately placed grab bars, towel dispensers, and directional signs; adjusting the force needed to open doors; creating an appropriate slope for ramps; installing accessible toilet stalls and ensuring that toilet seats were at the correct height; ensuring the appropriate height for lab counters and drinking fountains; making lecture halls, gymnasiums, and auditoriums fully accessible for wheelchair users; installing handrails; and creating more van-accessible parking (Jimenez & Rosynsky, 2013; U.S. Attorney's Office, 2013).

This evidence suggests that although the law clearly specifies the types of environmental modifications that are required to enable students with disabilities to negotiate college and university campuses, many institutions have not made the necessary changes.

Organizational Environment

Organizational aspects of the environment include policies and practices to which students must adhere, the way decisions are made, how resources are distributed, and what actions are rewarded (C. Strange, 2000). These aspects of the environment, as well as the extent to which flexibility is allowed in implementing them, affect innovation, efficiency, morale, and quality of performance within the organization (Hage, 1980). The extent to which policies and procedures affecting students with impairments are reasonable and flexible certainly influences the experiences of these students.

A significant policy affecting students with impairments is the requirement that to receive services, students must inform their college of their disability, request specific academic accommodations, and provide documentation to support their request (J. K. Seale, 2006). As J. K. Seale (2006) noted, having to disclose their disability to others to receive assistance and support is an uncomfortable process for students with impairments and can influence how they feel about the campus as a whole. Fortunately, amendments to the ADA that went into effect in 2008 have loosened the requirements for documentation (Association on Higher Education and Disability, 2012b). The Association on Higher Education and Disability (AHEAD) offered an explanation of how these changes in the ADA should be used when working with disabled college students. Of particular importance is the statement that "no legislation or regulations require that documentation be requested or obtained in order to demonstrate entitlement to legal protections because of disability and seek reasonable accommodations" (para. 2). Nevertheless, "entities can require documentation though they are not obligated to do so," but a request for documentation must be "reasonable and limited to the need for the modification, accommodation, or auxiliary aid or service requested" (note x). So as this directive pointed out, it is up to institutional officials, not the government, to decide if they wish to ask students with impairments for documentation. AHEAD went on to argue for the use of common sense, previous practice in school systems, and student statements to determine students' ability to benefit from accommodations rather than expensive testing that can create an inequitable situation for poor students. Unfortunately, far too many colleges and universities still require testing and other forms of documentation from students requesting services.

A 2012 report of the U.S. Government Accountability Office (GAO) indicated that practices can have a negative effect on students with disabilities even before admission. Many parents of disabled students stated to investigators that they had trouble securing information they needed about services offered to disabled students on college campuses (Moran, 2012). The report also noted that agencies providing various services to disabled students, such as Vocational Rehabilitation Services and the Social Security Administration, lack compatible goals for students and often failed to collaborate with each other to ensure a smooth transition process for disabled students from high school to college (U.S. GAO, 2012). On a positive note, a small change that will make a meaningful difference for students who are blind or have low vision was recently made by the U.S. Department of Education, which has agreed to make student loan information more accessible by providing documents in braille and large print and ensuring that its website is compatible with accessible technology (Thomason, 2014b).

Lennard J. Davis (2011), a leading historian of disability, pointed out that laws designed to provide disabled individuals with equal opportunities in higher education settings have done little to change the academic culture and practices of colleges and universities regarding disabled people. He stressed, "Although higher education has improved in providing accommodations and services to students with disabilities since the Americans with Disabilities Act (ADA), it has lagged very far behind in recognizing and incorporating disability across the curriculum" (L. J. Davis, 2011, para. 18). He also noted that college brochures and websites seldom include pictures or discussion of individuals with disabilities. Not seeing oneself represented in course work sends a message to students with disabilities that they are not a legitimate part of society. Their exclusion from pictures of campus activities also supports the idea that the institution does not want to acknowledge the existence of disabled students.

Within the classroom, several practices create a hostile environment for disabled students. One practice that is exclusionary for Black students who are d/Deaf is assuming that American Sign Language (ASL) is universal. In effect, Black Sign Language, which was developed in schools for Black d/Deaf children in the South, is quite different from ASL, which was based on French Sign Language (Landecker, 2014). For instance, Black Sign Language is more theatrical and uses more space than ASL. In addition to Black Sign Language, other sign language subcultures (Landecker, 2014) deserve attention, especially as increasing numbers of international students are attending U.S. universities. Another problematic practice for many students with disabilities is use of strict classroom attendance policies. For students who are chronically ill, such policies pressure them to attend classes when doing so is physically a struggle; for those who have suppressed immune systems, having classmates attend classes when they are sick exposes them to illnesses that may put them at great risk (Potter, 2014).

Another concern is the failure of colleges and universities to prepare students with disabilities for employment after college (Dowrick, Anderson, Heyer, & Acosta, 2005). Dowrick et al. (2005) found that students with disabilities were concerned about the lack of internships and programs to assist them with the school-to-work transition. (See Chapter 15 for further discussion of this issue and ways to address it.)

Perhaps the most egregious practice that students with disabilities experience is the failure of universities to provide them with equipment and accommodations to which they are legally entitled. Institutional agents often counter that while the federal government mandates accommodations, they do not have the funding, from state government in the case of public schools or other sources in the case of private schools, needed to comply with these mandates. However, educational leaders who believe in social justice will prioritize ensuring that all students can attend their institution. When lawsuits are the only recourse that disabled students have to obtain accommodations that are necessary for them to succeed in college, such as the interpreters and transcription services two deaf students needed to complete medical school (Beck, 2013, 2014; Biemiller, 2013; Freedman, 2014; Mangan, 2013) or accessible technology to complete readings and assignments (Parry, 2010a, 2010c, 2011), disabled students will certainly experience the environment as hostile. Potter (2014) urged students with disabilities to carefully consider the accessibility of the physical plant of the college and how effectively the college works with disabled students before choosing to attend a particular institution.

Institutional policies and practices have an impact on all college students; however, their effects on students with disabilities are often different because they are members of a nondominant population that is often overlooked in the policies and practices that target those who are "normal." Institutional agents must broaden their understanding of ways of doing things to include the ways that enable all students, including students with disabilities, to do things. Institutions must also be aware of federal legislation enabling students with disabilities to succeed in higher education and ensure that their policies are in line with this legislation.

The Human Aggregate

The human aggregate refers to the "collective characteristics of people in an environment" (C. Strange, 2000, p. 21). How a person experiences the environment is dependent on the degree to which the person is similar to other people in the environment (C. Strange, 2000). Disabled students often constitute a small minority surrounded by nondisabled students, faculty, and staff whose ways of moving, behaving, and learning are considered "normal." Since students with functional limitations do things differently, they often are viewed and treated differently from others, which can lead to feelings of isolation that can cause impaired students to leave the institution (C. Strange, 2000).

Nondisabled Students

How their peers feel about disabled students has a major effect on how they treat these students since attitudes motivate the behaviors in which individuals engage (Olkin, 2012; Shannon, Schoen, & Tansey, 2009). Research has suggested that individuals' attitudes toward those with disabilities are often negative and based on stereotypes (Hayashi & May, 2011; Shannon et al., 2009). For instance, many people believe "that all individuals with disabilities are dependent, isolated, and emotionally unstable" (McCaughey & Strohmer, 2005, p. 90). Negative attitudes such as these create major barriers for successful integration of disabled people into society in general and college in particular (Shannon et al., 2009).

Bruder and Mogro-Wilson (2010) surveyed 881 students at a northeastern university and found that while most nondisabled students reported positive attitudes toward disabled students, they also stated that their interactions with these students were limited and uncomfortable. While 72% of the undergraduate students in the study reported feeling admiration for disabled persons, 79% reported feelings of "pity…, awkwardness, and/or embarrassment…when encountering a person with a disability" (p. 7). Twenty-five percent of the students in the study by Baker, Boland, and Nowik (2012) admitted that they chose "their words carefully" when they were around disabled students, but only 5% indicated that they were uncomfortable sitting next to a disabled person. However, students also reported having limited interaction with disabled individuals (Bruder & Mogro-Wilson, 2010). Almost half of the students (45%) in Bruder and Mogro-Wilson's study stated that they had not socialized with any disabled students. So while the results regarding the attitudes of nondisabled college students toward those with disabilities are mixed, they all suggest that most nondisabled students have very little social interaction with disabled students.

Often the first characteristic people see when first meeting a physically disabled student is the student's impairment, which they generally view as negative (Olkin, 2012). Nondisabled individuals tend to assume that disabilities explain other characteristics of an individual, such as their work habits, intelligence, and personality (Olkin, 2012). In a study in which McCaughey and Strohmer (2005) had college students generate characteristics associated with various categories of impairments (e.g., spinal cord injury, hearing impairment, schizophrenia), the students included phrases that were generally misconceptions, overgeneralizations, and pejorative in nature. In addition, since attractiveness is a value that influences individuals' perceptions of others, disabled students whose impairments affect their appearance are doubly affected by the first impressions of nondisabled individuals (Olkin, 2012).

Man, Rojahn, Chrosniak, and Sanford (2006) studied romantic attraction to peers with disabilities, giving 123 college students packets with photographs (head shots) of 16 individuals of various ethnic backgrounds, along with a biographical sketch positively describing each individual; half were described as people with a disability and half as nondisabled persons. Each student was asked to rate the attractiveness of each opposite-sex photo and complete scales measuring human motivations (e.g., power, independence, curiosity) and level of discomfort interacting with disabled individuals. While students were more attracted to those of the same race, disability did not play a significant role in attraction. However, level of discomfort in social interactions with individuals with disabilities did influence romantic attraction to disabled people. The motivational value of curiosity was associated with a tendency to find disabled individuals attractive, while the value of family suggested a tendency to find nondisabled individuals attractive, so it seems that personal values play a role in whether an individual finds a disabled peer to be romantically attractive. The authors recommended that the study be replicated with different disabilities, pictures of the entire person, and implicit measures to determine if these factors would influence the results.

In a replication and extension of the Man et al. (2006) study, Rojahn, Komelasky, and Man (2008) used the same procedures as did Man et al. (2006) but added the Implicit Association Test (IAT) to determine participants' implicit attitudes toward disability. As in the Man et al. (2006) study, there were no differences in explicit ratings of romantic attraction based on whether the person in the photograph had a disability; however, the IAT revealed that students were significantly more attracted to the photographs of nondisabled persons than persons with disabilities, suggesting that students may have responded as they did about attraction to avoid appearing prejudiced with regard to disability (Rojahn et al., 2008).

In a third study regarding attitudes toward intimacy with individuals who have impairments, Marini, Chan, Feist, and Flores-Torres (2011) explored 408 nondisabled undergraduate students' attitudes toward someone who used a wheelchair. Participants were most willing to have a friendship with a person who used a wheelchair, followed by a dating relationship, and least likely to have a marriage relationship. The differences were significant. Women were more likely than men to engage in each type of relationship; the differences were small and nonsignificant for friendship, larger and significant for dating, and largest and significant for marriage. The same significant pattern of differences existed for those who had an existing relationship with a person with a disability versus those who did not have such a relationship. Those who indicated that they would not date or marry a person who used a wheelchair (33% of the participants) most often offered the following reasons for their reluctance: too much work would be required to take care of the person (23%), social awkwardness (22%), the person would often be ill (21%), and the person would not be sexually satisfied by a person with a disability (20%). Thus, misconceptions of persons with disabilities seemed to play a major role in why nondisabled students did not wish to engage in intimate relationships with individuals who were disabled.

Social context can have a significant impact on attitudes toward people with disabilities (Shannon et al., 2009). The situation in which interaction between disabled and nondisabled individuals occurs can either decrease anxiety, leading to more positive attitudes toward disabled people, or increase anxiety, resulting in the development of avoidance and other defense mechanisms among nondisabled individuals to lessen their discomfort (Shannon et al., 2009). For instance, Shannon et al. found that undergraduates majoring in human service fields held more positive attitudes toward individuals with disabilities than students whose majors were not in human service areas, suggesting that academic coursework can lead to changes in attitudes toward individuals with disabilities.

Hergenrather and Rhodes (2007) examined differences in attitudes toward people with disabilities based on social distance, which they defined as the degree of intimacy in a relationship. Attitudes of students in a convenience sample of approximately 1,000 undergraduate students at a large southern U.S. university toward disabled individuals were most positive in work settings, followed by marriage settings, and least positive in the context of dating. The authors claimed that this order parallels the social distance of these settings from least intimate to most intimate. Women's attitudes were more positive than men's attitudes toward people with disabilities in all three settings. The authors did indicate that the findings of their study should be interpreted cautiously since the sample was homogeneous, the measure used did not distinguish among impairments or specify type or frequency of interaction, and the self-reported answers may have been biased in favor of social desirability.

Social power, defined as the ability to create changes in situations or people, has the potential to affect the development of positive or negative attitudes toward individuals with disabilities (Shannon et al., 2009). For instance, both Shannon et al. (2009) and Hayashi and May (2011) found that undergraduates who had had a professor with a visible impairment demonstrated more positive attitudes toward individuals with disabilities than students who had not had a professor with a visible impairment. Both Shannon et al. and Hayaski and May also found that the extent of contact with disabled individuals by itself did not affect attitudes of students, even when the contact was with a close relative or peer, indicating that it was expert power within an academic setting that seemed to make a difference. Hayaski and May also reported that women had more positive attitudes toward people with disabilities than did men, there was no correlation between attitudes and age, and attitudes did not differ between those who had a disability and those who did not. Based on their study, Hayashi and May argued that disabled faculty and other disabled persons in positions of authority can help students to recognize that negative stereotypes of people with disabilities are not necessarily accurate and that individuals with disabilities can succeed in influential work settings.

Studies indicate that nondisabled students are uncomfortable with disabled students, particularly those whose appearance does not fit the mainstream because of physical impairments. These differences make many nondisabled students uncomfortable and contribute to their avoidance of social interaction with disabled students. As a result, they often base their opinions of disabled students on misinformation or stereotypes that reinforce the attitudes they already have. Finding ways of encouraging positive social contact between students with disabilities and those without disabilities is paramount in changing negative attitudes of nondisabled students.

Faculty

Perhaps the most important people affecting both the classroom environment and the success of disabled students in college are their faculty. Although faculty are legally obligated to provide needed academic accommodations to disabled students, their actions and attitudes toward doing so vary (Skinner, 2007). As discussed further in Chapter 9, faculty interactions with disabled students and their willingness to provide necessary accommodations to assist these students play an important role in faculty members' success in working with disabled students and in the students' feelings about their overall campus experience (Baker et al., 2012). A number of researchers have explored faculty attitudes, knowledge, experience, and actions in regard to disability.

Faculty Attitudes. Researchers have examined the attitudes of faculty members toward disabled students themselves and about providing students with accommodations to perform more effectively in classes. In a survey conducted by Bruder and Mogro-Wilson (2010), a large majority (83%) of faculty expressed admiration for students with disabilities, but 61% also indicated that they felt pity, as well as awkwardness or embarrassment, when they encountered a disabled student. A significant minority of the faculty (18%) in Bruder and Morgo-Wilson's study were unsure of how to interact with disabled students.

Most faculty reported that they believed students who disclosed to them that they had learning disabilities (C. Murray, Wren, & Keys, 2008). They were also generally willing to make certain types of accommodations for disabled students, such as provision of note takers, taped lectures, and oral or untimed tests (Baker et al., 2012; C. Murray, Wren, & Keys, 2008; Skinner, 2007) and to provide support for disabled students (C. Murray, Wren, & Keys, 2008). However, faculty were often neutral or disagreed with providing major accommodations, such as alternate or extra-credit assignments, alternative test formats, or course alternatives (C. Murray, Wren, & Keys, 2008; Skinner, 2007) that some felt would compromise academic rigor (C. Murray, Wren, & Keys, 2008). Skinner (2007) noted that "the frequency of *neutral* responses for accommodations and the lukewarm faculty attitudes toward course alternatives are cause for concern [especially when disabled students] already struggle with self-advocacy and self-determination" (p. 43).

Skinner (2007) found that faculty members in his study from the school of business were neutral about accommodations overall, although faculty from other schools were willing to provide them. In C. Murray, Wren, and Keys's (2008) study, faculty in computer science, telecommunications, and information systems (CTI), education, music, and theatre were more willing to provide exam accommodations than faculty in commerce and liberal arts and sciences. Faculty in liberal arts and sciences and commerce were also more likely to report that resource constraints prevented them from making accommodations more than faculty in other schools. In two different studies, school of education faculty members demonstrated the highest level of support for disabled students (C. Murray, Wren, & Keys, 2008; Skinner, 2007). C. Murray, Wren, and Keys's (2008) results also suggested that women faculty were generally more positive about working with disabled students than were men faculty, while junior-level faculty were more willing to make accommodations for disabled students and encourage students with learning disabilities to disclose their impairments than were senior-level faculty (C. Murray, Wren, & Keys, 2008).

In an interesting study at a large southwestern university, Barnard, Stevens, Oginga Siwatu, and Lan (2008) found that as faculty attitudes toward diversity become more positive, their attitudes toward individuals with disabilities become less positive, indicating that faculty in this study may consider disability as an individual difference rather than an aspect of diversity. As such, faculty may see disability as a problem rather than a positive component of student diversity. The results of this study warrant further study. If it is replicated, diversity training should be designed to include an examination of disability as a positive aspect of diversity in which disabled students are seen as an asset rather than a burden.

Faculty Knowledge. The knowledge that faculty have about disabilities, disability law, and services provided to disabled students in college varies. In Baker et al.'s (2012) study, faculty indicated that they understood the concept of disability but did not have much familiarity with disability-related regulations, suggesting that not much progress has been made since the implementation of the ADA in familiarizing faculty with their legal responsibilities when working with disabled students. However, Baker et al. did find that 71% of the faculty in their study were familiar or very familiar with on-campus services for disabled students. In the study by C. Murray, Wren, and Keys (2008), faculty believed that they were knowledgeable about learning disabilities. However, they reported that they did not know enough to make exam and teaching accommodations that were appropriate for learning-disabled students.

Faculty Experience. A number of theorists have argued that exposure to disabled individuals enables faculty to work more effectively with disabled students and leads to more positive attitudes toward them (Huger, 2011). Baker et al. (2012) found that a large minority of faculty (39%) in their study at a small women's college had never or only sometimes interacted with a disabled individual, and almost half (49%) of the faculty members indicated that they or a close friend or family member had a disability. Similarly, half of the faculty members at a large northeastern U.S. university (51%) indicated that they had close friends or family members with disabilities while 5% had a disability themselves (Bruder & Mogro-Wilson, 2010). Almost half of the faculty in Bruder and Mogro-Wilson's (2010) study reported that they had not socialized with anyone with a disability during the previous 30 days, while only 8% of the faculty had socialized with three or more people with disabilities during the same period. When Baker et al. (2012) asked faculty how often they had had experience with disabled students in their classroom, 68% indicated they had limited experience, 27% said they had a large amount of experience, and 5% said they had had no experience.

Most faculty had received no professional development or other training regarding how to work with disabled students. Baker et al. (2012) reported that 17% of faculty had received professional development on this topic, another 44% had been offered training but did not take advantage of the opportunity, and 38% had never been offered such training. Adjunct faculty members, in particular, receive very little training regarding how to work with disabled students (Medina, 2011).

C. Murray, Wren, and Keys (2008) reported that faculty members who were knowledgeable about learning disabilities were more likely to invite students to inform them of their disabilities and provide accommodations than faculty who had less knowledge. Similarly, C. Murray, Lombardi, Wren, and Keys (2009) found that faculty who had received training about disabilities were more willing to provide accommodations and held more positive attitudes about disabled students than faculty who had no training. Most effective were workshops and courses, although reading books and articles and consulting websites also had some positive effects. Time spent in training and satisfaction with the training were both correlated with positive attitudes.

Faculty Actions. Attitudes, knowledge, and experience may all influence how faculty treat disabled students personally and in the classroom. For example, 25% of the faculty in the study by Baker et al. (2012) admitted that they "choose their words carefully" if disabled students are present. In Bruder and Mogro-Wilson's (2010) study, only 24% of the faculty indicated that they included discussion of disability-related topics into their classes, and 45% believed that such topics were irrelevant to the classes they taught. Being around faculty who are personally uncomfortable in their presence and ignore their social identity in class can certainly create a challenge for disabled students.

Receiving appropriate accommodations is another important factor in the success of students with disabilities. The majority of faculty who participated in C. Murray, Wren, and Keys's (2008) study indicated that they had provided accommodations for disabled students, as did 65% of Bruder and Mogro-Wilson's (2010) faculty participants. Almost half (46%) of the faculty in Bruder and Mogro-Wilson's study waited for disabled students to ask them for an accommodation, while 18% made an announcement about accommodation availability at the beginning of the first class, and 18% included a statement in their syllabus about their accommodation policy. The majority of C. Murray, Wren, and Keys's faculty participants did not invite students to request necessary accommodations. On a positive note, only 7% of the faculty in Bruder and Mogro-Wilson's study viewed making accommodations as inconvenient and believed that they were disruptive and unfair to other students in the class.

Research indicates that many faculty have little knowledge about disabled students or disability-related regulations. Nor did they know disabled people or have much experience working with college students with disabilities. Perhaps as a result, many faculty are uncomfortable with disabled students and awkward when interacting with them, although most faculty members are cognitively aware that these students deserve the accommodations they ask for and view their ability to succeed in a positive light.

Social Construction of Disability

"The subjective views or social constructions of environmental participants" make up the socially constructed environment (C. Strange, 2000, p. 22). Perceptions that faculty, staff, and able-bodied students have about the experiences of impaired individuals play an important role in the extent to which they intervene to improve the environment for these students.

Nondisabled Students

When nondisabled students were asked to evaluate the treatment that students with disabilities received on campus, responses were mixed. Based on a study of faculty and students at a small women's liberal arts college, Baker et al. (2012) found that only 31% of the students viewed the environment for disabled students as being favorable. While 45% of the students in Bruder and Mogro-Wilson's (2010) study thought that disabled students had equitable social opportunities on campus, 20% did not think disabled students had the same opportunities as other students, and 35% of the nondisabled students were unsure if there were equitable opportunities. About half of the nondisabled students (49%) believed that the university did a poor to fair job of including disabled students in social organizations and cocurricular activities (Bruder & Mogro-Wilson, 2010).

With regard to classroom experiences, most nondisabled students (63%) believed that disabled students were treated fairly (Bruder & Mogro-Wilson, 2010). In the study by Baker et al. (2012), however, fewer than half of the students (42%) believed that disabled students received the accommodations that they needed to succeed in the classroom. Only 12% of the students, though, believed that disabled students were treated differently by both their classmates and their faculty (Baker et al., 2012). When asked in the same study if teachers focused more on disabled students, more students (25%) agreed with this statement. Most students in this study, though, did not believe that having disabled students in the classroom was distracting (93%) or caused discipline problems (99%). On a positive note, 73% of the students believed that having students with disabilities in the classroom taught students that being different was okay, and 78% of the students believed that disabled students' presence helped students to be more accepting of others (Baker et al., 2012).

Shifting to beliefs about the abilities of disabled students, 87% of the students in the study by Baker et al. (2012) believed that disabled students were just as capable academically as nondisabled students. Three-fourths of the students (76%) in this study felt that disabled students would be able to handle the demands of a job in their field. However, in a study examining undergraduate students' responses to disability accommodation requests in the workplace, attitudes of the participants regarding disabilities and their perceptions of disabled people played a significant role in whether they felt that granting accommodations to students with impairments was appropriate and in how they would treat and regard persons who received accommodations (Carpenter & Paetzold, 2013). These findings are important to keep in mind when employing students who need accommodations in work-study positions or other part-time employment on campus, as well as later in the workplace.

To summarize, most nondisabled students appear to believe that disabled students are treated fairly and that having disabled students in their classrooms helps to promote positive impressions of these students. Readers need to keep in mind, however, that perceptions of the experiences of disabled students by nondisabled students are often based on minimal contact and knowledge about how disabled students are actually treated.

Faculty

Researchers have determined that faculty members have varying perceptions of the environment affecting disabled students. In a study conducted at a small women's college on the East Coast, 56% of the faculty believed that the climate for disabled students was favorable; however, the mean rating ($M = 3.44$ out of 5) was only neutral about the climate's favorability (Baker et al., 2012). In regard to how disabled students were treated on campus, Bruder and Mogro-Wilson (2010) reported that only 34% of the faculty in their study believed that these students were treated fairly, 7% believed they were not treated fairly, and 59% were not sure. By contrast, Baker et al. (2012) found that a large majority of the faculty in their study believed that nondisabled students (89%) and faculty (82%) treated disabled students similarly to other students. However, in Bruder and Mogro-Wilson's (2010) study, 18% of the faculty believed that colleges and universities were doing only a poor to fair job of ensuring that students with disabilities had the opportunity to engage in social activities and join clubs and organizations, while slightly more faculty (25%) thought institutions were doing a good to excellent job in this area and 58% were not sure. Baker et al. (2012) found that only 30% of the faculty in their study believed that disabled students were satisfied with their college experience overall. The large number of faculty who indicated they did not know what the campus climate was like for disabled students is telling.

In the classroom, 55% of the faculty in Bruder and Mogro-Wilson's (2010) study thought disabled students were treated equitably, while 40% were not sure. The faculty believed that the university could do a better job of providing an inclusive climate for disabled students by providing better accessibility (37%), providing more accommodations and support (22%), improving transportation services (19%), improving services for students with disabilities (13%), increasing awareness of issues students with disabilities face (6%), and providing more opportunities for students with disabilities (3%).

In C. Murray, Wren, and Keys's (2008) study, faculty indicated that they did not think that resource constraints stopped them from providing appropriate accommodations. However, only 12% of Bruder and Mogro-Wilson's faculty participants thought that they themselves needed to make changes to improve the experiences of disabled students. In Baker et al.'s (2012) study, 67% of the faculty believed that disabled students received the accommodations that they needed in the classroom.

Baker et al. (2012) found that 25% of the faculty in their study believed that disabled students have difficulty learning and concentrating. However, 74% of the faculty in Baker et al.'s study felt that disabled students were just as capable of meeting the academic demands of college as nondisabled students. Faculty in C. Murray, Wren, and Keys's (2008) study also expected students with learning disabilities to perform similarly to nondisabled students. Therefore, the specific impairment the student has may affect beliefs that faculty hold.

Like nondisabled students, most faculty appear to believe that disabled students receive the services and accommodations required to allow them to achieve success in college. However, many faculty indicate that they are not aware of how disabled students experience the campus or whether the services they receive are adequate. This finding suggests that faculty would benefit from more information about the disabled students with whom they work and the services that will enable them to be successful in higher education.

Creating Campus Environments That Support Students With Impairments

More research is needed to understand how the campus environment affects aspects of the lives of college students with impairments. Specifically, researchers should examine how various types of educational settings affect the experiences of these students. Studies are needed comparing the environments of two-year colleges to those of four-year colleges, as well as those of small private colleges and large public universities on outcomes such as persistence and success rates, along with factors contributing to each of these outcomes (Mamiseishvili & Koch, 2011). With such data, interventions can be tailored to specific types of institutions of higher education and the students they enroll.

The studies that we have reviewed in this chapter suggest that much work is needed to improve the campus environment for students with disabilities. We next present a number of the recommendations researchers have offered regarding the physical, organizational, and human aggregate components of the campus environment.

Changing the Physical Environment

To ensure academic success, retention, and social integration of students with impairments, institutions must ensure that all physical aspects of the campus are accessible to students with disabilities. Matt's opening quote suggests that Michigan State does a particularly good job of modifying the physical environment of the residence hall rooms so that students with disabilities have a comfortable and workable space in which to live. Mamiseishvili and Koch (2011), S. E. Burgstahler (2008f), Goldstein (2008), and Kalivoda (2009) offered suggestions for using universal design principles in relation to the physical environment. Examples of universally designed physical spaces on college campuses can be found in Gilbert (2013), Salmen (2011), and Goldstein (2008).

Planning, Policies, and Evaluation. Planning ahead was one of the specific strategies Michigan State used to ensure that the residence hall rooms for incoming disabled students were designed for comfortable living and ease of use. Planning ahead by using universal design principles allows students, faculty, and staff to immediately feel comfortable in the environment and avoids the need to request special accommodations. It also saves the cost of retrofitting spaces. Whenever plans for creating or remodeling buildings or landscape architecture are under consideration, diversity of the users of the space should be considered to ensure that all people have access to and feel included in the environment. One way to ensure that a wide variety of users can successfully adjust to a particular space is to include representatives from various populations, including individuals with a variety of impairments, in the planning process. Another way to ensure that the campus is universally designed is to develop a policy that requires that any equipment, furniture, and other products purchased by the college or university be accessible and that disability-related issues be considered when evaluating the usefulness and workability of physical settings.

Appearance. While the appearance of the campus generally does not affect its accessibility, it does affect the campus climate. The design of the campus environment helps to ensure that all students, staff, faculty, and visitors feel welcome. To create an inclusive environment, designers need to be sure that the environment appeals to individuals from a broad range of cultures, with various abilities and other personal characteristics. For example, having an accessible playground for children in the vicinity of family housing would welcome adult students who have children with disabilities.

Entrances and Routes of Travel. The main entrance to a building may be its most important feature. Because alternative accessible entrances often are hard to find, universal design advocates that all main entrances to buildings be accessible to individuals who use wheelchairs. Having to separate from a group of friends or business colleagues to enter through an alternative accessible entrance can cause a person to feel lower in status than people who can use the main entrance.

Gently sloping sidewalks up to a level entrance are much more inclusive than ramps and steps that segregate individuals who use wheelchairs or other assistive mobility devices. Those who are designing entrances should ensure that they are barrier free; take into account site conditions, building context, and desired user experience; and consult building codes. Goldstein (2008) offered the Erb Memorial Union Amphitheater at the University of Oregon-Eugene as an example of a well-designed accessible building. The sidewalk leading to this building follows a curve outside the amphitheater, with one fork gently sloping upward to the upper floor of the amphitheater and another fork sloping down to a plaza and the lower floor of the building. In addition to being wheelchair accessible, the paths are barrier free for visually impaired visitors and offer clear sight lines to enable individuals with hearing impairments to read lips and see the body language of others on the path.

As noted in this example, paths should be clear of objects that might interfere with travel, such as tree branches or waste cans, and should not change directions abruptly or unpredictably. Entryways should be sheltered from the elements, and entrances should have outdoor lights with motion sensors nearby; motion sensors to open exterior doors should be close to the entrance as well. Convenient, wheelchair-accessible parking spaces, including extra-wide spaces for vans that have wheelchair lifts or ramps, should be located near building entrances and travel routes. Finally, large-print, high-contrast directional signs to and throughout the physical environment, such as those on the campus of the University of Minnesota, should be provided to enable students to easily find accessible entrances and other campus locations.

M. Peña (personal communication, August 5, 2016) pointed out that vacation sites often provide destination maps that include a "walk score" indicating the distance to an attraction from the hotel or parking lot. She suggested that campus accessibility maps place a "mobility score" between parking lots, student housing, and the main administrative offices on campus. What appears to be accessible may not be for someone with a particular kind of mobility disability. For instance, during the winter when people have to contend with snow and ice, parking lots could have a lower mobility score than they do at other times of the year. A new student or community member coming onto campus could then determine the parking lots or other spaces that are best to avoid based on their winter mobility score.

Classrooms. Classroom goals include maximizing contact between students and faculty, enhancing active learning among students through group interaction, and promoting a collaborative and inclusive atmosphere among students. To achieve these goals, classrooms must be designed to enable faculty to use a wide variety of learning strategies. Flexibility in design is the key to inclusivity and encourages student participation.

Classroom Design. Classroom space greatly affects interaction. For example, a room that is wider than it is deep enables all students to be closer to the instructor than deeper rooms allow. Whenever possible, floors should be on one level. To accomplish this goal, the University of Connecticut School of Business used chairs and tables that increased in height from the front to the back of the room rather than constructing a tiered floor. Aisles should be wide enough to allow students and faculty to move easily. Wheelchair users should be able to navigate throughout the room and sit wherever they wish. In large lecture halls with a tiered seating configuration, multiple entrances should enable individuals with mobility impairments to access both the teaching area and various seating levels. Spaces for wheelchairs should be spread around the hall to allow for choice of sight lines.

Furniture. To ensure that people of all sizes are comfortable, furniture and equipment should be selected to accommodate the "tallest and smallest" persons (Goldstein, 2008, p. 204), as well as those who are obese. Since it is difficult to find classroom chairs that are comfortable for all people, designers should attempt to find chairs on which components can be adjusted in a variety of ways, such as adjusting the seat height, arm height, and arm length. If such chairs cannot be found, providing chairs of various sizes may be a feasible alternative. Classroom furniture also should be movable to allow various configurations and student groupings.

Tables provide better work spaces than tablet arms attached to chairs. Chairs with tablet arms limit seating choices for left-handed students, and the arms fail to provide enough space for many individuals to sit comfortably in a seat or enough surface area to work with all the materials that students need in many classes. Table height should be adjustable, and the legs should be positioned at the farthest ends of the table and be either T-shaped or L-shaped to allow sufficient legroom and room to slide a wheelchair under the table.

Goldstein (2008) pointed out the importance of applying universal design principles to furniture for the instructor, including an adjustable-height podium, a table at least 60 inches wide by 24 inches deep, and adjustable seating. Controls for classroom technology used by the instructor must also be universally designed and easy to use at both a standing and sitting level.

Sound and Lighting. Classroom engagement is enhanced when the noise level is kept to a minimum, nonfluorescent lights are used so that students can see clearly, and other sensory modifications are made. These factors are particularly important for individuals with vision and hearing loss. As much as possible, classrooms should be located away from noisy areas in the building. The use of hard-surfaced ceiling materials will help to reflect sound downward. A wireless microphone will enable the instructor to move around the room to interact with students without compromising sound quality, and assistive listening devices should be available for individuals with hearing loss.

Flexibility is the key to creating effective lighting in classrooms, particularly when a great deal of technology is used. For viewing media presentations, a zoning system that allows lights in specific areas of the room to be turned off or on is helpful. A minimal number of control switches with standard layouts in every classroom on campus can increase ease of use for students and faculty. The controls should be clearly labeled and easy to see in the dark. Outlets and light switches with dimmers should be positioned so they can be reached from standing and sitting positions.

Restrooms. For individuals who use wheelchairs, have limited body strength, or have minimal use of arms, hands, or fingers, readily available accessible restrooms are a necessity on college and university campuses. Necessary features include enough clear space in the restroom itself and in the toilet stalls to enable a wheelchair user to maneuver; light switches, soap dispensers, hand dryers, and paper dispensers at a height that can be reached when seated or standing; levers for sink handles; and sinks that are high enough for wheelchairs to slide underneath so the fixtures can be reached. The entryway to the restroom should allow for entry without a door or have an automatic door opener for the outside door.

Information Resources and Technology. In addition to ensuring that technology itself is accessible, its location must be convenient and accessible as well. Computers in labs, offices, libraries, and other campus locations should be positioned so that all individuals can access them. All locations must have adjustable seating and lighting, and computers should be positioned at heights that those using wheelchairs can access.

Other sources of information, such as projection screens, whiteboards, and bulletin boards, should also be positioned so that they are visible to every student. Publications that are placed in information kiosks, on tables, or on counters must be reachable from seated or standing positions. Signage should be placed at a height that all individuals can read. Universities and colleges must also be sure to provide all information in various formats so that it can be accessed by individuals who are blind or have low vision or learning impairments.

Safety. Ensuring safety for every member of the college or university community is an important goal of universal design. All spaces should be designed to minimize the risk of injury. For example, nonslip walking surfaces should be provided both inside and outside buildings. In areas of the country with severe winter weather, snow and ice removal should be a top priority, with preference given to the routes and parking lots that students and staff with mobility impairments use. Students in one study noted that snow was often shoved from parking lots into disabled parking spaces and that they often feared getting stuck in the snow on sidewalks on their way to class (Evans, Assadi, Herriott, & Varland, 2004). Emergency systems that incorporate audio and visual warnings should be used in all buildings, especially in single residence hall rooms.

Accommodation. Many institutions of higher education have campuses that were built long before the concept of universal design was introduced, and their complete renovation may not be feasible. Colleges and universities can provide access to programs located in inaccessible buildings in a number of ways: (a) advertise that access to the program is available and provide contact information to arrange access; (b) provide a phone and phone numbers in an accessible location to call offices located in inaccessible spaces; (c) request that a conference room be made available on the first floor to meet with students in a building that is otherwise not accessible; (d) provide access to all departmental information on a website; and (e) communicate to all faculty and staff that it is their responsibility to provide equal access to all people, even if it is not convenient (Kalivoda & Totty, 2003).

Roufs (2012) identified a number of changes to the physical environment that would assist students and employees who are d/Deaf or hard of hearing—for example:

- Induction looping in classrooms and other spaces. These devices receive sound, filter out background noise, and relay the sound directly to hearing devices.

- Acoustical modifications such as carpet, cloth drapes, and fabric-covered room dividers.
- Seating arrangements that encourage closer interaction between faculty and students.
- Telephone systems that offer amplification or devices that translate the conversation into readable captions on the phone or a computer screen.
- Oval conference tables to allow better eye contact and easier lipreading.

Policy Implementation

Colleges and universities must also ensure that the policies they implement are fair and inclusive of all students. Inequitable and emotionally burdensome policies can contribute to negative perceptions that some students have of the institution they are considering attending or already attending. In addition, government agencies and colleges and universities should work together to develop compatible policies and procedures to assist youth in the transition from high school to college (U.S. GAO, 2012). Methods must be developed to increase awareness among families, high school teachers, and resource providers of services available to assist students who are transitioning from high school to college (U.S. GAO, 2012).

Studies are needed to investigate the "psychological, emotional, and economic impact" (Denhart, 2008, p. 494) of testing on students with learning disabilities and other forms of impairments that are not apparent. Research has indicated that such testing is quite upsetting for many students (see Chapter 9). Many students prefer to forgo accommodations in order to avoid having to undergo diagnostic testing. Studies are also needed to determine if some aspects of diagnostic testing and special accommodations can be replaced by implementing universal design practices in and out of the classroom (Denhart, 2008).

Institutional staff, and particularly disability resource providers, must stay current on legislation related to students with disabilities and guidelines for implementing new laws (see Chapter 3). In particular, institutional staff should become familiar with and implement the guidelines for accommodation requests recently developed by the AHEAD (2012b) that use the principle of common sense rather than extensive diagnostic testing to determine whether students are eligible for disability resources and accommodations.

Faculty Development

Since faculty play an important role in the experiences disabled students have in college, ensuring that faculty are knowledgeable about their obligations to provide an equitable learning environment for these students is a responsibility of institutions of higher education. University-wide training is needed to raise awareness of faculty regarding various types of disabilities and how they affect the learning processes of students with disabilities (Barnard et al., 2008; Denhart, 2008; Kalivoda, 2009; Rutgers University, 2012). Such training should be grounded in principles of social justice that focus on ensuring that the environment is inclusive of all students.

Institutions must find ways to encourage faculty to take a more inclusive view of disability as part of diversity and adopt more inclusive attitudes toward students with disabilities (Barnard et al., 2008). Steps for doing so include developing awareness in faculty of their own attitudes and beliefs and how their beliefs can affect their behavior; encouraging faculty to be committed to social justice, including achieving equity and equality for all people; and encouraging faculty to value and encourage open-mindedness.

A pretraining assessment of faculty knowledge and attitudes can be helpful in planning training and in evaluating learning after the training (Vogel, Holt, Sligar, & Leake, 2008). Disability training programs for faculty have been found to be most effective if they include a number of different types of training and are relatively long in duration (C. Murray et al., 2009). Participants report being more satisfied with longer, more multifaceted programs than brief programs. C. Murray et al. (2009) recommended implementing a training program designed for a small group of faculty who would then train other faculty in their departments or programs. Faculty in one study preferred web-based training since it is accessible whenever it is convenient and they can return to the information later if they need to (Vogel et al., 2008). Web-based training has also been shown to be effective in changing the attitudes of faculty about students with disabilities, particularly faculty who are men (Junco & Salter, 2004; Vogel et al., 2008).

In addition to formal faculty training sessions, disability resource websites should include videos, articles, and web links targeted to faculty that provide information about working with students with disabilities (C. Murray et al., 2009). Information about disability resources and strategies for implementing universal design also can be offered at department meetings, faculty orientation programs, and other faculty development events (C. Murray et al., 2009).

Changing Attitudes

In addition to faculty attitudes and behavior, studies we reviewed underscored the importance of peer attitudes in creating a welcoming environment. Interventions that contribute to changing student attitudes toward individuals with disabilities therefore must be implemented on college campuses. An effective and valuable way of increasing awareness of disability and the needs and concerns of students with disabilities is to include disability under the umbrella of diversity (Kalivoda, 2009; Rutgers University, 2012). Courses and course units on disability should be a part of multicultural education on campus. Diversity awareness programs sponsored by student affairs divisions must also include disability. Until such time as disability is seen as an important social identity and given the weight of other identities, such as race, gender, and social class, it will not be given serious attention in or out of the classroom.

Opportunities for interaction between nondisabled students and students who are disabled are important in changing the perceptions that each group holds of the other (Mamiseishvili & Koch, 2011). Faculty can encourage both academic and social integration among students with and without disabilities by incorporating cooperative learning activities. Students with disabilities should also be encouraged to join peer study groups, learning communities, first-year seminars, and other academic activities in which social interaction with peers and faculty take place. In addition to academic interaction among students, staff should encourage students with disabilities to get involved in cocurricular activities and to engage in informal interaction with faculty and peers (Mamiseishvili & Koch, 2011).

Many people use and advocate simulations as part of awareness training to effect attitude change regarding disability, believing that it provides nondisabled students with a sense of what it is like to be disabled (Evans et al., 2005; Lewis, 2011). However, daily experience of having a disability can never be simulated in the very short time periods that simulations are given. In reality, the experience is more like the first few moments after students become disabled and realize that they cannot see or hear or will have to use a wheelchair. Feelings toward impairment change significantly as disabled individuals learn more about their impairments and how to manage them. Students in simulations, however, are often left with feelings of powerlessness, fear, and panic that most disabled students quickly overcome. The experience tends to reinforce negative assumptions about disability as participants focus on what they cannot do rather than what they can do (Ostiguy, Peters, & Shlasko, 2016). Better ways of building awareness among nondisabled individuals might be listening to a panel of disabled students discuss their experiences or viewing a video about the lives of disabled individuals in different settings.

While most interventions designed to create attitude change are awareness programs or training sessions for specific groups of students such as residence life staff or student organization leaders, Lundberg, Zabriskie, Smith, and Barney (2008) found that recreation programs on college campuses can also promote attitude change. In their study, nondisabled students who participated in wheelchair sports along with students with disabilities experienced interacting on an equal "playing field" (p. 72) while becoming aware of how wheelchairs work and possible concerns such as fit and comfort, stability in the chair, and differences in use between daily life and sports. The participants also realized that wheelchair sports were fun. Gillies and Dupuis (2013) reported that opportunities for both disabled and nondisabled students to engage in sports and recreation broke down stereotypes and increased positive perceptions of people with disabilities.

To close this chapter, we consider how these recommended changes can help to create a socially just campus environment.

Creating a Socially Just Campus Environment

As an increasing number of students with disabilities enter college, providing accessible campus environments must be institutional priorities (Hayashi & May, 2011; Mamiseishvili & Koch, 2011). To create an equitable and inclusive environment in which students with disabilities can grow as people as well as succeed academically, disability resource offices and institutions as a whole must adopt a social justice philosophy and base their initiatives on it (see Chapter 2). An inclusive, universally designed campus environment, based on a social justice approach, enables students with disabilities to smoothly and seamlessly engage with the community without requiring extensive preplanning (Huger, 2011; See Chapter 10 for a discussion of universal design.)

Such an approach must have buy-in from those in power on the campus, starting with the senior executive officer. Under the leadership of this individual and other campus leaders, goals for the college or university related to inclusion of students and faculty with disabilities must be institutionalized, with those in positions of power providing strong leadership to ensure that those goals are achieved (Hayashi & May, 2011).

Institutions must also have a campuswide commitment to accessibility and inclusion (Huger, 2011). Disability resource staff cannot be the sole staff working with students with disabilities. Matt, in the opening quotation to this chapter, noted the importance of working with staff in other offices to create access. There must be collaboration across student services and with faculty to address the needs of these students, as well as collaboration with outside service providers, such as vocational rehabilitation counselors who assist some disabled students with vocational planning and financial support (Mamiseishvili & Koch, 2011). In this collaborative process, an important role of disability resource staff is to provide guidance on how various components of the institution can work together to create an inclusive campus environment.

The complete inclusion of students with disabilities into campus life is the responsibility of the entire campus community, including disability resource providers, student services staff and other administrators, faculty, and student leaders (Huger, 2011). Disability resource providers can assist students in becoming more integrated into the general campus and offer suggestions to other institutional personnel in making the campus environment friendlier. They also must stay up-to-date regarding new legislation to ensure that the campus is complying with federal and state laws; provide training to faculty and staff about disability concerns, terminology, and best practices; and partner with institutional technology services to ensure that all technology is accessible (Huger, 2011).

Student services staff and other administrators must be familiar with how students with disabilities interact with their offices and how to work effectively with them, including providing alternative services such as the web or the phone; make sure the physical space of their offices is accessible; work to minimize barriers to the use of programs and services; collaborate with disability resource staff to make sure they are aware of the needs of the student population and appropriate terminology; visually represent people with disabilities in publications; and practice nondiscriminatory hiring practices (Huger, 2011).

Faculty can use inclusive educational practices and universal instructional design principles discussed in Chapter 12. They also can use readings that include references to people with disabilities, classroom examples that mention people with disabilities, and invited guest speakers who have various types of impairments (Huger, 2011). Issues of disability should be included in the curriculum in fields such as history, literature, sociology, education, nursing, and rehabilitation (Hayashi & May, 2011). The social construction of disability and a social justice approach to disability also need to be taught in relevant classes.

Student leaders should be educated on the diverse needs and abilities of students with disabilities; hold events and meetings in accessible locations; bring speakers to campus to raise disability awareness; encourage participation of all students in organizations and activities; promote dialogue on campus about inclusion, stereotyping, and prejudice; and explore ways to structure the social integration of students with disabilities (Huger, 2011).

Disability resources need to be funded and staffed at higher levels than they currently are so that students receive more individualized attention than they get now (Rutgers University, 2012). Individualized services for students with specific disabilities are needed rather than assuming that a generalist approach to working with students with disabilities will create an environment inclusive of all such students (Oguntoyinbo, 2012). Students with autism, learning impairments, attention deficit hyperactivity disorder, brain injuries, and other specific impairments have unique situations that must be addressed by staff members who are knowledgeable about those impairments (Pope, 2013). Offering services tailored to each individual can also be valuable for recruiting and retaining students with particular impairments (Oguntoyinbo, 2012). Financial support for students with these types of impairments also is needed since currently only students who can afford to pay for individualized services themselves can receive them due to the high cost of such services (Pope, 2013).

Conclusion

Colleges and universities, by following ADA, Section 504, and ADAAA requirements, but stopping short of creating truly inclusive, accessible, and welcoming campus environments, foment ableist attitudes. An ableist environment is laden with assumptions about what is normal or desirable, and these assumptions disadvantage disabled students. As Denhart (2008) stated, "The finest accommodations based on the most sophisticated science will have no value if intolerance denies their use" (p. 495). Constructing physical environments that are fully accessible and organizational environments that are completely fair and just for individuals with all types of impairments is critically important. Even more important is ensuring that the human aggregates of colleges and universities are educated, aware, and accepting of people from all backgrounds, including disabled students, faculty, and staff.

Discussion Questions

1. What areas of your campus create the greatest environmental barriers to individuals with physical impairments? Learning disabilities? Psychological disabilities?

2. What systems are in place on your campus to address environmental barriers? How are people with disabilities included in those systems?

3. How might existing policies or procedures that contribute to organizational environmental barriers for people with disabilities be altered to create a more inclusive environment?

4. How does the social construction of disability contribute to environmental barriers? How can the social construction of disability be leveraged to provide greater access?

CHAPTER NINE

THE CAMPUS CLIMATE

People's judgment about disability is different on this campus in comparison to others.... I think that if you have an architectural environment where people with disabilities are always having to ask for assistance or may not be able to accomplish something as fast as their able-bodied counterparts you eventually gradually begin to believe the stereotypes that are out there.... The flip side of that is that on this campus you know people don't see people with disabilities as being all that slow or different or whatever and I think that they develop a much more positive attitude.... The experience that we have tried to [provide] our students is—we get them here on this campus where they are no longer the only kid [with a disability] in school.... And that is the kind of thing that we try to do here—to help them feel like they are not the only ones in the world and then to show them how they can be valuable in ways that they have not thought of and then they begin to carve their own rock at that point.

—Jeff, former director of the Office of Disability Services at Wright State University

An article in the publication *New Mobility* stressed that along with the academic and social aspects of a college, the success and happiness of disabled students in college is dependent on how disability-friendly the campus is ("Disability Friendly Colleges," 1998). According to Hannah (2012), the Wright State campus, which enrolls over 500 disabled students a year, has been rated among the top five disability-friendly campuses in the United States

We acknowledge with gratitude the assistance of Susan R. Rankin in providing portions of her data set and analyses, as well as descriptions of her methods, for use in this chapter.

in *College Success for Students with Physical Disabilities* (Wise Tiedemann, 2012). Factors contributing to the rating include accessible housing; accessible transportation; underground tunnels between buildings; and the availability of personal attendants, adaptive sports, and online guidance to help students prepare for college. Certainly the attitudes demonstrated by the Wright State staff also contribute to the friendliness of this institution.

The previous chapter considered specific environmental variables that contribute to the climate. In this chapter, we explore how students perceive and experience that environment as a whole, referred to as the campus climate—a more formal label for its friendliness—and the effects that the climate has on disabled college students. Our discussion is limited to colleges and universities that have actual physical campuses, although we acknowledge that online colleges and programs are enrolling students with disabilities in increasing numbers and do have climates that affect their students. We include in our discussion specific strategies for improving the climate and directly supporting disabled students. Following a literature review and analysis, we present a summary of a recent large multicampus study of campus climate experienced by students with disabilities. We also present a model for transforming the climate affecting college students with disabilities.

Definition of *Climate*

The climate of the college campus consists of "the current attitudes, behaviors, and standards [of faculty, staff, administrators, and students concerning] the access for, inclusion of, and level of respect for individual and group needs, abilities, and potential" (Rankin & Reason, 2008, p. 264). This conceptualization of climate focuses on the experiences of individuals and social identity groups on campus, as well as the quality and extent of interaction among various groups and individuals. Each of these factors is apparent in Jeff's description of the Wright State campus provided at the start of this chapter.

Viewed through the ableist lens that is part of the social justice model, students with disabilities are often discriminated against and oppressed by individuals who have more power and legitimacy in the environment, including college administrators, faculty, and nondisabled students (Evans, 2008; Rauscher & McClintock, 1997). Institutional structures, policies, and norms create environments having barriers to the success of students with disabilities. Finally, the attitudes and behaviors of these campus stakeholders, as well as the policies and structures they construct, contribute to the climate that impaired students must deal with as part of their college experience (Griffin, Peters, & Smith, 2007). An ableist perspective is laden with assumptions about what is normal or desirable, and these assumptions disadvantage disabled students (Castañeda et al., 2012). (See Chapter 2 for more information regarding the social justice model of disability.)

The Campus-Based Experiences of Impaired Students

The climate of a college or university is based on how students with disabilities view their interactions with faculty, staff, and nonimpaired students. In addition, students with different forms of impairment often have views about one another that are ableist. Finally, because of the oppression they experience, students with disabilities also internalize negative views of themselves, which shape how they feel about the climate, a pattern to which Jeff alluded in the opening quote. Disabled students' perceptions of the climate have a major impact on their behavior, satisfaction, persistence, and ultimate success in higher education (C. Strange, 2000). A number of researchers have examined how they perceive their experiences in college and how various factors contribute to their feelings and behaviors in the college setting. We review these studies in this section.

Overall Challenges

Studies conducted in different locations and using various methodologies have underscored the difficulties that students with disabilities have experienced in college. For example, using an online survey that included 53 self-identified disabled students who volunteered following an e-mail invitation, Baker, Boland, and Nowik (2012) found that half of the students indicated that their greatest challenge was in the academic arena. Twenty-eight percent said that their greatest challenge was in the physical environment, 6% in social interactions, and 16% in the psychological area. Despite noting these challenges, over half of the respondents did indicate that they were satisfied with their experiences as a disabled student in college (Baker et al., 2012). Students in this study were not asked to indicate their specific impairment.

In a study in which a similar research question was asked but a qualitative methodology was used, 16 students, most of whom had nonapparent impairments, kept journals for 10 weeks about barriers they experienced on a daily basis in college (Hong, 2015). Hong's participants provided responses that were quite different from those obtained by Baker et al. (2012). Students most frequently discussed situations in which they perceived that faculty members treated them in ways that were unfair and emotionally distressing, particularly when they revealed their impairments and sought accommodations (Hong, 2015). The students in Hong's study also viewed academic advisors as a barrier in that they lacked knowledge of their needs as students with disabilities and were unresponsive to them as people; only 1 student out of 16 indicated that she had a positive relationship with her advisor. The participants indicated that they felt a need to prove themselves in every situation and used words such as *stressful*, *upsetting*, and *frustrating* to describe their daily experiences (p. 217).

The contrasting findings of Baker et al. (2012) and Hong (2015) may be due to the differing methodologies they used. In Baker et al.'s study, participants were provided with general labels (e.g., *academic*, *social*) to use in describing their challenges, while in Hong's study, they used their own words to write about their challenges and wrote about them over a period of time rather than responding at one specific time as in Baker et al.'s study. Since students in the Baker et al. study were not asked to identify their impairments, it is not possible to tell if their impairments differ from those of students in Hong's study.

As we will discuss in Chapter 15, many students come to college with little understanding of what to expect. As a result, they are often surprised and disappointed by the challenges they experience. As a first step, students should be provided with information about disability resources and the accessibility of the campus before they begin college so they know whom to contact and what to expect (Mamiseishvili & Koch, 2011). Educational programs, advising, and career counselors can assist students with disabilities to establish a clear sense of purpose and encourage them to persist in college and achieve their academic goals (Mamiseishvili & Koch, 2011). Interventions such as self-advocacy workshops and conflict resolution skills training can help students with disabilities learn to stand up for themselves (Mamiseishvili & Koch, 2011). Athletic and recreational activities are helpful to all students since they enhance quality of life, offer stress relief, contribute to a sense of community, help develop leadership skills, and foster teamwork and team building (Gillies & Dupuis, 2013).

Experiences with Faculty

Students with disabilities often view faculty as creating barriers that prevent them from receiving the educational opportunities that other students have in college. In the study conducted by Baker et al. (2012), about 25% of the students with disabilities agreed or strongly agreed that they were hesitant or afraid of talking with their professors about accommodations, and one-third of the students felt that their professors would think differently about them if they knew they were disabled.

In a focus group study involving disabled students at universities in 10 states carried out by Dowrick, Anderson, Heyer, and Acosta (2005), participants reported that faculty frequently questioned whether students with disabilities deserved the accommodations they requested, and as a result, the disabled students felt stigmatized. Disabled students, particularly those with learning impairments and other nonevident impairments, reported that they had encountered faculty who refused to provide them with accommodations and were unfamiliar with the rights of students with disabilities (Dowrick et al., 2005). Similarly, in a phenomenological study involving college students with learning disabilities, 10 of 11 participants reported that they were often misunderstood by faculty when they asked for accommodations, with faculty viewing them as "lazy or lacking effort" (Denhart, 2008, p. 493), similar to the findings of Hong (2015). Nine of the participants were reluctant to ask for accommodations, feeling as if asking for them was "giving in" (Denhart, 2008, p. 492) and led to their being seen as "different" and "inferior" (p. 492). However, almost half of the participants in Baker et al.'s (2012) study thought that their professors were familiar with referral procedures for students who needed accommodations, indicated that their professors were willing to make accommodations, and believed that the accommodations were helpful.

That faculty can have an incredibly positive impact on students can be seen in this statement that a Deaf student made about his professor: "[He] believed in me so much that I began to believe in myself.... He is a person who cares about student success more than anything else" (Abdul-Alim, 2012, para. 13). Students with disabilities have also attributed academic success to mentoring relationships with faculty members (Rutgers University, 2012). Faculty should be encouraged to take on mentoring roles with disabled students and assist them in learning how to negotiate the campus, join peer groups and organizations, and develop effective study skills.

Faculty and staff with disabilities, in particular, can be effective role models of success in the academic community. They can also engage in helpful communication with disabled students as "insiders" who have themselves experienced many of the same issues as the students (Denhart, 2008; Kalivoda, 2009). To ensure that disabled mentors are available to disabled students, institutions must hire more faculty and staff with disabilities in visible and prominent positions. To do so, college and university leaders need to modify problematic work environments to ensure that positions are accessible to any potential faculty or staff member who is interested in applying (Hayashi & May, 2011; Kalivoda, 2009; See Chapter 7 for further discussion of the experiences of faculty and staff with disabilities.)

In combination, studies indicate great variability in the experiences disabled students have with faculty, but at best, only half of faculty seem well prepared to support the success of these students. These findings underscore the need for appropriate training of faculty and graduate students who strive to become faculty. This training should inform faculty and potential faculty of the legal requirements for providing accommodations to students with disabilities, as well as building awareness of both the challenges and the academic and personal potential of students with disabilities. Such training could be built into new faculty and graduate teaching assistant training at the beginning of the academic year and offered as online training to all faculty throughout the year. Many universities require that all faculty and staff complete online sexual harassment training; a similar policy could be implemented for training related to disability.

Experiences with Disability Resource Office Staff

Another contrast is evident in how students with disabilities view the assistance they receive from disability resource staff. Some of the students in Denhart's (2008) study viewed the learning disabilities specialist on their campus "as a transformative figure" (p. 491) who intervened when they had problems with faculty. One student from that study reflected, "I don't know what I would have done if there wasn't someone like her there" (p. 491). Similarly, students in Dowrick et al.'s (2005) study also noted the importance of disability resource staff, who provided a "human connection" (p. 43) to the institution, but they pointed out the need for more staff to better serve individual students and for better cooperation among student support services as a whole. They also stressed that the focus of services should be "on each individual's needs rather than on a formula according to the individual's disability" (Dowrick et al., 2005, p. 44). In Hong's (2015) study, 14 of the 16 students with impairments indicated that they felt intimidated and uncomfortable using disability resources. They reported being confused about the process that was necessary to receive services and were overwhelmed when staff expected them to know what accommodations they needed and how to advocate for themselves (Hong, 2015).

These reactions suggest the importance of having appropriately trained staff who can work effectively with disabled students, taking into consideration their varying levels of self-awareness and self-efficacy. Similar to faculty, disability resource staff play an important role in mentoring students with disabilities, encouraging their involvement on campus, and providing information about how to negotiate the challenges they may face. Too often, especially at smaller colleges, student affairs generalists are assigned responsibility for disability resources as part of their duties and have no experience or training in this area. Ensuring that training is provided in such situations is critical. Online educational programs such as those provided by the University of Connecticut can be a valuable asset to disability resource staff who need training to carry out their responsibilities effectively. Membership and regular attendance at the Association on Higher Education and Disability (AHEAD), a professional association for disability resource providers, is also of great value. Institutional leaders must also recognize that implementing environmental adjustments to ensure that all students receive equitable educations requires more trained staff members than most colleges and universities now provide, and financial support must be provided for appropriate staffing levels in disability resource offices (DROs).

These data also support the need for transition planning to inform students of what to expect from disability resource offices and how to access services. It is the responsibility of higher education institutions to provide this information to all students entering the higher education institution, since some students may not have received services while in high school but could benefit from supports in college. Information can be provided through orientation programs and summer communication to entering students. The data also suggest the value of informing students earlier about their specific impairments and the accommodations they warrant, which can be done by including students in discussions of their individual educational plans in K-12 educational settings. (See Chapter 15 for further discussion of transition planning.)

Experiences with Peers

Peers also play an important role in whether impaired students perceive the college climate as inclusive. Students with learning differences (LD) commented on the value of having an LD community group with whom they could discuss issues and find validation (Denhart, 2008). Many campuses, however, do not have formal groups of this kind. While Dowrick et al.'s (2005) participants used other students with impairments as resources to obtain information about available services, they indicated that they had trouble meeting people and making friends because of their disabilities. Hong's (2015) participants never mentioned interactions with other disabled students. Students in the studies by Dowrick et al. (2005) and Hong (2015) reported feeling constantly stigmatized by nonimpaired peers, including those who believed that disabled students who received accommodations were getting special treatment and who ostracized impaired students when they found out about their disability. In contrast, many of the students with impairments in Baker et al.'s (2012) study did not think that nondisabled students treated them differently from any other student but, again, there is no information on the types of impairments students in that study had.

Since peer support is important to all students, and students with disabilities have reported difficulty in making friends and finding support groups, establishing peer support groups such as the one Denhart (2008) mentioned though the DRO can be of great value for students with specific impairments and disabled students in general. Development of communities of students with disabilities can provide disabled students with support in building identity, developing strategies, and speaking on behalf of themselves (Denhart, 2008).

Providing educational programs for nonimpaired students about disabilities and including the study of disabled people as an oppressed group in multicultural classes can help to create more positive attitudes toward students with disabilities. Faculty can also be of assistance by forming randomly selected small groups for class discussion and for assignment completion that most likely will include students with disabilities and those without. Such groups will enable students to get to know each other while completing a common task, which may lead to greater contact among students outside the class. Recruiting and admitting greater numbers of disabled students, as Wright State has done, also increases the opportunity for students with disabilities and students who are not disabled to have more contact with each other, which normalizes the experience of going to college and interacting with other students on campus, regardless of their ability status.

The Impact of Climate on Disabled Students

While a number of researchers have examined factors that contribute to the ableist climate that many disabled students face on college campuses, fewer have examined the actual impact climate has on these students. Studies and examples that are available indicate that a negative climate created by the attitudes and behaviors of faculty, staff, and other students can cause students with disabilities to internalize stereotypes and negative qualities that others attribute to them.

That students with disabilities are affected by an oppressive campus climate is evident from reading several studies and newspaper articles. Using an ableist lens, Hutcheon and Wolbring (2012) conducted in-depth interviews with eight college students who identified as having a variety of apparent and nonapparent impairments to determine how they made meaning of their college experiences. One of the five themes the authors identified was hegemonic ableism. All of the students in this study demonstrated internalized ableism, including beliefs that some disabilities are more acceptable than others and that society rejects physical and mental differences among people. Similarly, Madriaga (2007) determined from life history interviews with 21 disabled students that when the atmosphere of the learning environment was negative, students "internalized [their] impairment as [their] problem, not the problem of others" (p. 407).

In several studies, impaired students have reported feeling stigmatized by faculty and nondisabled students if they were open about their disabilities and need for accommodations to succeed academically (Denhart, 2008; Dowrick et al., 2005; Hong, 2015). To avoid the stigma associated with disclosing their disabilities, many students refused to ask for accommodations (Denhart, 2008) or waited several weeks into the semester or just before final exams to determine if they could get through the class without accommodations (Hong, 2015). Even among the disabled students in Baker et al.'s (2012) study, the results of which were more positive than those of other studies, 75% of the participants stated that they did not disclose their impairments to other students, while 61% did not tell their professors that they had impairments. Approximately 44% of the students indicated that they never talked to their faculty members about accommodations at the beginning of the semester, while 64% said they sometimes or always spoke to their professors at some later time in the semester. Similarly, in a study involving a large national sample of students with disabilities, 15% of the participants reported that they never talked to faculty outside class or took part in study groups (Mamiseishvili & Koch, 2011). While none of these researchers examined the actual academic performance of students who did not disclose their impairments or use accommodations, one can assume that not having accommodations would at least make the students' academic work more difficult to complete and lengthen the time it took them to finish it.

In several court cases, students whose accommodations were withheld, resulting in their inability to start or complete coursework, sued for their rights. In a 2014 case involving a student at Palmer College of Chiropractic in Davenport, Iowa, a blind student who had been accepted and was enrolled in the college had to leave Palmer when the college refused to provide a sighted reader to assist him in reading x-rays to determine treatment plans for patients (Thomason, 2014a). In a similar case, a hearing-impaired student at Creighton University's Medical School was denied the hearing-assistance technology recommended by his audiologist and otolaryngologist (Beck, 2013, 2014; Mangan, 2013). The alternatives the school provided did not adequately accommodate his disability. He then purchased the equipment himself to complete his first two years of medical school. He had to take a leave of absence, however, when Creighton refused to provide an interpreter to assist him in communicating with his patients or allow him to pay for one himself (Beck, 2013, 2014; Mangan, 2013). In another case, a deaf student was admitted to Pacific Northwest University of Health Science's medical program in 2013 after an interview in which he proved that he could complete an integrated teamwork component with the assistance of an interpreter (Freedman, 2014). He agreed to defer his enrollment for a year to allow time for the school to arrange for the aids and services he needed. However, in April 2014, the university withdrew his admission, citing "concerns about patient safety in clinical situations, compromised educational experiences for classmates and an expected inability to finish performance exams in time" (Freedman, 2014, para. 7). Another case, settled in December 2015, involved a hard-of-hearing Licensed Practical Nurse with over 14 years of nursing experience who was admitted to Terra State Community College's Licensed Practical Nurse to Registered Nurse program. Soon after her admission, the college required that she prove that she could hear in order to remain in the program. They also refused to provide any type of aids or accommodations to her (National Association of the Deaf, 2015a). In each of these cases, the courts eventually ruled in favor of the student, although Creighton appealed the federal court ruling, arguing that the necessary accommodations, at a cost of around $300,000, would be an undue hardship for the college (Beck, 2014). Creighton later withdrew their appeal (Grossman, Colker, & Simon, 2015).

These examples demonstrate the seriousness of the ramifications of how students are treated on college campuses. Students can experience psychological reactions such as internalized ableism, self-doubt, fear, and stress caused by faculty and administrative attitudes and actions. The negative attitudes that these authority figures present, such as assuming that impaired students are lazy, incompetent, or cheaters, can lead to serious emotional outcomes for students. Another potential outcome is reluctance to ask for any kind of accommodation, which in turn often leads to illness and exhaustion, inability to fully participate in college classes and activities, and doing poorly in their courses.

When students do ask for accommodations, if those accommodations are denied and the student believes the denial is unjustified, the student has the right to file an appeal through the institutional grievance process. As noted in Chapter 3, all institutions receiving federal funds must have a published grievance process for accommodations. In addition, individuals with disabilities who are denied accommodation have the right to file a grievance with the Office of Civil Rights either in place of or in conjunction with an institutional grievance. Individuals are also entitled to file a separate discrimination grievance if they believe that their accommodations were not implemented as the result of identity-based discrimination.

For students with disabilities whose accommodations are denied, the outcome can be not only emotionally costly and have a profound academic impact, but also have a financial impact. These students may have to provide their own accommodations (e.g., purchase software, hire an interpreter) if they can raise the money or leave school and give up their dream of an education and career. A final option for those who can afford it is to sue the institution, hoping that the courts will support the individual's right to an equitable education, as outlined in Section 504 of the Rehabilitation Act and the Americans With Disabilities Act.

Studying Campus Climate

As the literature reviewed in this chapter illustrates, many factors contribute to campus climate, and students on various campuses perceive the environment differently. Understanding the climate of a specific campus is critical to ensure that it is effectively meeting the needs of the students with disabilities who are enrolled. Systematic climate assessments can be conducted in a number of ways using a variety of methods, including standardized climate assessment instruments, institution-specific climate assessments, and consultant-tailored climate assessments.

Standardized Climate Assessments

Standardized assessment instruments have the advantage of having been validated in previous studies to ensure that the instrument consistently measures what it is designed to measure. They can be useful in comparing a current assessment with previous ones on other campuses. However, the wording used is general in nature and may not fit the terminology used on a specific campus. It is also not possible to ask questions about specific aspects of the environment in which campus administrators may be interested. Two standardized assessment instruments are available for those who prefer to use instruments that have been validated in a broad range of studies.

AHEAD Program Evaluation Tools. The Association on Higher Education and Disability (AHEAD) has developed a set of online program evaluation tools to provide DROs with information regarding their campus climate as perceived by key target groups: faculty, administrators, and students with disabilities.

For a fee based on the cost of services, AHEAD (2014c) hosts the questionnaires on its server, conducts the data collection, cleans the data, and provides summaries of the results, as well as the raw data for further analysis by the institution.

College Students with Disabilities Campus Climate Survey. Using a theoretical model of disabled student success based on previous research as a foundation, A. Lombardi, Gerdes, and Murray (2011) developed the College Students with Disabilities Campus Climate survey, which has three components: individual actions such as self-efficacy and self-advocacy, postsecondary supports such as disability services and faculty teaching practices, and social supports including family and peer support. At a public research university in the northwestern United States, 197 students with disabilities, 70% of whom identified as having a learning disability, completed the survey to determine its reliability and validity. A factor analysis identified nine reliable factors across the three areas: peer support, using accommodations, disability services, self-advocacy, family support, campus climate, faculty teaching practices, faculty attempts to minimize learning barriers, and stigmatization of disability (A. Lombardi et al., 2011). Although the instrument needs further validation, initial results suggested that it may be helpful in developing data-based interventions to improve student outcomes and campus climate.

Institution-Specific Assessments

While an institution-specific climate assessment is much more time-consuming than a standardized instrument such as those just discussed, it can be more powerful since items can be tailored specifically for the institution on which the climate assessment is being conducted. Stodden, Brown, and Roberts (2011) described the process of conducting an institution-specific climate assessment with the purpose of determining the extent to which programs meet their stated objectives and what needs to be done to make programs more effective. To conduct a comprehensive assessment, data need to be collected from many sources, including faculty, students, facilities personnel, admissions and records offices, research units, and other institutional entities that work with or affect students with disabilities (Stodden et al., 2011).

Before constructing a climate assessment instrument, those involved in the process must agree on their objectives and how they are going to use the data, as well as the factors they will assess. An inclusive climate assessment should examine the physical environment, accessibility of teaching and learning strategies, and available support systems (Stodden et al., 2011).

Other aspects of the campus such as technology, communication, academic and workplace policy, and curricular environments also contribute to the climate and should be assessed. A climate assessment consists of three phases: preassessment, during which the climate assessment instrument is developed; assessment, when selected respondents complete the instrument; and postassessment, when the results are analyzed and evaluated and reports of the results are prepared and shared with various audiences to facilitate planning for changes suggested by the results (Stodden et al., 2011).

Consultant-Tailored Assessment

Frequently campus officials want to construct an institution-specific assessment but do not have the time or expertise to do so with assurance that they will be able to obtain the information they desire. Consultants are available to assist with such a project. For example, Susan R. Rankin and her associates have conducted numerous climate assessments across the United States for diverse colleges and universities (Rankin & Associates Consulting, 2012b). Rankin and Associates Consulting works with staff from each institution to tailor assessment instruments to fit the specific campus and address the questions and concerns in which the institution's assessment team is interested (Rankin & Associates Consulting, 2012a). The following discussion provides an overview of a multi-institutional assessment that Rankin and Associates conducted, highlighting the campus climate for students with disabilities.

Methods. All students of a 13-campus university system were invited to respond to an anonymous online questionnaire; 51,452 students completed at least 50% of the questionnaire and were included in the final data set. The complete survey had 93 questions, most of which were answered on a 5-point scale. As noted in Chapter 7, the data set had some limitations, including self-selection of the participants and the inability to generalize the findings to the entire population of students with disabilities in the university system. Survey data were analyzed to compare the responses (in raw numbers and percentages) of various groups. Descriptive statistics were calculated by salient group memberships (e.g., by gender, race/ethnicity, campus/location, position) to provide additional information regarding participant responses.

Results. Of the total number of students in the sample (51,452), 18.8% (9,682) reported that they had at least one disability/condition that affected learning, working, or living activities. The largest number of students with disabilities indicated that they had a mental health/psychological condition

($n = 3{,}546$; 36.7%) followed by low vision ($n = 2{,}173$; 22.5%), attention deficit hyperactivity disorder ($n = 1{,}729$; 17.9%), medical condition ($n = 1{,}632$; 16.9%), learning disability ($n = 754$; 7.8%), hard of hearing ($n = 649$; 6.7%), speech/communication condition ($n = 486$; 5.0%), physical/mobility condition not affecting walking ($n = 446$; 4.6%), physical/mobility condition affecting walking ($n = 402$; 4.2%), Asperger's/autism spectrum ($n = 207$; 2.1%), acquired/traumatic brain injury ($n = 188$; 1.9%), deaf ($n = 49$; 0.5%), and blind ($n = 41$; 0.4%). The number of students with mental health/psychological conditions is much larger than in other studies reviewed for this chapter and suggests that the number of students with this type of disorder now attending college is rapidly increasing. Also, an anomaly among studies is the extremely low number of students with learning disabilities. No explanation for this difference is immediately apparent, but it may suggest that either the climate is challenging for students with learning disabilities or the admissions process is exclusionary in some way.

Three survey questions asked about students' comfort with the climate on campus, in their academic departments, and in their classes. For each of these questions, responses of *very comfortable* and *comfortable* were combined, as were responses of *very uncomfortable* and *uncomfortable*. Seventy-five percent of the students with disabilities indicated that they were comfortable or very comfortable on the campus, while 85.2% of students without disabilities indicated they were comfortable or very comfortable; thus, while most students with disabilities were comfortable on campus, students without disabilities were meaningfully more comfortable on campus than students with disabilities (all differences discussed in this section are statistically significant).

Within their academic department, 72.6% of the students with disabilities reported being comfortable or very comfortable, while among students without disabilities, 82.4% indicated that they were comfortable or very comfortable. Thus, both groups reported a slightly lower level of comfort within their academic department than on the campus as a whole; students with disabilities were still meaningfully less comfortable in their academic departments than were students without disabilities.

With regard to classroom climate, 67.4% of students with disabilities reported that they were comfortable or very comfortable, while among students without disabilities, 71.6% reported being comfortable or very comfortable. The same patterns appeared in the responses for this question, with students overall being less comfortable in the classroom than in their academic department and the campus as a whole, and students with disabilities being less comfortable in the classroom than students without disabilities.

Rankin also asked students whether they had personally experienced any exclusionary, intimidating, offensive, or hostile conduct. Among students with disabilities, 20.3% reported that they had experienced such conduct but that it had not interfered with their ability to work or learn, and 13.4% reported that they had experienced this type of behavior and that it had interfered with their ability to work or learn. In comparison, 12.6% of the students without disabilities indicated that they had experienced such behavior, but it had not interfered with their ability to work or learn, and 4.5% reported that they had experienced such behavior and it had affected their ability to work or learn. As with the previous questions, students with disabilities reported meaningfully more experiences of harassment and more experiences that interfered with their learning or working than students without disabilities. In this case, however, a greater percentage of students with disabilities reported harassing or bullying behaviors: over one-third of the students with disabilities responded in this way. (While we present the data from this assessment in aggregate form, it is important to recognize that each student with a disability has a unique experience on campus.)

Students with disabilities were asked to rate the campus climate for individuals who have four specific types of impairments. Of the responding students with psychological health issues, 65.0% rated the climate as respectful or very respectful; 20.1% did not know how to rate it. For students with physical health issues, 74.4% rated the climate as respectful or very respectful; 17.0% did not know how to rate it. For students with learning disabilities, 67.7% rated the climate as respectful or very respectful; 21.1% did not know how to rate the climate. For individuals with physical disabilities, 70.8% of the students with disabilities rated the climate as respectful or very respectful; 21.1% did not know how to rate the climate for this population. As with the previous question, students with disabilities viewed the climate as less respectful for people with psychological issues than for people with other types of impairments, and a large percentage of these students did not know how to rate the climate for students with specific types of impairments. The large percentage of students with disabilities who indicated that they did not know how welcoming the climate was for students with different types of disabilities suggests that students may be aware only of how they and students with similar impairments experience the climate. Therefore, when students with disabilities report on the climate, they may really be taking only their own experience or those of others with a similar impairment into consideration. The generalizability of their responses, then, may be questionable, and the need for representative samples of students with disabilities in quantitative studies is underscored.

Rankin's assessment instrument contained two scales, *academic success* and *intent to persist,* which were supported through factor analysis. There was a significant difference in the test for means for undergraduate students by disability status for both *intent to persist* and *academic success.* The differences in means for *academic success* (−3.70) and *intent to persist* (−1.17) suggest that undergraduate students with no impairment perceived greater academic success and viewed themselves as more likely to persist than undergraduate students with disabilities. There was also a significant difference in the test for means for graduate/professional students by disability status for both *intent to persist* and *academic success.* The differences in means for *academic success* (−4.99) and *intent to persist* (−2.85) suggest that graduate and professional students with no impairment perceive greater academic success and viewed themselves as more likely to persist than graduate and professional students with an impairment. These findings support those of other researchers (see Chapter 14). Further studies are needed to determine if perceptions of specific aspects of the campus climate are related to academic success and intent to persist for students with disabilities.

In comparison with other studies discussed in this chapter, students with disabilities in this climate assessment appeared to be somewhat more comfortable with aspects of the climate. These findings may be unique to the setting, as this university system is located in a rather liberal part of the United States where people may be more accepting of students with disabilities. The low numbers of students with learning disabilities may also play a role. More large studies such as this one are needed in other parts of the country and in various types of institutions to verify these results. Climate assessments that are designed by external consultants, in conjunction with individual colleges and universities and university systems, can be especially helpful to disability researchers since they yield large data sets that can be broken down to assess the responses of specific subgroups of students.

Transforming the Campus Climate

While the research discussed in this chapter provides a much-needed introduction to the climate that students with disabilities experience on college campuses, more research is needed to gain a comprehensive understanding of the impact that both positive and negative campus climates have on students with various types of impairments in order to develop strategies to improve the climate and ensure the success and satisfaction of these students. Larger-scale quantitative studies need to be carried out to verify the existence of discrimination against students with disabilities, as reported in many of the small studies reviewed for this chapter (Denhart, 2008). Qualitative studies are also necessary to examine the nature and context of the discrimination that students with disabilities experience (Denhart, 2008) in order to create conditions that will help to overcome discrimination and stereotyping, leading to welcoming and supportive campus climates. Participatory action research holds much promise for creating positive change in specific settings, as Gillies and Dupuis (2013) demonstrated.

Based on the results of a participatory action research study they led, Gillies and Dupuis (2013) presented a framework for creating a campus culture of inclusion based on guiding principles and characteristics that are necessary to create a welcoming campus climate. In the study, a research team made up of representatives of the community investigated the climate by interviewing students, staff, key administrators, and alumni (Gillies & Dupuis, 2013). After analyzing and reviewing the data, the team arrived at six principles required to create an inclusive campus culture.

1. *Provide access for all.* This principle consists of "a commitment to identify and alleviate physical, social and systemic obstructions to meaningful community engagement" (Gillies & Dupuis, 2013, p. 198).
2. *Value the diversity and uniqueness of all.* This principle requires that the university move beyond just accommodating people to valuing all people and recognizing that each person has important gifts to share with the community. As Gillies and Dupuis stated, "People [must be] seen as holistic beings with many facets to their identity" (p. 198).
3. *Value interdependence and social responsibility.* By including this principle, Gillies and Dupuis recognized that inclusive "communities … genuinely want to help others, because they feel that they have a responsibility to those around them" (p. 199).
4. *Value diverse knowledge bases, voices, and perspectives.* Gillies and Dupuis stressed that in welcoming educational climates, "all community members, particularly those in power, … actively respond to the ideas, perspectives and viewpoints of others" (p. 199).
5. *Value the power of learning and education as tools for growth and change.* In inclusive campus climates, "learning extends beyond the classroom and is related to all aspects of campus life" (Gillies & Dupuis, 2013, p. 199).
6. *Value the whole person.* On a welcoming college campus, "opportunities for physical activity, leisure, social interaction, meaningful engagements and personal development are a critical component of wellness and quality of life" (Gillies & Dupuis, 2013, p. 199).

Intertwined Characteristics

In addition to ensuring that the campus climate is based on the six guiding principles, three intertwined characteristics are also needed to create an inclusive culture: "(1) an interconnected campus community, (2) a supportive and enabling campus community, and (3) an informed campus community" (Gillies & Dupuis, 2013, p. 200). *An interconnected campus community* fosters interconnections between those who have the power to implement policies and those who must adhere to them. In this type of system, middle managers help to bridge the divide between those at the top who make decisions and those at the bottom who are affected by those decisions. An interconnected campus community also develops synergistic partnerships between on-campus and off-campus entities. Synergistic partnerships involve people coming together and collectively using their abilities and strengths to develop joint solutions or responses that are better than the ones individuals could generate independently. As a staff member stated in Gillies and Dupuis's (2013) study, "It all comes down to relationships" (p. 201).

A *supportive and enabling campus community* considers "the physical, psychological and social needs of its members" (Gillies & Dupuis, 2013, p. 202). Higher education leaders can be supportive and enabling by addressing three aspects of the environment. First, they need to ensure that all aspects of the campus are accessible. One student in the participatory action research study pointed out, "The basic accessibility issues need to be targeted first before you can make somebody feel included. Because for someone to feel like, included, they have to be able to get to the location or wherever they're going, right?" (Gillies & Dupuis, 2013, p. 202).

Second, *the campus must be safe, supportive, and welcoming* (Gillies & Dupuis, 2013). Along with physical, academic, and technological barriers to inclusion, social barriers must also be eliminated. Inclusion results when members of the community, particularly those in power, are sensitive to the needs of others and act in ways that make them feel welcome. Diversity within a community must also be apparent to produce a space that is welcoming and inclusive; a visibly diverse community lessens feelings of otherness and stigma associated with having a disability. When students with disabilities are visible, others in the community see the realities of the lives of these students and awareness of their capabilities is raised.

Third, a *supportive and enabling community* must provide opportunities for disabled students to be engaged socially (Gillies & Dupuis, 2013). Disabled students who do not form friendships become isolated and fail to participate in social activities. Social engagement is critical for personal development, well-being, and support. Activities, residence life, and other student affairs staff should plan a variety of social, solitary, active, and spectator events to engage disabled students with different interests and needs and provide them with any supports they need to participate.

An informed campus community "(1) continually learns about the needs and preferences of community members, (2) effectively informs the community of [programs] and services, (3) provides learning opportunities for the community, and (4) ensures service providers are informed, trained and qualified" (Gillies & Dupuis, 2013, p. 204). Campus respondents need to be aware of ways the campus environment can be adjusted to better serve students with disabilities. Channels for obtaining information and feedback can be formal (e.g., advisory committees, student councils) or informal (e.g., individual feedback from students with disabilities, rates of attendance at programs). Members of the disabled student population must know how to provide requests and feedback to decision makers, and methods of gathering information must be accessible to all students with all types of impairments. Marketing of programs and services must also be targeted to students with disabilities in ways that they can access. In addition, disability resources and student affairs staff, as well as faculty, must be sensitive to the importance of students with disabilities taking care of themselves in all aspects of their lives—social, physical, emotional—rather than focusing exclusively on their academic pursuits. Staff, administrators, faculty, and nondisabled students must be provided with opportunities to learn about the lives of individuals with disabilities through awareness programming, media presentations, and story sharing. Finally, service providers must be qualified, trained in the areas of diversity awareness and sensitivity to difference, and informed of the ongoing and changing needs and concerns of the disabled students with whom they are working.

Putting the Framework into Action

Changing the culture of an institution is not easy (Gillies & Dupuis, 2013). It takes time, resources, and willingness to change. Change theory, such as the Probability of Adoption to Change model developed by Creamer and Creamer (1990), can be helpful in systematically working through implementation of new approaches to enhance institutional culture. In addition, the following process introduced by Gillies and Dupuis (2013) is useful for implementing and maintaining an inclusive climate over time:

> (1) create a vision for the future, (2) construct a plan to achieve the vision, (3) secure funds to put the plan in place, (4) be proactive to make change happen, (5) reach beyond compliance and (6) think critically and measure actions against the vision. (Gillies & Dupuis, 2013, p. 207)

Creating a vision is most effective when it is a shared community process. Similarly, planning must be done systematically and carefully by community representatives to ensure that all components of the college or university are addressed, including academic curriculum and instruction, cocurricular activities, and support services. To ensure that funding is always available for needed changes as they arise, it is best to work physical, academic, technological, and social accessibility improvements into the ongoing budget of the institution. In addition, campus communities must be proactive to anticipate changes that will become necessary as issues and the campus population change. Complying with legal requirements should be the very minimum expectation of an institution; communities that go beyond what is required to provide a truly welcoming and comfortable campus create "a culture of genuine compassion and inclusion" (Gillies & Dupuis, 2013, p. 207). Finally, to sustain an inclusive climate, an educational institution's leaders must critically consider the steps it has taken and compare them against their original goals. Assessment of the environment leading to future planning and ongoing change to meet the emerging needs of the community should occur regularly. This framework is extremely helpful for communities that are working toward "the development and sustenance of social conditions within which all persons have the greatest opportunity to realize their potentialities, both as unique individuals and as members of great communities and societies" (C. R. Williams, 2008, pp. 6–7).

Conclusion

Rachel Adams (2011) wrote in the *Chronicle of Higher Education*, "When our campuses tolerate, but do not welcome, people with disabilities, they undermine the values of democracy, justice, and intellectual freedom that are the core values of higher education" (para. 12). As Jeff discussed in the opening quotation in this chapter, the climate of a college or university campus is the key factor through which students with disabilities determine whether they are wanted, valued, and welcomed on the campus and thereby whether the core values of higher education are upheld. Those who experience a positive, inclusive climate are more likely to be happy, satisfied, and successful, factors that contribute to their obtaining college degrees and leading fulfilling lives. Educators have an obligation to these students to create a climate that will ensure these outcomes.

Discussion Questions

1. How might you assess the climate of your campus? What environmental strengths and weaknesses do you expect may be revealed?
2. In what ways do you see the climate of your campus affecting students with disabilities?
3. How might the campus begin to improve the campus climate over the next six months, one year, five years?

CHAPTER TEN

UNIVERSAL DESIGN

I've been to swimming events and ... there's nowhere to sit for a wheelchair, there's not enough room for anybody to sit in a wheelchair. There're windows on the north side of the building on the side of the pool on the second floor that you can look down into but ... you don't get the whole feeling of what's going on because you're on a total separate floor from where the pool is.

—Jessica, undergraduate student

I was going to join the Biology, Zoology, and Genetics club but a lot of their activities are like canoeing and hiking and stuff like that and it would be interesting to be in that club but I wouldn't be able to participate in a lot of the activities and so it would be kind of boring.

—Courtney, undergraduate student

The quotations that introduce this chapter were taken from a study of factors that affected the level of involvement of college students with disabilities for which Nancy interviewed several students who used wheelchairs (Evans, Assadi, Herriott, & Varland, 2004). These students readily identified barriers to involvement. Sometimes the barriers were physical, and other times they were primarily psychological. Jessica and Courtney's statements reflect the need to create inclusive campus environments for students with disabilities.

Researchers have found that perceptions of the campus environment and involvement in social activities, along with academic support, are related to success for students with disabilities (H. Belch, 2011; A. Lombardi, Gerdes, & Murray, 2011) as well as to social adjustment and retention (K. S. Adams

& Proctor, 2010; H. Belch, 2011; Shepler & Woosley, 2012). In order to get the most out of their college experiences, students with disabilities need not only to advocate for themselves (Barber, 2012; A. Lombardi et al., 2011; Test, Fowler, Wood, Brewer, & Eddy, 2005) but also be able to engage in campus environments that take into consideration full inclusion both in and out of the classroom (H. Belch, 2011; C. Strange, 2000). Unfortunately, many students with disabilities are not taught how to advocate for themselves and therefore do not make use of accommodations provided by disability resource offices (DROs; A. Lombardi et al., 2011). Other students prefer not to disclose their disabilities because of the stigma attached to disability (Barnard-Brak, Lechtenberger, & Lan, 2010).

Universal design (UD) helps to ensure the provision of inclusive, flexible, and supportive learning environments for students with disabilities, as well as students from other diverse populations (Thompson, 2012). Universal design requires that educators examine and change their approaches rather than shift the burden of adjustment to students who do not engage their environments in normative ways (Higbee, 2012). As D. H. Rose and Meyer (2002) stated, "Barriers to learning are not inherent in the capacities of learners, but instead arise in learner's interactions with inflexible educational materials and methods" (p. vi). A major advantage of the use of UD in higher education is that many environmental barriers are identified and eliminated in the design process so that students do not need to individually ask for special accommodations to succeed in college (Barnard-Brak et al., 2010; Thompson, 2012).

In this chapter, we examine the concept of UD and its application to various aspects of the campus environment. We start by discussing the meaning of UD and explore its origins and development and its various uses within higher education settings. Next, we examine an important application of UD: UD in instructional settings. Finally, we explore the relationship of UD and social justice. At the end of the chapter, we describe programs that provide resources and materials to assist college and university staff in developing universally designed initiatives to ensure that all students, staff, and faculty have opportunities to be involved, comfortable, and successful within the campus environment.

Principles of Universal Design

Universal design provides not only access but also nondiscriminatory inclusion. While UD emerged as a method to address the needs of individuals with disabilities (D. Rose, 2000), architects who developed the concept stressed that inclusively designed buildings and products that are accessible to individuals with disabilities also benefit others, particularly the elderly, children, and people who have temporary disabilities (Silver, Bourke, & Strehorn, 1998). Its usefulness to individuals with strollers, shopping carts, bicycles, luggage, and heavy equipment also became apparent (D. Rose, 2000). Arvid Osterberg, professor of architecture at Iowa State University, who teaches and advocates for UD, prefers the term *design for all people* and stresses that inclusive design should be accessible and comfortable for everyone (J. Miller, 2011, p. 9).

Staff of the Center for Universal Design (CUD), made up of architects, engineers, product designers, and environmental designers, defined *universal design* as "the design of products and environments to be useable by all people, to the greatest extent possible, without the need for adaptation or specialized design" (CUD, 2008b, n.p.). They presented a list of seven principles that can guide evaluation of existing designs; be referred to when buildings and products are in the process of development; and educate architects, product designers, and the public about factors that should be included in accessible buildings, products, and environments (CUD, 2008a). Although they were originally intended for use in the design of physical environments and products, these principles have been widely used to guide applications in instruction, program design, services, information technology, and inclusion (S. E. Burgstahler, 2008b). The seven principles are:

1. *Equitable use.* "The design is useful and marketable to people with diverse abilities" (CUD, 2008d, para. 4).
2. *Flexibility in use.* "The design accommodates a wide range of individual preferences and abilities" (CUD, 2008d, para. 6).
3. *Simple and intuitive use.* "Use of the design is easy to understand, regardless of the user's experience, knowledge, language skills, or current concentration level" (CUD, 2008d, para. 8).
4. *Perceptible information.* "The design communicates necessary information effectively to the user, regardless of ambient conditions or the user's sensory abilities" (CUD, 2008d, para. 10).
5. *Tolerance for error.* "The design minimizes hazards and the adverse consequences of accidental or unintended actions" (CUD, 2008d, para. 12).
6. *Low physical effort.* "The design can be used efficiently, comfortably, and with a minimum of fatigue" (CUD, 2008d, para. 14).
7. *Size and space for approach and use.* "Appropriate size and space is provided for approach, reach, manipulation, and use, regardless of user's body size, posture, or mobility" (CUD, 2008d, para 16).

The major underlying premise of UD, according to Thompson (2012), is to design products, buildings, and teaching approaches to be accessible to all people without need for modification and to determine the goals of a project and provide a variety of ways in which to meet those goals so that individuals with disabilities do not need to seek special accommodations after the fact. Imrie and Reyes (2009) stressed that an important aspect of UD is its avoidance of discriminatory design features that draw attention to a person's impairment, such as having to ask ahead of time for an electronic version of materials that will be used in class or having to use a separate ramped entrance while those without impairments enter through the main entrance that has stairs.

The Evolution From Barrier-Free Design to Universal Design

The concept of barrier-free design, the precursor of UD, was introduced in the early 1970s by architect, disability advocate, polio survivor, and wheelchair user Ron Mace (CUD, 2008c, 2008e). Mace's vision for an environment that all people could navigate was based on his own experience as a student at North Carolina State University, from which he graduated in 1966 (Fleischer & Zames, 2001). While there, Mace had to be carried up and down stairs to attend classes and was unable to use the men's restroom because his wheelchair was too wide to fit through the entrance. He vowed to use his training as an architect to alleviate such conditions.

Barrier-free design focused on making the environment accessible specifically for individuals with physical disabilities. Several factors came together in the 20th century that led to the development of this approach (CUD, 2008c; D. M. Johnson & Fox, 2003). First, the number of people living with disabilities increased as a result of healthier living, better sanitation, better medical care, and the eradication of many diseases that previously had led to early death. Children who survived chronic illnesses began to live longer and as greater numbers of people lived into their 80s and beyond, they were likely to develop serious impairments. In addition, soldiers who fought in 20th-century wars were more likely to survive with impairments than soldiers had in previous centuries (CUD, 2008c).

Second, increased numbers of individuals with disabilities, particularly veterans, organized the disability rights movement to change public policy so that they could live and work alongside able-bodied individuals (CUD, 2008c; Imrie & Reyes, 2009). A focus of their efforts was creation of barrier-free environments that would enable them to travel, live on their own, enroll in college, and work rather than being institutionalized.

Third, federal legislation, which resulted from the efforts of people with disabilities and their advocates, prohibited discrimination against people with disabilities and enabled them to live active lives (CUD, 2008c). This legislation included the Architectural Barriers Act of 1968, Section 504 of the Rehabilitation Act of 1973, and the Americans With Disabilities Act of 1990 (ADA; Imrie & Reyes, 2009). Much of this legislation focused on removing architectural barriers that prohibited individuals with impairments from entering workplaces and educational environments (CUD, 2008c).

Although legislation was put in place to remove architectural barriers and prevent institutions of higher education from turning away students with disabilities who wished to enroll, colleges and universities were slow to implement the requirements of disability-related legislation because of the cost of removing barriers and existing negative attitudes regarding the capabilities of people with disabilities (Kalivoda, 2009). As Nichols and Quaye (2009) pointed out, "From the outset of their educational experiences, students with disabilities face myriad difficulties in culturally exclusive classrooms and physically inaccessible campus environments that reflect the expectation of assimilation to dominant norms and practices, rather than the environment accommodating to student needs" (p. 51).

While, in theory, legislation enabled students with disabilities to obtain a college education and individuals with disabilities to obtain employment on college campuses, in reality, significant barriers to enrollment, learning, and campus involvement (e.g., physical layout, architectural design, lack of accessible transportation, normative curricular design, rigid teaching and testing methods) often prevented students from attending college, being engaged in campus activities, and succeeding academically (Pliner & Johnson, 2004). Similar issues kept persons with disabilities from being hired for campus-based employment (Kalivoda, 2009).

The ADA broadened the idea of barrier-free design to address the needs of individuals with a variety of impairments rather than focusing solely on the needs of wheelchair users (Imrie & Reyes, 2009). As a result, colleges and universities began providing accommodations for students experiencing various types of disabilities—for example, extended time on tests and distraction-free testing environments, as well as relocation of classes scheduled in inaccessible classrooms, accessible on-campus housing, ramped entrances to buildings, and accessible restrooms in buildings on campus (Kalivoda, 2009).

While these adjustments did enable students with disabilities to attend college, they raised a number of concerns among proponents of UD, including these:

- Accommodations separated students with disabilities from other students (Imrie & Reyes, 2009). For instance, students with disabilities were often segregated from other students (e.g., they had to use a separate route to enter buildings; arrange for testing in a different, quiet location; live on a special residence hall floor).
- Accommodations called attention to the individual's impairment (Hernandez, 2010; Higbee, 2012). As a result, many students were uncomfortable seeking services when they knew this would lead to others' becoming aware of their impairment.
- People often criticized the appearance of poorly designed building adaptations (Imrie & Reyes, 2009).
- Most accommodations focused on providing access for individuals who used wheelchairs while discounting other types of disabilities (Imrie & Reyes, 2009).
- Students from low-income backgrounds often could not afford expensive testing to document invisible disabilities (Higbee, 2012). Since such testing was often requested before providing accommodations and many institutions had no provisions to conduct the testing themselves, students with invisible disabilities, such as learning impairments or attention deficit disorder, often were unable to secure accommodations.

To address these issues, Mace and his colleagues expanded the idea of barrier-free environments created specifically for people with disabilities to that of universally designed environments that would benefit all people (CUD, 2008e). Universal design eliminated the segregation of people with disabilities that barrier-free environments created. It was also less expensive, more attractive, and label free (CUD, 2008c).

First applied to architectural design and the built environment, the concept of UD was next used to modify and develop products and technology in educational settings (S. E. Burgstahler, 2008b). Products such as large pens that could be gripped easily by those with limited hand movement and high-contrast labels for use by those with visual impairments were among the first objects designed specifically for individuals with disabilities. Later, products and technology were adapted so that all people, including those with disabilities, could use them. Voice recognition software embedded in computers is an example of UD since it can be helpful to individuals with stronger auditory than visual learning skills as well as students with visual impairments. (We discuss the use and modification of technology in more detail in Chapter 11.)

A number of researchers have used UD concepts to improve instruction and eliminate the need for most instructional accommodations (e.g., S. E. Burgstahler & Cory, 2008; Center for Applied Special Technology, 2012a; Higbee, 2012; Silver et al., 1998). We review three frequently used approaches—universal design for learning (UDL), universal instructional design (UID), and universal design for instruction (UDI)—later in this chapter and examine classroom applications in more detail in Chapter 12.

Universal design principles and procedures have also been applied to campus environments outside the classroom (S. E. Burgstahler & Cory, 2008). In particular, these principles have been used to create more welcoming and inclusive student services applications that enable students with disabilities to experience all aspects of college, cocurricular as well as academic (S. E. Burgstahler, 2008e, 2012b). (We discuss these applications in Chapters 14 and 15.)

Application of Universal Design in Higher Education

Kalivoda (2009) stressed that "in seeking to understand and engage people with disabilities in campus life … ensuring true connectedness is a primary goal" (p. 19). Since faculty, staff, and students at colleges and universities have a wide range of abilities and approaches to learning, including physical, visual, hearing, learning, attention, and communication differences, UD is a particularly valuable vehicle for achieving this goal (S. E. Burgstahler, 2008b; Salmen, 2011). Modifications that are made using a UD process benefit all people on campus, not just those who have impairments (S. E. Burgstahler, 2008c). For example, automatic door openers are convenient for staff who are moving heavy equipment on a cart and individuals who are exiting a building with their arms full, as well as those using wheelchairs or walkers.

For UD to make a positive difference, users must consider the specific aspects of their institution, including its size, type (e.g., residential or commuter), and specific programs (Salmen, 2011). Universal design can be (and should be) applied to any product, service, or aspect of the campus environment (S. E. Burgstahler, 2008b). All campus personnel participate in creating a welcoming and inclusive environment, starting with administrators who have the power to establish policy and procedures, architects who design the physical spaces that enable interactions to occur, and faculty members who create classroom culture and learning opportunities (DO-IT, 2009). Student affairs staff and other employees also play an important role in creating a holistic experience for students that enables them to be involved in activities and events on campus beyond the classroom (S. E. Burgstahler, 2008f; Evans et al., 2004).

Many factors can influence the extent to which a campus uses and accepts UD, particularly the attitudes about disability that administrators, student affairs staff, faculty members, and instructional technology staff responsible for its implementation and promotion hold and demonstrate (Kalivoda, 2009). Individuals who view disability as an environmental barrier that the college or university is responsible for addressing are much more likely to welcome UD as a potential solution than are individuals who believe that disability is an individual's problem to solve (S. E. Burgstahler, 2008b). In this section, we examine the process of implementing UD in college and university settings and the settings in which this concept is applied (see Table 10.1).

S. E. Burgstahler (2008b) stressed that the ability of students to persist in college, succeed academically, and have a positive, well-rounded college experience is contingent on the institution providing an environment that is "welcoming, inclusive, and usable for everyone" (p. 17). Successfully applying UD principles to all aspects of the campus setting will help to ensure that such an environment is created.

S. E. Burgstahler (2008b) listed some of the many settings in which UD can be used to increase accessibility for all people on campus, such as curriculum design, instruction, career services, tutoring and learning centers, conference exhibits, museums, computer labs, and web pages. S. E. Burgstahler (2007) noted the importance of applying UD in higher education in four broad settings: services, information technology, physical spaces, and instruction. We discuss the first three of these topics briefly in this chapter; each of them is covered in some depth in separate chapters in this book (Chapters 13 and 14, Chapter 11, and Chapter 8). We include a more exhaustive examination of the use of UD in instructional settings in the final section of this chapter and explore instructional strategies based on these models in Chapter 12.

Services

Feeling welcomed and being successful and happy in college requires more than adjustments in a student's academic environment. A significant part of the college experience occurs outside the classroom. To experience

TABLE 10.1. A PROCESS OF UNIVERSAL DESIGN
IN HIGHER EDUCATION

Universal Design Implementation Steps	Implementation Process Example
1. Identify the environment to be adapted.	New academic building being constructed on campus.
2. Identify stakeholders.	Users of the future building: faculty, staff, students, visitors to campus, invited lecturers, and others.
3. Involve stakeholders.	Invite a range of future users/stakeholders to join the consultation, review, and implementation process through a dedicated committee, open forums, and soliciting ongoing feedback.
4. Identify standards and guidelines to guide the implementation process.	S. E. Burgstahler (2008b) recommended creating campus-specific guidelines or selecting existing standards and "integrat[ing] them with other best practices within the field" (p. 13). The identified stakeholders should be involved in this creation process.
5. Apply identified standards and guidelines.	Throughout the design, building, and furnishing stages, as well as in the creation of policies for use, apply the standards identified in step 4.
6. Identify gaps in design and plan for individual modifications or accommodations.	Universal design allows use by the widest range of individuals possible; however, accommodation will still be necessary for some individuals to ensure access. Identify potential barriers, and plan for individual modifications or accommodations.
7. Train stakeholders and support use.	Provide training related to institutional goals regarding accessibility and inclusion. Ensure that the training includes policies and procedures to ensure that new barriers are not created.
8. Evaluate and implement necessary changes.	Create an ongoing process to evaluate the effectiveness of the design. Individual needs, building use patterns, best practices, and maintenance may all present the need for change or opportunities to improve the design.

Source: Content drawn from S. E. Burgstahler (2012a).

well-rounded and fulfilled lives, students must have opportunities to take part in cocurricular activities, clubs and organizations, and, if they desire and the campus offers it, residence living. They must also have access to student services that will enhance their academic experiences and future planning, such as advising, tutoring centers, career centers, study-abroad opportunities, and other support services.

Taking a UD approach to create services that are accessible to all students without requiring documentation or disclosure would enable institutions of higher education to embrace a socially just approach to accessibility rather than requiring students with disabilities to prove they are worthy of services provided automatically to nondisabled students (Higbee & Barajas, 2007). In addition, when UD principles are used to design facilities and services, they are available to individuals with a broad range of abilities, impairments, ages, reading levels, cultures, sizes, and other characteristics (S. Burgstahler, 2012; S. E. Burgstahler, 2008e, 2012c). (Chapters 14 and 15 provide information on the application of UD to student services in general, as well as specific areas, including admissions and orientation, residence life, student organizations and involvement, career development, and counseling.)

Information Technology

When considering technology in relation to students with disabilities, two factors must be considered: (a) how to provide access to information for students with disabilities through the use of specialized technology and (b) the needs of these students to have access to the technology that all students on campus use. Given the pervasive use of technology today, students must be able to access and employ effectively the forms of technology used in society in general and also specific technology that relates to their majors (S. E. Burgstahler, 2008f). As S. E. Burgstahler (2008f) pointed out, "Depending on how it is implemented, IT [information technology] can either level the playing field or further widen the gap in educational attainment between individuals of minority groups (e.g., individuals with disabilities, people from poor communities) and those of the majority" (p. 213).

Adaptive technology—existing technology that has been modified so that all students can use it (CUD, 2008b)—includes features such as text-to-speech capability added to computers or captioned videotapes, both of which aid, for example, students who communicate in languages other than English, as well as students with visual and hearing impairments. In addition, assistive technology—specialized software and hardware such as alternative keyboards and mouse options or equipment that allows students to issue computer commands with their heads—has been created specifically to enable individuals with disabilities to use IT to function more effectively in their physical and educational environments (S. E. Burgstahler, 2008f; D. M. Campbell, 2004). (We examine all forms of information technology, including assistive and adaptive technology, in Chapter 11.)

Physical Spaces

The concept of UD was developed by architects who saw the importance of making buildings accessible to individuals with disabilities (CUD, 2008b, 2008c). Ensuring that campus buildings and other aspects of the physical environment are accessible, welcoming, and equitable to all people remains an important focus for higher education since individuals studying and working on college campuses are increasingly diverse with regard to abilities and characteristics (Goldstein, 2008). Poorly designed environments create barriers that prevent individuals from accessing particular spaces, and it is the environment that must be modified to be accessible and inclusive (S. E. Burgstahler, 2008d).

In addition to being the equitable thing to do, the ADA requires that every new or remodeled building be made accessible for individuals with physical impairments (Goldstein, 2008). The more recent 2008 Americans With Disabilities Act Amendments Act (ADAAA) requirements are even more specific with regard to accessibility requirements (Gilbert, 2013). However, as Mace explained when he introduced the UD concept, merely following mandated building codes and regulations does not guarantee full access by all people (S. E. Burgstahler, 2008d). Incorporating UD principles into any building or remodeling project ensures that the requirements of laws and regulations, such as the ADA, will be met at the same time that the usability of the campus environment is improved for the entire college or university community (Goldstein, 2008; Salmen, 2011). (See Chapter 8 for further discussion of ways in which the physical environment can be modified using UD principles.)

Universal Design in Instruction

Instruction is a complicated process that has many components. S. E. Burgstahler (2008c) listed the following aspects of instruction that should be considered when attempting to create an inclusive and accessible classroom learning environment:

- Class climate
- Interaction
- Physical environments and products
- Delivery methods
- Information resources and technology
- Feedback
- Assessment
- Accommodation

When UDI methods are implemented, students with disabilities no longer have to approach the instructors for each of their classes to arrange personal accommodations (Silver et al., 1998); similarly, faculty do not have to arrange separate accommodations for each student who requests them (W. M. Hadley, 2011). In addition, other students in their classes also benefit from modifications, such as untimed exams administered through an online course management system and study guides, which may better match their learning styles (Silver et al., 1998). The goal of UDI is to move from meeting the minimum legal requirements for accessibility to providing inclusion and equal access to learning for all students (Silver et al., 1998).

While there are a number of different applications of UD principles, the basic concepts associated with the application of UD to instruction are proactivity, flexibility, and inclusivity (D. M. Johnson & Fox, 2003; Orr & Hammig, 2009). Three popular approaches for using UD in classroom settings are UDL (Center for Applied Special Technology, 2012a), UID (Higbee & Goff, 2008; Silver et al., 1998), and UDI (S. E. Burgstahler & Cory, 2008; McGuire & Scott, 2006). Although these three strategies are not identical, the practices associated with them are similar with regard to curricula, teaching techniques, and assessment strategies (S. E. Burgstahler, 2008c).

Universal Design for Learning

Universal design for learning (UDL) was developed by the Center for Applied Special Technology (CAST) as part of a cooperative agreement with the U.S. Department of Education (D. H. Rose, Harbour, Johnston, Daley, & Abarbanell, 2006). CAST is a nonprofit organization that engages in research, development, and implementation of UD principles in education. Its guidelines are derived from learning settings rather than from architecture or product design.

In the early 1990s CAST began to recognize that traditional learning tools, especially books, presented barriers for students with physical, sensory, and cognitive impairments that were equivalent to the barriers that stairs presented to people with mobility impairments (D. Rose, 2000). The CAST staff sought ways to enhance the development of educational curricula, including educational goals, methods, materials, and assessments, to enable all learners to gain knowledge, skills, and excitement for learning through reducing barriers and providing support for learning while maintaining high academic standards (CAST, 2012a). As D. H. Rose et al. (2006) pointed out, "UDL requires that we not only design accessible information, but also an accessible pedagogy" (p. 136).

Unlike deficit-based models, UDL is based on the premise that individuals possess a wide variety of skills, interests, and needs as they approach learning

(CAST, 2012a). Drawing on cognitive neuroscience research, educators determined that every individual's way of learning is different (Hackman & Rauscher, 2004; Meyer & Rose, 2000). Individuals' strengths, weaknesses, and intelligence types determine their learning styles (Meyer & Rose, 2000). Abilities, disabilities, and preferences all influence how individuals learn best (Meyer & Rose, 2000).

Impairments within the recognition networks include learning disabilities such as dyslexia and sensory disabilities such as blindness that prevent individuals from being able to take in information through traditional means, such as books or slide presentations (Meyer & Rose, 2000; D. H. Rose et al., 2006). UDL guidelines (CAST, 2012a) provide examples of how curricular materials can be presented in a variety of media so that individual learners can select a version that best addresses their needs and abilities.

Many learning impairments are associated with strategic networks, including those related to forming letters, spelling, doing arithmetic, planning projects, and organizing material (Meyer & Rose, 2000; D. H. Rose et al., 2006). UDL guidelines (CAST, 2012b) offer options for physical action, expression, communication, and executive functions using multimedia and Internet programs based on UDL principles. Such approaches can provide a variety of supportive learning techniques and practice strategies to guide learners who need assistance in developing their skills in these areas.

Affective networks dictate what factors motivate and engage learners (D. H. Rose et al., 2006). The UDL guidelines (CAST, 2012b) offer different approaches to encourage students, keep them on task and interested, introduce new material and concepts, and provide feedback. These strategies provide the variety and flexibility needed to engage students with diverse affective systems (Meyer & Rose, 2000). The CAST guidelines also suggest a variety of ways of presenting content using various media and teaching approaches that also contribute to the flexibility needed to appeal to different students.

Research has indicated that three major networks in the brain influence learning: *recognition networks*, which determine how individuals take in and organize information; *strategic networks*, which determine how learners plan and organize tasks and ideas; and *affective networks*, which determine what motivates, challenges, and engages learners (CAST, 2012a). These three networks work together in learning, with each network contributing essential aspects (D. H. Rose et al., 2006). This framework suggests what factors must be considered to ensure that learning is accessible for all students. As D. H. Rose and his colleagues (2006) succinctly explained,

> It is not enough merely to make classrooms or textbooks accessible. Successful learning environments require attention to three things: providing information and informational supports that are accessible to all students, providing ways of acting on information that are

accessible to all students, and providing ways of engaging and motivating learning that are accessible to all students. The UDL principles reflect those three aspects in the design of learning environments. (p. 138)

As a result, learning opportunities must be presented in ways that address these differences. These findings were used in the development of UDL, which was designed to guide educators in determining goals for learning, developing materials and strategies for instruction, and assessing student achievement (CAST, 2012a; Hackman & Rauscher, 2004).

Universal design for learning is based on three basic guidelines that address each of the three networks (CAST, 2012b). The first guideline is *multiple means of engagement*, which provides options for (a) self-regulation, (b) sustaining effort and persistence, and (c) recruiting interest. Application of this guideline contributes to the development of purposeful, motivated learners.

The second guideline is *multiple means of representation*, which provides learners with a variety of ways to take in information and knowledge (CAST, 2012b). Strategies for gathering information include providing options for (a) comprehension; (b) language, mathematical expressions, and symbols; and (c) perception. Use of this guideline helps to develop resourceful, knowledgeable learners.

The third guideline is *multiple means of action and expression*, which allows students to demonstrate their learning in a variety of ways, including options for (a) executive functions, (b) expression and communication, and (c) physical action (CAST, 2012b). Adherence to this guideline contributes to the development of strategic, goal-directed learners. The order of the UDL guidelines was reorganized in 2014 (see Figure 10.1) to provide more effective guidance regarding how to incorporate them in the curriculum (CAST, 2012b).

Universal Instructional Design

Universal instructional design was introduced in elementary and secondary education, where UD principles were applied to educational materials (Silver et al., 1998). The Council for Exceptional Children (1998) defined UID "as the design of instructional materials and activities that allow learning goals to be achieved by individuals, despite wide differences in abilities" (cited in Ouellett, 2004, p. 136). UID was initially applied to educational materials to enable K-12 students with sensory impairments to be able to access information (Silver et al., 1998). For example, sounds were made louder for students who had difficulty hearing, and text was enlarged so that students with visual impairments could read it. As teachers became aware of students' different

FIGURE 10.1. GUIDELINES FOR UNIVERSAL DESIGN FOR LEARNING

Universal Design for Learning Guidelines

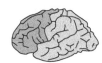

Provide Multiple Means of
Engagement
Purposeful, motivated learners

Provide Multiple Means of
Representation
Resourceful, knowledgeable learners

Provide Multiple Means of
Action & Expression
Strategic, goal-directed learners

Provide options for self-regulation
+ Promote expectations and beliefs that optimize motivation
+ Facilitate personal coping skills and strategies
+ Develop self-assessment and refection

Provide options for comprehension
+ Activate or supply background knowledge
+ Highlight patterns, critical features, big ideas, and relationships
+ Guide information processing, visualization, and manipulation
+ Maximize transfer and generalization

Provide options for executive functions
+ Guide appropriate goal-setting
+ Support planning and strategy development
+ Enhance capacity for monitoring progress

Provide options for sustaining effort and persistance
+ Heighten salience of goals and objectives
+ Vary demands and resources to optimize challenge
+ Foster collaboration and community
+ Increase mastery-oriented feedback

Provide options for language, mathematical expressions, and symbols
+ Clarify vocabulary and symbols
+ Clarify syntax and structure
+ Support decoding text, mathematical notation, and symbols
+ Promote understanding across languages
+ Illustrate through multiple media

Provide options for expression and communication
+ Use multiple media for communication
+ Use multiple tools for construction and composition
+ Build fluencies with graduated levels of support for practice and performance

Provide options for recruiting interest
+ Optimize individual choice and autonomy
+ Optimize relevance, value, and authenticity
+ Minimize threats and distractions

Provide options for perception
+ Offer ways of customizing the display of information
+ Offer alternatives for auditory information
+ Offer alternatives for visual information

Provide options for physical action
+ Vary the methods for response and navigation
+ Optimize access to tools and assistive technologies

learning styles and began adjusting their teaching approaches to meet each student's needs, UID principles were used to create flexible curriculum materials and activities (D. M. Johnson & Fox, 2003; Ouellett, 2004).

Silver et al. (1998) modified UID for use in higher education. Similar to its use in K-12 classrooms, the focus of UID in higher education classrooms centers on expanding teaching methods and materials to enable students from diverse backgrounds to have equal access to learning (Pliner & Johnson, 2004), while also complying with the requirements of the ADA (Hackman & Rauscher, 2004). Higbee (2009) stressed that the term *universal* in UID refers to access. In creating a course or curriculum, educators using UID principles must first consider the diverse social identities of all the students who could enroll and their various learning needs; they then create teaching approaches to best meet those needs (Higbee, 2012). An important goal of UID is to reduce the need for individual accommodations, particularly methods that separate students with disabilities from other students in the class (Higbee, 2009).

Another benefit of UID is that the responsibility for meeting the needs of students with disabilities is under the purview of the faculty (Hackman & Rauscher, 2004; Silver et al., 1998). As Hackman and Rauscher (2004) pointed out, while disability resource providers continue to work with disabled students, when faculty use UID principles, DRO staff can focus on disabled students with unique and complex needs that require more time and knowledge.

UID proponents also promote the collaboration of students and faculty in course design, website content, assessment techniques, and other learning strategies (Hackman & Rauscher, 2004; Pliner & Johnson, 2004). As such, UID gives

> all students the option to choose to learn in the manner that best accommodates their own ways of knowing, and also provides the opportunity to demonstrate what they have learned through mechanisms that showcase their strengths, not their perceived deficiencies. No exceptions are being made because the same choices are being provided for everyone and *everyone* benefits. (Higbee, 2012, para. 13)

Principles of UID were implemented in a federally funded project, Curriculum Transformation and Disability, at the University of Minnesota (J. A. Fox, Hatfield, & Collins, 2003). Both Chickering and Gamson's (1987) Seven Principles for Good Practice in Undergraduate Education and the principles developed at the Center for Universal Design (2008c) at North Carolina State University (discussed earlier in the chapter) served as a foundation for the UID principles (J. A. Fox et al., 2003; Higbee, 2012). Faculty and staff at a number of midwestern colleges and universities learned, used, and tested these principles as part of the Curriculum Transformation and Disability project (J. A. Fox et al., 2003). The UID principles (Higbee, 2009, pp. 66–70) are:

- *Creating a respectful and welcoming classroom climate for learning.* Examples include greeting students at the classroom door at they arrive, learning the names of students in the class, making sure that appropriate language is used, and seeing that ground rules are established for class discussion.

- *Determining the essential components of a course, curriculum, or program.* This practice enables instructors to evaluate students fairly.
- *Communicating clear expectations.* Expectations should be discussed with students both orally and in writing regarding how their work will be evaluated and what behaviors are expected in the classroom.
- *Designing teaching methods that consider diverse teaching styles, abilities, ways of knowing, and previous experience and background knowledge.* Use diverse ways of presenting material and assessing learning; address the various needs, learning styles, abilities, previous experience, and backgrounds of students.
- *Exploring the use of natural supports for learning, including technology, to enhance opportunities for all learners.* Such tools as study guides, discussion groups, handouts, and practice tests benefit all students. When using technology, educators must be aware of its limitations as well as its benefits (see Chapter 11).
- *Creating multiple ways for students to demonstrate their knowledge.* Possibilities include writing papers, giving speeches, and developing multimedia projects.
- *Providing constructive feedback.* Feedback provided in many formats—verbal and written—helps students to connect their learning and become aware of their own growth.
- *Promoting interaction among and between faculty and students.* Informal interaction helps faculty know their students and gives students a sense that their instructors care about them as people. Such methods as journals, e-mail communications, and face-to-face discussion can personalize a class. Small group discussion and group assignments help students learn about each other and overcome misconceptions they may have about individuals who are different from them.

As Higbee (2009) noted, UID requires a great deal of thinking and planning to determine what techniques are appropriate given the class makeup to ensure that all students feel welcome and included. In the process, instructors become more intentional and reflective while developing their pedagogical abilities (Higbee, 2012; Pliner & Johnson, 2004). In addition, the time invested in developing UID strategies during course planning can save time in the long run by avoiding the necessity of arranging individual accommodations for students at the last minute (Higbee, 2009).

Evidence exists that UID works. A fall 2006 study involving University of Minnesota faculty who took part in a 2006 summer institute on UID found that 92% of students without disabilities and 90% of students with disabilities passed courses taught by faculty trained in the use of UID (Higbee, 2009). In universally designed courses taught by these faculty, 29 of 31 students with disabilities did not need any additional accommodations. A study involving faculty from across the United States who were involved in 2006 and 2007 UID seminars revealed that 89% of students with disabilities and 95% of students without disabilities passed courses taught by faculty trained in UID (Higbee, 2009). These faculty also reported that overall pass rates and student evaluations were higher for these courses than for courses they taught before learning about UID.

Universal Design for Instruction

A research team at the Center on Postsecondary Education and Disability (CPED) at the University of Connecticut (UConn) and the staff of the Disabilities, Opportunities, Internetworking, and Technology Program (DO-IT) at the University of Washington each developed models that they both called universal design for instruction (UDI), based on the seven principles of UD developed by CUD (2008d) presented already in this chapter (S. E. Burgstahler, 2008b; McGuire & Scott, 2006). The purpose, goals, processes, and outcomes of each version were very similar, but some differences, noted in the following discussion, do exist.

The goal of researchers developing the UDI at UConn was to address the diverse learning needs of students from a variety of backgrounds entering higher education in the 21st century (McGuire & Scott, 2002). Similarly, the DO-IT team's goal was "to maximize the learning of students with a wide range of characteristics by applying UD principles to all aspects of instruction" (S. E. Burgstahler, 2012a, n.p.) The developers of the UDI from both groups assumed that "diversity in learners [is] the norm" (McGuire & Scott, 2002, p. 27). Rather than focusing on the "average" student, instructors using the UDI model take into consideration the differing abilities, learning styles, cultures, native language, and other characteristics that students exhibit (S. E. Burgstahler, 2012a).

The UDI models were designed to assist faculty in the proactive design of inclusive curricula, course delivery, and assessment techniques (S. E. Burgstahler, 2008c; McGuire & Scott, 2006; Scott, McGuire, & Shaw, 2003). Both sets of developers believed that anticipating the needs of a wide variety of learners and using inclusive instructional techniques rather than adjusting classes after the fact to meet the needs of individual students could save time and ensure the maintenance of academic standards (McGuire & Scott, 2002;

McGuire, Scott, & Shaw, 2003; Scott et al., 2003). The UDI models allow students to use a variety of methods both to learn and demonstrate their learning, "including reading, listening, viewing, manipulating, experimenting, discussing, [and] responding to questions, each of which are available in formats accessible to all students" (S. E. Burgstahler, 2008c, p. 24).

The UConn Model. In the early 1990s, UConn received a federal grant for a project to ensure that students with learning disabilities received equal access to learning in college by using UD in the classroom (McGuire et al., 2003). Three principles guided their work: (a) key stakeholders, such as students with disabilities, disability resource providers, faculty, and administrators had input; (b) recommendations were based on research findings; and (c) strategies for faculty development had administrative support and faculty involvement (McGuire et al., 2003). First, the CPED staff completed an extensive review of literature on UD, as well as on effective teaching for students in general and for students with learning disabilities specifically (Scott, et al., 2003). CPED then conducted several studies to establish the construct validity of the UDI model, including studies of the perceptions of students with learning disabilities, faculty who had been honored for excellent teaching, and disability service providers (Embry, Parker, McGuire, & Scott, 2005). In addition, learning communities based on UDI principles and consisting of faculty, administrators, and DRO staff were established on five different types of campuses to review and discuss the principles and their utility in various campus settings (McGuire & Scott, 2006). These studies and others led to the determination that the UDI principles provide a flexible foundation to guide faculty in course design and delivery (McGuire & Scott, 2006). (More details on the development and validation process can be found in Embry et al., 2005, and McGuire & Scott, 2006.)

The UDI model developed at UConn consists of nine principles; the first seven were those developed by CUD (2008d) and adapted for instructional use by CPED. The other two principles, added by the CPED staff, were based on concepts drawn from the education literature on effective learning (R. A. Shaw, 2011). Table 10.2 lists the UDI principles, and provides definitions and examples of each in practice, as developed at UConn.

To address the varying needs of faculty with regard to enhancing their teaching, the CPED-developed UDI principles were written so that both the tone and content would provide faculty with assistance in melding aspects of instruction, such as selection of course materials, instructional delivery, and assessment of student learning, to address the needs of a diversity of learners (Scott et al., 2003). Faculty can also use the principles to assess their own

TABLE 10.2. THE NINE PRINCIPLES OF UNIVERSAL DESIGN FOR INSTRUCTION: CPED VERSION

Principle	Definition	Examples	Rationale
Principle 1: Equitable use	Instruction is designed to be useful to and accessible by people with diverse abilities. Provide identical means of use for all students whenever possible, and equivalent means of use when not.	Provision of class notes online.	Comprehensive notes can be accessed in the same manner by all students, regardless of hearing ability, English proficiency, learning or attention disorders, or note-taking skill level. In an electronic format, students can use whatever individual assistive technology is needed to read, hear, or study the class notes.
Principle 2: Flexibility in use	Instruction is designed to accommodate a wide range of individual abilities.	Use of varied instructional methods (lecture with a visual outline, group activities, use of stories, or web-based discussions).	Provides different ways of learning and experiencing knowledge.
Principle 3: Simple and intuitive	Instruction is designed in a straightforward and predictable manner, regardless of the student's experience, knowledge, language skills, or current concentration level.	Provision of a grading rubric for exams, papers, or projects; a syllabus with comprehensive and accurate information; or a handbook guiding students through difficult homework assignments.	Clearly lays out expectations for student performance.
Principle 4: Perceptible information	Instruction is designed so that necessary information is communicated effectively to the student, regardless of ambient conditions or the student's sensory abilities.	Selection of textbooks, reading material, and other instructional supports in digital format or online.	Students with diverse needs (e.g., vision, learning, attention, English as a Second Language) can access materials through traditional hard copy or with the use of various technological supports (e.g., screen reader, text enlarger, online dictionary).
Principle 5: Tolerance for error	Instruction anticipates variation in individual student learning pace and prerequisite skills.	Structuring a long-term course project so that students have the option of turning in individual project components separately; provision of online practice exercises.	Provides the opportunity for students to receive constructive feedback and for integration into the final product; allows for supplemental material in addition to classroom instruction.

(continued)

TABLE 10.2. (CONTINUED)

Principle	Definition	Examples	Rationale
Principle 6: Low physical effort	Instruction is designed to minimize nonessential physical effort in order to allow maximum attention to learning. *Note:* This principle does not apply when physical effort is integral to essential requirements of a course.	Allow students to use a word processor for writing and editing papers or essay exams.	Facilitates editing the document without the additional physical exertion of rewriting portions of text—helpful for students with fine motor or handwriting difficulties or extreme organization weaknesses, while providing options for those who are more adept and comfortable composing on the computer.
Principle 7: Size and space for approach and use	Instruction is designed with consideration for appropriate size and space for approach, reach, manipulations, and use regardless of a student's body size, posture, mobility, and communication needs.	In small class settings, use a circular seating arrangement.	Allows students to see and face speakers during discussion—important for students with attention deficit disorder or who are d/Deaf or hard of hearing.
Principle 8: A community of learners	The instructional environment promotes interactions and communication among students and between students and faculty.	Structuring study groups, discussion groups, e-mail lists, or chat rooms; learning students' names or individually acknowledging excellent performance.	Fosters communication among students in and out of class; makes personal connection with students and incorporates motivational strategies to encourage student performance.
Principle 9: Instructional climate	Instruction is designed to be welcoming and inclusive. High expectations are espoused for all students.	A statement in the class syllabus affirming the need for class members to respect diversity and encouraging students to discuss any special learning needs with the instructor; highlight diverse thinkers who have made significant contributions to the field or share innovative approaches developed by students in the class.	Establishes expectations of tolerance; encourages students to be open with the instructor; demonstrates to students that their efforts are appreciated.

Source: Content drawn from Scott et al. (2003, p. 374).

teaching practices to determine the extent to which they are taking student diversity into consideration when they are developing or revising a course. In addition, those responsible for faculty professional development can use the UDI principles developed at UConn to structure sessions on designing inclusive instructional practice and ways to advance learning in diverse educational environments (Scott et al., 2003).

The DO-IT Model. Unlike the UConn model, DO-IT determined that the CUD (2008d) UD principles could be applied to instructional materials and environments without modification or addition of education-specific principles. They used the eight-step implementation process discussed previously in the chapter to apply the principles to various aspects of instruction. In Table 10.3, we list the principles and abbreviated definitions found in S. E. Burgstahler (2012c). We then provide examples of their use in practice. While using the CUD model in professional development sessions, they found some of the terminology used in this model was difficult for educators to grasp (S. E. Burgstahler, 2008c). Faculty desired applications for specific aspects of instruction.

To address this need, the DO-IT team developed checklists that outlined how the UID model could be used in the overall design of instruction, as well as particular aspects of instruction, such as creating an inclusive climate in the classroom, delivering instruction, providing feedback, and assessing learning (S. E. Burgstahler, 2008c, 2012a). The UDI Checklist of Instructional Practices was field-tested at 20 institutions of higher education across the United States and modified based on the feedback received (S. E. Burgstahler, 2012a).

We discuss practical examples of classroom uses of the various instructional models and techniques in Chapter 12.

Critiques of Universal Design and Universal Design for Learning

One substantial critique of UD is the rejection of principles of adaptable design (e.g., assistive technology) and accessible design (e.g., design features explicitly for people with disabilities). Erkilic (2012) stated, "UD asks users with diverse abilities to adapt or modify themselves to the 'designed-for-all products.... With this approach, it is not the physical environment but individual bodies, able-bodied or disabled, that are to be 'adaptable' when using UD products" (p. 185). This critique parallels those of other researchers and practitioners who believe that the broad nature of the goals of UD, which make it understandable and marketable to a wider audience, limit

TABLE 10.3. APPLICATIONS OF THE SEVEN PRINCIPLES OF UNIVERSAL DESIGN TO INSTRUCTION: DO-IT MODEL

Universal Design Principle	Definition	Example
Equitable use	A wide range of users of diverse abilities are able to use the product with a similar experience and without significant need for adaptation or accommodation.	Professors post their lecture notes in an accessible document for the course to access before the class period.
Flexibility in use	Individuals can use the product in a range of ways based on their preference.	Students can access the notes before class for a preview of topics, during class to add their own notes, or after class as a tool for review. Students can read the notes online, print them out, or listen to them with a text-to-speech program.
Simple and intuitive	The use is intuitive and does not require significant instruction for use. Unnecessary steps are not included in the process for use.	Notes should be posted in a format that does not require formatting, should be easy to find and navigate, and should be organized in a clear manner. For example, notes could be uploaded using the course management tool and labeled according to the course date to which they correspond, or they can be e-mailed directly to students at a set time with a consistent subject line.
Perceptible information	Information provided should be clear, and the content conveyed should not change based on the individual's sensory ability or the conditions under which the information is accessed.	The layout of the notes and the naming convention clearly denote the most important points of the lecture. Areas of discussion may be denoted to prepare students for difficult material. Information should be the same regardless of whether the student is reading the notes online, in a print format, or listening using text-to-speech software.

TABLE 10.3. (*CONTINUED*)

Universal Design Principle	Definition	Example
Tolerance for error	A user's mistakes are easily corrected and do not affect the user's ability to complete the task.	If students access the wrong document, they can easily navigate to the correct document or return to the previous page.
Low physical effort	The use of the product should not require undue physical effort. It should be usable regardless of energy levels and by individuals with a wide range of physical, sensory, or motor abilities.	The notes should be intuitive and easy to navigate. For example, headers and styles should be used in creating notes in order for individuals with limited mobility or using a text-to-speech program to access the material seamlessly.
Size and space for approach and use	The product should be usable by people having a wide range of heights and weights and by those who access it using a variety of mobile devices.	If a computer station is available in the classroom, there should be appropriate space for approach by individuals with a variety of mobility levels (e.g., manual chair, crutches, scooter). In the case of course notes, modifications to size of text, background color, and other features should be available. The notes should not be posted in a format that inhibits these modifications.

Source: Some content drawn from S. E. Burgstahler (2012a).

the impact it has to address specific issues faced by people with disabilities, particularly people with multiple targeted identities. Dolmage (2005) argued that in order to address the limitations of UD, people with disabilities must be "[in] the role not of consumers but of innovators or co-creators [which] can circumvent medical-model thinking, confront paternal attitudes and shift entrenched roles and stereotypes" (para. 13). As a result, individuals with disabilities of multiple types should be included in all stages of the planning and development of designs for new built environments on campus and be asked for feedback when considering modifications to existing environments.

Ostiguy, Peters, and Shlasko (2016) noted that UD should be expanded and clarified to "account for other forms of difference between people's minds, bodies, and experiences, including race, gender identity and expression, class, intellectual differences and body sizes/shapes" (p. 323). As we noted in Chapter 5, ableism intersects in multiple ways with other identities and is often masked by classism or other –isms. Critics question if "UD has the power to change the sociopolitical problems of 'equality'" (Erkilic, 2012, p. 197), especially because UD does not address the attitudinal and social environmental issues that individuals with targeted identities face. In order to have a socially just approach to UD, "UD should extend beyond matters of physical access and learning access" (Ostiguy et al., 2016, p. 323) presented by interactions between the designed environment and disability or age.

Universal design does not explicitly require feedback from users of the built environment, and UDL does not incorporate student evaluation or input in the design process or course revisions (Dolmage, 2005). In addition, UDL "presupposes that instructors have the awareness, skills, and expertise to produce designs that will be appropriate for people with diverse access requirements" (Ostiguy et al., 2016, p. 323). In order to address these critiques and to use UD as a socially just pedagogical approach, institutions and individual instructors must build multiple points for feedback into courses in order for student voices, particularly those with disabilities, to be represented in the construction of the syllabus and pedagogy (Dolmage, 2005).

Universal Design and Social Justice

Social justice provides an important rationale for implementing UD. A social justice approach requires recognition of both environmental conditions that create inaccessible college campuses and internal beliefs and attitudes that exclude and demean individuals with disabilities (Evans, 2008; Lindburg, 2012). Universal design interventions grounded in social justice should be based on three principles (Evans, 2008; Hackman & Rauscher, 2004; J. R. Johnson, 2010; Pliner & Johnson, 2004; Shakespeare, 2014):

1. Understanding of the role that power and privilege have played in excluding nondominant groups, including students with disabilities, from higher education
2. Affirmation that individuals are unique and worthy of respect from those around them, and that their voices should be included in any discussion of issues that affect them

3. Recognition that disability is largely an environmental condition—although aspects of individual impairments can play a role in disability—and that the environment needs to be changed to provide equitable educational opportunities for all students

Unfortunately, most programs for students with disabilities have been designed to meet legislative dictates rather than to create a truly inclusive, welcoming, and equitable learning environment (Hackman & Rauscher, 2004; Pliner & Johnson, 2004). Students with disabilities have rarely been included in discussions of their needs (Hackman & Rauscher, 2004). For example, the method that most institutions use to meet ADA compliance requires students with disabilities to arrange individual accommodations to negotiate classrooms, academic requirements, campus activities, and all other aspects of campus life further disadvantages these students because it adds steps for them to access education (Thompson, 2012). Under such regulations, power and privilege remain in the hands of university service providers and faculty (J. R. Johnson, 2010).

Consider Jessica and Courtney, the students quoted at the start of the chapter. Both experienced barriers that might have been addressed through UD or a socially just architectural design based partially on input from individuals with disabilities. Jessica experienced barriers in attending swimming events because of the built physical environment that separated her from other spectators and physically removed her from the same space as the event she wanted to attend. If the pool had been constructed with UD in mind, there would have been consideration for wheelchair users like Jessica in the construction of the event seating. Courtney felt a barrier to participation in many organizations as a result of the unintentional implicit social messages regarding who was welcomed in the group because of the routine events in which the organization participated.

Universal design based on social justice principles empowers students like Jessica and Courtney since they can independently and safely navigate a physical environment from which barriers have been removed. In addition, UID, which provides various methods of accessing classroom material and completing learning activities, enables students to learn in ways that accommodate their needs and empower them to be active participants without disclosing their impairments (Hackman & Rauscher, 2004; Pliner & Johnson, 2004). By providing different ways of accessing information that any student can use, implementation of UD in instruction also destigmatizes learning differences and helps to create a welcoming environment in which students are accepted as individuals and valued for what they can teach others (Hackman & Rauscher, 2004).

Resources for Additional Information

A number of federally funded programs and centers mentioned in this chapter offer comprehensive information and training materials related to universal design. The CUD, housed in the College of Design at North Carolina State University, offers information, conducts research, and provides training and assistance to those interested in learning more about the application of UD to products and built environments (CUD, 2008a). (The CUD URL is http://www.ncsu.edu/ncsu/design/cud/.)

CAST has been a leader in the development and dissemination of products and information related to the application of UDL principles to instruction and technology, principally for K-12 settings (Pliner & Johnson, 2004). The National Center on Universal Design for Learning, an offshoot of CAST, supports implementation of UDL in educational settings by sharing information and providing resources to educators (CAST, 2012a). Its staff has produced videos, presentations, web-based materials, and articles that are available in its resource library. (The CAST URL is http://www.udlcenter.org/.)

The DO-IT Center at the University of Washington focuses on improving success rates of individuals with disabilities in higher education and work settings. Now funded by the U.S. Department of Education, Washington State, and the National Science Foundation, its role has grown to include fostering the success of students with disabilities in challenging academic programs, particularly in the STEM areas of science, technology, mathematics, and engineering; promote UD applications in higher education; and make UD-based educational materials more readily available to college and university faculty and staff. DO-IT's educational focus includes information technology, student services, instruction, and redesign of physical spaces. DO-IT offers videos, books, and training materials, as well as free printed publications, on a wide variety of topics related to UD and disability in higher education. (The DO-IT URL is http://www.washington.edu/doit/Resources/udesign.html.)

The CPED at the University of Connecticut was one of the first centers to implement UDI in higher education settings (R. A. Shaw, 2011). Its staff is currently working on a project, UDI Online, to assist faculty who are preparing online and blended classes and want to incorporate UDI principles in their work. They provide online instruction on UDI principles as well as many examples. (The UDI Online URL is http://www.udi.uconn.edu.)

The Institute for Human Centered Design (IHCD) in Boston, Massachusetts, founded under the name Adaptive Environments in 1978, provides technical assistance to domestic and international organizations on UD. It also offers individualized design consulting services, provides training to leverage the expertise of user/experts (people with disabilities) in reviewing existing environments, and hosts a compilation of resources on its website. (The IHCD Online URL is www.humancentereddesign.org.)

The Equity and Excellence (E&E) in Higher Education project at the University of Massachusetts–Boston has examined factors that can block attempts to implement UD in instruction and has developed tools to address these barriers (R. A. Shaw, 2011). The E&E project has a core team whose members work with small groups of faculty regularly throughout a semester to learn and implement UD principles in their courses. These faculty then mentor colleagues at their home campuses in following semesters. (The E&E URL is http://www.eeonline.org.)

A similar model was used at the University of Minnesota (Higbee & Goff, 2008). Called the PASS-IT project, it ran for several years, training numerous faculty and staff over the course of three summers and disseminating information about UID through two books, journal articles, and many conference presentations. Although funding for this project was not renewed, its materials are still available and are valuable to those who wish to learn about how UID can be used in instruction, as well as student services (See http://cehd.umn .edu/passit/docs/PASS-IT-Book.pdf.)

Individuals who are seeking comprehensive training in UD may wish to consider Landmark College's one-year Certificate in Universal Design: Technology Integration, which is designed for professionals in the fields of education, technology, and support services who wish to gain an in-depth understanding of UD in instruction, assistive technology, and neurodevelopmental conditions that affect learning such as dyslexia, attention deficit hyperactivity disorder, and autism spectrum disorder (Shmulsky, 2013). Courses can be taken for graduate credit or noncredit and are taught using online instruction with a short residency requirement. (See www.landmark.edu/academics/ degree-and-credit-options/certificate-program/ for more information.)

Conclusion

All students, faculty, and staff should have the opportunity to participate fully and succeed while enrolled in or working at colleges and universities. Universal design provides a means for individuals with disabilities to engage in equitable ways in their academic pursuits, personal development, and social interactions. When institutions address barriers to participation proactively by implementing UD principles, individuals who have impairments are saved the hassle and possible embarrassment of having to reveal their impairments and ask for accommodations to enable them to succeed in all aspects of life on a college campus.

To ensure that UD is used in a socially just manner, individuals who are responsible for the UD process must be aware of the ways in which power and privilege can influence the decisions that are made and the changes that are implemented; they must respect students and faculty with disabilities as equals and ensure that they have meaningful input into any design project; and they must recognize that it is campus environments rather than individuals with disabilities that need to be changed. If these factors are taken seriously, UD can be a powerful vehicle for institutional transformation.

Discussion Questions

1. How can the seven UD principles be used to evaluate existing programmatic and educational environments?
2. In what ways are you using UD in your work? How could you include more of those practices?
3. How do you interpret and reconcile the differences between UDL, UDI, and UID?

CHAPTER ELEVEN

ASSISTIVE AND LEARNING TECHNOLOGY

Oh. My god. Between a significant head start from the weekend and the time Read and Write Gold saved me, I'm done with all the textbook reading assigned for this WEEK. The time it took me to complete the chapter for economics was cut to a quarter of what it has taken me every week this semester, and psychology was cut to a third. You know what I'm gonna do tomorrow? I'm gonna go to International Soccer Club, which I have skipped for the past 3 weeks to study. THIS IS MAGNIFICENT.

—Ryan, first-year student with learning disabilities

Ryan has highlighted the impact that assistive technology can have on the academic pursuits of people with disabilities and also has pointed out the emotional and social impact assistive technology can provide. Assistive technology is "any service piece of equipment, or product system, whether acquired commercially or off the shelf, modified, or customized, that is used to increase, maintain, or improve the functional capabilities of individuals with disabilities" (Technology-Related Assistance for Individuals with Disabilities Act of 1988 as cited in D. M. Campbell, 2004, p. 168). Assistive technology can improve the autonomy, independence, and productivity of many individuals with disabilities. Furthermore, these devices can often provide greater access without accommodation or disclosure to multiple people.

Similar to Ryan, we (the authors of this book) also use technology as modification or to support our social, employment, and academic environments. Kirsten is dyslexic and processes information best in an auditory capacity. Kirsten's spelling is abysmal, she skips small words in her writing, and she often must reread printed text several times out loud for editing purposes. With the use of a screen reader or another text-to-speech software, Kirsten is able to comprehend the material more quickly and completely on a first "listen" than she would with an initial "read." She is also able to use headphones to hear what she writes without disturbing colleagues at work or strangers in a coffee shop by talking to herself. Autumn uses a transcutaneous electrical nerve stimulation (TENS) machine, originally designed to relieve muscular pain, as a grounding device to interrupt panic and anxiety. This device can be discreetly worn in most settings and allows Autumn to manage symptoms of her generalized anxiety disorder without having to separate herself from her colleagues or peers. As Autumn's example demonstrates, technology has multiple uses and can be adapted to fit the individual.

Building on these examples, in this chapter we outline several forms of assistive technology and describe the considerations of using technology to support individuals with disabilities in the living and learning environment. We discuss the benefits that technology provides to students with disabilities and the problems associated with inaccessible technology in the learning environment. To inform this conversation, we describe three types of design mechanisms—accessible, adaptive, and universal—as a way of categorizing and understanding assistive technology. Then we review guidelines for accessible design and describe how these apply to educational software and websites. We discuss technology as an accommodation for students with disabilities and outline high-, middle-, and low-technology options that address various functional limitations. Next, we outline legal requirements associated with technology use in higher education, including Section 508, the Americans With Disabilities Act (ADA), and the Telecommunications Act of 1996. We conclude by providing an eight-step plan for creating an accessible campus technology culture.

History of Assistive Technology

From a historical perspective, assistive devices typically were developed for small audiences of individuals with specific disabilities (Center for Universal Design [CUD], 2010). During the 1980s, manufacturers began to develop devices and products that a wide range of people, including the elderly and people with disabilities (CUD, 2010) could use. This rise in development coincided with the growing awareness of disability rights and protections under Section 504 and the ADA. With the 1998 passage of and 2004 amendments to the Technology Related Assistance for Individuals with Disabilities Act (Tech Act), technology use increased among K-12 students. As a result of the Tech Act and the emphasis on technology in individual education plans (IEPs) at the secondary level, many individuals are entering postsecondary institutions with previous experience in using assistive technology; consequently, student requests for assistive technology are substantially increasing (Ofiesh, Rice, Long, Merchant, & Gajar, 2002).

Assistive technology encompasses a broad category of devices that serve users in a multitude of ways. Under principles of universal design (see Chapter 10), many assistive technology products are of use not only to disabled people but also provide benefits to nondisabled users. Examples of assistive products that can be useful to individuals with impairments include these:

- *Assistive listening devices* that amplify and transmit voices to any place in a room
- *Closed captioning* that provides access to television or movies by displaying the audio portion using text on the screen
- *Alternative text* that provides audiotaped, braille, or digital text versions of written material
- *Cognitive aids*—programs that provide spelling/thesaurus/dictionary functions (Kalivoda, Totty, & Higbee, 2009)

These technology products make it easier for individuals with a wide range of abilities and those whose abilities deteriorate over time to complete residential, administrative, and academic tasks (D. M. Johnson & Fox, 2003; Yearns, 2004). They also provide individuals with disabilities greater autonomy and fuller access to the residential, cocurricular, administrative, employment, and academic environments on college campuses.

Accessible, Adaptive, and Universally Designed Technology

Within the context of assistive technology, a distinction exists among three types of design: accessible design, adaptable design, and universal design (J. Seale, 2004). *Accessibly designed* technology is compliant with legal requirements and codes for accessibility. It often includes technology that was separately designed to provide "features for 'special' user groups" (J. Seale, 2004, p. 59). *Adaptable design* refers to technology that has a standard design that can be individually modified as needed for individuals with disabilities. *Universal design* refers to the design of products that take into account the widest range of abilities when being designed and implemented so that they "can be used and experienced by people of all abilities, to the greatest extent possible, without adaptation" (J. Seale, 2004, p. 59). In the following sections, we discuss how each of these design typologies can be used to support the learning and life goals of students with disabilities.

Accessibly Designed Technology

Accessible design is guided by principles that are legally mandated and provide standards for the minimum acceptable usability; the Access Board is a governmental agency that maintains information regarding the latest standards and legal requirements. *Accessible design* may also mean a design that is created to be compatible with adaptive technology devices (Field & Jette, 2007a). For example, many common technology products, such as Microsoft PDF, are accessibly designed, and students with disabilities can use adaptive technology devices (e.g., screen readers) to access the content.

The principles of accessible design provide substantial increases in the usability of technology by individuals with disabilities; however, many of the principles require disabled students to use features that are in addition to those used by nondisabled users. Furthermore, these technology products often require the creator to know how to make products with accessibility and compatibility in mind, and in practice, this requirement renders many accessible and legally compliant products inaccessible to a wide number of users. For instance, if Kirsten created a PDF of her lecture notes but did not take steps to ensure that the text and images were screen reader accessible, her lack of knowledge, skills, or time would render the PDF inaccessible to students with disabilities in her class. Although accessible technology is an important first step, it represents minimum compliance and may not provide enhanced use for all individuals with disabilities (Erlandson, 2008).

Adaptively Designed Technology

Unlike the legally mandated accessibly designed technology that we described in the previous section, adaptively designed technology is typically an additional product that individuals with disabilities employ to use technology. *Adaptive technology* refers to devices or products that "make an inaccessible mainstream or general use device useable by a person with a disability" (Field & Jette, 2007a, p. 187). Frequently, accessible and adaptive design products work in complementary fashion. For instance, although a PDF can be accessibly designed, individuals with print-related or visual disabilities can access it independently only through the use of adaptive technology such as a screen reader, for example, Job Access With Speech (JAWS) or Window-Eyes. Additional examples of adaptive technology include a refreshable braille display, literacy technology, or a hearing loop system.

Although adaptive technology provides access, these devices often must be purchased by the user and come at a substantive additional cost beyond that incurred by the inaccessible technology. For example, Kurzweil is adaptive literacy software that reads text out loud. It is proprietary and only individuals with a documented disability may use it. This product can be used in conjunction with accessible technology products, such as Microsoft PDF, to read information that is not accessible to viewers with print or visual disabilities. To give readers a sense of the costs associated with adaptive technology, a single web license of Kurzweil in 2016 costs $700 per year, and a site-wide license that would cover an entire postsecondary institution costs a minimum of $4,000 per year (all costs in U.S. dollars; Kurzweil, n.d.). Obviously, the additional fiscal costs of adaptive technology can be prohibitive for many students with disabilities.

Universally Designed Technology

Universally designed technology has built-in features that make it usable by students with various types of impairments (Kalivoda et al., 2009). Universally designed technology differs from assistive technology in that it is not legally required and goes beyond adaptive design because it is built into the technology product. Universally designed technology has features that benefit all users, not just students with disabilities. For example, captioning may offer the greatest benefit to students with hearing and learning disabilities, but seeing and hearing information at the same time can assist nondisabled students in learning and understanding information. Features such as these may be especially useful for students for whom English is an additional language. Additional examples of universally designed products are simple devices such as pencil grips, weighted writing utensils, magnifying glasses, kitchen utensils, garden tools, shop tools, and office tools (D. M. Campbell, 2004; Yearns, 2004), as well as newer technologies such as voice input devices, assistive listening devices, specialized software, alternative keyboards, and real-time captioning (D. M. Johnson & Fox, 2003).

When universally designed technology works well, people frequently do not notice the access it provides. Individuals who have used a restroom in an airport in the United States and most other countries may not perceive that they do not need to open doors to enter the bathroom itself, but all individuals appreciate the fact that they move through a short hallway with a privacy wall rather than trying to juggle luggage and open a door at the same time.

Universal design addresses the stigma associated with disability by allowing the widest range of individuals, including those with hidden, undocumented, or undiagnosed disabilities, to access information without accommodation. For example, universal features such as in-classroom captioning or text and streaming video that can be downloaded from the Internet by any student enables students with disabilities to choose when to share their disabilities while ensuring that they have the necessary support to learn (Ruffins, 2011). Other examples of universally designed technology include video presentations that have captions, operating systems with an option to enlarge characters on the screen, text-to-voice software built directly into the product, and programs installed on all computers that help students organize materials from class lectures (S. E. Burgstahler, 2008f; D. M. Campbell, 2004; Kalivoda et al., 2009).

Guidelines for Accessible Design

Technology use in the classroom and learning environment has increased exponentially, and it is important that institutions of higher education implement practices for designing and purchasing accessible technology and resources. Guidelines for accessible design, established in 1992 by key stake-holders, including the technology industry, consumers, government, and researchers, are organized by function and address cognitive, sensory, physical, language, and seizure disorders (S. E. Burgstahler, 2008f). These guidelines include:

- *Output/displays*, which refer to all means of presenting information to the user, such as auditory and visual output
- *Input/controls*, which include keyboards and other ways of communicating to the product, such as being able to reach and operate the controls
- *Manipulations*, which include being able to perform required actions, such as inserting a disk, loading a tape, or changing an ink cartridge
- *Documentation*, which refers to operating instructions, including being able to access and understand the instructions
- *Safety*, which refers to alarms and other protections from harm, such as being able to perceive warnings and use products without harming oneself or others

We briefly address how these five guidelines can be applied to educational software and web accessibility to support individuals with disabilities in the learning environment.

Educational Software

Accessibility must be considered when designing, choosing, and purchasing educational software. Educational software is a broad category of technology that includes learning management systems (e.g., Blackboard), platforms used to host online courses (e.g., Moodle), catalog management and course registration software (e.g., CourseLeaf), software packages used within a course (e.g., statistical software such as SPSS), and textbooks. Decisions about the accessibility of educational software directly affect the learning of students. For example, Julie, a visually impaired student who uses JAWS or Kurzweil to access course materials, was taking a statistics class where the software used (MiniTab) was not accessible. Therefore, she was required to learn an accessible statistical program (STATA) without the support of the peers in her class and the course material resources designed to teach that program. She also was restricted to what computer she could use because the STATA licenses are limited. Furthermore, the individual STATA license cost the disability resource office (DRO) over $500, which would have been an avoidable cost if the college simply had researched and used accessible technology in the learning environment. Accessible software is an important topic from the perspectives of student learning, social justice, and cost.

A full review of educational technology is beyond the scope of this book, and we direct readers to the Center for Applied Special Technology (CAST), a leader in the area of research and development. For example, CAST developed a prototype for electronic books that is accessible to students with learning, physical, and sensory impairments rather than just one type of impairment (D. Rose, 2000). It has also employed universal design principles in its learning materials, classroom teaching methods, and assessment techniques. Readers who visit CAST's website (http://www.cast.org/) can use screen reader technology that is built directly into the web page with the read-out-loud function in the upper right-hand corner. This type of integration is a socially just practice that postsecondary institutions should use on their own web pages.

Web Accessibility

The World Wide Web Consortium (W3C), the organization that is responsible for development and maintenance of the web, is committed to ensuring that the web is accessible to everyone (S. E. Burgstahler, 2008f). As part of its Web Accessibility Initiative (WAI), the W3C produced an international set of guidelines, Web Content Accessibility Guidelines (WCAG 2.0), which outline how to make the web accessible to a wide range of individuals with disabilities (Caldwell, Cooper, Guarino Reid, & Vanderheiden, 2008). The WCAG 2.0 includes "overall principles, general guidelines, testable success criteria, and a rich collection of sufficient techniques, advisory techniques, and documented common failures with examples, resource links, and code" (p. 4). These guidelines are vital to individuals with disabilities, but they also improve usability for web users in general. Four principles underscore the guidelines for accessibility. The web must be:

- *Perceivable:* "Users must be able to perceive the information being presented" (W3C, 2013, p. 2).
- *Operable:* "Users must be able to operate the interface" (W3C, 2013, p. 2).
- *Understandable:* "Users must be able to understand the information as well as the operation of the user interface" (W3C, 2013, p. 2).
- *Robust:* "Users must be able to access the content as technologies advance" (W3C, 2013, p. 2).

Web designers should attempt to follow 12 web content accessibility guidelines related to these four principles to ensure accessibility for individuals with various disabilities (Caldwell et al., 2008). In Table 11.1 we outline the 12 guidelines and describe the impact of these guidelines on web accessibility within the postsecondary environment.

Practitioners, faculty, and information technology (IT) professionals who want to assess if their websites meet WCAG 2.0 guidelines are able to use testable success criteria to objectively determine if web content conforms to each of the 12 guidelines. Each criterion is written as a true or false statement against which specific web content is tested to determine how well people with various disabilities can use the content for its intended purposes (W3C, 2013). For example, the success criterion for Guideline 1.1 regarding text alternatives is: "All non-text content that is presented to the user has a text alternative that serves the equivalent purpose" (Caldwell et al., 2008, p. 6). Following this test criterion, any photos or graphics on websites should include a detailed alternative text description to aid users with visual impairments. When website content is being tested for accessibility, people with disabilities should be included among those doing the testing.

WCAG 2.0 provides a wide variety of techniques for meeting each of the guidelines and success criteria (Caldwell et al., 2008). The WACG 2.0

TABLE 11.1. WEB CONTENT ACCESSIBILITY GUIDELINES

Guideline	Impact
1. Provide alternate text for images or graphics.	All nontext items must have a text descriptor that can be changed into other formats such as braille, speech, or large print. This alternate text should include descriptive identification and include information that describes the purpose of the original object.
2. Provide alternatives for time-based media.	This includes alternatives for audio- or video-only media and may include captions, audio descriptions, and sign language.
3. Create content that can be presented in different ways without changing the information or structure.	Meaningful sequencing and related information should not be altered. Instructions should not rely solely on sensory characteristics (e.g., size, shape).
4. The content should be easily distinguishable to make it easier for users to see and hear content.	Use of color should not be the only means of conveying information. Users should be able to stop or pause audio and should be able to change the level of contrast and type size. For visual presentations, there should be no more than 80 characters of width, text should not be justified, and there should be at least 1.5 line spacing and additional spacing between paragraphs.
5. All functionality must be accessible from a keyboard.	Content should be operable through a keyboard interface and should not require timing for individual keystrokes. There should be no keyboard trap that limits the areas of the functionality that are accessible by the keyboard.
6. Users must have enough time to read and use content.	Timings should be adjustable, or the user should be able to turn off the time limit. Users should also be able to pause, stop, or hide any blinking or scrolling content. Users should also not lose data after reauthenticating a session.
7. Content should not be designed in a way that causes seizures.	Content on web pages should not flash more than three times in any 1-second period.
8. Users should have a way to navigate and find content.	Pages should have titles that describe the topic or purpose, and the page should be able to be navigated sequentially. Headings and labels should describe a topic or purpose and should be used to organize the content. Users should also be able to bypass content that is repeated on multiple web pages. Users should be able to locate a web page in a set of web pages in multiple ways. In a set of multiple web pages, users should be able to find information regarding their location.

(continued)

TABLE 11.1. (*CONTINUED*)

Guideline	Impact
9. Text-based content should be understandable and readable.	Information should be able to be disseminated in a way that can be programmatically determined. Users should be able to have a way to identify definitions of words, phrases, or abbreviations used in an unusual way. A mechanism should be available for assistance with pronunciation of words.
10. Web pages should be operable in predictable ways.	The context of the content should not change based on the settings of the user. Web pages that are part of a set of pages should use consistent navigation and identification of various parts.
11. Assistance for input should be available to help users correct errors.	Errors should be described to a user in text when identified. Instructions should be available to correct errors and reduce the likelihood of user error. Submissions should also be reversible, have data that can be checked, and/or that asks for confirmation after review.
12. Developers should create compatible technology.	Content should be compatible with current technologies (including assistive technology) and should be maximized for compatibility with future updates.

techniques include directions for accomplishing specific actions on the web, such as adding links to take users to specific locations, providing a movie with extended audio descriptions, and so forth (Cooper, Guarino Reid, Kirkpatrick, Connor, & Vanderheiden, 2013). WCAG 2.0 also provides two categories of techniques: those that are *sufficient* for meeting the success criteria and those that are *advisory*; they go beyond what is necessary to meet the criteria in order to address the guidelines more effectively or to address accessibility barriers that are not included in the success criteria. For example, a website that is sufficient will provide closed captioning in English for prerecorded audio, whereas a website that is advisory will provide captioning in all languages for which there are audio tracks. Under a socially just paradigm, we advocate that postsecondary institutions follow advisory success criteria.

Technology as an Accommodation

DROs frequently use technology as an accommodation for students with disabilities. Many assistive technology devices that were developed to support a particular group of individuals with a specific disability are now being used by individuals across disability type (Ofiesh et al., 2002). For instance, speech recognition programs were developed for individuals with a visual or mobility impairment, but now they also benefit students with learning disabilities and some students with attention deficit disorder/attention deficit hyperactivity disorder (Roberts & Stodden, 2014). In fact, the greatest benefits of assistive technology (AT) use are often experienced by those with the most severe learning disabilities (Higgins & Raskind, 1997; Roberts & Stodden, 2014), and the benefits go beyond academic achievement to include increased self-esteem and self-confidence (Roberts & Stodden, 2014). The successful application of assistive technology across disability types has led researchers to suggest that postsecondary institutions and service providers "encourage the use of AT devices for individuals with disabilities based on the functional limitations and characteristics presented by the individual and not necessarily by the general characteristics of a specific type of disability" (Ofiesh et al., 2002, p. 100). We provide examples of high-, middle-, and low-level technology accommodations and their associated functional limitations in Table 11.2.

Barriers and Inaccessible Technology

Students are entering postsecondary education with a greater knowledge of technology resources available to them, yet attitudinal barriers, financial constraints, and a lack of knowledge or training may limit access. In a study conducted by Sharpe, Johnson, Izzo, and Murray (2005), 17% of students with disabilities reported that they "were not provided with a specific type of [assistive technology], which they considered necessary to meet their education needs in the postsecondary setting" (p. 9). Research indicates that disability service providers limit the number of assistive technology options available to students based on the devices and software that the provider is comfortable with rather than making decisions based on effectiveness or research (Ofiesh et al., 2002). As a result, some DROs have a small number of assistive technology devices available for student use. Under a social justice paradigm, staff members of these offices need to be familiar with a number of assistive technology devices, institutions must provide the necessary technical support, and devices or programs that students find beneficial from K-12 education should be considered in the postsecondary environment.

Assistive technology is costly, and there is a relationship between "frequency, use and overall expense" (Sharpe et al., 2005, p. 8). Technology programs and devices that are more costly to the individual student are less frequently used. However, when postsecondary institutions covered the cost

TABLE 11.2. EXAMPLES OF ASSISTIVE TECHNOLOGY COMMONLY USED BY STUDENTS IN HIGHER EDUCATION

Functional Impact of Disability	Level of Technology		
	Specialized or High	Mainstream or Mid	Human Alternative or Low
Writing (e.g., dysgraphia)	Speech-to-text (Read/ Write Gold or Dragon Naturally Speaking)	Built-in speech-to-text (Chrome voice recognition or I-Pad voice dictation)	Scribe
Vision (e.g., low vision or blind)	Text-to-speech (Kurzweil) Screen reader (JAWS) Braille embosser	Built-in text-to-speech Large print	Reader Raised graphics created with puffy paint or putty
Hearing (e.g., hard of hearing or deaf)	Assistive listening devices (FM or induction loop) TTY (text) telephone	Closed captioning Visual emergency alert system (strobe fire alarm)	Sign language interpreter
Fine motor function and dexterity	Eye tracking	Adaptive keyboard	Adaptive grip Adaptive switches, handles, and other devices
Focus and attention in the classroom (e.g., ADHD, social anxiety disorder)	Smart pen	Built-in note taking and recording software	Clipboard with fine sandpaper to provide biofeedback in writing Manipulatives
Focus and attention in studying or homework (e.g., ADHD)	Graphic organizers (Read and Write Gold)	Phone/computer timer FocusBooster app	Concept mapping with flash cards Stopwatch or timer
Physically attending class (e.g., chronic illness, autoimmune)	Shared whiteboard software for class notes and group work	Skype or GoToMeeting to "attend" classroom sessions Online courses	Recording of course content for later playback or supplemental notes

of accessing the technology, student use substantively increased; students also used technologies provided by the institution (regardless of complexity) more frequently than those of a similar cost that they had to purchase themselves (Sharpe et al., 2005).

Students with disabilities have complex intersecting identities and "women, low-income populations, and members of historically oppressed racial and ethnic groups" are the most likely to have limited access to a variety of technologies (Duquaine-Watson, 2008, p. 441). As a result, institutions that wish to support their students with disabilities who also have high financial need may want to consider options for making assistive technology available for students who may not be able to purchase a device or software on their own. Institutions can employ a variety of methods to address financial barriers facing students in a socially just capacity by creating lending libraries for devices or purchasing site and take-home licenses for software.

Some students with disabilities may not enter higher education with experience using technology as an accommodation due to funding limitations within their K-12 district or because the student recently acquired or was recently diagnosed with a disability. In these instances, disability resource providers should also consider options to ensure that students who are using a new assistive technology are properly trained. Learning a new educational tool, even one that is necessary for access, can be a difficult task for any individual and may greatly affect a student's academic progress if the student is asked to use an unfamiliar program without support (Ofiesh et al., 2002; Sharpe et al., 2005). A significant majority (84%) of students reported that they had learned how to use their assistive technology device on their own or with the assistance of a family member and that they would have liked training from a professional (Sharpe et al., 2005). Technology is dynamic; it is important that professionals supporting students with disabilities regularly provide ongoing support with periodic check-ins (Ofiesh et al., 2002). Following a socially just paradigm, postsecondary institutions must provide assistive technology training for students, faculty, and staff.

Failure to consider accessibility when incorporating technology into the campus environment can also lead to barriers. For example, although there has also been a rise in IT and purchasing departments rapidly buying new and "better" products for classroom consumption, individuals with disabilities rarely review these products. Therefore, new technology products are frequently assessed only for accessibility based on their compliance with current legal guidance (Dahlstrom, 2012) rather than their functional accessibility from a user perspective.

The effects of inaccessible technology are both academic and emotional. Academically, the accessibility of technology is critical for students with a number of impairments, particularly students who are blind or have low vision. As an example, a Southern University student stated in her lawsuit against the university that she experienced "embarrassment, humiliation and inability to participate in classroom instruction to the same degree as students without disabilities" (Crisp, 2014, para. 10) because of technology that did not meet ADA requirements. Similarly, a blind Arizona State student, commenting about a new Facebook application for students on his campus, stated, "Basically, I'm locked out" (Parry, 2010e, para. 4). What particularly bothered this student and many others was the attitude of technology companies that failed to even consider making their products accessible, as well as college administrators who did not consider accessibility when purchasing new equipment (Parry, 2010e). Such attitudes consistently send messages that disabled students are not wanted on college campuses, which is harmful as research demonstrates that a supportive, welcoming, and engaging campus climate is important to the retention and success of all students, including those with disabilities (see Chapter 14).

Legal Requirements for Technology and Postsecondary Education

Technology use by students, faculty, and staff, in and out of the classroom, continues to rise. Yet technology found to be inaccessible includes online courseware (Parry, 2010c, 2010e), course management software (National Federation of the Blind, 2010; Parry, 2010d), websites (National Federation of the Blind, 2010; Parry, 2010b, 2010d; Thomason, 2014a, 2014b), e-readers (Parry, 2010a, 2010e; Turner, 2010), and library catalogs (National Federation of the Blind, 2010; Parry, 2010d). In the following sections, we discuss legal requirements associated with technology use in higher education. (We have described this emerging legal topic in Chapter 3.)

Section 508

Section 508 of the Rehabilitation Act of 1973 requires that any IT that is developed, purchased, or used by federal agencies be accessible to people with disabilities (Harper & DeWaters, 2008). Accessible products must provide the same level of access to those with disabilities as to those without disabilities. This access may be provided by the initial technology or through adaptive technology or accommodation. Some educational institutions have voluntarily adopted the standards of Section 508. While universal design of instructional technology and websites ensures that all students have access to information (D. M. Campbell, 2004), many institutions of higher education still view universal design as too costly and complex to consider (G. Williams, 2010). As a result, many colleges and universities have poorly designed websites that are difficult for most students, let alone students with disabilities, to use (G. Williams, 2010). Both Ruffins (2011) and G. Williams (2010) argued, however, that providing accessible websites and technology is neither complicated nor expensive if one is familiar with the resources available. As noted in Chapter 3 and in the consent decree between the Department of Justice and Miami University

(U.S. DOJ, 2016), addressing the inaccessibility of websites and web materials continues to be an issue for many institutions.

The ADA and Telecommunications Act of 1996

The ADA mandates that colleges and universities ensure that students with disabilities have access to the same information as all other students through the provision of assistive technology (D. M. Campbell, 2004). In addition, the Americans With Disabilities Act Amendments Act (ADAAA) revisions require that information provided over public address systems and in assembly areas, as well as video relay systems, are all accessible via captioning (Gilbert, 2013). Any time that technology is upgraded, institutions are legally required to ensure that the new product either improves accessibility or is compatible with existing assistive technology (S. E. Burgstahler, 2008f). (We provided a detailed discussion of legal issues, including the Department of Justice's Dear Colleague letter on "Effective Communication," Office for Civil Rights letters, and court cases in relation to postsecondary institutions and the use of inaccessible technology by third-party vendors in Chapter 3.)

Students are frequently talking, texting, using social media, and accessing the Internet with their phones, and the link between social media and smartphones has brought telecommunications products into the classroom. Federal laws have mandated the development and use of accessible telecommunications devices (S. E. Burgstahler, 2008f). This legislation is designed to protect the access of individuals with impairments that affect their ability to communicate in person or by telephone (e.g., deafness, hearing loss, lack of hand function, blindness and impaired sight, and inability to speak). The ADA requires that all users be able to access all communications from all campus programs and services; Section 255 of the Telecommunications Act of 1996 mandates that all telecommunications equipment and service providers ensure that their products and services are accessible to individuals with disabilities (S. E. Burgstahler, 2008f).

Universally designed telecommunication goes beyond legal requirements to take into consideration individuals who do not speak English and those who have a wide range of sensory and physical impairments that interfere with their ability to communicate effectively. Hence, postsecondary institutions must consider telecommunications as part of their technology access planning.

Campus Accessibility Planning

It is imperative that the individuals who create and develop new technology and the postsecondary institutional representatives who use and purchase technology are aware of disability compliance. A 2008 study conducted by the

Enabling Technology Laboratory found that individuals who do not work in functional areas that are directly affected by legal mandates or institutional compliance are not likely to think about the design features that are necessary to ensure access for individuals with disabilities and may think of these features "as something nice to do for people with disabilities if development time and costs allow" (Erlandson, 2008, p. 10). As a result, many individuals making purchases of institutional education technology (e.g., faculty, technology offices, purchasing departments) do not evaluate technology for compliance and may make the mistake of purchasing inaccessible technology for their department, division, classroom, or campus.

While legal requirements for accessibility are mandated by a number of federal agencies and laws, many products are still being developed without accessibility features. Proprietary companies have little incentive to develop accessible products, and the implementation of regulations has little impact "if enforcement is lax or if the perceived real or opportunity costs of complying are higher than the costs (e.g., fines) of not complying" (Field & Jette, 2007a, p. 203). Companies also often prioritize features that are likely to "have a significantly greater profit potential" (Field & Jette, 2007a, p. 203). This prioritizing of profitable features can be seen in the development of early e-readers such as the Kindle. It was not until after numerous lawsuits and pressure from educational institutions that Kindle updated its technology to have built-in accessible features and to support adaptive technology so that individuals with visual impairments or who have other print disabilities could independently access text-to-speech content.

Unfortunately, proprietary companies are not the only entities that oppose accessible technology. Legislation introduced in the 2014 session of the U.S. Congress would have required that instructional materials and other technology used on college campuses be accessible to students, faculty, and staff with visual disabilities or that materials that are "substantially equivalent" to those offered to nondisabled students be available (O'Neil, 2013; Stratford, 2014, para. 2). However, the American Council on Education and several other higher education organizations opposed the proposed bill, arguing that it would be impossible for higher education institutions to meet the standards and that the bill would have a negative effect on the development and use of new technology (Koenig, 2014). The National Federation of the Blind strongly supported this legislation, stressing the importance of guidelines that would assist institutions in making purchasing decisions and prevent lawsuits when technology is not accessible (Koenig, 2014; Riccobono, 2014; Stratford, 2014). The congressional session ended prior to action on this legislation, indicating that the perceived cost of accessible technology is a contested issue.

Individuals making purchasing decisions for colleges and universities often are not aware of the lack of compliance by design companies and lack of support from organizations like the American Council on Education. As a result, many purchasers make the assumption that a product will be accessible to all users even though this is often not the case. In addition, the same prioritization of features may occur when purchasers are deciding between two products. Purchasers and institutions of higher education should be aware, however, that as we discussed in Chapter 3, many recent court cases have focused on institutional purchases and use of inaccessible products.

The ADA requires that all colleges and universities have a campus accessibility plan for technology (DO-IT, 2009). Learning about existing accessible technology in order to develop such a plan can be the first step to overcoming attitudinal resistance to universally designed technology. Furthermore, having a campuswide plan is one method for promoting proactive compliance and ensuring standardization across institutional silos. University regulations that require their purchasing agents to buy only accessible products can also put pressure on companies to develop more, better, and less expensive technology products that are universally designed (Azevedo, 2012). From a socially just perspective, we strongly advocate that campuses develop and use a campus accessibility plan that focuses on universal design and includes students, faculty, and staff with disabilities in the testing of all products before purchasing decisions are made.

Eight Steps to Creating an Accessible Campus Technology Culture

Creating a campus culture that stresses universal design of IT requires strong leadership, vision, collaboration, adequate budget, committed personnel, technical standards, clear policies, staff training, accountability, and enforcement (S. E. Burgstahler, 2008f; Harper & DeWaters, 2008). Institutions interested in developing a positive campus culture can use the WAI, which has created resources to support implementing web accessibility standards (Brewer, Horton, & Participants of the Education and Outreach Working Group, 2002). The WAI process has eight steps: (1) establish responsibilities, (2) conduct an initial assessment, (3) develop an institutional policy, (4) develop initial and ongoing promotion plans to increase awareness of the institution's IT accessibility policy, (5) provide training, (6) develop accessible websites and software, (7) promote IT accessibility awareness, and (8) monitor IT accessibility (S. E. Burgstahler, 2008f). It is important to note that creating an accessible campus technology culture is an ongoing process because technology is rapidly changing. The following sections address each of these eight steps in detail.

Establish Responsibilities

Establishing clear responsibilities for the review, purchase, implementation, and maintenance of technology that is accessible (Step 1) is important. These responsibilities should not be solely assigned to an individual but rather should include collaboration across multiple disciplines. These collaborations should at minimum include representation from the DRO, IT, and an upper-level administrator with oversight of purchasing and policy development. A prominent spokesperson (e.g., the provost) advocating for accessible technology and including access-based responsibilities directly on position descriptions are particularly helpful strategies to ensure responsibilities for technology access are clearly delineated.

Conduct an Initial Assessment

Institutions should conduct an initial assessment of the current accessibility of technology on campus (Step 2). This assessment should be comprehensive and review IT, technology hardware in campus labs, websites, and environmental technology such as door openers and elevators. The assessment should also determine the level of awareness, knowledge, and skills within the campus community regarding the need for accessible technology and the expertise of technology professionals.

The goal of this initial assessment is to create a plan for campus improvement. Consistent staffing, student voice, and creating a culture of inclusion are important components. Therefore, the individuals who will be responsible for implementing changes should be engaged in this initial assessment. We also advocate for using the assessment process as a method for developing leadership skills and mentoring students with disabilities; therefore, undergraduate and graduate students should be included in the initial assessment committee or working group.

Develop an Institutional Policy and Promotion Plan

The initial assessment should reveal if the campus has an existing policy for technology accessibility. If such a policy does not exist, the institution should establish (Step 3) and promote (Step 4) a policy that provides recommendations and requirements for technology purchasing, development, and usage. If the campus has an existing policy, information from the initial assessment should be used to update or revise this policy so that additional access topics or areas that were discovered during the assessment are included in an updated policy. As part of this process, the institution should create an accessibility statement that is both a visible commitment to community members and an article that can be referenced during the licensing of all electronic resources that the institution is considering purchasing or when the institution is accepting bids for review.

Institutional technology policies should be comprehensive and include learning platforms, software packages, websites, and hardware. The content of the policy should establish a minimum level of accessibility that all purchases must meet. We encourage institutions and readers to use the 12 guidelines described earlier in this chapter and outlined in Table 11.1 as a template for evaluating accessibility. Furthermore, as part of the comprehensive accessibility policy, institutions should require a review of the Voluntary Product Accessibility Template (VPAT) for all products prior to purchasing. A VPAT can be requested from all technology developers, and a blank VPAT can be accessed through the U.S. Department of State (IMPACT Outreach Center, 2015). Buyers can identify potential accessibility issues by consulting product disclosures; purchasers then can negotiate for updated and more accessible content. Because the VPAT is a standardized template that all developers easily can use to check accessibility, its use also will encourage proprietary developers to pay greater attention to accessibility in the development process.

Provide Training

Campus administrators and staff responsible for technology accessibility should arrange to offer training (Step 5) for a wide variety of groups on campus related to accessibility. These trainings should meet the individual and departmental needs of faculty, technology staff, disability resource staff, and other administrators. Training should be included that is tailored to anyone who is creating technology content (e.g., departmental web administrators, faculty managing online course content) and whenever possible should be integrated into existing training related to technology. If they do not already, institutions with computer science and human-computer interactions courses should consider incorporating this training and applicable accessibility principles into their instruction, as should degrees in educational technology.

Develop Accessible Websites and Software

Many campuses develop in-house websites and software platforms. These programs should be designed to meet the accessibility standards that the institution has developed (Step 6). Accessible websites include features such as skip to content, alternative text, captioned videos, and correctly titled links that open in the same tab of the browser. Universal design and accessibility should be a priority for the development of these products, and any technology development teams on campus should be provided with training.

Promote IT Accessibility Awareness

Accessibility of technology and any relevant policies should be incorporated into information related to technology (Step 7). The policy should be linked on appropriate websites and should be readily accessible to individuals looking for information related to campus accessibility. The University of Washington (2015) maintains a resource bank of IT policies that policy developers in higher education can reference. Trainings related to accessible technology should be widely advertised and made available to a wide variety of campus constituents. This promotion of accessibility as a key priority of the institution will encourage campus members to be compliant with the policy and will help to create a campus culture where accessibility is considered a key component of all technological aspects of the institution.

Monitor IT Accessibility

Institutions should create a plan for monitoring and periodic review of implemented technology (Step 8). This monitoring may include replacing outdated hardware, routinely updating existing software, and considering when to make new purchases. Technology advances occur rapidly, and institutions that fail to develop a plan for monitoring technology and reviewing updated legal guidance will quickly find themselves out of compliance. If close monitoring is not implemented, slow or out-of-date technology may result in the same barriers for students with disabilities as the limitations created by inaccessible technology. Similar to the initial assessment, responsibility for ongoing monitoring should be highly visible, part of individual job descriptions, and shared across multiple community members so that the necessary time and resources are allocated to this step.

Conclusion

With the increase in online, blended, and computer-mediated instruction, technology is quickly becoming a staple of all students' educational experiences. Clear legal mandates and industry guidelines exist for making technology accessible, adaptable, and universally designed. Individuals with responsibility for technology should develop institutional policies that foster a climate of technology inclusion by requiring that any technology purchased for the institution be accessible to all students, staff, and faculty and that faculty and staff refrain from using technology that is inaccessible to individuals with disabilities (Office for Civil Rights, 2010; O'Neil, 2013; Turner, 2010). Furthermore, new institutions of higher education and new programs being established in existing institutions must have services that adequately support students with disabilities, such as universally designed IT and other assistive technology accommodations necessary for academic success (Freedman, 2014). From a socially just perspective, institutions should be proactive and use accessible technology as a method for making institutions welcoming to students with disabilities.

Discussion Questions

1. Many colleges have outdated accessibility and purchasing policies for technology. What campus constituents should participate in updating (or creating) such policies?
2. What examples of technology are being used in your office or classroom? How might these technologies facilitate or inhibit accessibility?
3. Can you think of examples where the same technology both facilitates access for some people and inhibits access for others? How might you address multiple technological needs in a universally designed way?
4. What technology challenges do you see your institution facing? How might these be addressed?

CHAPTER TWELVE

CLASSROOM INSTRUCTIONAL INTERVENTIONS

My current department is wonderful. The full-time faculty and deans are committed to professional development of part-time faculty. This institution has teaching as its central mission with great folks in the Center for Teaching and Learning. However, the opportunities for training do not focus on universal design. Rather, the current faculty development is really centered on how to teach online classes or learn blackboard. This is unfortunate because we are an open enrollment institution and I have students with a wide range of abilities taking my classes. Our institution is lucky; the folks in the disability resource office are very knowledgeable and helpful. Yet part-time faculty are paid based on the amount of time they spend in the classroom only. We have no stipend for curriculum development or revisions—so there is little incentive to learn about or implement universal design, especially if you are teaching several classes per semester on multiple campuses. Part-time or adjunct faculty are the new faculty majority, and making sure these individuals get training on universal design is important.
—Kirsten, adjunct faculty

Increasing numbers of students with disabilities, particularly those with learning disorders, are attending college as a result of more effective services to aid high school students in transitioning to college, greater awareness of resources available to them in college, and the increasing necessity of a college education to widen their employment options (McGuire & Scott, 2002). Along with more students with disabilities, the overall population of students entering college is becoming increasingly diverse. Today's college student population includes adult learners, part-time students, students from diverse ethnic and racial backgrounds (McGuire & Scott, 2002), first-generation students, poor students, and international students. As a result, faculty require tools to address the different needs, learning styles, priorities, and goals of learners who are new to higher education (McGuire & Scott, 2002).

While more students with disabilities have been enrolling in college as a result of the factors McGuire and Scott (2002) listed, retention and graduation rates are problematic, with many students leaving college before graduation, especially in their first year (Orr & Hammig, 2009). Orr and Hammig (2009) identified several factors that may contribute to high attrition rates among students with disabilities, including poor academic preparation during their K-12 education, lack of support to students in their transition from high school to college, inadequate disability support services in college, and ignorance among faculty regarding ways to support students with disabilities. Universal design-based instruction provides effective strategies for working with students with disabilities, as well as diverse students from varied backgrounds, to increase their success in college as well as their sense of inclusion.

In this chapter, we examine current classroom practices that increase access and inclusion and explore the implications of universal design (UD)-based instruction for the education of students with disabilities and other nontraditional learners. As noted in Chapter 10, there are at least three types of UD–based instruction: UD for instruction (UDI), universal instructional design (UID), and UD for learning (UDL). In this chapter we specify a specific type of UD-based instructional method when it is cited in an article we are referencing. Otherwise, we use the phrase *UD-based instruction* when a particular type is not specified or when we are addressing these instructional principles generally.

Current Practice

The services that many colleges and universities offer to students with disabilities are based on a traditional rehabilitation-oriented functional limitations model (Linton, Mello, & O'Neill, 1995), as described in Chapter 2. The focus of these services is on seeing that students with disabilities receive accommodations that meet the requirements of the Americans With Disabilities Act (ADA) and are appropriate for their individual impairment, such as extended time on tests for students with learning disabilities, captioned videos for students who are d/Deaf, or lab tables at an appropriate height to enable a person using a wheelchair to roll up to it and reach lab equipment. Disability resource officers generally must certify that students' impairments require such accommodations and ensure that faculty are notified of the necessary accommodation by the student and carry it out (Sahlen & Lehmann, 2006). As such, current classroom practice with regard to students with disabilities has been largely remedial, one-on-one in nature, and time-consuming.

In addition, as Ouellett (2004) pointed out, few instructional faculty and graduate teaching assistants have any knowledge of how to work effectively with students with disabilities, and they have not received any training about how to create inclusive classroom environments. In a more recent study by Baker, Boland, and Nowik (2012), faculty indicated that they were not very familiar with regulations regarding how to work with students with disabilities, and most faculty in a study by C. Murray, Flannery, and Wren (2008) revealed that they did not know enough to design accommodations appropriate for a student with a learning disability. In Baker et al.'s (2012) study, only 17% of the faculty had received professional development related to working with disabled students in the classroom. Scott et al. (2003) also indicated that "college faculty have typically focused on content rather than pedagogy, raising concerns about their willingness and ability to provide effective instruction, especially for those with disabilities" (p. 370). Later studies by C. Murray, Flannery, and Wren (2008) and Medina (2011) suggested that many faculty still do not have the training or experience to provide effective instruction to students with disabilities.

As untenured junior faculty begin their careers and senior faculty retire, higher education institutions have the opportunity to shift toward emphasizing and rewarding effective instruction (Scott, McGuire, & Shaw, 2003). Some centers for improvement in teaching, such as the Center for Teaching and Learning at Iowa State, are now offering information about how to work with diverse students and UD-based instructional practices to assist faculty who wish to better serve all of their students. In addition, many colleges and universities are linking the work of centers for improvement in teaching and disability resource offices (DROs; Thousand, Villa, & Nevin, 2010). This collaborative work, as well as requirements for training included in many lawsuit settlements (see Chapter 3), is leading to increased education for faculty on the concepts of UD-based instruction and accommodating students with disabilities. In this chapter, we offer additional ideas that can be helpful in this endeavor.

Accommodations

Research is lacking on empirically sound best practices for disability accommodations that meet individual needs (Hatcher & Waguespack, 2004). While additional research is being conducted, educators and practitioners are left to implement accommodations as best they can. Adding to this lack of knowledge, many educators at the college level feel the same tension as educators in the K-12 system with regard to providing adequate support and access for students with disabilities without providing an unfair advantage to these students over their peers. Research is also lacking concerning which accommodations might actually present an unfair advantage if implemented incorrectly (Hatcher & Waguespack, 2004).

Traditionally offered accommodations typically provide only minor adjustments and, due to the fear of providing an undue advantage, many educators and practitioners err on the side of providing conservative accommodations rather than making major adjustments (Orr & Hammig, 2009). These traditional accommodations include extended time, alternate versions of textbooks, and use of a supplemental note taker. These approaches were developed when very few students with disabilities were accessing postsecondary education and do not take into account the changing demographics of higher education.

Less traditional accommodations, such as flexibility with attendance, remote access to lectures, and emotional support animals are controversial topics on many college campuses. These accommodations may be incredibly beneficial for students accessing higher education with multiple chronic illnesses or psychiatric disabilities that would have historically limited educational opportunities. However, these accommodations may also pose logistical challenges and in some instances or environments be truly unreasonable (e.g., a cow as an emotional support animal in an 8×8 single residence hall room or absences resulting in missing more than a third of course content). Decisions regarding the reasonableness of an accommodation should be made on a case-by-case basis and not be based on assumptions related to the size (or breed) of the animal or the mode by which all students will meet the course learning objectives. Although these accommodations are less common, they are not as a whole less valid as possible adjustments for an individual or more likely to be abused, concerns often cited by faculty and staff.

In addition, accommodations are provided only to students who let disability resource staff and faculty know they have a disability and seek support (Orr & Hammig, 2009). The individual accommodation approach may have seemed best practice when students with disabilities, especially those with learning disabilities, were only a small, and often unseen, cohort of college students. As Scott et al. (2003) pointed out, "Today, growing numbers of students with hidden disabilities combined with students at risk for academic failure require new approaches to provide accessible and effective instruction for this diverse cohort of college learners" (p. 370). The numbers have grown significantly since Scott et al.'s article was published; the National Center for Education Statistics (2016b) reported that 11.1% of college students had some sort of disability, double the numbers from the mid-1990s.

Problems with Current Services

Within the context of traditional accommodations for students with disabilities, a number of issues have become apparent, particularly as the number of students disclosing their disability status to institutions increases. Under the ADA, institutions are required to provide "otherwise qualified" individuals with reasonable accommodation; however, many faculty do not receive training to help them understand and/or implement accommodations in the classroom (Medina, 2009; C. Murray, Flannery, & Wren, 2008; Salzberg et al., 2002). As a result of the significant role that faculty play in implementing accommodations, disability personnel are often tasked with providing training and faculty outreach pertaining to "legal mandates, compliance requirements, and office procedures" (Scott et al., 2003, p. 371). This approach fails to address the deeper systemic issues of equity, privacy, and inclusion when it comes to students with disabilities. Increasing the reliance of these students on support services, modifications, and accommodations has not fostered effective learning or positive outcomes (Mamiseishvili & Koch, 2011; C. Murray, Lombardi, & Kosty, 2014).

Inequity. At a national conference of the Education Policy Institute in 2010, disability advocates shared their frustration that so little had been done to include students with disabilities in the conversation about access and equity in higher education (Hernandez, 2010). They pointed out how few outreach efforts targeted this underserved population and how limited funding was for such efforts. There has also been an increased acknowledgment of the need for a more collaborative approach to working with faculty, not just on legal compliance but also on effective instruction as a more proactive and powerful approach to providing equity within educational access (Scott et al., 2003). Unfortunately, even with greater levels of educational access, students with disabilities are still confronted with the inequity of a system that continues to put these students in a position of "other," where their disability status is made known to their faculty, setting them apart from their classmates, and where accommodations such as extended time on examinations typically leave these student conspicuously absent during those exams.

Required Disclosure. Students who wish to receive accommodations are required to disclose their disability status to not only the disability office staff but also to their faculty through the delivery of accommodation notices. For some students, this required disclosure serves as a barrier to receiving services and access. For other students, it may serve to limit their own self-reliance and suggest that they are "different" from other students (Scott et al., 2003).

Exclusion. As McGuire and Scott (2006) stated, "While it may sound radical, the time has come to move the paradigm relating to instructional access from accommodation to full inclusion" (p. 124). Inclusion cannot be achieved through the current system of individual accommodations. It must be achieved through the implementation of universally designed learning environments. Colleges and universities that fail to modify their curricular pedagogy are creating systems of exclusion that are as substantial as those presented by the absence of ramps, curb cuts, and other recognizable examples of universally designed physical environments.

Barriers to Change

Unfortunately, barriers to implementation of UD in instruction are prevalent (S. E. Burgstahler, 2008a). S. E. Burgstahler (2008a) listed the following: legislation, awareness, attitudes, diversity efforts, reluctance to change, cost, and market forces. We discuss a number of these factors in this section.

S. E. Burgstahler (2008a) suggested that legislation can be a positive or negative force. It is inhibiting if the institution focuses only on meeting the minimum requirements of the ADA rather than attempting to see how addressing the access and inclusion of students with disabilities connects with achieving the overall goals and values of the institution.

Awareness and attitudes also inhibit the development of UD (S. E. Burgstahler, 2008a). One of the most important factors in UD-based instruction is personal support and attention from faculty (Bremer, 2003–2004). Research focused on students with learning disabilities, for example, has "shown that the faculty-student relationship is important to student success" (Orr & Hammig, 2009, p. 182) and "the success of college students with LD is directly influenced by their perception of faculty support" (p. 182). However, as discussed in Chapters 8 and 9, many faculty are unwilling to provide encouragement to students or to modify their teaching procedures to assist them. Often faculty are unaware of the principles associated with UD and do not believe they have the time to learn about them (Izzo, Murray, & Novak, 2008). Moriarty (2007) found that community college instructors in science, technology, engineering and mathematics (STEM) fields were more supportive of inclusive teaching and more knowledgeable about teaching techniques that are helpful to students with disabilities than faculty in four-year colleges and universities; however, she discovered similar barriers to inclusive practice: "lack of an inclusive mindset, lack of knowledge about pedagogy, high teaching loads, and lack of time for instructional development" (p. 264), in addition to lack of institutional support.

The extent to which institutions are addressing diversity efforts in general and have expanded their understanding of diversity to include disability also has an effect on whether UD principles are welcomed on campus (S. E. Burgstahler, 2008a). Not only can UD be beneficial to students with disabilities, but it is also of significant value to students from other diverse backgrounds.

In addition to the attitudinal barriers that faculty may present for students with disabilities, many faculty and administrators are also change aversive and will find excuses to maintain the status quo (S. E. Burgstahler, 2008a). Indeed, the one-on-one nature of accommodations that are emphasized by current university structures place significant time constraints on both the instructor and the learner, with varying levels of effectiveness related to these individual interventions.

D. H. Rose, Harbour, Johnston, Daley, and Abarbanell (2006) found that as a result of the "emphasis on the disabilities in students, not enough [attention was placed] on the disabilities in the learning environment" (p. 150). As a result, very few techniques for large-scale curricular changes "on the level of courses, departments, or universities" (D. H. Rose et al., 2006, p. 150) are being explored by the majority of individual faculty, departments, or institutions. In addition to time, the cost of training and resources is often also used as an excuse for failure to consider such changes (S. E. Burgstahler, 2008a). Cost may have been a factor in the lack of training in UD available to faculty at Kirsten's institution, as she reported in the opening scenario. Finally, lack of emphasis by purchasing agents on the need for accessible technology and other equipment that will enhance the use of UD-based instructional principles is also an inhibitor of change (S. E. Burgstahler, 2008a).

Addressing Barriers

As Moriarty (2007) pointed out, "The priorities and policies that institutions set around time and resources are critical to the implementation of new instructional practices" (p. 263). Arendale and Poch (2008) as well as S. E. Burgstahler (2008a) suggested means for encouraging the implementation of UD principles. They point out that having support and leadership from top-level administrators and respected faculty is critical when attempting to gain acceptance of new practices on campus, such as UD-based instruction. Institutional leadership can use their authority in forming a team of individuals with vested interests in implementing UD-based instruction.

Arendale and Poch (2008) noted that one way of establishing the need for the implementation of UD-based instruction is through surveys of current students with disabilities. (See Chapter 9 for further discussion of assessment approaches.) Reporting on the growing number of students with disabilities, assessing their academic needs, and determining how well those needs are being met can raise awareness among various campus constituents, especially if a variety of methods, such as presentations, websites, print, and video, are used. Data from a pilot implementation project can also demonstrate the value of UD in instruction. Having DRO staff charged with providing training to faculty can make use of the knowledge that these staff possess. Other offices that offer professional development, such as faculty development offices or centers for teaching and learning, should also include UD-based instruction as part of their regular offerings (Finn, Getzel, Asselin, & Reilly, 2008). Tailoring training to different audiences, such as administrators and faculty members in various departments, helps each constituent group understand the value of implementing UD-based instruction. Providing incentives to faculty who complete training, such as travel stipends, summer salary, or a course release, can encourage faculty to take part in training sessions or pilot programs. As Kirsten noted in the opening scenario, such incentives should be available to both full- and part-time faculty, particularly given the increasing numbers of part-time faculty teaching in community colleges that enroll a large number of students with disabilities. Finally, implementing policies that require purchase of universally designed products, especially technology, underscores the importance of ensuring that UD-based instruction principles are put into practice.

Effective Classroom Practices

While UD-based instruction is not yet being implemented on a large scale, researchers are exploring the effects of classroom interventions on all learners, including those with disabilities. Orr and Hammig (2009) conducted a comprehensive analysis of research on the pedagogical techniques associated with UD principles. This study highlighted the work presented in 38 articles that focused on students with disabilities, 23 of which specifically addressed educational outcomes for students with learning disabilities. They identified five distinct categories that were associated with instructional UD that they recommended as inclusive teaching practices in postsecondary education: "(a) backward design, (b) multiple means of presentation, (c) inclusive teaching strategies and learner supports (d) inclusive assessment, and (e) instructor approachability and empathy" (p. 185).

Backward Design

Backward design, a concept associated with UDL, refers to formulating goals and objectives; determining essential components of the course based on these goals; and then determining course content, methods, and expectations based on the goals and essential components (Ouellett, 2004; D. H. Rose & Meyer, 2002). This technique benefits all students since the goals are clearly presented and all students are being evaluated on factors that are made clear to them, usually on the course syllabus (Orr & Hammig, 2009).

Backward design requires faculty to think through the course from start to finish, ensuring that all components align with the course objectives. This planning allows faculty to be able to provide students with detailed syllabi, course reading lists, and clear expectations for all course components. J. Madaus, Scott, and McGuire (2003) found that explicit expectations and clear directions were important factors in all students' success. They also found that follow-through on the components of the syllabus was important for students to feel confident in the faculty member's support of their learning. Inconsistency was viewed as a "barrier to learning" (p. 2) and negated the positive effects of a clear syllabus.

Using surveys, focus groups, and case studies, researchers have found that students with disabilities value detailed syllabi, the provision of reading lists prior to the beginning of the semester, explicit expectations, and clear information about requirements (Orr & Hammig, 2009), actions associated with backward design. In two case studies that Orr and Hammig reviewed, students' success improved when backward-design principles were used (Brothen & Wambach, 2003; Sullivan, 2005).

Multiple Means of Presentation

Backward design also allows faculty to consider implementing UD components into each section of the course and use multiple means of presenting information. S. E. Burgstahler (2008c) found that considerations for the dissemination of content were an important component of implementing UD in the classroom. S. E. Burgstahler (2008c) cited the work of a group of researchers who met in 1997 to determine ways of using UD in curriculum development. They identified steps for course design to ensure multiple means of presenting content for the greatest understanding by students. These steps included providing text in a digitally accessible format; captioning any audio or audio-visual materials used in the course; providing alternate text or descriptions for images and graphics; and providing cognitive supports such as scaffolding learning, summarizing complex ideas, incorporating in-class practice, and providing assessments to build on background knowledge. These steps encourage instructors to vary their presentation of material and provide digital, visual, and auditory options for students to engage with content throughout the course.

Inclusive Teaching Strategies and Learner Supports

We have already noted that the demographics of higher education continue to evolve, and each year an increasingly diverse student body is admitted to institutions across the country. The role of the college faculty is to teach "these diverse students and, indeed, all students in the classroom as effectively as possible without compromising academic standards and expectations" (Scott et al., 2003, p. 374). Individualized accommodations are no longer the most effective way to meet the needs of many learners, especially given the increasing numbers of students with disabilities and other at-risk students entering college. The same UD components for instruction that benefit many students with disabilities also provide support for students from other underrepresented populations in higher education.

Scott et al. (2003) noted that many exemplary teachers who are being recognized for their effectiveness in teaching are "already using many inclusive practices in their classrooms, though they are not calling their instruction approaches UDI" (p. 377). These inclusive practices include many strategies that faculty are adopting as best practices. One example is providing course information in an electronic format so that students can access it at a pace that is best suited for their learning and in the size, contrast, and format that best meets their needs (Pliner & Johnson, 2004).

Faculty can also include a wide variety of other instructional techniques to support a diverse population of learners in the classroom. For instance, lecture often presents "a number of accessibility barriers to students with LD" (Orr & Hammig, 2009, p. 189). Orr and Hammig found that the strategies that provided the greatest positive outcomes for learners with LD included providing guided lecture notes and using the pause procedure—pausing periodically for discussion and "immediate free recall" (p. 189). Another helpful technique is monitoring the speed of presentation and lecture to support all learners, including those with slower processing speeds and those who struggle with note taking and listening simultaneously (Fuller, Healey, Bradley, & Hall, 2004). Other strategies include providing ample time for students to view visual materials, providing lecture notes or slides in advance, and providing a supplemental set of notes or a lecture guide for all students. Another technique is to "employ a concrete-to-abstract sequence that starts with a demonstration or activities using manipulatives" (Sullivan, 2005, p. 207). This technique allows students' learning to progressively increase and will engage students who struggle to grasp abstract concepts. Students also experienced strong positive gains when study aids for outside reading were provided, including "graphic organizers … reading guides, chapter outlines, and study guides" (Orr & Hammig, 2009, p. 190).

In addition to reviewing strategies for lecture and improving students' participation with the assigned readings, Orr and Hammig (2009) reviewed research on providing writing assistance to students and found that breaking down large assignments, providing writing prompts far in advance, and "embedding some level of course-specific writing support" (p. 190) into the class structure was valuable for learners.

Faculty will also find that students benefit from being provided opportunities "for guided practice prior to independent practice" (Sullivan, 2005, p. 207). Just as students benefit from having guided lecture and reading opportunities, they will also experience greater learning gains when taught how to practice in effective ways. This practice may include allowing students the opportunity to verbalize their thought process and learning to their peers or to offer in-class writing that requires students to explain the solution to a particular problem.

Inclusive Assessment and Evaluation

Multiple means of presentation is an important component of UDL, as is providing multiple means for students to represent their learning. Assessments and evaluation are considered an important component of education and are used to measure students' learning. Due to the impact of various impairments on the reproduction of learned material, one UD component for learning is to vary the ways in which students can show their learning. Assessments should be both accessible and reviewed for validity for as wide a range of students as possible (Bremer, 2003–2004). Research conducted by Dolan, Hall, Banerjee, Chun, and Strangman (2005), which was based on statewide assessments, suggested that all students, including those with disabilities, "may perform significantly better on tests applying UD principles than traditionally designed tests" (p. 7).

Fink, cited by R. A. Shaw (2011), suggested the use of assessment techniques that help maintain the flow of the class and do not penalize students with slow processing ability. Fink's ideas included posting questions on the course website and having students either e-mail or post their answers on the site, using class discussion as a means of determining comprehension of the topics covered and including questions on the syllabus with dates on which responses are to be submitted. Sullivan (2005) suggested the inclusion of "short in-class assessments with open resources, extended at-home tasks, journal writing, oral presentation of problems, focused writing that described process and understanding and small projects with presentations" (p. 208) in order to provide varied means for instructors to assess the learning of students.

In addition, Dolan et al. (2005) found that technology was an important component to consider as a "key enabler [of UD] due to its inherent flexibility" (p. 7). They recommended the use of text-to-speech supports for testing to allow all users to take exams in a self-paced, multimodal, and adaptive environment. Dolan et al. (2005) found that students who accessed materials using text-to-speech support "scored significantly higher on computer-based tests that provided large print, extra spacing, and recorded human voice compared to standard paper-based delivery" (p. 8).

Instructor Approachability and Empathy

As discussed in Chapter 9 on campus climate, how faculty treat students plays an important role in students' success and adjustment (Mamiseishvili & Koch, 2011; C. Murray et al., 2014). When faculty do not value inclusivity, they are less likely to adjust their pedagogy to take into account the needs of all students and to ensure that they feel welcomed in the class (Moriarty, 2007). Fuller et al. (2004) noted specific exclusionary behaviors that faculty can demonstrate, including "an unwillingness to allow their lecture to be tape-recorded, ... having unrealistic expectations about the amount of new reading that students could reasonably manage during a taught session, or failing to provide user-friendly handouts" (p. 311). Students' feelings of exclusion can be multiplied if there is minimal or no institutional support (through training or time) for faculty to develop inclusive practices and implement UD-based instruction.

Graham-Smith and Lafayette (2004) cited the theoretical work of Chickering (1969), who stressed the importance of a sense of belonging to the success and development of students in college. Graham-Smith and Lafayette reported that "faculty relationships are known to have a pivotal effect on whether at risk students, like students with disabilities, are embraced in the college environment" (p. 1). To encourage feelings of inclusion in the classroom, faculty can greet students as they enter the classroom, provide one-on-one attention to students, add encouraging feedback to assignments that will be returned to students, and in other ways show students that their presence in the class matters. In addition, Izzo et al. (2008) pointed out the value of faculty modeling "positive regard" (p. 67) for others who are from different racial, gender, or cultural backgrounds and share their expectation that "prejudice and ridicule will not be tolerated" (p. 67). For specific examples of instructional strategies associated with each of the categories of effective classroom practices that Orr and Hammig (2009) offered, see Table 12.1.

TABLE 12.1. EFFECTIVE CLASSROOM PRACTICES GUIDED BY UNIVERSAL DESIGN FOR LEARNING

Backward Design	Multiple Means of Presentation	Inclusive Learner Supports	Inclusive Assessment	Instructor Approachability
Begin course with the course objectives and essential components of the course.	Include descriptions or alternate text for images and graphics.	Scaffold learning and summarize big ideas.	Vary means of assessing students' learning.	Include a statement regarding accessibility and accommodation on syllabus and course materials.
Clearly define expectations for the course.	Include captions for any audiovisual material.	Offer structured learning/study supports until students learn positive learning habits.	Use short in-class assessments.	Provide accommodations approved through the DRO.
Provide detailed syllabi and course reading lists.	Provide a range of digital, visual, and auditory options for students to engage with content.	Present material at a speed that allows all learners to process the information provided in lecture.	Use journaling or reflective writing.	Incorporate components of UDL in course design and implementation.
Select accessible course materials or identify them early enough to be converted.	Have supplemental course notes or recordings available to all students.	Provide opportunities for students to verbalize their learning process to other students.	Use technology to allow students to post answers to discussion questions or pose discussion questions in advance.	Attend trainings and professional development opportunities on disability and UD.
Provide multiple means of presentation and assessment.	Provide visual materials in a high-contrast format (e.g., black text on white background).	Allow students to show their learning in writing.	Include questions on syllabus with date that answers are to be submitted.	
Provide course materials in an online format.		Structure learning from concrete to abstract.	Provide detailed assignment prompts on the syllabus.	
		Use manipulatives.		

Practices of Specific Academic Disciplines

While they may comprehend the overall concepts of UD-based instruction, many classroom teachers have trouble translating the concepts into specific techniques they can use in their academic disciplines. Some suggestions that faculty have offered appear to work regardless of discipline. For example, faculty participating in the Ivy Access Initiative (R. A. Shaw, 2011) found that online chat rooms or asynchronous bulletin boards increased the willingness of quiet or shy students who normally do not speak in class to participate using online methods. Ivy Access Initiative faculty also recommended having accessible course websites and using accessible in-class media (R. A. Shaw, 2011). Arries (1999) allowed students with disabilities who wished to complete tests in a quiet atmosphere to take them in a different room. This strategy for assessment seems to be helpful for many students with learning impairments and attention deficit disorders. To create a socially just environment, any student should have this opportunity so that students with disabilities are not singled out from others in the class.

Some disciplines, however, require specific strategies suited to the kind of material that is part of the curriculum of that area. World languages, STEM fields, and fine arts are particularly challenging for students with various disabilities. Instructors who have been part of various initiatives focused on incorporating UD-based instruction, such as the Ivy Access Initiative (R. A. Shaw, 2011), the PASS-IT project (Higbee & Goff, 2008), and others have provided guidance for instructors in these disciplines. While not a comprehensive list of universally designed strategies covering every subject, the activities discussed in this section and listed in the tables that follow may provide ideas for teachers in various disciplines.

The website Merlot Elixr (CSU Center for Distributed Learning, 2009–2010a) provides almost 100 case studies and sample lesson plans from different subject areas that are based on UDL principles. The website is highly interactive, presenting material in written, auditory, and visual ways. It is an excellent resource for classroom teachers and those engaged in professional development of educators.

World Languages

World languages can be particularly difficult for students with disabilities, especially for those who have learning impairments that manifest as problems with language processing (Arries, 1999). Handle (2004) provided a number of suggestions for incorporating UID into the study of world languages. She noted that UID principles can be most effectively incorporated into a communicative approach to language teaching in which the emphasis is on speaking the language rather than writing or reading it. Arries (1999) also identified several strategies that were helpful to students with learning disabilities in his world languages classes. He found it useful for disability resource staff to serve as consultants to faculty by providing input on the specific needs of students with disabilities while world languages faculty identified strategies for teaching language that might best meet those needs (Arries, 1999). Table 12.2 provides some strategies for use in world language classrooms.

STEM Disciplines

Despite the encouragement that students are given to enter STEM majors and the career availability in STEM fields, many students with disabilities are discouraged by barriers they perceive to success in this area (Street et al., 2012). Faculty in STEM fields will find that students experience greater gains when allowed to progress from concrete concepts to "representational phases with specific examples and diagrams" (p. 207) followed by abstracted generalizations. Street et al. (2012) found that peer-led team learning (PLTL), a national STEM peer mentoring model, was more effective for students with disabilities when the peer mentors were taught the principles of UDL than it was when the mentors did not use these principles.

Derntl and Motschnig-Pitrik (2007), from the University of Vienna, Austria, provided an excellent framework and suggestions for including UD (which they call universal access) in engineering education. They also conducted a study that demonstrated that students in universally designed engineering classes developed greater social and communicative skills, as well as personal dispositions and intuitions, than students who took engineering classes that did not incorporate UD. The gains in knowledge and intellect were similar for both groups. This study, which was not limited to students with disabilities, demonstrated that UD principles can benefit all engineering students.

The Disabilities, Opportunities, Internetworking, and Technology Program (DO-IT), which is located at the University of Washington, has had a large grant from the National Science Foundation since 2002 entitled the Alliance for Students with Disabilities in Science, Technology, Engineering, and Mathematics to prepare students with disabilities for study and employment in STEM fields using UD techniques (S. E. Burgstahler & Bellman, 2016). Under the auspices of DO-IT, S. E. Burgstahler (2015) has published an online book, *Making STEM Accessible to Postsecondary Students with Disabilities*, that includes valuable information regarding STEM education for disabled students. Strategies employed by R. A. Shaw (2011) and others teaching STEM subjects are provided in Table 12.3.

TABLE 12.2. LEARNING STRATEGIES FOR WORLD LANGUAGE CLASSROOMS

Strategy	Purpose	Source
Use a communicative approach that focuses on contextual, real-world language use: hands-on activities (e.g., games, group work, pair pictures with vocabulary, use grab bags containing cultural items), problem solving drawing on previous knowledge, open-ended questioning, use of target language, and introducing nonlinguistic aspects of language.	Accommodate new information gained from active engagement into previous way of thinking; address different types of learning.	Handle (2004); Richards & Rogers (2001)
Accessible website with web-based tools (e.g., study guides, digitized audio files of text-based materials, digitized video clips of native speakers; links to websites in target language or highlighting target culture); materials should be accessible using adaptive technologies such as screen readers.	Provide continual access to course materials; use concrete methods for presenting materials.	Handle (2004)
Make instruction multimodal (e.g., role plays, Velcro cards, website searches in target language).	Address different learning approaches.	R. A. Shaw (2011)
Use flash cards to introduce new vocabulary; color-code vowels.	Learn correct pronunciation and improve listening comprehension; reinforce phonetic code.	Arries (1999)
Use pictures from magazines or hand-drawn images with color-coded labels and group oral repetition or words.	Reinforce vocabulary acquisition and pronunciation.	Arries (1999)
Have students work in small groups. Encourage students to applaud when other students are successful in presenting work.	Create a supportive atmosphere.	Arries (1999)
Videotape students' presentations.	Students can see progress and areas needing improvement.	Arries (1999)
Use a variety of assessment approaches (e.g., written assignments, oral cassettes, tests with extra time for all students).	Address various learning approaches.	Handle (2004)

TABLE 12.3. LEARNING STRATEGIES FOR STEM DISCIPLINES

Mathematics		
Learning Strategy	**Purpose**	**Source**
Verbalize a commitment to diversity, universal access, and equity on the first day of class.	Reduce anxiety and create a welcoming environment.	Duranczyk & Fayon (2008)
Specifically define and describe unfamiliar mathematical words and concepts.	Clarity.	R. A. Shaw (2011)
Pause between meaningful concepts and make eye contact.	Stress key concepts, assess understanding.	R. A. Shaw (2011)
Use activity-based, discovery-based, and learner-centered strategies.	Promote independent thinking and require sustained effort.	Duranczyk & Fayon (2008)
Emphasize process rather than correct answers.	Focus on concepts rather than computation.	Duranczyk & Fayon (2008)
Use small groups in class and study groups outside class.	Provide flexibility and natural supports for students.	Duranczyk & Fayon (2008)
Present or have students present how their cultures use probability concepts in work and play.	Demonstrate cultural sensitivity.	Duranczyk & Fayon (2008)
Vary type and length of activities, reflection, and skill building.	Increase memory and meaning making.	Duranczyk & Fayon (2008)
Have students verbally or visually demonstrate their thinking process in solving problems.	Help students formalize what makes sense and what does not; help them use more of their physical senses to enhance memory paths.	Duranczyk & Fayon (2008)
Use instructor-prepared handouts with key mathematical concepts drawn from texts rather than complete text.	Material is more concise and readable.	Sullivan (2005)
Use multiple assessment techniques integrated into the teaching and learning process (e.g., questions for students to answer as the instructor moves through the class period).	Ensure equal access and equity; reduce student anxiety.	Duranczyk & Fayon (2008); Kinney & Kinney (2008)
Use students' assessment results to adjust methods and materials.	Ensure continuous improvement of methods and materials.	Duranczyk & Fayon (2008)
Use rubrics to assess activities, assignments, exams, and presentations.	Create a venue for presenting clear expectations, feedback, and assessment.	Duranczyk & Fayon (2008)

TABLE 12.3. (*CONTINUED*)

Science

Learning Strategy	Purpose	Source
At beginning of class, overview key concepts and reasons they are important.	Provide context for understanding daily class lectures.	R. A. Shaw (2011)
Start the unit with a short in-class essay of what students know about the topic.	Allow students who write better than they talk to share knowledge, which enhances participation.	R. A. Shaw (2011)
Use two projectors, and leave each slide on screen for a period of time long enough for students to copy material.	Give students time to absorb and copy down information presented.	R. A. Shaw (2011)
Create, use, and post computer animation modules.	Illustrate important concepts.	R. A. Shaw (2011)
Use a combination of online simulations, songs, video animations, kinesthetic modeling, and traditional and digital text.	Communicate difficult concepts in a variety of ways.	Staskowski, Hardin, Klein, & Wozniak (2013)
Create work groups by random assignment.	Make lab assignments more accessible.	Bremer (2003–2004)

Engineering

Learning Strategy	Purpose	Source
Use information system tools in assessment.	Improve the accessibility of assessment instruments.	Variawa & McCahan (2010)
Create engaging learning environments, and encourage students to identify and solve problems in their communities.	Immerse students in real-life, meaningful situations and encourage active participation.	Basham & Marino (2013); Derntl & Motschnig-Pitrik (2007)
Use evidence-based teaching practices, guided inquiry, and instructional scaffolding.	Break down the complexity of problem solving.	Basham & Marino (2013)
Use captioned videos and films, along with visual, aural, and tactile instructional demonstrations.	Enhance students' content knowledge and meta-cognitive skills.	Basham & Marino (2013)
Have students use graphic organizers to visually represent concepts.	Encourage systems thinking.	Basham & Marino (2013)
Use collaborative whole-team projects.	Encourage collaborative team-based skills.	Basham & Marino (2013); Derntl & Motschnig-Pitrik (2007)

(*continued*)

TABLE 12.3. (*CONTINUED*)

Engineering		
Learning Strategy	**Purpose**	**Source**
Provide opportunities for students to practice face-to-face and online communication in assignments using small group work, e-mail, text messages, and Facebook.	Develop communication skills in multiple settings.	Basham & Marino (2013); Derntl & Motschnig-Pitrik (2007)
Use strategies such as think-alouds to model behavior.	Model ethical thinking and rationalizations.	Basham & Marino (2013)
Use video games to solve engineering problems.	Visualize problems and techniques to solve them.	Basham & Marino (2013)
Have students propose or choose problems to work on.	Ensure that all students feel included.	Derntl & Motschnig-Pitrik (2007)
Involve students in determining curricular design and assessment strategies through the use of learning contracts.	Ensure that learning is tailored to students' skills and interests, and help students take responsibility for their learning.	Derntl & Motschnig-Pitrik (2007)
Brainstorm course goals and expectations with students.	Help to build trust among students and between students and instructor.	Derntl & Motschnig-Pitrik (2007)
Publish all relevant information and content on an accessible web-based platform.	Enhance students' ability to understand and access course information.	Derntl & Motschnig-Pitrik (2007)
Employ self-evaluation and peer evaluation of learning.	Encourage students to take responsibility for their learning.	Derntl & Motschnig-Pitrik (2007)

Fine Arts

Because the arts are sensory in nature, many arts educators assume that students who have sensory impairments will be unable to successfully participate in their classes (Glass, Meyer, & Rose, 2013). However, Straus (2011), writing about music, pointed out that "the range of human hearing is wider than generally recognized—the boundary between normal and abnormal hearing is a construction, a fiction.... In fact, there are many kinds of bodies, many kinds of brains, and many kinds of musical hearing" (p. 180). For instance, Dohn, Garza-Villarreal, Heaton, and Vuust (2012) noted that individuals on the autism spectrum are much more likely to have perfect pitch as musicians than other individuals. Those with vision and mobility impairments also "see" and "move," just not in ways that nondisabled people expect. Universal design encourages arts educators to expand their definition of "normal" while using their creativity to engage students in unique ways. Furthermore, postsecondary institutions that are solely focused on art or design (e.g., Milwaukee Institute of Art and Design) may inherently challenge the "normal" within society as part of their academic and curricular focus. Art is frequently a method of critiquing the status quo, and as such, the value of normalcy is fundamentally diminished within a postsecondary environment that values, rewards, and fosters a culture of creativity.

Table 12.4 offers a number of suggestions of ways that educators in visual arts, dance, music, and theatre can use UDL principles in particular to increase options for representation, expression, and engagement, thereby changing people's minds regarding the definition of art and the skills needed to become an artist (Glass et al., 2013).

Glass et al. (2013) also discussed ways that the arts can be used to enhance learning in other disciplines. By varying how ideas are presented, students can find their own preferred path. For example, an event from history might be presented through art (e.g., a painting of an event), theatre (e.g., a skit depicting the event), oral language (e.g., a novel with the event as the context), or choral music (e.g., telling the story). (See Tables 12.2 and 12.3 for uses of the arts in world languages and STEM fields.) Studies of the influence of arts activities on learning outcomes demonstrate the effectiveness of different arts forms on reading comprehension, nonverbal reasoning, expressive skills, creativity, and problem solving (Glass et al., 2013).

Alternative Instructional Approaches

Research and development of instructional strategies and implementation of UD for learning has largely centered on traditional classroom settings. However, various institutional structures and educational opportunities may require adaptation of the traditional instructional techniques, as we discuss in this section.

Large Lecture Classes

Many large institutions offer large lecture courses that traditionally have provided fewer opportunities for students to engage in classes beyond listening

TABLE 12.4. LEARNING STRATEGIES FOR FINE ARTS

Visual Arts

Learning Strategy	Purpose	Source
Have students describe what they see in a piece of art and then reflect on what and how they were paying attention during a timed period; group reports out experiences. Repeat timed periods of looking and sharing multiple times.	Learn to comprehend, become more comfortable with complex and varied interpretations and meaning-making strategies. Co-construct rich and layered understanding of the art.	Glass et al. (2013)
Provide artistic examples from different cultures that deal with multicultural issues.	Help students expand their repertoire of approaches to art and confront their own beliefs.	James & Kader (2008)
Show the work of artists with disabilities.	Provide role models for students with disabilities.	James & Kader (2008)
Make explicit connections between the arts and other subjects, such as sociology and history.	Ground images in facts and well-developed theories rather than myths and stereotypes.	James & Kader (2008)
Develop assignments that explicitly help students to attend to visual information; analyze relationships within a composition; and make interpretive connections to ideas, experiences, and emotions.	Slow students down so they can really think about artistic images and objects.	James & Kader (2008)
Use assignment guidelines to provide structure but allow students to go in directions relevant to their expressive needs.	Help students to go beyond their own preconceived creative limits.	James & Kader (2008)
Use exercises and assignments that use a variety of modes of representation (e.g., verbal, aural, visual, and kinesthetic).	Help students learn in ways that make sense to them and expand their repertoires.	James & Kader (2008)
Model risk taking and vulnerability; value the diverse products that students develop.	Encourage creativity.	James & Kader (2008)
Have students use their own abilities and limitations as part of the content of the work.	Help students create work that is distinctive and meaningful.	James & Kader (2008)
Alternate among individual, partnered, small group, and all-class levels of involvement.	Create bridges for students to feel confident in their own ideas and to risk sharing their ideas with classmates.	James & Kader (2008)

TABLE 12.4. (*CONTINUED*)

Dance and Theatre

Learning Strategy	Purpose	Source
Integrate dancers with and without disabilities into a piece that uses various mobility devices to explore movement.	Leverage individual variability to expand understanding of dance.	Glass et al. (2013)
Use games and routines for ensemble building.	Foster a sense of community; minimize threats; optimize challenge; focus on collaborative work.	Glass et al. (2013)
Use warm-ups, circle exercises, and improvisation activities.	Help students pay attention, support each other, and work as a team.	Glass et al. (2013)
Work together as an ensemble.	Optimize motivation and promote expectations that actors are all in it together.	Glass et al. (2013)

Music

Learning Strategy	Purpose	Source
Pay attention and respond to the many ways that people hear, think, and do things; acknowledge the limitations of normal hearing; do not assume what people can and cannot do.	Avoid "normalizing" people with disabilities.	Straus (2011); Dohn et al. (2012)
Color-code notes.	Help differentiate notes and the roles they play in harmony.	CSU (2009–2010b)
Make connection between music terminology and how it sounds in practice by identifying a note on the board, talking about it, playing it.	Experiential process helps to remove the abstract component in theory classes.	CSU (2009–2010b)
Use physical movement.	Feeling changes in tones helps to internalize them.	CSU (2009–2010b)
Sing in music theory class.	Make connection between what they hear and theory, which allows them to participate.	CSU (2009–2010b)
Have students complete multiple drill sheets.	Low-stakes assessment to check for understanding.	CSU (2009–2010b)

and taking notes. While large lecture classes may offer unique challenges to incorporating UD-based instruction and limit a faculty member's ability to engage individually with learners, R. A. Shaw (2011) offered suggestions on incorporating UDI into large classrooms. Many of the suggestions are variations on UDI techniques and best practices for inclusion already discussed in the chapter. R. A. Shaw (2011) suggested that faculty consider videotaping or recording course lectures for students to review at their own pace, requiring students to post their notes from lecture to share with their peers, and creating small groups for "collaborative note-taking" (p. 28) to encourage peer reinforcement of material. These techniques not only support students who may need supplemental notes or additional review but will also help all students learn and practice more effective note-taking skills.

Computer-Mediated and Web-Based Instruction

B. G. Wilson, Ludwig-Hardman, Thornam, and Dunlap (2004) found that "some aspects of diversity (such as gender, age, ethnicity, [and] learning challenge/disability... are masked in an online setting" (p. 7), which can distance students from the learning environment. As discussed in Chapters 5 and 6, the masking of these identities can make it less obvious that particular learners' needs are not being addressed, which may lead to implications for full participation in online and blended courses. B. G. Wilson et al. stated that individuals at the greatest disadvantage in these settings "include those not fluent in reading and writing; those unskilled in independent problem solving; and those lacking prior knowledge of the subject matter" (p. 7).

S. E. Burgstahler (2008c) found that many educational learning platforms and distance learning courses unintentionally erect barriers for individuals with disabilities. These barriers are often the result of the communication methods used in the course. The instructor should ensure that communication methods used in the course (e.g., blogs, bulletin boards) are accessible to potential students with all types of disabilities. Universal design-based instruction can be used to mitigate these barriers and should be built into specific assignments for students. For example, if working in small groups is selected as a general teaching strategy for an assignment in an online course, students could be told that the first order of business for their group is to select a communication method through which everyone can actively participate in group meetings (S. E. Burgstahler, 2008c).

For some disciplines, computer-mediated instruction may be useful for specific classroom learners. Kinney and Kinney (2008) found that computer-mediated mathematics courses may help a wide variety of learners because of the flexibility to move at their own pace and the increased one-on-one time with the instructor. Computer-mediated classrooms that incorporate learning modules can provide immediate feedback on learning activities. However, Kinney and Kinney found that while some students greatly benefited from computer-mediated learning, other students were able to engage more deeply with material in traditional lecture-style courses. Kinney and Kinney suggested that institutions offer multiple options for each course to allow learners the choice among computer-mediated, online, and traditional lecture courses. As a result, instructors of computer-mediated courses, developers of online courses, and college administrators determining which courses to offer should pay close attention to instructional strategies and environments that engage a range of learners and allow for one-to-one engagement between instructors and students to assist those who may be most affected, positively and negatively, by these learning environments. (See Chapter 11 for more information on the use of technology for access.)

Learning Communities

Jehangir (2003) found that participation in learning communities can have results similar to the implementation of UID and "can facilitate achievement among all students" (p. 88). The recent rise in learning communities reflects the shift in higher education from a teaching-focused to a learning-focused environment. Learning communities place an emphasis on cooperative learning and facilitate "interdependence between instructors and students" (p. 88), which can improve access for multiple types of learners.

The emphasis on cooperative learning and the interdependence of class participants can enhance the trust that students have for their instructors (Jehangir, 2003; B. G. Wilson et al., 2004). Researchers (Fuller et al., 2004; Moriarty, 2007; B. G. Wilson et al., 2004) have found that students with disabilities experience greater success in courses where they have a trusting relationship with the instructor and they feel comfortable articulating their needs. B. G. Wilson et al. (2004) found that the "design and details of the course and messages sent from the instructor" (p. 9) can lead to high variance in the levels of safety and trust that students feel in the classroom.

Learning communities may also be the ideal environment for institutions to begin to implement UID components. Jehangir (2003) found that the greater trust between students and instructor led to an environment where creativity of expression flourished and all members became responsible for creating accessible environments and presentations. This flexibility of expression allowed faculty experimenting with UD the space to try new ways of engaging and supporting students in sharing concerns if a method did not work for their learning needs (Jehangir, 2003).

Study-Abroad and Faculty-Led International Programs

Soneson and Cordano (2009) found that several student populations have been and continue to be underrepresented in study-abroad programming. These groups "include students of color, students with disabilities, and gay, lesbian, bisexual and transgender students, and over traditional age students" (p. 270). These populations need special consideration and support as more and more institutions begin to consider and implement required study-abroad experiences for graduation and as the number of courses including a faculty-led abroad component become more prevalent. Universal design may be a key consideration for institutions expanding their programming abroad by using a framework for analyzing sites based on their ability to meet the needs of a wide range of students (Soneson & Cordano, 2009).

At the same time that institutions are considering study-abroad experiences as an essential component for graduation, institutions have interpreted past legal cases as removing institutions' "legal obligation of assuring equitable access for students with disabilities on study abroad programs" (Soneson & Cordano, 2009, p. 271). As is discussed in Chapter 3, this interpretation may not be accurate or in line with social justice approaches for inclusion of students with disabilities. However, the resulting tension for educational environments and students with disabilities wishing to study abroad is leading to an increase in one-on-one counseling by disability resource and study-abroad office staff with students who have access considerations for studying abroad.

Institutions, particularly those surveying potential study-abroad locations, should consider adopting an assessment of the physical, educational, and social environment of the site for accessibility. This assessment can then be used to develop a plan for universally designed programs, even in locations that may have seemingly inherent limitations. The same components that enhance domestic classroom experiences, such as backward design, may have a pronounced impact for all learners in abroad environments. Specific components that should be assessed in order to enhance accessibility include the residential environment (e.g., location of rooms, emergency alert options, way-finding signage, and variation of housing options), the classroom environment (e.g., equipment, location, and furniture), and excursions (e.g., transportation, availability of health providers, and residential accommodations).

Experientially Based Practicums, Clinical Experiences, and Internships

Many institutions, particularly those with professional programs (e.g., law, medical fields, engineering, teacher training programs, student affairs preparation programs, social work, counseling), are increasingly requiring practical experiences in order to prepare students for the workforce and to gauge a student's preparedness to work in the field. Concerns related to a student's successful employment are often intermixed into discussions of practical or clinical experiences. However, Pardo and Tomlinson (1999) emphasized that university and college programs are academic in nature, and as a result, institutions cannot make admission or retention decisions "based on a hypotheses [*sic*] of how well the student will do in the future job market" (p. 24) or in a practical environment. Pardo and Tomlinson also pointed out that a few institutions have begun to require the first practical experience early in a student's career (e.g., second year as opposed to the third or fourth year) in order to help students who are not successful in the work environment, even with reasonable accommodations, or those who determine they do not enjoy the practical applications of the field, to explore other career paths before dedicating substantial time or money to the program.

For successful integration of students with disabilities into practicum and field placements, collaboration and communication between the DRO staff, the corresponding academic department faculty and advisors, and the site coordinators is essential. This collaboration will allow the institution to provide clear guidance to students seeking accommodations regarding how those accommodations are made available and whom they must contact to ensure those accommodations are put into place. Milani (1996) stated, "It is meaningless for an institution to make internship opportunities off-campus available to students without ensuring that those internships are, in fact, accessible through accommodations to qualified students" (p. 1039).

Colleges should develop policies and protocols for accommodating students in internships and practicums that are required as a part of successful completion of the program or are offered for credit. Accommodations in these environments have been widely interpreted to be the responsibility of the institution, and institutions should expect to be asked to provide accommodations (Milani, 1996). Internships and practicums that enhance the learning of students or are affiliated with the institutional program but are not for credit may require accommodations that are offered by the host site or are a blend of accommodations on the part of the host site and institution. Institutional staff should inquire about accommodations that are offered and identify a host employee responsible for arranging accommodations, often someone housed in human resources, when vetting potential internship and practicum sites for students. These inquiries should be considered a substantial criterion for developing a relationship with the host site staff alongside an analysis of the learning that would take place at the host site.

Tribal Education

With sponsorship from the National Science Foundation, the College of Menominee Nation is spearheading a program to explore the use of UD in tribal education (College of Menominee Nation, 2012). In May 2013, the college hosted a two-day seminar for 61 tribal educators from 30 colleges and universities focused on addressing individual differences in learning using UD principles. They are now sponsoring an online circle via a Facebook group of tribal college educators who are invited to share successes and challenges in using UDI.

Conclusion

Universal design-based instruction can be used effectively with other interactive approaches in the higher education classroom, such as cooperative learning and computer-assisted instruction (Silver, Bourke, & Strehorn, 1998). In most cases, the use of UD-based instruction enables students with disabilities to actively participate in courses without having to ask for accommodations (R. A. Shaw, 2011). As a result, these students' classroom experience is similar to that of other students, in that they are not required to go through the stressful and humiliating process of seeking out special accommodations from professors who often do not understand the accommodation process or the need for accommodations. Universal design-based instruction also benefits other students with diverse backgrounds and needs, such as those for whom English is a second language, those who must miss class for legitimate reasons, those at different levels of familiarity with the subject matter, and those with learning styles that may not match the teaching style of the instructor.

In addition to aiding students in learning, UD principles help instructors develop their teaching skills (R. A. Shaw, 2011). The first step in UD is determining the essential components of the course and the course objectives. Universal design helps instructors to carefully evaluate these critical course components and how to meet the objectives of the course using creative and effective instructional techniques and assessment methods that enable students to demonstrate their actual learning. Finally, by eliminating the need to set up individual accommodations, UD-based instruction saves time that faculty, disability providers, and students can use productively in other activities.

Discussion Questions

1. What barriers to changing current classroom practices and accommodation processes exist on your campus? How might you address those barriers?
2. Several discipline-specific approaches to UD-based instruction have been identified in the chapter. How might you adapt those approaches to other fields of study?
3. How can UD-based instruction improve access to specialized programs (e.g., study abroad, internships)?

PART FOUR

SERVING STUDENTS

CHAPTER THIRTEEN

DISABILITY RESOURCE OFFICES

This week, I had a student, their roommate, and a cat to support. I am becoming known on campus by my relationship to animals.

—Autumn, coordinator of disability resources

I received an email with attachment this morning at 8 a.m. from Professor Carter. The email only says, "Here is something for Sara (a student who uses the DRO)." As I rush to convert the attached document, I see that this "MAY" look like a test. I reply back to Professor Carter's message asking for clarification if it is a test or assignment. Of course, Professor Carter can't answer me because this class started at 8 a.m., so he is teaching. I wait.

—Sandra, academic support and assistive technologist

The introductory quotations, uttered in relation to a roommate conflict arising from a residential accommodation for an emotional support animal and a last-minute alternate format request from a faculty member, offer humorous and pithy examples of the diversity that disability resource providers encounter daily at work. Place yourself in Autumn's shoes, contemplate the various stakeholders (e.g., custodial staff, dining services, faculty members, legal counsel, parents, roommates, resident assistant, residence life director, feline, student), imagine their concerns, and consider policy or legal implications related to the request for an emotional support cat living in the residence hall. In addition, remember that Autumn's solution needs to provide access; respect the rights of others; follow federal, state, and local legal precedent; adhere to institutional policy; and be presented in a manner that is diplomatically palatable to the stakeholders involved. This scenario illustrates why it is important that disability resource providers have strong problem-solving skills and provides a glimpse into the wide range of topics related to ensuring access.

In this chapter, we build on the real-world experiences of disability resource providers to examine current practices and socially just approaches to addressing disability in higher education. We start by discussing the inauguration of disability resources on college campuses. Then we provide an overview of the services offered today, including professional standards and philosophical implications for practice. We categorize the activities associated with these offices as administrative, service provision, or outreach (Funckes, Kroeger, Loewen, & Thornton, n.d.d) and describe specific tasks that fall under each of these categories. We conclude by looking to the future and focusing on how practitioners can advocate for social justice.

Historical Overview of Disability Resources

A historical perspective on disability resources is valuable because history provides insight into attitudes and expectations, "illustrating the things to be avoided" (P. Murray, 1988, p. 93) and offering a deeper understanding of people. Postsecondary support services began to increase after World War II with the advent of a disability resource program at the University of Illinois to assist veterans studying under the G.I. Bill (Dean, 2009). The expansion of resources for students with disabilities occurred after 1973 (Hall & Belch, 2000) when Section 504 (Pub. L. 93–112) of the Rehabilitation Act required that institutions receiving federal funding "provide nondiscriminatory, equal access to programs and facilities for individuals with disabilities" (Dean, 2009, p. 196). Consequently, the field of disability resources developed in response, accommodating the influx of students with disabilities (Dean, 2009).

From 1973 to 2000, four key historical events shaped the evolution of disability resources as a professional field. First, in 1975 the Education for All Handicapped Children Act (Pub. L. 94–142) provided a legal mandate for free and appropriate K-12 education. Although not formally directed at the postsecondary setting, this legislation had an indirect and time-delayed effect by creating a larger group of students seeking access to higher education (Ryan & McCarthy, 1994b). Second, in 1977, the Association on Higher Education and Disability (AHEAD) was formed and became the first professional organization for "individuals involved in the development of policy and in the provision of quality services to meet the needs of persons with disabilities involved in all areas of higher education" (AHEAD, 2014a, para. 1). Third, in 1985 the U.S. Department of Education recognized the importance of data on students with disabilities and sponsored the National Longitudinal Transition Study (NLTS) to gather nationally representative information about children receiving special education services (Newman, Wagner, Cameto, Knokey, & Shaver, 2010), which allowed for data-based policy and practice decisions. Fourth, in 1990 the Americans With Disabilities Act (ADA; Pub. L. 101–336) was passed. This legislation expanded the mandates found in Section 504 (Pub. L. 93–112) to a wider range of institutions and imposed direct financial penalties for discriminatory practices (Gehring, Osfield, & Wald, 1994).

Consequently, the 1990s saw an increase in professional staff and offices that provided services to students with disabilities in higher education. However, due to the emerging nature of the field, many disability resource practitioners were housed within other units, such as counseling centers, dean of students, "special population" function areas, and, in a few cases, under the auspices of academic affairs with academic assistance programs. In some cases, the responsibility for providing accommodations was tacked on to an existing position with little additional financial support or adequate training. As the number of students with disabilities grew, so did the importance of understanding and addressing issues related to access.

Disability Resources Today

In 2000, the U.S. Department of Education continued to recognize the importance of data on disabled students and sponsored the National Longitudinal Transition Study-2 as a follow-up to the 1985 NLTS study. Professional organizations evolved as well. To handle the increase in students with disabilities on campuses, AHEAD and the Council for the Advancement of Standards in Higher Education developed professional indicators and program standards for disability resource practitioners; these standards recognized that the concept of disability, legal parameters, and administrative duties are constantly evolving (Harbour, 2009). Since 2000, many colleges and universities have developed a disability resource office (DRO) as a specific administrative unit to address accommodations.

In September 2008, the ADA was reauthorized by Congress as the Americans With Disabilities Act Amendments Act (ADAAA; Pub. L. 110–325), and changes became effective January 2009. The ADAAA addressed court rulings that limited the definition of *disability* and reaffirmed the promise of equal access in higher education for persons with disabilities (Simon, 2011).

Furthermore, the Office for Civil Rights and the U.S. Department of Justice jointly recognized the increasing role that technology plays in accessing higher education via a "Dear Colleague"(advisory memos from the federal government) letter and mandated that students with disabilities have "equal access to emerging technology in university and college classrooms" (Office of Civil Rights, 2010, para. 7).

These social, institutional, professional, and legal changes have created a culture that focuses on access, inclusion, and an understanding that disability work is the responsibility of all units on campus rather than those that have a defined responsibility to oversee DROs (S. R. Jones, 1996). As institutions work toward an inclusive climate for students with disabilities, the work of DROs has shifted toward a social justice framework.

Institutional Characteristics and Disability Resources

Institutional characteristics play an important role in shaping the type of work disability service practitioners engage in. Like any other field, standards and values occur on a continuum, and DROs are as diverse as the institutional cultures they are embedded within and the types of students whom they serve. Kalivoda and Totty (2003) noted, "Programming design for disability services ... varies widely just as size and characteristics of institutions vary" (p. 267). For instance, returning to the topic of emotional support animals, a disability resource provider at a two-year public institution that does not offer on-campus housing would not experience Autumn's conundrum of a residential feline.

Institutional characteristics can be conceptualized in a variety of manners, including Carnegie classification, enrollment size, geographic location, residential or commuting campus, public or privately funded, minority serving, nonprofit or for-profit mission, open access or selective admissions, and two-year or four-year degree focus. Type of degree granted is particularly important, as the overwhelming majority of students with disabilities who are enrolled in postsecondary education attend two-year colleges (Newman, Wagner, Cameto, & Knokey, 2009; Sanford et al., 2011). In addition, the presence of online classes and distance education has significantly increased, creating a myriad of technology-related access issues for disability resource providers at institutions with a strong online focus. (We discuss different types of institutions in Chapter 6 and accessible technology in Chapter 11.) Each institution has unique characteristics that will shape the DRO; "therefore, it is important to design institution-specific interventions when engaging students with disabilities" (K. Brown & Broido, 2015, p. 189).

Professional Standards

Professional standards provide one avenue of guidance for disability resource practitioners cultivating a socially just campus. AHEAD and CAS are two organizations that offer professional standards.

AHEAD's code of ethics emphasizes educational excellence, integrity, confidentiality, respect, participation in professional activities, and maintenance of clear policies (AHEAD, 1996). As a professional organization, AHEAD assists practitioners by providing guidance on documentation practices to support accommodation requests (AHEAD, 2012b). It also outlines tangible guidelines through the development of standards that address administration, service, consultation, collaboration, awareness, and professional development (AHEAD, 2014b, 2014d).

In conjunction with the guidance above, AHEAD offers eight program standards for DROs that are "intended to enhance service provision for college students with disabilities by directing program evaluation and development efforts, improving personnel preparation and staff development... [and] expanding the vision of disability services at the postsecondary level" (AHEAD, 2014a, para. 1). Specifically, the DRO is responsible for "*providing services that promote access to the campus community*" (AHEAD, 2014a, p. 3). Disability resource practitioners serve as advocates, provide guidance on pertinent campus committees, and create programs that educate the campus community. In addition, disability resource staff members are responsible for determining appropriate academic accommodations, maintaining records, and collaborating with faculty to ensure a balance between reasonable accommodations and academic quality. DRO staff should employ a service model that encourages student self-determination and independence and develop, review, and revise policies to ensure equal access. Disability resource providers are also responsible for collecting service data, assessing programs, and evaluating student satisfaction. Administratively, the DRO staff members are responsible for fiscal or budgetary management, collaborating with campus constituents to ensure that institutional purchases are accessible, and providing university staff and faculty with training and development.

The second professional organization, CAS, provides guidelines for the purpose of "fostering and enhancing student learning, development, and achievement and in general to promote good citizenship" (Council for the Advancement of Standards in Higher Education, 2013, para. 6). To this end, the CAS Standards outline 14 key areas for disability resources: mission, program, leadership, human resources, ethics, legal responsibilities, equity and access, diversity, organization and management, campus and external relations, financial resources, technology, facilities and equipment, and assessment and evaluation. Written in collaboration with an AHEAD contributor, most of the CAS Standards align with the ethical, professional, and program standards described above. For example, Dean (2009) asserted the mission of disability resources is to "ensure equal access for students with disabilities to all curricular and co-curricular opportunities offered by the institution" (p. 198). The ideals of equal access to the educational community are common philosophical themes for both professional organizations.

Philosophical Components of Disability Resources

Philosophical approaches to disability resources and the associated institutional support for students with disabilities occur on a continuum (Kurth & Mellard, 2006). Unfortunately, at the most rudimentary level, DROs function as an institutional compliance mechanism for federal regulations; this practice is coupled with a philosophical system that functions solely under the letter of the law. In contrast, DROs that operate under the spirit of the law focus on access, equity, and social justice. Kurth and Mellard (2006) explained the influence of philosophy on service provision:

> Institutions that provide equal access by the letter of the law, (i.e., primarily to avoid lawsuits) exhibit a philosophy that may not be verbalized on a campus but is felt and observed, and ultimately limits the success potential of a college and its students. Colleges that embrace the spirit of the law, on the other hand, are likely to invest in an accommodation process that considers the entire context of student life, individual functional needs, trade-offs between the immediate and long-term costs and benefits, and incorporates system wide universal design concepts. (p. 83)

Philosophically, from a social justice perspective, the ADA and subsequent legislation is a floor, not a ceiling, relative to true inclusion for persons with disabilities. We encourage institutions to embrace the spirit of the law by defining *disability* as something other than "non-normalcy" or "devalued differences" (Titchkosky, 2011, pp. 5–6), incorporating disability into diversity initiatives, educating the campus community (R. Cunningham, personal communication, October 27, 2014), and challenging institutionalized ableism.

Conceptual Models of Disability That Inform Disability Resources

The conceptualization and meanings of disability that DRO professionals implicitly or explicitly hold influence the types of services the DRO provides (Guzman & Balcazar, 2010). Guzman and Balcazar (2010) examined the prevalence of three theoretical models among disability service professionals and found that participants were more likely to use an individual/medical approach than a universal design or social model in the majority of service areas (e.g., advocacy, access, consultation, accommodations, and policies). Participants who had more years of experience working as disability service professionals were more likely to use universal design or social models, whereas DRO practitioners with less experience were more likely to employ an individual/medical model.

DRO professionals play a critical role in articulating a conceptualization or model of disability to the students they work with and the broader campus community. Pragmatically, in their daily work, disability resource practitioners often find themselves operating simultaneously in multiple models. Broader societal perceptions of impairment and disability, combined with the current legal structure for obtaining accommodations in postsecondary education, subsequent professional guidelines (e.g., AHEAD, 2012b), and a focus on creating inclusive and welcoming campuses require practitioners to negotiate a balance between functional limitations, social construction, and social justice paradigms.

Historically, the functional limitations model was a foundation for procedures that disability resource providers use to administer accommodation requests. In order to access accommodations under both Section 504 and the ADA, students had to prove that they had "a physical or mental impairment which substantially limits one or more … major life activities" (Section 504, 1973, n.p.; ADA, 2010a). Prior to the ADAAA, this initial step required students to furnish the disability service provider with written documentation from a physician confirming they had a physical or mental impairment. After the ADAAA was enacted in 2009, this strict standard of requiring third-party medical documentation and assessing functional limitations as prerequisites for accessing accommodations has shifted toward a more balanced approach that gives greater weight to student self-report, observations made by the disability service professional, previous experiences, and incorporation of a variety of documentation (AHEAD, 2012b). However, because of this historical precedent and the broader culture of medicalization (Titchkosky, 2007), a component of disability resource providers' practice still engages with the broader culture that views disability as a functional limitation or problem that requires a solution.

Many disability resource practitioners also recognize that legal parameters and medical definitions of disability are inherently social constructions. As outlined in Chapter 3, seasoned practitioners have witnessed numerous changes in the legal constructs associated with Section 504, the ADA, subsequent court cases, OCR letters, and, most recently, the ADAAA. Changes to the legal definition of "a person with a disability" over the past 40 years exemplify the law as a social construction. Originally motivated by demands to provide services for military veterans, Section 504 (Pub. L. 93–112) of the Rehabilitation Act of 1973 defined a person with a disability, as "any individual who (a) has a physical or mental impairment which substantially limits one or more of such person's major life activities, (b) has a record of such an impairment, or (c) is regarded as having such an impairment" (29 U.S.C. § 794). This definition was reaffirmed by Congress in 1990 with the ADA, and then substantially narrowed by multiple court cases over a 19-year period (Simon, 2011). Effective in 2009, the ADAAA (Pub. L. 110–325) broadened who is considered to have a disability under the law (Simon, 2011) and reduced the amount of documentation individuals are required to offer when establishing that they have a disability (Heyward, 2011). These legal changes provide an example of how the law is socially constructed and demonstrate how social constructions have significant consequences for students accessing accommodations by shaping which students qualify and what actions students have to take in order to access accommodations.

Similarly, as medical research and technology progress, socially constructed or shared understandings of disease and etiology change. Experienced disability resource practitioners have observed changes in medical definitions of specific disabilities with subsequent revisions to the *Diagnostic and Statistical Manual of Mental Disorders* (DSM; American Psychiatric Association, 1994, 2000, 2013). For example, the definition and etiology of *autism* has changed significantly from 1943 when Leo Kanner used the term to describe children who lacked the ability to form relationships with others (Ghaziuddin, 2005; Heflin & Alaimo, 2007). From the 1940s to the 1960s, medical literature focused on psychological factors as the cause of autism; it was believed that healthy children were born into environments where they did not feel love (Heflin & Alaimo, 2007) and "refrigerator mothers" were blamed for lacking maternal affection and emotional competence (Bettelheim, 1967). In the mid-1970s and 1980s, the focus shifted away from environmental causes toward the idea that children are born with autism, and in the early 1990s, autism was initially included in the DSM-IV (American Psychiatric Association, 1994). Since this inclusion, the definition of autism has changed from a set of pervasive developmental disorders including Asperger's syndrome (American Psychiatric Association, 2000) to a broad spectrum that affects individuals with varying severity (American Psychiatric Association, 2013; Caruso, 2010).

Beyond socially constructed meanings, the methods used to address impairments are also advancing rapidly with new technological developments (e.g., advances in cochlear implants). Hence, practitioners recognize that in many cases, the medical definitions of disability and treatment for impairments are inherently social constructions and therefore it is imperative to focus on student self-report, DRO practitioner observations, and barriers in the environment when designing accommodations.

Disability resource providers also operate in a social justice paradigm by "ensuring that students with disabilities have equal access to educational opportunities available to all other students" (Duffy & Gugerty, 2005, pp. 89–90) and by being aware of and actively combating social inequality and stereotypes. Goodley (2011) summarized social inequity: "To be disabled evokes a marginalized place in society, culture, economics and politics" (p. 1). Individuals with disabilities are frequently viewed through a stereotypical lens of charity that results in patronizing or paternalistic treatment. Alternatively, people with disabilities are expected to comply with "the common-sense assumption of the good of overcoming" (Titchkosky, 2007, p. 143), resulting in expectations to surmount barriers, become a heartwarming success story, or even attain prestige as a supercrip. To combat inequality and stereotypes, the tenets of inclusion, agency, and voice are critical for practitioners operating in a socially just paradigm. Disability resource practitioners enact these tenets by supporting student agency, advocating for inclusive practices and policies, educating the campus community, and modeling social justice in their daily interactions. In addition, campuses are microcosms housed within a larger society, and practitioners work to deconstruct stereotypes by advocating for a campuswide understanding of ability as something that occurs on a continuum and potentially affects all people over the course of their lives.

The DRO and disability resource practitioners play an important role in promoting socially just and progressive models and understandings of disability. The philosophical and theoretical perspectives that practitioners hold are vital to working effectively with students and educating the broader campus community. (For further discussion regarding conceptual models of disability, see Chapter 2.)

Core Activities of Disability Resource Offices

The core activities of a DRO can be categorized in several ways. Funckes et al. (n.d.d) offered a concise and well-articulated typology that consists of service provision, administration, and outreach. Here, we build on the three broad categories that Funckes et al. (n.d.d) provided and extend their conceptualization (see Table 13.1) by including key areas of assessment, campus accessibility audits, budget, and supervision. We also modify their framework, collapsing

TABLE 13.1. CORE ACTIVITIES OF A DISABILITY RESOURCE OFFICE

Category	Components
Service provision	Communicating the accommodations process Assessing and maintaining documentation Facilitating accommodations
Administration	Advocacy Assessment Budgeting Grievance process Hiring and supervision Language and branding
Outreach	Campus climate and accessibility audits Collaborative programs Educational events Transition assistance DRO website and campus technology access Student engagement and development

some tasks into larger themes to broadly capture the accommodations process and additional administrative tasks. In doing this, we acknowledge the "inevitable tradeoffs in inquiry" (Weick, 1979, p. 35) that occur when using models to conceptually frame programs and advocate for an understanding of the core activities as conceptual categories with overlapping areas of commonality rather than distinct silos. Frequently, work in one of these core areas will inform or engage activities in another area. Although the law informs DRO work, we limit the description of legal topics within this section (see Chapter 3 for a full discussion of legal issues).

Service Provision

Disability resource professionals support appropriate educational accommodations for students enrolled in classes at their postsecondary institution. Depending on the structure of the institution, DROs may also be responsible for providing campus accessibility services for community members visiting the institution (e.g., interpreters for graduation ceremonies), facilitating work-related accommodations for employees (Duffy & Gugerty, 2005), or administering broader campus services (e.g., testing centers). In this chapter, we focus on the core task of providing accommodations to students and outline the three components of service provision as communicating the process for requesting reasonable accommodations, assessing and maintaining accommodation-related documentation, and facilitating accommodations.

Communicating the Accommodations Process. Disability resource practitioners are responsible for communicating the process of requesting reasonable accommodations at their institution. Actions that students are required to take in order to identify themselves to the institution as students with disabilities and request accommodation cannot be overly burdensome, and the process must ensure that students receive accommodations in a timely fashion. The accommodations process needs to be clearly outlined on the DRO website and communicated to campus partners through additional methods, such as sample syllabi statements for faculty members, marketing at new student orientation, and accessibility statements on campus technology web pages.

Disability resource practitioners may occasionally update or modify the accommodations process to take advantage of changes in technology, remain in compliance with legal requirements, or fit within new institutional processes. For example, in an attempt to conserve resources or streamline the communication process, an institution may switch from providing paper accommodation letters to an electronic notification system. Any changes to the process of requesting and receiving reasonable accommodations should be clearly and broadly advertised, and information about the changes should be easily accessible.

Assessing and Maintaining Documentation. Each institution sets its own documentation process, and disability resource practitioners must consistently apply the same protocol for every student. To assist with this process, AHEAD provided guidance and professional standards. We concur with the objectives outlined by AHEAD (2012b) and advocate for a socially just approach to documentation assessment that views students through a holistic lens and trusts students as people who are experts on their own lives rather than assigning expertise to a third party with medical authority. A holistic assessment process may involve reviewing external documentation including, but not limited to, individual educational plans (IEP) from high school, parental communication, accommodations from previous standardized testing (e.g., Compass, ACT, or SAT), and medical documentation (both historic and current).

A socially just assessment process also includes a detailed and structured interview with the student, which serves as the primary source of information for determining accommodations. This narrative intake process allows the DRO professional to gain an understanding of students' views of their histories, current functioning, strengths, weaknesses, multiple identities (see Chapters 5 and 6), and previously successful or unsuccessful accommodation strategies. In some cases, an accurate assessment of documentation will require that the DRO practitioner request that students provide additional information regarding how they are currently affected by a functional limitation or disability, which may include using more traditional medical reports as a secondary source of documentation. Many disability resource practitioners have advanced academic training, such as a master's degree in rehabilitation counseling, that enables the practitioner to interpret documentation submitted by third parties and make assessments. A full review of documentation guidance is not possible within this chapter; interested readers are encouraged to consult AHEAD (2012b) for further direction.

Disability resource practitioners maintain documentation and student records in a confidential, secure, accurate, and organized manner. They keep copies, either electronic or paper, of the documentation that students provide and return the originals to the student. Documents on file with the DRO are considered part of a student's academic record and protected under the Family Educational Rights and Privacy Act (FERPA, 1974: 34 CFR § 99.31). Therefore, many DRO offices use a FERPA waiver to provide a student with the opportunity to have the practitioner speak about the student's academic record with others (e.g., a parent).

Over the course of a student's academic career, disability resource practitioners may have several interactions with the student. Hence, these practitioners should create their own case notes to summarize and document student meetings, e-mail, and third-party interactions. Keeping accurate documentation of student interactions allows practitioners to remember what was previously communicated to a student, provides an audit trail in the event a grievance is filed, and allows the professional to support the student as a unique individual, which is particularly challenging for practitioners with large caseloads.

Facilitating Accommodations. A significant component of disability resource providers' work is to facilitate accommodations through an interactive process that actively engages the student in the request for accommodations. As discussed in Chapter 3, accommodations are reasonable changes or modifications that provide a level playing field; accommodations do not fundamentally alter academic standards or provide personal services. When facilitating accommodations from a social justice perspective, it is imperative to present accommodations as a means of providing equal access and removing barriers within the environment. DRO practitioners should resist conceptualizing accommodations from a limitation-based perspective or see accommodations as giving students extra help.

There is a lack of national data on student perceptions about or satisfaction with accommodations. However, limited institution-specific surveys found that the majority of students reported they were satisfied with academic accommodations, on average ranking each of the 16 specific accommodations (e.g., assistive reading technology) above a 3 on a 4-point Likert-type scale (Reinschmiedt, Sprong, Dallas, Buono, & Upton, 2013).

Newman et al. (2011) documented the frequency of accommodations for students identified as disabled in high school. Nationally, the most common type of accommodation is additional time to complete exams; 79% of students used this modification (Newman et al., 2011). Other accommodations that are frequently used included assistive technology (37%); additional time for or modified assignments (23%); a different test setting (19%); a note taker (17%); physical adaptions to the classroom (10%); large print, books on tape, or braille materials (8%); and early registration (3%; Newman et al., 2011).

A more nuanced understanding of the types of accommodations that disability service practitioners facilitate is helpful to comprehend the daily work of DRO staff. To that end we build on existing work (Duffy & Gugerty, 2005; Hart, Grigal, & Weir, 2010) to offer a framework that provides examples of accommodations for students with disabilities in postsecondary education (see Table 13.2). This framework provides general examples; the specific accommodations that DRO staff coordinate will vary significantly depending on the institution type, geographic region, and student population. This framework is not intended to be exhaustive; further supplements would include more detailed descriptions of residential accommodations, service animals, access to the social environment (e.g., sporting events and student organizations), and assistive technology. Although we group accommodations into four areas of access (instructional, academic policy, testing, and environmental/physical) for conceptual ease, categories of access are not mutually exclusive and frequently overlap.

Disability resource practitioners facilitate accommodations in an individualized manner based on the student's functional limitations, the student's preference, environmental barriers, and the academic standards or fundamental components of a course. These practitioners determine accommodations by "drawing a direct line between an impairment (e.g., low vision), a major life activity (e.g., seeing), and the accommodation (e.g., document conversion)" (Duffy & Gugerty, 2005, p. 95). Accommodations are tailored to the student and the environmental barriers rather than broadly linked to a disability typology or category. For example, not every student with dyslexia will access the course material equitably with the accommodation of extended exam

TABLE 13.2. EXAMPLES OF ACCOMMODATIONS FOR STUDENTS WITH DISABILITIES

Instructional	Academic Policy	Testing	Environmental/Physical
Advanced receipt of syllabus/handouts	Course substitution for required courses (e.g., math or world language)	Allow student to mark responses on the test rather than a Scantron form	Accessible campus transportation (e.g., bus or shuttle service)
Course materials in alterative format	Flexible attendance with professor approval	Breaks during testing	Accessible websites and learning management systems (e.g., Blackboard)
FM listening device	Priority or early registration	Dictate exam answers to scribe or tape	Accessible parking
Grammar/spell checker	Reduced course load	Document conversion (e.g., audio or braille)	Pre-plating meals (for people with food allergies)
Kurzweil Reader or e-reader		Extended exam time (e.g., 1.5 times)	Captioning for lectures and videos
Livescribe pen use		Increased size of text and response bubbles	Computer-assisted transcription or Communication Access Realtime Translation (CART)
Note taker		Oral exam format	Ensuring proper and timely snow removal
Outline or notes from professor		Reader to verbalize directions and questions on the exam	Ensuring proper curb cuts and audio pedestrian crossing
Priority or preferential seating		Room with minimal distractions	Laboratory assistance
Record lecture		Separate room for testing	Physical access (e.g., doorways and bathrooms)
Screen text enlarger (e.g., zoom text)		Use of word processor for written responses	Residence hall bed shakers and emergency lights
Screen-reader-accessible technology (e.g., JAWS)			Sign language interpreting (including at campus events)
Textbooks and instructional material in braille			Single residence hall room
Textbooks in alternative text or format			
Use of laptop computer or calculator			

time or a quiet testing environment. Each academic course is also unique in the intended learning outcomes and technical standards; extended exam time may be completely appropriate in one class and inappropriate for the technical standards or learning outcomes of another. A student may also experience functional limitations associated with two or more different medical diagnoses; for example, a dyslexic student may also experience visual impairment. Therefore, practitioners facilitate accommodations in an individualized manner, consider a variety of factors in the accommodations process, and document "the rational for accommodations decisions" (Duffy & Gugerty, 2005, p. 95).

Facilitating accommodations extends beyond the classroom. For instance, access to technology, websites, and learning management systems is imperative. (We discuss this further in Chapter 11.) In addition, disability resource practitioners support students by facilitating accommodations for study abroad, internships, the campus social environment, and practicum experiences. Under a social justice paradigm, students with disabilities have the same access to learning, social, and developmental opportunities that all other students do.

The process of facilitating accommodations requires that disability resource practitioners are problem solvers and collaborative relationship builders. As Autumn's quote about the residential emotional support cat indicates, practitioners often troubleshoot a variety of situations. Problems may occur when students do not request accommodations, are unaware of institutional policies, or enter the accommodations process as a last recourse. In these situations, the disability resource practitioner acts as an educator, mediator, and cross-campus collaborator. Problems may also arise with approved student accommodations that are not executed properly. For instance, an interpreter for an important lecture course may fall ill, a textbook may be extremely difficult to locate in alternative format, or an instructor may forget to drop off the exam at the testing center, leaving an anxious student without a test to take. In all of these situations, the disability resource practitioner works to find creative solutions—for example, locating a replacement interpreter on short notice or providing captioned notes for the lecture, asking colleagues in the library or at a different institution to assist with locating the textbook, and calling the professor with a reminder about the missing exam.

Administration

Broadly conceptualized, administrative tasks incorporate advocacy, assessment, budgeting, grievance process, hiring and supervision, and language and branding. Other administrative components include where the DRO is located in the institutional structure (e.g., academic affairs or student affairs), where the office is physically located on campus, and if disability resources is a stand-alone unit or part of a broader administrative department focused on student academic support or underrepresented student populations.

Generally DROs are housed within student affairs (58%) or located within academic affairs (24%); a small but growing number of DROs (7%) are found in counseling or academic advising units (Kasnitz, 2011). The vast majority of campuses (83%) use a centralized DRO model, where one office provides services for the entire campus. Other administrative options are a decentralized office with disability services embedded within a college (3%) or a partially centralized office (8%). A small minority of institutions (5%) do not have any DRO on their campus (Kasnitz, 2011). Duffy and Gugerty (2005) outlined the benefits and drawbacks of centralization and institutional location; they concluded that campus culture and politics play an important role and that "the best answer is that a disability services program should be located in a unit that wants it" (p. 93). We agree that administrative location is important and advocate for a structure that places DROs directly under the purview of the president or provost as one method of communicating the importance of access to the broader campus community.

Advocacy. Advocacy is the process by which an individual or group attempts to influence policy decisions and resource allocation (Funckes, Kroeger, Loewen, & Thornton, n.d.a). Advocacy for a socially just understanding of disability takes many forms. Disability resource practitioners advocate with faculty members to encourage the use of universal design and inclusive classroom practices. Practitioners also advocate with administrators to make sure that the institution invests in accessible technology, plans for physically accessible buildings, and allocates the appropriate budget to support accommodations. Disability resource practitioners support students by providing programs that promote self-advocacy and cultivate transferable skills. Practitioners also serve as advocates to the broader campus community, building collaborations around students, promoting a socially just understanding of disability, helping the community examine and change social constructions that are limiting or biased, and providing education about the intersectional nature of ability, disability, and other forms of identity (see Chapter 5).

Disability resource practitioners advocate for an accessible campus by providing services that go beyond legally required reasonable accommodations. For example, the DRO staff may take a socially just view to leveling financial inequality by providing more expensive technology-related tools (e.g., Livescribe pens, which provide synchronized audio and pdf text) on a semester loan program. Although personal equipment associated with short-term functional limitations or short-term disability legally is the student's responsibility, a socially just institution could recognize that many students and campus visitors would benefit from a program that provides short-term loan of commonly used mobility devices such as wheelchairs or crutches. These are two examples of programs that disability resource practitioners can implement to promote campus access, demonstrate a socially just awareness of the financial limitations many college students face, and educate the community about the fluctuating or temporary nature of ability.

Assessment. Assessment is a way to operationalize excellence, with the goal of using data to inform decision making by "gathering of information concerning the functioning of students, staff, and institutions of higher education" (Astin, 2002, p. 2). The purpose of assessment is to provide a data-driven method to improve educational programs (Palomba & Banta, 1999). For example, student satisfaction data can be used to indicate areas for service improvement (Duffy & Gugerty, 2005; Reinschmiedt et al., 2013), institutional data regarding student-to-staff caseload ratios can be compared to national benchmarks (e.g., Harbour, 2009; Kasnitz, 2011), and budgetary information can be used to advocate for funding for additional personnel (Duffy & Gugerty, 2005). In addition, practitioners use assessment data to communicate the role DROs play in promoting "student retention, academic success, and program completion" (Duffy & Gugerty, 2005, p. 109).

Assessment frequently is a part of academic programs, yet nonacademic units sometimes struggle with conceptualizing and measuring their contributions or view assessment as a tedious and time-consuming activity (Duffy & Gugerty, 2005). A collaborative approach to assessment is one method to address challenges related to data analysis skills, feasibility, and time constraints. For example, disability resource practitioners can work collaboratively with partners in the office of institutional research to track student retention, transfer, and graduation data. Practitioners can build disability into a campuswide environment assessment process to determine and evaluate "how the various elements and conditions of the college campus milieu affect student learning and growth" (Upcraft & Schuh, 1996, p. 167). Finally, disability resource practitioners evaluate how the DRO is meeting office and divisional outcomes. For practitioners seeking guidance, M. K. Brown (1994) described assessment for nonacademic units, and Astin (2002) provided an applicable model focused on inputs, environments, and outcomes.

Budgeting. The DRO should track and manage administrative and accommodations-related expenses. Because issues of access are not limited to a particular department or division, several budgeting models exist, ranging from institutions that use department-specific funding to a larger university-wide model. Harbour (2009) provided fiscal data for approximately 420 postsecondary institutions. The average budget for DROs housed in student affairs was $277,150 ($SD$ = $364,999); the average for DROs housed in academic affairs was $126,696 ($SD$ = $189,118). When interpreting these data, it is important to note that larger institutions usually had larger budgets and, conversely, smaller institutions usually had smaller budgets (Harbour, 2009). In addition, the type of accommodations provided also influenced budget size. The vast majority of accommodations are relatively inexpensive (e.g., the average annual cost of note taking in the University of Wisconsin system was $183 per full-time student); however, the cost of interpreting or captioning services is significantly greater (Duffy & Gugerty, 2005). Duffy and Gugerty (2005) advocated for a budgeting model that tracks fixed and variable expenses in a separate manner, noting that this "allows a clear understanding of actual costs for direct services and actual costs for staffing and infrastructure" (p. 108). Specific examples are not within the scope of this chapter. We direct interested readers to Duffy and Gugerty (2005), who provided an excellent discussion on predicting direct service expenses.

Grievance Process. Institutions must have a written grievance policy and appeals process that is impartial and timely (Duffy & Gugerty, 2005). In some instances, the DRO handles the institutional ADA appeals process; in other cases, this responsibility falls under the purview of human resources or legal services. Regardless of where the grievance process falls in the institutional structure, each institution must have a designated ADA and Section 504 compliance officer, an individual who responds to the Office for Civil Rights in the event that a formal complaint is filed. It is imperative that the grievance process is clearly explained in writing, published in multiple places, easily accessible to students, not unduly burdensome, and followed carefully. Due to the increasing legal and compliance aspects of DRO work, practitioners may want to consider purchasing professional liability insurance through their professional organizations (e.g., AHEAD, ACPA, NASPA) to provide additional coverage in the event of a lawsuit. This coverage may provide peace of mind for practitioners.

Hiring and Supervision. A socially just approach begins with a job description that frames access in the language of equity rather than deficiency or limitations (Funckes, Kroeger, Loewen, & Thornton, n.d.b). During the hiring process, institutions should advertise the position in a variety of ways with the goal of having a diverse selection of candidates in the hiring pool. As an advocate for access and social justice on campus, the hiring process embodies equal opportunity. In support of this, recent AHEAD survey data indicated that approximately 34% of individuals working in DROs self-reported having a disability, 81% are female, and 14% were nonwhite (Kasnitz, 2011). Bachelor's degrees are held by 13% of disability resource practitioners, 69% have a master's degree, and 10% a doctoral degree (Kasnitz, 2011).

The optimal number of professional staff working in the DRO depends on student use, resources of the postsecondary institution, and other campus services (e.g., tutoring center). Duffy and Gugerty (2005) noted that "a common ratio of professional staff to students is 1:100" (p. 105), but different student populations require varying levels of support. Harbour (2009) wrote that DRO offices housed in student affairs had significantly larger staffs (an average of eight staff members, $SD = 12$) than do DRO offices located in academic affairs (an average of four staff members, $SD = 6$). A generalized best practice is for the office to have as many staff as are necessary to complete tasks in a thorough and timely manner.

It is imperative that all employees working in the DRO have access to and support for professional development opportunities. Depending on the employees' needs, professional development can include conference support for staff, the opportunity to present on-campus for graduate student interns, or the ability to develop transferable skills for undergraduate student workers. Due to several emerging legal issues (see Chapter 3), professional development is an important component of social justice at all supervisory levels.

Language and Branding. As indicated in the Introduction, there are various preferences surrounding person-first and disability-first language. Hall and Belch (2000) stated, "Human dignity can be achieved by using person-first language that emphasizes the individual and not the disability" (p. 11). In contrast, Collier (2012) posited that "sticking a word in the shadow of a noun can create the impression that there is something inherently wrong with it, that it should be hidden" (p. E939). Hutcheon and Wolbring (2012) offered a third option: they advocated for the term *ability-diverse students* (p. 40). Linguistic nuances are also impairment specific; for example, Robertson and Ne'eman (2008) used identity-first language (e.g., *autistic people*) because the international autistic self-advocacy community prefers it. We acknowledge Biklen's (2005) conclusion—"There is no agreement about best language" (p. 12)—and advocate for the use of the student's preferred language when engaging in individual interactions.

The office title is an important area where language and branding apply. DROs are called by a wide range of names (Harbour, 2009, p. 144). Nationally, according to Kasnitz (2011), "Disability Services" (31%) is the most commonly used nomenclature; also used are "Office for Students with Disabilities" (11.5%), "Disabled Support Services" (10.4%), and "Disability Resource Center" (8.7%).

When selecting an office name, it is important to clearly communicate the office purpose in a large bureaucratic structure that is frequently difficult for new students and their parents to navigate and use language that reflects a socially just mission. When choosing a name, the following issues should be considered: the population being served (students, faculty, staff, visitors); the breadth of services (disability, testing accommodations, test proctoring, academic support services); the history of the institution (donors and alumni); and logistical considerations (accessible student services or similar variations result in an unfortunate acronym). For example, if the office serves faculty, staff, and other employees, then including the word *student* in the title does not make good sense. The office name may also communicate additional linguistic meaning regarding ability and disability. There is no one correct answer to this linguistic quandary, and some practitioners have devised creative compromises such as using *disability access resources* to strike a balance between easily identifiable services and placing emphasis on facilitating access.

The DRO mission statement is a second area where language and branding are important. "A mission statement is an action-oriented statement that describes how a vision will be achieved," according to Funckes, Kroeger, Loewen, and Thornton (n.d.c, para. 1). A mission statement provides direction, outlines priorities, and is "intimately linked" with assessment (Palomba & Banta, 1999, p. 3). Frequently, mission statements for DROs focus on legal compliance or a service-based model for students with disabilities. Socially just mission statements make disability a campuswide responsibility and "explicitly recognize the power of design to include or exclude and frame access as an environmental concern rather than an individual problem" (Funckes et al., n.d.c, para. 3). Practitioners interested in creating a socially just mission can switch from a statement that addresses accommodating students to a focus on the DRO playing a leadership role "in creating a more inclusive campus" (Funckes et al., n.d.c, para. 4).

Outreach

Outreach is an important component of disability resource practitioners' work because it involves expanding the mission of social justice to a broader community. Outreach activities include campus climate and accessibility audits, collaborative programs, educational events, transition assistance, DRO website and campus technology access, and student engagement and development.

Campus Climate and Accessibility Audits. Historically underrepresented groups experience an unwelcoming environment when they first enter higher education (Hall & Belch, 2000). The overall campus climate is important when creating a disability-friendly environment, and "the top ranked campuses focused on programmatic access rather than physical access" (K. Wilson, Getzel, & Brown, 2000, p. 37). Ableism plays a powerful role in creating welcoming or unwelcoming educational environments (K. Brown & Broido, 2015), and research indicates that students with disabilities perceived their campus environments as significantly less supportive than their peers without disabilities (Hedrick, Dizén, Collins, Evans & Grayson, 2010). Campus climate audits are one method of assessing the social context for students with disabilities. Campus accessibility audits are access-specific assessments, generally conducted by skilled third-party providers, that evaluate the environment based on standards for barrier-free design and technology. Accessibility audits allow campuses to systematically plan for the elimination of physical, technological (see Chapter 11), and architectural barriers and to design buildings and choose technology that supports the success of all members of the campus community.

Collaborative Programs. Disability resource practitioners collaborate with a variety of campus and community partners to support accessibility. Collaboration takes several forms, including committee service, informal networking, cross-campus outreach programs, and community education events. DRO staff frequently engage with professionals in the dean of students office, veterans services, TRIO programs, residence life, human resources, legal counsel, admissions, and technology services offices. Positive or reward-based programs, such as an annual award for faculty and staff who are supportive of disabled students, are another method of collaboration.

External community agencies that DRO staff collaborate with include vocational rehabilitation, disability-specific organizations (e.g., American Council of the Blind, Pepnet2), high school counselors, and community-based organizations. Campus-community hybrid programs that promote access are also increasing. One example of an access-driven hybrid program is the Cutting Edge Program (n.d.) at Edgewood College, which provides individuals with intellectual disabilities an age-appropriate peer experience located on a college campus, where the students are part of a cohort model and take specially tailored classes.

Educational Events. Education of others about disability is one of the most important pieces of student academic success (Kurth & Mellard, 2006). Disability resource practitioners engage campus partners by providing training for faculty, staff, and students regarding appropriate language and terminology, best practices for managing accommodations, updates on recent legislation, access to technology, and suggestions for increasing access to offices and services.

Students with disabilities reported significantly higher levels of faculty interaction than nondisabled peers on NSSE benchmark scores (Hedrick et al., 2010) and perceived faculty members' attitudes and behavior as playing a role in their academic success (Kurth & Mellard, 2006). Although faculty reported a willingness to provide accommodations, the level of faculty knowledge regarding disability-related issues varies (Vogel, Leyser, Burgstahler, Sligar, & Zecker, 2006). Furthermore, faculty members often are not acquainted with disability resources and accommodations strategies (S. E. Burgstahler, 2002; K. Wilson et al., 2000), and they expressed concerns regarding the need for training and disability-specific information (Vogel et al., 2008).

Similar to interaction with faculty members, students with disabilities perceived staff members as playing a role in their success (S. Burgstahler & Moore, 2009), and the vast majority of university staff are supportive of accommodations (C. Murray, Flannery, & Wren, 2008). However, students with disabilities reported that support personnel generally took a "reactive rather than proactive" approach (S. Burgstahler & Moore, 2009, p. 164), and staff members expressed a need for training, professional development, and support strategies (C. Murray, Flannery, & Wren, 2008). Key areas of training for staff members are technology, legal requirements, campus resources, and methods for interacting with students who do not have apparent disabilities (S. Burgstahler & Moore, 2009).

Education of faculty and staff members can occur in a variety of formats, including workshops and training, one-on-one conversations, and web-based supports (e.g., sample syllabi statements and videos), and the educational content and methods used will vary with institution-specific needs and resources. Disability resource practitioners need to be flexible and creative in their educational programs to address the ever-changing nature of academic work. Specifically, numerous institutions are increasingly using adjunct or part-time faculty; these instructors are paid on a class-by-class basis, have limited time on campus, and may not be included in faculty orientation. In addition, much of the classroom teaching at large research institutions may be done by nontenured academic staff or graduate assistants. Disability resource providers should seek out all faculty and staff, regardless of status or employment type, and creatively provide educational information.

Transition Assistance. Students will navigate at least two different types of transitions during their college experience. All students will navigate the transition into and out of college; many students will also navigate the transition from one institution to another. The transition from high school into postsecondary education involves significant legal, academic, and social changes. We describe legislative changes in Chapter 3 and transitions broadly in Chapter 15; here we focus on changes in student self-identification and awareness of services as those directly affect disability resource practitioners.

National data indicate that the number of students who self-identify as disabled and used accommodations decreased significantly between high school and college. "Almost two-thirds (63 percent) of postsecondary students who were identified by their secondary school as having a disability did not consider themselves to have a disability by the time they had transitioned to postsecondary school" (Newman et al., 2011, p. 31). In addition, 9% of high school students who identified as a person with a disability chose not to disclose this to their college or university (Newman et al., 2011). Only 28% of students who had a disability in high school notified their postsecondary school, either before or after enrollment (Newman et al., 2011). It is important to note that these data reflect only high school students; they do not include returning adult learners or individuals who may have acquired functional limitations after high school.

Another transition-related issue is that individuals who support students through the transition process (e.g., parents and high school counselors) are not fully aware of the services that postsecondary institutions offer. The result is that students are unaware of services and programs before admission. Practitioners operating in a socially just framework can help students navigate the transition by publicizing services to parents, educating high school representatives, and being visible during admissions and orientation processes.

In stark contrast to the ample data regarding the transition into postsecondary education, limited research exists on transitions associated with transferring or graduation. Given that the vast majority of students with disabilities are enrolled at two-year institutions, information on transfer experiences is an important area for future research. The transition out of college to a career or graduate school is an equally important and relatively unexplored area of transition.

DRO Website and Campus Technology Access. The DRO website is an important component of the campus disability narrative. In their discourse analysis of postsecondary DRO websites, Lester, Dostal, and Gabriel (2013) found that some DROs used language to indicate the office existed because of the law, and in these instances "the university's obligation resides not with defending students' rights, but in protecting the integrity of institutional objectives" (p. 52). In contrast, other offices "presented their existence as being about something far more than a law, as they sought to become a space of inclusion and diversity" (Lester et al., 2013, p. 52). Lester et al. (2013) concluded that the type of language used on DRO websites can "function to police" or limit individual and collective diversity (p. 53); therefore, the content and tone of the DRO website should be inclusive and welcoming. Furthermore, campus community members view the DRO website as a hub of expertise, and it is imperative that the website promote and advocate social justice.

One of the most critical areas for advancing student access is through close collaboration with technology services to ensure that campuswide platforms such as websites, course management tools, and e-mail systems are accessible to all users. It is imperative that disability staff be included in the conversation as campuses are using student portals for registration, course management, and other aspects of student records. Videos must be captioned, and website content must be screen reader accessible. Website and online course accessibility topics are described in greater depth in Chapters 11 and 12.

Student Engagement and Development. The engagement of students with disabilities is one of the most important pieces of student academic success (Kurth & Mellard, 2006). Pascarella and Terenzini (2005) provided strong evidence for the importance of out-of-class engagement as a means to support college retention. Using nationally representative longitudinal survey data, Mamiseishvili and Koch (2011) found a significant relationship between social integration and persistence for students with disabilities. Specifically, socially engaged students with disabilities were almost 10% more likely to persist from their first to their second year of college when compared to their uninvolved classmates (Mamiseishvili & Koch, 2011).

Depending on institutional characteristics, there are several ways to conceptualize cocurricular engagement. For example, living in a campus residence hall was a statistically significant and meaningful predictor of retention of students with disabilities between their first and second years of college (Mamiseishvili & Koch, 2011). Students attending community colleges placed value on the availability of supports for independence, such as transportation and accessible seating, and indicated that a sense of belonging was important (Kurth & Mellard, 2006). Disability resource practitioners can facilitate student development by creating socially just events that move beyond "disability" or "deficiency-centered" programming. Examples of these include programs that target leadership and self-advocacy, community service, student organizations, skills acquisition, and cultural programming.

Considerations for the Future of Disability Resources

Considerations for future disability practitioners fall into areas of funding, politics, law, data collection, research, constructions of disability, and continuing education. Disability resource practitioners will continue to face constraints associated with limited resources. Future practitioners will need to be savvy advocates, budgeters, and negotiators as neoliberalism grows, budget cuts continue, and the fiscal landscape of higher education becomes increasingly politicized. Currently, legal precedent shapes the work of disability resource practitioners; as the law continues to evolve, future practitioners will need to stay abreast of changes and advocate for a socially just understanding of disability rather than a legal system driven by functional limitations.

Future disability resource practitioners must advocate for research on important topics that are notably absent from the existing literature. For example, although data from the U.S. Department of Education (Newman et al., 2009; Wagner, Newman, Cameto, Garza, & Levine, 2005) provide useful information about students with disabilities in nonprofit postsecondary education, these statistics "do not reflect all students with disabilities" (K. Brown & Broido, 2015, p. 189). Rather, NLTS data include only students identified during high school. It is imperative that future research defines disability as a variable that changes over the life course and incorporates students who are not currently represented in NLTS data, including students diagnosed in college, students who experience a life event that leads to impairment before or during college enrollment (e.g., military service), returning adult students, and students who attend for-profit institutions.

Future practitioners play an important role in shaping campus conversations around ability. These conversations manifest in several forms, from questioning bureaucratic segregation, to understanding ethics of inclusion, to developing nonbinary perceptions of ability. Although centrally located DROs are common and this institutional structure provides administrative visibility, siloed services segregate students. Titchkosky (2007) critiqued the bureaucratic practices of developing an office to serve specific populations as "ordering inclusion" (p. 141), and Scotch (2001b) explained that a "separate community of people with disabilities continues to be reinforced by 'special' service strategies and the stigma that pervades our culture" (p. 389). Practitioners must challenge the pervasive mind-set that *disabled students belong to the DRO* by advocating that all campus members are responsible for access.

Future disability resource practitioners should also work to challenge the constructions of disability as a dichotomous and detrimental identity. Titchkosky (2007) explained, "Disability is constantly put into the form of a devalued binary partner to valued notions such as ability, normality, or even, naturalness" (p. 210). Future practitioners, working to build a socially just campus, must challenge the notion of disability as less than by starting a critical discourse and promoting the idea that ability is on a continuum and changes throughout the life course.

Continuing education is imperative for disability practitioners. For practitioners interested in a broader overview of disability services in higher education, including a strong grounding in universal design of instruction, the University of Connecticut Neag School of Education offers a 12-credit online certificate program in postsecondary disability services. Included among the four required courses is a practicum that includes a face-to-face meeting with the student's cohort and faculty. The Center on Disability Studies at the University of Hawaii at Manoa offers several disability studies courses and an online graduate-level certificate in disability and diversity studies. Both programs are designed to prepare individuals who are disability resource professionals or wish to work in DROs, as well as other higher education professionals who collaborate with disability resource staff.

Conclusion

In this chapter, we have attempted to balance a socially just future with a pragmatic view of the lived experience of disability resource practitioners who work in an educational environment distinguished by shrinking budgets and competing political interests. Our goal in writing this chapter was to be clear that issues exist, describe what institutions are legally required to do, and advocate for best practices that constantly move toward a social justice approach. Social justice is not easy in any setting, but the goals of social justice are worth striving for.

Discussion Questions

1. Collaborations between an institution's DRO and other campus units typically focus on facilitating access and accommodations. How might those collaborations be extended to other functions of the DRO?
2. How can models of disability (discussed in Chapter 2) inform the services that DROs provide?
3. Identify three disability-related issues on your campus about which you could partner with the DRO and serve as an advocate for change. What tangible steps could you take to become an advocate?
4. In your current position, do you hire or supervise student workers or professional staff with disabilities? What types of professional development opportunities do you provide to develop and cultivate transferable skills? Can you identify barriers to employment that might discourage or prevent people with disabilities from applying for jobs in your functional area?
5. In this chapter, we describe the importance of transition into college, between colleges for transfer students, and into graduate school or career paths. What are some ways that you can partner with professionals in the DRO on your campus to create programs that help students with disabilities navigate transitions?

CHAPTER FOURTEEN

STUDENT AFFAIRS

I signed a contract that was supposed to be an ADA apartment. To me an ADA apartment is something that is accessible, things that I can get to whenever I need to be alone, not to have someone there all the time. . . . I get out there, I can't access my refrigerator. . . . I couldn't access anything in my cupboards. When I first moved in there was a bar, like a food bar like type thing, that was in the middle of my kitchen. So I lived there probably a month before I got them to move it. . . . I couldn't get into my building until February because the doors were too heavy; it didn't have an automatic door. . . . I have an aide that lives with me and like for instance to get in the building, I had to knock on my window and . . . she'd have to be there [and come and let me in].

—Joe, undergraduate student with a disability

In this chapter, we build on the real-world experiences of student affairs practitioners to examine current practices and socially just approaches to engaging and supporting students with disabilities in higher education. We start by discussing current research on the role student affairs plays in the retention and graduation of students with disabilities and describe how knowledge about disability must be a part of student affairs training and decision making. Then we focus on how student affairs practitioners can use universal design (UD) principles and advocate for social justice. We conclude by synthesizing the literature on students with disabilities in 11 key functional areas: advising, athletics and recreational sports, campus health and counseling centers, campus safety, dining and events, facilities management, foundation and alumni relations, identity-based centers, residence life, student involvement, and student conduct. Throughout this chapter, we interweave quotes from students with disabilities (in Evans, Assadi, Herriott, & Varland, 2004), to give voice to the importance of a welcoming environment and an inclusive community.

Persistence, Retention, and Graduation of Students With Disabilities

Completion of college is vital; postsecondary education improves the overall quality of life and disrupts the school-to-prison pipeline for youth with disabilities (National Council on Disability, 2015). Given the positive correlation between a bachelor's degree and employment for individuals with disabilities (Dowrick, Anderson, Heyer, & Acosta, 2005), it is imperative to examine factors that explain divergent retention and graduation rates. We described individual factors earlier in this book; here, we focus on student affairs and discuss the interplay between personal and institutional factors as important considerations for student retention and graduation (S. Burgstahler, 2014; Mamiseishvili & Koch, 2011; Pingry O'Neill, Markward, & French, 2012).

The research on retention and graduation of students with disabilities has provided mixed results, partly because studies employ different operational definitions of *disability* (Stapleton et al., 2014; K. Brown & Broido, 2015) and partly because studies do not track access to accommodations with the same precision or reliability as other retention variables (e.g., socioeconomic status; Trammell, 2009). In general, research studies where students self-identify have found comparable grade point averages (GPA; K. S. Adams & Proctor, 2010), similar rates of transfer from community colleges to four-year institutions (Ponticelli & Russ-Eft, 2009), similar rates of completion for associate's degrees (Ponticelli & Russ-Eft, 2009), and no difference in retention and graduation rates between students with disabilities and those without (Wessel, Jones, Markle, & Westfall, 2009). However, national longitudinal surveys that have identified students with disabilities based on high school records (e.g., Mamiseishvili & Koch, 2012; Newman et al., 2011) have found that students with disabilities earn fewer credits and have higher rates of nonpersistence and lower graduation rates. Research that has considered broader factors, including family income and access to postsecondary education, such as the U.S. Bureau of Labor Statistics (2015), has found that "persons with a disability are less likely to have completed a bachelor's degree or higher than those with no disability" (p. 1).

Students with disabilities provide many of the same reasons for educational nonpersistence and stopping out of college as students without disabilities, such as financial problems (I. H. Lee, Rojewski, Gregg, & Jeong, 2015), personal problems, GPA, or work (Barber, 2012). Similar to their nondisabled peers, women with disabilities are more likely to graduate than men with disabilities (Pingry O'Neill et al., 2012). Among students with disabilities, lower family income and attendance at a high-poverty high school decreases access to and success in college (Madaus, Grigal, & Hughes, 2014). In comparison to continuing-generation students with disabilities, first-generation students with disabilities had lower GPAs, less family support, and higher levels of financial stress (A. R. Lombardi, Murray, & Gerdes, 2012).

However, students with disabilities also address additional concerns that affect retention and graduation. Specifically, stigma (Goffman, 1963; Gruttadaro & Crudo, 2012; Markoulakis & Kirsh, 2013; Trammell, 2009) and the "stress of school, health, problems with medications, and weather conditions" influenced the enrollment of students with disabilities (Wessel et al., 2009, p. 117). Further disability-specific challenges include a lack of awareness of accommodations and academic supports, limited self-advocacy skills, and additional financial costs associated with paying for disability-related expenses (Mamiseishvili & Koch, 2011).

Accommodations are vital to the academic success of most students with disabilities (Denhart, 2008; Kim & Lee, 2016; Mamiseishvili & Koch, 2011; Newman et al., 2009; Van Hees, Moyson, & Roeyers, 2015). Students who used accommodations in the first year were more likely to persist than students who did not use accommodations (Mamiseishvili & Koch, 2011), and use of testing and course accommodations (e.g., extended exam time) were significant predictors of GPA for students with disabilities (Kim & Lee, 2016). In spite of the important role that appropriate accommodations play in retention, students with disabilities identified accessing accommodations as a major barrier in their transition to postsecondary education (Cawthon & Cole, 2010), and many students sought services only in response to an academic crisis (Lightner, Kipps-Vaughan, Schulte, & Trice, 2012). Specifically, stigma is an important factor in accessing accommodations; in one study, 45% of the students who stopped attending college due to mental health–related reasons reported that they did not receive accommodations and 50% did not access mental health services or supports (Gruttadaro & Crudo, 2012). Hence, connecting students with student affairs–related services, including the disability resource office (DRO), financial aid, student health and counseling, first-year programs, transition support, and student involvement early in their career may be important factors in mitigating these concerns. Facilities management will play a crucial role in making sure that weather does not impede access, particularly for students with mobility impairments.

There is a correlation between type of impairment and the persistence of students with disabilities (Mamiseishvili & Koch, 2011; Pingry O'Neill et al., 2012). In particular, first-year students with chronic illness reported greater rates of loneliness and isolation (Herts, Wallis, & Maslow, 2014), and first-year students with nonapparent disabilities "have lower academic and social self-concepts at the start of college than do students in the overall population" (Higher Education Research Institute, 2011, p. 1). Of the 24% of first-to-second-year students who did not persist in Mamiseishvili and Koch's (2011) research, students with orthopedic or physical impairments (30%) and those in the category of "other disabilities" (e.g., brain injury, developmental disability, speech and language impairment, and other conditions not specified in the survey; 36%) had the highest percentage of stopping out. Students least likely to stop out were those with dyslexia (14%) and those with health impairments (18%).

A second study (Pingry O'Neill et al., 2012) used a more general categorization of impairment types and found that "students with physical disabilities were more likely to graduate than students with cognitive or mental disabilities" (p. 32). Unfortunately, as we described further in Chapter 4, there are several difficulties with categorization and conceptualization of disability type, and these processes have implications for the literature base. Specifically, there is a paucity of research on disability as a co-occurring phenomenon (e.g., a visually impaired student might also have anxiety). Because quantitative statistical decisions frequently overlook the importance of multiple forms of impairment by forcing each student into only one category, it is difficult to ascertain the retention or graduation rate of students with co-occurring disabilities.

Important factors that affect the persistence of students with disabilities include academic engagement (I. H. Lee et al., 2015), social integration (H. A. Belch, 2004; DaDeppo, 2009; Paul, 2000), and campus climate (K. Brown, Peña, & Rankin, in press). Students with disabilities who participated in academic activities (e.g., study groups, informal meetings with faculty, meetings with academic advisors) were significantly less likely to leave after their first year (22%) than students who were not academically integrated (31%; Mamiseishvili & Koch, 2011). Furthermore, students with greater academic engagement were "more likely to enroll and persist in their degree program" (I. H. Lee et al., 2015, p. 78). However, as we detail in Chapter 15, students with disabilities will have had less access to college preparatory courses in high school (Shifrer, Callahan, & Muller, 2013). As a result, they might be at an academic disadvantage in college. The empirical literature on academic engagement for disabled students is limited (Kimball, Wells, Ostiguy, Manly, & Lauterbach, 2016). This is an important area of future research.

There is a paucity of research on social integration for students with disabilities (D. W. Leake & Stodden, 2014). The literature on campus support services for students with disabilities typically focuses on accommodations, academics, and legal compliance to the detriment of social involvement (Gillies & Dupuis, 2013). The limited existing research indicates that after controlling for GPA and other common characteristics, social integration remains a significant predictor of intent to persist for students with learning disabilities (DaDeppo, 2009), and the expectations of students with disabilities regarding involvement with campus organizations was a significant factor in predicting their social integration (Shepler & Woosley, 2012).

For first-year students with disabilities, the ability to self-advocate, which is vital in accessing accommodations, is connected to sense of belonging (Vaccaro, Daly-Cano, & Newman, 2015). Students with disabilities may face additional hurdles, such as making nondisabled students feel comfortable during social interactions (Myers & Bastian, 2010). Given the importance of social integration to retention for the broader student population (Pascarella & Terenzini, 2005), student affairs practitioners can work to make all areas of the campus inclusive and welcoming.

The literature on campus climate for students with disabilities indicates that students face an unwelcoming and chilly campus climate (Beilke & Yssel, 1999) and barriers due to ableism (Hutcheon & Wolbring, 2012). Students may experience the campus climate, including classroom comfort, comfort with faculty members, peer interactions, and bullying, differently depending on their type of impairment (K. Brown et al., in press). Furthermore, students with poor adjustment profiles gave lower campus climate ratings (C. Murray, Lombardi, & Kosty, 2014). In their review of the literature, Kimball et al. (2016) noted that existing campus climate models "pay only scant attention to the relationship between disability and institutional climate" (p. 107). Student affairs professionals play critical roles in shaping the experience of disabled students by ensuring that their departments are welcoming and comfortable (see Chapter 9).

Importance of Knowledge About Disability in Student Affairs

> I would like for there to be more tolerance of invisible disabilities. Sometimes I hand them my SAAR [disability documentation] and they look at me and I don't look disabled so I must not be, or something.
>
> —*Kelli, undergraduate student with a disability*

As Kelli's quotation indicates, many student affairs practitioners are not knowledgeable about disability-related topics, including the fact that many types of impairments are not apparent. While practitioners working in a wide range of student affairs areas generally hold positive attitudes toward students with disabilities, a significant number of practitioner respondents indicated they required training and professional development on disability and how to support students with disabilities (Aune & Kroeger, 1997; C. Murray, Flannery, & Wren, 2008), and students with disabilities reported that college faculty and academic staff lacked disability knowledge (Barber, 2012).

This gap in knowledge may occur because published scholarship on disability is limited within higher education (E. V. Peña, 2014), and postsecondary institutions are "designed without regard to students with disabilities, creating a situation where such students continue to be marginalized through add-on programs" (S. E. Burgstahler & Cory, 2008, p. 576). Hence, student affairs graduate programs may not integrate disability within their curriculum, and "student affairs units may opt out of addressing questions from disabled students, referring them back to the disability office as if it were a primary care entity" (Ashmore & Kasnitz, 2014, p. 24). Given the paucity of information about disability in the published literature and many graduate training programs, we start by explaining how different disability models hold unique implications for practitioners; we then advocate for including disability in staff training and diversity initiatives, and focus on how UD fits within student affairs.

How disability is conceptualized influences institutional structures, policies, and practices (Ashmore & Kasnitz, 2014). We remind readers of the models of disability presented in Chapter 2 and suggest a review of Table 2.1 before continuing with this chapter.

Student affairs practitioners need to be aware of the necessity of, and strategies for, creating inclusive environments. Unfortunately, practitioners often lack knowledge about accommodations, legal requirements, inclusive language, and hidden forms of impairment (S. Burgstahler & Moore, 2009). Therefore, all staff members (paraprofessional and professional) should be trained to know human, technological, and physical resources commonly used by disabled students and how to make a referral by calling on the appropriate campus resources. Furthermore, staff must be educated on the importance of confidentiality about disability status and the consequences of disclosing this information without the student's permission.

Hiring qualified individuals with apparent and nonapparent disabilities is one method of creating a campus community that values diversity. Proactive hiring practices demonstrate an inclusive environment and provide students with the opportunity for mentoring and role models. Moreover, students with disabilities should be encouraged to apply for paraprofessional staff and leadership positions. Given that students with disabilities are less likely to have prior work or leadership experience (Getzel, 2008), some students might benefit from encouragement to apply, and their credentials should be evaluated in light of their prior opportunity for involvement.

Universal Design in Student Affairs

Practitioners can use UD principles to create facilities and services that are available to individuals with a broad range of abilities, impairments, ages, cultures, and other characteristics (S. Burgstahler, 2012, 2014; S. E. Burgstahler, 2008e). As we described in Chapter 10, the foundational aspects of UD are equitable use; flexibility in use; simple and intuitive; perceptible information; tolerance for error; low physical effort; and size and space for approach and use. S. E. Burgstahler (2008e) and S. Burgstahler (2012) stressed that UD of all student services is a long-term process to be carried out in small steps, prioritized based on the requirements of one's campus. Arendale and Poch (2008) offered stages for implementing UD principles:

1. Determine areas that are most problematic for students with disabilities.
2. Conduct and evaluate a pilot program that uses UD principles.
3. Build on pilot data to present a comprehensive model for implementing UD, including necessary staff training.
4. Have the entire staff adopt the new approach, and recognize staff for doing so.

Practitioners consider five components of student services when applying principles of UD: (a) planning, policies, and evaluation; (b) staff training; (c) information resources and technology; (d) physical environments and products; and (e) events and programming (S. E. Burgstahler, 2007). We next provide examples of how practitioners can incorporate UD in their work.

Planning, Policies, and Evaluation

It is imperative that practitioners consider the diversity of the student population when planning and evaluating services. This can be done by including a general statement regarding access in all informational materials and involving students with impairments, as well as students with other diverse backgrounds, in the planning and review processes. It is the responsibility of practitioners to ensure that evaluation methods (e.g., surveys) are accessible.

Staff Training

It is crucial that professional and paraprofessional staff members are prepared to work with all students. Inclusive staff training addresses disability-related topics such as accommodations, inclusive language, and communication etiquette (e.g., speak directly to students rather than to their interpreters or personal aides).

Information Resources and Technology

Practitioners are responsible for ensuring that information and technology is accessible to all students, including both print-based and web-based resources (Luna, 2014). As we described in Chapter 11, departmental websites must follow accessibility guidelines; print materials should be available in alternative formats; videos need to be captioned; and social media accounts (e.g., Facebook, Twitter, LinkedIn, Instagram), cloud-based storage or file sharing (e.g., Google Docs, Dropbox, and Box), and mobile technology (e.g., apps such as the University of Wisconsin-Madison's Mobile-UW) must all be accessible.

Physical Environment and Products

Practitioners are responsible for ensuring the accessibility, comfort, and safety of all services. For example, signage should be high contrast, large print, and in braille; aisles should be wide and kept clear for wheelchair users and students of size; building entrances should be accessible from all directions; and sidewalks and parking lots should be cleared of snow and ice.

Events and Programming

It is essential that all staff and students have access to events sponsored by the institution. This means that events have to be scheduled in spaces that are accessible to individuals who use wheelchairs, information about accommodations is provided on advertisements, and if an event is off campus, there is accessible transportation. It is important that campus programming appeals to the variety of students in the campus community, and as such, some events should be of specific interest to students with disabilities and represent the variety of their lives. Pragmatically, this means that practitioners rethink icebreakers and other social orientation programs so as not to exclude students with mobility, social, communication, or developmental disabilities (Wolf & Brown, 2014).

Functional Areas in Student Affairs

For this chapter, we selected 11 critical areas of student affairs and describe existing research, or the lack thereof, regarding students with disabilities in those areas. (We address functional areas related to transitions, such as admissions, orientation, study abroad, and career services, in Chapter 15.) Although we address each functional area as a discrete unit, we recognize that there are substantial overlaps between functional areas and stress that collaboration among campus units is critical to engaging students with disabilities.

Advising

> The [music] advisor[s] ... really helped me. They knew exactly what they needed to do and always thought ahead like ordering buses and stuff like that.
>
> —*Courtney, undergraduate student with a mobility impairment*

There is little empirical literature on academic advising or general advising for students with disabilities. One notable exception found that meeting with an academic advisor was positively associated with persistence for students with disabilities who attended two-year institutions (Mamiseishvili & Koch, 2012). Disability knowledge and awareness, UD principles, and accessible technology are three important areas for advisors to be familiar with.

Advisors need to have knowledge and awareness of disability-related topics so that they can assist students with creating degree plans, cultivating value-added experiences (e.g., study abroad, internships, and undergraduate research), and developing transferable skills (e.g., networking). An awareness of ableism is important so that advisors do not inadvertently, subtly, or actively reproduce social stigma and limiting views. An example of subtle discrimination is when an advisor does not discuss competitive internships, particularly those located outside the institution's geographic area (e.g., at a federal agency in Washington, DC) with disabled students because of assumptions about accommodation cost or ability to succeed.

At times, the Family Educational Rights and Privacy Act (FERPA) places academic advisors in a difficult situation; advisors frequently guide students regarding the types of classes and number of credits to take, yet unless students self-disclose or have visible impairments, FERPA policies may prevent the advisor from knowing about their disability. Therefore, concepts of UD are invaluable for advisors since they may be helping students select classes without knowing the student uses accommodations (e.g., reduced course load).

Accessible technology is also imperative for academic advising. Specifically, many institutions use a degree audit reporting system that allows students to view how their classes meet specific degree requirements. Frequently this report uses colors such as green or red to distinguish between requirements that the student has fulfilled and those the student has yet to complete. As Luna (2014) pointed out, the use of red and green colors as indicators can create difficulties for students who are color-blind or have other visual impairments.

Athletics and Recreational Sports

> Football games and stuff I feel comfortable because I'm with my friends and they sit me right next to the student section, the handicapped section, right next to the student section, so we all kind of blend in.
>
> —*Jason, undergraduate student with a disability*

Athletics is a broad term that includes attendance at athletic events, participating in intermural or recreational activities, and competing in divisional sports. (We discuss student athletes in Chapter 6.) As Jason's quote at the start of this section describes, athletic events are important for cultivating engagement and a sense of belonging. Athletic events and facilities need to be technically and practically accessible to ensure comfort and inclusion for students, faculty, staff, and community members with disabilities. For example, Ohio State University captions football and basketball games (National Association of the Deaf, 2010). Communication access is important because "deaf and hard of hearing spectators are legally entitled to all of the benefits of sporting events, including understanding announcements, play by play commentaries, referee calls, and the highly spirited school songs so integrated in the ultimate sport fan experience" (National Association of the Deaf, 2010, para. 3).

Participation in intermural or recreational opportunities offers disabled students several benefits, including wellness, increased sense of self-esteem and independence, and leadership skills (U.S. Government Accountability Office, 2010), and participation in adaptive sport is correlated with a higher quality of life (Groff, Lundberg, & Zabriskie, 2009; Yazicioglu, Yavuz, Goktepe, & Tan, 2012). Research finds that for individuals with physical impairments, participation in recreational activities results in increased confidence and expanded social interactions and friendships (Blinde & McClung, 1997). Additional benefits include greater levels of competence, goal attainment, and social integration (Blinde & Taub, 1999); opportunities to develop or redefine a stigmatized identity (Lundberg, Taniguchi, McCormick, & Tibbs, 2011); and lower scores of depression (Paulsen, French, & Sherrill, 1991). Participation in intermural sports is positively related to higher rates of first- to second-year persistence for students with disabilities (Mamiseishvili & Koch, 2011). Research on the experience of college students with physical disabilities and their involvement in a collegiate athletic club found that participants created or strengthened friendships, had higher levels of social interactions, and reported greater levels of independence and self-confidence (Wessel, Wentz, & Markle, 2011). Furthermore, for nondisabled students, participation in wheelchair-adaptive sports promotes disability awareness and decreases fear of interaction with wheelchair users (Lundberg et al., 2008).

Yet in spite of the clear benefits, students with disabilities frequently face challenges, including inaccessible campus fitness centers, limited opportunities to participate in competitive or recreational athletics (e.g., quad rugby or wheelchair basketball), and a lack of adapted and universally designed fitness equipment (Springer, 2014). For example, only 15 institutions offer adaptive athletics programs (Wheelchair and Ambulatory Sports, n.d.), and only 11 of these institutions offer varsity disabled sports (Lum, 2007). Some of the most common problems associated with implementing inclusive recreational and competitive athletics are a lack of financial resources, ableist attitudes, and limited staffing. However, "under Section 504 and its implementing regulations, institutions must afford disabled students an equal opportunity to participate in physical education, athletic, and recreational programs" (Kaplin & Lee, 2013, p. 1356). Furthermore, the Office for Civil Rights (OCR) issued a "Dear Colleague" letter that addressed equal athletic opportunities for students with disabilities. Although this letter focused on elementary and secondary schools, the OCR clearly stated, "Students with disabilities at the postsecondary level must also be provided an equal opportunity to participate in athletics, including intercollegiate, club, and intramural athletics" (2013a, p. 2).

Campus Safety

"The ADA requires that emergency evacuation procedures for individuals with disabilities be reviewed so that access to evacuation in the event of an emergency is assured" as Armstrong, Lewis, Turingan, and Neault (1997, p. 21) noted. It is imperative that all students and employees with disabilities that would affect their ability to respond in the event of a campus emergency have evacuation plans. Evacuation plans are designed in consultation with the individual, and all relevant parties (e.g., residence life, emergency services, employing units, DRO) need to have knowledge of the plan.

An important aspect of emergency planning involves the creation and/or designation of areas of refuge in campus buildings. Areas of refuge "consist of an accessible space, separated from the rest of the building by fire-resisting materials and fire doors that limit the passage of fire and smoke" (Proulx, 2002, p. 6). Areas of refuge are required under the ADA for buildings or portions of buildings without an accessible exit route; however, these are a best practice for all buildings to assist with the evacuation of people with disabilities (Proulx, 2002). Areas of refuge should have access to two-way communication so that users are able to contact support, closed-circuit TV to provide monitoring from a separate location, chairs for individuals to sit, windows to provide reassurance, and clear signage so that individuals know where the area of refuge is located (Proulx, 2002). It is important to identify a fire warden for each building to assist with evacuation. (Interested readers can review the most recent international building code and consult Rowland, White, Fox, and Rooney, 2007, for an overview of evacuation processes or K. M. Christensen, Blair, and Holt, 2007, for further reading on ADA accessibility requirements, including emergency alarms and egress windows.)

Campus Health and Counseling Centers

You know, if somebody has cancer, they are going to talk about it. But if somebody has depression, it's just, "Oh, everybody gets down sometimes." If somebody has generalized anxiety, then it's, "Oh everybody has stress; just deal with it." You see all over these ribbons that they have for breast cancer and for AIDS, and they have all of the awareness campaigns. You don't see that for mental illness. You don't see anything. What you do see is the little Zoloft guy bouncing around on commercials saying, "Oh, do you feel blue?"

—Jamal, undergraduate student with a mental health disability

Research on students with disabilities and their use of campus wellness or physical health services for routine health care (e.g., visiting a nurse practitioner for strep throat or getting an annual flu shot) is nonexistent. Given that health services may be a significant support, particularly for students with long-term, chronic health conditions, this is an important area of future research. Access to quality health care, including pharmaceutical services at a reasonable cost, is a critical consideration for administrators. Both health and counseling centers need to assess the accessibility of their facilities, use of UD strategies, and interpreter availability.

The literature on counseling centers is more robust, in part because the number of students with mental health concerns is growing on college campuses and mental health concerns can lead to disabling impairments. (See Chapter 4 for a discussion of prevalence, relationship to disability, and risk factors.) Counseling centers also serve students with other types of disabilities who are addressing transition, stress, wellness, and personal or academic difficulties. At some institutions, practitioners within the counseling center may collaborate with the DRO to offer low-cost diagnostic testing and disability assessment (e.g., Woodcock Reading Mastery Tests—Revised) for students who did not receive a diagnosis during K-12 education but report experiencing learning difficulties.

Counseling centers have a range of visibility and collaboration within the campus community; therefore, practitioners within each counseling center will take a slightly different approach to engaging with the campus community and students with disabilities. For example, practitioners in highly embedded centers will naturally have closer working relationships with a variety of units (e.g., residence life) and cross-campus teams (e.g., behavior threat team), whereas practitioners in siloed centers will have to make intentional collaboration efforts.

In working with students with disabilities, it is important for practitioners to know when and how to make referrals to the counseling center on campus or, if their institution does not have this service, to connect the student with community-based resources. It is also imperative that student affairs practitioners know their institution's policies because many colleges place a limit (e.g., 10 hours per semester) on the number of counseling sessions each student can receive before referring the student to a community care setting (E. Klingensmith, personal communication, March 14, 2015). Furthermore, in a cost-savings measure, some institutions are outsourcing their counseling services to for-profit agencies in the geographic region; smaller institutions may contract with larger universities within the geographic area for health and counseling services. In their review of the literature, Markoulakis and Kirsh (2013) found that students had difficulties navigating dispersed services due to a lack of service coordination between campus units and/or community mental health providers. Therefore, practitioners can provide a bridge between campus departments and develop community-based networks.

Students with disabilities may seek services from the counseling center for a variety of reasons. Here we discuss stigma, family environment, alcohol or drug abuse, partner violence, and trauma. (We direct readers who are interested in ethical counseling practices for students with disabilities to Palombi and Mundt, 2006, and Palombi, 2010.)

Although disability stigma exists in a variety of situations, students face unique challenges addressing stigma within the postsecondary setting. Students with mental health impairments (Markoulakis & Kirsh, 2013) and other types of disability (Trammell, 2009) experience disability stigma in a variety of formats, including loneliness, social isolation, exclusion from academic opportunities, limited career-related activities, and denial of accommodations (Gruttadaro & Crudo, 2012). Unfortunately, faculty members are more likely to hold negative attitudes toward students with mental health impairments than those with other types of disabilities (Sniatecki, Perry, & Snell, 2015).

Similarly, students with learning or cognitive impairments may have to combat negative assumptions about their right to be in college or their ability to learn.

The family environment is an important component of social support (Heiman & Berger, 2008), and students with disabilities may seek assistance from the counseling center to address their parental relationships. Students may have overprotective parents who use disability as a method of preventing their child from functioning autonomously. Students with overprotective parents might be navigating lower expectations or limited independence (Sanders, 2006) and a lack of respect for their choices (Hitchings et al., 2001). Students may also seek assistance in coping with parents who do not support their personal or academic aspirations, as parents are not immune to stigma or negative interpretations of disability, and therefore they may have lower expectations for their children (Shifrer, 2013).

Students with disabilities, and particularly those with nonapparent disabilities, are at greater risk for increased alcohol use (Higher Education Research Institute, 2011). However, this risk might be masked; the literature on alcohol use shows an increase in consumption for the general student population while attending postsecondary education (Wolf, Simkowitz, & Carlson, 2009b). Much of the empirical research on alcohol use among college students with disabilities is based on the National Longitudinal Study of Adolescent to Adult Health (Add Health) that tracks secondary students in grades 7 to 12 or data from the American College Health Association–National College Health Assessment (ACHA-NCHA II). ACHA-NCHA II data indicate the percent of students consuming alcohol in the past 30 days is similar (83% disabled; 81% not disabled; Bernert, Ding, & Hoban, 2012). Blanco et al. (2008) also found consistent rates of alcohol use (80%) between students with and without disabilities.

In their analysis of ACHA-NCHA II data, Bernert et al. (2012) found that about 35.4% of students without disabilities reported marijuana use in the past month, whereas 44.2% of students with one disability and 49.5% of students with co-occurring disabilities indicated marijuana use. Major depression, which can be a disabling condition, was significantly associated with frequent marijuana use by undergraduate students (Keith, Hart, McNeil, Silver, & Goodwin, 2015). Currently the majority of research focuses on factors such as gender, race, and fraternity and sorority membership; hence, there is limited information about disability beyond analysis of ACHA-NCHA II data. As the legalization of marijuana in the United States changes, research priorities may also shift.

Students with co-occurring disabilities are at greater risk for alcohol and drug use. Bernert et al. (2012) found that students with two or more disabilities "had a higher percentage of engagement in substance use behaviors than did those with one disability or with no disability" (p. 465). In comparison to their nondisabled peers, students with co-occurring disabilities were 9.76 times more likely to report an addiction diagnosis (Bernert et al., 2012).

Disability status is a significant risk factor for intimate partner violence (D. L. Smith, 2008). Scherer, Snyder, and Fisher (2013) found that female students with disabilities (20.4%) were almost twice as likely to experience partner violence when compared to female students without disabilities (11.1%). Furthermore, male college students with disabilities also experience partner violence at a greater rate (11.7%) than their male peers without disabilities (6.7%). The most common type of partner violence for students with disabilities (men and women) was psychological victimization, followed by physical and sexual violence (Scherer et al., 2013).

Survivors of trauma, including veterans and sexual assault survivors, are growing populations on campus. We described the literature on veterans with disabilities in Chapter 6. The limited literature on sexual assault indicates that college students with disabilities experience higher rates of victimization (Cantor et al., 2015), and undergraduate students who self-identify as disabled (9.3%) were almost twice as likely to report unwanted sexual contact than their peers without disabilities (4.6%; K. Brown et al., in press; see Chapter 5). It is probable that these rates are higher because sexual assault is viewed as a private topic that is frequently associated with shame, guilt, embarrassment, or anger; therefore, victims may be unwilling to disclose (Sable, Danis, Mauzy, & Gallagher, 2006). Students with developmental disabilities (B. Stevens, 2012) or autism spectrum disorder (ASD; K. Brown et al., in press) may be at greater risk for sexual assault due to social and emotional functional limitations. Furthermore, the mistaken belief that disabled individuals are asexual (Irvine, 2005), a corresponding lack of sex education (Koller, 2000), and the relationship between actual sexual knowledge and increased risk of victimization (Brown-Lavoie, Viecili, & Weiss, 2014) place disabled students at higher risk.

Dining and Event Services

> You're stuck all the way in the back of [the theater] so you don't get to see. So if it wasn't for [my boyfriend] wanting to go, I probably wouldn't go just because it's really bad seating and if it's for something that wouldn't be packed, I feel kind of weird sitting all the way in the back and everybody would be in the front.
>
> —*Clare, undergraduate student who uses a wheelchair*

Collaboration between dining services and the DRO is vital. Student accommodations to address both dietary needs and physical access are individualized (see Chapter 13). Examples of dining-related accommodations can include meal plan adjustments for specific dietary requirements, the use of service dogs in dining facilities, access to a private space for food preparation to accommodate allergies, communication of the menu in an alternative format for students who are visually impaired, and modifications that address architectural barriers.

Food allergies are an important consideration for dining services. According to data from the National Health Interview Survey conducted in conjunction with the Centers for Disease Control and Prevention, 5.1% of children have food allergies, and these numbers are increasing (Jackson, Howie, & Akinbami, 2013). The U.S. Department of Justice (2013a) found that the Americans With Disabilities Act (ADA) may cover food allergies and has provided guidelines for accommodation. At the time of writing, the extent of university responsibilities was not clear, but Lesley University, as an example, provides allergy- and gluten-free foods in its dining halls and also allows students to preorder allergen-free meals (U.S. Department of Justice, 2013a).

Unlike many other units that primarily serve the internal campus community, dining and event services also have legal obligations under Section 504 of the Rehabilitation Act. These obligations necessitate that campus dining and event services ensure that events open to the public, which may include the campus dining hall, are not only accessible to students, faculty, and staff but are also accessible to campus visitors. Campus units responsible for providing access to the public should receive training on the accommodation process for campus visitors.

Campus events (e.g., commencement) must be accessible, and socially just institutions go beyond compliance to create a welcoming environment for all participants. In order to facilitate this, the planning committee for large campus events such as graduation should include a staff member from the DRO. Issues of accessible seating, sign language interpreting, ramps, live captioning, accessible loading zones, accessible parking, large-print programs, and signage are just some of the considerations that event planners address. (We direct interested readers to S. N. Friedman, Berger, and Parks, 2014, for further information on accessibility guidelines.)

Facilities Management

> I'm stuck inside when it snows; I can't leave. I tried my freshman year here and I'll never do it again.... Some days I sit at home and think, "Okay, what's campus going to be like?" and sometimes the sidewalks on campus aren't plowed until midafternoon so I don't risk it. If it looks bad outside my door, I just stay because it's too big of a risk.
>
> —*Joe, undergraduate student with a mobility impairment*

The literature on facilities, grounds, and parking is limited, particularly in regard to student affairs interventions. In many ways, these functional areas are frequently ignored or presented as silos external to the realm of student affairs. However, collaboration across campus constituents is imperative to support students with disabilities, and accessible facilities are critical prerequisites that allow students to participate in student affairs programming and services. We address the physical campus environment in Chapter 8; here we focus on accessibility of student affairs buildings, parking, and snow removal.

All physical spaces operated by student affairs, including residence halls, multicultural spaces, offices, dining facilities, recreation facilities, computer labs, kitchens, laundry, child care facilities, and common areas, need to be accessible and inclusive. New buildings must be constructed to ADA standards; however, as we described in Chapter 3, under the letter of the law, these standards provide only a minimum. Creating student affairs facilities that are inclusive requires attention to details beyond those specified by ADA Accessibility Guidelines (ADAAG; U.S. Access Board, 2002). To achieve a socially just level of access, practitioners work closely with facilities management and disability consultants when considering renovations or construction of spaces. Welcome desks and office spaces should be designed to be wheelchair accessible for not only office visitors but also for staff who may require an accessible work space. Also, as discussed in Chapter 5, care should be given to spaces of cultural significance to ensure the accessibility of programs that provide support to individuals from multiple minoritized identities.

Under the ADA Accessibility Guidelines, institutions have to provide enough accessible parking spaces, and these spaces have to be sufficiently dispersed across the campus to provide access in a meaningful manner. It is also important that accessible parking spaces are well maintained during winter months, and facilities management staff are diligent in snow removal not only from accessible parking spaces but also from accessible paths leading to and from those spaces.

Foundation and Alumni Relations

There is a paucity of literature on cultivating relationships with donors or alumni in relation to programs for students with disabilities. However, in a climate of increasing tuition costs and declining state appropriations, institutions benefit from cultivating donors and developing long-term socially just relationships with alumni. The limited literature on disability-specific funding strategies describes the use of external funding and gifts to support endowed scholarships for students with disabilities, promote study abroad, procure naming rights, and fund new building construction (S. N. Friedman et al., 2014). For example, the McBurney Center for Disabilities at the University of Wisconsin-Madison was founded by the family of an alumnus, Floyd Mike McBurney, with the goal of "improving access for students with disabilities long before the passage of any federal legislation requiring campus access" (McBurney, n.d., para. 5). Additional ways to develop relationships include placing a "make a gift" link on the DRO website or incorporating an alumni profile in the DRO newsletter. Not all gifts need to be financial; time and access to resources are also valuable. DRO staff can work with alumni to build networking events, career mentoring, and internships for students with disabilities.

Alumni services would be wise to remember that disability is fluid and ever changing over the life span; therefore, alumni who are currently able-bodied may not retain these corporal capacities, and many alumni consider legacy or larger donations later in life. Therefore, it is imperative to make alumni events welcoming and inclusive by providing accommodations.

From a social justice perspective, gifts are used to add to existing scholarships or develop new programs, not shirk institutional budgetary responsibilities by using donations to meet ADA compliance standards, provide reasonable accommodations, or renovate buildings that are not up to code. It is imperative that images of disability are included within the campus community and that this is done in a manner that is socially just rather than pejorative, reinforcing of ablest stereotypes, or tokenizing. For example, an alumni profile on a music student who is also visually impaired should focus on her postgraduate career rather than detailing hardships, impairments, or otherwise differentiating alumni with disabilities from other alumni.

Identity-Based Centers and Services

Disability is frequently conceptualized as part of diversity and is often included within the framework of multicultural competence in student affairs, yet there is a paucity of literature on the relationship between the DRO and identity-based services such as multicultural student services, Black student unions, Chicanx and Latinx centers, adult student services, women's centers, or LGBTQ centers. It is important that programming locations and the physical location of identity-based centers are accessible spaces because students with disabilities hold multiple and intersectional identities (see Chapter 5) and underrepresented students with disabilities report gaining support from peers and faculty with similar backgrounds (Dowrick et al., 2005). Practitioners working at larger, decentralized, or siloed institutions can build relationships with the DRO to intentionally bridge the gap between functional areas.

Residence Life

> I've been a Cyclone [the Iowa State University mascot] since I was little [laughs], you know. I've always wanted to come down here [Ames, Iowa] and then when I saw they had accessible living I was sold, I was on my way, I signed the paper.
>
> —*Samantha, undergraduate student with a mobility impairment*

The residential experience is an important part of social integration for students with disabilities. Living in residence halls has a positive influence on students' retention from the first to the second year of college (Mamiseishvili & Koch, 2011). Socially just institutions use principles of UD so that facilities are inclusive, regardless of the ability status of students currently living in a specific building. Inclusive environments are imperative because many different people access this space, including off-campus students with disabilities who are visiting their friends and students' family members with disabilities. Residence halls are also places of employment for staff (e.g., custodians) and administrators with disabilities.

Accessible housing should be placed as close to academic and frequently used service buildings as possible, and students' choices of living accommodations have to be comparable to the choices afforded to nondisabled students. If academic programs have a residential component, the program must accommodate students with disabilities within housing unless doing so would result in a fundamental alteration of the nature of the program. In collaboration with the DRO, residence life should maintain clearly publicized policies and deadlines for requesting housing accommodations. "Those deadlines should not be absolute; rather, they should be seen as a date by which a request for an accommodation has the best chance of being considered reasonable" (Coolbaugh, 2014, p. 160). Residence life staff also need to understand that accessibility is not just bathrooms and doorways; as Joe described in the quote at the start of this chapter, all features (e.g., ability to use the kitchen) of a living area are important.

In the next section, we discuss assistance and service animals, personal care assistants, and specialized housing requests as three types of accommodations. We also discuss disability-themed housing as an important avenue of connecting with other disabled students.

Assistance and Service Animals. Although service animals and emotional support animals (ESAs) share some similarities, primarily that they are both animals, there are also substantial differences (see Chapter 3). Therefore, residence life staff should work closely with the DRO to develop two policies, one for service animals and one for ESAs, and treat ESA accommodations requests on a case-by-case basis. Both animal policies should be clearly articulated and easily accessible.

Service animal and ESA etiquette is an important topic for staff training. Staff should understand and be able to educate their residential community that service animals are working and the dog is not to be touched or distracted without first receiving permission from its owner. ESAs are newer, and a formal etiquette protocol is not well established in the literature; we encourage staff and students with ESAs to mirror the service animal etiquette to avoid confusion, limit liability, and avoid detrimental consequences for service animals. Staff training also addresses stereotypes, including support for students with nonapparent disabilities. For example, ESAs often provide support for students with psychiatric disabilities, and it is important that staff training reduce implicit bias that can affect the treatment of students with hidden disabilities, including questioning the use of an ESA.

Personal Care Assistants. In some cases, students with disabilities employ personal care assistants (PCAs) to support their independent living by accompanying the student in the same residential space. Residence life policies for PCAs should include a background check, appropriate access to common space, overnight lodging within the same residential space, and parking, even if the PCA is not an enrolled student (DO-IT, 2012). The research indicates that students who use PCAs gain important skills when they hire, train, and supervise PCAs in residential living, and the shift from family care management to personal care management is an important transition (Burwell, Wessel, & Mulvihill, 2015). Specifically, students learned how to (a) manage time in relation to aid availability for daily functions and social activities, (b) train attendants, (c) become comfortable with having strangers assist with daily living activities (e.g., showering), (d) address poor performance of care assistants, and (e) transfer responsibility from parents (Burwell et al., 2015). Residence life staff should be trained on PCA policies and be aware that students who employ PCAs will have housing-related accommodations and will likely be transitioning from family members as care providers to PCA services.

Specialized Housing Environments. Specialized housing environments encompass a wide range of individualized accommodations, including single living spaces, air-conditioning, substance-free housing, physical accessibility features, or an exemption from college-owned housing. Students may also request social accommodations (e.g., early move-in).

Single rooms are a commonly requested accommodation, and demand often greatly exceeds institutional capacity. Single rooms are an accommodation used to address a variety of functional limitations in the living-learning environment. Some situations in which a single room might be a reasonable accommodation are when a student's disability-related equipment (in particular, motorized wheelchairs or scooters) requires sufficient space to turn and cannot be accommodated in a double room. Students with severe social-anxiety disorder may request a space without other people, and it may be reasonable to provide a single for a student with a severe sleep disorder who requires increased quiet to achieve adequate sleep or may require sleep at different times of the day. However, in many situations, students with disabilities can live in double rooms. A quiet and distraction-free environment is not a reason to grant a single room, as no rooms in a residence hall can reasonably be considered distraction free, and noise-cancelling headphones and libraries provide alternatives. The limited availability of single rooms encourages DRO and residence life staff to be creative problem solvers.

Students with a wide variety of physical disabilities, including asthma, severe allergies, vocal chord dysfunction, sleep disorders, seizures, and migraines, may request a residence hall that is air-conditioned or designated as substance-free in order to limit exposure to environmental triggers (e.g., dust, pollen, or heat) or to decrease the likelihood of late-night disruptions or second-hand smoke. Air-conditioned housing requests can be accommodated through UD by making all buildings air-conditioned or retroactive processes by placement in a specific residence hall or the installation of individual air-conditioning units. Students who are recovering from addiction may also request an environment without the use of substances, and institutions can create specific living communities that are substance free by choice rather than solely through a campus policy. Students may require an accommodation for a room that includes traditional physical accessibility features (e.g., a door opener). Common examples of physical accessibility accommodations include students with mobility impairments requiring housing on the first floor with a door opener that is located in a building with an elevator, in order to access laundry, lounges, and other amenities. Students with chronic fatigue may benefit from a residence building that is centrally located on campus to reduce transition time to classes and other campus buildings. Students with hearing impairments may require placement in a room with a strobe alarm and bed shaker to alert them in the event of a fire. Each student's accommodations are unique, and residence life staff should collaborate closely with the DRO and the student.

Students may also request an exemption from living in the housing environment. An exemption may be reasonable for a student who requires 24-hour assistance and would benefit from living with a family member off campus, for a student in recovery who may be prone to relapse in the residence halls, or for a student with immune deficiency where communal living poses an increased health risk. All institutions need clear policies and procedures that outline exemption policies. Institutions with a substantive number of disability-based exemptions from housing may choose to use review boards to handle requests. Review boards allow for the inclusion of professionals (e.g., physicians) and may provide a greater level of credibility, as well as an additional layer of appeal if the director of housing or DRO director is not a board member.

Accommodations related to the social environment are also important. These requests may include early access to the residence halls in order to avoid the bustle of move-in day or greater control and autonomy in the selection of a roommate. Students with obsessive-compulsive disorder, major anxiety, ASD, or personality disorders may benefit from accommodations that reduce the likelihood of being overstimulated or exposure to environmental triggers.

Disability-Themed Housing. Beyond the accommodations process, some students may find it beneficial to reside in a disability-themed living-learning or special interest community. Many students with disabilities were isolated in high school and had minimal interactions with other people who share their impairment; getting to know other students with similar experiences can be empowering.

It is important to note that disability-themed housing is not mandatory or segregated; rather it is a space for people who experience stigma to connect with others and even explore disability as an area of academic study. One particularly successful example of disability-focused housing is the Beckwith residential support services program at the University of Illinois, which provides accommodations for students who use PCAs for activities of daily living. This living option provides single rooms with multiple accessibility features, support in supervising PCAs, disability-related transition planning, a mentoring program, accessible gym facilities, and assistance in the adjoining dining hall.

Student Involvement

> The main reason why I get involved in extracurricular activities is to grow myself and find out more about me in different situations.
>
> —*Robin, undergraduate student with a learning disability*

Student involvement takes many shapes and forms across campus, from sorority and fraternity life to service-learning to political activism. In this chapter, we focus on the substantive areas of undergraduate research and student organizations. We direct interested readers to K. Brown and Broido

(2015) for further reading on engagement and postsecondary students with disabilities.

Undergraduate Research. Undergraduate research is an opportunity for students to engage with faculty members, develop critical thinking skills, foster public speaking and analytical writing, and develop an application portfolio for graduate school. Unfortunately, the research on students with disabilities participating in undergraduate research programs is scarce. Ableism is present within many scientific communities, and students may have difficulty accessing laboratory facilities or research opportunities in science disciplines (e.g., chemistry) and health care professions (e.g., nursing). Resources for students and practitioners in this area include the American Chemical Society and its Committee on Chemists with Disabilities (ACS-CWD, n.d.) and the American Association for the Advancement of Science (AAAS). AAAS's Project on Science, Technology and Disability publishes a resource directory of scientists and engineers who have disabilities (AAAS, n.d.a) and hosts "Entry Point!", a program that identifies and recruits students with disabilities studying science, engineering, mathematics, and computer science for internships and co-op opportunities (AAAS, n.d.b). It is imperative to foster research skills and encourage students with disabilities to participate in undergraduate research as a method of promoting engagement and diversifying future faculty.

Student Organizations. There is limited empirical literature on students with disabilities and their involvement in student organizations, either disability focused or otherwise. Although involvement in student organizations is generally considered a positive or value-added part of the college experience, students with disabilities may face barriers to inclusion. For example, not all activities that student organizations take part in are accessible to students with mobility impairments, and students with ASD may not find large group interactions comfortable (K. R. Brown & Coomes, 2015). Furthermore, students with learning disabilities often spend more time on academic tasks (e.g., studying) than their nondisabled peers do, resulting in fewer opportunities for cocurricular activities (Markoulakis & Kirsh, 2013; May & Stone, 2010). Student affairs practitioners play an important role in making sure that organizations and activities under their purview are accessible to all students. In addition, it is important that disability resource providers seeking to start or maintain disability-specific student organizations take a nondeficit-based approach to programming and activities (K. R. Brown & Coomes, 2015). For instance, educational programming for an autism-based student group could focus on "learning e-mail etiquette" (a skill all students and many professionals would benefit from) rather than "improving social skills."

Student Conduct

Administrators who address student code-of-conduct issues face complex and difficult decisions. An extensive discussion of risk management or law is beyond the scope of this chapter; interested readers are directed to B. A. Lee and Abbey (2008), Stuart (2012), or Kaplin and Lee (2013). Here, we briefly describe legal guidelines, discuss harm to self or others and medical marijuana, and conclude with the potential for UD in conduct policies.

Legal Guidelines. As we outlined in Chapter 3, the law (e.g., ADA and Section 504) provides foundational legal protection for students with disabilities. Specifically, institutions may not discriminate against students with disabilities as part of the conduct process (Kaplin & Lee, 2013). This means that administrators cannot treat a student with a disability differently than they would treat a student who does not have a disability, and institutions must apply disciplinary procedures in a uniform manner (Gelpi, 2015a, 2015b). Furthermore, administrators who are considering disciplinary actions must engage in an interactive process, provide accommodations, and follow due process (Kaplin & Lee, 2013). For example, students who are d/Deaf or hard of hearing must have access to an interpreter or their preferred means of facilitated communication for all conduct meetings and disciplinary hearings. Students also have responsibilities under the law, and although disability "can be considered a mitigating factor during sanctioning" (Hudson & Janosik, 2014, p. 181), students are "not entitled to appeals or readmission hearings solely on the basis of new evidence of previously undiagnosed or undisclosed disabilities" (Hudson & Janosik, 2014, pp. 180–181). We summarize additional relevant case law and OCR letters in Table 14.1.

Harm to Self or Other. Although there is a wide breadth of student conduct violations (e.g., plagiarism, drug or alcohol use, and falsifying evaluations), a substantive portion of the existing literature and case law focuses on students who threaten to harm themselves or others, and these conduct violations are frequently associated with students who have mental health or psychiatric disabilities. Prior to 2010, many institutions employed policies that viewed a direct threat to harm oneself in the same manner as a threat to harm others. However, this changed in September 2010, when the U.S. Department of Justice "narrowed the definition of 'direct threat' to an individual who is a threat to others but not to him or herself" (Kaplin & Lee, 2013, p. 1177). Hence, institutional policies that address student conduct violations associated with "direct threat" can only be applied in situations where the student is threatening to harm others (OCR, 2011a). The OCR's letter to Case Western Reserve University (2011a)

TABLE 14.1. RELEVANT CASE LAW AND OFFICE FOR CIVIL RIGHTS LETTERS PERTAINING TO STUDENT CONDUCT

Effect on Educational Institution or Student	Resolution or Letter	Citation
Institutions can deny participation if the student exhibits significant unsafe behavior over an extended period of time even with the provision of reasonable modifications, auxiliary aids, or services.	Letter to Glendale Community College	OCR (2003)
Disclosure of disability after the fact does not require the institution to mitigate sanctions; "the purpose of the ADA is not to give a second or third chance to one who commits misconduct" (para. 30).	*Bhatt v. University of Vermont*	*Bhatt v. University of Vermont* (2008)
Institutions must have an individualized process to assess whether a student poses a direct threat to the health or safety of others before prohibiting participation in a program.	Letter to Doane College	OCR (2009)
Students are responsible for notifying conduct officials of their disability and providing appropriate documentation. Conduct processes are confidential, so staff in the DRO may not be aware, informed, or able to share information. Students cannot make a claim about disability after the conduct process has concluded.	*Toth v. Slippery Rock University of Pennsylvania*	*Toth v. Slippery Rock University of Pennsylvania* (2010)
The standard of "direct threat" applies to situations where a student poses a significant risk to the health or safety of others. "Any determination that a person poses a direct threat to others is made through an individualized assessment based on reasonable judgment relying on the most current medical knowledge of the individual or the best available objective evidence" (OCR, 2011a, p. 7).	Letter to Case Western	OCR (2011a)
The institution cannot require that students who take leave for mental health reasons provide documentation demonstrating that they are not a direct threat as a condition of reenrollment; doing so is discriminatory because it assumes that all students with mental health issues are a direct threat regardless of previous actions.	Letter to Case Western	OCR (2011a)
Institutions cannot have suspension policies for students with physical or mental disabilities that are different from suspension policies for nondisabled students. All students must be afforded due process in a timely manner.	Letter to Farmingdale State College	OCR (2011b)

TABLE 14.1. (*CONTINUED*)

Effect on Educational Institution or Student	Resolution or Letter	Citation
Students cannot violate the code of conduct, including interrupting university business.	Letter to University of Michigan—Dearborn	OCR (2011c)
The institution may suspend students for behavior related to their disabilities, as long as the suspension was not because of the students' disabilities or stereotypes about their disabilities.	Letter to University of Michigan—Dearborn	OCR (2011c)
The institution's grievance procedure must be easily accessible and incorporate appropriate due process standards, including adequate notice and appropriate contact information.	Letter to University of Michigan—Dearborn	OCR (2011c)
Institutions cannot have policies that subject students with mental health impairments (or students who are regarded as having mental health impairments) to different requirements than students without disabilities. Specifically, with respect to attendance and readmission, unless the university is able to demonstrate that the student posed a direct threat to the health or safety of others, it cannot require that students with mental health disabilities follow different procedures or meet different requirements to start attending the institution again (e.g., obtain a note from their private physician recommending the student return to class).	Letter to Western Michigan University	Cited in Gelpi (2015a)
Although students can advocate for reasonable accommodations, they cannot do so in a manner that is threatening or abusive to members of the campus community.	Letter to Ivy Tech Community College	Gelpi (2015a); OCR (2013b)
Institutions "may establish rules to maintain a safe and orderly environment and may discipline a student even if the misconduct resulted from disability when the misconduct violates an essential conduct code provision" (Gelpi, 2015b, p. 10).	Letter to Southwestern College	Cited in Gelpi (2015b)
The postsecondary institution is not required to excuse past conduct of a student with a disability.	*J.A.M. v. Nova Southeastern University*	*J.A.M. v. Nova Southeastern University* (2015)

is particularly instructive regarding the definition of direct threat and the assessment process:

> The "direct threat" standard applies to situations where a university proposes to take adverse action against a student whose disability poses a significant risk to the health or safety of others. A significant risk constitutes a high probability of substantial harm and not just a slightly increased, speculative, or remote risk, in determining whether a student poses a direct threat, the University must make an individualized assessment, based on a reasonable judgment that relies on current medical knowledge or on the best available objective evidence, to ascertain: the nature, duration, and severity of the risk; the probability that the potential injury will actually occur; and whether reasonable modifications of policies, practices, or procedures will sufficiently mitigate the risk. The student must not be subject to adverse action on the basis of unfounded fear, prejudice and stereotypes related to his disability or perceived disability. (p. 3)

Furthermore, the OCR (2011a) clarified actions that the institution can take as part of the readmission process for a student who has been found to be a direct threat. Educational institutions can require that students document the steps that they took to address and reduce the previous threat prior to readmission. "However," according to the OCR, "educational institutions cannot require that a student's disability-related behavior no longer occur, unless that behavior creates a direct threat that cannot be eliminated through reasonable modifications" (pp. 3–4).

In the event that a student's actions are harmful to self or disruptive to university business (e.g., learning), the institution may sanction the student in accordance with its conduct code. However, with harm to self, the OCR has made it clear in successive letters to several schools (see Table 14.1) that unless the student presents a "direct threat," the institution cannot stipulate different requirements for readmission for students with mental health disabilities or students who are regarded as having mental health disabilities, in comparison to students without disabilities. Regardless of disability, this area of student conduct is difficult for administrators to address because the consequences of handling a situation poorly can be devastating.

Medical Marijuana. Student affairs practitioners working in states that have legalized marijuana for medical or recreational purposes will face an inconsistency between state and federal law. Staying within the scope of this book, we limit our discussion to medical marijuana and the associated conduct policies in regard to students with disabilities. We also note that marijuana laws (medical and recreational) are relatively new, and thus the courts provide limited guidance. Nevertheless, practitioners can use three legal precedents to inform conduct decisions. First, as we outlined in Chapter 3, under the

ADAAA, impairments related to alcoholism and drug addiction may be covered as a disability only if the individual is in recovery and not currently using alcohol or drugs. Second, in *Coates v. Dish Network* (2015), the Colorado Supreme Court upheld the termination of an employee with a documented disability who was using medical marijuana, noting that the supremacy clause (U.S. Const., art. VI, § 2) establishes that the federal Constitution (and federal law) takes precedence over state laws. Third, the majority of postsecondary institutions receive federal funding (e.g., financial aid, federal grants), and these institutions must follow federal regulations or lose that funding. The legalization of medical marijuana in specific states is a new area of the law, and although current indications are that student codes of conduct follow federal policy, there is a possibility that will change. Practitioners will want to work closely with legal counsel to remain updated.

Universal Design in Conduct Policies. As we outlined above, conduct policies cannot legally discriminate against or treat students with disabilities differently from students without disabilities. Administrators must follow the same process for all students, provide reasonable accommodations within the conduct process, ensure due process and confidentiality, and maintain detailed written documentation (Hudson & Janosik, 2014). Sanctions based on behavior and conduct policies need to be applied in a consistent manner to all members of the campus community. All students, regardless of disability, are entitled to access resources including counseling and legal representation.

Socially just conduct practices go beyond legal compliance to incorporate UD and address the stigma frequently associated with disability. Here, we draw on the theoretical paradigms outlined in Chapter 2 and principles of UD outlined in Chapter 10 to provide examples of how the conduct process and policies can be modified:

- Consider the student within a learning framework and as a member of the campus community.
- Decrease the stigma associated with disability by providing a visible and accessible method for students with disabilities to disclose this information as part of the conduct process.
- Write conduct policies in a manner that limits ambiguity and provides concrete, explicit directions so that students with functional limitations associated with abstract processing (e.g., ASD) are able to understand institutional expectations (K. R. Brown & Coomes, 2015).
- Practitioners need to be aware of the judgments, stigmas, and stereotypes they bring about disability from our broader society into the conduct process.

- Following principles of UD, the conduct process should allow students different ways to express what they have learned.
- The conduct process should be designed in a straightforward and predictable manner, regardless of the student's experience, knowledge, or language skills.

Conclusion

Knowledge and awareness of disability-related issues are imperative in student affairs. However, as we illustrated in this chapter, there is limited existing research on key functional areas, including student organizations, activities, and undergraduate research. Student affairs professionals consider structural, programmatic, behavioral, and attitudinal implications for disability within their own practice, unit, division, and institution as they work to create a more socially just living and learning environment for students with disabilities.

Discussion Questions

1. From an intersectional perspective, consider how different social identities (e.g., gender, sexual orientation, age, race, family income, parents' education) might enhance or mitigate the relative effects of a disability on an individual. How can you apply this knowledge to specific student affairs functional areas?
2. As a student conduct officer, consider your current procedures. Then, based on the information presented in this chapter, identify two areas that could be changed to support students with disabilities at your institution.
3. Consider your residence life training process. What information is provided about students with disabilities? What changes need to be made?
4. Select the functional area of student affairs that you currently work in (or would like to work in). Then identify how you could implement concepts of UD in this area.
5. What are the challenges associated with being a student at an institution where services and functional units exist in silos? How could you, as a student affairs professional, mitigate or work to reduce those barriers?

CHAPTER FIFTEEN

TRANSITIONS AND STUDENT AFFAIRS

I met with another student today, Bill, who had an IEP throughout secondary education, but could not tell me a single thing about his disability. Bill did not have any idea of what accommodations would provide him access and no understanding of his disability or the process for receiving accommodations in college.... The only reason he made his way to me was because a faculty member walked him to my office after he completed less than 50% of the exam during the class period.
—Autumn, coordinator of disability resources

Bill is just one of more than a dozen students whom Autumn has worked with in the past few years who received little or no high school transition planning. Bill's individualized education plan (IEP), which he had his high school fax to Autumn, stated that he received educational testing in third grade and was diagnosed with dyslexia and dysgraphia. Bill used accommodations throughout his education but did not receive updated diagnostic testing as part of his transition planning; he had expected that in college he would continue to receive the same set of supports. Bill said that he had met with a counselor once, early in his high school career, but he had no recollection of meeting with a counselor in the previous two years.

In this chapter, we address issues related to transitions for students with disabilities. Korbel, McGuire, Banerjee, and Saunders (2011) asserted, "Transitions begin well before matriculation and include strategies to assist students as they exit the collegiate environment. Therefore institutions must plan ahead for such transitions, creating partnerships across the university that are intentional about collaborating to design meaningful programs" (p. 40).

Transitions span the life course. Here we examine three distinct yet interrelated types of change that students experience: entering, during, and leaving higher education.

Entering Postsecondary Education

Students with disabilities take varied routes to accessing postsecondary education; we describe entry from secondary education, after military service, and as an adult learner. Then we discuss challenges and supports associated with the transition into postsecondary education. We conclude by focusing on admissions, financial aid, and orientation programs as important areas of support.

Points of Entry

In describing three different forms of entry to higher education, we encourage readers to be aware that these are not distinct. For example, many returning veterans are also adult learners, and they may be returning to higher education a second time—either to complete a bachelor's degree that they started directly after high school or to begin graduate work. Furthermore, although we present these entrances as discrete instances, students may enter and exit higher education numerous times.

Entering From K–12. Student affairs practitioners must be aware that students who enter postsecondary education directly from the K-12 system are navigating legal differences and varying levels of transition planning. The transition to postsecondary education for students with disabilities involves changing from a legal framework that mandates protection under the Individuals With Disabilities Education Act (IDEA) to a legal framework focused on equal access as stipulated by the Americans With Disabilities Act (ADA), subsequent Americans With Disabilities Act Amendments Act (ADAAA), and subpart E of Section 504 (see Chapter 3). Students and parents will notice this transition in three critical areas. First, students change roles; they move from passive and uninvolved bystanders to active and independent actors who are responsible for securing their own accommodations through self-advocacy. Second, as the locus of responsibility shifts, parents have significantly less involvement in the process. Third, although students with disabilities and their parents may expect the same types and levels of services to be available in the postsecondary setting, many students who received services in K-12 face a reduction in eligibility. In particular, students with learning disabilities or executive functioning impairments may enter college without strong organizational or time management skills as much of their study planning was done for them in high school (W. M. Hadley & Satterfield, 2013). Since personal assistants and time management are not accommodations in postsecondary education, incoming college students should understand their legal rights, develop self-advocacy skills, and learn how to disclose and discuss their disabilities. These skills should be included within high school transition planning (Eckes & Ochoa, 2005).

Transition planning is mandatory in the K-12 system under the Individuals With Disabilities Educational Improvement Act (IDEIA) 2004 amendment, which includes revisions to address transition. Daly-Cano, Vaccaro, and Newman (2015) emphasized that it is a violation of "IDEA/IDEIA if students have not been provided with supports; to identify their strengths and areas of need; to set goals and make plans to achieve them; and to know their rights, if any… as they move out of secondary education" (p. 214). As illustrated in the story at the start of this chapter and in Chapters 5 and 6, transition planning for students entering colleges may vary widely, and students from secondary schools with limited financial and staff resources often receive less transition planning. J. W. Madaus, Grigal, and Hughes (2014) found that poverty influences the expectations and thus the actions of educators working with students with disabilities who wish to participate in higher education. Diminished expectations of students with disabilities with marginal socioeconomic resources often lead to minimal transitional support. Hence, student affairs practitioners must be aware that not all students with disabilities have the same access to transition support, even if this support is legally mandated.

The number of students with disabilities who actively participate in high school transition planning is shockingly low. Studies conducted by Hitchings et al. (2001) and Cole and Cawthon (2010, 2015) found that less than 10% of secondary students with disabilities reported having transition or college preparation–related meetings in high school. The type of disability with which a student has been diagnosed also factors into access to transition planning. Janiga and Costenbader (2002) found that limited transition planning may be especially prevalent for students with learning disabilities (LD) because "high school personnel hold the misconception that LD is such a mild disability that these students can succeed without assistance" (p. 464). However, Janiga and Costenbader reminded us that learning disabilities often span an individual's lifetime, and many students who do not experience transition planning struggle in their initial academic endeavors. Furthermore, students leaving the K-12 system may have undiagnosed or undocumented disabilities and therefore have never received an IEP or transition support. Under a social justice paradigm, student affairs practitioners must be aware that stereotypes about disability and access to resources in K-12 education affect the transition experience.

As noted in Chapter 13, while self-advocacy and self-determination are considered important for students with disabilities, institutions of higher education cannot expect that all students with disabilities will enter with a mastery of either of these skills (Eckes & Ochoa, 2005). Disability resource providers should implement processes that facilitate the development of self-advocacy skills over time. The narrative intake process discussed in Chapter 13 provides students with the opportunity to articulate the effects of their disability, as well as to note accommodations that have previously been successful for them. This process should be structured so that it provides students with questions that prompt reflection and develop a deeper understanding of disability for students like Bill in the example from the opening of this chapter. Examples of questions that facilitate reflection include asking students to describe in their own words their disability and its effects on accessing the college environment; asking for a list of accommodations, assistive technology, or academic assistance they have previously used; and asking students to think about activities they hope to participate in at college (e.g., employment, study abroad, athletics) and if they anticipate any barriers to participating in those activities. Disability resource providers could also use a form or questionnaire that encourages students to self-reflect about the specific effects of their disability (see Table 15.1). Disability resource office (DRO) staff also should not limit these questions to the start of a student's career but instead check in frequently (e.g., a week after the semester starts, after midsemester assessments, at the close of the semester, in each subsequent semester) to help students develop a fluency in describing their disability and provide ample opportunity for students to self-advocate if the accommodations are not working.

The role of parents in higher education and the relationship between parents and colleges continues to evolve, and many institutions are grappling with when and how to involve parents in student concerns. The federal Family Educational Rights and Privacy Act (FERPA) protects the educational records of all students and as a result limits what educators can share with parents without a release of information in place (Family Policy Compliance Office, 2015). This regulation does not mean, however, that institutions of higher education should completely exclude family members from their students' college experiences.

Parental involvement can be an important factor in the transition of some students with disabilities to college, and DRO staff should consider their philosophy on parent involvement. For example, the vast majority of students who registered with the DRO before the start of their first semester indicated that their parents played an active role in that decision (Lightner, Kipps-Vaughan, Schulte, & Trice, 2012). Furthermore, postsecondary institutions have an obligation to educate and prepare parents for their student's

TABLE 15.1. FUNCTIONAL EFFECTS OF DISABILITY-SELF REPORT FORM

Task	No Impact	Minimal Impact	Moderate Impact	Significant Impact	Comments
Attention/concentration					
Taking notes					
Starting, organizing, and completing tasks					
Interacting with others					
Following verbal directions					
Following written directions					
Seeing					
Hearing					
Understanding visual information					
Memorizing information					
Understanding auditory information					
Putting thoughts into writing					
Using my hands					
Speaking clearly					
Sitting for long periods					
Moving around (standing/walking)					
Tolerating stress					
Motivation					
Finishing tests on time					
Spelling					
Writing					
Reading at a standard rate					
Understanding what I read					
Doing math calculations					
Doing math word problems					
Managing time					
Studying					
Other (please list)					
Other (please list)					
Other (please list)					

transition (K. R. Brown & Coomes, 2015). The education can facilitate ongoing parental involvement and reduce unrealistic expectations of the DRO and the institution. K. R. Brown and Coomes noted that "best practices balanced family support with empowering the student and recognized that this experience is also a change and an educational opportunity for [parents]" (p. 474). In addition, Dallas, Ramisch, and McGowan (2015) recommended that colleges consider "family involvement during the transition to college in order to help answer [disability service providers'] questions and gauge [students'] level of self-advocacy skills, [their] knowledge of … diagnosis, specific reactions to stress/changes, [and] level of independent living skills" (pp. 136–137). These practices can help to engage the student, provide disability resource providers with a broader picture of the student's skills, and make the family feel as though their student is supported and understood.

Entering From Military Service. Not all students with disabilities will enter college immediately following secondary education. As discussed in Chapter 6, veteran students with disabilities represent a growing population in higher education and require institutions to prepare adequate support systems to assist with the transition from active duty to higher education. Students with disabilities who enter postsecondary education following military service may have skills and resources that their traditionally aged peers lack; however, they may also experience other challenges as the result of their disability and veteran status (Burnett & Segoria, 2009). The unique experiences of student veterans with disabilities require that student affairs practitioners take "a new approach to service delivery" (p. 53).

Veterans with disabilities frequently must address different functional limitations, recent onset of disabilities, and ongoing medical care when compared to their disabled peers without military service experience. Approximately 20% of military veterans returning from foreign service are diagnosed with post-traumatic stress disorder or major depression (Ackerman, DiRamio, & Garza Mitchell, 2009; Hoge, Auchterlonie, & Miliken, 2006; J. W. Madaus et al., 2009; Murphy, 2011). In addition, returning veterans experience greater rates of traumatic brain injury, loss of limbs, or other physical impairments when compared to the general population (Ackerman et al., 2009; J. W. Madaus et al., 2009). Student veterans may also "have cognitive disabilities such as learning disabilities (LD) or attention deficit/hyperactivity disorder (ADHD) that existed prior to military service" (J. W. Madaus et al., 2009, p. 14). As a result, a significant population of student veterans may be eligible for services and supports from the DRO. However, "in many instances, the evaluations, diagnoses, and documentation necessary to establish a student veteran's disability issues and to review and assess their accommodation needs may be tied-up in our government's bureaucracy" (Shackelford, 2009, p. 37).

Student veterans may require ongoing health care while enrolled in post-secondary education. Yet Veterans Affairs (VA) policies are often complex, and access to health care may be delayed due to long waiting lists. Due to challenges with receiving documentation and health care in a timely manner, Shackelford (2009) recommended that resource practitioners receive VA-specific training and institutions adapt a creative approach to implementing programs so that postsecondary supports are not delayed.

In addition to delays in documentation and health care, "the standards used by the military in determining disability for the purposes of separation and benefits, as well as the standards used by Veterans Affairs to review disability claims, are different from the definition of disability in Section 504 and the ADA" (U.S Department of Education, 2008, p. 2). In general, when determining disability status, the military requires a much greater level of impairment than the ADA does. Therefore, veterans may qualify as students with disabilities by postsecondary standards and at the same time fail to meet the military definition for benefits. This is why J. W. Madaus et al. (2009) stressed that it is important for disability resource providers to take note of, and rely on, their standard procedures for reviewing documentation. It also is important that staff members in Veteran Services offices be aware of the less stringent criteria under the ADA, so they can broaden the range of students they refer to the DRO.

Furthermore, Burnett and Segoria (2009) noted, "Returning veterans with physical and/or psychological injuries do not typically identify themselves as someone who would qualify to receive support and reasonable accommodations through a DSS program" (p. 54). As a result, disability resource practitioners and other student affairs providers should explore options to combat this perception. These options may include partnering heavily with the veteran student affairs office or resource center on campus, creating an affinity group for veterans with disabilities (Murphy, 2011), developing a relationship with the local veterans affairs office, and/or hiring a veteran to work in the DRO to provide outreach to this population (Burnett & Segoria, 2009; J. W. Madaus et al., 2009; Shackelford, 2009). In addition, concerns over privacy and potential impact on future employment are common reasons why veterans are reluctant to disclose or seek disability accommodations (Burnett & Segoria, 2009). In particular, veterans who are interested in postgraduation employment in private or public sector security (e.g., FBI) or foreign affairs service work may face background checks as part of the employment process. Disability resource practitioners should take steps to assure veterans that the DRO can provide a high level of confidentiality and that the institution will not release disability status to employers conducting background checks without the veteran's permission.

Veteran students with disabilities may experience cultural adjustment when entering postsecondary education. Ackerman et al. (2009) found that this adjustment could often be attributed to a combination of returning from a long break from education and posttraumatic stress disorder. One veteran in this study explained, "What made it hard was my attention span and patience were very short, so sitting in class...became very hard to do" (p. 10). Veteran students with disabilities also described the difficulties they experienced moving from the structured environment and hierarchy of the military to the campus environment "where there was no chain of command from which to get answers" (Ackerman et al., 2009, p. 11). Training for faculty and staff on issues facing student veterans (Elliot, Gonzalez, & Larsen, 2011; American Council on Education, 2008) and accommodations that address emotional triggers students may experience when the course content includes references to war, politics, and/or violence are important for the successful transition of veterans to college.

Entering as an Adult Learner. Research on the transition to postsecondary education for adult learners with disabilities is nonexistent. Anecdotally, many of these students may enter via the two-year system, and a substantial number will claim multiple minoritized identities. Similar to nondisabled adult learners, adult students with disabilities may face stressors associated with family responsibilities and concurrent employment (see Chapter 6). Adult learners enter or return to postsecondary education for a variety of reasons, including job retraining, unemployment or underemployment, the desire to change career fields, and lifelong learning goals. Many adult learners with disabilities will not have access to IEP plans from high school and may also lack a medical diagnosis from a practitioner, or if a medical diagnosis was made, the documentation could be dated or a product of military service. Furthermore, as functional limitations are frequently acquired with the aging process (e.g., hearing loss), adult learners may be addressing recent onset and the transition to being disabled. Given the complex nature of disability over the life span and the increasing value of postsecondary education in a global economy, the transition for adult learners with disabilities is an important area for future research.

Challenge and Support

Students with disabilities face transition challenges that their nondisabled peers frequently do not navigate (Getzel, 2008; Hong, 2015). These challenges may include insufficient academic preparation, greater expectations for self-awareness and self-advocacy, health concerns, and an unwelcoming campus climate. Although postsecondary disability practitioners are often aware of transition challenges, students may not fully identify difficulties until they have experienced academic or social problems (Janiga & Costenbader, 2002).

Academic Preparation. Students with disabilities do not always get appropriate support from teachers and counseling staff at their secondary school (Garrison-Wade & Lehmann, 2009). Garrison-Wade and Lehmann found that secondary counselors had "minimal expectations for students with disabilities in terms of continuing on to college" (p. 429), and these biases affected the secondary courses in which students with disabilities were placed. The participants noted feeling insufficiently prepared for their introductory college courses or starting with significantly lower-level course work than their peers. For some students, insufficient preparation meant greater academic difficulty during the first year of college or a longer time to degree completion, or both. Student affairs practitioners should understand that students with disabilities might face discriminatory attitudes and enter postsecondary education with limited college preparatory or advanced placement courses. Postsecondary institutions can address inadequate academic preparation by providing targeted summer courses designed to bridge the secondary-to-postsecondary experience and address underpreparation in critical areas such as writing, math, and reading.

Self-Awareness and Advocacy. Self-awareness, self-assessment, and the ability to explain functional limitations in relation to the learning and living environment are critical parts of transition planning. However, these skills are not consistently taught in secondary education, and in fact, many parents do this work for their children. Barnard-Brak, Sulak, Tate, and Lechtenberger (2010) found that "students with disabilities, especially those with non-visible disabilities such as learning disabilities, may be unable to explain the depth of their disability or the manner in which it may affect their classroom participation or academic performance" (p. 141). This phenomenon is especially prevalent for students who were not actively engaged in the accommodation and transition process during secondary education or are not comfortable with their disability status (Barnard-Brak et al., 2010). Adult learners may face further challenges in that they are unaware of their learning style and learning needs because they have taken an extended break from an academic learning environment.

Postsecondary institutional policies expect students with disabilities to be able to explain their functional limitations and self-advocate, skills that may be underdeveloped (Janiga & Costenbader, 2002). During secondary education, students have structured support from administrators, educators, and family members who navigate the request for accommodations. Hence, when students enter postsecondary education, they are unsure of the supports they should request and unable to articulate their accommodation requests (C. Murray, Lombardi, & Kosty, 2014). Development of self-advocacy skills is especially vital for students whose functional limitations may directly affect their communication skills. For example, K. R. Brown and Coomes (2015) noted that "due to social limitations, the transition to a system of self-advocacy was particularly difficult for students with [autism spectrum disorder]" (p. 473) and recommended "social coaching, role modeling, patience, and attentiveness" (p. 473) as important practices associated with cultivating self-advocacy skills. Disability resource providers can support students by explaining how individual accommodations benefit the student, reviewing how to discuss accommodations with faculty members, and employing role modeling to teach the use of accommodations.

Health Concerns. Health concerns are not frequently discussed in secondary transition planning but can have significant bearing on students, particularly those with specialized health care requirements. As such, postsecondary institutions should make relevant health care information available to students and their families so that they can make informed decisions about whether the geographic location and resources of the institution can support the postsecondary goals of the student (Repetto, Jaress, Lindsey, & Bae, 2016). The office of admissions should accurately portray the level of academic, technological, physical, and social support available to students. Overselling an institution's ability to support specialized health care during the admissions or recruitment process is detrimental to students and their families, who deserve accurate information to determine which institutions can best fit their specific health-related concerns.

Health-related concerns pose challenges to social integration for students with disabilities. First-year students with chronic health conditions reported significantly higher levels of loneliness than their first-year peers without chronic conditions (Herts, Wallis, & Maslow, 2014). Chronically ill students also report feeling isolated from similar peers; over half (57%) did not know other chronically ill students at their postsecondary institution (Herts et al., 2014). Preorientation or intentional programming during orientation can address disability-specific issues by creating groups for students to connect with others who share similar functional limitations (e.g., a group for students with chronic illness). In addition, student affairs providers can use technology and social media to create social communities that foster student interaction without the requirement of attending group meetings or participating in physically demanding activities.

Environmental Change and Campus Climate. Environmental differences between secondary and postsecondary education also present challenges for students with disabilities (Janiga & Costenbader, 2002). These postsecondary differences include larger class sizes, greater independence and unstructured time, increased social distraction, fewer evaluations and assessments, and projects that span the course of a semester and require independent and ongoing work (Garrison-Wade & Lehmann, 2009; Janiga & Costenbader, 2002). Students may be unprepared for the loss of their support network, such as family and friends (Janiga & Costenbader, 2002), and expect faculty and staff to provide highly structured support, such as demonstrating how students should complete assignments or class requirements (Garrison-Wade & Lehman, 2009). Practitioners can support students and their families by developing programs (e.g., disability orientation or bridge programs) that educate incoming students about academic expectations in a postsecondary environment and describe available support programs.

Campus climate also plays a role in the transition of students with disabilities: it influences students' initial adjustment to campus (C. Murray et al., 2014) and longer-term comfort (K. Brown, Peña, & Rankin, 2015). C. Murray et al. identified three levels of adjustment (poor, average, and high) and found that adjustment level was related to campus climate; students reporting poor adjustment also indicated they were uncomfortable and found campus to be unsupportive. About one-third of students with disabilities in C. Murray et al.'s study reported scores associated with poor initial adjustment, while only one-tenth reported high adjustment scores. Notably, initial adjustment was not related to high school GPA, amount of time spent studying, support received from disability services, use of accommodations, or financial stress. K. Brown et al. found that not all students with disabilities reported similar campus climate experiences, and students with ASD reported greater satisfaction with their classroom interactions and lower satisfaction with cocurricular aspects of the campus climate.

Lack of Research. While researchers have identified several challenges that students with disabilities face, there is a paucity of research on effective support programs. The limited existing research indicates that proactive connections with the DRO are important for academic success. Students with learning disabilities who engaged with DRO during the transition from high school had better academic performance than students who waited until after their first year to seek support (Lightner et al., 2012). Furthermore, students who sought DRO services later in their academic career did so in response to poor academic performance, including failing exams or courses and low first-semester

GPA (Lightner et al., 2012). In addition, alumni with disabilities identified the ability to understand their disability and advocate for the accommodations they would benefit from as critical to their postsecondary success (Barber, 2012). Given the likelihood that students will enter with disparate levels of secondary transition planning and postsecondary preparation, evidenced-based practices and transition support is clearly an area that needs future research.

Student Affairs Functional Areas

Admissions, financial aid, and orientation programs are three functional areas that are critical for a successful transition into higher education. Although we present these in distinct subsections, all three functional areas must work collaboratively across institutional silos.

Admissions. Student affairs professionals working in recruitment and admissions need to consider nondiscrimination in the admissions process, accessibility of promotional materials and events, and inclusion of disability as a visible part of the campus community. As noted by Kaplin and Lee (2013), it is illegal for postsecondary institutions to use admissions criteria to screen out students with disabilities. (We discuss disability discrimination in the admissions process further in Chapter 3.) Beyond legal compliance, admissions offices should include information regarding disability resources during the admissions process and should offer the chance to interact with practitioners in the DRO during the campus visit. Admissions office staff also should ensure that their websites, preadmission communication, application forms, and recruitment activities are accessible and that a clear process exists for requesting necessary accommodations to participate in these activities.

Similarly, all promotional materials and events, including websites, social media accounts, videos, and photos, must be accessible and welcoming to a variety of students with disabilities. Postsecondary institutions must caption videos, provide photo descriptions, and employ accessible technology (see Chapter 11 for further description). Institutions should also consider the explicit and implicit messages sent during recruitment in order to attract and matriculate students with disabilities. Explicitly, marketing materials should include images of current students with disabilities as a means of supporting the diversity that students with disabilities bring to the campus environment. Implicit methods (e.g., diversity statements and staff disability knowledge across the institution; Korbel et al., 2011) and conspicuous senior leadership support (Martin et al., 2011) are powerful ways to send messages of inclusion.

Admissions and enrollment policies also communicate inclusion and exclusion. Many institutions strongly encourage prospective first-year students to visit campus, but that same push is not implemented for transferring students. Because many students with disabilities start their postsecondary career at two-year institutions, Zubernis, McCoy, and Snyder (2011) suggested that admissions office staff encourage transfer and nontraditional students to visit campus. Admissions office personnel can also support veterans with disabilities by implementing flexible application and entry deadlines to accommodate delays caused by military time lines (e.g., delayed release) and training that overlaps with the beginning of the semester (Murphy, 2011).

Financial Aid. For many students and their families, financial aid is a significant factor in the college decision process. Students with disabilities face unique considerations as they may be more likely to enroll on a part-time basis (Kimball, Wells, Ostiguy, Manly, & Lauterbach, 2016) and may have medical or assistive technology–related expenses that students without disabilities do not need to consider. J. W. Madaus et al. (2014) discussed personal care attendants, special equipment, transportation, and medical expenses as additional disability-related costs associated with college attendance. From a social justice perspective, expenses that are disability related factor into a student's complete college expenses, and these costs should be included in the FAFSA for review by financial aid administrators.

Information about federal grants, state grants, scholarships, and student loans must be clearly communicated during the admissions process. Specifically, students and their families should be informed that students are required to maintain satisfactory academic progress to retain federal financial aid (e.g., Federal Pell Grant, Federal Work Study, or Federal Perkins Loan) eligibility (Federal Student Aid, n.d.). Financial aid staff should also "clarify any impact a particular academic accommodation might have on a student's academic program, including taking a reduced course load or the option to take one or more classes on a pass-or-fail basis" (Soneson & Fisher, 2011, p. 61). Under a social justice paradigm, colleges and universities will want to assess their institutional grant and scholarship requirements and, where possible, develop provisions for funding when students with disabilities would benefit from a lighter credit load. Residential colleges that have full-time-enrollment policies should develop and use a policy for students with disabilities that allows for part-time enrollment and includes the provision of financial aid. Institutions should also consider policies for flexible disbursement of funds for student veterans and methods to address later payment of tuition and fees caused by federal government delays in issuing military benefits (Murphy, 2011).

Orientation Programs. Postsecondary institutions can use existing orientation programs to highlight a commitment to students with disabilities, address questions related to transition prior to the student's arrival on campus, encourage disability disclosure early in the student's college career, and navigate transitions. Nondisability-specific program staff should include the DRO in all resource fairs, hire students with disabilities as orientation leaders, and develop (or expand existing) bridge programs to include students with disabilities. Beyond modifying existing programs, disability-specific orientation and summer bridge programs are additional ways colleges and universities are supporting students with disabilities (M. W. Hadley, 2007).

In addition to the broader category of students with disabilities, several subpopulations benefit from targeted orientation. Martin et al. (2011) noted the need for colleges to offer STEM (science, technology, engineering, and mathematics) preorientation for students with disabilities as a method of addressing their underrepresentation in the sciences (Martin et al., 2011; National Science Foundation, 2015). Furthermore, STEM preorientation programs for students with disabilities are crucial in reducing the self-selection of students out of STEM fields (Martin et al., 2011). African American students with disabilities (Banks, 2014) and first-generation college students (Padgett, Johnson, & Pascarella, 2012) experienced difficulties in the transition process due to a lack of adequate information about disability services and difficulty in creating strong support networks. Hence, building collaborative bridge programs with offices designed to support diverse students (e.g., TRIO or student support services) is important social justice work.

Cross-campus collaboration during the admissions and orientation process is key in order "to increase the success rate for students with disabilities" (Del Rey, 2014, p. 149). A siloed approach where disability resources, residence life, counseling, and other key areas that support students with disabilities are not involved or represented during admissions and orientation led to a more difficult transition for students with disabilities (Kezar, 2005), whereas preadmissions strategies that included an intentional partnership between the DRO and offices of admissions, financial aid, orientation, and public relations increased the visibility and success of disabled students (Korbel et al., 2011). A cross-campus approach may include providing information related to the transition process for students with disabilities, the use of peer mentors during admissions and orientation sessions (Getzel, 2008), or a specific training module in collaboration with disability resources that addresses advocacy skills and the accommodations process and builds academic self-confidence (Chiba & Low, 2007).

Transitions During Postsecondary Education

Students with disabilities will not only experience transitions entering postsecondary education, but will also navigate periods of change during the course of their college career. These transitions may include the transfer from one institution to another, the development of greater assistive technology independence, and study abroad. We describe three specific functional areas that directly support these transitions. However, taking a holistic perspective, the effects of transitions during college influence many areas with which practitioners in residence life, student engagement, health, and counseling should familiarize themselves.

Transferring Institutions

Many transfer students start their college education at a two-year or community college (Monroe, 2006). Specifically, two-year colleges offer a variety of benefits including open admissions policies, a teaching focus, lower tuition, closer proximity to home, transfer articulation agreements with four-year institutions, and, in some cases, smaller class sizes. These benefits attract a substantial number of students with disabilities.

There is limited research on the experience of transfer students with disabilities or evidenced-based practices to support this transition. In one notable exception, Ponticelli and Russ-Eft (2009) found that students with disabilities who received orientation and assessment were more likely than students with disabilities who did not receive orientation and assessment to transfer. Furthermore, the proportion of transfer courses taken and the proportion of credits completed were the strongest predictors of whether students with disabilities transferred (Ponticelli & Russ-Eft, 2009). Given the number of disabled students who start at two-year institutions, this topic merits future research.

Students with disabilities who transfer from two-year colleges to four-year institutions may face challenges associated with a shift in academic standards. Monroe (2006) found that 79% of transfer students from community colleges "experienced a drop in grades" (p. 37), which Monroe attributed to difficulty with adjustment to their new institution. Adjustments experienced by transfer students may include larger classes, changes in student-teacher interaction, and heavier course loads (Monroe, 2006), as well as modifications in the types of accommodations provided (Becerra, 2006). Specifically, students frequently assume that all the accommodations they received at their two-year institution will be honored at the new four-year institution; however, this assumption is not guaranteed (Beccerra, 2006). Because many two-year colleges are open enrollment, they see greater numbers of students with disabilities. The DRO staff at these colleges often provide extensive support services and accommodations (G. Johnson, Zascavage, & Gerber, 2008; Mamiseishvili & Koch, 2012); hence, "the level of independence expected at a four-year institution may be a difficult adjustment for students with disabilities" (Zubernis et al., 2011, p. 4). Students who transfer later in their academic career may experience higher expectations for independence and self-advocacy, since many four-year institutions require upper-class students to be self-sufficient (Zubernis et al., 2011). As a result, students may be caught off guard when transitioning to a new institution or may experience stress and worry related to a loss of accommodations. From a social justice perspective, disability service practitioners should provide each transfer student with an individualized assessment of the student's self-advocacy skills and clearly explain the accommodations process.

Transfer student orientation programs are one way that institutions can support students with disabilities (Becerra, 2006; Zubernis et al., 2011). Effective transfer student orientation must consider the experiences and accommodation requirements of students with disabilities and older students rather than simply replicating the same types of education and activities used for incoming first-year students. Transfer student orientation should also create systems to bridge the gaps between institutions (Becerra, 2006) by extending beyond a half-day or one-day event to include follow-up meetings and activities that support full integration within the campus community (Zubernis et al., 2011).

Assistive Technology Independence

When students start their partnership with the DRO, assistive technology providers may work closely with students to identify the most appropriate technology to support their learning goals (Getzel, 2008). Generally, assistive technology practitioners help students navigate unfamiliar technology, educate the students and faculty about how to use assistive technology in the classroom, and provide accommodations such as converting textbooks and other materials into alternative formats. Practitioners also assist students as they explore and develop competency with technology options that were not available in secondary education. Students may require support connecting with vocational rehabilitation in order to apply for financial support for their technology accommodations.

During the middle years of the students' postsecondary education, the assistive technology staff may begin to transfer more technology responsibilities to the student. Getzel (2008) found that "students need opportunities to try the technology in order to learn how to correctly use it and to determine if it is suitable, both for short-term and long-term needs" (p. 212). Hence, many DRO staff develop a plan for slowly weaning students off direct assistive technology support as students develop familiarity and skills to navigate assistive technology independently. This transition to assistive technology autonomy prepares the student for life after graduation. These changes may include students taking on responsibility for running optical character recognition on their own documents for compatibility with screen reader technology, discussing technology with their faculty, and identifying if they require additional technology programs. The transition must be facilitated and supported; this process needs to have cocreated goals and clear expectations for independence. For example, when responsibility for the conversion of materials is transferred from the DRO to the student, staff should hold training sessions and clearly communicate dates so the student is not caught unprepared. It is important to understand that the goal of assistive technology independence is not to reduce work for DRO staff or avoid providing reasonable accommodations. Rather, this is a process by which students are trained to develop and procure their own assistive technology resources so that they can function independently after graduation.

If the transition to technology autonomy is successful, students in their final year of postsecondary education may require very little support from the assistive technology office as they are developing skills for self-accommodation after college. DRO staff, however, may schedule meetings with students to help them plan for technology-related aspects of the transition to work or graduate education.

In order to facilitate the technology transition, student affairs professionals need an "awareness of the ways in which technology has transformed and continues to shape postsecondary education" (Korbel et al., 2011, p. 38). Following Roessler and Kirk (1998), practitioners should develop a systematic method of evaluating the technology requirements of students throughout their postsecondary career. This process involves identifying students who would benefit from additional training and the development of educational programs to foster independent technology use. From a social justice perspective, staff and faculty of postsecondary institutions should support the long-term career goals of students with disabilities by focusing on how classroom technology can be employed in the workplace and teaching students how to request employment-related accommodations.

Study Abroad

Many institutions emphasize the education of students as global citizens. Study abroad is a common avenue to attain global competence. Over the past two decades, the number of students studying abroad has more than tripled, and some undergraduate programs have incorporated study abroad as a graduation requirement for all students (Roach, 2013; Soneson & Cordano, 2009). In the 2013–14 academic year, 14.8% of U.S. domestic students studied abroad during their bachelor's degree program (Institute of International Education, 2015a). Of the students who choose to study abroad, the percent of students with disabilities has increased in the past eight years, from 2.6% in the 2006–7 academic year to 5.7% in the 2013–14 academic year (Institute of International Education, 2015b). However, the overall rate of participation in study abroad for students with disabilities remains substantially lower than for their nondisabled peers (Matthews, Hameister, & Hosley, 1998). In addition, in an examination of study abroad by type of impairment, students with learning disabilities account for about half of all students with disabilities who study abroad, whereas students with physical disabilities decreased participation from 8.0% in the 2006–7 academic year to 4.7% in the 2013–14 academic year (Institute of International Education, 2015b).

Several factors are related to the relatively low proportion of students with disabilities studying abroad. College and university study-abroad staff may lack consistent processes for recruiting and advising students with disabilities and often have insufficient knowledge about the accessibility of study sites for these students (D. Johnson, 2000). Students with disabilities face additional considerations, including determining if they can access medical care, accommodations (e.g., sign language interpreting), transportation, and housing, as well as funding for additional disability-related expenses. Students may also face discriminatory attitudes or actions in the admissions process.

Under a social justice paradigm, students with disabilities should have access to the benefits associated with study abroad. Furthermore, McLean, Heagney, and Gardner (2003) urged that "as global educational opportunities expand, the implications for students with a disability must also be considered; not to do so is potentially discriminatory, as it restricts the employment options for students with a disability and impedes their opportunities for success" (p. 226). Institutional staff can take several steps toward creating equal access to study abroad. First, staff of postsecondary institutions will need to move beyond legal compliance, as the ADAAA does not generally extend beyond the United States, to focus on social justice by providing accommodations for students who study abroad. Second, institutional staff should market study abroad in an inclusive and welcoming manner (see Table 15.2). Third, in order to avoid making discriminatory decisions on

TABLE 15.2. STRATEGIES TO ENCOURAGE STUDY ABROAD FOR STUDENTS WITH DISABILITIES

Strategy	Rationale
Clearly communicate the accommodations process for study abroad.	Students can adapt to changes with advance notice and are not set up to expect more than a site or institution can provide. Students also know whom to work with to arrange appropriate accommodations.
Include students with visible disabilities in marketing and promotion, and market the stories of individuals with a wide range of disabilities.	Students may self-select out of study-abroad experiences based on misconceptions that they will not be able to successfully travel abroad. Images and testimonials from fellow students with disabilities help individuals imagine themselves studying abroad and can increase interest and enrollment in these programs.
Hold educational sessions about study abroad as collaboration between the study-abroad office and the DRO.	Students may not be sure whether to seek resources for travel abroad with accommodations from disability resources or from study abroad. Information sessions can show the collaboration between these offices, as well as help students see study abroad as an encouraged option for them in their educational career.
Develop a mentoring program that pairs students with disabilities who have returned from study abroad with students preparing for departure.	This may help students to prepare for their study-abroad experience and have realistic expectations of systems or supports that may be different while abroad. It will also help students learn of other students with disabilities who have successfully managed their disabilities (and others' perceptions of their disability) while abroad.
Indicate which programs are in countries with legislation similar to the ADA (e.g., the United Kingdom).	This will allow students who require substantial accommodation in some environments or who are nervous about travel abroad to pick a program in a country with greater protections or similar supports to those available in the United States.
Indicate programs where specific medications (e.g., Adderall) are illegal to use or possess.	This will allow students time to work with their providers to discuss alternatives or to identify programs in which their medication needs and educational interests can both be met.
Start the planning process early.	Early preparation for a new program sponsored by the institution allows for planning for anticipated accommodation needs or to review in-country resources necessary to distribute to students with physical, psychiatric, or learning needs abroad. This will be especially important for students who may need additional time to arrange the necessary

(continued)

TABLE 15.2. (*CONTINUED*)

Strategy	Rationale
	accommodations or require alternatives from their typical supports while abroad (e.g., paperwork for service animals to travel abroad may take several months or even years or may not be possible in some locations).
Provide resources on cultural perceptions of disability in host countries.	Not all countries have perceptions of people with disabilities that are similar to those in the United States. Early preparation for students will help them to understand cultural norms that they may experience or need to navigate as they relate to their disability.

applications for study-abroad sites, disclosure information "should always be collected after a student's acceptance into a particular program" (Soneson & Fisher, 2011, pp. 64–65). Fourth, study-abroad practitioners must strategically develop relationships with students, the DRO, and their overseas program colleagues to develop strategies to support students with disabilities.

Student affairs practitioners can support students with disabilities as they transition into, during, and out of their study-abroad experience. Students with disabilities may require assistance in choosing a study-abroad program and geographic location that will meet their accommodation requests and provide sufficient access. The process of selecting a study-abroad program is unique to each student, and access to medical care and medication, food allergies, public transit, duration of the program, cost of the program, language of instruction, disability legislation of the host country, and fit of the study-abroad program with academic requirements needed for graduation are some of the factors that practitioners and students should take into consideration. Students with specific accommodations (e.g., accessible housing, use of a service animal, alternate formatted materials) may require additional information and detailed research when choosing a program.

Preparing students for the new cultural experiences is another critical component of the predeparture planning (Soneson & Cordano, 2009). Students should learn about the cultural expectations of their host country and community, as well as set goals for individual learning. In some cases, practitioners in the DRO and study-abroad office, in collaboration with host country partners, may need to prepare for reasonable accommodations abroad (e.g., scheduling interpreters). Students also should consider and address predeparture health and travel planning. There are six key areas for consideration:

1. Explore resources that support study abroad for students with disabilities (e.g., Mobility International [miusa.org]) to learn location- and impairment-specific considerations.
2. Discuss routine medications and health care while abroad with a medical provider.
3. Update or obtain vaccinations required for travel to and within the host country.
4. Explore student health insurance and research international insurance coverage for general medical issues and disability-specific health care.
5. Research local disability organizations or specialized services that may be available while abroad.
6. Explore options of inter- and intracountry travel while abroad and determine if additional preparation is needed (e.g., paperwork for service animals).

Student affairs practitioners in the DRO, academic or major advising, and study abroad should schedule check-in e-mail or video and audio contact at least once per semester with all students studying abroad to address any transition problems (e.g., culture shock) and discuss pertinent topics (e.g., course registration for the following semester).

Students who return to the United States after prolonged travel, such as a semester or year abroad, may experience reverse culture shock. Student affairs practitioners should be aware that reintegration is challenging at times, particularly if students feel that they are isolated or unable to share their study-abroad experience with peers and family. In addition, students who experienced greater autonomy and independence and who "enjoyed greater accommodation and more positive social interactions at the host site than at home" (Soneson & Fisher, 2011, p. 70) may require greater support in transitioning back to their domestic campus. Staff in the study-abroad office and DRO can collaborate to provide resources for students with disabilities who have returned from abroad, including discussing how transferable skills learned abroad relate to future employment goals or graduate education. Practitioners can also build a network of students with disabilities who have studied abroad as a method of encouraging future participation and promoting this value-added experience as realistic.

Exiting Postsecondary Education

Transitions occur across a continuum, and although the transition into college is frequently focused on, the transition out of college is equally, if not more, important. Until 2012, the Association on Higher Education and

Disability (AHEAD) professional standards did not address career transition for students with disabilities. It still is only minimally addressed by encouraging disability professionals to consult with other campus departments such as career services. Furthermore, the topic of transition to graduate school is notably absent within the existing standards (AHEAD, 2012a) and body of research. As a result, there has been less of a focus on the development of career and graduate preparation than on other areas of postsecondary support for students with disabilities. Here, we describe challenges and supports associated with the transition into career and graduate school programs. We specifically highlight career services as an important functional area for both undergraduate and graduate students.

Career Transition

Students with disabilities experience fewer postgraduation career options than their nondisabled peers. According to the U.S. Bureau of Labor Statistics (2015), people with disabilities had a significantly lower rate of employment in 2014 than people without disabilities, regardless of education level. Specifically, for individuals with disabilities, 16.1% who graduated from high school, 23.8% of individuals with an associate's degree or some college, and 28.5% of individuals with a bachelor's degree or higher were employed. These percentages are in comparison to individuals without disabilities who were employed at a rate of 66.4% for individuals with a high school diploma, 73.3% of those with an associate's degree or some college, and 78.3% of individuals with a bachelor's degree or higher. Furthermore, college graduates with disabilities face an earnings gap (Dickinson & Verbeek, 2002) and are more likely to hold part-time employment in comparison with nondisabled peers (U.S. Bureau of Labor Statistics, 2015).

When interpreting these data, it is important to note that the Bureau of Labor Statistics uses the Current Population Survey's definition of a *disability*, which is "people who have physical, mental, or emotional conditions that cause serious difficulty with their daily activities" (p. 5). As we discuss in Chapter 2, many students may not view themselves as disabled, and students with some types of disabilities who qualify for reasonable accommodations under the ADA (e.g., learning disabilities) may not meet the Current Population Survey definition of *disability*. It is likely that the number of students with disabilities entering the workforce is higher than these statistics indicate.

Students with disabilities may have unique circumstances that influence their approach to career development. For example, students with behavioral-based functional limitations may benefit from additional support preparing for interviews, which often have rigid expectations of proper etiquette. Students with disabilities have also reported that stress associated with schoolwork, health problems—including waiting until they had received further information about medical conditions or had received specific treatments (e.g., organ transplant)—and the need to find an internship or employment located on a bus route, led them to an intentional delay in career development (Aune & Kroeger, 1997). Students with lower GPAs might have limited internship opportunities and require additional support during the application process (Getzel, 2008).

Students with disabilities expressed several concerns regarding how disability could affect their transition to employment (Hennessey, Roessler, Cook, Unger, & Rumrill, 2006). Students were worried about (a) being treated fairly when they apply for jobs; (b) understanding the risks and benefits of disclosing their disability status to their employer; (c) presenting themselves positively in job interviews; (d) knowing how to identify and discuss employment accommodations with their employer; and (e) knowing how to conduct informational interviews, write résumés, and access career services. Students with disabilities experience stigma in securing employment that has "very little to do with their training since they are in fact college graduates" (p. 127) and instead is the result of stereotypes (e.g., high cost of accommodations, productivity) on the part of potential employers (Roessler, Hennessey, Hogan, & Savickas, 2009).

Helm (2012) interviewed students with psychiatric disabilities who were about to graduate about their employment-seeking plans. She found that most still did not have clear career goals and had not had meaningful interactions with the staff of their campus career services offices. Furthermore, the seniors knew little to nothing about how the ADA would apply to their future employment. All participants were concerned about potential employers' stigmatization of psychiatric disabilities; consequently, most were not planning to disclose their disability in the hiring process. Helm suggested that career development offices do targeted outreach to students with psychiatric disabilities and provide education about their rights under the ADA.

Students with disabilities have less career exposure when compared with their nondisabled college-educated peers (Getzel, 2008). Getzel (2008) found that "prior to entering college, students with disabilities typically have limited career development activities and little or no meaningful work experience, which results in difficulties when deciding on a career" (p. 212). For many students with disabilities, career exploration, including volunteering, begins during college. J. W. Madaus (2006) found that early exposure to work environments through internships, on-campus employment, and research opportunities are critical because they allow "students the opportunity to assess the impact [of disability] in varying environments, to judge the need for accommodations, to validate areas of interest and strengths" (p. 87). Korbel et al. (2011) and McConnell et al. (2013) expanded on this point, recommending that students experience internships in order to match their skills with potential career paths and to network with potential employers and recommenders. Hence, proactive and specialized career development is imperative for students with disabilities. A good example of this is the state of California's WorkAbility IV grant program, which provides college students with disabilities at multiple California State University campuses with career planning, employment preparation, assistance with work site transition, and federal employment advising.

Mentorship is another important component of the career process; S. Burgstahler (2001) indicated that mentorship increased necessary career skills, as well as knowledge of accommodations and legal rights, while Noonan et al. (2004) found that mentorship was also a valuable social support. Furthermore, alumni with disabilities who were currently employed stated that postsecondary education was important to their career success (Lindstrom, Doren, & Miesch, 2011), and students identified mentoring relationships with faculty, staff, or within their social circle as critical (Barber, 2012). Unfortunately, there is limited research on evidenced-based mentoring practices; in their review of the literature, S. Brown, Takahashi, and Roberts (2010) found only four peer-reviewed studies that addressed career mentorship for students with disabilities.

Postsecondary institutional administrators often assume that general career service practitioners have adequate knowledge to assist students with disabilities in the job search process (McConnell et al., 2013). Unfortunately, generic job search strategies do not take into consideration functional limitations or proactively address discriminatory hiring practices—for example, stereotypes or assumptions about what types of work individuals with disabilities can perform (Lindsay, 2010). Practitioners cannot simply apply traditional career development theories to students with disabilities; rather, practitioners must understand how the presence of a disability may alter underlying assumptions or compromise theoretical application (Enright, Conyers, & Szymanski, 1996).

Career services practitioners should avoid making assumptions about what students with disabilities can or cannot do, address attitudinal barriers about disability by educating employers, gain knowledge about disability by working with individuals in the community who are disabled (Aune & Kroeger, 1997), identify internships that are on bus routes, create mentoring programs for students with disabilities, make sure that career services marketing material is accessible, and reach out to students with disabilities through collaboration with the DRO. In order for career services to be able to support students with disabilities, professionals need to receive training on accessibility and accommodation in the workplace and employment barriers that people with disabilities face. At the departmental level, career services professionals should assess the accessibility of their advertisements and measures taken to recruit students with disabilities. It is also imperative that the department be in an accessible building with adaptive equipment (Enright et al., 1996).

DRO and career center staff need to collaborate and develop a comprehensive, disability-specific approach to career transition (Getzel, 2008). National surveys indicate that only between 26% (Raue & Lewis, 2011) and 32% (K. Brown, in press) of postsecondary institutions offer career services or placement strategies that are targeted for students with disabilities. A comprehensive, disability-specific approach to career advising includes educating students about the process for determining accommodation support in the workplace, demonstrating how to network, addressing the effects of disability on the application process, and how to respond to illegal questions (Roessler et al., 2009). A postgraduation survey of alumni with disabilities found that institutions could improve the career transition by providing internships, mentoring programs, specific courses related to disability and the transition to employment, providing more information about the ADA and rights of workers with disabilities, follow-up with graduates through support or transition groups, and postgraduation access to career services (J. W. Madaus, 2006). Hennessey et al. (2006) suggested several career-related interventions, including

> credit-bearing coursework, written materials on employment laws and policies, self-advocacy training, group and individual career counseling, community-based internship programs, mentoring from student and business leaders, job-seeking skills training, and interview skills training. Referrals to existing community resources such as the state Vocational Rehabilitation program are also key components of career services for students with disabilities. (p. 50)

Barber (2012) found that only 20% of graduated students with disabilities reported using career services; the practices recommended here may help students with disabilities find career services to be a more valuable resource.

Graduate School Preparation

There is a paucity of evidence-based research on the transition to graduate or professional school for students with disabilities. The limited exceptions to this trend indicate that students struggle with the independence required to conduct graduate research (Lovitts, 2008) and students with disabilities may struggle because they do not know what to expect in the new environment (Adelman & Wren, 1990). Students with learning disabilities may be particularly affected as graduate education requires use of skills in writing and reading that may be affected by functional limitations and, in general, there are fewer support services or accommodations available at the graduate level (Booren & Hood, 2007).

Similar to faculty and staff with disabilities, data regarding national trends on graduate students with disabilities are limited. According to the National Postsecondary Aid Study, "about 8% of master's students and 7% of doctoral students in the 2007–2008 academic year had some type of disability" (N. E. Bell, 2011, para. 3). Science, technology, engineering, and mathematics (STEM) fields had even fewer students with disabilities, with only 4% of master's students and 1.5% of doctoral graduates identifying as disabled (National Science Foundation, 2015).

Students with disabilities wishing to take part in graduate or professional education face several challenges. Many graduate and most professional schools require standardized testing as an aspect of admissions. It is imperative that students be familiar with the process for requesting accommodations on standardized exams (e.g., GRE, LSAT, MCAT) because each agency has unique requirements and time lines (Korbel et al., 2011). In addition, testing agencies often have more stringent documentation requirements than the student's postsecondary institution, and many students who received undergraduate testing accommodations may not qualify. DRO staff and academic advisers should stay up-to-date on testing accommodation requirements, especially in light of the U.S. Department of Justice (2014d) consent decree that "requires comprehensive reforms to [Law School Admission Council]'s policies and ends its 'flagging' or annotating, LSAT score reports for test takers with disabilities who receive extended time as an accommodation" (para. 1). Although the 2014 consent decree eliminates discriminatory practices that single out students who use testing accommodations, the effect of this legal action on stringent documentation requirements remains unknown at this time.

Students with disabilities face difficulty and discrimination in the hiring process, even after obtaining a graduate degree. For example, a national survey of physical therapy graduate programs found only 29.4% of program faculty thought that students with physical disabilities (e.g., hearing loss) who completed their program would have the same job opportunities as nondisabled students (Hinman, Peterson, & Gibbs, 2015). Therefore, career transition programs are also imperative for graduate students with disabilities.

Conclusion

In general, there is a dearth of research on postsecondary transitions for students with disabilities, and very few studies focus on supporting students who study abroad, continue on to graduate school, or enter the workforce. Given the disadvantages students with disabilities face, particularly when exiting postsecondary education, from a social justice perspective, institutions should engage in a review of current services in order to create a collaborative, systemwide approach to transition planning that works to address stigma and inequality in the broader society. This collaborative approach and reduction of institutional silos is important for supporting diverse populations of students with disabilities with the multiple transitions they will experience during the course of postsecondary education.

Discussion Questions

1. What transitional supports are available for students with disabilities on your campus? What transitional supports discussed in this chapter that are not already available to your students could be of benefit to them?
2. In what ways can the principles of universal design be incorporated into transitional periods to benefit all students on campus?
3. Are there additional experiences that are unique to your campus that may present additional transitional issues for students with disabilities?
4. What offices would need to collaborate in order to enhance existing transition services or implement new services for students with disabilities entering your institution? Exiting the institution?

CONCLUSION: A SOCIAL JUSTICE APPROACH TO DISABILITY IN HIGHER EDUCATION: STRATEGIES FOR INCLUSION

All bodies are unique and essential. All bodies are whole. All bodies have strengths and needs that must be met. We are powerful not despite the complexities of our bodies, but because of them. We move together, with no body left behind. This is disability justice.
—Patty Berne (cited in Lamm, 2015)

Historically, higher education has defined itself by whom it excludes rather than by whom it includes (Carlson, 2016); prestigious institutions are those having the lowest admissions rates, for example. A social justice approach inverts this perspective. We argue that higher education institutions are at their best when they invite, welcome, and adapt to the broadest possible range of individuals who can contribute to and meet the standards of education institutions, recognizing the discriminatory history of determining for minoritized others their (in)ability to contribute and benefit.

As we examine the research we and others have conducted and the vast stacks of books and articles we have reviewed in writing this book, it is clear that colleges and universities are not yet the inclusive, accessible, engaging places for people with disabilities that a social justice approach calls for. We believe there is a need for a specific articulation of what a social justice approach to disability in higher education entails. Informed by our readings and research, and in particular by previous writings about social justice approaches to disability (Griffin, Peters, & Smith, 2007), critical disability theory, and the disability justice movement, we argue that in the context of higher education, a social justice approach to disability must include the following elements:

- A focus on the ways power and privilege shape the lives of disabled and nondisabled people in higher education
- An explicit recognition of the dangers of presuming that typical ways of doing, being, learning, teaching, thinking, feeling, moving, and communicating are preferable and encouragement of a diversity of approaches that support the success of all individuals
- Attention to and acceptance of the diversity of experience within disability communities, in terms of intersecting social identities and the multiple ways in which particular forms of disability are experienced, both between people and over the course of a given individual's experience of impairment
- Acceptance that all people are interdependent and rejection of independence as a desired outcome
- Attention to the impacts of people's physical bodies and minds on the experience of disability, in addition to and in interaction with the environment (e.g., social, cultural, and economic)
- Recognition that a social justice approach to disability in higher education must attend to the influence of disability and ableism not just on students but also on staff and faculty
- Advocacy for inclusion and equity in access to and within all higher education settings

A social justice approach to disability directly challenges the ableism prevalent in society, which manifests on higher education campuses as well. K. Brown and Broido (2015) called on higher education professionals to "identify and address ways in which ableism shapes the experiences of members of our campus communities" (p. 187). While there are multiple definitions of *ableism*, we concur with F. K. Campbell (2009), who wrote "that a chief feature of an ableist viewpoint is a belief that impairment or disability (irrespective of 'type') is inherently negative and should the opportunity present itself, [should] be ameliorated, cured, or indeed eliminated" (p. 5). Although we recognize that impairment in many cases can be painful and limiting (Shakespeare, 2014), we also recognize it as an inherent part of human diversity and believe that impairment can be a point of identity, community, and meaning. We share Hehir's (2002) assertion about K-12 schooling—"progress toward equity is dependent first and foremost on the acknowledgement that ableism exists in schools" (p. 22)—and believe the statement is equally applicable in higher education.

Strategies for Creating More Socially Just Campuses

Understandings of disability in higher education and in the larger society are evolving rapidly. Over the five years we have been writing this book, we have seen significant expansion of the range and complexity of thinking, practice, and research about disability. Yet we still see much room for continued development. A social justice approach to disability in higher education offers multiple implications for practice, research, and policy development. While in the preceding chapters we have addressed population- or topic-specific implications, here we present 10 implications that have broad applicability across higher education contexts. Each of these implications integrates multiple aspects of the framework for a social justice approach to disability in higher education presented earlier in this chapter.

Challenge Assumptions About Normality

Colleges and universities still function under the assumption that there are singular right or best ways to learn, teach, communicate, move, and work (Evans, Forney, Guido, Patton, & Renn, 2010), thereby "privilege[ing] those who carry out these functions as prescribed and oppress[ing] those who use other methods" (p. 242). If we, as Hehir (2002) suggested, "encourage disabled students to develop and use skills and modes of expression that are most effective and efficient for them" (p. 22), we inherently question the assumption that what is normal or typical is innately better or more desirable.

While standardization might in some cases seem to be more economically efficient than allowing for a range of ways to do things, it has significant costs in the ways it limits the ability of all people to perform at their best. Not just allowing for but expecting and encouraging all people to do things in ways most effective for them will create more inclusive, just campus environments. Universities in many ways espouse a value for the exceptional and the unusual, especially in creative activity and scholarship; expanding the range of settings in which different approaches are valued will both enhance social justice on campus and promote the exceptionalism that makes universities distinctive.

Conduct More, Better, and Broader Research

As noted throughout this book, research on disability in higher education is, as a whole, limited, dated, and compromised by paradigmatic and procedural limitations (Stapleton et al., 2014; E. V. Peña, 2014; Vaccaro, Daly-Cano, & Newman, 2015). In 1992, Oliver argued that existing research did not "accord with disabled people's own explanations of the problems of disability" (p. 108). Much of disability research still is based on medical or rehabilitation models, giving little attention to environmental considerations or the perspectives of disabled participants (K. Brown, Broido, Stapleton, Evans, & Peña, 2016). Critical scholarship in higher education rarely addresses disability; for example, the recent and otherwise excellent *Critical Approaches to the Study of Higher Education: A Practical Introduction* (Martinez-Alemán, Pusser, & Bensimon, 2015) has no discussion of disability.

In addition to paradigmatic and methodological limitations, much of the research on disability in higher education is narrowly focused. Much of it is atheoretical or presumes that all participants with the same disability label have the same experiences. Researchers tend to focus on a limited range of outcomes, paying little attention to the lived experiences of people with disabilities. Many of the topics discussed in this book are underresearched, including how students experience transitions into and out of higher education, how people who have additional minoritized identities experience disability, and the experiences of faculty and staff with disabilities. Research on these and many other topics would allow policy and practice to be informed by data rather than by best guesses or anecdote.

Foreground the Experiences of People With Disabilities

Research on disability in higher education should highlight the experiences of university members with disabilities, as should policy and practice decisions. Shakespeare (2006b) wrote, "So central is the concept of 'nothing about us, without us' that Charlton (1998) use[d] it as the title of his study of the worldwide disability movement" (p. 185). Colleges and universities perpetuate beliefs common in the larger society that disabled people lack the knowledge or objectivity to determine for themselves what they need, what are the most appropriate or effective accommodations, and how best to build inclusive communities. While we believe there are important roles for nondisabled people to play in these decisions, none should be made without serious consideration of the input of people with a wide range of impairments and functional limitations, to best address the diverse experiences of the disability community.

Recognize the Multifaceted Nature of Disability

It is important to recognize that disability is simultaneously political, social, economic, psychological, and biological. In addition, disability is experienced by people of particular genders, races and ethnicities, sexual orientations, religions, economic statuses, and other salient experiences and identities. Recognizing the complexity of all members of higher education communities, including those with disabilities, will lead to movement toward more socially just campuses. While doing so, it is important to avoid a "double-deficit" approach, presuming that disabled and otherwise minoritized individuals are defined by their limitations rather than by their talents. Looking for assets and strengths arising from people's experiences, without romanticizing or heroicizing disabled people, is an appropriate approach.

Recognition that people with disabilities are simultaneously people with other social identities means that curricula and programming serving other populations are always also in service of people with disabilities so long as those programs are accessible. Collaboration with and support across other identity- and experienced-based campus organizations and service offices (e.g., the Multicultural Resource Center, the Women's Center, the Veterans Center) will help develop a more socially just campus.

Support Disabled People Who May Not Need or Request Accommodations

Disability in the context of higher education is addressed most often as a technical problem (Michalko, 2002)—as something needing to be accommodated so that disabled students, staff, and faculty can be productive in the same ways as their nondisabled peers. This perspective is limited in at least four distinct ways. First, it removes from awareness those who are disabled but do not need academic or workplace accommodations. Second, this approach ignores the ways in which the experience of disability is shaped by other aspects of identity and experience. Third, it presumes that existing normative ways of being productive in higher education are the most desirable way to function. Finally, it disregards the social, political, and cultural aspects of disability. A social justice perspective calls for recognition of the multiple ways disabled people contribute to their campuses and how their experiences are shaped by the environment and their impairments, whether or not they identify themselves to their institutions as disabled. All disabled members of university communities have the right to participate in and benefit from disability community and advocacy.

Center Universal Design

> Universal design is a matter of simple justice.
>
> *—Hehir (2002, p. 29).*

Rather than reacting to the accommodation requirements of individual students, a truly inclusive environment prepares for and welcomes a diverse student population. As campuses begin to ensure that all instruction and services are accessible to the broadest range of ways of taking in, processing, and communicating knowledge, the need for individual accommodations will diminish and learning can become, as described in Chapter 10, "universal." This approach creates campuses in which "environments and activities are designed in such a way that they are accessible to anyone, regardless of the person's functional limitations" (Aune, 2000, p. 57), providing "access to all people in advance rather than after the fact" (Kalivoda & Totty, 2003, p. 217).

Although universal design is typically thought of as a classroom strategy, it also applies to student development programs and services (e.g., S. Burgstahler & Moore, 2009; Higbee, 2009), institutional and departmental websites (e.g., Harper & DeWaters, 2008), residence halls (e.g., Wisbey & Kalivoda, 2008), and administrative planning (e.g., Arendale & Poch, 2008). Higbee (2003) outlined nine universal design principles of student development programs and services: create welcoming spaces; develop, implement, and evaluate pathways for communication; promote interaction among students and between staff and students; ensure equal opportunities for learning and growth; communicate clear expectations; use methods that consider diverse learning styles; provide natural supports for learning; ensure confidentiality; and define service quality. Although many of these universal design principles sound very similar to other guidelines for good practice, applying them focuses on inclusion as the unifying goal and makes them unique (Higbee, 2003).

Treat Disability as a Campuswide Responsibility

Inclusive campuses are everyone's responsibility: the president's, the parking officers', the orientation leaders', the maintenance staff's, the faculty's, the finance and budget officer's, the disability resource staff's, the residence hall directors'. Disability resource office (DRO) staff can provide direction and leadership for institutions as they commit to a culture shift to facilitate the full participation of all students, including those with disabilities. However, a social justice commitment leads to the recognition that universally designed and inclusive campuses require the engagement of all members of the community. Like other forms of campus culture, such an approach works best when it is supported from both the bottom up and the top down.

It is important to understand how the politics and organizational structures of higher education affect service to students with disabilities. Although DROs are as different as the institutions and students they serve (Harbour, 2009), institutional commitment to disability is a critical component of a diverse campus. As highlighted in Chapter 13, it is critical that directors of DROs embrace a social justice perspective. They must have skills not just of assessing the needs of and supporting disabled students, but also of advocating for the structural, cultural, financial, and policy changes required to create inclusive campuses that value and support multiple ways of contributing to the success of campuses and their constituents.

J. T. Brown (1994) outlined three key considerations when assessing institutional commitment to disability. First, J. T. Brown noted the importance of upper-level leadership in creating a welcoming environment. "As with the commitment to diversity in general, an institutional commitment to serving students with disabilities must emanate from the highest levels of the administrative hierarchy" (J. T. Brown, 1994, p. 99). Second, J. T. Brown (1994) pointed out the significance of community orientation and campus collaboration; he stated, "The commitment to diversity extends beyond a single office devoted to meeting the needs of a specific minority group on campus" (p. 103). J. T. Brown (1994) also highlighted the effect of policy and organizational structures in creating supportive environments, stating: "Attitudes toward individuals with disabilities can be influenced by policies, procedures, and initiatives supported by both academic and student affairs divisions" (p. 99). J. T. Brown suggested that one method to address institutional commitment to students with disabilities was to create a campuswide committee composed of staff, faculty, and students to address disability issues such as access and removal of barriers.

The campuswide responsibility for disability extends beyond awareness and acceptance of people with disabilities as part of the campus community. It means that advocating for inclusive, affirmative practices and policies is also everyone's responsibility. While disabled members should be affirmed and supported in advocating for inclusive communities (and, as noted in Chapter 15, may need assistance in developing the skills and confidence to do so, given that disabled young people rarely are taught self-advocacy), advocacy needs to happen at both the unit level and the senior leadership level.

Consider Additional Perspectives on Disability

Practitioners who work to create more inclusive, just campuses are informed by many sources: direct experience, conferences and workshops, electronic mailing lists, and practitioner-oriented journals and newsletters, among others. We strongly encourage practitioners also to pay attention to the ideas arising in other arenas, particularly those of the disability justice movement and the academic field of disability studies.

As we make this recommendation, we remain conscious of the critique raised by Nomy Lamm (2015):

> A lot of white disabled people are using the term [*disability justice*] without knowing exactly what it means. In fact, they are often using it to advance their careers as academics and consultants, instead of listening to and amplifying the voices of people of color in the movement. (para. 7)

We know that a book such as this one, focused on access to some of the most privileged institutions in society, can never fully claim to be part of the disability justice movement. Simultaneously, we recognize the parallels between a social justice and a disability justice approach and are indebted to the writings of disability justice activists that have shaped our thinking in writing this book. We believe that college and university members who seek to create socially just campuses have much to learn from the arguments and methods of disability justice activists.

Similarly, we advocate that practitioners attend to the arguments and critiques made by academics working in disability studies. Disability studies theorists study

> the social meanings, symbols, and stigmas attached to disability identity and [ask] how they relate to enforced systems of exclusion and oppression, attaching the widespread belief that having an able body and mind determines whether one is a quality human being. (Siebers, 2015, p. 224)

While at times quite abstract, many of the ideas that disability studies theorists raise have applicability to higher education practice as well as to disability advocacy.

Foster Disability Culture

Because of the combination of multiple factors, few campuses have formal or informal mechanisms that bring people with disabilities together for cultural and political support. These factors include federal privacy laws such as the Health Insurance Portability and Accountability Act and the Family Educational Rights and Privacy Act, which make it challenging to proactively identify students with disabilities. Understaffing, limited budgets, and a narrow focus on academic accommodations within DROs preclude many of these offices from taking on this role. Because disabled students, staff, and faculty are not treated as a minoritized group (as are Latinx or women students, staff, and faculty) on many campuses means they do not have designated cultural space, programming, or staff support. Finally, many college- and university-associated individuals with disabilities are reluctant to identify as part of a stigmatized group. These factors converge to make it difficult for disabled university students, faculty, and staff to identify each other; recognize their shared experiences; and understand how they could benefit from collective support and activism.

But there are campuses where disabled students and their allies have created communities that provide peer education, support, and advocacy, in some cases supported by physical space and staff members (Broido & Stygles, 2016). An incomplete list of such institutions includes the University of California Berkeley, Syracuse University, and the University of Illinois at Urbana-Champaign, and, particularly for D/deaf and hard-of-hearing students, Gallaudet University, California State University at Northridge, and the Rochester Institute of Technology. We encourage more campuses to expand their disability resources to support a cultural approach to disabled students rather than a restricted focus on accessibility.

Consider Disability in Campus Internationalization Efforts

While in this book we have kept a close focus on U.S. higher education, we recognize that countries around the world have disabled students, staff, and faculty in their higher education institutions. We are aware that our focus, while necessary to keep this book to a reasonable length, has excluded important information about disability in higher education worldwide. Indeed, "when 80 percent of disabled people live in developing countries, many in poverty, it seems essential to reframe what has largely been a Western understanding of what it means to be disabled" (Yelling Clinic, n.d., para. 1).

International students and faculty who come to the United States with preexisting disabilities or who acquire them while here may bring with them meaningfully different understandings of and responses to impairment and disability (Awoniyi, 2014). Simultaneously, we should encourage students with disabilities to study abroad, working to ensure that all sites are accessible, as discussed in more detail in Chapter 15.

Conclusion

We call readers' attention to the epigraph at the start of this chapter. If higher education administrators, staff, and faculty are to enact social justice on their campuses, they can do so only if they understand that all members of their community are unique and essential. They must recognize that the interaction of people's individual talents, strengths, and complexities strengthens their ability to foster the expansion, integration, and application of knowledge in service of the larger society. Disabled people are integral to this effort, as are all members of every community.

REFERENCES

Abberley, P. (1987). The concept of oppression and the development of a social theory of disability. *Disability, Handicap & Society, 2*(1), 5–19.

Abdul-Alim, J. (2012, November 16). *Outstanding professors honored at Thursday ceremony in Washington.* Retrieved from http://diverseeducation.com/article/49540

Abes, E. S., Jones, S. R., & McEwen, M. K. (2007). Reconceptualizing the Model of Multiple Dimensions of Identity: The role of meaning-making capacity in the construction of multiple identities. *Journal of College Student Development, 48*(1), 1–22.

Abram, S. (2003). Americans with Disabilities Act in higher education: The plight of disabled faculty. *Journal of Law & Education, 32*, 1–20.

ACCESS Project. (2010). *Disability information for faculty.* Colorado State University. Retrieved from http://accessproject.colostate.edu/disability/

Ackerman, R., & DiRamio, D. (2009). Editor's notes. In R. Ackerman & D. DiRamio (Eds.), *Creating a veteran-friendly campus: Strategies for transition success* (New Directions for Student Services, no. 126, pp. 1–3). San Francisco, CA: Jossey-Bass.

Ackerman, R., DiRamio, D., & Garza Mitchell, R. L. (2009). New directions for transitions: Combat veterans as college students. In R. Ackerman & D. DiRamio (Eds.), *Creating a veteran-friendly campus: Strategies for transition success* (New Directions for Student Services, no. 126, pp. 5–14). San Francisco, CA: Jossey-Bass.

Adams, K. S., & Proctor, B. E. (2010). Adaptation to college for students with and without disabilities: Group differences and predictors. *Journal of Postsecondary Education and Disability, 22*(3), 166–184.

Adams, M., Bell, L. A., & Griffin, P. (2007). Preface. In M. Adams, L. A. Bell, & P. Griffin (Eds.), *Teaching for diversity and social justice* (pp. xv–xvii). New York, NY: Routledge.

Adams, R. (2011, November 6). Bring down the barriers—Seen and unseen. *Chronicle of Higher Education.* Retrieved from http://chronicle.com/article/Bring-Down-the-Barriers-Seen/129648/?sid=at&utm_source=

Adelman, P. B., & Wren, C. T. (1990). *Learning disabilities, graduate school, and careers: The student's perspective.* Unpublished manuscript, Barat College, Lake Forest, IL.

Adreon, D., & Durocher, J. S. (2007). Evaluating the college transition needs of individuals with high-functioning autism spectrum disorders. *Intervention in School and Clinic, 42*(5), 271–279.

Advisory Commission on Accessible Instructional Materials in Postsecondary Education for Students with Disabilities. (2011). *Report of the Advisory Commission on Accessible Instructional Materials in Postsecondary Education for Students with Disabilities.* Retrieved from http://www2.ed.gov/about/bdscomm/list/aim/meeting/aim-report.pdf

Affirmative Action and Nondiscrimination Obligations of Contractors and Subcontractors Regarding Individuals with Disabilities, 41 C.F.R. § 60–741 (2015). Retrieved from https://www.law.cornell.edu/cfr/text/41/part-60–741

Albrecht, G. L., Seelman, K. D., & Bury, M. (Eds.). (2001a). *Handbook of disability studies.* Thousand Oaks, CA: Sage.

Albrecht, G. L., Seelman, K. D., & Bury, M. (2001b). Introduction: The formation of disability studies. In G. L. Albrecht, K. D. Seelman, & M. Bury (Eds.), *Handbook of disability studies* (pp. 1–8). Thousand Oaks, CA: Sage.

Altman, B. M. (2001). Disability definitions, models, classification schemes, and applications. In G. L. Albrecht, K. D. Seelman, & M. Bury (Eds.), *Handbook of disability studies* (pp. 97–122). Thousand Oaks, CA: Sage.

American Association for the Advancement of Science. (n.d.a). *Project on science, technology and disability.* Retrieved from http://www.aaas.org/page/finding-aid-aaas-project-science-technology-and-disability#Scope and Contents

American Association for the Advancement of Science. (n.d.b). *Entry point!* Retrieved from http://www.aaas.org/program/entrypoint

American Association of University Professors. (2012, January). *Accommodating faculty members who have disabilities.* Retrieved from http://www.aaup.org/report/accommodating-faculty-members-who-have-disabilities

American Association of University Professors. (n.d.). *About the AAUP.* Retrieved from http://www.aaup.org/about-aaup

American Chemical Society-Chemists with Disabilities. (n.d.). *Chemists with disabilities.* Retrieved from http://www.acs.org/content/acs/en/about/governance/committees/cwd.html

American College Health Association. (2014). *National College Health Assessment Spring 2014 reference group data report.* Retrieved from http://www.acha-ncha.org/docs/ACHA-NCHA-II_Reference Group_DataReport_Spring2014.pdf

American Council of the Blind. (n.d.). *Mission.* Retrieved from http://www.acb.org/

American Council on Education. (2008). *Serving those who serve: Higher education and America's veterans.* Retrieved from http://www.acenet.edu/Content/NavigationMenu/ProgramsServices/MilitaryPrograms/serving/index.htm

American Immigration Council. (2014). *Two years and counting: Assessing the growing power of DACA.* Retrieved from http://www.immigrationpolicy.org/special-reports/two-years-and-counting-assessing-growing-power-daca

American Psychiatric Association. (1994). *Diagnostic and statistical manual of mental disorders* (4th ed.). Washington, DC: Author.

American Psychiatric Association. (2000). *Diagnostic and statistical manual of mental disorders* (4th ed., text rev.). doi:10.1176/appi.books. 9780890423349

American Psychiatric Association. (2013). *Diagnostic and statistical manual of mental disorders* (5th ed.). doi:10.1176/appi.books. 9780890425596.514988

Americans With Disabilities Act. (2010a). *Equal opportunities for individuals with disabilities,* 28 C.F.R § 12112. Retrieved from https://www.ada.gov/pubs/adastatute08.htm#12112

Americans With Disabilities Act. (2010b). *Nondiscrimination on the basis of disability in state and local government services.* 28 C.F.R § 35.151. Retrieved from https://www.ada.gov/regs2010/titleII_2010/titleII_2010_regulations.htm

Americans With Disabilities Act. (2010c). *Removal of barriers.* 28 C.F.R § 36.304. Retrieved from https://www.ada.gov/reachingout/t3regl4.html

Americans With Disabilities Act Amendments Act of 2008. (2008). Public Law 110–325, 122 Stat. 3553.

Americans With Disabilities Act of 1990. (1991). Pub. L. No. 101–336, § 2, 104 Stat. 328.

Anastasiou, D., & Kauffman, J. M. (2011). A social constructionist approach to disability: Implications for special education. *Exceptional Children, 77*(3), 367–384.

Anderson, R. C. (2006). Teaching (with) disability: Pedagogies of lived experience. *Review of Education, Pedagogy, and Cultural Studies, 28*(3–4), 367–379.

Anderson, R. C. (2007). Faculty members with disabilities in higher education. In M. L. Vance (Ed.), *Disabled faculty and staff in a disabling society: Multiple identities in higher education* (pp. 183–200). Huntersville, NC: Association on Higher Education and Disability.

Ankeny, E. M., & Lehmann, J. P. (2010). The transition lynchpin: The voices of individuals with disabilities who attended a community college transition program. *Community College Journal of Research and Practice, 34*(6), 477–496.

Annamma, S. A., Connor, D., & Ferri, B. (2013). Dis/ability critical race studies (DisCrit): Theorizing at the intersections of race and dis/ability. *Race, Ethnicity, and Education, 16*(1), 1–31.

Antonetta, S. (2007). *A mind apart: Travels in a neurodiverse world.* New York, NY: Penguin.

Architectural Barriers Act. (1968). Pub. L. 94–541, 42 U.S.C. 4151.

Arendale, D., & Poch, R. (2008). Using universal design for administrative leadership, planning, and evaluation. In J. L. Higbee & E. Goff (Eds.), *Pedagogy and student services for institutional transformation: Implementing universal design in higher education* (pp. 419–436). Minneapolis: Center for Research on Developmental Education and Urban Literacy, College of Education and Human Development, University of Minnesota. Retrieved from http://cehd.umn.edu/passit/docs/PASS-IT-Books.pdf

Armstrong, W. B., Lewis, M., Turingan, M., & Neault, L. C. (1997). *Americans with Disabilities Act (ADA): City College self-evaluation study.* San Diego, CA: San Diego Community College District. (ERIC Document Reproduction Service No. ED413972).

Arries, J. F. (1999). Learning disabilities and foreign languages: A curriculum approach to the design of inclusive courses. *Modern Language Journal, 83*(1), 98–110.

Artiles, A., & Ortiz, A. A. (2002). English language learners with special education needs: Contexts and possibilities. In A. J. Artiles & A. A. Ortiz (Eds.), *English language learners with special education needs: Identification, assessment, and instruction* (pp. 3–28). Crystal Lake, IL: Center for Applied Linguistics and Delta Systems.

Ashmore, J., & Kasnitz, D. (2014). Models of disability in higher education. In M. L. Vance, N. E. Lipsitz, & K. Parks (Eds.), *Beyond the Americans with Disabilities Act: Inclusive policy and practice for higher education* (pp. 21–34). Washington, DC: NASPA-Student Affairs Administrators in Higher Education.

Associated Press. (2011, February 15). Virginia University named in lawsuit alleging poor access for disabled. *Diverse Education.* Retrieved from http://diverseeducation.com/cache/print.php?articleID=14766

Association on Higher Education and Disability (AHEAD). (1996). *Code of ethics.* Retrieved from http://www.ahead.org/learn/resources

Association on Higher Education and Disability (AHEAD). (2012a). *AHEAD professional standards.* Retrieved from https://www.ahead.org/uploads/docs/resources/AHEAD_Professional_Standards.doc

Association on Higher Education and Disability (AHEAD). (2012b, April). *Supporting accommodation requests: Guidance on documentation practices.* Retrieved from http://www.ahead.org/resources/documentation-guidance

Association on Higher Education and Disability (AHEAD). (2014a). *About AHEAD.* Retrieved from http://www.ahead.org/about

Association on Higher Education and Disability (AHEAD). (2014b). *Professional standards.* Retrieved from http://www.ahead.org/learn/resources

Association on Higher Education and Disability (AHEAD). (2014c). *Program evaluation tools.* Retrieved from https://www.ahead.org/program_eval_tools

Association on Higher Education and Disability (AHEAD). (2014d). *Program standards.* Retrieved from http://www.ahead.org/learn/resources

Astin, A. W. (2002). *Assessment for excellence: The philosophy and practice of assessment and evaluation in higher education.* Westport, CT: Oryx Press.

Aune, B. (2000). Career and academic advising. In H. Belch (Ed.), *Serving students with disabilities* (New Directions in Student Services, no. 91, pp. 55–67). San Francisco, CA: Jossey-Bass.

Aune, B. P., & Kroeger, S. A. (1997). Career development of college students with disabilities: An interactional approach to defining the issues. *Journal of College Student Development, 38*(4), 344–356.

Awoniyi, B. (2014). Engaging international students with disabilities. In M. L. Vance, N. E. Lipsitz, & K. Parks (Eds.), *Beyond the Americans with Disabilities Act: Inclusive policy and practice for higher education* (pp. 171–177). Washington, DC: NASPA-Student Affairs Administrators in Higher Education.

Azevedo, A. (2012, November 7). Campus leaders speak out on value of keeping tech accessible. *Chronicle of Higher Education.* Retrieved from chronicle.com/blogs/wiredcampus/…/40852?cid=pm&utm_source=pm&utm_medium=en

Badger, N. (2009). Determination points the way for others: Congenital vision impairment. In J. L. Higbee & A. A. Mitchell (Eds.), *Making good on the promise: Student affairs professionals with disabilities* (pp. 89–93). Lanham, MD: American College Personnel Association and University Press of America.

Baker, K. Q., Boland, K., & Nowik, C. M. (2012). Survey of faculty and student perceptions of persons with disabilities. *Journal of Postsecondary Education and Disability, 25*(4), 309–329.

Baldridge, D. C., & Swift, M. L. (2013). Withholding requests for disability accommodation: The role of individual differences and disability attributes. *Journal of Management, 39*(3), 743–762.

Ball-Brown, B., & Frank, Z. L. (1993). Disabled students of color. In S. A. Kroeger (Ed.), *Responding to disability issues in student affairs* (New Directions for Student Services, no. 64, pp. 79–88). San Francisco, CA: Jossey-Bass.

Banks, J. (2014). Barriers and supports to postsecondary transition: Case studies of African American students with disabilities. *Remedial and Special Education, 35*(1), 28–39.

Banton, M., & Hirsch, M. M. (2000). *Double invisibility: Report on research into the needs of Black disabled people in Coventry.* Coventry, England: Warwickshire County Council.

Barber, P. (2012, September). College students with disabilities: What factors influence successful degree completion? A case study. *Disability and Work.* Joint publication from the John J. Heldrich Center for Workforce Development and the Kessler Foundation. Retrieved from http://www.heldrich.rutgers.edu/sites/default/files/products/uploads/College_Students_Disabilities_Report.pdf

Baril, A. (2015). Needing to acquire a physical impairment/disability: (Re)thinking the connections between trans and disability studies through transability. *Hypatia, 30*(1), 30–48.

Barnard, L., Stevens, T., Oginga Siwatu, K., & Lan, W. (2008). Diversity beliefs as a mediator to faculty attitudes toward students with disabilities. *Journal of Diversity in Higher Education, 1*(3), 169–175.

Barnard-Brak, L., Lechtenberger, D., & Lan, W. Y. (2010). Accommodation strategies of college students with disabilities. *Qualitative Report, 15*(2), 411–429.

Barnard-Brak, L., Sulak, T., Tate, A., & Lechtenberger, D. (2010). Measuring college students' attitudes toward request accommodations: A national multi-international study. *Assessment for Effective Intervention, 35*(3), 141–147.

Barnartt, S. N., & Scotch, R. K. (2001). *Disability protests: Contentious politics, 1970–1999.* Washington, DC: Gallaudet University Press.

Barnes, C. (1991). *Disabled people in Britain and discrimination.* London, England: Hurst.

Basham, J. D., & Marino, M. T. (2013). Understanding STEM education and supporting students through universal design for learning. *Teaching Exceptional Children, 45*(4), 8–15.

Batavia, A., & Schriner, K. (2001). The Americans With Disabilities Act as an engine of social change models of disability and the potential of a civil rights approach. *Policy Studies Journal, 29*, 690–702.

Baynton, D. C. (2001). Disability and the justification of inequality in American history. In P. K. Longmore & L. Umansky (Eds.), *The new disability history* (pp. 33–57). New York: New York University Press.

Baynton, D. C. (2009). Oralism. In S. Burch (Ed.), *Encyclopedia of American disability history* (vol. 2, pp. 679–681). New York, NY: Facts on File.

Becerra, M. M. (2006). *Making the transition: The educational experiences of students with disabilities who transfer from community college to California State University, Sacramento.* Retrieved from http://scholarworks.calstate.edu/bitstream/handle/10211.9/1259/Maricela.pdf?sequence=1

Beck, M. A. (2013, December 22). *Creighton University must accommodate deaf student.* Retrieved from http://diverseeducation.com/article/59654/

Beck, M. A. (2014, June 8). *Creighton University appeals order favoring deaf student.* Retrieved from http://diverseeducation.com/article/64754/

Bedrossian, L. (2016). Coordinate accommodations for pregnant women with campus Title IX officials. *Disability Compliance for Higher Education, 21*(10), 6.

Beilke, J. R., & Yssel, N. (1999). The chilly climate for students with disabilities in higher education. *College Student Journal, 33*(3), 364–371.

Bernert, D. J., Ding, K., & Hoban, M. T. (2012). Sexual and substance use behaviors of college students with disabilities. *American Journal of Health Behavior, 36*(4), 459–471.

Bettelheim, B. (1967). *The empty fortress: Infantile autism and the birth of the self.* New York, NY: Free Press.

Biemiller, L. (2013, December 23). Deaf medical student must be offered more assistance, judge rules. *Chronicle of Higher Education.* Retrieved from http://chronicle.com/blogs/ticker/jp/deaf-medical-student-must-be-offered-more-assistance-judge-rules

Belch, H. (2011). Understanding the experiences of students with psychiatric disabilities: A foundation for creating conditions of support and success. In M. S. Huger (Ed.), *Fostering the increased integration of students with disabilities* (New Directions for Student Services, no. 134, pp. 73–94). San Francisco, CA: Jossey-Bass.

Belch, H. A. (2004). Retention and students with disabilities. *Journal of College Student Retention, 6,* 3–22.

Bell, L. A. (2013). Theoretical foundations. In M. Adams, W. J. Blumenfeld, C. R. Castañada, H. W. Hackman, M. L. Peters, & X. Zúñiga (Eds.), *Readings for diversity and social justice* (3rd ed., pp. 21–26). New York, NY: Routledge.

Bell, N. E. (2011). *Data sources: Graduate students with disabilities.* Retrieved from http://cgsnet.org/ data-sources-graduate-students-disabilities

Berne, P. (2015, June 10). *Disability justice—A working draft.* Retrieved from http://sinsinvalid.org/ blog/disability-justice-a-working-draft-by-patty-berne

Bertrand, M., & Mullainathan, S. (2004). Are Emily and Greg more employable than Lakisha and Jamal? A field experiment on labor market discrimination. *American Economic Review, 94*(4), 991–1013.

Bhaskar, R. (1998). General introduction. In M. Archer, R. Bhaskar, A. Collier, T. Lawson, & A. Norrie (Eds.), *Critical realism: Essential readings* (pp. ix–xxiv). New York NY: Routledge.

Bhatt v. The University of Vermont, 958 A.2d 637 (Vermont S. Ct. 2008).

Bickenbach, J. E., Chatterji, S., Badley, E. M., & Üstün, T. B. (1999). Models of disablement, universalism and the international classification of impairments, disabilities and handicaps. *Social Science and Medicine, 48,* 1173–1187.

Biklen, D. (2005). *Autism and the myth of the person alone.* New York: New York University.

Blanchett, W. J. (2006). Disproportionate representation of African American students in special education: Acknowledging the role of white privilege and racism. *Educational Researcher, 35*(6), 24–28.

Blanco, C., Okuda, M., Wright, C., Hasin, D. S., Grant, B. F., Liu, S. M., & Olfson, M. (2008). Mental health of college students and their non–college-attending peers: Results from the National Epidemiologic Study on Alcohol and Related Conditions. *Archives of General Psychiatry, 65*(12), 1429–1437. doi:10.1001/archpsyc.65.12.1429

Blanks, A. B., & Smith, J. D. (2009). Multiculturalism, religion, and disability: Implications for special education practitioners. *Education and Training in Developmental Disabilities, 44*(3), 295–303.

Blanks, J., & Hughes, M. S. (2013). Double consciousness: Postsecondary experiences of African American males with disabilities. *Journal of Negro Education, 82*(4), 368–381.

Blinde, E. M., & McClung, L. R. (1997). Enhancing the physical and social self through recreational activity: Accounts of individuals with physical disabilities. *Adapted Physical Activity Quarterly, 14,* 327–344.

Blinde, E. M., & Taub, D. E. (1999). Personal empowerment through sport and physical fitness activity: Perspectives from male college students with physical and sensory disabilities. *Journal of Sport Behavior, 22*(2), 181–202.

Booren, L. M., & Hood, B. K. (2007). Learning disabilities in graduate school: Closeted or out in the open? *Observer, 20*(3). Retrieved from http://www.psychologicalscience.org/index.php/ publications/observer/2007/march-07/learning-disabilities-in-graduate-school-closeted-or-out-in-the-open.html

Brake, D. (1994). Legal challenges to the educational barriers facing pregnant and parenting adolescents. *Clearinghouse Review, 28,* 141.

Brault, M. W. (2012). *Americans with disabilities: 2010* (pp. P70–P131). Washington, DC: U.S. Department of Commerce, Economics and Statistics Administration, and U.S. Census Bureau. Retrieved from http://www.census.gov/prod/2012pubs/p70-131.pdf

Bremer, C. D. (2003–2004). Universal design in secondary and postsecondary education. *Impact, 16*(3). Minneapolis: Institute on Community Integration and the Research and Training

Center on Community Living, College of Education and Human Development, University of Minnesota. Retrieved from http:/ici.umn.edu/products/impact/163/over3.html

Brewer, Horton, & Participants of the Education and Outreach Working Group. (2002). *Web accessibility initiative*. Retrieved from https://www.w3.org/WAI

Bricher, G. (2000). Disabled people, health professionals and the social model of disability: Can there be a research relationship? *Disability & Society, 15*(5), 781–793.

Brockelman, K. F. (2009). The interrelationship of self-determination, mental illness, and grades among university students. *Journal of College Student Development, 50*(3), 271–286.

Broido, E. M. (2006). *Diabetes as case study: Experiences of students with disabilities.* Paper presented at the American College Personnel Association conference, Indianapolis, IN.

Broido, E. M., & Stygles, K. S. (2016). *Developmental outcomes of students' disability leadership and activism.* Paper presented at the ACPA: College Student Educators International Conference, Montreal, Canada.

Bronfenbrenner, U. (1979). *The ecology of human development: Experiments by nature and design.* Cambridge, MA: Harvard University Press.

Bronfenbrenner, U. (1993). The ecology of cognitive development: Research models and fugitive findings. In R. H. Wozniak & K. W. Fischer (Eds.), *Development in context: Acting and thinking in specific environments* (pp. 3–44). Hillsdale, NJ: Erlbaum.

Bronfenbrenner, U. (1995). Developmental ecology through space and time: A future perspective. In P. Moen & G. H. Elder Jr. (Eds.), *Examining lives in context: Perspectives on the ecology of human development* (pp. 619–647). Washington, DC: American Psychological Association.

Brothen, T., & Wambach, C. (2003). Universal instructional design in a computer-based psychology course. In J. L. Higbee (Ed.), *Curricular transformation and disability: Implementing universal design in higher education* (pp. 7–21). Minneapolis: Center for Research on Developmental Education and Urban Literacy, General College, University of Minnesota. Retrieved from http://cedh.umn.edu/CRDEUL/books-ctad.html

Brown, J. T. (1994). Effective disability support service programs. In D. Ryan & M. McCarthy (Eds.), *A student affairs guide to the ADA and disability issues* (pp. 98–110). Washington, DC: National Association of Student Personnel Administrators.

Brown, K., & Broido, E. M. (2015). Engagement of students with disabilities. In S. Quaye & S. Harper (Eds.), *Student engagement in higher education: Theoretical perspectives and practical approaches for diverse populations* (2nd ed., pp. 187–207). New York, NY: Routledge.

Brown, K., Broido, E., Stapleton, L., Evans, N., & Peña, E. (2016, November). *Disability research: Frameworks for qualitative inquiry.* Paper presented at the Association of the Study of Higher Education Conference, Columbus, OH.

Brown, K., Peña, E. V., & Rankin, S. (in press). Unwanted sexual contact: Students with autism and other disabilities at greater risk. *Journal of College Student Development.*

Brown, K., Peña, E., & Rankin, S. (2015, November). *Academic success and unfriendly turf: Campus climate for students with autism spectrum disorder.* Paper presented at the Association of the Study of Higher Education Conference, Denver, CO.

Brown, K. R. (in press). Accommodations and support services for students with autism spectrum disorder: A national survey of disability resource providers. *Journal of Postsecondary Education and Disability.*

Brown, K. R., & Coomes, M. D. (2015). A spectrum of support: Current and best practices for students with autism spectrum disorder (ASD) at community colleges. *Community College Journal of Research and Practice, 40*(6), 465–479. doi:10.1080/10668926.2015.1067171

Brown, L. (2014). Disability in an ableist world. In C. Brown (Ed.), *Criptiques* (pp. 37–46). Retrieved from https://criptiques.files.wordpress.com/2014/05/crip-final-2.pdf

Brown, M. K. (1994). Developing and implementing a process for the review of nonacademic units. In J. Stark & A. Thomas (Eds.), *Assessment and program evaluation* (pp. 445–463). Needham Heights, MA: Simon & Schuster.

Brown, S. E. (2008). Breaking barriers: The pioneering disability students services program at the University of Illinois, 1948–1960. In E. H. Tamura (Ed.), *The history of discrimination in U.S. education: Marginality, agency, and power* (pp. 165–192). New York, NY: Palgrave Macmillan.

Brown, S. E., Takahashi, K., & Roberts, K. D. (2010). Mentoring individuals with disabilities in post-secondary education: A review of the literature. *Journal of Postsecondary Education and Disability, 23*(2), 98–111.

Brown, V., & Nichols, T. R. (2012). Pregnant and parenting students on campus policy and program implications for a growing population. *Educational Policy, 27*(3), 499–530.

Brown v. Board of Education, 347 U.S. 483 (1954).

Brown-Lavoie, S. M., Viecili, M. A., & Weiss, J. A. (2014). Sexual knowledge and victimization in adults with autism spectrum disorders. *Journal of Autism and Developmental Disorders, 44*(9), 2185–2196.

Browne, M. N., Morrison, V., Keeley, B., & Gromko, M. (2010). Obesity as a protected category: The complexity of personal responsibility for physical attributes. *Michigan State University Journal of Medicine and Law, 14*, 1. Retrieved from LexisNexis Academic database.

Bruder, M. B., & Mogro-Wilson, C. (2010). Student and faculty awareness and attitudes about students with disabilities. *Review of Disability Studies, 6*(2), 3–13.

Bryan, W. V. (1996). *In search of freedom: How persons with disabilities have been disenfranchised from the mainstream of American society.* Springfield, IL: Charles C. Thomas.

Bryan, W. V. (2002). *Sociopolitical aspects of disabilities: The social perspectives and political history of disabilities and rehabilitation in the United States.* Springfield, IL: Charles C. Thomas.

Bryan, W. V. (2010). Struggle for freedom: Disability rights movements. In M. Adams, W. J. Blumenfeld, C. Castañeda, H. W. Hackman, M. L. Peters, & X. Zúñiga (Eds.), *Readings for diversity and social justice* (2nd ed., pp. 464–469). New York, NY: Routledge.

Bryan, W. V. (2013). Struggle for freedom: Disability rights movements. In M. Adams, W. J. Blumenfeld, C. Castañeda, H. W. Hackman, M. L. Peters, & X. Zúñiga (Eds.), *Readings for diversity and social justice* (3rd ed., pp. 468–474). New York, NY: Routledge.

Burch, S. (2001). Reading between the signs: Defending Deaf culture in early twentieth-century America. In P. K. Longmore & L. Umansky (Eds.), *The new disability history: American perspectives* (pp. 214–235). New York: New York University Press.

Burch, S., & Sutherland, I. (2006). Who's not here yet? American disability history. *Radical History Review, 94*, 127–147.

Burgstahler, L. C., Crawford, L., & Acosta, J. (2001). Transition from two-year to four-year institutions for students with disabilities. *Disability Studies Quarterly, 21*(1). Retrieved from http://dsq-sds.org/article/view/253

Burgstahler, S. (2001). A collaborative model to promote career success for students with disabilities. *Journal of Vocational Rehabilitation, 16*, 209–215.

Burgstahler, S. (2012). *Universal design: Process, principles, and applications.* Retrieved from http://www.washington.edu/doit/universal-design-process-principles-and-applications

Burgstahler, S. (2014). Universal design in higher education. In M. L. Vance, N. E. Lipsitz, & K. Parks (Eds.), *Beyond the Americans with Disabilities Act: Inclusive policy and practice for higher education* (pp. 35–48). Washington, DC: NASPA-Student Affairs Administrators in Higher Education.

Burgstahler, S., & Moore, E. (2009). Making student services welcoming and accessible through accommodations and universal design. *Journal of Postsecondary Education and Disability, 21*(3), 151–174.

Burgstahler, S. E. (2002). Accommodating students with disabilities: Professional development needs of faculty. In C. M. Wehlburg & S. Chadwick-Blossy (Eds.), *To improve the academy: Resources for faculty, instructional, and organizational development* (vol. 21, pp. 151–183). Bolton, MA: Anker Publishing Company.

Burgstahler, S. E. (2007). *Applications of universal design in education.* Seattle: University of Washington. Retrieved from http://www.washington.edu/doit/Brochures/Academics/app_ud_edu .html

Burgstahler, S. E. (2008a). Promoters and inhibitors of universal design in higher education. In S. E. Burgstahler & R. C. Cory (Eds.), *Universal design in higher education: From principles to practice* (pp. 279–283). Cambridge, MA: Harvard University Press.

Burgstahler, S. E. (2008b). Universal design in higher education. In S. E. Burgstahler & R. C. Cory (Eds.), *Universal design in higher education: From principles to practice* (pp. 3–20). Cambridge, MA: Harvard University Press.

Burgstahler, S. E. (2008c). Universal design of instruction: From principles to practice. In S. E. Burgstahler & R. C. Cory (Eds.), *Universal design in higher education: From principles to practice* (pp. 23–43). Cambridge, MA: Harvard University Press.

Burgstahler, S. E. (2008d). Universal design of physical spaces: From principles to practice. In S. E. Burgstahler & R. C. Cory (Eds.), *Universal design in higher education: From principles to practice* (pp. 187–197). Cambridge, MA: Harvard University Press.

Burgstahler, S. E. (2008e). Universal design of student services: From principles to practice. In S. E. Burgstahler & R. C. Cory (Eds.), *Universal design in higher education: From principles to practice* (pp. 167–175). Cambridge, MA: Harvard University Press.

Burgstahler, S. E. (2008f). Universal design of technological environments: From principles to practice. In S. E. Burgstahler & R. C. Cory (Eds.), *Universal design in higher education: From principles to practice* (pp. 213–224). Cambridge, MA: Harvard University Press.

Burgstahler, S. E. (2012a). *Equal access: Universal design of instruction.* Seattle, WA: DO-IT, University of Washington. Retrieved from http://www.washington.edu/doit/equal-access-universal-design-instruction

Burgstahler, S. E. (2012b). *Equal access: Universal design of student services.* Retrieved from http://www.washington.edu/doit/Brochures/Academics/equal_access_ss.html

Burgstahler, S. E. (2012c). *Universal design in postsecondary education: Process, principles, and applications.* Seattle, WA: DO-IT, University of Washington. Retrieved from http://www.washington .edu/doit/universal-design-postsecondary-education-process-principles-and-applications (Original version 2008).

Burgstahler, S. E. (2015). *Making STEM accessible to postsecondary students with disabilities.* Retrieved from http://www.washington.edu/doit/making-stem-accessible-postsecondary-students-disabilities

Burgstahler, S. E., & Bellman, S. (2016, March). AccessStem resources promote change. *DO-IT News.* Retrieved from http://www.washington.edu/doit/accessstem-resources-promote-change

Burgstahler, S. E., & Cory, R. C. (Eds.). (2008). *Universal design in higher education: From principles to practice.* Cambridge, MA: Harvard Education Press.

Burke, E. P. (1995). *Improving the implementation of the Individuals with Disabilities Education Act: Making schools work for all of America's children.* Washington, DC: National Council on Disability.

Burnett, S. E., & Segoria, J. (2009). Collaboration for military transition students from combat to college: It takes a community. *Journal of Postsecondary Education and Disability, 22*(1), 53–58.

Burwell, N. R., Wessel, R. D., & Mulvihill, T. (2015). Attendant care for college students with physical disabilities using wheelchairs: Transition issues and experiences. *Journal of Postsecondary Education and Disability, 28*(3), 293.

Button v. Board of Regents of University and Community College System of Nevada, 289 F.3d 964 (9th Cir. 2008).

Byrom, B. (2001). A pupil and a patient. In P. K. Longmore & L. Umansky (Eds.), *The new disability history: American perspectives* (pp. 133–156). New York: New York University Press.

Caldwell, B., Cooper, M., Guarino Reid, L., & Vanderheiden, G. (Eds.). (2008). *Web Content Accessibility Guidelines (WCAG) 2.0.* Retrieved from http://www.w3.org/TR/WCAG20/#guidelines

Campbell, D. M. (2004). Assistive technology and universal instructional design: A postsecondary perspective. *Equity & Excellence in Education, 37*(2), 167–173.

Campbell, F. K. (2009). *Contours of ableism: The production of disability and abledness.* New York, NY: Palgrave MacMillan.

Cantor, D., Fisher, B., Chibnali, S., Townsend, R., Lee, H., Bruce, C., & Thomas, G. (2015). *Report on the AAU campus climate survey on sexual assault and sexual misconduct.* Retrieved from https://www.aau.edu/uploadedFiles/AAU_Publications/AAU_Reports/Sexual_Assault _Campus_Survey/AAU_Campus_Climate_Survey_12_14_15.pdf

Carlson, S. (2016, May 6). Should everyone go to college? *Chronicle of Higher Education,* pp. A23–A25.

Carodine, K., Almond, K. F., & Gratto, K. K. (2001). College student athlete success both in and out of the classroom. In M. F. Howard-Hamilton & S. K. Watt (Eds.), *Student services for athletes* (New Directions for Student Services, no. 93, pp. 9–33). San Francisco, CA: Jossey Bass.

Carpenter, N. C., & Paetzold, R. L. (2013). An examination of factors influencing responses to requests for disability accommodations. *Rehabilitation Psychology, 58*(1), 18–27.

Caruso, D. (2010). Autism in the U.S.: Social movement and legal change. *American Journal of Law & Medicine, 36,* 483–539.

Castañeda, C., Hopkins, L. E., & Peters, M. L. (2013). Ableism: Introduction. In M. Adams, W. J. Blumenfeld, C. Castañeda, H. W. Hackman, M. L. Peters, & X. Zúñiga (Eds.), *Readings for diversity and social justice* (3rd ed., pp. 461–468). New York, NY: Routledge.

Castañeda, C., & Peters, M. L. (2000). Ableism: Introduction. In M. Adams, W. J. Blumenfeld, C. Castañeda, H. W. Hackman, M. L. Peters, & X. Zúñiga (Eds.), *Readings for diversity and social justice* (pp. 319–323). New York, NY: Routledge.

Catlin, J. H., McCabe-Miele, G., Bowen, I., & Babbit, E. M. (2010). *Surviving an ADA accessibility audit: Best practices for policy development and compliance.* Retrieved from National Association of College and University Attorneys website: http://www.higheredcompliance.org/resources/ resources/xxiii-10–06–61.doc

Cawthon, S. W., & Cole, E. V. (2010). Postsecondary students who have a learning disability: Student perspectives on accommodations access and obstacles. *Journal of Postsecondary Education and Disability, 23*(2), 112–128.

Center for Applied Special Technology (CAST). (2012a). *About UDL.* Retrieved from http://www .udlcenter.org/aboutudl/whatisudl

Center for Applied Special Technology (CAST). (2012b). *UDL guidelines: Theory and practice version.* Retrieved from http://www.udlcenter.org/aboutudl/udlguidelines_theorypractice

Center for Managing Chronic Disease. (n.d.). *What is chronic disease?* University of Michigan. Retrieved from http://cmcd.sph.umich.edu/what-is-chronic-disease.html

Center for Universal Design (CUD). (2008a). *About the Center.* Retrieved from http://www.ncsu .edu/ncsu/design/cud/about_us/about_us.htm

Center for Universal Design (CUD). (2008b). *About UD.* Retrieved from http://www.ncsu.edu/ ncsu/design/cud/about_ud/about_ud.htm

Center for Universal Design (CUD). (2008c). *History of universal design.* Retrieved from http://www .ncsu.edu/ncsu/design/cud/about_ud/udhistory.htm

Center for Universal Design (CUD). (2008d). *The principles of universal design.* Retrieved from http://www.ncsu.edu/ncsu/design/cud/about_ud/udprinciplestext.htm

Center for Universal Design (CUD). (2008e). *Ronald L. Mace: 1941–1998.* Retrieved from http://www.ncsu.edu/ncsu/design/cud/about_us/usronmace.htm

Center for Universal Design (CUD). (2010). *History of universal design.* Retrieved from www.ncsu .edu/project/design-projects/udi/center-for-universaldesign/history-of-universal-design

Cerney, J. (2013). Historical and cultural influences in deaf education. In M. Adams, W. J. Blumenfeld, C. Castañeda, H. W. Hackman, M. L. Peters, & X. Zúñiga (Eds.), *Readings for diversity and social justice* (3rd ed., pp. 474–478). New York, NY: Routledge.

Charlton, J. I. (1998). *Nothing about us without us: Disability oppression and empowerment.* Berkeley, CA: University of California Press.

Cheatham, G. A., & Elliott, W. (2013). The effects of family college savings on postsecondary school enrollment rates of students with disabilities. *Economics of Education Review, 33,* 95–111.

Chen, R. K., Brown, A. D., & Kotbungkair, W. (2015). A comparison of self-acceptance of disability between Thai Buddhists and American Christians. *Journal of Rehabilitation, 81*(1), 52–62.

Chiba, C., & Low, R. (2007). A course-based model to promote successful transition to college for students with learning disorders. *Journal of Postsecondary Education and Disability, 20*(1), 40–53.

Chickering, A. W. (1969). *Education and identity.* San Francisco, CA: Jossey-Bass.

Chickering, A. W., & Gamson, Z. F. (1987). Seven principles for good practice in undergraduate education. *AAHE Bulletin, 397,* 3–7.

Choose your parents wisely: Parenting in America. (2014, July 26). *Economist, 412*(8897). Retrieved from http://www.economist.com/news/united-states/21608779-there-large-class-divide-how-americans-raise-their-children-rich-parents-can

Christensen, K. M., Blair, M. E., & Holt, J. M. (2007). The built environment, evacuations, and individuals with disabilities: A guiding framework for disaster policy and preparation. *Journal of Disability Policy Studies, 17*(4), 249–254.

Christiansen, J. B. (2009). Deaf president now! In S. Burch (Ed.), *Encyclopedia of American disability history* (vol. 1, pp. 244–246). New York, NY: Facts on File.

Christiansen, J. B., & Leigh, I. W. (2009). Cochlear implants. In S. Burch (Ed.), *Encyclopedia of American disability history* (vol. 1, pp. 192–194). New York, NY: Facts on File.

Chronology. (2009). In S. Burch (Ed.), *Encyclopedia of American disability history* (vol. 1, pp. xxiv–lvi). New York, NY: Facts on File.

Church, T. E. (2009). Returning veterans on campus with war related injuries and the long road back home. *Journal of Postsecondary Education and Disability, 22*(1), 43–52.

Ciuffreda, K. J., & Kapoor, N. (2012). Acquired brain injury. In M. B. Taub, M. Bartuccio, & D. Maino, (Eds.), *Visual diagnosis and care of the patient with special needs* (pp. 95–100). Philadelphia, PA: Wolters Kluwer Health/Lippincott Williams & Wilkins.

Clark, A. E., & Pryal, K. R. G. (2015). Where Title IX meets Title II. *Chronicle of Higher Education.* Retrieved from https://chroniclevitae.com/news/864-where-title-ix-meets-title-ii

Class v. Towson University, No. 15–1811 (4th Cir. Nov. 13, 2015).

Coates v. Dish Network, 350 P.3d 849 (Co. 2015).

Cole, E. V., & Cawthon, S. W. (2015). Self-disclosure decisions of university students with learning disabilities. *Journal of Postsecondary Education and Disability, 28*(2), 163–179.

Colker, R., & Grossman, P. (2014a). *The law of disability discrimination for higher education professionals.* New Providence, NJ: LexisNexis.

Colker, R., & Grossman, P. (2014b). *The law of disability discrimination: 2014 supplement.* New Providence, NJ: LexisNexis. Retrieved from http://www.lexisnexis.com/store/images/Supplements/35542014SupplementSummerReadingList_3.pdf

College of Menominee Nation. (2012). *Universal design.* Retrieved from http://www.menominee.edu/universal_design.aspx?id=1637

Collier, R. (2012). Person-first language: Laudable cause, horrible prose. *CMAJ: Canadian Medical Association Journal, 184*(18), E939-E940. doi:10.1503/cmaj.109–4338

Collins, M. E., & Mowbray, C. T. (2008). Students with psychiatric disabilities on campus: Examining predictors of enrollment with disability support services. *Journal of Postsecondary Education and Disability, 21*(2), 91–104.

Colorado Asset. (2015–2016). *How to get started.* Retrieved from http://ciccoloradoasset.org/

Colorado Department of Education. (2012). *Twice-exceptional students: Gifted students with disabilities* (4th ed.). Retrieved from https://www.cde.state.co.us/sites/default/files/documents/gt/download/pdf/level_1_resource_handbook_4th_ed_10–2–12.pdf

Connor, D. J., & Gabel, S. L. (2013). "Cripping" the curriculum through academic activism: Working toward increasing global exchanges to reframe (dis)ability and education. *Equity & Excellence in Education, 46*(1), 100–118.

Convention in brief. (2006). Prepared by the UN Web Services Section, Department of Public Information. Retrieved from http://www.un.org/disabilities/convention/convention.shtml

Cook v. State of Rhode Island, Dept. of MHRH, 10 F.3d 17, 20–21 (1st Cir. 1993); Brief of Plaintiff-Appellee at 9–10, Cook, 10 F.3d 17 (No. 93–1093).

Coolbaugh, E. A. (2014). Accessible on-campus living. In M. L. Vance, N. E. Lipsitz, & K. Parks (Eds.), *Beyond the Americans with Disabilities Act: Inclusive policy and practice for higher education* (pp. 159–163). Washington, DC: NASPA-Student Affairs Administrators in Higher Education.

Cooper, M., Guarino Reid, L., Kirkpatrick, A., Connor, J. O., & Vanderheiden, G. (2013). *Techniques for WCAG 2.0.* Retrieved from www.w3.org/TR/WCAG20-TECHS/

Copley, T. Y. (2011, November 1). *What disability justice has to offer social justice.* Retrieved from http://www.grassrootsfundraising.org/2011/11/11–3-what-disability-justice-has-to-offer-social-justice-by-theo-yang-copley/

Corker, M. (1998). Disability discourse in a postmodern world. In T. Shakespeare (Ed.), *The disability reader: Social science perspectives* (pp. 221–233). New York, NY: Cassell.

Corker, M. (1999). Differences, conflations and foundations: The limits to "accurate" theoretical representation of disabled people's experience? *Disability & Society, 14*(5), 627–642.

Corker, M., & Shakespeare, T. (2002). Mapping the terrain. In M. Corker & T. Shakespeare (Eds.), *Disability/postmodernity: Embodying disability theory* (pp. 1–17). New York, NY: Cassell.

Corrigan, P. W. (2005). *On the stigma of mental illness: Practical strategies for research and social change.* Washington, DC: American Psychological Association.

Corrigan, P., Markowitz, F. E., Watson, A., Rowan, D., & Kubiak, M. A. (2003). An attribution model of public discrimination towards persons with mental illness. *Journal of Health and Social Behavior, 44*, 162–179.

Cortiella, C. (2009). New federal law promotes success in postsecondary education for students with disabilities. *Exceptional Parent Magazine*. Retrieved from http://www.ahead.org/aff/virginia/Exceptional%20Parent%20Magazine%20article%20on%20HEOA.pdf

Costa-Black, K. M., Feuerstein, M., & Loisel, P. (2013). Work disability models: Past and present. In P. Loisel & J. R. Anema (Eds.), *Handbook of work disability: Prevention and management* (pp. 71–93). New York, NY: Springer.

Council for the Advancement of Standards in Higher Education. (2013). *Disability resources and services*. Retrieved from http://standards.cas.edu/getpdf.cfm?PDF=E86A6AC1-C709-8EBF-8697C7CA1D64DA2D

Council for Exceptional Children. (2008). *Higher Education Opportunity Act Reauthorization: Summary of selected provisions for individuals with exceptionalities and the professionals who work on their behalf*. Arlington, VA: Author.

Creamer, D. G., & Creamer, E. G. (1990). Use of a planned change model to modify student affairs programs. In D. G. Creamer & Associates, *College student development theory and practice for the 1990s* (pp. 181–192). Alexandria, VA: American College Personnel Association.

Crisp, E. (2014, July 12). SU settles lawsuit over accessibility complaints. *Baton Rouge Advocate*. Retrieved from http://theadvocate.com/home/9631084–125/su-settles-lawsuit-over-accessibility-complaints

Crowley, J. (2014). Asylum for the deaf and dumb. *Disability History Museum*. Retrieved from http://www.disabilitymuseum.org/edu/essay.html?id=3

CSU Center for Distributed Learning. (2009–2010a). *Merlot Elixr case stories: Disciplines*. Retrieved from http://elixr.merlot.org/case-stories/disciplines

CSU Center for Distributed Learning. (2009–2010b). *Merlot Elixr: Teaching music theory*. Retrieved from http://elixr.merlot.org/case-stories/understanding—meeting-students-needs/universal-design-for-learning-udl/teaching-music-theory

Cutting Edge Program. (n.d.). *The Cutting Edge program*. Retrieved from http://www.edgewood.edu/Prospective-Students/Cutting-Edge

DaDeppo, L. M. (2009). Integration factors related to the academic success and intent to persist of college students with learning disabilities. *Learning Disabilities Research & Practice, 24*(3), 122–131

Dahlstrom, E. (2012). *ECAR study of undergraduate students and information technology, 2012* (Report). Louisville, CO: EDUCAUSE Center for Applied Research.

Dallas, B. K., Ramish, J. L., & McGowan, B. (2015). Students with autism spectrum disorders and the role of family in postsecondary settings: A systematic review of the literature. *Journal of Postsecondary Education and Disability, 28*(2), 135–147.

Daly-Cano, M., Vaccaro, A., & Newman, B. (2015). College student narratives about learning and using self-advocacy skills. *Journal of Postsecondary Education and Disability, 28*(2), 213–227.

Danermark, B. (2002). Interdisciplinary research and critical realism: The example of disability research. *Alethia, 5*(1), 56–64.

Danermark, B., Ekström, M., Jakobsen, L., & Karlsson, J. C. (2002). *Explaining society: Critical realism in the social sciences*. New York, NY: Routledge.

Danermark, B., & Gellerstedt, L. C. (2004). Social justice: Redistribution and recognition—a non-reductionist perspective on disability. *Disability & Society, 19*(4), 339–353.

DAV. (n.d.). *History: Wars and scars*. Retrieved from https://www.dav.org/learn-more/about-dav/history/

Davidson, J., & Henderson, V. L. (2010). "Coming out" on the spectrum: Autism, identity and disclosure. *Social & Cultural Geography, 11*(2), 155–170.

Davis, L. (2002). *Bending over backwards: Disability, dismodernism and other difficult positions*. New York: New York University Press.

Davis, L. J. (2006). Constructing normalcy: The bell curve, the novel, and the invention of the disabled body in the nineteenth century. In L. J. Davis (Ed.), *The disability studies reader* (2nd ed., pp. 3–16). New York, NY: Rutledge.

Davis, L. J. (2011, September 25). Why is disability missing from the discourse on diversity? *Chronicle of Higher Education*. Retrieved from http://chronicle.com/article/Why-Is-Disability-Missing-From/129088/?sid=at&utm_source

Davis, L. J. (2015a). *Enabling acts: The hidden story of how the Americans with Disabilities Act gave the largest U.S. minority its rights*. Boston, MA: Beacon Press.

Davis, L. J. (2015b, July 23). Where's the outrage when colleges discriminate against students with disabilities? *Chronicle of Higher Education*. Retrieved from chronicle.com/article/where-s-the-Outrage-When/2317991/

Dean, L. A. (Ed.). (2009). *CAS Professional Standards for Higher Education* (7th ed.). Washington, DC: Council for the Advancement of Standards in Higher Education.

de Lorenzo, D. (2009). Gallaudet University. In S. Burch (Ed.), *Encyclopedia of American disability history* (vol. 2, pp. 394–396). New York, NY: Facts on File.

Del Rey, J. L. (2014). Transition to college. In M. L. Vance, N. E. Lipsitz, & K. Parks (Eds.), *Beyond the Americans with Disabilities Act* (pp. 145–150). Washington, DC: NASPA-Student Affairs Administrators in Higher Education.

Denhart, H. (2008). Deconstructing barriers: Perceptions of students labeled with learning disabilities in higher education. *Journal of Learning Disabilities, 41*(6), 483–497.

Dente, C. L., & Coles, K. P. (2012). Ecological approaches to transition planning for students with autism and Asperger's syndrome. *Children & Schools, 34*(1), 27–36.

Department of Fair Employment and Housing and the United States v. LSAC, No. CV 12–1830-EMC (N.D. Cal. May 20, 2014). Retrieved from http://www.ada.gov/dfeh_v_lsac/lsac_consentdecree.htm

Dermott, E., & Pomati, M. (2015). "Good" parenting practices: How important are poverty, education and time pressure? *Sociology, 1*, 1–18. doi:0038038514560260

Derntl, M., & Motschnig-Pitrik, R. (2007, October). *Inclusive universal access in engineering education*. Paper presented at the 37th ASEE/IEEE Frontiers in Education Conference, Milwaukee, WI. Retrieved from http://citeseerx.ist.psu.edu/viewdoc/download?doi=10.1.1.132.1630&rep=rep1&type=pdf

Dickinson, D. L., & Verbeek, R. L. (2002). Wage differentials between college graduates with and without learning disabilities. *Journal of Learning Disabilities, 35*(2), 175–184.

Did Bryn Mawr engage in fat shaming? (2015, February 2). *Inside Higher Education*. Retrieved from https://www.insidehighered.com/quicktakes/2015/02/02/did-bryn-mawr-engage-fat-shaming

Dill, B. T., & Zambrana, R. E. (2009). *Emerging intersections: Race, class and gender in theory, policy, and practice*. New Brunswick, NJ: Rutgers University Press.

DiRamio, D., & Spires, M. (2009). Partnering to assist disabled veterans in transition. In R. Ackerman & D. DiRamio (Eds.), *Creating a veteran-friendly campus: Strategies for transition and success* (New Directions for Student Services, no. 126, pp. 81–88). San Francisco, CA: Jossey-Bass.

Disability. (2015, September). Oxford English Dictionary. Oxford University Press. Retrieved from http://www.oxforddictionaries.com/us/definition/english/handicap

Disability culture. (n.d.). Retrieved from https://drc.uic.edu/disability-culture-2/

Disability friendly colleges. (1998, September 1). *New mobility*. Retrieved from http://www.new mobility.com/1998/09/disability-friendly-colleges/

Dohn, A., Garza-Villarreal, E. A., Heaton, P., & Vuust, P. (2012). Do musicians with perfect pitch have more autism traits than musicians without perfect pitch? An empirical study. *PLoS ONE, 7*(5), 1–8. doi:10.1371/journal.pone.0037961

DO-IT. (2009). *Self-examination: How accessible is your campus?* Seattle, WA: University of Washington.

DO-IT. (2012). *Equal access: Universal design of housing and residential life*. Retrieved from http://www.washington.edu/doit/equal-access-universal-design-housing-and-residential-life

Dolan, R. P., Hall, T. E., Banerjee, M., Chun, E., & Strangman, N. (2005). Applying principles of universal design to test delivery: Read-aloud on test performance of high school students with learning disabilities. *Journal of Technology, Learning, and Assessment, 3*(7), 4–32.

Dolmage, J. (2005). Disability studies pedagogy, usability and universal design. *Disability Studies Quarterly, 25*(4). Retrieved from http://dsq-sds.org/article/view/627/804

Dona, J., & Edmister, J. H. (2001). An examination of community college faculty members' knowledge of the Americans with Disabilities Act of 1990 at the fifteen community colleges in Mississippi. *Journal of Postsecondary Education and Disability, 14*(2), 91–103.

Dong, S., & Lucas, M. S. (2014). Psychological profile of university students with different types of disabilities. *Journal of College Student Development, 55*(5), 481–485. doi:10.1353/csd.2014.0044

Dowrick, P. W., Anderson, J., Heyer, K., & Acosta, J. (2005). Postsecondary education across the USA: Experiences of adults with disabilities. *Journal of Vocational Rehabilitation, 22*, 41–47.

Drum, C. E. (2009). Models and approaches to disability. In C. E. Drum, G. L. Krahn, & H. Bersani Jr. (Eds.), *Disability and public health* (pp. 27–44). Washington, DC: American Public Health Association and American Association on Intellectual and Developmental Disabilities.

Duffy, J. T., & Gugerty, J. (2005). The role of disability support services. In E. E. Getzel & P. Wehman (Eds.), *Going to college: Expanding opportunities for people with disabilities* (pp. 89–115). Baltimore, MD: Brookes.

Duke, T. S. (2011). Lesbian, gay, bisexual, and transgender youth with disabilities: A meta-synthesis. *Journal of LGBT Youth, 8*(1), 1–52.

Dunlavey, R., Magliulo, M., & Marotta, E. A. (2009). Sheltered workshops. In S. Burch (Ed.), *Encyclopedia of American disability history* (vol. 3, pp. 823–824). New York, NY: Facts on File.

Dunn, D. S., & Burcaw, S. (2013). Disability identity: Exploring narrative accounts of disability. *Rehabilitation Psychology, 58*(2), 148–157.

Duquaine-Watson, J. M. (2008). Computing technologies, the digital divide, and "universal" instructional methods. In J. L. Higbee & E. Goff (Eds.). *Pedagogy and students services for institutional transformation: Implementing universal design in higher education* (pp. 437–450). Minneapolis, MN: Center for Research on Developmental Education and Urban Literacy, College of Education and Human Development, University of Minnesota.

Duranczyk, I. M., & Fayon, A. K. (2008). Successful undergraduate mathematics through universal design of essential course components, pedagogy, and assessment. In J. Higbee & E. Goff (Eds.). *Pedagogy and student services for institutional transformation: Implementing universal design in higher education* (pp. 137–153). Minneapolis, MN: Center for Research on Developmental Education and Urban Literacy, College of Education and Human Development, University of Minnesota. Retrieved from http://cehd.umn.edu/passit/docs/PASS-IT-Books.pdf

Duval v. County of Kitsap, 260 F.3d 1124 (3d. Cir. 2001).

Dyer, S. (2011). *An overview of ADAAA and other disability legislation compliance issues* [White paper]. Retrieved from http://www.ok-ahead.org/ADAAAwhitepaper.pdf

Easton, G. (2010). Critical realism in case study research. *Industrial Marketing Management, 39*(1), 118–128.

Eblin, L. (1988, July 25). Let's put people first, and disability second [Letter to the editor]. *Business Week*, p. 8.

Eckes, S., & Ochoa, T. (2005). Students with disabilities: Transitioning from high school to higher education. *American Secondary Education, 33*, 6–20.

Educating the senses: The 19th century awakes to reform. (2014). *Disability Museum History*. Retrieved from http://www.disabilitymuseum.org/dhm/edu/cluster.html?cluster_id=24

Education for All Handicapped Children Act of 1975, Pub. L. No. 94–142, 89 (1975).

Edwards, R. A. R. (2001). "Speech has an extraordinary humanizing power": Horace Mann and the problem of nineteenth century American deaf education. In P. K. Longmore & L. Umanky (Eds.), *The new disability history: American perspectives* (pp. 58–82). New York: New York University Press.

Edyburn, D. L. (2010, Winter). Would you recognize universal design for learning if you saw it? Ten propositions for new directions for the second decade of UDL. *Learning Disability Quarterly, 33*, 33–41.

Elhoweris, H., Whittaker, C., & Salend, S. J. (2007). Addressing the religious and spiritual diversity of students with disabilities and their families. *Multiple Voices, 10* (1&2), 1–7.

Elliott, M., Gonzalez, C., & Larsen, B. (2011). U.S. military veterans transition to college: Combat, PTSD, and alienation on campus. *Journal of Student Affairs Research and Practice, 48*(3), 279–296.

Embry, P. B., Parker, D. R., McGuire, J. M., & Scott, S. S. (2005). Postsecondary disability service providers' perceptions about implementing universal design for instruction (UDI). *Journal of Postsecondary Education and Disability, 18*(1), 34–38.

Engle, J., & Tinto, V. (2008). *Moving beyond access: College success for low-income, first-generation students.* Retrieved from http://files.eric.ed.gov/fulltext/ED504448.pdf

Enright, M. S., Conyers, L. M., & Szymanski, E. M. (1996). *Journal of Counseling & Development, 75*, 103–114.

Erevelles, N., & Minear, A. (2010). Unspeakable offenses: Untangling race and disability in discourses of intersectionality. *Journal of Literary & Cultural Disability Studies, 4*(2), 127–146.

Erickson, A. R. (2008). Challenges in advising ESL students with learning disabilities. *Academic Advising Today, 31*(1). Retrieved from http://www.nacada.ksu.edu/Resources/Academic-Advising-Today/View-Articles/Challenges-in-Advising-ESL-Students-with-Learning-Disabilities.aspx

Erickson, W., Lee, C., & von Schrader, S. (2015). *Disability statistics from the 2013 American Community Survey (ACS).* Ithaca, NY: Cornell University Employment and Disability Institute. Retrieved from www.disabilitystatistics.org

Erkilic, M. (2012). Conceptual challenges between universal design and disability in relation to the body, impairment, and the environment: Where does the issue of disability stand in the philosophy of UD? *Middle East Technical University Journal of the Faculty of Architecture, 28*(2), 181–203.

Erlandson, R. (2008). *Universal and accessible design for products, services, and processes.* Boca Raton, FL: CRC Press.

Evans, N. J. (2008). Theoretical foundations of universal instructional design. In J. L. Higbee & E. Goff (Eds.), *Pedagogy and student services for institutional transformation: Implementing universal design in higher education* (pp. 11–23). Minneapolis, MN: University of Minnesota, Center for Research on Developmental Education and Urban Literary, College of Education and Human Development.

Evans, N. J., Assadi, J. L., & Herriott, T. K. (2005). Encouraging the development of disability allies. In R. D. Reason, E. M. Broido, T. L. Davis, & N. J. Evans (Eds.), *Developing social justice allies* (New Directions for Student Services, no. 110, pp. 67–79). San Francisco, CA: Jossey-Bass.

Evans, N. J., Assadi, J., Herriott, T., & Varland, C. (2004, April). *Compliance is not inclusion: Social integration of students with disabilities.* Paper presented at the American College Personnel Association Annual Convention, Philadelphia, PA.

Evans, N. J., & Broido, E. M. (2011, November 14). *Social involvement and identity involvement of students with disabilities.* Poster presented at the Association for the Study of Higher Education conference, Charlotte, NC.

Evans, N. J., Forney, D. S., Guido, F. M., Patton, L. D., & Renn, K. A. (2009). *Student development in college: Theory, research, and practice* (2nd ed.). San Francisco, CA: Jossey-Bass.

Evans, N. J., & Herriott, T. K. (2009). Philosophical and theoretical approaches to disability. In J. L. Higbee & A. A. Mitchell (Eds.), *Making good on the promise: Student affairs professionals with disabilities* (pp. 27–40). Lanham, MD: American College Personnel Association and University Press of America.

Fair Housing Amendments Act of 1988. 42 U.S.C.A. §§ 3601–3631

Family Educational Rights and Privacy Act of 1974 (FERPA), 20 U.S.C. § 1232g.

Family Policy Compliance Office. (2015). *Family Educational Rights and Privacy Act (FERPA).* Retrieved from http://www2.ed.gov/policy/gen/guid/fpco/ferpa/index.html

Federal Student Aid. (n.d.). *Staying eligible.* Retrieved from https://studentaid.ed.gov/sa/eligibility/staying-eligible#meet-basic-criteria

Field, M. J., & Jette, A. M. (2007a). Assistive and mainstream technologies for people with disabilities. In M. J. Field & A. M. Jette (Eds.), *The future of disability in America* (pp. 183–221). Washington, DC: National Academies Press.

Field, M. J., & Jette, A. (Eds.). (2007b). *The future of disability in America.* Washington, DC: National Academies Press.

Figueroa, R. A. (2002). Toward a new model of assessment. In A. J. Artiles & A. A. Ortiz (Eds.), *English language learners with special education needs: Identification, assessment, and instruction* (pp. 51–64). Crystal Lake, IL: Center for Applied Linguistics and Delta Systems.

Fine, M., & Asch, A. (2000). Disability beyond stigma: Social interaction, discrimination, and activism. In M. Adams, W. J. Blumenfeld, R. Castañeda, H. W. Hackman, M. L. Peters, & X. Zúñiga (Eds.), *Readings for diversity and social justice* (pp. 330–339). New York, NY: Routledge. (Reprinted from *Journal of Social Issues, 44,* 3–21, 1998)

Finkelstein, V. (1980). *Attitudes and disabled people: Issues for discussion.* New York, NY: World Rehabilitation Fund.

Finn, D. E., Getzel, E. E., Asselin, S. B., & Reilly, V. (2008). Implementing universal design: Collaboration across campus. In S. E. Burgstahler & R. C. Cory (Eds.), *Universal design in higher education: From principles to practice* (pp. 267–277). Cambridge, MA: Harvard University Press.

Fleischer, D. Z., & Zames, F. (2001). *Disability rights movement: From charity to confrontation.* Philadelphia, PA: Temple University Press Press.

Fleischer, D. Z., & Zames, F. (2011). *The disability rights movement: From charity to confrontation* (2nd ed.). Philadelphia, PA: Temple University Press.

Florey, A. T., & Harrison, D. A. (2000). Informal accommodation requests from employees with disabilities: Multistudy evidence on willingness to comply. *Academy of Management Journal, 43*(2), 224–233.

Forber-Pratt, A. J., & Aragon, S. R. (2013). A model of social and psychosocial identity development for postsecondary students with physical disabilities. In M. Wappett & K. Arndt (Eds.), *Emerging perspectives on disability studies* (pp. 1–22). New York, NY: Palgrave Macmillan.

Foucault, M. (1977). *Discipline and punish: The birth of the prison* (A. Sheritan, Trans.). New York, NY: Vintage.

Foucault, M. (1980). *Power/knowledge: Selected interviews and other writings, 1972–1977*. New York, NY: Pantheon.

Fougeyrollas, P., & Beauregard, L. (2001). Disability: An integrative person-environment social creation. In G. L. Albrecht, K. D. Seelman, & M. Bury (Eds.), *Handbook of disability studies* (pp. 171–194). Thousand Oaks, CA: Sage.

Fowler v. Westminster College of Salt Lake, 2:09-cv-00591, No. 271 (D. Utah, 2012).

Fox, J. A., Hatfield, J. P., & Collins, T. C. (2003). Developing the curriculum transformation and disability workshop model. In J. L. Higbee (Ed.), *Curriculum transformation and disability: Implementing universal design in higher education* (pp. 7–39). Minneapolis, MN: Center for Research on Developmental Education and Urban Literacy, College of Education and Human Development, University of Minnesota.

Fox, R. (2014, June 17). Too fat to be a scientist? *Chronicle of Higher Education*. Retrieved from http://www.chronicle.com/blogs/conversation/2014/06/17/too-fat-to-be-a-scientist/

Fraley, S. S., Mona, L. R., & Theodore, P. S. (2007). The sexual lives of lesbian, gay, and bisexual people with disabilities: Psychological perspectives. *Sexuality Research and Social Policy, 4*(1), 15–26.

Franke, A. H., Bérubé, M. F., O'Neil, R. M., & Kurland, J. E. (2012). Accommodating faculty members who have disabilities. *Academe, 98*(4), 1–13.

Freedman, E. (2014, August 12). Diverse docket: Deaf student wins admittance to medical school. *Diverse*. Retrieved from http://diverseeducation.com/article/66304/

Friedman, S. (1993). Accommodation issues in the work place for people with disabilities: A needs assessment in an educational setting. *Disability, Handicap, & Society, 8*(1), 3–23.

Friedman, S. N., Berger, E. C., & Parks, K. (2014). Beyond the minimum innovations and partnerships. In M. L. Vance, N. E. Lipsitz, & K. Parks (Eds.), *Beyond the Americans with Disabilities Act: Inclusive policy and practice for higher education* (pp. 127–133). Washington, DC: NASPA-Student Affairs Administrators in Higher Education.

Frum, J. L. (2007). Postsecondary educational access for undocumented students: Opportunities and constraints. *American Academic, 3*(1), 81–108.

Fuecker, D., & Harbour, W. S. (2011). UReturn: University of Minnesota services for faculty and staff with disabilities. In W. S. Harbour & J. W. Madeus (Eds.), *Disability services and campus dynamics* (New Directions for Higher Education, no. 154, pp. 45–54). San Francisco, CA: Jossey-Bass.

Fujiura, G. T., & Rutkowski-Kmitta, V. (2001). Counting disability. In G. L. Albrecht, K. D. Seelman, & M. Bury (Eds.), *Handbook of disability studies* (pp. 69–96). Thousand Oaks, CA: Sage.

Fuller, M., Healey, M., Bradley, A., & Hall, T. (2004). Barriers to learning: A systemic study of the experience of disabled students in one university. *Studies in Higher Education, 29*(3), 303–318.

Funckes, C., Kroeger, S., Loewen, G., & Thornton, M. (n.d.a). *Refocus: Advocacy*. Retrieved from http://www.projectshift-refocus.org/advocacy.htm

Funckes, C., Kroeger, S., Loewen, G., & Thornton, M. (n.d.b). *Refocus: Job descriptions*. Retrieved from http://www.projectshift-refocus.org/job.htm

Funckes, C., Kroeger, S., Loewen, G., & Thornton, M. (n.d.c). *Refocus: Mission statement*. Retrieved from http://www.projectshift-refocus.org/mission.htm

Funckes, C., Kroeger, S., Loewen, G., & Thornton, M. (n.d.d). *Refocus: Viewing the work of disability services differently*. Retrieved from http://www.projectshift-refocus.org/index.htm.

Gable, S. L. (2001). I wash my face with dirty water. *Journal of Teacher Education, 52*(1), 31–47.

Garland, J. L. (2015). Commuter students with disabilities. In J. P. Biddix (Ed.), *Understanding and addressing commuter student needs* (New Directions for Student Services, no. 150, pp. 57–67). San Francisco, CA: Jossey-Bass.

Garlow, S. J., Rosenberg, J., Moore, J. D., Haas, A. P., Koestner, B., Hendin, H., & Nemeroff, C. B. (2008). Depression, desperation, and suicidal ideation in college students: Results from the American Foundation for Suicide Prevention College Screening Project at Emory University. *Depression and Anxiety, 25*(6), 482–488.

Garrison-Wade, D. F., & Lehmann, J. P. (2009). A conceptual framework for understanding students' with disabilities transition to community college. *Community College Journal, 33*(5), 415–443.

Gehring, D. D., Osfield, K. J., & Wald, J. (1994). Legal, ethical, and policy implications of the Americans with Disabilities Act. In D. Ryan & M. McCarthy (Eds.), *A student affairs guide to the ADA and disability issues* (pp. 1–14). Washington, DC: National Association of Student Personnel Administrators.

Gelpi, A. (2015a). OCR rulings summary. *Disability Compliance for Higher Education, 20*(10), 10–12.

Gelpi, A. (2015b). OCR rulings summary. *Disability Compliance for Higher Education, 20*(11), 10–12.

Gerschick, T. J., & Miller, A. S. (1994). Gender identities at the crossroads of masculinity and physical disability. *Masculinities, 2*(1), 34–55.

Getzel, E. E. (2008). Addressing the persistence and retention of students with disabilities in higher education: Incorporating key strategies and supports on campus. *Exceptionality, 16*(4), 207–219.

Ghaziuddin, M. (2005). *Mental health aspects of autism and Asperger syndrome.* Philadelphia, PA: Jessica Kingsley.

Gilbert, M. (2013, March 11). Schools make adjustments to comply with updated standards to make campuses more accessible to the disabled. *Diverseeducation.com.* Retrieved from http://diverseeducation.com/article/51840

Gildersleeve, R. E., Rumann, C., & Mondragón, R. (2010). Serving undocumented students: Current law and policy. In J. Price (Ed.), *Understanding and supporting undocumented students* (New Directions for Student Services, no. 131, pp. 5–18). San Francisco, CA: Jossey-Bass.

Gill, C. J. (1995). A psychological view of disability culture. *Disability Studies Quarterly, 15*(4), n.p.

Gillies, J., & Dupuis, S. L. (2013). A framework for creating a campus culture of inclusion: A participatory action research approach. *Annals of Leisure Research, 16*(3), 193–211.

Glass, D., Meyer, A., & Rose, D. H. (2013). Universal design for learning and the arts. *Harvard Educational Review, 83*(1), 98–119.

Gluck, E. B., & Dermott, J. (2011). Accommodation service and assistance animals on campus: Making heads or tails of the ADA, FHA, and Section 504. *National Association of College and University Attorneys (NACUA) Notes 9*(8), Retrieved from http://csd.uconn.edu/wp-content/uploads/sites/607/2014/04/nacua4.pdf

Goffman, E. (1963). *Stigma: Notes on the management of spoiled identity.* Englewood Cliffs, NJ: Prentice Hall.

Goldman, A. S., Schmalstieg, E. J., Freeman, D. H., Jr., Goldman, D. A., & Schmalstieg, F. C., Jr. (2003). What was the cause of Franklin Delano Roosevelt's paralytic illness? *Journal of Medical Biography, 11*, 232–240.

Goldstein, E. (2008). Applications of universal design to higher education facilities. In S. E. Burgstahler & R. C. Cory (Eds.), *Universal design in higher education: From principles to practice* (pp. 199–212). Cambridge, MA: Harvard University Press.

Goodley, D. (2004). Who is disabled? Exploring the scope of the social model of disability. In J. Swain, S. French, C. Barnes, & C. Thomas (Eds.), *Disabling barriers—Enabling environments* (2nd ed., pp. 118–124). London, England: Sage.

Goodley, D. (2011). *Disability studies: An interdisciplinary introduction.* London, England: Sage.

Goodwin, S. A., & Morgan, S. (2012, May–June). Chronic illness and the academic career: A hidden epidemic in higher education. *Academe.* Retrieved from http://www.aaup.org/article/chronic-illness-and-academic-career

Goren, W. D. (2016, July 8). ADA and ADA related cases at the Supreme Court: Where they have been and what is next [Web log post]. Retrieved from www.williamgoren.com/blog/2016/07/08/ada-ada-related-cases-supreme-court-historical-where-they-have-been-whats-next/

Goss, D. (2001). Chasing the rabbit: Metaphors used by adult learners to describe their learning disabilities. *Adult Learning, 12*(2), 8–9.

Graham-Smith, S., & Lafayette, S. (2004). Quality disability support for promoting belonging and academic success within the college community. *College Student Journal, 38*(1), 90–100.

Greenwood, S. C. & Wright-Riley, L. (2007). Adapting to Parkinson's disease: Two tales. Faculty members with disabilities in higher education. In M. L. Vance (Ed.), *Disabled faculty and staff in a disabling society: Multiple identities in higher education* (pp. 235–242). Huntersville, NC: Association on Higher Education and Disability.

Greytek, E. A., Kosciw, J. G., & Diaz, E. M. (2009). *Harsh realities: The experiences of transgender youth in our nation's schools.* New York, NY: GLSEN.

Griffin, P., Peters, M. L., & Smith, R. M. (2007). Ableism curricular design. In M. Adams, L. A. Bell, & P. Griffin (Eds.), *Teaching for diversity and social justice* (2nd ed., pp. 335–358). New York, NY: Routledge.

Groff, D. G., Lundberg, N. R., & Zabriskie, R. B. (2009). Influence of adapted sport on quality of life: Perceptions of athletes with cerebral palsy. *Disability and Rehabilitation, 31*(4), 318–326. doi:10.1080/09638280801976233

Grossman, P., Colker, R., & Simon, J. (2015). *The law of disability discrimination for higher education professionals: 2014–2015 supplement.* New Providence, NJ: LexisNexis. Retrieved from http://www.lexisnexis.com/store/catalog/booktemplate/productdetail.jsp?pageName=relatedProducts&catId=&prodId=prod20900324#

Gruttadaro, D., & Crudo, D. (2012). *College students speak: A survey report on mental health.* Retrieved from http://www.nami.org/getattachment/About-NAMI/Publications-Reports/Survey-Reports/College-Students-Speak_A-Survey-Report-on-Mental-Health-NAMI-2012.pdf

Guckenberger v. Boston University, 974 F. Supp. 106 (D. Mass. Aug. 15, 1997).

Guzman, A., & Balcazar, F. E. (2010). Disability services' standards and the worldviews guiding their implementation. *Journal of Postsecondary Education and Disability, 23*(1), 48–62.

Hackman, H. W. (2008). Broadening the pathway to academic success: The critical intersections of social justice education, critical multicultural education, and universal instructional design. In J. L. Higbee & E. Goff (Eds.), *Pedagogy and student services for institutional transformation: Implementing universal design in higher education* (pp. 25–48). Minneapolis, MN: University of Minnesota, Center for Research on Developmental Education and Urban Literacy, College of Education and Human Development.

Hackman, H. W., & Rauscher, L. (2004). A pathway to access for all: Exploring the connections between universal instructional design and social justice education. *Equity & Excellence in Education, 37*(2), 114–123.

Hadley, M. W. (2007). The necessity of academic accommodations for first-year college students with learning disabilities. *Journal of College Admission, 195*, 9–13.

Hadley, W. M. (2011, August 24). Universal design: Creating a learning environment for all students. *Net results: Critical issues for student affairs practitioners.* Retrieved from http://www.naspa.org/membership/mem/pubs/nr/PrinterFriendly.cfm?id=1804

Hadley, W. M., & Satterfield, J. W. (2013). Are university students with learning disabilities getting the help they need? *Journal of the First-Year Experience & Students in Transition, 25*(1), 113–123.

Hage, J. (1980). *Theories of organizations: Forms, process, and transformation.* New York, NY: Wiley.

Hahn, H. (1985). Disability policy and the problem of discrimination. *American Behavioral Scientist, 28,* 293–318.

Hahn, H. (1988). The politics of physical differences: Disability and discrimination. *Journal of Social Issues, 44*(1), 39–47.

Hahn, H. (1991). Alternative views of empowerment: Social services and civil rights. *Journal of Rehabilitation, 57*(4), 17–19.

Hahn, H. (1994). The minority group model of disability: Implications for medical sociology. *Research in the Sociology of Health Care, 11,* 3–24.

Hahn, H. D., & Belt, T. L. (2004). Disability identity and attitudes toward cure in a sample of disabled activists. *Journal of Health and Social Behavior, 45,* 453–464.

Halfon, N., & Newacheck, P. W. (2010). Evolving notions of childhood chronic illness. *Journal of the American Medical Association, 303*(7), 665–666.

Hall, L. M., & Belch, H. A. (2000). Setting the context: Reconsidering the principles of full participation and meaningful access for students with disabilities. In H. A. Belch (Ed.), *Serving students with disabilities* (New Directions for Student Services, No. 91, pp. 4–17). San Francisco, CA: Jossey-Bass.

Halpern v. Wake Forest University Health Sciences, 669 F.3d 454 (4th Cir. 2012).

Handicaprice. (2011). Retrieved from http://www.snopes.com/language/offense/handicap.asp

Handle, D. (2004). Universal instructional design and world languages. *Equity & Excellence in Education, 37,* 161–166.

Hannah, J. (2012, February 28). Wright State named one of nation's top disability-friendly schools. *Wright State NewsRoom.* Retrieved from http://webapp2.wright.edu/web1/newsroom/2012/02/28/wright-state-named-one-of-nations-top-disability-friendly-schools/

Harbour, W. S. (2008). *Final report: The 2008 biennial AHEAD survey of disability services and resource professionals in higher education.* Huntersville, NC: Association on Higher Education and Disability.

Harbour, W. S. (2009). The relationship between institutional unit and administrative features of disability services offices in higher education. *Journal of Postsecondary Education and Disability, 21*(3) 138–154. Retrieved from http://www.ahead.org/publications/jped

Hardiman, R., Jackson, B., & Griffin, P. (2007). Conceptual foundations for social justice education. In M. Adams, L. A. Bell, & P. Griffin (Eds.), *Teaching for diversity and social justice* (2nd ed., pp. 35–66). New York, NY: Routledge.

Hardiman, R., Jackson, B. W., & Griffin, P. (2013). Conceptual foundations. In M. Adams, W. J. Blumenfeld, C. R. Castañada, H. W. Hackman, M. L. Peters, & X. Zúñiga (Eds.), *Readings for diversity and social justice* (3rd ed., pp. 26–35). New York, NY: Routledge.

Harker, Y. S. (2015). Fat rights and fat discrimination: An annotated bibliography. *Legal Reference Services Quarterly, 34*(4), 293–323.

Harley, D. A., Nowak, T. M., Gassaway, L. J., & Savage, T. A. (2002). Lesbian, gay, bisexual, and transgender college students with disabilities: A look at multiple cultural minorities. *Psychology in the Schools, 39*(5), 525–538.

Harper, K. A., & DeWaters, J. (2008). A quest for website accessibility in higher education institutions. *The Internet and Higher Education, 11,* 160–164.

Hart, D., Grigal, M., & Weir, C. (2010). Expanding the paradigm: Postsecondary education options for individuals with autism spectrum disorders and intellectual disabilities. *Focus on Autism and Other Developmental Disabilities, 25,* 134–150. doi:10.1177/1088357610373759

Hartley, M. T. (2010). Increasing resilience: Strategies for reducing dropout rates for college students with psychiatric disabilities. *American Journal of Psychiatric Rehabilitation, 13*(4), 295–315.

Hatcher, S., & Waguespack, A. (2004). Academic accommodations for students with disabilities. In A. S. Canter, L. Z. Paige, M. D. Roth, I. Romero, & S. A. Carroll (Eds.), *Helping children at home and school II: Handouts for families and educators* (S8–1–4). Bethesda, MD: NASP Publications.

Hayashi, R., & May, G. E. (2011). The effect of exposure to a professor with a visible disability on students' attitudes toward disabilities. *Journal of Social Work in Disability & Rehabilitation, 10*(1), 36–48. doi:10.1080/1536710X.2011.546300

Hedrick, B., Dizén, M., Collins, K., Evans, J., & Grayson, T. (2010). Perceptions of college students with and without disabilities and effects of STEM and non-STEM enrollment on student engagement and institutional involvement. *Journal of Postsecondary Education and Disability, 23*(2), 129–136.

Heflin, L. J., & Alaimo, D. F. (2007). *Students with autism spectrum disorders: Effective instructional practices.* Columbus, OH: Pearson.

Hehir, T. (2002). Eliminating ableism in education. *Harvard Educational Review, 72*(1), 1–32.

Heiman, T., & Berger, O. (2008). Parents of children with Asperger syndrome or with learning disabilities: Family environment and social support. *Research in Developmental Disabilities, 29*(4), 289–300.

Helm, S. C. (2012). *Career development and employment concerns of employment-seeking students with psychiatric disabilities* (Doctoral dissertation). University of Tennessee, Knoxville, TN. Retrieved from http://trace.tennessee.edu/utk_graddiss/1304

Hennessey, M. L., Roessler, R., Cook, B., Unger, D., & Rumrill, P. (2006). Employment and career development concerns of postsecondary students with disabilities: Service and policy implications. *Journal on Postsecondary Education and Disability, 19*(1), 39–55.

Henry, W. J., Fuerth, K., & Figliozzi, J. (2010). Gay with a disability: A college student's multiple cultural journey. *College Student Journal, 44*(2), 377–388.

Herek, G. M., Capitanio, J. P., & Widaman, K. F. (2003). Stigma, social risk, and health policy: Public attitudes toward HIV surveillance policies and the social construction of illness. *Health Psychology, 22*(5), 533.

Hergenrather, K., & Rhodes, S. (2007). Exploring undergraduate student attitudes toward persons with disabilities: Application of the Disability Social Relationship Scale. *Rehabilitation Counseling Bulletin, 50*(2), 66–75.

Hernandez, A. (2010, April 10). Conference panelists: Disabled students would benefit from universal instruction design. *Diverse Education.* Retrieved from http://diverseeducation.com/cache/print.php?articleID=13700

Herts, K. L., Wallis, E., & Maslow, G. (2014). College freshmen with chronic illness: A comparison with healthy first-year students. *Journal of College Student Development, 55*(5), 475–480.

Hewitt, L. E. (2011). Perspectives on support needs of individuals with autism spectrum disorders: Transition to college. *Topics in Language Disorders, 31*(3), 273–285.

Heyward, S. (2011). Legal challenges and opportunities. In W. S. Harbour & J. W. Madaus (Eds.), *Disability and campus dynamics* (New Directions for Higher Education, No. 154, pp. 55–64). San Francisco, CA: Jossey-Bass.

Hickel, K. W. (2001). Medicine, bureaucracy, and social welfare: The politics of disability compensation for American veterans of World War I. In P. K. Longmore & L. Umansky (Eds.), *The new disability history: American perspectives* (pp. 236–267). New York: New York University Press.

Hickel, R. K. (2001). American disability policy in the twentieth century. In P. K. Longmore & L. Umansky (Eds.), *The new disability history: American perspectives* (pp. 375–392). New York: New York University Press.

Higbee, J. L. (2003) Universal design principles of student development programs and services. In J. L. Higbee & E. Goff (Eds.), *Implementing universal design in higher education* (pp. 255–266). Minneapolis, MN: Center for Research on Developmental Education and Urban Literacy, College of Education and Human Development, University of Minnesota. Retrieved from http://conservancy.umn.edu/handle/11299/5356

Higbee, J. L. (2009). Implementing universal instructional design in postsecondary courses and curricula. *Journal of College Teaching and Learning, 6*(8), 65–77.

Higbee, J. L. (2012). Creating a culture of inclusion: Respectful, intentional, reflective teaching. In *Expanding the frame: Applying universal design in higher education (part III). ACPA Developments, 10*(3). Retrieved from http://www2.myacpa.org/developments/fall-2012/creating-a-culture-of-inclusion-respectful-intentional-reflective-teaching

Higbee, J. L., & Barajas, H. L. (2007). Building effective places for multicultural learning. *About Campus, 12*(3), 16–22.

Higbee, J. L., & Goff, E. (2008). *Pedagogy and student services for institutional transformation: Implementing universal design in higher education.* Minneapolis, MN: Center for Research on Developmental Education and Urban Literacy, College of Education and Human Development, University of Minnesota. Retrieved from http://cehd.umn.edu/passit/docs/PASS-IT-Books.pdf

Higbee, J. L., & Mitchell, A. A. (Eds.). (2009). *Making good on the promise: Student affairs professionals with disabilities.* Lanham, MD: American College Personnel Association and University Press of America.

Higgins, E., & Raskind, M (1997). The compensatory effectiveness of optical character recognition/speech synthesis on reading comprehension of postsecondary students with learning disabilities. *Learning Disabilities, 8*(2), 75–87.

Higher Education Opportunity Act of 2008, Pub. L. No. 110–315 (2008).

Higher Education Research Institute. (2011). *College students with "hidden" disabilities: The Freshman Survey Fall 2010.* Los Angeles, CA: University of California at Los Angeles. Retrieved from http://www.heri.ucla.edu/PDFs/pubs/briefs/HERI_ResearchBrief_Disabilities_2011_April_25v2.pdf

Hinman, M. R., Peterson, C. A., & Gibbs, K. A. (2015). Prevalence of physical disability and accommodation needs among students in physical therapy education programs. *Journal of Postsecondary Education and Disability, 28*(3), 309–328.

History of NTID. (n.d.). National Technical Institute for the Deaf [website]. Retrieved from www.ntid.rit.edu/history

Hitchings, W. E., Luzzo, D. A., Ristow, R., Horvath, M., Retish, P., & Tanners, A. (2001). The career development needs of college students with learning disabilities: In their own words. *Learning Disabilities Research & Practice, 16*(1), 8–17.

Hoge, C. W., Auchterlonie, J. L., & Miliken, C. S. (2006). Mental health problems, use of mental health services, and attrition from military service after returning from deployment to Iraq or Afghanistan. *Journal of the American Medical Association, 295*, 1023–1032.

Hong, B. S. S. (2015). Qualitative analysis of the barriers college students with disabilities experience in higher education. *Journal of College Student Development, 56*(3), 209–226.

Howarth, J. W. (2007–2008). Recruiting sexual minorities and people with disabilities to be dean. *Seattle University Law Review, 31,* 751–763.

H.R. Rep. No. 93–500, 1973.

Hudson, R. L., & Janosik, S. M., (2014). Student conduct and disability. In M. L. Vance, N. E. Lipsitz, & K. Parks (Eds.), *Beyond the Americans with Disabilities Act: Inclusive policy and practice for higher education* (pp. 179–183). Washington, DC: NASPA-Student Affairs Administrators in Higher Education.

Huger, M. S. (2011). Fostering a disability-friendly institutional climate. In M. Huger (Ed.), *Fostering the increased integration of students with disabilities* (New Directions for Student Services, no. 134, pp. 3–11). San Francisco, CA: Jossey-Bass.

Humphrey, L., Clifford, D., & Morris, M. N. (2015). Health at every size college course reduces dieting behaviors and improves intuitive eating, body esteem, and anti-fat attitudes. *Journal of Nutrition Education and Behavior, 47*(4), 354–360.

Hunt, J., & Eisenberg, D. (2010). Mental health problems and help-seeking behavior among college students. *Journal of Adolescent Health, 46*(1), 3–10.

Hutcheon, E. J., & Wolbring, G. (2012). Voices of "disabled" post secondary students: Examining higher education "disability" policy using an ableism lens. *Journal of Diversity in Higher Education, 5*(1), 39–49.

Hux, K., Bush, E., Zickefoose, S., Holmberg, M., Henderson, A., & Simanek, G. (2010). Exploring the study skills and accommodations used by college student survivors of traumatic brain injury. *Brain Injury, 24*(1), 13–26.

Iantaffi, A. (1996). Women and disability in higher education: A literature search. In L. Morley & V. Walsh (Eds.), *Breaking boundaries: Women in higher education* (pp. 180–186). Bristol, PA: Taylor & Francis.

Iezzoni, L. I., McCarthy, E. P., Davis, R. B., & Siebens, H. (2000). Mobility problems and perceptions of disability by self-respondents and proxy-respondents. *Medical Care, 38*(10), 1051–1057.

I-graduate. (2015). *International student barometer: Fall 2015.* Retrieved from https://www.uc.edu/content/dam/uc/international/docs/international_student_barometer.pdf

Imrie, R. (1997). Rethinking the relationships between disability, rehabilitation, and society. *Disability and Rehabilitation, 19*(7), 263–271.

Imrie, R., & Reyes, M. G. (2009). Universal design. In S. Burch (Ed.), *Encyclopedia of American disability history* (vol. 3, pp. 919–921). New York, NY: Facts on File.

Individuals with Disabilities Education Improvement Act, P.L. 108–446 20 U.S.C. § 1400 (2004).

Institute of International Education. (2015a). *Open doors report, fast facts.* Retrieved from http://www.iie.org/Research-and-Publications/Open-Doors/Data/Fast-Facts#.VzKu0fkrLIU

Institute of International Education. (2015b). Students with disabilities, 2006/07–2013/14. *Open doors report on international educational exchange.* Retrieved from http://www.iie.org/opendoors

Irvine, A. (2005). Issues in sexuality for individuals with developmental disabilities: Myths, misconceptions, and mistreatment. *Exceptionality Education Canada, 15*(3), 5–20.

Izzo, M. V., Murray, A., & Novak, J. (2008). The faculty perspective on universal design for learning. *Journal of Postsecondary Education and Disability, 21*(2), 60–72.

Jackson, K. D., Howie, L. D., & Akinbami, L. J. (2013) *Trends in allergic conditions among children: United States, 1997–2011. NCHS data brief, no. 121.* Hyattsville, MD: National Center for Health Statistics.

J.A.M. v. Nova Southeastern University Inc., No. 0:15-cv-60248 (S.D. Fla. August 12, 2015).

James, P., & Kader, T. (2008). Practicing universal instructional design in visual art courses. In J. Higbee & E. Goff (Eds.), *Pedagogy and student services for institutional transformation:*

Implementing universal design in higher education (pp. 87–105). Minneapolis: Center for Research on Developmental Education and Urban Literacy, College of Education and Human Development, University of Minnesota. Retrieved from http://cehd.umn.edu/passit/docs/PASS-IT-Books.pdf

Janiga, S. J., & Costenbader, V. (2002). The transition from high school to postsecondary education for students with learning disabilities: A survey of college service coordinators. *Journal of Learning Disabilities, 35*(5), 462–468, 479.

Jehangir, R. R. (2003). Charting a new course: Learning communities and universal design. In J. L. Higbee (Ed.), *Curriculum transformation and disability: Implementing universal design in higher education* (pp. 79–92). Minneapolis, MN: Center for Research on Developmental Education and Urban Literacy, College of Education and Human Development, University of Minnesota.

Jemtå, L., Fugl-Meyer, K. S., Öberg, K., & Dahl, M. (2009). Self-esteem in children and adolescents with mobility impairment: Impact on well-being and coping strategies. *Acta Paediatrica, 98*, 562–572.

Jenkins, S. R., Belanger, A., Londoño Connally, M., Boals, A., & Durón, K. M. (2013). First-generation undergraduate students' social support, depression, and life satisfaction. *Journal of College Counseling, 16*, 129–142.

Jernigan, K. (2009, March). The pitfalls of political correctness: Euphemisms excoriated. *Braille Monitor*. Retrieved from https://nfb.org/images/nfb/publications/bm/bm09/bm0903/bm090308.htm

Jimenez, D. M., & Rosynsky, P. T. (2013, January 23). Oakland: Mills College settles disability access dispute with federal government. *San Jose Mercury News*. Retrieved from www.mercurynews.com/breaking-news/ci_22434749/oakland-mills-college-settles-disability-access-dispute-federal

Johnson, D. (2000). Enhancing out-of-class opportunities for students with disabilities. In H. Belch (Ed.), *Serving students with disabilities* (New Directions in Student Services, no. 91, pp. 41–53). San Francisco, CA: Jossey-Bass.

Johnson, D. M., & Fox, J. A. (2003). Creating curb cuts in the classroom: Adapting universal design principles to education. In J. L. Higbee (Ed.), *Curricular transformation and disability: Implementing universal design in higher education* (pp. 7–21). Minneapolis, MN: Center for Research on Developmental Education and Urban Literacy, General College, University of Minnesota.

Johnson, G., Zascavage, V., & Gerber, S. (2008). Junior college experience and students with learning disabilities: Implications for success at the four-year university. *College Student Journal, 42*, 1162–1168.

Johnson, J. R. (2010). Universal instructional design and critical (communication) pedagogy: Strategies for voice, inclusion, and social justice/change. *Equity & Excellence in Education, 37*(2), 145–153.

Johnson, S. G., & Fann, A. (2015). Deaf and hard of hearing students' perceptions of campus administrative support. *Community College Journal of Research and Practice, 40*(4), 1–13.

Johnson Santamaria, L., Fletcher, T. V., & Bos, C. S. (2002). Effective pedagogy for English language learners in inclusive classrooms. In A. J. Artiles & A. A. Ortiz (Eds.), *English language learners with special education needs: Identification, assessment, and instruction* (pp. 3–28). Crystal Park, IL: Center for Applied Linguistics and Delta Systems.

Johnstone, C. J. (2004). Disability identity: Personal constructions and formalized supports. *Disability Studies Quarterly, 24*(4). Retrieved from http://dsq-sds.org/article/view/880/1055

Jones, K. H., Domenico, D. M., & Valente, J. S. (2006). Incidence of pregnant and parenting teens with disabilities within FACS programs. *Journal of Family and Consumer Sciences Education, 24*(2), 24–35.

Jones, L. E. (2012). The framing of fat: Narratives of health and disability in fat discrimination litigation. *New York University Law Review, 87*, 1996–2039.

Jones, S. R. (1996). Toward inclusive theory: Disability as a social construction. *NASPA Journal, 33*, 347–354.

Jones, S. R., & Abes, E. (2013). *Identity development of college students: Advancing frameworks for multiple dimensions of identity.* Hoboken, NJ: Wiley.

Junco, R., & Salter, D. W. (2004). Improving the campus climate for students with disabilities through the use of online training. *NASPA Journal, 41*(2), 263–276.

Kafer, A. (2013). *Feminist, queer, crip.* Bloomington, IL: Indiana University.

Kalivoda, K. S. (2009). Disability realities: Community, culture, and connection on college campuses. In J. L. Higbee & A. A. Mitchell (Eds.), *Making good on the promise: Student affairs professionals with disabilities* (pp. 3–25). Lanham, MD: American College Personnel Association and University Press of America.

Kalivoda, K. S., & Totty, M. C. (2003). Disability services as a resource: Advancing universal design. In J. L. Higbee (Ed.), *Curriculum transformation and disability: Implementing universal design in higher education* (pp. 187–201). Minneapolis, MN: Center for Research on Developmental Education and Urban Literacy, General College, University of Minnesota.

Kalivoda, K. S., Totty, M. C., & Higbee, J. L. (2009). Appendix E: Access to information technology. In J. L. Higbee & A. A. Mitchell (Eds.), *Making good on the promise: Student affairs professionals with disabilities* (pp. 226–232). Lanham, MD: American College Personnel Association and University Press of America.

Kaplin, W. A., & Lee, B. A. (2013). *The law of higher education* (5th ed.). San Francisco, CA: Jossey-Bass.

Kasnitz, D. (2011). *Preliminary report & chartbook: The 2010 biennial AHEAD survey of disability service and resource professionals in higher education.* Huntersville, NC: Association on Higher Education and Disability.

Keith, D. R., Hart, C. L., McNeil, M. P., Silver, R., & Goodwin, R. D. (2015). Frequent marijuana use, binge drinking and mental health problems among undergraduates. *American Journal on Addictions, 24*(6), 499–506.

Kerka, S. (2002). Teaching adults: Is it different? Myths and realities. *Clearinghouse on Adult, Career, and Vocational Education, 21.* Retrieved from http://files.eric.ed.gov/fulltext/ED468614.pdf

Kerschbaum, S. L., Garland-Thompson, R., Oswal, S. K., Vadali, A., Ghiacuic, S., Price, M., … Samuels, E. (2013, December 9). *Faculty members, accommodation, and access in higher education.* Retrieved from http://profession.commons.mla.org/2013/12/09/faculty-members-accommodation-and-access-in-higher-education/

Kezar, A. (2005). Redesigning for collaboration with higher education institutions: An exploration into the developmental process. *Research in Higher Education, 46*(7), 831–860.

Kim, W. H., & Lee, J. (2016). The effect of accommodation on academic performance of college students with disabilities. *Rehabilitation Counseling Bulletin, 60*(1), 40–50. Retrieved from http://doi.org/10.1177/0034355215605259

Kimball, E. W., Wells, R. S., Ostiguy, B. J., Manly, C. A., & Lauterbach, A. A. (2016). Students with disabilities in higher education: A review of the literature and an agenda for future research. In M. B. Paulsen (Ed.), *Higher education: Handbook of theory and research* (vol. 31, pp. 91–156). Cham, Switzerland: Springer International Publishing.

Kinney, D. P., & Kinney, L. S. (2008). Computer-mediated learning in mathematics and universal instructional design. In J. Higbee & E. Goff (Eds.). *Pedagogy and student services for institutional transformation: Implementing universal design in higher education* (pp. 155–163). Minneapolis, MN: Center for Research on Developmental Education and Urban Literacy, College of Education and Human Development, University of Minnesota. Retrieved from http://cehd.umn.edu/passit/docs/PASS-IT-Books.pdf

Koenig, R. (2014, September 30). For bill on disabled access to online teaching materials, the devil's in the details. *Chronicle of Higher Education*. Retrieved from chronicle.com/blogs/wired campus/for-bill-on-disabled-access-to-online-teaching-materials-the-devils-in-the-details/5465/

Koller, R. A. (2000). Sexuality and adolescents with autism. *Sexuality and Disability, 18*(2), 125–135.

Korbel, D. M., McGuire, J. M., Banerjee, M., & Saunders, S. A. (2011). Transition strategies to ensure active student engagement. In M. S. Huger (Ed.), *Fostering the increased integration of students with disabilities* (New Directions for Student Services, no. 134, pp. 35–46). San Francisco, CA: Jossey-Bass.

Kozol, J. (1992). *Savage inequalities: Children in America's schools*. New York, NY: Crown.

Kraus, A. (2008). *The sociopolitical construction of identity: A multidimensional model of disability* (Doctoral dissertation). University of Arizona, Tucson. Retrieved from http://arizona.open repository.com/arizona/bitstream/10150/193722/1/azu_etd_2625_sip1_m.pdf

Krause, M., & Richards, S. (2014). Prevalence of traumatic brain injury and access to services in an undergraduate population: A pilot study. *Brain Injury, 28*(10), 1301–1310.

Kübler-Ross, E., & Kessler, D. (2005). *On grief and grieving: Finding the meaning of grief though the five stages of loss*. New York, NY: Scribner.

Kuchmas et al. v. Towson University et al., No. RDB 06–3281 (D. Md. 2006).

Kudlick, C. J. (2001). The outlook of *The Problem* and the problem with the *Outlook*: Two advocacy journals reinvent blind people in turn-of-the-century America. In P. K. Longmore & L. Umansky (Eds.), *The new disability history: American perspectives* (pp. 187–213). New York: New York University Press.

Kulkarni, M. (2013). Help-seeking behaviors of people with disabilities in the workplace. *Employee Responsibilities and Rights Journal, 25*(1), 41–57. doi:10.1007/s10672-012-9202-x

Kuppers, P., & Wakefield, M. (2009). Disability culture. In S. Burch (Ed.), *Encyclopedia of American disability history* (vol. 1, pp. 269–274). New York, NY: Facts on File.

Kurth, N., & Mellard, D. (2006). Student perceptions of the accommodation process in postsecondary education. *Journal of Postsecondary Education and Disability, 19*(1), 71–84.

Kurzweil. (n.d.). *Kurzweil store*. Retrieved from https://www.kurzweiledu.com/store.php

Ladau, E. (2014). What should you call me? I get to decide: Why I'll never identify with person-first language. In C. Brown (Ed.), *Criptiques* (pp. 47–56). Retrieved from https://criptiques.files .wordpress.com/2014/05/crip-final-2.pdf

Lamm, N. (2015, September 2). *This is disability justice*. Retrieved from http://thebodyisnot anapology.com/magazine/this-is-disability-justice/

Lampros, A. (2011, May 11). *UC Berkeley launches groundbreaking disability research*. Retrieved from http://newscenter.berkeley.edu/2011/05/11/uc-berkeley-launches-groundbreaking-disability-research-initiative/

Landecker, H. (2014, January 9). A deaf linguist explores Black American sign language. *Chronicle of Higher Education*. Retrieved from http://chronicle.com/a-deaf-linguist-explores-black-american-sign-language/33817?cid=at&utm_source+at&utm_medium=en

Lange, K. W., Reichl, S., Lange, K. M., Tucha, L., & Tucha, O. (2010). The history of attention deficit hyperactivity disorder. *ADHD Attention Deficit and Hyperactivity Disorders, 2*(4), 241–255.

Leake, D. (2015). Problematic data on how many students in postsecondary education have a disability. *Journal of Postsecondary Education and Disability* (1), 73–87.

Leake, D. W., & Stodden, R. A. (2014). Higher education and disability: Past and future of underrepresented populations. *Journal of Postsecondary Education and Disability, 27*(4), 399–408.

Lee, B. A., & Abbey, G. E. (2008). College and university students with mental disabilities: Legal and policy issues. *Journal of College and University Law, 34*, 349–392.

Lee, I. H., Rojewski, J. W., Gregg, N., & Jeong, S. O. (2015). Postsecondary education persistence of adolescents with specific learning disabilities or emotional/behavioral disorders. *Journal of Special Education, 49*(2), 77–88.

Leigh, I. W. (2009). *A lens on deaf identities.* New York, NY: Oxford University Press.

Leland and Fair Housing Council of Oregon v. Portland State University, 3:12-cv-00911-SI (Feb. 13, 2014).

Lerner, C. (2004). "Accommodations" for the learning disabled: A level playing field or affirmative action for elites? *Vanderbilt Law Review, 57*, 1041–1122.

Lester, J. N., Dostal, H., & Gabriel, R. (2013). Policing neurodiversity in higher education: A discourse analysis of the talk surrounding accommodations for university students. In C. D. Herrera & A. Perry (Eds.), *Ethics and neurodiversity* (pp. 52–66). Newcastle, England: Cambridge Scholars Press.

Lewin, K. (1935). *A dynamic theory of personality: Selected papers.* New York, NY: McGraw-Hill.

Lewin, K. (1936). *Principles of topological psychology.* New York, NY: McGraw-Hill.

Lewis, J. L. (2011). Student attitudes toward impairment: An assessment of passive and active learning methods in urban planning education. *Teaching in Higher Education, 16*(2), 237–249.

Li, L., & Moore, D. (1998). Acceptance of disability and its correlates. *Journal of Social Psychology, 138*, 13–25.

Lightman, E., Vick, A., Herd, D., & Mitchell, A. (2009). "Not disabled enough": Episodic disabilities and the Ontario Disability Support Program. *Disability Studies Quarterly, 29*(3). Retrieved from http://dsq-sds.org/article/view/932/1108

Lightner, K. L., Kipps-Vaughan, D., Schulte, T., & Trice, A. D. (2012). Reasons university students with a learning disability wait to seek disability services. *Journal of Postsecondary Education and Disability, 25*(2), 145–159.

Lindburg, J. J. (2012). Creating a culture of inclusive leadership: The intersection of student affairs and universal design. *ACPA Developments, 10*(3). Retrieved from www2.myacpa.org/developments/fall-2012/creating-a-culture-of-inclusive-leadership-the-intersection-of-student-affairs-and-universal-design

Lindsay, S. (2010, November). Discrimination and other barriers to employment for teens and adults with disabilities. *Disability and Rehabilitation*, 1–11.

Lindstrom, L. Doren, B., & Miesch, J. (2011). Waging a living: Career development and long-term employment outcomes for young adults with disabilities. *Council for Exceptional Children, 77*(4), 423–434.

Linton, S., Mello, S., & O'Neill, J. (1995). Disability studies: Expanding the parameters of diversity. *Radical Teacher, 47*(Fall), 4–10.

Llewellyn, A., & Hogan, K. (2000). The use and abuse of models of disability. *Disability & Society, 15*(1), 157–165.

Logue, L. M. (2009). Civil War. In S. Burch (Ed.), *Encyclopedia of American disability history* (vol. 1, pp. 181–183). New York, NY: Facts on File.

Loisel, P., Anema, J. R., Feuerstein, M., Pransky, G., MacEachen, E., & Costa-Black, K. M. (2013). Preface. In P. Loisel & J. R. Anema (Eds.), *Handbook of work disability: Prevention and management* (pp. ix–xiii). New York, NY: Springer Science+Business Media.

Loisel, P., & Côté, P. (2013). The work disability paradigm and its public health implications. In P. Loisel & J. R. Anema (Eds.), *Handbook of work disability: Prevention and management* (pp. 59–67). New York, NY: Springer Science+Business Media.

Lombardi, A., Gerdes, H., & Murray, C. (2011). Validating an assessment of individual actions, postsecondary supports, and social supports of college students with disabilities. *Journal of Student Affairs Research and Practice, 48*(1), 107–126.

Lombardi, A. R., Murray, C., & Gerdes, H. (2012). Academic performance of first-generation college students with disabilities. *Journal of College Student Development, 53*(6), 811–826.

Lombardo, P. A. (2008a). Disability, eugenics, and the culture wars. *Saint Louis University Journal of Health Law & Policy, 2*(57), 57–79.

Lombardo, P. A. (2008b). *Three generations, no imbeciles: Eugenics, the Supreme Court, and Buck v. Bell.* Baltimore, MD: John Hopkins University Press.

Longmore, P. K. (2003). *Why I burned my book and other essays on disability.* Philadelphia, PA: Temple University Press.

Longmore, P. K. (2009). Disability rights movement. In S. Burch (Ed.), *Encyclopedia of American disability history* (vol. 1, pp. 280–285). New York, NY: Facts on File.

Longmore, P. K., & Umansky, L. (2001). Disability history: From the margins to the mainstream. In P. K. Longmore & L. Umansky (Eds.), *The new disability history: American perspectives* (pp. 1–29). New York: New York University Press.

Lovett, B. J. (2010). Extended time testing accommodations for students with disabilities: Answers to five fundamental questions. *Review of Educational Research, 80*(4), 611–638.

Lovitts, B. E. (2008). The transition to independence research: Who makes it, who doesn't, and why. *Journal of Higher Education, 79*(3), 296–325.

Lowery, S. E., Kurpius, S. E. R., Befort, C., Blanks, E. H., Sollenberger, S., Nicpon, M. F., & Huser, L. (2005). Body image, self-esteem, and health-related behaviors among male and female first year college students. *Journal of College Student Development, 46*(6), 612–623.

Loy, B. (2015). *Workplace accommodations: Low cost, high impact.* Retrieved from https://askjan.org/media/downloads/LowCostHighImpact.pdf

Lum, L. (2007). Got game. *Diverse Issues in Higher Education, 23*(25), 24–26.

Luna, R. (2014). Accessible technology in student affairs. In M. L. Vance, N. E. Lipsitz, & K. Parks (Eds.), *Beyond the Americans with Disabilities Act: Inclusive policy and practice for higher education* (pp. 51–67). Washington, DC: NASPA-Student Affairs Administrators in Higher Education.

Lundberg, N. R., Taniguchi, S., McCormick, B. P., & Tibbs, C. (2011). Identity negotiating: Redefining stigmatized identities through adaptive sports and recreation participation among individuals with a disability. *Journal of Leisure Research, 43*(2), 205–225.

Lundberg, N. R., Zabriskie, R. B., Smith, K. M., & Barney, K. W. (2008). Using wheelchair sports to complement disability awareness curriculum among college students. *Schole: A Journal of Leisure Studies and Recreation Education, 23,* 61–74

Lutz, B. J., & Bowers, B. J. (2007). Understanding how disability is defined and conceptualized in the literature. In A. E. Dell Orto & P. W. Power (Eds.). *Psychological and social impact of Illness and disability* (5th ed., pp. 11–21). New York, NY: Springer. (Reprinted from *Rehabilitation Nursing, 28,* 74–78, 2003).

MacKinnon, F. J. D., Broido, E. M., & Wilson, M. E. (2004). Issues in student affairs. In F. MacKinnon (Ed.), *Rentz's student affairs practice in higher education* (3rd ed., pp. 387–402). Springfield, IL: Charles C. Thomas.

Madaus, J., Scott, S., & McGuire, J. (2003). *Barriers and bridges to learning as perceived by postsecondary students with learning disabilities* (Rep. No. 01). Storrs: University of Connecticut, Center on Postsecondary Education and Disability.

Madaus, J. W. (2000). Services for college and university students with disabilities: A historical perspective. *Journal of Postsecondary Education and Disability, 14*(1), 4–21.

Madaus, J. W. (2006). Improving the transition to career for college students with learning disabilities: Suggestions from graduates. *Journal of Postsecondary Education and Disability, 19*(1), 85–93.

Madaus, J. W. (2011). The history of disability services in higher education. In W. S. Harbour & J. W. Madaus (Eds.), *Disability services and campus dynamics* (New Directions for Higher Education, no. 154, pp. 5–15). San Francisco, CA: Jossey-Bass.

Madaus, J. W., Grigal, M., & Hughes, C. (2014). Promoting access to postsecondary education for low-income students with disabilities. *Career Development and Transitions for Exceptional Individuals, 37*(1), 50–59.

Madaus, J. W., Miller, W. K., II, & Vance, M. L. (2009). Veterans with disabilities in postsecondary education. *Journal of Postsecondary Education, 22*(1), 10–17.

Madigan, J. C. (2005). The intersection of gender, race, and disability: Latina students in special education. *Multiple Voices for Ethnically Diverse Exceptional Learners, 8*(1), 45–60.

Madriaga, M. (2007). Enduring disablism: Students with dyslexia and their pathways into UK higher education and beyond. *Disability & Society, 22*(4), 399–412.

Mamiseishvili, K., & Koch, L. C. (2011). First-to-second-year persistence of students with disabilities in postsecondary institutions in the United States. *Rehabilitation Counseling Bulletin, 54*(2), 93–105.

Mamiseishvili, K., & Koch, L. C. (2012). Students with disabilities at 2-year institutions in the United States: Factors related to success. *Community College Review, 40*(4), 320–339.

Man, M., Rojahn, J., Chrosniak, L., & Sanford, J. (2006). College students' romantic attraction toward peers with physical disabilities. *Journal of Developmental and Physical Disabilities, 18*(1), 35–44. doi:10.1007/s10882–006–9004-x

Mangan, K. (2013, January 15). Hearing-impaired student's case against medical school may proceed, court rules. *Chronicle of Higher Education.* Retrieved from http://chronicle.com/article/Hearing-Impaired-Students/136681/?cid=at&utm_source=at&utm_medium=en#top

Manus, G. (1975). Is your language disabling? *Journal of Rehabilitation, 41*(5), 35.

Marini, I., Chan, R., Feist, A., & Flores-Torres, L. (2011). Student attitudes toward intimacy with persons who are wheelchair users. *Rehabilitation Education, 25*(1–2), 15–26.

Markoulakis, R., & Kirsh, B. (2013). Difficulties for university students with mental health problems: A critical interpretive synthesis. *Review of Higher Education, 37*(1), 77–100.

Marks, D. (1997). Models of disability. *Disability and Rehabilitation, 19,* 85–91.

Marks, D. (1999). *Disability: Controversial debates and psychosocial perspectives.* London, England: Routledge.

Martin, J. K., Stumbo, N. J., Martin, L. G., Collins, K. D., Hedrick, B. N., Nordstrom, D., & Peterson, M. (2011). Recruitment of students with disabilities: Exploring science, technology, engineering and mathematics. *Journal of Postsecondary Education and Disability, 24*(4), 285–299.

Martinez-Alemán, A. M., Pusser, B., & Bensimon, E. M. (2015) *Critical approaches to the study of higher education: A practical introduction.* Baltimore, MD: Johns Hopkins University Press.

Masala, C., & Petretto, D. R. (2008). From disablement to enablement: Conceptual models of disability in the 20th century. *Disability and Rehabilitation, 30*(17), 1233–1244.

Masinter, M. R. (2015). Justice Department settlement gives new power to campuses over emotional support animals. *Disability Compliance for Higher Education, 21*(5), 6–7.

Massachusetts Department of Public Health. (2009). *The health of lesbian, gay, bisexual and transgender (LGBT) persons in Massachusetts.* Retrieved from http://www.masstpc.org/wp-content/uploads/2012/10/DPH-2009-lgbt-health-report.pdf

Matthews, P. R., Hameister, B. G., & Hosley, N. S. (1998). Attitudes of college students towards study abroad: Implications for disability service providers. *Journal of Postsecondary Education and Disability, 13*(2), 67–77.

Matthews v. NCAA, 179 F. Supp. 2d 1209 (E.D. Wash. 2001).

May, A. L., & Stone, C. A. (2010). Stereotypes of individuals with learning disabilities: Views of college students with and without learning disabilities. *Journal of Learning Disabilities, 43*(6), 483–499.

McBurney (n.d.). *McBurney Center for Disability: Our history.* Retrieved from http://mcburney.wisc .edu/information/history/index.php

McCarthy, H. (2003). The disability rights movement: Experiences and perspectives of selected leaders in the disability community. *Rehabilitation Counseling Bulletin, 46*(4), 209–223.

McCaughey, T. J., & Strohmer, D. C. (2005). Prototypes as an indirect measure of attitudes toward disability groups. *Rehabilitation Counseling Bulletin, 48*(2), 89–99.

McConnell, A. E., Martin, J. E., Juan, C. Y., Hennessey, M. N., Terry, R. A., el-Kazimi, N. A., ... & Willis, D. M. (2013). Identifying nonacademic behaviors associated with post-school employment and education. *Career Development and Transition for Exceptional Individuals, 36*(3), 174–187.

McGregor, K. K., Langenfeld, N., Horne, S., Oleson, J., Anson, M., & Jacobson, W. (2016). The university experiences of students with learning disabilities. *Learning Disabilities Research & Practice, 31*(2), 90–102.

McGuire, J. M., & Scott, S. S. (2002). Universal design for instruction: A promising new paradigm for higher education. *Perspectives, 28*, 27–29.

McGuire, J. M., & Scott, S. S. (2006). Universal design for instruction: Extending the universal design paradigm to college instruction. *Journal of Postsecondary Education and Disability, 19*(2), 124–134.

McGuire, J. M., Scott, S. S., & Shaw, S. F. (2003). Universal design for instruction: The paradigm, its principles, and products for enhancing instructional access. *Journal of Postsecondary Education and Disability, 17*(1), 11–21.

McLean, P., Heagney, M., & Gardner, K. (2003). Going global: The implications for students with a disability. *Higher Education Research and Development, 22*(2), 217–228.

Meade, T., & Serlin, D. (2006, Winter). Editors' introduction. *Radical History Review, 94*, 1–8.

Medina, B. (2011, October 16). Adjunct professors often lack training in how to handle disabilities in the classroom, experts say. *Chronicle of Higher Education.* Retrieved from http://chronicle .com/article/Adjunct-Professors-Often-Lack/129436/

Meekosha, H. (2006). What the hell are you? An intercategorical analysis of race, ethnicity, gender and disability in the Australian body politic. *Scandinavian Journal of Disability Research, 8*(2–3), 161–176.

Meekosha, H., & Shuttleworth, R. (2009). What's so "critical" about critical disability studies? *Australian Journal of Human Rights, 15*(1), 47–75.

Mercer, G. (2002). Emancipatory disability research. In C. Barnes, M. Oliver, & L. Barton (Eds.), *Disability studies today* (pp. 228–249). Malden, MA: Polity Press.

Mershon v. St. Louis University, 442 F.3d 1069 (8th Cir. 2006).

Meyer, A., & Rose, D. H. (2000). Universal design for individual differences. *Educational Leadership, 58*(3), 39–43.

Mezey, S. (2009). Americans with Disabilities Act (1990). In S. Burch (Ed.), *Encyclopedia of American disability history* (vol. 1, pp. 47–50). New York, NY: Facts on File.

Michalko, R. (2002). *The difference that disability makes.* Philadelphia, PA: Temple University Press.

Michigan Paralyzed Veterans of American and the United States v. The University of Michigan and The Regents of the University of Michigan, No. 07–11702 (Eastern District of Michigan. March 10, 2008). Retrieved from http://www.ada.gov/umichstadium.htm

Mikelson, J. D. (2014). Wounded warriors. In M. L. Vance, N. E. Lipsitz, & K. Parks (Eds.), *Beyond the Americans with Disabilities Act: Inclusive policy and practice for higher education* (pp. 85–96). Washington, DC: NASPA-Student Affairs Administrators in Higher Education.

Milani, A. A. (1996). Disabled students in higher education: Administrative and judicial enforcement of disability law. *Journal of College and University Law, 22*(4), 989–1043.

Milchus, K., & Grubbs, R. L. (2007). Work experiences of educators with disabilities. In M. L. Vance (Ed.), *Disabled faculty and staff in a disabling society: Multiple identities in higher education* (pp. 243–252). Huntersville, NC: Association on Higher Education and Disability.

Miller, J. (2011, September). "Design for all people." *Des Moines Register fiftysomething*, pp. 9–10.

Miller, R. A. (2015). "Sometimes you feel invisible": Performing queer/disabled in the university classroom. *Educational Forum, 79*(4), 377–393.

Mills v. Board of Education of District of Columbia, 348 F. Supp. 866 (D.C. 1972).

Minaire, P. (1992). Disease, illness and health: Theoretical models of the disablement process. *Bulletin of the World Health Organization, 70*, 373–379.

Mingus, M. (2011). *Changing the framework: Disability justice. How our communities can move beyond access to wholeness.* Retrieved from https://leavingevidence.wordpress.com/2011/02/12/changing-the-framework-disability-justice/ (Reposted from the November 2010 *RESIST Newsletter*)

Mingus, M. (2014). Reflection toward practice: Some questions on disability justice. In C. Brown (Ed.), *Criptiques* (pp. 107–114). Retrieved from https://criptiques.files.wordpress.com/2014/05/crip-final-2.pdf

Mobility International USA. (2016a). *Statistics: International students who use disability services report satisfaction.* Retrieved from http://www.miusa.org/resource/tipsheet/international studentstats

Mobility International USA. (2016b). *Coming to the U.S.A.* Retrieved from http://www.miusa.org/plan/coming-to-usa

Monroe, A. (2006). Non-traditional transfer student attrition. *Community College Enterprise, 12*(2), 33–54.

Moos, R. H. (1976). *The human context: Environmental determinants of behavior.* New York, NY: Wiley.

Moran, R. E. (2012, July 12). *Better federal coordination could lessen challenges in the transition from high school (GAO-12-594).* Retrieved from http://www.gao.gov/products/GAO-12-594

Morgan, J. J., Mancl, D. B., Kaffar, B. J., & Ferreira, D. (2011). Creating safe environments for students with disabilities who identify as lesbian, gay, bisexual, or transgender. *Intervention in School and Clinic, 47*(1), 1–11.

Moriarty, M. (2007). Inclusive pedagogy: Teaching methodologies to reach diverse learners in science instruction. *Equity & Excellence in Education, 40*(3), 252–265.

Moya, P. M. L. (2000). Introduction. In P. M. L. Moya & M. R. Hames-García (Eds.), *Reclaiming identity: Realist theory and the predicament of postmodernism* (pp. 1–26). Berkeley, CA: University of California.

Muccigrosso, L., Scavarda, M., Simpson-Brown, R., & Thalacker, B. E. (1991). *Double jeopardy: Pregnant and parenting youth in special education.* Reston, VA: Council for Exceptional Children.

Murphy, M. P. (2011). *Military veterans and college success: A qualitative examination of veteran needs in higher education.* Retrieved from https://libres.uncg.edu/ir/uncg/f/Murphy_uncg_0154D_10816.pdf

Murphy v. United Parcel Service, 527 U.S. 516 (1999).

Murray, C., Flannery, B. K., & Wren, C. (2008). University staff members' attitudes and knowledge about learning disabilities and disability support services. *Journal of Postsecondary Education and Disability, 21*(2), 73–90.

Murray, C., Lombardi, A., & Kosty, D. (2014). Profiling adjustment among postsecondary students with disabilities: A person-centered approach. *Journal of Diversity in Higher Education, 7*(1), 31–44.

Murray, C., Lombardi, A., Wren, C. T., & Keys, C. (2009). Associations between prior disability-focused training and disability-related attitudes and perceptions among university faculty. *Learning Disability Quarterly, 32,* 87–102.

Murray, C., Wren, C. T., & Keys, C. (2008). University faculty perceptions of students with learning disabilities: Correlates and group differences. *Learning Disability Quarterly, 31,* 95–113.

Murray, P. (1988). The study of the history of disability services: Examining the past to improve the present and the future. *Australia and New Zealand Journal of Developmental Disabilities, 14*(2), 93–102.

Myers, K. A., & Bastian, J. J. (2010). Understanding communication preferences of college students with visual disabilities. *Journal of College Student Development, 51*(3), 265–278.

NAAFA. (n.d.). *Healthy at every size.* Retrieved from http://www.naafaonline.com/dev2/education/haes.html

Nagi, S. Z. (1965). Some conceptual issues in disability and rehabilitation. In M. B. Sussman (Ed.), *Sociology and rehabilitation* (pp. 100–113). Washington, DC: American Sociological Association.

Nario-Redmond, M. R., Noel, J. G., & Fern, E. (2013). Redefining disability, re-imagining the self: Disability identification predicts self-esteem and strategic responses to stigma. *Self and Identity, 12*(5), 1–21. doi:10.1080/15298868.2012.681118

National Association of the Deaf. (2010). *Score for accessibility: OSU to provide in-stadium captions.* Retrieved from http://nad.org/news/2010/11/score-accessibility-osu-provide-stadium-captions

National Association of the Deaf. (2015a, December 8). *Judgment entered against college in discrimination case filed by nursing student who is hard of hearing.* Retrieved from https://nad.org/blogs/12/08/2015/judgment-entered-against-college-discrimination-case

National Association of the Deaf. (2015b). *NAD sues Harvard and MIT for discrimination in public online content.* Retrieved from http://nad.org/news/2015/2/nad-sues-harvard-and-mit-discrimination-public-online-content

National Association to Advance Fat Acceptance. (n.d.). *About us.* Retrieved from http://www.naafaonline.com/dev2/about/index.html

National Center for Education Statistics. (2015). *Digest of education statistics, 2013* (NCES 2015–011). Retrieved from https://nces.ed.gov/fastfacts/display.asp?id=60

National Center for Education Statistics. (2016a). *Characteristics of postsecondary students.* Retrieved from: http://nces.ed.gov/programs/coe/indicator_csb.asp

National Center for Education Statistics. (2016b). *Fast facts: Students with disabilities.* Retrieved from https://nces.ed.gov/fastfacts/display.asp?id=60

National Collegiate Athletic Association. (2015). *NCAA sports medicine handbook.* Retrieved from http://www.ncaapublications.com/productdownloads/MD15.pdf

National Council on Disability. (2015). *Breaking the school-to-prison pipeline for students with disabilities.* Retrieved from https://www.ncd.gov/publications/2015/06182015

National Federation of the Blind. (2010, November 11). *Penn State discriminates against blind student and faculty.* Retrieved from http://www.nfb.org?nfb/NewsBot.asp?MODE=VIEW&ID=702

National Institute on Drug Abuse. (2010). *Is drug addiction a mental illness?* Retrieved from http://www.drugabuse.gov/publications/research-reports/comorbidity-addiction-other-mental-illnesses/drug-addiction-mental-illness

National Science Foundation. (2010). *Doctorate recipients from U.S. universities: 2009.* Retrieved from www.nsf.gov/statistics/nst11306/nsf11306.pdf

National Science Foundation, National Center for Science and Engineering Statistics. (2015). *Women, minorities, and persons with disabilities in science and engineering: 2015* (Report NSF 15–311). Arlington, VA. Retrieved from http://www.nsf.gov/statistics/wmpd/

Newman, L., Wagner, M., Cameto, R., & Knokey, A. M. (2009). *The post-high school outcomes of youth with disabilities up to 4 years after high school. A report from the National Longitudinal Transition Study-2 (NLTS-2).* Prepared for the U.S. Department of Education (NCSER2009–3017). Retrieved from http://www.nlts2.org/reports/2009_04/nlts2_report_2009_04_complete.pdf

Newman, L., Wagner, M., Cameto, R., Knokey, A. M., & Shaver, D. (2010). *Comparisons across time of the outcomes of youth with disabilities up to 4 years after high school. A report of findings from the National Longitudinal Transition Study (NLTS) and the National Longitudinal Transition Study-2 (NLTS-2).* Prepared for the U.S. Department of Education (NCSER2010–3008). Retrieved from http://www.nlts2.org/reports/2010_09/nlts2_report_2010_09_complete.pdf

Newman, L., Wagner, M., Knokey, A.-M., Marder, C., Nagle, K., Shaver, D., ... Schwarting, M. (2011). *The post–high school outcomes of youth with disabilities up to 8 years after high school. A report from the National Longitudinal Transition Study-2 (NLTS-2).* (NCSER 2011–3005). Menlo Park, CA: SRI International. Retrieved from http://files.eric.ed.gov/fulltext/ED524044.pdf

Nichols, A. H., & Quaye, S. J. (2009). Beyond accommodation: Removing barriers to academic and social engagement for students with disabilities. In S. R. Harper & S. J. Quaye (Eds.), *Student engagement in higher education: Theoretical perspectives and practical approaches for diverse populations* (pp. 39–60). New York, NY: Routledge.

Nielsen, K. (2012). *A disability history of the United States.* Boston, MA: Beacon Press.

Nocella, A. J., Jr. (2009). Disabling dis-ability: Re-building inclusive into social justice. *Theory in Action, 2*(1), 140–157. doi:10.3798/tia.1937–0237.08033

Noonan, B. M., Gallor, S. M., Henseler-McGinnis, N. F., Fassinger, R. E., Wang, S., & Goodman, J. (2004). Challenge and success: A qualitative study of the career development of highly achieving women with physical and sensory disabilities. *Journal of Counseling Psychology, 51*(1), 68–80.

North Dakota State University Women with Disabilities Task Force. (2012). *Faculty with disabilities survey results.* Retrieved from https://www.ndsu.edu/fileadmin/forward/documents/Faculty_with_Disabilities_Survey_March_2012.pdf

Norton, S. M. (1997). Examination accommodations for community college students with learning disabilities: How are they viewed by faculty and students? *Community College Journal of Research and Practice, 21*(1), 57–69.

Notalone.gov. (2015). *Sample language for interim and supportive measures to protect students following an allegation of sexual misconduct.* Retrieved from https://www.notalone.gov/assets/interim-and-supportive-measures.pdf

Office for Civil Rights. (2003). *Letter to Glendale Community College* (No. 09–02–2148). Retrieved from AHEAD Members Wiley OCR Database. Retrieved from http://ahead.wiley.com:8080/ahead/home

Office for Civil Rights. (2005). *Letter to Michigan State* (No. 15–04–2046). Retrieved from AHEAD Members Wiley OCR Database. Retrieved from http://ahead.wiley.com:8080/ahead/home

Office for Civil Rights. (2006a). *Letter to Loyola University Chicago* (No. 05–05–2139). Retrieved From AHEAD Members Wiley OCR Database. Retrieved from http://ahead.wiley.com:8080/ahead/home

Office for Civil Rights. (2006b). *Letter to University of Wisconsin-Milwaukee* (No. 05–06–2090). Retrieved from AHEAD Members Wiley OCR Database. Retrieved from http://ahead.wiley.com:8080/ahead/home

Office for Civil Rights. (2007). *Letter to Platt College* (No. 09–06–2113). Retrieved from AHEAD Members Wiley OCR Database. Retrieved from http://ahead.wiley.com:8080/ahead/home

Office for Civil Rights. (2009). *Letter to Doane College* (No. 07–09–2063). Retrieved from AHEAD Members Wiley OCR Database. Retrieved from http://ahead.wiley.com:8080/ahead/home

Office for Civil Rights. (2010). *Joint "Dear Colleague" letter: Electronic book readers* (No. 07–09–2063). Retrieved from http://www2.ed.gov/about/offices/list/ocr/letters/colleague-20100629.html

Office for Civil Rights. (2011a). *Letter to Case Western Reserve University* (No. 15–11–2024). Retrieved from AHEAD Members Wiley OCR Database. Retrieved from http://ahead.wiley.com:8080/ahead/home

Office for Civil Rights. (2011b). *Letter to Farmingdale State College* (No. 02–10–2176). Retrieved from AHEAD Members Wiley OCR Database. Retrieved from http://ahead.wiley.com:8080/ahead/home

Office for Civil Rights. (2011c). *Letter to University of Michigan–Dearborn* (No. 15–10–2105). Retrieved from AHEAD Members Wiley OCR Database. Retrieved from http://ahead.wiley.com:8080/ahead/home

Office for Civil Rights. (2013a). *Dear colleague letter: Students with disabilities in extracurricular athletics.* Retrieved from http://www2.ed.gov/about/offices/list/ocr/letters/colleague-201301-504.pdf

Office for Civil Rights. (2013b). *Letter to Ivy Tech Community College* (No. 05–13–2408). Retrieved from http://www2.ed.gov/about/offices/list/ocr/docs/investigations/more/05132408-a.pdf

Office for Civil Rights. (2013c). *Letter to South Carolina Technical College System* (No. 11–11–6002). Retrieved from http://www2.ed.gov/about/offices/list/ocr/docs/investigations/11116002-b.pdf

Office for Civil Rights. (n.d.). *Recent resolutions.* Retrieved from http://www2.ed.gov/about/offices/list/ocr/docs/investigations/index.html

Ofiesh, N., Rice, C., Long, E., Merchant, D., & Gajar, A. (2002). Service delivery for postsecondary students with disabilities: A survey of assistive technology use across disabilities. *College Student Journal, 36*(1), 94–109.

Oguntoyinbo, L. (2012, November 1). *Few schools offer extra services to those with learning disabilities.* Retrieved from http://diverseeducation.com/article/49200/Ohio Mechanics Institute. (n.d.). *Ohio mechanics institute.* Retrieved from www.ohiohistorycentral.org/w/Ohio_Mechanics_Institute?rec=782

Oliver, M. (1990). *The politics of disablement.* London, England: Macmillan.

Oliver, M. (1992). Changing the social relations of research production? *Disability, Handicap & Society, 7*(2), 101–114.

Oliver, M. (1996). Defining impairment and disability: Issues at stake. In C. Barnes & G. Mercer (Eds.), *Exploring the divide: Illness and disability* (pp. 29–54). Leeds, England: Disability Press.

Oliver, M. (2004). If I had a hammer: The social model in action. In J. Swain, S. French, C. Barnes, & C. Thomas (Eds.), *Disabling barriers—Enabling environments* (2nd ed., pp. 7–12). London, England: Sage.

Oliver, M. (2013). The social model of disability: Thirty years on. *Disability & Society, 28*(7), 1024–1026.

Olkin, R. (1999). *What psychotherapists should know about disability.* New York, NY: Guilford Press.

Olkin, R. (2011a). Academic leaders with disabilities: How do we know if we are winning when no one is keeping score? In J. L. Martin (Ed.), *Women as leaders in education: Succeeding despite inequity, discrimination, and other challenges* (pp. 201–217). Santa Barbara, CA: ABC-CLIO.

Olkin, R. (2011b). Disability: A primer for therapists. In E. M. Altmaier & J.-I. C. Hansen (Eds.), *The Oxford handbook of counseling psychology* (pp. 460–479). New York, NY: Oxford University Press.

Olkin, R. (2012). Disability: A primer for therapists. In E. M. Altmaier & J.-I. C. Hansen (Eds.), *The Oxford handbook of counseling psychology* (pp. 460–479). New York, NY: Oxford University Press. Retrieved from http://www.oxfordhandbooks.com/view/10.1093/oxfordhb/9780195342314.001.0001/oxfordhb-9780195342314 (Original work published 2011)

O'Neil, M. O. (2013, November 15). Bill would require instructional technology to be accessible to all. *Chronicle of Higher Education.* Retrieved from chronicle.com/blogs/wiredcampus/bill-would-require-instructional-technology-to-be-accessible-to-all/48383?cid=pm&utm_source=pm&utm_medium=en

Orbe, M. P. (2004). Negotiating multiple identities within multiple frames: An analysis of first-generation college students. *Communication Education, 53*(2), 131–149.

Orosco, M. J., & O'Connor, R. (2013). Culturally responsive instruction for English language learners with learning disabilities. *Journal of Learning Disabilities, 47*(6), 515–531.

Orr, A. C., & Hammig, S. B. (2009). Inclusive postsecondary strategies for teaching students with learning disabilities: A review of the literature. *Learning Disability Quarterly, 32,* 181–196.

Ostiguy, B. J., Peters, M. L., & Shlasko, D. (2016). Ableism. In M. Adams & L. A. Bell (Eds.), *Teaching for diversity and social justice* (3rd ed., pp. 299–337). New York, NY: Routledge.

O'Toole, C. J. (2004). The sexist inheritance of the disability movement. In B. G. Smith & B. Hutchison (Eds.), *Gendering disability* (pp. 294–300). New Brunswick, NJ: Rutgers University Press.

Ouellett, M. L. (2004). Faculty development and universal instructional design. *Equity & Excellence in Education, 37*(2), 135–144.

Padden, C. A., & Humphries, T. L. (1990). *Deaf in America.* Cambridge, MA: Harvard University Press.

Padgett, R. D., Johnson, M. P., & Pascarella, E. T. (2012). First-generation undergraduate students and the impacts of the first year of college: Additional evidence. *Journal of College Student Development, 53*(2), 243–266.

Pahulu v. University of Kansas, 897 F. Supp. 1387 (D. Kan. 1995).

Palomba, C. A., & Banta, T. W. (1999). *Assessment essentials: Planning, implementing, and improving assessment in higher education.* San Francisco, CA: Jossey-Bass.

Palombi, B. J. (2010). Disability: Multiple and intersecting identities: Developing multicultural competencies. In E. Cornish, B. Schreier, L. Nadkarni, L. Metzger, & E. Rodolfa (Eds.), *Handbook of multicultural counseling competencies* (pp. 55–92). Hoboken, NJ: Wiley.

Palombi, B. J., & Mundt, A. M. (2006). Achieving social justice for college women with disabilities. In R. Toporek (Ed.), *Handbook for social justice in counseling psychology: Leadership, vision and action* (pp. 170–184). Thousand Oaks, CA: Sage.

Pardo, P., & Tomlinson, D. (1999). *Implementing academic accommodations in field/practicum settings.* Unpublished manuscript, Disability Resource Center, University of Calgary, Calgary, Canada. Retrieved from https://www.mtroyal.ca/cs/groups/public/documents/pdf/implementing_accommodations.pdf

Parry, M. (2010a, June 29). Inaccessible e-readers may run afoul of the law, feds warn colleges. *Chronicle of Higher Education.* Retrieved from http://chronicle.com/blogs/wiredcampus/inaccesssible-e-readers-may-run-afoul-of-the-law-feds-warn-colleges/25191

Parry, M. (2010b, August 12). College web pages are "widely inaccessible" to people with disabilities. *Chronicle of Higher Education*. Retrieved from http://chronicle.com/blogs/wiredcampus/college-web-pages-are-widely-inaccessible-to-people-with-disabilities/26188

Parry, M. (2010c, November 12). ADA compliance is a "major vulnerability" for online programs. *Chronicle of Higher Education*. Retrieved from http://chronicle.com/blogs/wiredcampus/ada-compliance-a-major-vulnerability-for-online-programs/28136

Parry, M. (2010d, November 12). Penn State accused of discriminating against blind students. *Chronicle of Higher Education*. Retrieved from http://chronicle.com/blogs/wiredcampus/penn-state-accused-of-discriminating-against-blind-students/28154

Parry, M. (2010e, December 12). Colleges lock out blind students online. *Chronicle of Higher Education*. Retrieved from http://chronicle.com/article/Blind-Students-Demand-Access/125695/

Parry, M. (2011, October 11). QuickWire: Advocates for the blind resolve tech-accessibility dispute with Penn State. *Chronicle of Higher Education*. Retrieved from http://chronicle.com?blogs/wiredcampus/quickwire-advocates-for-the-blind-resolve-tech-accessibility-dispute-with-penn-state

Parsons, T. (1951). *The social system*. London, England: Routledge and Kegan Paul.

Pascarella, E. T., & Terenzini, P. T. (2005). *How college affects students: A third decade of research* (2nd ed.). San Francisco, CA: Jossey-Bass.

Patterson, L. (2009). Residential schools. In S. Burch (Ed.), *Encyclopedia of American disability history* (vol. 3, pp. 778–780). New York, NY: Facts on File.

Patton, L. D., Renn, K. A., Guido, F. M., & Quaye, S. J. (2016). *Student development in college: Theory, research, and practice* (3rd ed.). San Francisco, CA: Jossey-Bass.

Paul, S. (2000). Students with disabilities in higher education: A review of the literature. *College Student Journal, 34*(2), 200–211.

Paulsen, P., French, R., & Sherrill, C. (1991). Comparison of mood states of college able-bodied and wheelchair basketball players. *Perceptual and Motor Skills, 73*, 396–398.

Pelka, F. (2012). *What we have done: An oral history of the disability rights movement*. Amherst, MA: University of Massachusetts Press.

Peña, E. V. (2014). Marginalization of published scholarship on students with disabilities in higher education journals. *Journal of College Student Development, 55*, 30–40.

Peña, E. V., Stapleton, L. D., & Schaffer, L. M. (2016). Critical perspectives on disability identity. In E. S. Abes (Ed.), *Critical perspectives on student development theory* (New Directions for Student Services, no. 154, pp. 85–96.) San Francisco, CA: Jossey-Bass.

Peña, M., Thomas, P., Owen, L., Altman Bruno, B., Urvater, C., Howell, D. & Howell, P. (2016). *Size diversity in higher education*. Foster City, CA: National Association to Advance Fat Acceptance.

Pennsylvania Association for Retarded Children (PARC) v. Commonwealth of Pennsylvania, 343 F. Supp. 279 (E.D. Pa. 1972).

Pepnet2: Deaf and hard of hearing. (n.d.). *Mission*. Retrieved from http://www.pepnet.org/about-us/mission

Pernick, M. S. (2009). Eugenics. In S. Burch (Ed.), *Encyclopedia of American disability history* (vol. 1, pp. 333–335). New York, NY: Facts on File.

Pfeiffer, D. (2007). The disability paradigm. In A. E. Dell Orto & P. W. Power (Eds.), *Psychological and social impact of illness and disability* (5th ed., pp. 7–10). New York, NY: Springer. (Reprinted from *Journal of Disability Policy Studies, 11,* 98–99, 2000)

Pilgrim, D. (2014). Some implications of critical realism for mental health research. *Social Theory and Health, 12*(1), 1–21.

Pinder-Amaker, S. (2014). Identifying the unmet needs of college students on the autism spectrum. *Harvard Review of Psychiatry, 22*(2), 125–137.

Pingry O'Neill, L. N., Markward, M. J., & French, J. P. (2012). Predictors of graduation among college students with disabilities. *Journal of Postsecondary Education and Disability, 25*(1), 21–36.

Pliner, S. M., & Johnson, J. R. (2004). Historical, theoretical, and foundational principles of universal instructional design in higher education. *Equity & Excellence in Education, 37*(2), 105–113.

Ponticelli, J. E., & Russ-Eft, D. (2009). Community college students with disabilities and transfer to a four-year college. *Exceptionality, 17*(3), 164–176.

Pope, J. (2013, September 16). *New college options for students with disabilities.* Retrieved from http://diverseeducation.com/article/56019/?utm_campaign=Diverse

Porth, C. M. (2009). Concepts of health and disease. In C. M. Porth & G. Matfin (Eds.), *Pathophysiology: Concepts of altered health states* (8th ed., pp. 2–9). Philadelphia, PA: Wolters Kluwer Health/Lippincott Williams & Wilkins.

Potter, C. (2014, August 2). Do attendance policies discriminate against disability? *Chronicle of Higher Education.* Retrieved from http://chronicle.com/blognetwork/tenuredradical/2014/08/do-attendance-policies-discriminate-against-disability/

Potts, T., & Price, J. (1995). Out of the blood and spirit of our lives: The place of the body in academic feminism (pp. 102–115). In L. Morley & V. Walsh (Eds.), *Feminist academics: Creative agents for change.* London, England: Taylor and Francis.

Price, M. (2011). *Mad at school: Rhetorics on mental disability and academic life.* Ann Arbor, MI: University of Michigan.

Price, M. (2013, January). *Disclosure, crip time, policy, and stigma: A report on a study in progress.* Paper presented at the meeting of the Modern Language Association, Boston, MA. Retrieved from https://margaretprice.wordpress.com/presentations/

Proulx, G. (2002). *Evacuation planning for occupants with disability.* Ottawa: Fire Risk Management Program, Institute for Research in Construction, National Research Council Canada.

Pryal, K. R. G. (2014a, June 13). Disclosure blues: Should you tell colleagues about your mental illness? *Chronicle of Higher Education.* Retrieved from https://chroniclevitae.com/news/546-disclosure-blues-should-you-tell-colleagues-about-your-mental-illness

Pryal, K. R. G. (2014b, September 26). I'm not brave. *Chronicle of Higher Education.* Retrieved from https://chroniclevitae.com/news/722-i-m-not-brave

Puhl, R. M., & King, K. M. (2013). Weight discrimination and bullying. *Best Practice & Research Clinical Endocrinology & Metabolism, 27*(2), 117–127.

Purdie-Vaughns, V., & Eibach, R. P. (2008). Intersectional invisibility: The distinctive advantages and disadvantages of multiple subordinate-group identities. *Sex Roles, 59*(1), 377–391.

Pushkin v. Regents of the University of Colorado (10th Cir. 1981).

Putnam, M. (2005). Conceptualizing disability: Developing a framework for political disability identity. *Journal of Disability Policy Studies, 16*(3), 188–198.

Quick, D., Lehmann, J., & Deniston, T. (2003). Opening doors for students with disabilities on community college campuses: What have we learned? What do we still need to know? *Community College Journal of Research and Practice, 27*(9–10), 815–827.

Quinones v. University of Puerto Rico, et al., No. 14–1331, 2015 WL 631327, 2015 U.S. Dist. LEXIS 18319, 31 Am. Disabilities Case. (BNA) 471 (D.P.R. Feb. 13, 2015).

Rankin & Associates Consulting. (2012a). *Services.* Retrieved from www.rankin-consulting.com/services

Rankin & Associates Consulting. (2012b). *Staff.* Retrieved from www.rankin-consulting.com/staff

Rankin, S. R. (2003). *Campus climate for sexual minorities: A national perspective.* New York, NY: National Gay and Lesbian Task Force Policy Institute.

Rankin, S. R., & Reason, R. D. (2008). Transformational Tapestry Model: A comprehensive approach to transforming campus climate. *Journal of Diversity in Higher Education, 1*(4), 262–274. doi:10.1037/a0014018

Raue, K., & Lewis, L. (2011). *Students with disabilities at degree-granting postsecondary institutions* (NCES 2011–018). U.S. Department of Education, National Center for Education Statistics. Washington, DC: U.S. Government Printing Office.

Rauscher, L., & McClintock, M. (1997). Ableism curriculum design. In M. Adams, L. A. Bell, & P. Griffin (Eds.), *Teaching for diversity and social justice: A sourcebook* (pp. 198–229). New York, NY: Routledge.

Reid, D. K., & Knight, M. G. (2006). Disability justifies exclusion of minority students: A critical history grounded in disability studies. *Educational Researcher, 35*(6), 18–23.

Reinschmiedt, H. J., Sprong, M. E., Dallas, B., Buono, F. D., & Upton, T. D. (2013). Post-secondary students with disabilities receiving accommodations: A survey of satisfaction and subjective well-being. *Journal of Rehabilitation, 79*(3), 3–10.

Renn, K. A., & Arnold, K. D. (2003). Reconceptualizing research on peer culture. *Journal of Higher Education, 74*, 261–291.

Repetto, J. B., Jaress, J., Lindsey, J., & Bae, J. (2016). Investigation of health care components in transition IEPs. *Career Development and Transition for Exceptional Individuals, 39*(1), 4–11.

Riccobono, M. A. (2014, September 3). *Unachievable or unwanted: Why is ACE opposed to accessibility guidelines?* Retrieved from National Federation of the Blind website: https://nfb.org?blog/vonb-blog/unachievable-or-unwanted-why-ace-opposed-accessibility-guidelines

Richards, J. C., & Rogers, T. S. (2001). *Approaches and methods in language teaching: A description and analysis* (2nd ed.). Cambridge, England: Cambridge University Press.

Riddell, S., Baron, S., & Wilson, A. (2001). The significance of the learning society for women and men with learning disabilities. *Gender and Education, 13*(1), 57–73.

Ritchie, M. (2013). *Advising international students with disabilities.* Retrieved from http://www.nafsa.org/uploadedFiles/Chez_NAFSA/Find_Resources/Publications/Periodicals/Epublications/Advising%20Internlt%20Students%20w%20Disabilities.pdf

Roach, R. (2013). U.S. international education enrollment reaches all-time high. *Diverse Issues in Higher Education, 30*(23), 3.

Roberts, K. D., & Stodden, R. (2014). Research synthesis on assistive technology usage by people with learning disabilities and difficulties. *Review of Disability Studies: An International Journal, 1*(2). Retrieved from http://www.rds.hawaii.edu/ojs/index.php/journal/article/view/388

Robertson, S. M., & Ne'eman, A. D. (2008). Autistic acceptance, the college campus, and technology: Growth of neurodiversity in society and academia. *Disability Studies Quarterly, 28*(4). Retrieved from http://dsq-sds.org/article/view/146/146

Rocco, T. S., & Delgado, A. (2011). Shifting lenses: A critical examination of disability in adult education. In T. S. Rocco (Ed.), *Challenging ableism, understanding disability: Including adults with disabilities in workplace and learning spaces* (New Directions for Adult and Continuing Education, no. 132, pp. 3–12). San Francisco, CA: Jossey-Bass.

Rodas, J. M. (2016). Here there be monsters: Teaching disability studies at CUNY's Bronx Community College. *Transformations: The Journal of Inclusive Scholarship and Pedagogy, 25*(2), 189–198.

Roessler, R. T., Hennessey, M. L., Hogan, E. M., & Savickas, S. (2009). Career assessment and planning strategies for postsecondary students with disabilities. *Journal of Postsecondary Education and Disability, 21*(3), 126–137.

Roessler, R. T., Hurley, J. E., & McMahon, B. T. (2010). A comparison of allegations and reso- lutions involving issues of discharge versus constructive discharge: Implications for diversity management. *Advances in Developing Human Resources, 12*(4), 407–428.

Roessler, R. T., & Kirk, H. M. (1998). Improving technology training services in postsecondary education: Perspectives of recent college graduates with disabilities. *Journal of Postsecondary Education and Disability, 13*(3), 48–59.

Rojahn, J., Komelasky, K. G., & Man, M. (2008). Implicit attitudes and explicit ratings of romantic attraction of college students toward opposite-sex peers with physical disabilities. *Journal of Developmental and Physical Disabilities, 20*, 389–397. doi:10.1007/s10882-008-9108-6

Rolland, J. S. (1994). *Families, illness, and disability: An integrative treatment model.* New York, NY: Basic Books.

Rose, D. (with Meyer, A.). (2000). Universal design for learning. *Journal of Special Education Tech- nology, 15*(1), 67–70.

Rose, D. H., Harbour, W. S., Johnston, C. S., Daley, S. G., & Abarbanell, L. (2006). Universal design for learning in postsecondary education: Reflections on principles and their application. *Jour- nal of Postsecondary Education and Disability, 19*(2), 135–151.

Rose, D. H., & Meyer, A. (2002). *Teaching every student in the digital age: Universal design for learning.* Alexandria, VA: Association for Supervision and Curriculum Development.

Rose, S. F. (2012). The right to a college education? The GI Bill, Public Law 16, and disabled veterans. *Journal of Policy History, 24*(1), 26–52.

Ross-Gordon, J. M. (2011). Research on adult learners: Supporting the needs of a student popu- lation that is no longer nontraditional. *Peer Review, 13*(1), 26–29.

Rothblum, E. D., & Solovay, S. (Eds.). (2009). *The fat studies reader.* New York: New York University Press.

Rothstein, L. (2004). Disability law and higher education: A road map for where we've been and where we may be heading. *Maryland Law Review, 163*(1), 122–163.

Roufs, K. S. (2012, October 8). Let's break the silence on hearing loss. *Chronicle of Higher Education.* Retrieved from: http://chronicle.com/article/Lets-Break-the-Silence-on/134888/

Rousso, H. (2003). *Education for all: A gender and disability perspective.* Background paper pre- pared for the Education for All Global Monitoring Report 2003/2004, *The leap to equality.* Paris, France: Global Monitoring Report. Retrieved from http://unesdoc.unesco.org/images/0014/001469/146931ec.pdf

Rowland, J. L., White, G. W., Fox, M. H., & Rooney, C. (2007). Emergency response training prac- tices for people with disabilities: Analysis of some current practices and recommendations for future training programs. *Journal of Disability Policy Studies, 17*(4), 216–222.

Ruffins, P. (2011, May 5). Engineering universal access for learning. *Diverse Education.* Retrieved from http://diverseeducation.com/cache/print.php?articleId=15489

Rumann, C. B., & Hamrick, F. A. (2009). Supporting student veterans. In R. Ackerman & D. DiRamio (Eds.), *Creating a veteran-friendly campus: Strategies for transition success* (New Directions for Student Services, no. 126, pp. 25–34). San Francisco, CA: Jossey-Bass.

Rutgers University. (2012, October 23). *Rutgers study: For college students with disabilities, success linked to mentoring, self-advocacy and perseverance.* Retrieved from http://diverseeducation.com/article/48992/

Ryan, D., & McCarthy, M. (1994a). *A student affairs guide to the ADA and disability issues.* Washington, DC: National Association of Student Personnel Administrators.

Ryan, D., & McCarthy, M. (1994b). Introduction. In D. Ryan & M. McCarthy (Eds.), *A student affairs guide to the ADA and disability issues* (pp. vii-xi). Washington, DC: National Association of Student Personnel Administrators.

Sable, M. R., Danis, F., Mauzy, D. L., & Gallagher, S. K. (2006). Barriers to reporting sexual assault for women and men: Perspectives of college students. *Journal of American College Health, 55*(3), 157–162.

Safransky, R. J. (n.d.). Civil Rights Restoration Act of 1987. *Law and Higher Education.* Retrieved from http://lawhigheredu.com/31-civil-rights-restoration-act-of-1987.html

Saguy, A. C. (2013). *What's wrong with fat?* New York, NY: Oxford University Press.

Sahlen, C., & Lehmann, J. (2006). Requesting accommodations in higher education. *Teaching Exceptional Children, 38*(3), 28–34.

Saks, E. (2009, November 25). Mental illness in academe. *Chronicle of Higher Education.* Retrieved from http://chronicle.com/article/Mental-Illness-in-Academe/49233/?cid=vem

Salmen, J. P. S. (2011). Universal design for academic facilities. In W. S. Harbour & J. W. Madaus (Eds.), *Disability services and campus dynamics* (New Directions for Student Services, no. 134, pp. 13–20). San Francisco, CA: Jossey-Bass. doi:10.1002/ss.391

Salzberg, C. L., Peterson, L., Debrand, C. C., Blair, R. J., Carsey, A. C., & Johnson, A. S. (2002). Opinions of disability service directors on faculty training: The need, content, issues, formats, media, and activities. *Journal of Postsecondary Education and Disability, 15*(2), 101–114.

Samuels, E. J. (2003). My body, my closet: Invisible disability and the limits of coming-out discourse. *GLQ: A Journal of Lesbian and Gay Studies, 9*(1), 233–255.

Sanchez, N. F., Sanchez, J. P., & Danoff, A. (2009). Health care utilization, barriers to care, and hormone usage among male-to-female transgender persons in New York City. *American Journal of Public Health, 99*(4), 713–719.

Sanders, K. Y. (2006). Overprotection and lowered expectations of persons with disabilities: The unforeseen consequences. *Work, 27*(2), 181–188.

Sanford, C., Newman, L., Wagner, M., Cameto, R., Knokey, A., & Shaver, D. (2011). *The post-high school outcomes of young adults with disabilities up to 6 years after high school. Key findings from the National Longitudinal Transition Study-2 (NLTS2)* (NCSER 2011–3004). Menlo Park, CA: SRI International. Retrieved from http://ies.ed.gov/ncser/pubs/20113004/pdf/20113004.pdf

Santuzzi, A. M., Waltz, P. R., Finkelstein, L. M., & Rupp, D. E. (2014). Invisible disabilities: Unique challenges for employees and organizations. *Industrial and Organizational Psychology, 7*(2), 204–219.

Scambler, G., & Scambler, S. (2010). Introduction: The sociology of chronic and disabling conditions: Assaults on the lifeworld. In G. Scambler & S. J. Scambler (Eds.), *New directions in the sociology of chronic and disabling condition* (pp. 1–7). New York, NY: Palgrave Macmillan.

Scherer, H. L., Snyder, J. A., & Fisher, B. S. (2013). A gendered approach to understanding intimate partner victimization and mental health outcomes among college students with and without disability. *Women & Criminal Justice, 23*(3), 209–231.

Schriner, K., & Ochs, L. A. (2001). Creating the disabled citizen: How Massachusetts disenfranchised people under guardianship. *Ohio State Law Journal, 62*, 481–533.

Schur, L. (1998). Disability and the psychology of political participation. *Journal of Disability Policy Studies, 9*, 4–31.

Schur, L., Nishii, L., Adya, M., Kruse, D., Bruyère, S. M., & Blanck, P. (2014). Accommodating employees with and without disabilities. *Human Resource Management, 53*(4), 593–621.

Schwarz, R., & Terrill, L. (2000). *ESL instruction and adults with learning disabilities.* Washington, DC: Center for Applied Linguistics. Retrieved from http://www.cal.org/caela/esl_resources/digests/LD2.html

Schweik, S. M. (2009). *The ugly laws: Disability in public.* New York: New York University Press.

Scotch, R. K. (1988). Disability as the basis for a social movement: Advocacy and the politics of definition. *Journal of Social Issues, 44*(1), 159–172.

Scotch, R. K. (2001a). American disability policy in the twentieth century. In P. K. Longmore & L. Umansky (Eds.), *The new disability history: American perspectives* (pp. 375–392). New York: New York University Press.

Scotch, R. K. (2001b). *From good will to civil rights: Transforming federal disability policy* (2nd ed.). Philadelphia, PA: Temple University Press.

Scotch, R. K. (2009). Models of disability and the Americans with Disabilities Act. In R. M. Baird, S. E. Rosenbaum, & S. K. Toombs (Eds.), *Disability: The social, political, and ethical debate* (pp. 171–184). Amherst, NY: Prometheus. (Reprinted from *Berkeley Journal of Employment and Labor Law, 21*(1), 213–222, 2000).

Scott, S. S., McGuire, J. M., & Shaw, S. F. (2003). Universal design for instruction: A new paradigm for adult instruction in postsecondary education. *Remedial and Special Education, 24*, 369–379. doi:10.1177/07419325030240060801

Seale, J. (2004). The development of accessibility practices in e-learning: An exploration of communities of practices. *Research in Learning Technology, 12*(1), 51–63.

Seale, J. K. (2006). *E-learning and disability in higher education: Accessibility research and practice.* New York, NY: Routledge.

Section 504 of the Rehabilitation Act of 1973, 29 U.S.C. sec. 794. Retrieved from www.dol.gov/oasam/regs/statutes/sec504.htm

Shackelford, A. L. (2009). Documenting the needs of student veterans with disabilities: Intersection roadblocks, solutions, and legal realities. *Journal of Postsecondary Education and Disability, 22*(1), 36–42.

Shakespeare, T. (1994). Cultural representation of disabled people: Dustbins for disavowal? *Disability & Society, 9*(3), 283–301.

Shakespeare, T. (1996). Disability, identity, and difference. In C. Barnes & G. Mercer (Eds.), *Exploring the divide*. Leeds, England: Disability Press.

Shakespeare, T. (2006a). The social model of disability. In L. J. Davis (Ed.), *The disability studies reader* (2nd ed., pp. 197–204). New York, NY: Routledge.

Shakespeare, T. (2006b). *Disability rights and wrongs*. New York, NY: Routledge.

Shakespeare, T. (2014). *Disability rights and wrongs revisited* (2nd ed.). New York, NY: Routledge.

Shakespeare, T., & Watson, N. (1997). Defending the social model. *Disability & Society, 12*(2), 293–300.

Shannon, C. D., Schoen, B., & Tansey, T. N. (2009). The effect of contact, context, and social power on undergraduate attitudes toward persons with disabilities. *Journal of Rehabilitation, 75*(4), 11–18.

Shapiro, J. P. (1993). *No pity: People with disabilities forging a new civil rights movement*. New York, NY: Three Rivers Press.

Sharpe, M. N., Johnson, D. R., Izzo, M., & Murray, A. (2005). An analysis of instructional accommodations and assistive technologies used by postsecondary graduates with disabilities. *Journal of Vocational Rehabilitation, 22*(1), 3–11.

Shaw, R. A. (2011). Employing universal design for instruction. In M. S. Huger (Ed.), *Fostering the increased integration of students with disabilities* (New Directions for Student Services, no. 134, pp. 21–33). San Francisco, CA: Jossey-Bass. doi:10.1002/ss.392

Shaw, S. F. (2012). Disability documentation: Using all the data. *Journal of Postsecondary Education and Disability, 25*(4), 277–282. Retrieved from http://files.eric.ed.gov/fulltext/EJ1002152.pdf

Shepler, D. K., & Woosley, S. A. (2012). Understanding the early integration experiences of college students with disabilities. *Journal of Postsecondary Education and Disability, 25*(1), 37–50.

Sherry, M. (2007). (Post)colonizing disability. *Wagadu: Journal of Transnational Women's and Gender Studies, 4,* 10–22.

Shifrer, D. (2013). Stigma of a label: Educational expectations for high school students labeled with learning disabilities. *Journal of Health and Social Behavior, 54*(4), 462–480.

Shifrer, D., Callahan, R. M., & Muller, C. (2013). Equity or marginalization? The high school course-taking of students labeled with a learning disability. *American Educational Research Journal, 50*(4), 656–682.

Shigaki, C. L., Anderson, K. M., Howald, C. L., Henson, L., & Gregg, B. E. (2012). Disability on campus: A perspective from faculty and staff. *Work: A Journal of Prevention, Assessment & Rehabilitation, 42*(4), 559–571.

Shildrick, M. (2009). *Dangerous discourses of disability, subjectivity and sexuality.* Basingstoke, NY: Palgrave Macmillan.

Shildrick, M. (2012). Critical disability studies: Rethinking the conventions for the age of postmodernity. In N. Watson, A. Roulstone, & C. Thomas (Eds.), *Routledge handbook of disability studies* (pp. 30–41). London, England: Routledge.

Shlaes, J. L., Jason, L. A., & Ferrari, J. R. (1999). The development of the Chronic Fatigue Syndrome Attitudes Test: A psychometric analysis. *Evaluation & the Health Professions, 22*(4), 442–465. doi:10.1177/01632789922034400

Shmulsky, S. (2013, August 5). *New certificate offers educators edge on creating learning environments.* Retrieved from www.landmark.edu/news/new-certificate-offers-educators-edge-on-creating-learning-environments-whe

Shulman, D. (2002). Diagnosing learning disabilities in community college culturally and linguistically diverse students. *Journal of Postsecondary Education and Disability, 16*(1), 17–31.

Siebers, T. (2008). *Disability theory.* Ann Arbor, MI: University of Michigan Press.

Siebers, T. (2015). Disability trouble. In N. J. Hirschmann & B. Linker (Eds.). *Civil disabilities: Citizenship, membership, and belonging* (pp. 223–235). Philadelphia, PA: University of Pennsylvania.

Silver, P., Bourke, A. B., & Strehorn, K. C. (1998). Universal instructional design in higher education: An approach for inclusion. *Equity & Excellence in Education, 31*(2), 47–51.

Simon, J. A. (2000). Legal issues in serving students with disabilities in postsecondary education. In H. A. Belch (Ed.), *Serving students with disabilities* (New Directions for Student Services, no. 91, pp. 69–81). San Francisco, CA: Jossey-Bass.

Simon, J. A. (2011). Legal issues in serving students with disabilities in postsecondary education. In M. S. Huger (Ed.), *Fostering the increased integration of students with disabilities* (New Directions for Student Services, no. 134, pp. 95–107). San Francisco, CA: Jossey-Bass.

Skinner, M. E. (2007). Faculty willingness to provide accommodations and course alternatives to postsecondary students with learning disabilities. *International Journal of Special Education, 22*(2), 32–45.

Slone, M. B. (2007). Navigating the academy when your ship is thrown off course: The effects of multiple sclerosis on one college professor. In M. L. Vance (Ed.), *Disabled faculty and staff in a disabling society: Multiple identities in higher education* (pp. 269–271). Huntersville, NC: Association on Higher Education and Disability.

Smart, J. F., & Smart, D. W. (2006). Models of disability: Implications for the counseling profession. *Journal of Counseling & Development, 84,* 29–40.

Smith, D. L. (2008). Disability, gender and intimate partner violence: Relationships from the behavioral risk factor surveillance system. *Sexuality and Disability, 26*(1), 15–28.

Smith, S. R. (2009). Social justice and disability: Competing interpretations of the medical and social models. In K. Kristiansen, S. Vehmas, & T. Shakespeare (Eds.), *Arguing about disability: Philosophical perspectives* (pp. 15–29). New York, NY: Routledge.

Smith-Chandler, N., & Swart, E. (2014). In their own voices: Methodological considerations in narrative disability research. *Qualitative Health Research, 24*(3), 420–430.

Sniatecki, J. L., Perry, H. B., & Snell, L. H. (2015). Faculty attitudes and knowledge regarding college students with disabilities. *Journal of Postsecondary Education and Disability, 28*(3), 259–275.

Solovay, S. (2000). *Tipping the scales of justice: Fighting weight based discrimination.* Amherst, NY: Prometheus Books.

Soneson, H. M., & Cordano, R. J. (2009). Universal design and study abroad: (Re-)designing programs for effectiveness and access. *Frontiers: The Interdisciplinary Journal of Study Abroad, 18*(1), 269–288.

Soneson, H. M., & Fisher, S. (2011). Education abroad for students with disabilities: Expanding access. In M. S. Huger (Ed.), *Fostering the increased integration of students with disabilities* (New Directions for Student Services, no. 134, pp. 59–72). San Francisco, CA: Jossey-Bass.

Southeastern University Community College v. Davis, 442 U.S. 397 (1979).

Spade, D. (2011). *Normal life: Administrative violence, critical trans politics and the limits of the law.* Brooklyn, NY: South End Press.

Spencer, B., Barrett, C., Storti, G., & Cole, M. (2013). "Only girls who want fat legs take the elevator": Body image in single-sex and mixed-sex colleges. *Sex Roles, 69*(7–8), 469–479.

Springer, M. (2014). Accessible recreational and athletic opportunities. In M. L. Vance, N. E. Lipsitz, & K. Parks (Eds.), *Beyond the Americans with Disabilities Act: Inclusive policy and practice for higher education* (pp. 155–158). Washington, DC: NASPA-Student Affairs Administrators in Higher Education.

S. Rep. No. 93–318, at 70 (1973).

Stapleton, L. (2015). When being Deaf is centered: d/Deaf women of color's experiences with racial/ethnic and d/Deaf identities in college. *Journal of College Student Development, 56*(6), 570–586.

Stapleton, L., Peña, E. V., Brown, K. R., Stygles K., Broido, E. M., & Rankin, S. R. (2014, November). *Researching disability in higher education: Emerging perspectives.* Paper presented at the Association of the Study of Higher Education Conference, Washington, DC.

Staskowski, M., Hardin, S., Klein, M., & Wozniak, C. (2013). Universal Design for Learning: Speech-language pathologists and their teams making the Common Core curriculum accessible. *Seminars in Speech and Language, 33*(2), 111–129.

Stevens, B. (2012). Examining emerging strategies to prevent sexual violence: Tailoring to the needs of women with intellectual and developmental disabilities. *Journal of Mental Health Research in Intellectual Disabilities, 5*(2), 168–186.

Stevens, C. E. (2011). *Fat on campus: Students' experiences of sizist discrimination on college campus.* (Master's thesis). Ohio University, Athens, Ohio. Retrieved from https://etd.ohiolink.edu/!etd .send_file?accession=ohiou1312580170&disposition=inline

Stiker, H.-J. (1999). *A history of disability* (W. Sayers, Trans.). Ann Arbor, MI: University of Michigan Press.

Stodden, R. A., Brown, S. E., & Roberts, K. (2011). Disability-friendly university environments: Conducting a climate assessment. In W. S. Harbour & J. W. Madaus (Eds.), *Disability services and campus dynamics* (New Directions for Higher Education, no. 154, pp. 83–92). San Francisco, CA: Jossey-Bass.

Stover, M. (2010). These scales tell us that there is something wrong with you: How fat students are systemically denied access to fair and equal education and what we can do to stop this. *Southern California Law Review, 83,* 933–983.

Strahl v. Purdue University, 4:07-cv-61-AS (Dis. Court. Northern District. IN. 2009).

Strange, C. (2000). Creating environments of ability. In H. A. Belch (Ed.), *Serving students with disabilities* (New Directions for Student Services, no. 91, pp. 19–30). San Francisco, CA: Jossey-Bass.

Strange, C. C., & Banning, J. H. (2001). *Education by design: Creating campus learning environments that work.* San Francisco, CA: Jossey-Bass.

Stratford, M. (2014, September 19). Higher ed associations, disability rights groups clash over campus technology standards. *Inside Higher Ed.* Retrieved from https://www.insidehighered.com/news/2014/09/19/higher-ed-associations-disability-rights-groups-clash-over-campus-technology

Straus, J. N. (2011). *Extraordinary measures: Disability in music.* New York, NY: Oxford University Press.

Strauss, R. (1965). Social change and the rehabilitation concept. In M. B. Sussman (Ed.), *Sociology and rehabilitation* (pp. 1–34). Washington, DC: American Sociological Association.

Street, C. D., Koff, R., Fields, H., Kuehne, L., Handlin, L., Getty, M., & Parker, D. R. (2012). Expanding access to STEM for at-risk learners: A new application of universal design for instruction. *Journal of Postsecondary Education and Disability, 25*(4), 363–375.

Stuart, S. P. (2012). Hope and despondence: Emerging adulthood and higher education's relationship with its nonviolent mentally ill students. *Journal of College and University Law, 38,* 319–380.

Sullivan, M. M. (2005). Teaching mathematics to college students with mathematics-related learning disabilities: Report from the classroom. *Learning Disability Quarterly, 28*(3), 205–220.

Summers v. Altarum Institute Corp., No. 13–1645 (4th Cir. Jan. 23, 2014).

Susman, J. (1994). Disability, stigma and deviance. *Social Science & Medicine, 38*(1), 15–22. doi:10.1016/0277-9536(94)90295-X

Sutton v. United Airlines, 527 U.S. 471 (1999).

Szasz, T. (2002). The myth of mental illness. Retrieved from psychclassics.yorku.ca/Szasz/myth.htm (Reprinted from *American Psychologist, 15,* 113–118, 1960)

Tajfel, H. (1972). Social categorization. English manuscript of "La categorisation sociale." In S. Moscovici (Ed.), *Introduction a la Psychologie Sociale* (vol. 1, pp. 272–302). Paris, France: Larousse.

Taormina-Weiss, W. (2013). In pursuit of disability justice. Retrieved from www.disabled-world.com/editorials/justice.php

Test, D. W., Fowler, C. H., Wood, W. M., Brewer, D. M., & Eddy, S. (2005). A conceptual framework of self-advocacy for students with disabilities. *Remedial and Special Education, 26*(1), 43–54.

Thelin, J. R. (2004). *A history of American higher education.* Baltimore, MD: John Hopkins University Press.

Thelin, J. R. (2011). *A history of American higher education* (2nd ed.). Baltimore, MD: Johns Hopkins University Press.

Thomas, C. (1999). *Female forms: Experiencing and understanding female disability.* Buckingham, England: Open University Press.

Thomas, C. (2004). Disability and impairment. In J. Swain, S. French, C. Barnes, & C. Thomas (Eds.), *Disabling barriers—Enabling environments* (2nd ed., pp. 21–27). London, England: Sage.

Thomas, S. B. (2000). College students and disability law. *Journal of Special Education, 33,* 248–257.

Thomason, A. (2014a, June 27). Iowa court orders chiropractic college to accommodate blind students. *Chronicle of Higher Education.* Retrieved from http://chronicle.com/blogs/ticker/iowa-court-orders-chiropractic-college-to-accommodate-blind-students/80773?cid=pm&utm_source=pm&utm_medium=en

Thomason, A. (2014b, October 8). Education Dept. will make loan data more accessible to the blind. *Chronicle of Higher Education*. Retrieved from http://chronicle.com/blogs/ticker/education-dept-will-make-loan-data-more-accessible-to-the-blind/87677

Thompson, M. V. (2012). Creating a culture of inclusion: Shifting the disability frame. *ACPA Developments, 10*(1). Retrieved from http://www2.myacpa.org/developments/spring-2012/creating-a-culture-of-inclusion-the-disability-frame/2306

Thorne, S., McCormick, J., & Carty, E. (2009). Deconstructing the gender neutrality of chronic illness and disability. *Health Care for Women International, 18*(1), 1–16.

Thousand, J. S., Villa, R. A., & Nevin, A. I. (2010). The many faces of collaborative planning and teaching. *Theory Into Practice, 45*(3), 239–248.

Tidwell, R. (2004). The "invisible" faculty member: The university professor with a hearing disability. *Higher Education, 47*(2), 197–210.

Titchkosky, T. (2007). *Reading and writing disability differently: The textured life of embodiment*. Toronto, Ontario, Canada: University of Toronto Press.

Titchkosky, T. (2011). *The question of access: Disability, space, meaning*. Toronto, Ontario, Canada: University of Toronto Press.

Toth v. Slippery Rock University of Pennsylvania, Pa. Comm. 6A. 3d 1082 (2010).

Toyota Motor Manufacturing v. Williams, 584 U.S. 184 (2002).

Trainor, A., Murray, A., & Kim, H. (2016). English learners with disabilities in high school: Population characteristics, transition programs, and postschool outcomes. *Remedial and Special Education, 37*(3), 146–158.

Trammell, J. (2009). Postsecondary students and disability stigma: Development of the Postsecondary Student Survey of Disability-Related Stigma (PSSDS). *Journal of Postsecondary Education and Disability, 22*(2), 106–116.

Travers, J. C., Tincani, M., & Krezmien, M. P. (2013). A multiyear national profile of racial disparity in autism identification. *Journal of Special Education, 47*(1), 41–49.

Tregaskis, C. (2002). Social model theory: The story so far. *Disability and Society, 17*, 457–470.

Trent, J. W. (2009). Asylums and institutions. In S. Burch (Ed.), *Encyclopedia of American disability history* (vol. 1, pp. 72–74). New York, NY: Facts on File.

Tudge, J., Gray, J. T., & Hogan, D. M. (1997). Ecological perspectives in human development: A comparison of Gibson and Bronfenbrenner. In J. Tudge, M. Shanahan, & J. Valsiner (Eds.), *Comparisons in human development: Understanding time and context* (pp.72–105). New York, NY: Cambridge University Press.

Turner, D. (2010, June 30). Colleges instructed to make blind-friendly gadgets available to students. *Diverse Education*. Retrieved from http://diverseeducation.com/cache/print.php?articleID=13923

Underhile, R., & Cowles, J. R. (1998). Gay, lesbian, bisexual, and transgender students with disabilities: Implications for faculty and staff. In R. L. Sanlow (Ed.), *Working with lesbian, gay, bisexual, and transgender college students: A handbook for faculty and administrators* (pp. 171–177). Westport, CT: Greenwood Press.

Union of the Physically Impaired Against Segregation. (1976). *Fundamental principles of disability*. London, England: Author.

United Nations. (2008, May 5). Landmark UN treaty on rights of persons with disabilities enters into force. *Scoop Independent News*. Retrieved from www.scoop.co.nz/stories/WO0805/S00048.htm

United Nations General Assembly. (2007). *Convention on the Rights of Persons with Disabilities*. Retrieved from http://www.un.org/disabilities/default.asp?id=261

United States v. University of Nebraska, No. 4:11-CV-3209, 2013 (D. Neb. Apr. 19, 2013).

University of California, Office of the President (2014). *Campus climate study.* Retrieved from http://campusclimate.ucop.edu/index.html

University of Michigan, Services for Students with Disabilities (n.d.). *Register: Mobility impairment.* Retrieved from https://ssd.umich.edu/article/register-mobility-impairment

University of Minnesota Disability Resource Center. (n.d.). *Employee services.* Retrieved from https://diversity.umn.edu/disability/employeeservices

University of Washington. (2015). *Example policies in higher education.* Retrieved from www.washington.edu/accessibility/requirements/example-policies/

University of Washington DO-IT (Disabilities, Opportunities, Internetworking, and Technology) Program. (2014). *How are the terms deaf, deafened, hard of hearing, and hearing impaired typically used?* Retrieved from http://www.washington.edu/doit/Faculty/articles?86

Upcraft, M. L., & Schuh, J. H. (1996). *Assessment in student affairs: A guide for practitioners.* San Francisco, CA: Jossey-Bass.

U.S. Access Board. (2002). *Americans with Disabilities Act accessibility guidelines.* Retrieved from https://www.access-board.gov/guidelines-and-standards/buildings-and-sites/about-the-ada-standards/background/adaag

U.S. Attorney's Office, Northern District of California. (2013, January 23). *U.S. Attorney's Office reaches settlement with Mills College over compliance with Americans with Disabilities Act.* Retrieved from www.justice.gov/usao/can/news/2013/2013_01_23_millscollege.agreement.press.html

U.S. Bureau of Labor Statistics. (2015). *Persons with a disability: Labor force characteristics—2014.* (USDL-15–1162). Retrieved from http://www.bls.gov/news.release/pdf/disabl.pdf

U.S. Commission on Civil Rights (2000, October). *Sharing the dream: Is the ADA accommodating all?* Washington, DC: Author. Retrieved from www.usccr.gov/pubs/ada/main.htm

U.S. Const. art. VI, § 2.

U.S. Department of Education. (1995). *The civil rights of students with hidden disabilities under Section 504 of the Rehabilitation Act of 1973.* Retrieved from http://www2.ed.gov/about/offices/list/ocr/docs/hq5269.html

U.S. Department of Education. (2008). *So you want to go back to school.* Washington, DC: U.S. Government Printing Office. Retrieved from http://www.ed.gov/about/offices/list/ocr/letters/back-to-school-2008.html

U.S. Department of Education. (2015). *Nondiscrimination on the basis of handicap in programs or activities receiving federal financial assistance.* 34 C.F.R § 104.11. Retrieved from https://www2.ed.gov/policy/rights/reg/ocr/edlite-34cfr104.html

U.S. Department of Education. (2016). Federal TRIO programs [Home page]. Retrieved from http://www2.ed.gov/about/offices/list/ope/trio/index.html

U.S. Department of Housing and Urban Development. (2011, February). *Memo: New ADA regulations and assistance animals as reasonable accommodations under the Fair Housing Act and Section 504 of the Rehabilitation Act of 1973.* Retrieved from http://www.bazelon.org/LinkClick.aspx?fileticket=lhyaA_hRAoE=

U.S. Department of Justice. (1998). *Consent Decree, the United States of America v. National Collegiate Athletic Association,* No. 98–1290 (D.D.C. May 27, 1998). Retrieved from http://www.ada.gov/ncaa.htm#anchor369197

U.S. Department of Justice. (2013a). *Questions and answers about the Lesley University agreement and potential implications for individuals with food allergies.* Retrieved from http://www.ada.gov/q&a_lesley_university.htm

U.S. Department of Justice. (2013b). *Settlement agreement: United States Federal Government and Louisiana Tech University.* Retrieved from http://www.ada.gov/louisiana-tech.htm

U.S. Department of Justice. (2013c). *Settlement agreement: United States Federal Government and Mills College.* Retrieved from http://www.ada.gov/mills_college_sa/mills-college.htm

U.S. Department of Justice. (2014a). *Dear colleague letter: Effective communication.* Retrieved from http://www2.ed.gov/about/offices/list/ocr/letters/colleague-effective-communication-2014 11.pdf

U.S. Department of Justice. (2014b). *Effective communication.* Retrieved from http://www.ada.gov/ effective-comm.htm

U.S. Department of Justice. (2014c). *Frequently asked questions on effective communication for students with hearing, vision, or speech disabilities in public elementary and secondary schools.* Retrieved from http://www2.ed.gov/about/offices/list/ocr/docs/dcl-faqs-effective-communication-201411.pdf

U.S. Department of Justice. (2014d). *Law School Admission Council agrees to systemic reforms and $7.73 million payment to settle justice department's nationwide disability discrimination lawsuit.* Retrieved from http://www.justice.gov/opa/pr/law-school-admission-council-agrees-systemic-reforms-and-773-million-payment-settle-justice

U.S. Department of Justice. (2016). *Consent Decree, The United States of America and Dudley v. Miami University,* No. 1:14-cv-38 (D.D.C. October 17, 2016). Retrieved from https://www .ada.gov/miami_university_cd.html

U.S. Department of Justice v. The University of Nebraska at Kearney and the Board of Regents of University of Nebraska, No 4:11CV3209 (U.S. District Court for the District of Nebraska, September, 3, 2015). Retrieved from http://www.justice.gov/opa/file/767276/download

U.S. Equal Employment Opportunity Commission. (2009). *Americans with Disabilities Act: Questions and answers.* Retrieved from http://www.ada.gov/q&aeng02.htm

U.S. Equal Employment Opportunity Commission. (2011a). *The Americans With Disabilities Act: Applying performance and conduct standards to employees with disabilities.* Retrieved from https://www.eeoc.gov/facts/performance-conduct.html

U.S. Equal Employment Opportunity Commission. (2011b). *Resources for Human Development settles EEOC disability suit for $125,000.* Retrieved from https://www.eeoc.gov/eeoc/newsroom/ release/4–10–12a.cfm

U.S. Government Accountability Office. (2010, June). *Students with disabilities: More information and guidance could improve opportunity in physical education and athletics.* (Report No. GAO-10–519). Retrieved from http://www.gao.gov/assets/310/305770.pdf

U.S. Government Accountability Office. (2012, July). *Students with disabilities: Better federal coordination could lessen challenges in the transition from high school* (GAO-12–594). Retrieved from http://www.gao.gov/products/GAO-12–594

ushistory.org (2016). Economic growth and the early industrial revolution. *U.S. history online textbook.* Retrieved from http://www.ushistory.org/us/22a.asp

U.S. Social Security Administration. (n.d.). *Disability evaluation under Social Security: Listing of impairments—Adult listings (Part A).* Retrieved from http://www.ssa.gov/disability/profes sionals/bluebook/AdultListings.htm

Vaccaro, A., Daly-Cano, M., & Newman, B. (2015). A sense of belonging among college students with disabilities: An emergent theoretical model. *Journal of College Student Development, 56*(7), 670–686.

Vaccaro, A., Kimball, E. W., Wells, R. S., & Ostiguy, B. J. (2015). Researching students with disabilities: The importance of critical perspectives. In R. S. Wells & F. K. Stage (Eds.), *New scholarship in critical quantitative research—Part 2: New populations, approaches, and challenges* (New Directions for Institutional Research, no. 163, pp. 25–41). San Francisco, CA: Jossey-Bass.

Vance, M. L. (Ed.). (2007). *Disabled faculty and staff in a disabling society: Multiple identities in higher education.* Huntersville, NC: Association on Higher Education and Disability.

Vance, M. L., & Miller, W. K. (2009). Serving wounded warriors: Current practices in postsecondary education. *Journal of Postsecondary Education and Disability, 22*(1), 18–35.

Van Cleve, J. V. (2009). Communication debates. In S. Burch (Ed.), *Encyclopedia of American disability history* (vol. 1, pp. 203–204). New York, NY: Facts on File.

Van Hees, V., Moyson, T., & Roeyers, H. (2015). Higher education experiences of students with autism spectrum disorder: Challenges, benefits and support needs. *Journal of Autism and Developmental Disorders, 45*, 1673–1688.

Variawa, C., & McCahan, S. (2010). Universal design of engineering education. *Proceedings of the Canadian Engineering Education Association.* Retrieved from http://ojs.library.queensu.ca/index.php/PCEEA/article/viewFile/3146/3084

Vernon, A. (1998). Multiple oppression and the disabled people movement. In T. Shakespeare (Ed.), *The disability reader: Social science perspectives* (pp. 201–210). London, England: Cassell.

Vernon, A., & Swain, J. (2002). Theorizing divisions and hierarchies: Towards a commonality or diversity? In C. Barnes, M. Oliver, & L. Barton (Eds.), *Disability studies today* (pp. 77–97). Bodmin, Cornwall, England: MPG Books.

Vinson v. Thomas, 288 F.3d 1145 (9th Cir. 2002).

Vogel, S. A., Holt, J. K., Sligar, S., & Leake, E. (2008). Assessment of campus climate to enhance student success. *Journal of Postsecondary Education and Disability, 21*(1), 15–31.

Vogel, S. A., Leyser, Y., Burgstahler, S. E., Sligar, S., & Zecker, S. (2006). Faculty knowledge and practices regarding students with disabilities in three contrasting institutions of higher education. *Journal of Postsecondary Education and Disability, 18*, 109–123.

Wagner, M., Newman, L., Cameto, R., Garza, N., & Levine, P. (2005). *After high school: A first look at the postschool experiences of youth with disabilities.* Menlo Park, CA: SRI International. Retrieved from http://www.nlts2.org/reports/2005_04/nlts2_report_2005_04_complete.pdf

Waldron, J. J., & Dieser, R. B. (2010). Perspectives of fitness and health in college men and women. *Journal of College Student Development, 51*(1), 65–78.

Walker, N. (2013, August 16). *Throw away the master's tools: Liberating ourselves from the pathology paradigm.* Retrieved from http://neurocosmopolitanism.com/throw-away-the-masters-tools-liberating-ourselves-from-the-pathology-paradigm/

Walker, N. (2014, September 27). *Neurocosmopolitansm: Nick Walker's notes on neurodiversity, autism, and cognitive liberty.* Retrieved from http://neurocosmopolitanism.com/neurodiversity-some-basic-terms-definitions/

Ward, M. J. (2009). A personal perspective on historical views of disability. In C. E. Drum, G. L. Krahn, & H. Bersani (Eds.), *Disability and public health* (pp. 45–64). Washington, DC: American Public Health Association.

Warder, G. (2014). Horace Mann and the creation of the common school. *Disability History Museum.* Retrieved from http://www.disabilitymuseum.org/dhm/edu/essay.html?id=42

Warner, T. D., Dede, D. E., Garvan, C. W., & Conway, T. W. (2002). One size still does not fit all in specific learning disability assessment across ethnic groups. *Journal of Learning Disabilities, 35*(6), 500–508.

Webb, J. B., Fiery, M. F., & Jafari, N. (2016). "You better not leave me shaming!": Conditional indirect effect analyses of anti-fat attitudes, body shame, and fat talk as a function of self-compassion in college women. *Body Image, 18*, 5–13.

Weber, M. C. (1995). Disability discrimination by state and local government: The relationship between Section 504 of the Rehabilitation Act and Title II of the Americans with Disabilities Act. *William and Mary Law Review, 36*(3), 1089.

Wei, X., Wagner, M., Hudson, L., Jennifer, W. Y., & Javitz, H. (2015, April). The effect of transition planning participation and goal-setting on college enrollment among youth with autism spectrum disorders. *Remedial and Special Education, 1–12.* doi:10.1177/0741932515581495

Weick, K. E. (1979). *The social psychology of organizing* (2nd ed.). New York, NY: McGraw-Hill.

Wessel, R. D., Jones, D., Blanch, C. L., & Markle, L. (2015). Pre-enrollment considerations of undergraduate wheelchair users and their post-enrollment transitions. *Journal of Postsecondary Education and Disability, 28*(1), 57–71.

Wessel, R. D., Jones, J. A., Markle, L., & Westfall, C. (2009). Retention and graduation of students with disabilities: Facilitating student success. *Journal of Postsecondary Education and Disability, 21*(3), 116–125.

Wessel, R. D., Wentz, J., & Markle, L. L. (2011). Power soccer: Experiences of students using power wheelchairs in a collegiate athletic club. *Journal of Postsecondary Education and Disability, 24*(2), 147–159.

Wheelchair & Ambulatory Sports, USA. (n.d.). *University adapted athletics programs.* Retrieved from http://www.wasusa.org/universitiescolleges.htm

Whetzel, M. A., & Goddard, T. M. (2010). *Accommodating educators with disabilities.* Retrieved from https://askjan.org/media/downloads/Educators.docW

White, S. W., Ollendick, T. H., & Bray, B. C. (2011). College students on the autism spectrum: Prevalence and associated problems. *Autism, 15,* 683–701. doi:1362361310393363

White v. University of South Carolina-Columbia, 93 F. Supp. Ed 1293 (S. Carolina 1996).

Wilhelm, S. (2003). Accommodating mental disabilities in higher education: A practical guide to ADA requirements. *Journal of Law & Education, 32*(2), 217–237.

Wilson, B. G., Ludwig-Hardman, S., Thornam, C. I., & Dunlap, J. C. (2004). Bounded community: Designing and facilitating learning communities in formal courses. *International Review of Research in Open and Distance Learning, 5*(3), 2–22.

Wilson, K., Getzel, E., & Brown, T. (2000). Enhancing the post-secondary campus climate for students with disabilities. *Journal of Vocational Rehabilitation, 14,* 37–50.

Williams, C. R. (2008). Compassion, suffering and the self: A moral psychology of social Justice. *Current Sociology, 56*(1), 5–24. doi:10.1177/0011392107084376

Williams, G. (2010, December 13). Universal design, usability, and accessibility. *Chronicle of Higher Education.* Retrieved from http://chronicle.com/blogs/profhacker/universal-design-usability-andaccessibility/29501

Williams, J. B. (2010). *College and university administrators with disabilities: Experiences in the workplace* (Unpublished doctoral dissertation). Colorado State University, Fort Collins, CO.

Williams, S. J. (1999). Is anybody there? Critical realism, chronic illness, and the disability debate. *Sociology of Health and Illness, 21*(6), 797–819.

Winter, B. (2016, July 14). Accessible book treaty ratified. *Perkins School for the Blind Email Update.* Retrieved from http://www.perkins.org/stories/news/accessible-book-treaty-ratified?utm_campaign=infocus%20july2016&utm_source=in%20focus&utm_medium=email

Winter, J. A. (2003). The development of the disability rights movement as a social problem solver. *Disability Studies Quarterly, 23*(1), 33–58. Retrieved from www.cds.hawaii.edu/dsq

Wisbey, M. E., & Kalivoda, K. S. (2008). Residential living for all: Fully accessible and "liveable" on-campus housing. In J. L. Higbee & E. Goff (Eds.), *Pedagogy and student services for institutional transformation: Implementing universal design in higher education* (pp. 255–266). Minneapolis, MN:

Center for Research on Developmental Education and Urban Literacy, College of Education and Human Development, University of Minnesota. Retrieved from http://conservancy.umn.edu/handle/11299/5356

Wise Tiedemann, C. (2012). *College success for students with physical disabilities.* Waco, TX: Prufrock.

Wolf, L. E., & Brown, J. T. (2014). Fostering success for students with hidden disabilities. In M. L. Vance, N. E. Lipsitz, & K. Parks (Eds.), *Beyond the Americans with Disabilities Act: Inclusive policy and practice for higher education* (pp. 111–126). Washington, DC: NASPA-Student Affairs Administrators in Higher Education.

Wolf, L. E., Brown, J. T., & Bork, G. R. (2009) *Students with Asperger Syndrome: A guide for college personnel.* Shawnee Mission, KS: Autism Asperger.

Wolf, L. E., Simkowitz, P., & Carlson, H. (2009). College students with attention-deficit/hyperactivity disorder. *Current Psychiatry Reports, 11*(5), 415–421. doi:10.1007/s11920–009–0062–5

Wong v. Regents of University of California, No. 98–15757, 1999 U.S. App. (9th Cir. Sept. 16, 1999).

Wong v. Regents of University of California, 410 F.3d 1052 (9th Cir. June 7, 2005).

Wood, D. (2012). *Veterans' college drop-out rate soars.* Retrieved from http://www.huffingtonpost.com/2012/10/25/veterans-college-drop-out_n_2016926.html

Woodcock, K., Rohan, M. J., & Campbell, L. (2007). Equitable representation of deaf people in mainstream academia: Why not? *Higher Education, 53*(3), 359–379.

World Health Organization. (2002). *Towards a common language for functioning, disability, and health.* Geneva, Switzerland: Author. Retrieved from http://www.who.int/classifications/icf/icfbeginnersguide.pdf?ua=1

Wright v. Columbia University, 520 F. Supp. 789 (E.D. Pa. 1981).

W3C.(2013). *Understanding WCAG 2.0.* Retrieved from www.w3.org/TR/UNDERSTANDING-WCAG20/intro.html#introduction-fourprincs-head

Wurster, K. G., Rinaldi, A. P., Woods, T. S., & Ming Liu, W. (2013). First-generation student veterans: Implications of poverty for psychotherapy. *Journal of Clinical Psychology, 69*(2), 127–137.

Wyatt, L. C., Ung, T., Park, R., Kwon, S. C., & Trinh-Shevrin, C. (2015). Risk factors of suicide and depression among Asian American, Native Hawaiian, and Pacific Islander youth: A systematic literature review. *Journal of Health Care for the Poor and Underserved, 26*(2), 191–237.

Wynn v. Tufts University School of Medicine, 976 F.2d 791 (1st Cir. 1992).

Yazicioglu, K., Yavuz, F., Goktepe, A. S., & Tan, A. K. (2012). Influence of adapted sports on quality of life and life satisfaction in sport participants and non-sport participants with physical disabilities. *Disability and Health Journal, 5*(4), 249–253.

Yearns, M. H. (2004, May). *Universal design for better living: Better tools for everyday tasks.* Ames: Iowa State University Extension.

Yelling Clinic (n.d.). *Global disability studies.* Retrieved from http://www.katherinesherwood.com/yellingclinic/about.html

Young, N. K., Nakashian, M., Yeh, S., & Amatetti, S. (2006). *Screening and assessment for family engagement, retention, and recovery (SAFERR)* (DHHS Pub. No. 0000). Rockville, MD: Substance Abuse and Mental Health Services Administration. Retrieved from National Center on Substance Abuse and Child Welfare website: https://www.ncsacw.samhsa.gov/resources/SAFERR.aspx

Zeitlin, J. (2013, March). *Disability rights convention rejected by U.S. Senate.* The Leadership Conference on Civil and Human Rights/Leadership Conference Education Fund. Retrieved from http://www.civilrights.org/monitor/march-2013/disability-rights-convention.html?referrer=https://www.google.com/

Zola, I. K. (1993). Self, identity, and the naming question: Reflections on the language of disability. *Social Science & Medicine, 36*(2), 167–173.

Zubernis, L., McCoy, V. A., & Snyder, M. (2011). *Starting over again: Counseling considerations for transfer students in higher education.* Retrieved from http://counselingoutfitters.com/vistas/vistas11/Article_11.pdf

Zukle v. Regents of the University of California, 166 F.3d 1041 (9th Cir. 1999).

Zullig, K. J., & Divin, A. L. (2012). The association between non-medical prescription drug use, depressive symptoms, and suicidality among college students. *Addictive Behaviors, 37*(8), 890–899.

INDEX

Printed in the USA/Agawam, MA
February 26, 2024

861806.077